EYEWITNESS TRAVEL GUIDES

SWEDEN

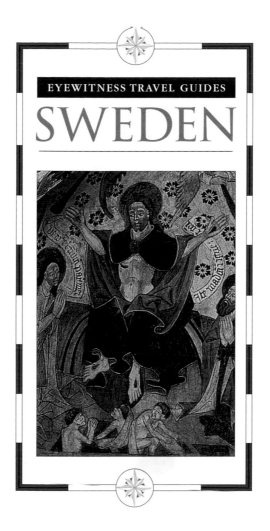

EYEWITNESS TRAVEL GUIDES

SWEDEN

DK

LONDON, NEW YORK,
MELBOURNE, MUNICH AND DELHI
www.dk.com

PRODUCED FOR DORLING KINDERSLEY BY
Streiffert Förlag AB, Stockholm

SENIOR EDITOR Bo Streiffert

PROJECT AND PICTURE EDITOR Guy Engström

ASSISTANT PICTURE EDITOR Ebba Mörner

MAIN CONTRIBUTORS Ulf Johansson, Mona Neppenström,
Kaj Sandell

PHOTOGRAPHERS Peter Hanneberg, Erik Svensson,
Jeppe Wikström

CARTOGRAPHER Stig Söderlind

ILLUSTRATORS Stephen Conlin, Gary Cross, Urban Frank,
Claire Littlejohn, Jan Rojmar, John Woodcock

ENGLISH TRANSLATION Kate Lambert, Stuart Tudball

EDITOR OF ENGLISH EDITION Jane Hutchings

Reproduced by Colourscan, Singapore
Printed and bound by South China Printing Co. Ltd., China

First American Edition, 2005
05 06 07 08 10 9 8 7 6 5 4 3 2 1

Published in the United States by DK Publishing, Inc.,
357 Hudson Street, New York, New York 10014

Copyright 2005 © Dorling Kindersley Limited, London

Published in Great Britain by Dorling Kindersley Limited.

ISSN 1542-1554

ISBN 0-7566-0913-5

**The information in every
DK Eyewitness Travel Guide is checked regularly.**
Every effort has been made to ensure that this book is as
up-to-date as possible at the time of going to press. Some details,
however, such as telephone numbers, opening hours, prices, gallery
hanging arrangements and travel information are liable to change.
The publishers cannot accept responsibility for any consequences
arising from the use of this book, nor for any material on third party
websites, and cannot guarantee that any website address in this book
will be a suitable source of travel information. We value the views
and suggestions of our readers very highly. Please write to:
Publisher, DK Eyewitness Travel Guides
Dorling Kindersley, 80 Strand, London WC2R 0RL, Great Britain

Summer-flowering cottongrass in
the mountains of Sylarna

CONTENTS

INTRODUCING SWEDEN

PUTTING SWEDEN ON
THE MAP *8*

A PORTRAIT OF
SWEDEN *10*

SWEDEN THROUGH
THE YEAR *26*

THE HISTORY OF
SWEDEN *30*

STOCKHOLM AREA BY AREA

STOCKHOLM AT A
GLANCE *46*

GAMLA STAN *48*

CITY *62*

Erik XIV's crown in the Treasury
at Stockholm's Royal Palace

◁ Skogavik nature reserve on Bullerö in the Stockholm Archipelago

SOUTHERN NORRLAND
246

NORTHERN NORRLAND
262

Cross-country skiers resting on
Åreskutan mountain *(see p259)*

TRAVELLERS' NEEDS

WHERE TO STAY *278*

WHERE TO EAT *290*

BLASIEHOLMEN AND
SKEPPSHOLMEN *72*

MALMARNA AND
FURTHER AFIELD *82*

STOCKHOLM STREET
FINDER *112*

Cheesecake with cloudberries, a
traditional Swedish dessert

SPORTS AND OUTDOOR
ACTIVITIES *314*

SURVIVAL GUIDE

PRACTICAL
INFORMATION *320*

TRAVEL INFORMATION
328

GENERAL INDEX *336*

ACKNOWLEDGMENTS
349

PHRASE BOOK *351*

STOCKHOLM TRANSPORT
MAP
Inside back cover

SHOPPING IN SWEDEN
304

ENTERTAINMENT IN
SWEDEN *310*

Inner courtyard of Läckö castle,
Västergötland *(see p220)*

SWEDEN AREA BY AREA

SWEDEN AT A GLANCE
120

EASTERN SVEALAND *122*

EASTERN GÖTALAND *140*

GOTLAND *158*

SOUTHERN GÖTALAND
170

GOTHENBURG *190*

WESTERN GÖTALAND *206*

WESTERN SVEALAND *228*

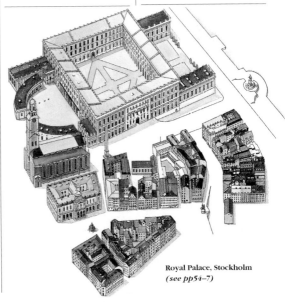

Royal Palace, Stockholm
(see pp54–7)

INTRODUCING
SWEDEN

PUTTING SWEDEN ON THE MAP 8-9
A PORTRAIT OF SWEDEN 10-25
SWEDEN THROUGH THE YEAR 26-29
THE HISTORY OF SWEDEN 30-43

Putting Sweden on the Map

THE KINGDOM OF SWEDEN is one of the largest
countries in Europe, covering 449,964 sq km
(173,730 sq miles). The most southerly point,
Smygehuk, lies at about the same latitude as
Edinburgh in Scotland, and the northernmost tip,
Treriksröset, is nearly 300 km (186 miles) north of
the Arctic Circle. Much of the country is habitable
thanks to the warming effects of the Gulf Stream.
As the crow flies, Sweden is 1,572 km (977 miles)
from south to north – the same distance as from
Smygehuk to Rome. Sweden shares a border with
Norway to the west and Finland to the east.
Denmark lies across the Kattegat to the southwest.

**Satellite photo of Stockholm and Mälardalen, with the
inlets of Bråviken and Slätbaken to bottom left**

NORWEGIAN SEA

NORTH SEA

NORWAY

Trondheim

Bergen

OSLO

Strömstad

SKAGERRAK

Kristiansand

Newcastle

Amsterdam

Gothenburg   Borås

Hirtshals

Hanstholm

Frederiks-
havn

Varberg

KATTEGAT

DENMARK   Halmstad

Grenå

Helsingborg
Helsingör

COPENHAGEN

Harwich

Esbjerg

Malmö

Kiel

0 kilometres	300
0 miles	200

KEY

✈	International airport
✖	Domestic airport
⛴	Ferry port
▬	Motorway
▬	Major road
▬	Train line
–·–	International border

◁ **Wall-hanging depicting *The Wedding in Cana and Jesus's Entry into Jerusalem*, 1781**

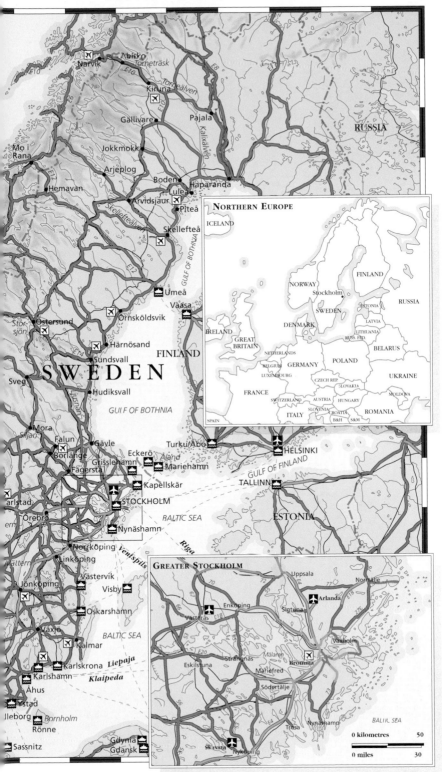

Narvik • Abisko • Torneträsk
E10
Kiruna
Gällivare • Pajala
Jokkmokk
Arjeplog
Boden • Haparanda
Hemavan • Arvidsjaur • Luleå
Piteå
Skellefteå
Mo i Rana
Umeå
Vaasa
Östersund • Örnsköldsvik
Stor-sjön
Härnösand
Sveg • Sundsvall
FINLAND
S W E D E N
Hudiksvall
GULF OF BOTHNIA
Mora
Falun • Gävle
Borlänge • Eckerö
Fagersta • Grisslehamn • Åland • Mariehamn
Turku/Åbo • HELSINKI
GULF OF FINLAND
Kapellskär
TALLINN
arlstad
STOCKHOLM
Örebro
BALTIC SEA
ESTONIA
Nynäshamn
Norrköping • Ventspils
Linköping • Riga
Jönköping • Västervik
Visby
Oskarshamn
Växjö
Kalmar
Karlskrona • Liepaja
Karlshamn • Klaipeda
Åhus
Ystad
lleborg • Bornholm
Rönne
Sassnitz
Gdynia
Gdansk

NORTHERN EUROPE

ICELAND

NORWAY
Stockholm
SWEDEN
FINLAND
RUSSIA
ESTONIA
LATVIA
DENMARK
LITHUANIA
RUSS. FED.
IRELAND
GREAT BRITAIN
NETHERLANDS
BELGIUM
LUXEMBOURG
GERMANY
POLAND
BELARUS
UKRAINE
CZECH REP.
SLOVAKIA
FRANCE
SWITZERLAND
AUSTRIA
HUNGARY
MOLDOVA
SLOVENIA
CROATIA
ROMANIA
SPAIN
ITALY
B&H
S&M

GREATER STOCKHOLM

Uppsala
Norrtälje
Enköping
Sigtuna
Arlanda
Västerås
Vaxholm
Mälaren
Eskilstuna
Strängnäs
Bromma
Mariefred
Södertälje
Nynäshamn
BALTIC SEA
Trosa
Skavsta
Nyköping

0 kilometres   50

0 miles   30

A PORTRAIT OF SWEDEN

SWEDES ARE PASSIONATE ABOUT NATURE and the outdoors, and justly so since their country contains some of Europe's last surviving areas of wilderness. As a nation, Sweden has built its wealth on its natural resources and the ingenuity of its engineers. It has a heritage rich in music, literature and folk traditions and its people have a deep-rooted sense of peace and democracy.

Few nations in Europe offer such an exceptionally diverse landscape, rich in flora and fauna, as Sweden. From north of the Arctic Circle the country stretches a lengthy 1,572 km (977 miles) south, a distance equal to almost half the length of Europe.

Elk

The extreme north is the land of the midnight sun, where daylight lasts for 24 hours in high summer, but is almost non-existent in mid-winter. Here, the mountains and tundra are home to the Sami (Lapp) people and their herds of reindeer. Moving southwards, the forests and wetlands of Norrland provide habitats for large numbers of elk and a thriving birdlife. In the far south, the rolling plains of Skåne and the area around the great lakes make good arable land. To the east, the green islands of the Stockholm archipelago contrast with the bare rocky outline of the west coast, but the waters around both offer a wide variety of marine life.

A COUNTRY SHAPED BY ICE

The mountain chain which runs along part of Sweden's border with northern Norway has several peaks more than 2,000 m (6,500 ft) high. It was formed when the ice which covered the country until 10,000 years ago retreated northwards, leaving its mark on the landscape as it shaped mountains and created

Start of the annual Vasaloppet race, which attracts more than 16,000 skiers

◁ Crown Princess Victoria and Princess Madeleine in national costume on Swedish Flag Day

L M Ericsson, setting Sweden on the path to industrialization by founding Ericsson in 1876

ridges. Several glaciers from this time still linger in the north.

THE CLIMATE

The warming effect of the Gulf Stream on Scandinavia gives Sweden a relatively mild climate for its northerly location. Cucumbers grow in the Torne Valley bordering Finland at a latitude which in Greenland is covered by ice.

However, because of the length of the country, the temperature in autumn and spring can vary by more than 20° C (68° F) from one end to the other. Northern Sweden holds the record for the coldest temperature of -53° C (-63° F), while Ultuna, near Uppsala, has recorded the highest summer temperature of 38° C (100° F).

Although there are occasional green winters in southern Sweden, heavy snowfalls can occur. The worst snowstorm took place in Skåne in February 1979, while the heaviest snowfall of 150 cm (5 ft) was on 4–5 December 1998 in Gävle in central Sweden.

SPACE FOR ALL

Sweden covers an area of 449,964 sq km (173,731 sq miles) and with just 9 million inhabitants and 20 people per sq km (52 per sq mile), Swedes have plenty of space. In the under-populated forested areas,

towns can be few and far between. Yet from the 1850s onwards, when increasing numbers of people were dependent on the land and a primitive agricultural system, Sweden couldn't feed its population. Emigration to North America was the way out and more than one million Swedes crossed the Atlantic.

Towards the end of the 19th century and thanks largely to the coming of the railways, Sweden began to exploit her rich natural resources. Forestry and copper industries were established and the rivers were harnessed to produce hydroelectricity. Large manufacturing companies began to develop, such as Ericsson, Volvo and Scania, all of which are still in operation today. The needs of industry led to a massive shift in population. Today 85 per cent of the Swedish population lives in the cities and less than 2 per cent is employed in agriculture.

In the post-war period the need for labour led to immigration rather than emigration. Flows of immigrants became even greater at the end of the 20th century with the arrival of refugees from the world's trouble spots. Sweden is now the most multicultural of the Nordic countries.

GOVERNMENT AND POLITICS

The Swedes have a strong sense of democracy and equality. Sweden is both a parliamentary democracy and a hereditary monarchy. As the head of state, the king has no political power, but he is considered to be an important representative of Sweden to the rest of the world and popular support for the monarchy is high. Carl XVI Gustaf is the descendant of one of Napoleon's marshals, Jean-Baptiste Bernadotte, who was chosen as the heir to the

Emblem of state

throne of the last of the Vasa kings, the childless Karl XIII. The Frenchman was crowned in 1818 as Carl XIV Johan, King of Sweden and Norway. Carl XVI Gustaf came to the throne in 1973 and married the German Silvia Sommerlath. Despite doubt over the king's choice of a commoner for his bride, Swedes soon took Queen Silvia to their hearts. The couple's eldest daughter, Crown Princess Victoria, is the heir to the throne.

Berry- and mushroom-picking in rural areas, with permission under Sweden's Right to Roam

Sweden's parliament, the Riksdag, has 349 members and is Sweden's legislative assembly. Elections are held every four years. At the same time, representatives are elected for 21 regional county councils and almost 300 municipalities.

Since World War II, a balance has prevailed between the socialist and non-socialist parties in parliament. With only a few exceptions, the Social Democrats, as the largest group, have governed, either alone or with smaller supporting parties. Generally, policy decisions such as neutrality and non-alliance, social welfare and equality between the sexes have had cross-party support. Taxation has reached record levels, but the majority of Swedes tend to believe that they get value for money. However, dramatic increases in welfare costs have forced cuts in health, education and social care.

The environment is a key issue. Swedes have a deep-rooted love of nature, enshrined in the Right to Roam, which guarantees free access to the forests and the countryside and the right to pick berries and mushrooms. There is widespread support for combating pollution. After the 1986 Chernobyl disaster in the former USSR, some parts of Sweden were affected by radioactive fallout, which for a time halted the consumption of reindeer meat and fish. This fuelled an already heated debate on nuclear power and a decision was taken to decommission nuclear power stations, but this has proved difficult to implement in a country so dependent on energy.

On the issue of religion, the link between church and state was dissolved in the year 2000. Sweden's Evangelical Lutheran Church is now one faith among several. Although 85 per cent of Swedes remain members, church visits are largely restricted to weddings, funerals and festivals. The Free Church movement is strong in parts of the country. Immigration has also led to many Catholic and Muslim communities being formed.

LANGUAGES AND DIALECTS

While Swedish is the dominant language, Finnish, Tornedalsfinska (the dialect of Finnish spoken in the Torne Valley), Sami and Romany are all official minority languages. The

The Swedish Parliament's plenary chamber in Stockholm, accommodating 349 members

largest of these is Finnish with around 20,000 speakers, while Sami is spoken by about 10,000 people. The majority are multilingual and Swedes in general are often fluent in English. Among immigrants, around 100,000 people have Arabic or Persian as their main language. Other major languages are Turkish, Serbo-Croat and Spanish.

Roxette, one of Sweden's most successful pop exports over the years

Despite the general use of standard Swedish, dialects flourish. Historical links with neighbouring countries can often be detected, for example between Skånska, the dialect spoken in Skåne, and Danish, and between Jämtska, the dialect heard in Jämtland, and Norwegian.

AN INFORMATION SOCIETY

Sweden has long been a nation of readers. Early investment in education and libraries provided a firm foundation and many of Sweden's most renowned 20th-century writers came from humble beginnings. Among those known internationally is the children's author Astrid Lindgren *(see p24)*.

Astrid Lindgren's Pippi Longstocking

Although radio, television and the Internet have become the main means of receiving news, 75 per cent of households take a daily newspaper. Swedes became keen users of the telephone early on, and today almost 90 per cent of the population has a mobile phone. Computer ownership and Internet usage are also among the highest in the world.

RICH CULTURE

Besides the many specialist museums in the cities, there are more than 1,000 rural museums reflecting local history and popular culture. Great interest is shown in art and handicrafts which can be seen in the countless galleries and shops.

Swedes are keen musicians: many play in local orchestras and large numbers sing in choirs. The country claims to have enough world-class opera soloists to form a choir of their own. Folk music and dancing enjoy a natural high season from Midsummer to the end of August. Recent decades have seen Swedish pop go global with Abba, the Cardigans and Roxette. Music producers and songwriters also attract international artists to Sweden and have turned pop music into a major export industry. The story of film history also has a Swedish chapter, thanks to stars such as Greta Garbo and Ingrid Bergman, and the director Ingmar Bergman.

A SPORTING NATION

Swedes enjoy being active and getting out into the countryside for recreation. Fishing is the nation's biggest hobby. More than half of all Swedes have access to a holiday cottage, with coastal and mountain areas the most popular locations. The long coastline, glorious archipelagos and numerous waterways have made Sweden a nation of sailors.

Interest in sport goes without saying, and for a small nation Sweden

has proud traditions, especially in winter sports. Skiing and ice hockey as well as football, handball, tennis, table tennis and golf, all set Swedish pulses racing, while swimming, athletics, boxing, water sports and motorsports also number several stars at international level *(see p25)*.

Ideal conditions for Sweden's sailing enthusiasts in sheltered archipelagos

SWEDEN ON THE WORLD STAGE

The neutrality which protected Sweden from two world wars has remained a guiding principle. Sweden did not join NATO, choosing instead to focus on its own defence and related industry. Despite its policy of non-alliance, the country's export of weapons is considerable.

Sweden has been a member of the EU since 1995 and elections to the European Parliament are held every five years. The attitude to the EU is divided: many people dislike the fact that laws and regulations are dictated increasingly from Brussels. In a referendum in 2003, the Swedes voted "no" to adopting the euro by a considerable majority.

Sweden is an enthusiastic advocate for the work of the UN. Its own Dag Hammarskjöld was a celebrated Secretary-General (1953–61), and Swedish troops have been involved in peace initiatives worldwide.

There have been many myths about the Swedes, who have done their best to shake off their image as a silent, boring, sex-mad nation. Honesty and inventiveness are considered among their most positive characteristics, and EU membership has made Swedes more outgoing internationally. The country comes under the global spotlight at the end of each year when the prestigious Nobel Prizes *(see p69)* for science and literature are awarded in Stockholm amid great pomp and ceremony.

In the years following World War II Sweden had an advantage over those European countries that had suffered during the conflict. It was then that the country's transformation into a welfare state became an example that others were to follow. The "Swedish model" of understanding and collaboration between employers, employees and trade unions also attracted attention.

Talk of cracks in the welfare system do little to cloud the fact that Swedes experience a high standard of living of which they are proud.

Nadine Gordimer receiving the Nobel Prize for Literature from King Carl XVI Gustaf in 1991

Landscape and Wildlife

SWEDEN HAS A REMARKABLY varied landscape. The flat arable land of Skåne in the south gives way to lakes and forests, rugged mountains, fast-flowing rivers and wild open moorland further north, leading to the Arctic tundra. Plant and animal species from both continental Europe and the Arctic thrive. Large areas of wilderness have become enclaves where endangered species such as bears and wolves, snakes and owls have been able to survive the pressure from civilization. The coastline, too, is immensely varied. Marine life is unique, as North Sea fish make their way into the brackish water of the Baltic and mix with species normally only found in fresh water.

Wolves *are a threatened species and, despite migration from neighbouring countries, there are only around 100 in Sweden.*

COASTS AND ISLANDS

Smooth rocks and sandy beaches dominate the west coast, where marine life includes saltwater fish such as cod and haddock. Freshwater pike and whitefish can be found off the northerly stretches of the east coast. On the limestone islands of Öland and Gotland orchid meadows flourish.

THE ARABLE SOUTH

The flat lands of Skåne with their fields of crops, willow windbreaks and half-timbered houses topped by storks' nests are a familiar image of Sweden. But just as typical are the stony pastures and juniper slopes of Småland surrounding red cottages, and the meadows and pasture lands of Mälardalen.

Seals *declined in number as a result of hunting, pollution and disease. But now populations of grey seals, ringed seals and harbour seals (pictured) are increasing, thanks to their protected status.*

Roe deer *were almost extinct in the early 19th century. Now they are so common in southern and central Sweden that they are known to raid local gardens in search of food.*

Sea eagles, *with a wing span of up to 250 cm (8 ft), are Sweden's largest birds of prey. They nest along the east coast and also on lakes in Lappland.*

Hedgehogs *rely on their 5,000 spines for protection and curl into a ball at the approach of danger. But this is of little effect against cars, and the popular door-step guest is in decline.*

SWEDEN'S FLORA

Considering Sweden's unusually rich flora, it is not surprising that the father of botany, Carl von Linné *(see p128)*, was born here. There are more than 2,000 species of flowers alone. After a long cold winter, nature explodes into life with a profusion of blooms, as in the orchid meadows of Öland. Swedes' love of wild flowers is illustrated by the maypoles and garlands used to celebrate Midsummer.

Wood anemones carpeting the forests signal the arrival of spring.

The red water-lily can only be found in some lakes in Tiveden National Park.

King Karl's Spire can grow 1 m (3 ft) tall – an impressive height for an orchid. It is most common in swampy mountain areas.

FORESTS

More than half of Sweden's land area is covered by forests, with deciduous trees in the south, coniferous forests with pines and spruce further north. Here lingonberries, blueberries and chanterelles grow. This is the home of elk and beaver, and forest birds such as capercaillies and black grouse.

THE FAR NORTH

The mountains and moorlands are characterized by their proximity to the Arctic. With late spring come the migratory birds such as hooper swans and the lesser white-fronted goose, and the mountain flora bursts into flower. Wolves, bears, wolverine and lynx inhabit the national parks.

The elk is the big game of the forest. Around 100,000 elk are killed in the annual hunting season and, despite the road warning signs, others die in accidents involving cars.

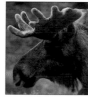

Reindeer live as domesticated animals in northern Sweden, farmed by Sami in the mountains and forests. In winter the herds move further south to graze.

The brown bear is the largest of Sweden's predators and can weigh up to 300 kg (660 lb). It may look slow, but it moves quickly and is dangerous if disturbed.

The ptarmigan lives above the tree line and is often encountered, as it is unafraid of mountain hikers. It follows the changing seasons with up to four changes of plumage.

Sweden's Wooden Houses

The quintessential image of Sweden is the red-and-white painted wooden cottage. Originally, wooden houses were not considered attractive so they were painted red to make them look as though they were built of brick, or yellow to represent stone, and this tradition has continued. Every building from the humblest hut to the most majestic mansion was made of timber from the large tracts of forest. Wood triumphs in the grandiose manor houses of Hälsingland and the decoratively carved merchants' homes of the Stockholm Archipelago. Even today, architects are developing innovative ways of using this classic material.

Bell Tower
Many 18th-century churches had wooden bell towers: Delsbo's, with its elegant onion cupola, dates from 1742.

Hut in Härjedalen
This simple log-built hut in the mountain pasture of Ruändan incorporates the centuries-old tradition of a grass roof.

Interlocking posts bind together the external and interior walls, while the façades are often boarded.

Skogaholm Manor
Built in the 1680s, this Carolian timber house from Närke was originally painted red. In the 1790s, it was given a yellow plaster façade and large windows in line with Gustavian style. More recently it was moved to the museum at Skansen.

The façade is clad in pine and painted with a copper-vitriol paint, known as Falu red, to prevent rotting.

HÄLSINGLAND'S MANOR HOUSES
Reaping the benefits from the lucrative 19th-century timber industry, the forest-owning farmers of Hälsingland built themselves extravagant manor houses. The size of house and magnificence of the painted portico reflected the owner's wealth and status. The interiors were often decorated with wall paintings.

Swedenborg's Pavilion
The miniature manor house of philosopher Emanuel Swedenborg (1688–1772). It is now at Skansen (see p92).

Societetshuset
Decorative wooden buildings, such as this club house for wealthy visitors to the seaside town of Marstrand (see p216), were a feature of the fashionable west coast bathing resorts in the late 19th century.

Modern Wooden Architecture

The Nordic Watercolour Museum in Skärhamn on the west coast opened in 2000. The Danish architects Bruun/Corfitsen have clad the building's steel and concrete shell with vertical wooden panels in red, using this traditional material in a public setting.

Wooden Lighthouse

Dating from 1840, the wooden lighthouse at Bonan also served as a pilot station. It marked the shipping route into Gävle. The building is now a museum.

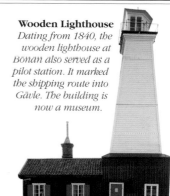

Two-storey houses are common in Hälsingland. The finest have an attic floor with half-windows.

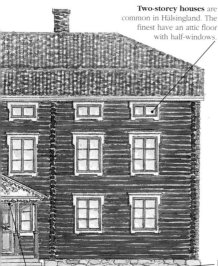

Merchant's House in the Archipelago

In the late 19th century Stockholm's upper middle classes spent their summers in the archipelago, where they built magnificent wooden villas with verandas, summer houses, bathing huts and boat houses.

Foundations are a course of cobblestones.

Porticoes and outer doors are particularly richly ornamented and painted. Other details include turned pillars, intricate woodcarving and elegant roofs. The designs vary from parish to parish.

Fishing Cottages at Kungshamn

In fishing villages on the rocky islands of Bohuslän, where space is tight, timber-clad houses in pastel shades crowd in higgledy-piggledy fashion around the harbours.

Decorative Woodwork

More expensive wooden houses dating from around 1900 were often a riot of fretwork and rich ornamentation, known as "carpenter's joy", on verandas, entrances and gables.

Traditions, Customs and Folklore

GLOBALIZATION AND THE gradual erosion of regional identity over the last 50 years have had a major impact on Swedish traditions and lifestyle. Much of the formerly rigid etiquette has been relaxed and today Swedes are more informal when it comes to dress and manners. At the same time, Swedes have become more interested in their roots, local customs, history and traditions. They are passionate about their little red cottages, the countryside, eating herring at Midsummer and the first fresh strawberries.

Folk musician

Sami in traditional costume for a celebratory occasion

FEASTS AND FESTIVITIES

CELEBRATING the high points of the year within the family has again become increasingly important, after a dismissive attitude towards tradition in the 1960s and 70s.

Many traditions have pagan origins, most of them related to the coming and going of seasons, and are an excuse to eat special treats and play games. The most important is Midsummer, the summer solstice feast. Along with dancing and games around the maypole, the light, short night (when all sorts of magic is in the air) can be marked by watching the sun set and rise a few hours apart (or hardly at all in the north). For those who go to bed it is the custom to pick seven different flowers in silence and place them under their pillow; their future partner will appear in their dreams. Walpurgis night, 30 April, is when the last day of winter is chased away with

huge bonfires, and songs and speeches welcome spring. Lucia Day, in December, is an intricate mix of pagan and Christian, a festival of light at the onslaught of darkness, which has adopted a Christian martyr as its symbol of hope and bringer of light. Every school, office and church has a Lucia, a girl dressed in white with a red ribbon around her waist symbolizing the martyr's blood, and a crown of candles on her head *(see p29)*.

Easter also has elements of old folk beliefs. Maundy Thursday is the day witches fly to Blåkulla *(see p154)* to dance with the devil. Today, children dress up, broomsticks and all, and give handmade Easter greetings cards in exchange for sweets. Christmas is preceded by the hectic run-up of Advent, when Swedes go partying and consume vast quantities of *glögg* (mulled wine usually mixed with cognac or vodka), *lussebullar* (saffron buns) and *pepparkakor* (ginger snaps).

DRESS AND ETIQUETTE

THOSE WHO OWN a folk costume take it out for midsummer, folk dances, weddings and other formal occasions. Each region has its own historic style and there is also a national dress *(see p10)*. The Sami have their own elaborate costumes.

At weddings people are expected to dress up, as specified on the invitation (white tie, black tie or suit). In everyday life, style is more casual, especially in summer.

Although Swedes are more easy-going these days, they are still fond of etiquette. It is important to know how to *"skål"*. Swedes first raise their glass to their female partner at the table, and then to the hostess. People look each other in the eye while raising their glass and saying *"skål"*, looking down as they drink and then re-establishing eye contact before putting down their glass. If the *skål* is communal, everyone has to look each person around the table in the eye before drinking.

Despite this interest in etiquette, Swedes tend not to observe minor courtesies such as holding open doors or apologizing when they bump into someone. They are very informal when addressing one another; everyone is on first name terms from the start, even when doing business.

SINGERS AND MUSICIANS

MORE THAN half a million Swedes sing in a choir, and their passion for song is reflected not just in singing

Midsummer celebrations with games and dancing round the maypole

at parties and the ever-increasing repertoire of drinking songs, but also in the popularity of singing together. There are few 50th birthday parties where each plate doesn't come with a songbook or where friends don't perform songs they have written themselves. Everyone is expected to know works by troubadour Carl Bellman and ballads by Evert Taube *(see p60).*

Folk music is played at clubs and there are festivals dedicated to folk instruments such as the accordion and hurdy-gurdy. Pageants and history plays have also seen a huge upturn in popularity in recent years.

A tournament during Medieval Week, a popular pageant in Visby

CLOSE TO NATURE

THE SWEDES' LOVE of nature is deeply rooted. Many feel, subconsciously, an almost spiritual affinity with the forest, mountains or the sea. Legends and folklore are often linked to nature and many mythical beings are part of country lore. Trolls dwell in the forest, as does the Skogsvrå or Huldra (siren), a beautiful young woman who lures men deeper and deeper into the woods and then, once they are lost, she turns around and all there is to be seen is a hollow tree. Women who stroll too far might hear a lovely tune drifting among the trees – that is Näcken, a handsome naked man, playing his fiddle in the middle of gushing streams

Painting depicting mythical beings in the forest

and, needless to say, it is best to stay away from him. Giants and dwarfs roam the mountains while elves dance in the meadows and marsh-lands. Some beings have adopted modern guises. The Tomte, who traditionally is a stern, grey little man guarding farmers' barns and livestock, has been transformed into a kindly distributor of Christ-mas gifts. In the countryside, however, a plate of Christmas porridge is left for him on the doorstep, just to be safe.

There is a strong aware-ness of the changing seasons, linked to how deeply Swedes long for the bright summer. Spring is a slow affair, build-ing up with the blossoming of one flower at a time, each one eagerly awaited. People know when each bloom is due, hence expressions like "between bird cherry and lilac" (ie "at end of May").

On a more practical note, it is easy to be physically close to nature thanks to the Right to Roam. This grants everyone access to all land, apart from the immediate surroundings of a house or farm *(see p314).* Many make the most of this resource, walking, camping, or going mushroom or berry-picking.

A COUNTRY COTTAGE

THE LITTLE RED cottage is the symbol of paradise. Maybe it is the Swedes' farm-ing roots combined with the

brief summer which makes having a holiday house in the countryside or out on an island such a major ambition.

When spring comes, people head out to tend their cottage gardens, and as the autumn nights draw in they are still at their cottages, curled up by the fire. Almost half the population have access to a summer cottage and 20 per cent own one of their own.

CULINARY TRADITIONS

PEOPLE ARE rediscovering old Swedish dishes and there has been something of a revival in *husmanskost* ("home-cooking"). Few, however, have time to prepare these at home on a daily basis, so childhood favourites such as *kalops* (a slow-cooked meat stew), *köttbullar* (meatballs, *see p293)* and freshly cleaned and fried herring fillets are now often enjoyed in restaurants.

Strawberry cream cake

Swedes drink lots of coffee, and at work the *fika paus* (coffee break) is strictly observed. In fact, *fika* is something everyone does, as proven by the large number of cafés even in small towns. To accompany coffee there is a great variety of *bullar* (buns), cakes, gateaux and biscuits. Home-made sponge cake layered with lots of whipped cream and straw-berries is a summer favourite, especially for birthdays.

Swedish Design

S WEDISH DESIGN first attracted international attention at the 1925 World Exhibition in Paris, when glassware in particular took the world by storm and the concept of "Swedish Grace" was launched. The nation's design tradition is characterized by simplicity and functionality, with a major emphasis on natural materials. Swedish designers and architects are renowned for creating simple, attractive, "human" objects for everyday use. The 20th century marked the beginning of a new golden age, in which Swedish design has won worldwide acclaim.

Stoneware, Hans Hedberg
Swedish ceramics from the 1940s, 50s and 60s, such as the stoneware egg, are popular with collectors around the world.

Armchair (1969), Bruno Mathsson
Bruno Mathsson, one of Sweden's most famous 20th-century furniture designers, is one of the creators of the style that became known as "Swedish Modern". He designed the first version of the Pernilla armchair in 1942.

Pale wood and simplicity is the concept most closely associated with Swedish style.

Rag rugs are an old Swedish weaving tradition adopted by Karin Larsson, whose skill as a textile designer is widely recognized.

Cabinet (1952), Josef Frank
Frank was born in Austria, but worked in Sweden, and was another disciple of the "Swedish Modern" style. He is best known for his printed textiles, but he also designed furniture.

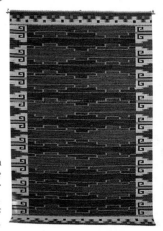

Carpet (1931), Märta Måås-Fjetterström
From 1919, Märta Måås-Fjetterström wove her famous rugs at her studio in Skåne. Her work was inspired by folklore and nature, and she created a design concept that was new but still firmly rooted in tradition.

Silver jug (1953)
Sigurd Persson
Persson has an unrivalled ability to handle metal. He made his mark on the history of design with his everyday industrial pieces and exclusive artworks.

Flowers and plants on a windowsill and no curtains typifies the Larssons' ideas on interior decoration.

Chair (1981), Jonas Bohlin
The Concrete *chair was the most talked about piece of Swedish furniture in the 1980s. A graduation project, it represented an entirely new approach to furniture design.*

Bookshelf (1989), John Kandell
The Pilaster *bookshelf stores books horizontally instead of vertically. The lines are simple and typically Scandinavian. The maker, Källemo, is one of Sweden's most unconventional furniture companies.*

CARL LARSSON'S SUNDBORN

The home created by the artist Carl Larsson (1853–1919) and his wife Karin *(see p237)* became a inspiration around the world when it featured in his watercolours series *A Home.* The mixture of old and new, pure clear colours, light and space and lots of plants was a clear expression of the "Beauty for All" movement.

Gustavian late 18th-century style elements have remained a strong feature in Swedish design through the centuries, but made an international comeback in the 1990s.

Vase, Ann Wåhlström
Wahlström is one of Kosta Boda's new generation of glass designers. Organic, warm and beautiful, Cyklon (1998) is an excellent example of contemporary Swedish glass.

WHERE TO SEE SWEDISH DESIGN

Asplund	**DesignTorget**
Sibyllegatan 31,	Vallgatan 14,
Stockholm. **Map** 2 E3.	Gothenburg.
Nationalmuseum	**Röhsska Museet**
Södra Blasieholmshamnen,	Vasagatan 37–39,
Stockholm. **Map** 4 D2.	Gothenburg.
Nordiska Museet	**David Design**
Djurgårdsvågen 6–16,	Stortorget 5,
Stockholm. **Map** 4 F1.	Malmö.
Svenskt Tenn	**Glassworks shops**
Strandvägen 5, Stockholm.	Various, Småland.
Map 2 E4.	*(See pp152–3).*

Famous Swedes

FOR A NATION with only 9 million inhabitants, a surprisingly large number of Swedes have made names for themselves abroad. They include scientists such as Anders Celsius, who gave us the temperature scale, Alfred Nobel, founder of the prize that bears his name, Dalarna artists Anders Zorn and Carl Larsson, the playwright August Strindberg and peacemaker Dag Hammarskjöld. In recent years, tennis players such as Björn Borg and Stefan Edberg, skiers, film-makers, writers of children's books and pop stars have all gained international acclaim.

Carl Larsson (1853–1919), loved for his paintings of Sundborn

August Strindberg, Sweden's influential dramatist and author

LITERATURE

THE FIRST SWEDISH AUTHORS to achieve international recognition were the late-19th-century writers Selma Lagerlöf *(see p232)* and August Strindberg. Lagerlöf's *Gösta Berling's Saga* (1891), set in her home province of Värmland, marked a turning point in modern Swedish novel-writing. She won the Nobel Prize in 1909, an honour not granted the titan August Strindberg (1849–1912), whose groundbreaking naturalistic plays, including *The Father* (1887), *Miss Julie* (1888), *The Dance of Death* (1901) and *A Dream Play* (1902), are still performed around the world.

In contemporary literature it is mainly detective and thriller writers who have gained an international readership. Jan Guillou's Carl Hamilton spy novels have attracted a wide audience largely thanks to films starring Stellan Skarsgård, while the detective stories of Henning Mankell (b. 1948), featuring Inspector Kurt Wallander, have become bestsellers in a number of countries. Astrid Lindgren heads the list of renowned Swedish children's authors, with characters such as Pippi Longstocking and Emil.

ART & ARCHITECTURE

SWEDEN'S AGE OF GREATNESS as the dominant power in northern Europe in the 17th century produced a flowering of art and architecture. Three generations of the Tessin family made their mark: Nicodemus Tessin the Elder (1615–81), who created the Baroque palace of Drottningholm, his son Nicodemus the Younger (1654–1728), who designed Stockholm's Royal Palace, and his grandson, Carl Gustaf (1695–1770), who was an artistic mentor to Gustav III and introduced the Rococo style to Sweden with Carl Hårleman. The sculptor and artist Johan Tobias Sergel (1740–1814) is another influential figure from the Gustavian period.

The period around 1900 was a golden age in Swedish painting. The best-known National Romantic artist was Anders Zorn (1860–1920) from Dalarna, whose paintings of female nudes in the landscape won acclaim. The Stockholm Archipelago featured in the work of Bruno Liljefors (1860–1939), whose lifelike animal paintings are beloved by Swedes. Carl Larsson's idyllic scenes from his Dalarna home, Sundborn, documented in the book *A Home* (1899), have become firm favourites in Sweden and abroad *(see p237)*.

Carl Milles (1875–1955) was one of Sweden's best-known sculptors internationally and several of his monumental works are on public display around Stockholm and at his former home, Millesgården, on the island of Lidingö *(see p95)*.

Architect Gunnar Asplund (1885–1940) was a pioneer of the Functionalist style in the 1920s and 30s, with works such as Stockholm's City Library *(see p99)* and Skogskyrkogården cemetery's crematorium *(see p105)*.

MUSIC

CLASSICAL SWEDISH MUSIC has not attracted major attention abroad, but opera singers have become big

ABBA, the most internationally successful Swedish pop group

names on the international stage. The "Swedish nightingale" Jenny Lind (1820–87) and Christina Nilsson (1843–1921) won international acclaim. They were followed by Birgit Nilsson (b. 1918), renowned for her interpretation of Wagner, while Jussi Björling (1911–60) was the great tenor of his age *(see p237)*.

Swedish pop music became a major export industry in the late 20th century, with the advent of groups such as ABBA, the Cardigans, Ace of Base, and the duo Roxette, all of which have had considerable success abroad.

FILM & PHOTOGRAPHY

SILENT FILMS soon became an important art form in Sweden and directors such as Victor Sjöström *(The Phantom Carriage,* 1920), and Mauritz Stiller *(Song of the Scarlet Flower,* 1918), got breaks in Hollywood. Stiller was responsible for launching the enigmatic Greta Garbo *(see p105),* later to star in *Anna Karenina* (1935) and *Camille* (1937). The next big star was Ingrid Bergman, forever remembered for her role in *Casablanca* (1943).

The film genius and multi-Oscar-winning director Ingmar Bergman became internationally synonymous with Swedish film in the 1950s and 60s. *The Seventh Seal* (1957), *The Virgin Spring* (1960), *The Silence* (1963) and *Fanny and Alexander* (1982) are among his masterpieces.

The art of photography has always played an important role in Sweden. Lennart Nilsson, with his voyages of discovery into the inner workings of mankind, such as in *A Child is Born* (1965), has attracted much attention.

Anna Lindh (1957–2003), murdered foreign minister

POLITICS OF PEACE

DAG HAMMARSKJÖLD was one of a line of Swedish peacemakers who have made their mark on world affairs. He became Secretary General of the United Nations in 1953 and was awarded the Nobel Prize for Peace in 1961 after his death in a plane crash during the Congo crisis.

Another Swedish diplomat who met an unfortunate fate was Raoul Wallenberg, who organized the rescue of 100,000 Hungarian Jews in World War II. In 1944 he was captured by the Russians and never seen again.

Ingrid Bergman (1915–82)

More recently, the gunning down in Stockholm of two prominent politicians and peace campaigners shocked the nation: prime minister Olof Palme in 1986 and foreign minister Anna Lindh in 2003.

SCIENCE & TECHNOLOGY

FOR A SMALL COUNTRY, Sweden has an unusually large number of genius inventors. The 18th century produced the father of botany, Carl von Linné *(see p128);* Anders Celsius, the man behind the temperature scale; and chemists Carl Wilhelm von Scheele, who discovered elements such as oxygen, nitrogen and chlorine, and Jöns Jacob Berzelius, who systematized chemistry and introduced chemical symbols. Inventors included John Ericsson (1803–89),

locomotive and screw-propeller designer and creator of the first modern naval war vessel *Monitor (see p235);* the telephone pioneer L M Ericsson (1846–1926); and the inventor of dynamite Alfred Nobel (1833–96), whose fortune was used to establish the prestigious Nobel Prize.

SPORT

INTEREST IN SPORT has always been strong in Sweden and the nation has had many international successes. Cross-country skiers such as Mora Nisse Karlsson, Sixten Jernberg, Gunde Svahn and Per Elofsson have Olympic medals under their belts; and in alpine skiing, no-one has yet eclipsed Ingemar Stenmark. Women's skiing was long dominated by Pernilla Wiberg, whose mantle has now been taken on by Anja Pärsson. Professional ice hockey players such as Peter Forsberg and Markus Näslund are among the foremost players in the North American National Hockey League.

Tennis greats have included Björn Borg, Mats Wilander and Stefan Edberg, while in table tennis Jan-Ove Waldner holds his own against the top Chinese players. The world's best woman golfer in 2003 was a Swede, Annika Sörenstam.

Swedish athletes have also reached the top, including high jumpers Kajsa Bergkvist and Stefan Holm.

Annika Sörenstam, the world's top female golfer, 2003

SWEDEN THROUGH THE YEAR

The crocus, a sign of spring

THANKS TO SWEDEN'S geographical location, it experiences wide variations in seasons and climate. Winter retains its icy hold on the north until May, when in the south Skåne is already basking in sunshine. Once spring gets going in the north and the days lengthen, nature soon catches up. Summers are pleasantly warm throughout Sweden and that is when Swedes head off into the countryside to swim and enjoy the outdoor life, often staying in a summer cottage.

The holiday period from June to August is the height of the tourist season, with the widest range of attractions on offer. In winter, Swedes make for the mountains, which see the first snowfall as early as November. They value their festivals, and events such as Christmas, New Year, Easter, Midsummer's Eve and Walpurgis are celebrated with enthusiasm.

An April start for the salmon fly-fishing season in Mörrum

SPRING

AFTER THE LONG, dark Swedish winter, spring makes a welcome appearance. In Skåne the migratory birds return and spring flowers bloom in March, while in the north it's mid-May before winter releases its hold. Traditionally eaten before Lent, the *semla* cream bun is a tempting treat. Walpurgis Night, on the last day of April, marks a farewell to winter with folk dancing, torchlight processions, student choirs, bonfires and fireworks.

Semla bun

MARCH

Vasa Ski Race *(early Mar)*. World famous long-distance ski race *(see p245)*.
Stockholm International Boat Show *(early Mar)*. The spring's major boat exhibition at Stockholm International Fairs in Älvsjö.

Spring Salon *(Mar)*. Annual art exhibition featuring new artists at Liljevalchs Konsthall in Djurgården, Stockholm.
Åselenappet *(end of Mar)*. Ice-fishing competition, the high point of the winter market in Åsele, Lapland.

APRIL

Start of Salmon Fishing Season, Mörrum *(1 Apr)*, Sweden's main salmon river *(see p187)*.
The "crane dance", Hornborgasjön *(mid-Apr)*. Several thousand cranes gather on the fields around this lake in Västergötland for their annual mating dance.
Walpurgis Night *(30 Apr)*. Around the country bonfires welcome spring, with students donning their white caps and making merry. In the student town of Uppsala, Walpurgis Night also includes fine student choirs, a river-rafting carnival and many other events.

MAY

May Day *(1 May)*. Workers' processions countrywide.
Linné's birthday, Stenbrohult *(23 May)*. The father of botany is commemorated at his childhood home in Småland.
Gärdet Kite Festival, Stockholm *(last weekend in May)*. The Arts College's spectacular kite competition. Great day for a picnic.
Elite Race *(last weekend in May)*. International trotting competition at Solvalla.
"Tjejtrampet", Gärdet *(last weekend in May)*. The 40-km (25-mile) women-only cycling competition.
Trollhättan waterfalls *(weekends in May)*. Magnificent falls, usually tamed by the power station, burst into life.

Walpurgis Night bonfire, at Riddarholmen, Stockholm

Midsummer celebrations at Skansen open-air museum, Stockholm

SUMMER

THE SCHOOL YEAR finishes in early June and summer comes into its own with Midsummer celebrations and dancing round the maypole. Evenings are often warm and the nights light, encouraging parties round the clock. In the far north the sun doesn't even set. July is traditionally the main holiday month and favourite spots can become crowded. But Sweden is big and there's room for everyone. The start of the school term at the end of August coincides with two popular culinary festivals celebrating crayfish and fermented Baltic herring.

JUNE

Stockholm Marathon *(first Sat in Jun).* One of the world's 10 biggest marathons with around 15,000 runners.
Archipelago Boat Day, Stockholm *(first Wed in Jun).* Classic steamboats assemble at Strömkajen for a round trip to Vaxholm.
National Day *(6 Jun).* Not a public holiday, National Day is celebrated around the country as Swedish Flag Day. The royal family attend the celebrations at Skansen in Stockholm.
Postrodden Mail Boat Race, Grisslehamn *(Sat before Midsummer).* Rowing race to the Åland islands following the old mail route.
"Vätternrundan" *(mid-Jun).* Classic cycling race 300 km (190 miles) round Lake Vättern with up to 17,000 participants, starting and finishing in Motala.

Midsummer's Eve *(penultimate Sat in Jun).* A major Swedish festival celebrated by dancing around a flower-bedecked maypole. Midsummer in Dalarna, Rättvik and Mora is especially rich in tradition with folk music and the wearing of colourful national costumes.

JULY

Gotland Race *(first week in Jul).* Major international sailing race around Gotland, starting and finishing in Sandhamn in the Stockholm Archipelago.
Skule Song Festival *(first weekend in Jul).* One of Sweden's largest singing festivals, held at the foot of the Skule mountain on the High Coast.
Hälsinge Hambo *(early Jul).* Folk-dancing competition in Hårga, Bollnäs and Arbrå, with the finals in Järvsö.
Vansbro Swim *(mid-Jul).* Up to 5,000 people take part in the 3-km (2-mile) swim in the Vanån and Västerdalälven rivers, starting in Vansbro.
Stånga Games, Gotland *(mid-Jul).* Events featuring Gotland sports such as Square-and-border-ball, The Stone, Gotlandic Pole Throwing and "Hook the Bottom".
Gammelvala Brunnskog, Värmland *(end of Jul).* Week-long festival celebrating the domestic skills of the past. Music, exhibitions, drama and local food.
Storsjöyran Festival *(end of Jul).* Week-long festival in "the Republic of Jämtland" with drama, exhibitions, films, and concluding with a

huge pop and rock festival.
Music in the Kingdom of Crystal, Småland's Glass-works *(end of Jul).* Folk music, choral singing, opera, wind bands and jazz in a charming setting.
Kukkolaforsen Whitefish Festival *(last weekend in Jul).* Celebrations in Sweden and Finland to mark the whitefish reaching the Torneälven river, which forms the border between the two countries. The fish are caught in large nets and eaten grilled or smoked.

AUGUST

Skänninge Market, Östergötland *(Thu after first Wed in Aug).* One of Sweden's most traditional markets, attracting 100,000 visitors to this medieval city.
Royal Philharmonic Orchestra Outdoor Concert, Stockholm *(2nd Sun in Aug).* This concert on the lawn outside Sjöhistoriska Museet is one of the highlights of the season.
Gotland Medieval Week *(early Aug).* Visby once more becomes a 14th-century Hanseatic city with tournaments, plays and music and participants in colourful medieval costumes.
Hjo Accordion Festival *(2nd weekend in Aug).* Accordion players meet in Hjo on the shores of Lake Vättern.

Crayfish

Crayfish and Fermented Herring *(end of Aug).* Although there is no longer a statutory start date for eating these national delicacies – accompanied by ice-cold schnapps, cheese and silly paper hats – this is when Swedes party the most.

Medieval Week tournament in Visby, Gotland

Beech forest in autumn at Söderåsen, Skåne

AUTUMN

THE NIGHTS may be drawing in, but the mornings are light and the days often crisp and clear. In late autumn deciduous trees provide a stunning display of colours. It's harvest time in the forests and countryside, and a wide variety of delicious edible mushrooms, as well as blueberries, lingonberries and the red-gold cloudberries of the northern marshes are all ripe for the picking.

SEPTEMBER

Oxhälja Market, Filipstad (early Sep). Traditional market in eastern Värmland.
Riddarfjärden Regatta (first weekend in Sep). Stockholmers line the quay to watch hundreds of fine old wooden boats compete.

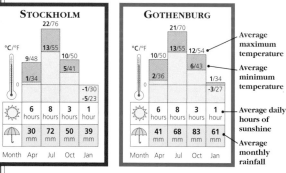

Chanterelles

Swedish Trotting Derby, Jägersro (Sep). Sweden's top four year-olds compete for the derby title on the trotting track in Malmö.
Halland Salmon Festival (end Sep). In celebration of salmon, the pride of the province, the festival includes fishing, best salmon dish competitions and the crowning of the Salmon King.

OCTOBER

Lidingö Race (first weekend in Oct). The world's largest cross-country race, with tens of thousands of competitors, including elite runners, senior citizens and children.
Harvest Festival, Öland (early Oct). Sweden's biggest harvest festival takes place over four days around Michaelmas, with more than 1,000 events attracting 200,000 visitors to enjoy local food, concerts and exhibitions.
Umeå International Jazz Festival (end Oct). Leading jazz festival, first staged in the 1960s.

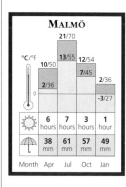

STOCKHOLM

	22/76		
°C/°F	13/55	10/50	
9/48		5/41	
1/34			
0			-1/30
			-5/23

☼	6 hours	8 hours	3 hours	1 hour
☂	30 mm	72 mm	50 mm	39 mm

| Month | Apr | Jul | Oct | Jan |

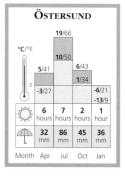

GOTHENBURG

	21/70		
°C/°F	13/55	12/54	
	10/50	6/43	
2/36			1/34
0			-3/27

☼	6 hours	8 hours	3 hours	1 hour
☂	41 mm	68 mm	83 mm	61 mm

| Month | Apr | Jul | Oct | Jan |

• Average maximum temperature
• Average minimum temperature
• Average daily hours of sunshine
• Average monthly rainfall

Climate

Considerable variations in climate from north to south sometimes result in southern Sweden having no snow and temperatures above freezing in winter, while the north is blanketed in thick snow. The differences are less extreme in summer. The effect of the North Atlantic and the Gulf Stream is felt on the west coast in mild damp winds and the highest rainfall.

MALMÖ

	21/70		
°C/°F	13/55	12/54	
	10/50	7/45	
2/36			2/36
0			-3/27

☼	6 hours	7 hours	3 hours	1 hour
☂	38 mm	61 mm	57 mm	49 mm

| Month | Apr | Jul | Oct | Jan |

ÖSTERSUND

	19/66		
°C/°F		10/50	
	5/41	6/43	
0			1/34
-3/27			-6/21
			-13/9

☼	6 hours	7 hours	2 hours	1 hour
☂	32 mm	86 mm	45 mm	36 mm

| Month | Apr | Jul | Oct | Jan |

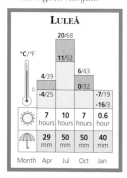

LULEÅ

	20/68		
°C/°F		11/52	
	4/39	6/43	
0			0/32
-4/25			-7/19
			-16/3

☼	7 hours	10 hours	7 hours	0.6 hour
☂	29 mm	50 mm	50 mm	40 mm

| Month | Apr | Jul | Oct | Jan |

WINTER

WHILE CHRISTMAS does not always go hand in hand with snow in southern Sweden, there are plenty of opportunities for ice-skating and there's always a chance of a white January. The mountains become a paradise for skiers, while snow cannons help out elsewhere if nature isn't up to the job. From the first day of Advent, the Christmas season is in full swing, culminating in present-giving on Christmas Eve. Restaurants enjoy their busiest time and Lucia processions brighten the winter darkness.

NOVEMBER

Gustav Adolf Day *(6 Nov).*
Gothenburg celebrates the royal founder of the city on the anniversary of his death *(see p195).*
St Martin's Day *(10–11 Nov).*
Roast goose and "black soup" containing goose blood are served at parties for St Martin of Tours and Martin Luther.

DECEMBER

Nobel Day *(10 Dec).* The year's Nobel Prize laureates are honoured in a ceremony at Konserthuset (Concert Hall) and a banquet in Stadshuset (City Hall) attended by the King and Queen.
Lucia Celebrations *(13 Dec).*
Sweden's chosen Lucia, with her girl attendants and "star boys", serves the Nobel laureates morning coffee with saffron buns and

performs traditional songs. In the evening a Lucia procession winds through the capital to celebrations and fireworks at Skansen. Similar Lucia processions take place throughout Sweden and, on a smaller scale, in many homes and schools.
Christmas Markets throughout Sweden *(from early Dec).* The markets at Skansen and Stortorget in Stockholm are particularly atmospheric.
Christmas *(24–26 Dec).*
Filled with traditions, Christmas is the most important Swedish holiday. The main

Lucia, the "Queen of Light", with her attendants at Skansen

event is Christmas Eve when an abundant *smörgåsbord* is followed by gifts. Christmas Day often begins with a church service.
New Year *(31 Dec–1 Jan).*
People go out on the town. Celebrations are televised from Skansen, including a traditional midnight reading of Tennyson's *"Ring out wild bells..."* Church bells peal and there are spectacular fireworks displays.

Northern Lights over Jokkmokk on a cold winter night

JANUARY

Hindersmässan *(end Jan).*
Market in Örebro dating back to medieval times.
Ice Globe Theatre, Jukkasjärvi *(mid Jan).*
Shakespeare season opens at the theatre in ice *(see p272).*

FEBRUARY

Jokkmokks Winter Market *(first weekend in Feb)*
Colourful festival with traditional market, Sami reindeer sledding and races.
Gothenburg Boat Show *(early Feb).* New boats on show at the Swedish Exhibition Centre in Gothenburg.
Vikingarännet *(as soon as the ice holds).* Long-distance ski race over 80 km (50 miles) on Lake Mälaren from Uppsala to Stockholm.
Globen Gala *(2nd half of Feb).* Athletes converge on Globen arena for this top indoor competition.

PUBLIC HOLIDAYS

New Year's Day (1 Jan)
Epiphany (6 Jan)
Good Friday (Mar/Apr)
Easter Monday (Mar/Apr)
Ascension Day (6th Thu after Easter)
Labour Day (1 May)
Whit Monday (May/Jun)
Midsummer (Jun)
Christmas Day (25 Dec)
Boxing Day (26 Dec)

Frozen Riddarfjärden in Stockholm as a winter park

THE HISTORY OF SWEDEN

DESCRIBED IN THE 4TH CENTURY BC *as a land of frozen seas and midnight sun, this northerly nation of reindeer herders also produced the fearsome Viking traders of the 9th century. By the 17th century, Sweden, in its Age of Greatness, ruled supreme over the Baltic region. Vanquished by Russia in 1809, the country adopted a more peaceful role and today is heavily engaged in world affairs.*

In the last 100,000 years, Sweden has been covered by thick inland ice on at least three occasions. As the ice retreated northwards for the last time in approximately 12,000 BC, nomadic reindeer hunters moved in to use the newly revealed land, but it was not until 6500 BC that Sweden was entirely free of ice.

Rune stone, 9th century

Farming was gradually adopted in southern Sweden from 4000 BC, while hunting continued to remain prevalent in the inland areas of Norrland for a long time to come. The first examples of domestic pottery date from this period and burial mounds appeared in the southern provinces.

Finds from the Bronze Age (1800–500 BC) bear witness to increased contact with the outside world. A chieftain society based on power and social alliances began to develop. Magnificent bronze objects, huge burial mounds and cairns with grave goods as well as rock carvings date from this period *(see p212).*

The transition to the Iron Age in 500 BC saw the first written accounts about Scandinavia. In the 4th century BC the Greek explorer and trader, Phytheas of Massilia, described the journey to "Thule", with its frozen seas and midnight sun. In his *Germania* (AD 98), the Roman Tacitus refers to the *"sviones"* as a powerful people with strong men, weapons and fleets.

With the growth of the Roman Empire, links with the Continent increased and numerous finds show evidence of trade with Rome via the many German tribes in the area north of the Rhine. The fall of Rome and the subsequent period of population migrations saw the rise of small kingdoms across Europe. In Sweden there was a kingdom centred on Uppsala where large *kungshögar* (King's Mounds) can still be seen today *(see p129).*

From 800 until Christianity reached Sweden in the mid-11th century, the Vikings took the world by storm. As traders, settlers and plunderers, they set sail in search of land, slaves and treasure. They carried out raids throughout Europe, sailed as far as Baghdad and even reached America. Christian monks wrote of attacks on rich monasteries and towns. But the Vikings were more than wild barbarians. They were also hard-working farmers, traders, experienced sailors, craftsmen and shipbuilders.

TIMELINE

12 000 BC	4000 BC	2000 BC	AD	500	1000
c. 12,000 BC Thick ice covers the country. As the ice retreats, reindeer herders gradually move into the southernmost coastal area	**1500 BC** Regional provinces build barrows and cairns to powerful men and women		**500 BC** Early Iron Age; a worsening climate and a decline in agriculture	*Viking ship c. 980*	
4000 BC Farming is gradually adopted in the south of the land	**3700 BC** Burials take place in chambered mounds, creating the first monuments in the Swedish countryside	**1800 BC** Bronze objects start to be made in Sweden along continental lines	**AD 98** Tacitus refers to the *sviones* in his writings	**800** The Viking period begins and the trading centre of Birka in Lake Mälaren is founded	

◁ *Gustav Vasa* **(1523–60), painting by Cornelius Arendtz**

Christianity and the Birth of a Kingdom

During the 11th and 12th centuries several families from different provinces battled for power over the central part of what is known today as Sweden. The country was more like a federation of self-governing provinces, a number of which, for a limited time, had influence over those around them.

Little is known of the kings and chieftains in the early Middle Ages other than brief mentions in sagas. In the 11th century, King Olof Skötkonung (d. 1020) was converted to Christianity and was baptized in 1008, along with his sons Anund Jakob (d. 1050) and Edmund the Old (d. 1060). Thereafter power passed to the Stenkil family, which had strong links with Västergötland where the Christian church had gained the most influence.

Birger Jarl's seal

The church and the gradual transition to Christianity underway in the 12th century were vital to the growing power of the king. The priests brought with them an administrative tradition, a civil service and a rational system for regulating property. The church also reinforced the strength of the king ideologically through the idea that his power was derived from God.

Once the Stenkil dynasty came to an end around 1120, the royal houses of Västergötland (Erik) and Östergötland (Sverker) battled for supremacy. Both families died out in the first half of the 13th century at the time when the power of the *riksjarl* (earl) was at its height. The *riksjarl* was the king's most important statesman and the position gained greater influence through Birger Magnusson, known as Birger Jarl, who became *riksjarl* in 1248 under King Erik Eriksson. Until his death in 1266, Birger Jarl was the de facto wielder of power in Sweden, which by then had developed into a medieval kingdom similar to those elsewhere in Europe.

The Hanseatic League and the Bjälbo Dynasty's Power Struggle

The 13th century saw the founding of many of the medieval towns still standing today. Documents show that Stockholm existed as a town in 1252, four years after Birger Jarl became *riksjarl*. In 1289 it was described as the largest town in Sweden, but it was not yet a capital city. Its importance lay in its role as a trading centre, particularly for the German Hanseatic League, during the 14th century. The Hanseatic League had previously established a base in Visby on Gotland, which was one of its most important centres. In some places, the Hansa influence was so great that the king had to prevent Germans from holding more than half of the leading positions in the town.

Through Birger Jarl's son, Valdemar, elected king in 1250, power passed to

King Olof Skötkonung's baptism at Husaby well in Västergötland, 1008

Timeline

	1080 Pagan revolt replaces the Christian, Inge the Elder, by the Svea family, who choose Blot-Sven as king	1143 Alvastra monastery in Östergötland is founded by Cistercians	*Birger Jarl*	1248 Birger Jarl is *riksjarl*, the king's foremost statesman
	1100	**1150**	**1200**	**1250**
1008 Olof Skötkonung is baptized a Christian in Västergötland	1101 The meeting of the three kings in Kungahälla sets the borders of the Nordic countries	1130 Östergötland chief Sverker the Elder elected king	1222 The last of the Sverker dynasty, Johan Sverkersson, dies and is succeeded by Erik Eriksson	1250 Erik Eriksson is succeeded by Valdemar Birgersson, son of Birger Jarl and first of the Folkung dynasty

the Bjälbo dynasty. Valdemar was replaced after a revolt by his brother Magnus Ladulås who was elected king in 1275. During Magnus's reign, Swedish legislation was reformed and the Ordinance of Alsnö of 1280 granted the nobility and church far-reaching privileges and freedom from taxation.

The king's nickname, Ladulås (literally "lock barn"), is said to derive from his ban on nobles from helping themselves to sustenance from peasants' barns when travelling.

On Magnus' death in 1290, his son Birger was still a minor and Sweden was ruled by a regency. Once the king reached his majority in 1303, a power struggle broke out between Birger and his brothers, Dukes Erik and Valdemar. Sweden was divided between the brothers until in 1317 Birger invited Erik and Valdemar to a banquet at Nyköping Castle and had them both imprisoned and left to die. Soon, Birger himself was forced to flee the country after a revolt and Magnus Eriksson, the three year-old son of Duke Erik, was elected king of Sweden in 1319.

Magnus's rule was characterized by severe domestic opposition and financial problems. Sweden also suffered the Black Death in 1350 in which one-third of the population died. The crisis led to the Swedish nobles in 1363 appealing to the Duke of Mecklenburg, whose son Albrecht was hailed king of Sweden the following year.

THE KALMAR UNION

Albrecht of Mecklenburg came to the throne with the support of the nobility, who reacted with a revolt when he subsequently sought to wield his own power. The nobles were backed by Queen Margareta of Denmark-Norway and Albrecht was defeated at

Beheading of 100 members of the Swedish nobility in the Stockholm Bloodbath, 1520

Fallköping in 1389, after which Denmark, Norway and Sweden came under the rule of Denmark. At a meeting in Kalmar in 1397, Margareta's nephew, Erik of Pomerania, was crowned king of Denmark, Norway and Sweden, thus establishing the Kalmar Union, which lasted until 1523.

The unification period was characterized by conflict in Sweden. Under Erik of Pomerania there was great dissatisfaction with newly-introduced taxes. A peasant revolt, known as the Engelbrekt revolt after its legendary leader, led to Erik being deposed in 1439. The Kalmar Union was unable to control the Council of State or the castles, and Sweden lacked a recognized supreme authority. Subsequent Danish kings were recognized as rulers in Sweden only for a few years and in between the country was controlled by representatives of the nobility.

At the Battle of Brunkeberg in Stockholm in 1471, the Danish King Christian I sought to enforce his power in Sweden, but was defeated by the viceroy, Sten Sture the Elder. A new Danish crusade under Christian II in 1520 culminated in the notorious Stockholm Bloodbath in which 100 Swedish nobles were executed.

1275 Magnus Ladulås elected king of Sweden at Mora Stones	1349–50 Black Death rampages through Sweden	1364 Albrecht of Mecklenburg elected king of Sweden		1434 Engelbrekt leads revolt over the taxes and burdens imposed by the Kalmar Union
1300		**1350**	**1400**	**1450**
1280 Ordinance of Alsnö grants freedom from taxation to the nobility	1350 Magnus Eriksson's law applies throughout the land, although cities have their own laws		1397 The Kalmar Union unites the Nordic countries under Queen Margareta	1471 Sten Sture the Elder defeats Danish King Christian I at Brunkeberg	1520 Swedish nobles executed in the Stockholm Bloodbath

Queen Margareta

Gustav Vasa making his ceremonial entry into Stockholm, Midsummer Day, 1523

THE VASA ERA

Among the nobles fortunate to avoid execution in the Stockholm Bloodbath was the young Gustav Eriksson. At the end of 1520 Gustav organized an army to oust the Danish King Christian from Sweden. Gustav was successful and on 6 June 1523 – later to become Sweden's National Day – he was named king. On Midsummer Day the new monarch, Gustav Vasa, made his ceremonial entry into war-torn Stockholm.

When Gustav Vasa took the throne, he discovered a nation in financial crisis. He called on parliament to pass a controversial law transferring the property of the church to the state, which then became the country's most important source of economic power. Another important result of this policy was the gradual separation from Catholicism and the adoption of the Lutheran State Church, which was to remain tied to the state until 2000.

During his reign, Gustav Vasa implemented tough economic policies in order to concentrate central power in Stockholm. This effective dictatorship also resulted in the Swedish parliament's decision in 1544 to make the monarchy hereditary.

Descendants of Gustav Vasa oversaw the rise of Sweden into one of Europe's great powers. During the reign of Gustav's eldest son Erik XIV (r. 1561–69), there were wars against Denmark, Lübeck and Poland. His brothers dethroned him. Erik died in prison, possibly by eating pea soup poisoned by his brother Johan III. During the reign of Karl IX, the third son, Sweden waged war against Denmark and Russia.

Portrait of Erik XIV (1561)

GUSTAV II ADOLF AND KRISTINA

When the next king, Gustav II Adolf, came to power in 1611, Sweden was involved in wars against Russia, Poland and Denmark. This reign came to be as remarkable as that of his grandfather and under his rule Sweden steadily increased its influence over the Baltic region. It was also in the 17th

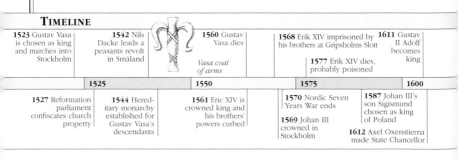

TIMELINE

1523 Gustav Vasa is chosen as king and marches into Stockholm	**1542** Nils Dacke leads a peasants revolt in Småland	*Vasa coat of arms*	**1560** Gustav Vasa dies	**1568** Erik XIV imprisoned by his brothers at Gripsholms Slott / **1577** Erik XIV dies, probably poisoned	**1611** Gustav II Adolf becomes king

1525	1550	1575	1600

1527 Reformation parliament confiscates church property	**1544** Hereditary monarchy established for Gustav Vasa's descendants	**1561** Eric XIV is crowned king and his brothers' powers curbed	**1570** Nordic Seven Years War ends / **1569** Johan III crowned in Stockholm	**1587** Johan III's son Sigismund chosen as king of Poland / **1612** Axel Oxenstierna made State Chancellor

century that Stockholm started to develop into the country's political and administrative centre. In 1630 Gustav II Adolf, with his influential chancellor Axel Oxenstierna, decided to intervene in the Thirty Years War *(see p36)*, first on the side of the Protestants, then in an alliance with France. Sweden had some military successes during the war, but paid a heavy price for winning the bloody battle at Lützen in 1632, as the king was killed in action.

Gustav II Adolf's only child, Kristina, came to the throne at the age of six. During her reign (1633–54), life at court was influenced by the world of science and philosophy. Kristina's reluctance to marry resulted in her cousin, Karl Gustav, becoming Crown Prince. Kristina abdicated and left for Rome, where she converted to Catholicism, a sensation at the time.

Young Karl XII with the widowed queen on his arm leaving the burning Tre Kronor Palace, 1697

Queen Kristina corresponding with leading scientists and philosophers of the time

THE CAROLIAN ERA

Karl X Gustav (1654–60) was the first of three Karls to reign. At the height of Sweden's era as a great power, he defeated Denmark by leading his army across the frozen waters of the Great Belt *(see p36)*, thus gaining Sweden's southernmost provinces. Karl XI (1660–97) secured the border and divided the land more evenly between crown, nobility and peasants.

While the body of Karl XI lay in state at Tre Kronor in 1697, a fire broke out which destroyed most of the building. The new monarch was the teenage Karl XII (1697–1718). He faced awesome problems when Denmark, Poland and Russia formed an alliance in 1700 with the aim of crushing the power of Sweden. Karl XII set off to battle.

Denmark and Poland were soon forced to plead for peace, but Russia was a harder nut to crack. A bold push towards Moscow was unsuccessful and the Swedish army suffered a devastating defeat at Poltava in Ukraine in 1709. This marked the beginning of the end of Sweden's Age of Greatness.

Karl XII, possibly the most written about and controversial Swedish monarch, returned to Sweden in 1715 after an absence of 15 years. His plans to regain Sweden's position of dominance never came to fruition and he was killed in Norway in 1718. Sweden was in crisis. Crop failures and epidemics had wiped out one third of the population and the state's finances were drained.

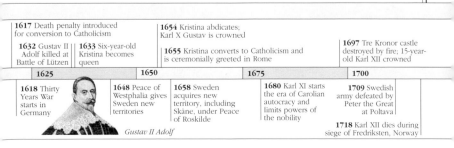

1625	1650	1675	1700

1617 Death penalty introduced for conversion to Catholicism

1632 Gustav II Adolf killed at Battle of Lützen

1633 Six-year-old Kristina becomes queen

1654 Kristina abdicates; Karl X Gustav is crowned

1655 Kristina converts to Catholicism and is ceremonially greeted in Rome

1697 Tre Kronor castle destroyed by fire; 15-year-old Karl XII crowned

1618 Thirty Years War starts in Germany

Gustav II Adolf

1648 Peace of Westphalia gives Sweden new territories

1658 Sweden acquires new territory, including Skåne, under Peace of Roskilde

1680 Karl XI starts the era of Carolian autocracy and limits powers of the nobility

1709 Swedish army defeated by Peter the Great at Poltava

1718 Karl XII dies during siege of Fredriksten, Norway

Sweden's Age of Greatness

FOR MORE THAN A CENTURY (1611–1721) Sweden was the dominant power in northern Europe, and the Baltic was effectively a Swedish inland sea. The country was at its most powerful after the Peace of Roskilde in 1658, when Sweden acquired seven new provinces. Outside today's frontiers, the Swedish Empire covered Finland, large parts of the Baltic states, and important areas of northern Germany. Over 111 years as a great power Sweden spent 72 of them at war, but the period also marked great cultural development and more efficient state administration. Treasures were brought back as trophies and grand palaces were built.

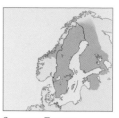

SWEDISH EMPIRE

☐ Sweden's empire after the Peace of Roskilde, 1658

The Tre Kronor Castle
Built as a defensive tower in the 1180s, the Tre Kronor castle was the seat of Swedish monarchs from the 1520s and became the administrative centre of the Swedish Empire. Named after the three crowns on the spire, it burned down in 1697.

The columns of troops
ride out over the shifting ice
towards Danish Lolland.

THE THIRTY YEARS WAR

A major European war raged from 1618–48, largely on German soil. Sweden entered the fray in 1630 and joined forces with France in 1631 against the Austrian Habsburgs. The Swedish army had been reorganized and rearmed by Gustav II Adolf and immediately had successes at the battles of Breitenfeld (1630) and Lützen (1632), where the king was killed in action.

Later the Swedes pressed into southern Germany and also captured Prague (1648). Rich cultural treasures were brought home from the war. In 1648 the Peace of Westphalia gave Sweden several important possessions in northern Germany.

The death of Gustav II Adolf at the Battle of Lützen in 1632

Stockholm in 1640
The city's transformation from a small medieval town into a capital city can be seen in the network of straight streets, similar to the present layout.

Karl XI's Triumphs
The ceiling painting in Karl XI's gallery at the Royal Palace (see p56) by the French artist Jacques Foucquet (1693) shows in allegoric form the king's victories at Halmstad, Lund and Landskrona.

Field Marshal Count Carl Gustav Wrangel *(see p127)*

Karl X Gustav himself leads the Swedish army of 17,000 men.

The Powerful Nobility
The nobility were very influential in the Empire era and many successful soldiers were ennobled. The Banér family coat of arms from 1651 is adorned by three helmets and barons' crowns.

Karl X Gustav
Portrait of Karl X Gustav (r. 1654–60) as a general. It was in this role that he became known throughout Europe during the final phase of the Thirty Years War.

CROSSING THE GREAT BELT
When Denmark declared war on Sweden in autumn 1657, the Swedish army was in Poland. Marching west, it captured the Danish mainland, but without the navy was unable to continue to Copenhagen. However, unusually severe weather froze the sea, making it possible for the soldiers to cross the ice of the Great Belt, and the Danes had to surrender.

Karl XII's Pocket Watch
The warrior king's watch-case dates from 1700. It shows the state coat of arms, as well as those of the 49 provinces that belonged to Sweden at that time.

Karl XII's Last Journey
After he was hit by a fatal bullet at Fredrikshald in Norway (1718), the king's body was taken first to Swedish territory then on to Uddevalla for embalming. Painting by Gustav Cederström (1878).

Gustav III with the white armband he wore when mounting his *coup d'etat* in 1772

THE AGE OF LIBERTY AND THE GUSTAVIAN ERA

A new constitution came into force in 1719 which transferred power from the monarch to parliament. As a result, Sweden developed a system of parliamentary democracy similar to that of Britain at the time.

The "Age of Liberty" coincided with the Enlightenment, with dramatic advances in culture, science and industry. The botanist Carl von Linné became one of the most famous Swedes of his time. Another was the scientist, philosopher and author Emanuel Swedenborg, who is thought to have influenced both Balzac and Baudelaire. The production of textiles expanded in Stockholm, and Sweden's first hospital was constructed on Kungsholmen.

Changes in the balance of power around 1770 gave the new king, Gustav III, an opportunity to strike in an attempt to regain his monarchical powers. On 19 August 1772 Gustav accompanied the guards' parade to the Royal Palace where, in front of his lifeguards, he declared his intention to mount a *coup d'etat*. The guards and other military units in Stockholm swore allegiance to the king, who tied a white handkerchief round his arm as a badge and rode out into the city to be acclaimed by his people. Absolute power had been restored.

Gustav III was influenced by the Age of Enlightenment and by French culture, which had a great effect on Swedish life *(see pp40–41)*. Over the years opposition grew to the king's powers, largely because of his costly war against Russia. In 1792 he was murdered by a nobleman during a masked ball at the Opera House.

Gustav III was succeeded by his son, Gustav IV Adolf. During his reign Sweden was dragged into the Napoleonic wars. After a war against Russia in 1808–9, Sweden lost Finland, which at the time accounted for one-third of Swedish territory. The king was deposed and went into exile.

THE ERA OF KARL JOHAN AND BOURGEOIS LIBERALISM

By the early 19th century the absolute powers of the monarch had been removed for all time, and the privileges

Napoleon's former marshal, Jean-Baptiste Bernadotte, as King Karl XIV Johan surrounded by his family

TIMELINE

1719 New constitution transfers power from the king to parliament	**1741** Carl von Linné appointed professor at Uppsala	**1754** Royal family moves into Royal Palace	**1780s** Immigrants given religious freedom		**1790** Sweden defeat Russia at the Battle of Svenskund **1792** Gustav III is murdered
1720	**1740**	**1760**		**1780**	**1800**
	1738 Parliamentary power is established in the Age of Liberty as the "Hat" party wins elections *Carl von Linné*		**1772** Gustav III crowned and mounts coup d'etat giving the king absolute power	**1786** Swedish Academy founded **1778** National costume decreed. Death penalty removed for some crimes	

Newspaper readers outside the *Aftonbladet* office in 1841

Denmark had to hand over Norway to Sweden. The Norwegians were reluctant to unite with Sweden, but after a display of military power in Norway, a union between the two countries was agreed which lasted from 1814 to 1905.

A long era of peace began, and with it came a dramatic increase in population, which grew by 1 million to 3.5 million by 1850. Many Swedes were driven into poverty because of the shortage of work. Mass emigration followed. From the 1850s to the 1930s about 1.5 million people left Sweden, mostly for North America.

of the aristocracy were undermined even more in 1809 with a new constitution that divided power between the king, the government and parliament.

With a new class structure and the effect of the French Revolution, a new middle class emerged which also wanted to be more influential. Altercations between middle-class liberals and the conservatives prevailed. One of the best-known newspapers founded at this time was the liberal mouthpiece, *Aftonbladet.*

Difficulties in finding a suitable new monarch led to the choice of one of Napoleon's marshals, Jean-Baptiste Bernadotte, who took on the Swedish name of Karl Johan. Founder of the present royal dynasty, Karl XIV Johan continued to speak French and never fully learned Swedish. His French wife, Desirée, found Stockholm a cultural backwater after Paris.

In 1813 a Swedish army, with Karl XIV Johan at its head, became involved in the final battle against Napoleon. The Battle of Leipzig ended in defeat for France, but more significantly for Sweden,

Swedes heading for a new life in North America

SOCIAL MOVEMENTS AND INDUSTRIALIZATION

As Sweden was transformed from an agricultural society into an industrialized country, the problems posed by the population surplus were gradually tackled. Its industrial revolution started around 1850, gathering momentum in the late 19th century, and the textile, timber and iron industries provided the main sources of employment. Here the early and fast development of a coherent railway network played an important role.

Social movements sprang up in the 19th century which still play an important role in Swedish life. One of the first was the temperance movement, which emerged from a background of alcohol abuse – in the 1820s annual consumption of spirits was 46 litres (80 pints) per person.

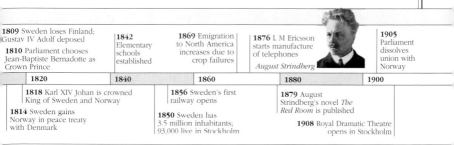

1809 Sweden loses Finland; Gustav IV Adolf deposed

1810 Parliament chooses Jean-Baptiste Bernadotte as Crown Prince

1842 Elementary schools established

1869 Emigration to North America increases due to crop failures

1876 L M Ericsson starts manufacture of telephones

August Strindberg

1905 Parliament dissolves union with Norway

1820	1840	1860	1880	1900

1818 Karl XIV Johan is crowned King of Sweden and Norway

1814 Sweden gains Norway in peace treaty with Denmark

1856 Sweden's first railway opens

1850 Sweden has 3.5 million inhabitants; 93,000 live in Stockholm

1879 August Strindberg's novel *The Red Room* is published

1908 Royal Dramatic Theatre opens in Stockholm

The Era of Gustav III

GUSTAV III (r. 1771–92) is one of the most colourful figures in Swedish history. The king's great interest in art, literature and the theatre made the late 18th century a golden age for Swedish culture, and several academies were founded at this time. After a bloodless revolution in 1772, Gustav III ruled with absolute power and initiated a wide-ranging programme of reform. But his attacks on the privileges of the nobility and his adventurous and costly foreign policy made him powerful enemies. In 1792 he was murdered during a masked ball at Stockholm's Opera House.

The Swedish Academy
The academy was founded by Gustav III in 1786 to preserve the Swedish language. Members received a token depicting the king's head at every meeting.

Gustav III's Coronation 1772
The coronation of the all-powerful monarch in Stockholm's cathedral was a magnificent ceremony, portrayed here by C G Pilo (1782). Every detail was overseen by Gustav himself, who used his flair for the dramatic in politics as well.

A courtier entertains by reading aloud.

Gustav III studies architectural designs.

The Battle of Svensksund
Gustav III was not known as a successful warrior king, but in 1790 he led the Swedish fleet to its greatest victory ever, when it defeated Russia in a major maritime battle in the Gulf of Finland.

COURT LIFE AT DROTTNINGHOLM
Hilleström's painting (1779) gives an insight into court life at Drottningholm, where the king resided between June and November. In what is now the Blue Salon, Gustav III and Queen Sofia Magdalena socialized with their inner circle. Behaviour was modelled on the French court and etiquette was even stricter at Drottningholm than at Versailles.

Life in the Inns
Stockholm abounded with inns, frequently visited by the city's 70,000 inhabitants. J T Sergel's sketch shows a convivial dinner party.

Murder at the Masked Ball

In 1792 Gustav III fell victim to a conspiracy at the Opera House. He was surrounded by masked men and shot by Captain Anckarström on the crowded stage. He died of his wounds 14 days later.

Gustav III's Mask and Cocked Hat

Despite his mask, Gustav III was easy to recognize since he was wearing the badges of two orders of chivalry. The drama intrigued the whole of Europe and inspired Verdi's opera Un Ballo in Maschera.

Flogging of the King's Murderer

Among the conspirators, only Anckarström was condemned to death. Before he was taken to his execution in Södermalm, he was flogged on three successive days on the square in front of Riddarhuset.

Queen Sofia Magdalena does her needlework.

Bust of Catherine the Great of Russia, the king's cousin

GUSTAVIAN STYLE

The mid-18th century saw the emergence of Neo-Classicism, with the focus on antiquities and Greek

ideals. Gustav III embraced this trend with great enthusiasm and supported the country's talented artists and authors. He established his own Museum of Antiquities *(see p57)* with marble sculptures which he brought home from Italy. In handicrafts, the sweeping lines of Rococo elegance were replaced by the stricter forms of what has become known as Gustavian Style. Rooms at the Royal Palace were renovated with decoration and furnishings adapted to suit this style.

Chair designed in Gustavian style

Swedish Court Costume

In 1778, Gustav III introduced a court costume, based on French lines, for daily wear at court, in order to restrain fashion excesses.

UNIVERSAL SUFFRAGE

Sweden's population reached 5 million around 1900, despite mass emigration to America. Many people moved to the towns to work in industry, and by the early 20th century Stockholm's population was about 300,000, a fourfold increase since the year 1800.

Increasing social awareness and the rise of the Social Democrat and Liberal parties in the early 20th century gave impetus to the demands for universal suffrage. Authors such as August Strindberg became involved. A political battle ensued which was not resolved until 1921, when universal suffrage was introduced for both sexes.

Another question which was hotly debated in the 19th century was the role of the king and the extent of his powers.

Branting and Gustav V in conversation, 1909

In his "courtyard speech" at the Royal Palace in 1914, King Gustav V called for military rearmament. This led to a constitutional crisis and the resignation of the Liberal government. After the 1917 election, the king had to accept a government which contained republican-friendly Social Democrats, including the future prime minister, Hjalmar Branting. By then it was parliament, not the king, that decided what sort of government Sweden should have.

THE GROWTH OF THE WELFARE STATE

In 1936 the Social Democrats and Farmers' Party formed a coalition which developed what was to become known as the welfare state. The Social Democrat prime minister, Per Albin Hansson (1885–1946), defined the welfare state as a socially conscious society with financial security for all. Reforms introduced under this policy included unemployment benefit, paid holidays and childcare. As a result, poverty in Sweden virtually disappeared during the 1930s and 1940s.

The right of everyone to good housing was also part of welfare state policy. Under the principle of "work-home-centre" a new Stockholm suburb, Vällingby, was built in the early 1950s. The idea was to transform the dormitory suburbs into thriving communities where people would both live and work. The concept was unsuccessful. It soon became apparent that the people who lived there still worked somewhere else, and vice versa. The great shortage of housing in the 1960s led to the "million" programme, which involved the building of a million homes in a very short time. These areas soon became known as the "new slums" despite high standards of construction.

Calls for democratic reforms in June 1917 led to riots like this one outside the parliament building in Stockholm

TIMELINE

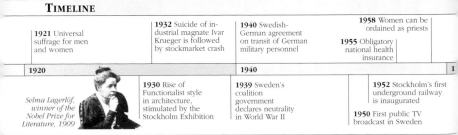

1921 Universal suffrage for men and women	**1932** Suicide of industrial magnate Ivar Krueger is followed by stockmarket crash	**1940** Swedish-German agreement on transit of German military personnel	**1958** Women can be ordained as priests
			1955 Obligatory national health insurance

1920		1940	

Selma Lagerlöf, winner of the Nobel Prize for Literature, 1909

1930 Rise of Functionalist style in architecture, stimulated by the Stockholm Exhibition	**1939** Sweden's coalition government declares neutrality in World War II	**1952** Stockholm's first underground railway is inaugurated
		1950 First public TV broadcast in Sweden

THE WAR YEARS

Sweden declared its neutrality during both World Wars I and II. Its policy of continuing to trade with nations involved in the conflict during World War I provoked a number of countries into imposing a trade blockade on Sweden. The situation became so serious that hunger riots broke out in some towns.

World War II proved an even more difficult balancing exercise for Swedish neutrality, largely because its Nordic neighbours were at war. Through a combination of luck and skill, Sweden remained outside the conflict, but the concessions it had to make were strongly criticized both nationally and internationally

Neutrality stamp issued in 1942

THE POST-WAR ERA

Although the Social Democrats dominated government from the 1930s to the 1970s, the socialist and non-socialist power blocs in Swedish politics have remained fairly evenly matched since World War II.

The policy of non-alignment has not proved an obstacle to Swedish involvement on the international scene, including the United Nations. The country has offered asylum to hundreds of thousands of refugees from wars and political oppression. Prime Minister Olof Palme (1927–86), probably the best-known Swedish politician abroad, was deeply involved in questions of democracy and disarmament, as well as the problems of the Third World. He was renowned for condemning undemocratic acts by right-wing and left-wing dictators. Palme's assassination on the streets of Stockholm in 1986 sent shock waves across the world. The murder has still not been solved.

Important changes took place during the closing decades of the 20th century. These included a new constitution in 1974 which removed the monarch's political powers. In 1995 Sweden joined the European Union after a referendum approved entry by a narrow majority. The start of the new millennium marked a change in the role of the church in Sweden, which severed its connections with the state after more than 400 years.

Sveavägen, the site of Palme's murder, 1986

As Sweden enters the third millennium, the country shows signs of economic downturn, even though most people still lead a good, socially secure life. Rapid technical developments and globalization have given Sweden new job opportunities and new inhabitants, as well as a leading international role in information technology.

The centre of Vällingby, which attracted attention among city planners worldwide in the 1950s

1967 Driving on the right introduced	**1980** New constitution gives women the right of succession to the throne	**2000** Öresund Bridge opens between Denmark and Sweden	**2003** Foreign Minister Anna Lindh murdered in Stockholm
1974 The monarch loses all political powers		**1986** Prime Minister Olof Palme murdered in Stockholm	

1980		2000

1964 Art exhibition at Moderna Museet shows works by Andy Warhol, Roy Lichtenstein and Claes Oldenburg	**1974** ABBA pop group wins Eurovision Song Contest	**1995** Sweden joins European Union	**2000** Swedish church separates from the state
	1973 Gustav VI Adolf dies and is succeeded by his grandson, Carl XVI Gustaf	*Crown Princess Victoria*	

STOCKHOLM
AREA BY AREA

STOCKHOLM AT A GLANCE 46-47
GAMLA STAN 48-61
CITY 62-71
BLASIEHOLMEN & SKEPPSHOLMEN 72-81
MALMARNA & FURTHER AFIELD 82-111
STOCKHOLM STREET FINDER 112-117

Stockholm at a Glance

STOCKHOLM HAS around 100 museums covering every conceivable subject, as well as buildings of historic and architectural interest, such as Stadhuset (City Hall). The museum collections range from the treasures and antiquities of Kungliga Slottet (the Royal Palace) to the latest in contemporary art at Moderna Museet and the spectacular *Vasa* warship at Vasamuseet. Open spaces abound, and it is even possible to swim in the heart of the city.

Hallwylska Palatset
Thanks to a methodical countess and her impeccable taste this lavishly decorated 1890s' palace has become a magnificent museum with 67,000 exhibit displayed in their original setting.

VASASTADEN

CITY

Stadshuset
This stunning building opened in 1923 is the seat of the capital's government and a symbol of Stockholm. It is also the venue for the annual Nobel Prize festivities.

KUNGS-
HOLMEN

0 metres   500

0 yards   500

GAML
STAN

Swimming in the City
During the summer, swimmers bathe in the clean, warm water (about 20 °C/68 °F) in the city centre. Långholmen (see p102) has sandy beaches and smooth rocks – an ideal setting for a dip.

Kungliga Slottet
In addition to its own attractions, the Royal Palace has four specialist museums: the Treasury, featuring Erik XIV's orb (1561), the Royal Armoury, Gustav III's Museum of Antiquities, and Tre Kronor Museum.

Nordiska Museet

This enormous building, opened in 1907, houses many different artifacts illustrating Swedish life and customs, including this coat of Count Axel von Fersen (1780s).

Nationalmuseum

The National Museum of Fine Arts, Sweden's largest art gallery, has superb collections of 17th- and 18th-century Swedish paintings, as well as handicrafts, 18th-century French and 17th-century Dutch art. Rubens's *Bacchanal on Andros* dates from the 1630s.

Skansen

The world's first open-air museum, founded in 1891, shows the Sweden of bygone days with farms and manor houses, urban scenes and craftspeople at work. Nordic fauna and flora are also on display.

ÖSTERMALM

DJURGÅRDEN

SKEPPS
HOLMEN

Moderna Museet

Paradise (1966) by Tinguely/de Saint Phalle marks the way to Moderna Museet, which houses remarkable collections of international and Swedish modern art.

ODER-
MALM

Vasamuseet

A fatal capsizal in 1628 and a successful salvage operation 333 years later gave Stockholm its most popular museum. The warship Vasa *is 95 per cent intact after painstaking renovation.*

GAMLA STAN

RELICS OF STOCKHOLM's early history as a town in the 13th century can still be found on Stadsholmen, the largest island in Gamla Stan (Old Town). The island is a huge area of historical heritage, with the many sights just a few metres apart.

The Royal Palace is the symbol of Sweden's era as a great power in the 17th and early 18th centuries *(see pp36–7)*, and its magnificent state rooms, apartments and artifacts are well matched to the Roman Baroque-style exterior. The historic buildings standing majestically

Anchor point on a palace façade

around Slottsbacken underline Stockholm's role as a capital city.

This area has a special atmosphere with much to offer: from the bustling streets of souvenir shops, bookstores and antique shops to elegant palaces, churches and museums. Many medieval cellars are now restaurants and cafés, while the narrow cobbled streets recall a bygone era.

Bridges lead to Riddarholmen, with its 17th-century palaces and royal crypt, and to Helgeandsholmen for the newer splendours of Riksdagshuset (the Parliament building).

SIGHTS AT A GLANCE

Palaces and Museums
Kungliga
  Myntkabinettet ❸
Livrustkammaren ❷
Medeltidsmuseet ⓰
Postmuseum ❿
*The Royal Palace
(Kungliga Slottet)
pp54–7* ❶

Public Buildings
Riddarhuset ⓮
Riksdagshuset ⓯

Historic Buildings
Tessinska Palatset ❹
Wrangelska Palatset ⓬

Streets and Squares
Evert Taubes Terrass ⓭
Mårten Trotzigs Gränd ❽
Stortorget ❻
Västerlånggatan ❾

Churches
Riddarholms-
  kyrkan ⓫
Storkyrkan ❺
Tyska Kyrkan ❼

KEY

▦	Street-by-Street map *See pp50–51*
⛴	Ferry landing point
Ⓣ	Tunnelbana station
🚌	Bus stop
Ⓟ	Parking

0 metres   250
0 yards   250

◁ **Prästgatan in Gamla Stan, with its yellow ochre plastering typical of the 18th century**

Street-by-Street: Slottsbacken

SLOTTSBACKEN IS MUCH MORE than just a steep hill linking Skeppsbron and the highest part of Gamla Stan (Old Town). It also provides the background for ceremonial processions and the daily changing-of-the-guard, and is the route for visiting heads of state and foreign ambassadors when they have an audience with the king at the Royal Palace. Alongside Slottsbacken the palace displays its most attractive façade, with the entrance to the Treasury (Skattkammaren), State Room (Rikssalen) and Palace Church (Slottskyrkan). Architect Nicodemus Tessin the Younger's ambition to make Stockholm a leading European city in architectural terms was realized in 1799 with the addition of the Obelisk.

The Olaus Petri statue by Storkyrkan stands in front of a tablet telling the cathedral's history since 1264.

Axel Oxenstiernas Palats (1653) is, for Stockholm, an unusual example of the style known as Roman Mannerism. For 30 years, Axel Oxenstierna (1583–1654) himself was a dominant figure in Swedish politics *(see p35)*.

Outer Courtyard

TRÅNGSUND

★ **Storkyrkan**
An impressive cathedral with a late Gothic interior, it is full of treasures from many different eras ❺

The Obelisk by Louis Jean Desprez was erected in 1799 to thank the citizens for supporting Gustav III's Russian war in 1788–90.

Stock Exchange
(see p54)

STOR–TORGET

STAR SIGHTS

★ Storkyrkan

★ Livrustkammaren

★ The Royal Palace

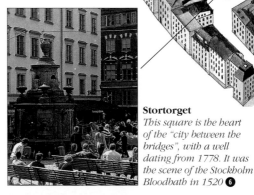

Stortorget
This square is the heart of the "city between the bridges", with a well dating from 1778. It was the scene of the Stockholm Bloodbath in 1520 ❻

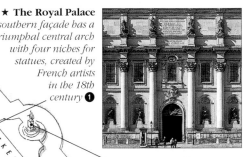

★ **Livrustkammaren**
Sweden's oldest museum displays royal weaponry, clothing and carriages from over five centuries. The picture shows Gustav II Adolf's stallion Streiff, from the battle of Lützen in 1632 ❷

LOCATOR MAP
See Street Finder map 3

Kungs-trädgården

★ **The Royal Palace**
The southern façade has a triumphal central arch with four niches for statues, created by French artists in the 18th century ❶

SKEPPSBRON

SLOTTSBACKEN

ÖSTERLÅNGGATAN

Gustav III's statue was sculpted by J T Sergel in 1799 in memory of the "gallant king" who was murdered in 1792.

↓ Slussen

KÖPMANGATAN

Köpmantorget with statue of St George Slaying the Dragon (1912).

Kungliga Myntkabinettet
In a 16th-century setting, the Royal Coin Cabinet has the world's largest stamped coin, from 1644 ❸

Finska Kyrkan, Slottsbacken's oldest building, dates from the 1640s. Originally a royal ballgames court for the palace, since 1725 it has been the religious centre for the Finnish community.

Tessinska Palatset
Built by and for Nicodemus Tessin the Younger, architect of the Royal Palace, in 1694–7, this palace has been the residence of the Governor of Stockholm County since 1968 ❹

| 0 metres | 100 |
| 0 yards | 100 |

KEY

– – – Suggested route

The Royal Palace ❶

See pp54–7.

Livrust-
kammaren ❷

Slottsbacken 3. **Map** 3 C2.
📞 08-519 555 44. 🚇 Gamla Stan.
🚌 2, 43, 55, 76. ⏰ Jun–Aug:
10am–5pm daily; Sep–May: 11am–
5pm Tue–Sun (Thu also 5–8pm).
🎧 📷 🚫 ♿ 🛍
🌐 www.livrustkammaren.se

SWEDEN'S OLDEST museum, Livrustkammaren (the Royal Armoury) was founded in 1633 and is full of *objets d'art* and everyday items used by the Royal Family over the past five centuries. The oldest exhibit is Gustav Vasa's crested helmet dating from 1548. The museum also houses a variety of royal items which illustrate events in Swedish history. Among them are Gustav II Adolf's stuffed stallion, Streiff, which he rode at the Battle of Lützen in 1632; Gustav III's costume from the notorious masked ball at which he was murdered in 1792; and Karl XII's blue uniform with the still muddy boots he was wearing when he died at the siege of Fredrikshald in Norway in 1718.

Coronation ceremonies are illustrated by costumes such as those worn by King Adolf Fredrik and Queen Lovisa Ulrika in 1751. The king's attire alone was adorned with some 2 kg (4 lb) of silver. The coronation carriage, originally

Sweden's first coin, struck in about AD 995

The coronation carriage of King Adolf Fredrik and Queen Lovisa Ulrika in Livrustkammaren

built in the 17th century, was modernized for this event. Its renovation in the 1970s took eight years and cost 700,000 kronor. The cellar vault, once used for firewood, is skilfully lit, providing an imaginative setting for the exhibits.

Kungliga Myntkabinettet ❸

Slottsbacken 6. **Map** 3 C3.
📞 08-519 553 00. 🚇 Gamla Stan.
🚌 2, 43, 55, 76. ⏰ 10am– 4pm
daily. 📷 by appointment. ♿
♿ 🍴 🛍 🏧
🌐 www.myntkabinettet.se

THE ROYAL COIN CABINET is a museum highlighting the history of money from the 10th century to the present day – from the little cowrie shell via the drachma and denarius to the current cash card. The museum also gives an insight into the art of medal design over the past 600 years and shows both traditional portrait medals and modern examples such as those that have been awarded to Nobel laureates. Visitors can also see the first Swedish coin, struck in the late 10th century by King Olof Skötkonung. Other rarities include Queen Kristina's coin from 1644, weighing 19.7 kg (43 lb) and reckoned to be the world's heaviest coin. From the island of Yap in Micronesia the museum has acquired the world's largest means of payment, a so-called "rai-stone" which greets visitors in the foyer.

The many sections in the museum include "The World's Money", "State Finance" and "Saving in a Piggy Bank and Bank". "Summa Summarum" is a section designed for children and illustrates the use of money in play and real life.

The elegant Baroque garden in Tessinska Palatset's courtyard

Tessinska Palatset ❹

Slottsbacken 4. **Map** 3 C3.
🚇 Gamla Stan. 🚌 2, 43, 55, 76.
⬤ to the public.

THE TESSIN PALACE at Slottsbacken is considered to be the most beautiful private residence north of Paris. It is the best-preserved palace from Sweden's era as a great power in the 17th century and was designed by and for Tessin the Younger (1654–1728), the nation's most renowned architect (see p24).

Completed in 1697, the building is located on a narrow site which widens out towards a courtyard with a delightful Baroque garden. The relatively discreet façade with its beautiful porch was inspired by the exterior design of Roman palaces. The decor and garden were influenced by Tessin's time in Paris and Versailles.

Tessin, who became a count and state councillor, spent large sums on the building's ornamentation. Sculptures and paintings were provided by the same French masters whose work had graced the Royal Palace. Later, however, his son, Carl Gustaf, had to sell the palace for financial reasons.

The building was acquired by the City of Stockholm as a residence for its governor in 1773. In 1968 it became the residence of the governor of the County of Stockholm.

Storkyrkan 5

Trångsund 1. **Map** 3 B3. 08-723
30 16. Gamla Stan. 7, 43, 55,
76. May–Aug: 9am–6pm daily;
Sep–Apr: 9am–4pm daily. 11am
Sat & Sun. Eng: Jul–Aug: 11am Fri.
Eng: Jul–Aug: 1pm, 4pm Mon–Fri, 2pm
Sat, noon Sun.

STOCKHOLM'S 700-year-old cathedral is of great national religious importance. It was from here that the Swedish reformer Olaus Petri (1493–1552) spread his Lutheran message around the kingdom. It is also used for royal ceremonies.

Originally, a small village church was built on this site in the 13th century, probably by the city's founder Birger Jarl. It was replaced in 1306 by a much bigger basilica, St Nicholas, which was altered over the centuries.

The Gothic character of the interior, acquired in the 15th century, was revealed in 1908 when, during restoration work, plaster was removed from the pillars, exposing the characteristic red tiling. The late Baroque period provided the so-called "royal chairs" and the pulpit, while the façade was adapted to bring it into keeping with the rest of the area around the Royal Palace. The 66-m (216-ft) high

Storkyrkan's façade in Italian Baroque style, seen from Slottsbacken

tower, added in 1743, has four bells, the largest of which weighs about 6 tons.

The cathedral houses some priceless artistic treasures, including *St George and the Dragon*, regarded as one of the finest late Gothic works of art in Northern Europe. The sculpture, situated to the left of the altar, was carved from oak and elk horn by Lübeck sculptor Bernt Notke. Unveiled in 1489, it commemorates Sten Sture the Elder's victory over the Danes in 1471 (*see p33*).

The Last Judgment (1696) is a massive Baroque painting by David Klocker von Ehrenstrahl. The 3.7-m (12-ft) high bronze candelabra before the altar, likely to be German, has adorned the cathedral for some 600 years. One of

the cathedral's most prized treasures is the silver altar, which gave the interior a completely new appearance in the 1650s. It was a gift from the diplomat Johan Adler Salvius.

The pews nearest to the chancel, the "royal chairs", were designed by Nicodemus Tessin the Younger in 1684 to be used by royalty on special occasions. In 1705, the pulpit was installed

Storkyrkan's silver altar (detail)

above the grave of Olaus Petri.

On 20 April 1535, a light phenomenon was observed over Stockholm – six rings with sparkling solar halos. *The Parhelion Painting*, recalling the event, hangs in Storkyrkan and is thought to be the oldest portrayal of the capital. It shows the modest skyline dominated by the cathedral, at that time still the basilica of St Nicholas.

The sculpture *St George and the Dragon* by Bernt Notke (1489) in Storkyrkan

The Royal Palace (Kungliga Slottet) ❶

Royal sceptre

DEFENSIVE INSTALLATIONS or castles have stood on the island of Stadsholmen ever since the 11th century. The Tre Kronor (Three Crowns) fortress was completed in the mid-13th century, but became a royal residence only during the following century. The Vasa kings turned the fortress into a Renaissance palace which burned to the ground in 1697. In its place the architect Nicodemus Tessin the Younger created a new palace in Baroque style with an Italianate exterior and a French interior toned down to suit Swedish tastes. The palace's 608 rooms were decorated by Europe's foremost artists and craftsmen. Adolf Fredrik was the first king to move into the palace, in 1754. It is no longer the king's private residence, but remains one of the city's leading sights.

★ Changing the Guard
Stockholm's most popular tourist event is the daily changing of the guard at midday in the Outer Courtyard.

Entrance to the State Apartments

The Western Staircase
Tessin was especially proud of the two staircases, made from Swedish marble and porphyry. On the western staircase stands a bust of the gifted architect.

★ The Hall of State
This opulent hall has an atmosphere of ceremonial splendour and forms an ideal setting for Queen Kristina's silver throne, probably the palace's most famous treasure.

The Guest Apartments

Entrance to Treasury and Royal Chapel

A ROYAL WORKPLACE

The king and queen have their offices at the palace, where they hold audiences with visiting dignitaries, and official ceremonies. They travel around the country attending special events, official openings and anniversaries, and they make regular State visits abroad. The king is well known for his interest in the environment while the queen is heavily involved with her work for children, especially the disabled.

King Carl XVI Gustaf and Queen Silvia

The Royal Chapel
This delightful little church has a rich interior decorated by many different artists. The pulpit is the work of J P Bouchardon.

STAR FEATURES

★ Karl XI's Gallery

★ The Hall of State

★ Changing the Guard

Gustav III's State Bedchamber
Sergel's bust of Gustav III (1779) stands in the room where the king died after being shot at the Opera House. The 1770s decor is by J E Rehn.

VISITORS' CHECKLIST

Gamla Stan. **Map** 3 B2
☎ 08-402 61 30. **Ⓣ** *Gamla Stan, Kungsträdgården.* 🚌 *2, 43, 55, 76.* **The Royal Apartments, The Treasury, Gustav III's Museum of Antiquities, Tre Kronor Museum** ☐ *May–Aug: 10am–4pm daily; Sep–Apr: noon–3pm Tue–Sun.* ● *during official functions of the Court.* 🎫 *for tours in English, call 402 61 30 for details.* 🎒 ⬛ 🅿 👟 **The Royal Chapel** ☐ *mid-Jun–mid-Aug: noon–3pm Wed & Fri; Mass 11am Sun.* ✝ *May–Aug: 11am Sun.* 🅿 👟 Ⓦ *www.royalcourt.se*

The Bernadotte Apartments are situated on the floor below Karl XI's Gallery.

Tre Kronor Museum entrance from Lejonbacken (see p57).

★ Karl XI's Gallery
One of the most magnificent rooms in the palace, this fine example of Swedish Late Baroque is used for banquets hosted by the king and queen. In the cabinet is this priceless salt-cellar dating from 1627–8.

Carl Hårleman played an important role in the design of the palace. His bust adorns this niche.

Logården is the terrace between the palace's east wings.

Livrustkammaren (see p52)

Gustav III's Museum of Antiquities
The museum's collection includes antique statues brought home by Gustav III from his journey to Rome.

Exploring the Royal Palace

THE PUBLIC AREAS of the Royal Palace allow visitors to walk through grand rooms of sumptuous furnishings and priceless works of art and craftsmanship. The Hall of State and the Royal Chapel are both characterized by their magnificent lavish decor and Gustav III's Museum of Antiquities contains ancient marble sculptures from the king's journey to Italy. The palace also houses the Treasury with the State regalia; the new Tre Kronor Museum, which depicts the palace before the 1697 fire; and the Livrustkammaren *(see p52)*.

The Pillar Hall in the Bernadotte Apartments with original decor

Karl XI's Gallery, the finest example of the Late Baroque period in Sweden

THE STATE APARTMENTS

THE ROYAL FAMILY has lived at Drottningholm Palace *(see pp106–9)* since 1982, but official functions still take place in the State Apartments, including banquets hosted by the king during visits by foreign heads of state. Other official dinners are held here, as well as the annual festivities in December to honour the Nobel laureates.

The dinners are served in Karl XI's Gallery, the finest example of Swedish Late Baroque, modelled on the Hall of Mirrors at Versailles. Each window is matched with a niche on the inner wall where some of the palace's priceless works of arts and crafts are exhibited. Most remarkable is the salt-cellar made from ivory and gilded silver designed by the Flemish painter Rubens (1577–1640). The room known as "The

King Karl XIV Johan's egg cup

White Sea" serves as a drawing room. Gustav III's State Bedchamber, where the king died after being shot at the Opera House in 1792 *(see pp40–41)*, is the height of Gustavian elegance. Along with Queen Sofia Magdalena's State Bedchamber, it was designed by the architect Jean Eric Rehn. The lintels on the doors to the Don Quixote Room, named after the theme of its tapestries, were made by François Boucher and are among the most treasured pieces.

THE GUEST APARTMENTS

AN IMPOSING part of the palace, these apartments are where visiting heads of state stay. The beautiful rooms include the Meleager Salon, where official gifts and decorations are exchanged, and a large bedroom with a sculpted and gilded bed. Other impressive rooms are the Inner Salon, whose decor was inspired by the excavations in Pompeii, and the Margareta Room, named after the present king's grandmother, which displays pictures painted by her.

The apartments contain remarkable works of craftsmanship by such 18th-century masters as Georg Haupt, Ephraim Ståhle and Jean-Baptiste Masreliez.

THE BERNADOTTE APARTMENTS

THIS MAGNIFICENT suite has earned its name from the gallery displaying portraits of the Bernadotte dynasty. The apartments have some notable ceiling paintings and mid-18th-century chandeliers, and are used for many a ceremonial occasion. The elegant Pillar Hall is the venue for investitures, and the East Octagonal Cabinet with probably the palace's best Rococo decor, is where the king receives foreign ambassadors. Along with the western cabinet, its interior has remained just as it was planned by Carl Hårleman more than 250 years ago.

Oscar II's very masculine Writing Room, dating from the 1870s, also looks much as it did in his day. However, the palace was kept up to date with the latest technical advances: electricity was installed in 1883, and the telephone only one year later.

THE HALL OF STATE

ROCOCO AND Classicism were brought together in perfect harmony by the architects Nicodemus Tessin the Younger and Carl Hårleman when they designed the two-storey Hall of State.

The Hall provides a worthy framework for Queen Kristina's silver throne, a gift for the coronation in 1650 and one of the most valuable treasures in the palace. The throne was given to the queen by Magnus Gabriel de la Gardie and was made in Augsburg by the goldsmith

Abraham Drentwett. The canopy was added 100 years later for the coronation of King Adolf Fredrik and was designed by Jean Eric Rehn.

The room is lavishly decorated. The throne is flanked by colossal sculptures of Karl XIV Johan and Gustav II Adolf, while those on the cornice symbolize Peace, Strength, Religion and Justice.

Until 1975 the Hall of State was the scene of the ceremonial opening of the Swedish Parliament (Riksdagen), which included a march past of the royal bodyguard in full regalia. It is now used for official occasions and, like the Royal Chapel, is a venue for summer concerts.

The Hall of State, the most important ceremonial room in the palace

THE ROYAL CHAPEL

It took 50 years to build the Royal Palace, and a lot of effort went into the interior decoration of the Royal Chapel. The work was carried out largely by Carl Hårleman under the supervision of Tessin. As with the Hall of State, the co-operation between the two produced a magnificent result, enhanced by the contributions of several foreign artists.

A number of remarkable artifacts have been added over the centuries. The most recent was a group of six 17th-century-style bronze crowns, as well as two crystal crowns, given by the Court to King Carl XVI Gustaf and Queen Silvia to mark their marriage in 1976.

It also has some rare relics of the original Tre Kronor

fortress: new benches that had been ordered by Tessin. They had been rescued during the palace fire in 1697 and preserved, but not put in the chapel until the 19th century. The benches were made by Georg Haupt, grandfather of the Georg Haupt who was to create some of the palace's most prized furnishings *(see p80)*.

GUSTAV III'S MUSEUM OF ANTIQUITIES

Opened in 1794 in memory of the murdered king, the Museum of Antiquities initially housed more than 200 exhibits, mainly acquired during Gustav's Italian journey in 1783–4 and then supplemented with more purchases at a later date.

In 1866 the museum's collection was moved to the city's National Museum *(see pp80–81)*. During the 1950s the main gallery was renovated, followed by the smaller galleries 30 years later, which enabled the collection to be returned to its original setting.

The most prized exhibits are in the main gallery, the best known being the sculpture of Endymion, the eternally sleeping young shepherd and lover of the Moon Goddess Selene. The 18th-century sculptor Johan Tobias Sergel is represented by *The Priestess*, ranked as the collection's second most important piece. She is flanked by two large candelabras.

THE TREASURY

At the bottom of 56 well-worn steps, below the Hall of State on the south side of the palace, is the entrance to the Treasury (Skattkammaren) where the State regalia, the most potent symbols of the monarchy, are kept. Occasionally, for an important event, King Erik XIV's crown, sceptre, orb and the keys of the kingdom are taken out of their showcase and placed beside the uncrowned King

Erik XIV's crown, made by Cornelis ver Weiden in Stockholm in 1561

Carl XVI Gustaf. The 1-m (3-ft) high silver baptismal font, which took the French silversmith Jean François Cousinet 11 years to make, is over 200 years old and is still used for royal baptisms. Hanging in the Treasury is the only undamaged tapestry among six dating from the 1560s, salvaged from the 1697 fire.

TRE KRONOR MUSEUM

The newest attraction at the Royal Palace is the Tre Kronor (Three Crowns) Museum, which is housed in the oldest parts of the ruined Tre Kronor fortress, preserved under the north side of the palace. About half of a massive 12th-century defensive wall and brick vaults from the 16th and 17th centuries provide a dramatic setting for the museum which illustrates the palace's history over almost 1,000 years.

Two models of the Tre Kronor fortress show changes made during the second half of the 17th century and how it looked by the time of the fire. Among items rescued from the ashes are a schnapps glass, amber pots and bowls made from mountain crystal.

A glass bowl in the Tre Kronor Museum, saved from the 1697 fire

The imposing Stock Exchange on the north side of Stortorget

Stortorget **6**

Map 3 B3. **T** *Gamla Stan.* ▦ *2, 3, 43, 53, 55,, 76.* **Nobelmuseet** **C** *08-23 25 06.* ○ *mid-May–mid-Sep: 10am–5pm Wed–Mon, 10am–8pm Tue; mid-Sep–mid-May: 11am–5pm Wed–Sun, 11am–8pm Tue.* ▣ ▨ ▧ ▯ ▧ ㋯ *www.nobel.se/nobelmuseum*

IT WAS NOT until 1778, when the Stock Exchange (Börsen) was completed, that Stortorget ("the big square") in the heart of the Old Town, acquired a more uniform appearance. Its northern side had previously been taken up by several buildings that served as a town hall. Since the early Middle Ages the square had been a natural meeting point with a well and marketplace, lined with wooden stalls on market days.

A pillory belonging to the jail, which was once on nearby Kåkbrinken, used to stand on the square. It is now in the Town Hall on Kungsholmen. The medieval layout is clear on Stortorget's west side, where

the red Schantzska Huset (No. 20) and the narrow Seyfridtska Huset were built around 1650. The Schantzska Huset remains unchanged and has a lovely limestone porch adorned with figures of recumbent Roman warriors. The artist Johan Wendelstam was responsible for most of the notable porches in the Old Town. The 17th-century gable on Grilska Huset (No. 3) is also worth a closer study. Today there are cafés and restaurants in some of the vaulted cellars.

The decision to construct the Stock Exchange was taken in 1667, but the many wars delayed the start of the building by 100 years. The architect was the young and talented Erik Palmstedt (1741–1803), who also created the decorative cover for the old well. Trading on the floor of the Stock Exchange ceased in 1990. In 2001 the **Nobelmuseet** was opened here to mark the centenary of the Prize *(see p69).* The exhibition explores the work and ideas of more than

700 creative minds by means of short films and original artifacts. On the upper floor, the Swedish Academy holds its ceremonial gatherings, a tradition maintained since Gustav III gave his inauguration speech here in 1786.

Tyska Kyrkan **7**

Svartmangatan 16. **Map** 3 B3. **C** *08-411 11 88.* **T** *Gamla Stan.* ▦ *3, 43, 46, 53, 55, 59, 76.* ○ *May–Sep: noon–4pm daily; Oct–Apr: noon–4pm Sat & Sun.* ✝ *11am Sun, German.* ▣ *by arrangement in Swedish & German.* ♿

THE GERMAN CHURCH is an impressive reminder of the almost total influence that Germany had over Stockholm during the 18th century. The Hanseatic League trading organization was in control of the Baltic and its ports, which explains why the basic layout of Gamla Stan resembled that of Lübeck. Germany's political influence was only broken after the Stockholm Bloodbath and Gustav Vasa's accession to the throne in 1523 *(see p34),* but its cultural and mercantile influence remained strong as German merchants and craftsmen settled in the city.

The church's congregation, which today has some 2,000 members, was founded in 1571. The present twin-aisle church was built in 1638–42, as an extension of a smaller church which the parish had used since 1576.

In German Late Renaissance and Baroque style, the interior has a royal gallery, added in 1672 for German members of

THE STOCKHOLM BLOODBATH

Stortorget is intimately linked with the Stockholm Bloodbath of November 1520. The Danish king, Christian II, besieged the Swedish Regent, Sten Sture the Younger, until he capitulated and the Swedes chose Christian as their king. The Dane promised an amnesty and ordered a three-day feast at Tre Kronor Fortress. Near the end of the festivities, the revellers were suddenly shut in and arrested for heresy. The next day more than 80 noblemen and Stockholm citizens were beheaded in the square.

Detail of a painting of the Bloodbath (1524)

The royal gallery in the 17th-century Tyska Kyrkan

the royal household. The pulpit (1660) in ebony and alabaster is unique in Sweden and the altar, from the 1640s, is covered with beautiful paintings surrounded by sculptures of the apostles and evangelists.

The sculptures on the south porch by Jobst Hennen date from 1643 and show Jesus, Moses and three figures portraying Faith, Hope and Love.

Mårten Trotzigs Gränd, the narrowest street in the city

Mårten Trotzigs Gränd **8**

Map 3 C4. Ⓣ *Gamla Stan.*
🚌 *3, 43, 46, 53, 55, 59, 76.*

A T ONLY 90 CM (3 ft) wide, Mårten Trotzigs Gränd is the city's narrowest street. Climbing up the 36 steps gives a good impression of how the various parts of the Old Town differ in height and how tightly the houses are packed together.

Mårten Trotzigs Gränd is named after a German merchant called Traubzich who owned two houses here at the end of the 16th century. After being fenced off at both ends for 100 years, the street was reopened in 1945.

Västerlånggatan **9**

Map 3 B3. Ⓣ *Gamla Stan.* 🚌 *3, 43, 46, 53, 55, 59, 76.*

O NCE A MAIN ROAD outside the city proper, built along parts of the original town wall, Västerlånggatan now runs through the heart

of the Old Town, and is usually thronging with people – tourists and locals – shopping or strolling. Starting at Mynttorget in the north, by the Chancery Office (Kanslihuset) and Lejonbacken, the lively and atmospheric street finishes at Järntorget in the south, where the export of iron was once controlled. On Järntorget is Bancohuset, which served as the headquarters of the State Bank from 1680 to 1906.

The building at No. 7 has been used by the Swedish Parliament since the mid-1990s. Its late 19th-century façade has a distinctive southern European influence.

No. 27 was built by and for Erik Palmstedt, who also designed the Stock Exchange and the well at Stortorget. No. 29 is a truly venerable building, dating from the early 15th century. The original pointed Gothic arches were revealed during restoration in the 1940s.

No. 33 is a good example of how new materials and techniques in the late 19th century made it possible to fit large shop windows into old houses. The cast-iron columns which can be seen in many other places also date from this period.

No. 68, Von der Lindeska House, has a majestic 17th-century façade and a beautiful porch with sculptures of Neptune and Mercury.

Postmuseum **10**

Lilla Nygatan 6. **Map** 3 B3.
📞 *08-781 17 55* Ⓣ *Gamla Stan.*
🚌 *3, 53.* 🕐 *11am–4pm Tue–Sun, Sep–Apr also Wed 4pm–7pm.*
📷 *by arrangement.* ♿ 🍴 🎁
🖥 *www.posten.se/museum*

A N ATTRACTION in itself, the Postmuseum building takes up a whole area bought by the Swedish Post Office in 1720. About 100 years later

Västerlånggatan, Gamla Stan's most popular shopping street

the majestic-looking Post Office was built, incorporating parts of the 17th-century buildings already there. Stockholm's only Post Office until 1869, it was turned into the Postal Museum in 1906.

Letters have been sent in Sweden, in an organized way, since 1636, and the museum's permanent exhibits include a portrayal of early "peasant postmen" fighting the Åland Sea in their boat *Simpan*. Also on display is the first post bus which ran in northern Sweden in the early 1920s

Mauritian stamp in the Postmuseum

and a stagecoach used in eastern Sweden.

The collection includes Sweden's first stamp-printing press and no less than four million stamps among which are the first Swedish stamps, produced in 1855. Also on show is "Penny Black", the world's first stamp dating from 1840, and some stamps issued by Mauritius in 1847.

There is a philatelic library holding 51,000 volumes and stamp collections, as well as computers and multimedia equipment for research. A special exhibition for children is on display in the basement.

Riddarholms-kyrkan ⓫

Birger Jarls Torg. **Map** 3 A3. 08-402 61 30. Gamla Stan. 3, 53. May–Aug: 10am–4pm daily, Sep: noon–3pm Sat & Sun. Eng: 1pm.

THIS CHURCH ON the island of Riddarholmen is best known as a place for royal burials. Its interior is full of ornate sarcophagi and worn gravestones, and in front of the altar are the tombs of the medieval kings Karl Knutsson and Magnus Ladulås.

Built on the site of the late 13th-century Greyfriars abbey, founded by Magnus Ladulås, the majestic brick church was gradually enlarged over the centuries. After a serious fire in 1835, it acquired its present lattice-work cast-iron tower.

Inside, the church is surrounded by splendid burial vaults dating back to the 16th century. The coffins rest on a lower level with space for a memorial above. The most recent was built in 1858–60 for the Bernadotte dynasty.

The vaults contain the remains of all the Swedish monarchs from Gustav II Adolf in the 17th century to the present day with two exceptions: Queen Kristina was buried at St Peter's in Rome in 1689 and Gustav VI Adolf, who was interred at Haga in 1973 *(see p96)*. The most magnificent sarcophagus is that of the 19th-century king, Karl XIV Johan, which had to be towed here by sledge from his porphyry workshops in northern Sweden.

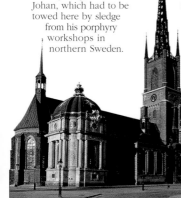

Riddarholmskyrkan and the external burial vault by Tessin and Hårleman

Wrangelska Palatset, a royal residence after the Tre Kronor fire of 1697

Particularly moving are the graves of royal children, including the many small tin coffins that surround the last resting place of Gustav II Adolf and his queen, Maria Eleonora.

Wrangelska Palatset ⓬

Birger Jarls Torg 16. **Map** 3 A3. Gamla Stan. 3, 53. to the public.

ONLY TWO PARTS of Gustav Vasa's fortifications from 1530 remain – Birger Jarl's Tower and the southernmost tower of what became the Wrangel Palace. Built as a residence for the nobleman Lars Sparre in 1652–70, it was remodelled a few decades later by Carl Gustaf Wrangel. A field marshal in the Thirty Years War, Wrangel chose Nicodemus Tessin the Elder as his architect. The result was Stockholm's largest privately-owned palace.

In 1697 the royal family moved into the palace after the Tre Kronor fortress *(see p54)* was ravaged by fire. It became known as the King's House, and it was here in the same year that the 15-year-old Karl XII took the oath of office after the death of his father. Gustav III was born here in 1746 and in 1792 his assassin was incarcerated in the dungeons. The Court of Appeal now uses this building, as well as Rosenhane Palace

(Birger Jarls Torg 10) and Hessenstein House (Birger Jarls Torg 2), built in 1630 by Bengt Bengtsson Oxenstierna.

Evert Taubes Terrass ⓭

Norra Riddarholmshamnen. **Map** 3 A3. Gamla Stan. 3, 53.

A STATUE OF Evert Taube, the much-loved troubadour and ballad writer, stands on the terrace below Wrangelska Palatset looking out over the waters of Riddarfjärden. In an ideal position, given the poet's close links to the sea, the bronze sculpture was created by Willy Gordon in 1990. Close by stands Christer Berg's granite sculpture *Solbåten* (Sun Boat), unveiled in 1966. Inspired by the shape of a shell, from some angles it also resembles a sail.

Evert Taube (1890–1976)

Riddarhuset ⓮

Riddarhustorget 10. **Map** 3 A3. 08-723 39 90. Gamla Stan. 3, 53. 11:30am–12:30pm Mon–Fri. by appointment. www.riddarhuset.se

OFTEN REGARDED as one of Stockholm's most beautiful buildings, Riddarhuset (House of Knights) stands on Riddarhustorget, the city's

centre until the 19th century. Built in 1641–7 on the initiative of the State Chancellor, Riddarhuset provided the knights with a base for meetings and events. The building is a supreme example of Dutch Baroque design by the architects Simon and Jean de la Vallée, Heinrich Wilhelm and Justus Vingboons.

Riddarhuset, built in the 17th century in imposing Dutch Baroque style

Over the entrance on the northern façade is the knights' motto *Arte et Marte* (Art and War) with Minerva, Goddess of Art and Science, and Mars, God of War.

The sculptures on the vaulted roof symbolize the knightly virtues. On the south side is *Nobilitas* (Nobility) holding a small Minerva and spear. She is flanked by *Studium* (Diligence) and *Valor* (Bravery). Facing the north is the male equivalent, *Honor*, flanked by *Prudentia* (Prudence) and *Fortitudo* (Strength).

Inside, a magnificent double staircase leads up to the Knights' Room. This has a painted ceiling by David Klöcker Ehrenstrahl (1628–98) and Riddarhuset's fore most treasure, a sculpted ebony chair, 1623. The walls are covered with coats of arms.

Riksdagshuset ⑮

Riksgatan 3 A. **Map** 3 B2. 08-786 40 00. ⓣ *Kungsträdgården.* 3, 43, 53, 62. *tours & meetings in the Chamber.* daily in summer; weekends in winter; ring for details. www.riksdagen.se

THE PARLIAMENT building (Riksdagshuset) and State Bank (Riksbank) on Helgeandsholmen were inaugurated in 1905 and 1906 respectively. In the 1970s and 1980s the

The new Parliament building, with the older building behind

two buildings were combined and restored and a modern extension built to house a new, single debating chamber. The chamber is truly Nordic in its decoration with benches of Swedish birch and wall-panelling in Finnish birch carved in Norway. A large tapestry, *Memory of a Landscape* (1983), by Elisabeth Hasselberg-Olsson, covers 54 sq m (581 sq ft) of wall and took 3,500 hours to make. Parliamentary debates can be watched from the public gallery.

The original two-chamber Parliament is used for meetings of the majority party. The former Upper House has three paintings by Otte Sköld (1894–1958); the other chamber contains works by Axel Törneman and Georg Pauli. Between the chambers is a 45-m (148-ft) long hall with an elegant display of coats of arms. The Finance Committee meets in the oak-panelled library surrounded by old prints and *Jugendstil* (Art Nouveau-style) lamps. Facing the Norrbro entrance is the original 1905 stairwell with columns, floor, steps and balusters in various marbles. The

present entrance was the State Bank's main hall until 1976 and contains paintings from the Parliamentary collection.

Medeltidsmuseet ⑯

Strömparterren, Norrbro. **Map** 3 B2. 08-508 317 90. ⓣ *Kungsträdgården.* 43, 62. *Jul & Aug: 11am–4pm Thu–Tue, 11am–6pm Wed; Sep–Jun: 11am–4pm Tue–Sun, (also 4–6pm Wed).* www.medeltidsmuseet.stockholm.se

Medieval stone head of Birger Jarl at Medeltidsmuseet

THIS FASCINATING museum of medieval Stockholm is built around some of the capital's archaeological remains, mainly parts of the city wall that date from the 1530s. They were discovered in 1978–80. Completely underground, the museum includes finds evoking Stockholm's early history. Among them is the 22-m (72-ft) long Riddarholm ship, dating from the 1520s, which was found off Riddarholmen in 1930.

The museum provides a good picture of Stockholm's early days. From the entrance, a 350-year-old tunnel leads into a reconstructed medieval world. There is a pillory in the square and gallows with the tools of the executioner's trade. The harbour has been recreated, with a quayside, jetties, boathouses and warehouses. As was the custom, a spruce wreath hangs outside the wine cellar to show that supplies of wine and beer have arrived from the Continent.

CITY

THE AREA KNOWN AS CITY today was where, in the mid-18th century, the first stone-built houses and palaces outside Gamla Stan started to appear for the burghers and nobility. After World War II, the run-down buildings around Hötorget were demolished to form what is now Sergels Torg; many homes were replaced by rather dreary office blocks.

In recent years, though, the area has livened up and become the true heart and commercial centre of Stock-

Street light near Kungliga Operan

holm. A hub for public transport and banking, City is the place for the best department stores and shopping malls, exclusive boutiques and nightspots. The centre also has some beautiful parks and pleasant squares which serve as popular meeting places. The unique landscape surrounding Stockholm permeates even City, offering sudden unexpected glimpses of water complete with bustling boat life and a string of anglers along the embankments.

SIGHTS AT A GLANCE

Museums
Armémuseum ⑭
Dansmuseet ⑤
Hallwylska Palatset ⑱
Medelhavsmuseet ⑥
Musikmuseet ⑮
Strindbergsmuseet
  Blå Tornet ⑪

Churches
Adolf Fredriks
  Kyrka ⑫
Jacobs Kyrka ③
Klara Kyrka ⑧

Squares
Kungsträdgården ②

Public Buildings
Arvfurstens Palats ⑦
Hovstallet ⑯
Kungliga Biblioteket ⑬
Nordiska Kompaniet ①

Theatres and Musical Stages
Konserthuset ⑩
Kulturhuset och
  Stadsteatern ⑨
Kungliga Dramatiska
  Teatern ⑰
Kungliga Operan ④

KEY

▢	Street-by-Street map See pp64–5
Ⓣ	Tunnelbana station
🚋	Tram stop
🚌	Bus stop
P	Parking

0 metres 500
0 yards 500

◁ **Sagerska Palatset, official residence of the prime minister, between Rosenbad (left) and Arvfurstens Palats**

Street-by-Street: Around Kungsträdgården

WITH A HISTORY GOING back to the 15th century, the King's Garden (Kungsträdgården) has long been the city's most popular meeting place and recreational centre. Both visitors and Stockholmers gather here for summer concerts and festivals, or just to enjoy a stroll under the lime trees. Around the park is a wealth of shops, including the upmarket department store Nordiska Kompaniet, boutiques, churches, museums and restaurants. A short walk takes you to Gustav Adolfs Torg, flanked by the Royal Opera House and other stately buildings, including the Swedish Foreign Office.

Dansmuseet
Anything connected with dance, such as costumes, stage-set sketches and posters for the famous Les Ballets Suédois, can be seen here ❺

★ Medelhavsmuseet
This museum near Gustav Adolfs Torg has vast collections from prehistoric cultures around the Mediterranean ❻

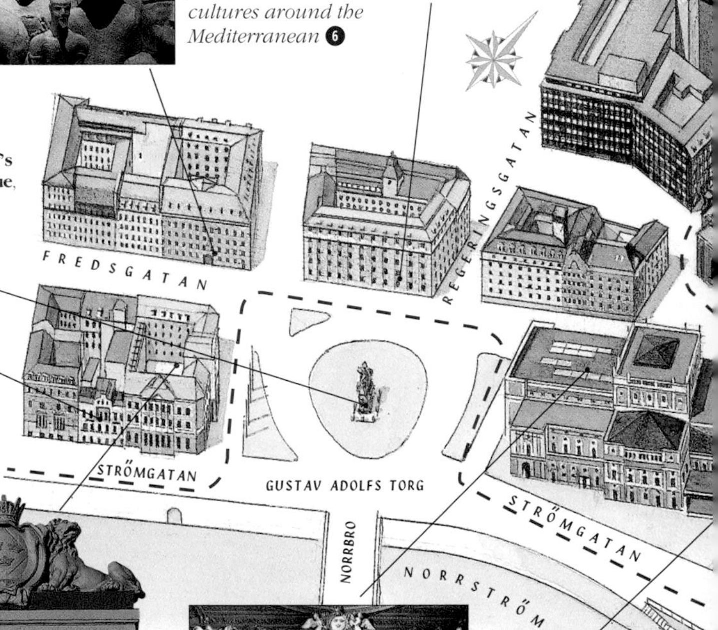

Gustav II Adolf's equestrian statue, designed by L'Archevêques, was unveiled in 1796.

Sagerska Palatset

FREDSGATAN

STRÖMGATAN

GUSTAV ADOLFS TORG

REGERINGSGATAN

STRÖMGATAN

NORRBRO

NORRSTRÖM

Opera-källaren
(see p294)

Arvfurstens Palats
The Swedish Foreign Office is based in this palace, built for Gustav III's sister Sofia Albertina in 1794 ❼

SOPHIA·ALBERTINA ÆDIFICAVIT·

★ Kungliga Operan
Built in 1898 with a magnificently ornate auditorium, the Royal Opera House replaced an earlier one from the time of Gustav III ❹

KEY

━ ━ ━   Suggested route

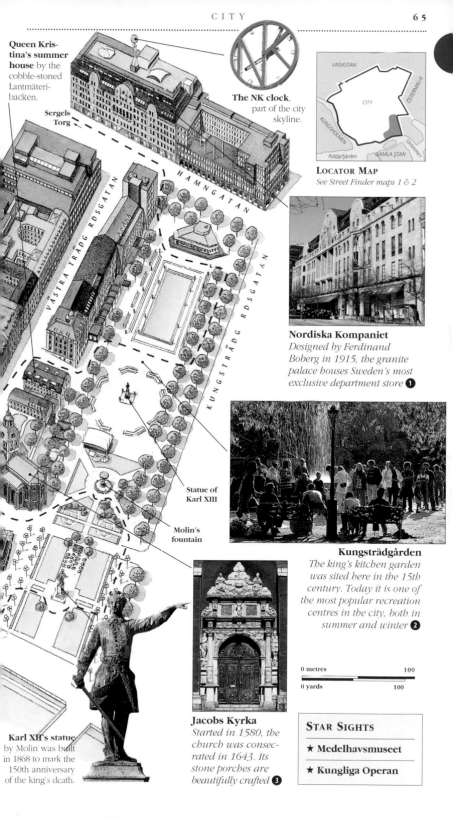

Queen Kristina's summer house by the cobble-stoned Lantmäteri-backen.

The NK clock, part of the city skyline.

Sergels Torg

HAMNGATAN

VÄSTRA TRÄDGÅRDSGATAN

KUNGSTRÄDGÅRDSGATAN

LOCATOR MAP
See Street Finder maps 1 & 2

VASASTAN

CITY

ÖSTERMALM

KUNGSHOLMEN

Riddarfjärden GAMLA STAN

Strömmen

Nordiska Kompaniet
Designed by Ferdinand Boberg in 1915, the granite palace houses Sweden's most exclusive department store **1**

Statue of Karl XIII

Molin's fountain

Kungsträdgården
The king's kitchen garden was sited here in the 15th century. Today it is one of the most popular recreation centres in the city, both in summer and winter **2**

0 metres	100
0 yards	100

Jacobs Kyrka
Started in 1580, the church was consecrated in 1643. Its stone porches are beautifully crafted **3**

Karl XII's statue by Molin was built in 1868 to mark the 150th anniversary of the king's death.

STAR SIGHTS

★ **Medelhavsmuseet**

★ **Kungliga Operan**

Nordiska Kompaniet ❶

Hamngatan 18–20. **Map** 2 D4. ☎ 08-762 80 00. ⊤ T-centralen. 🚌 2, 47, 55, 62, 69, 76. ◻ 10am–7pm Mon–Fri, 10am–6pm Sat, 10am–5pm Sun.

DESIGNED BY Ferdinand Boberg, the granite palace on Hamngatan houses the department store Nordiska Kompaniet (NK). Opened in 1915, NK was – and still is – aimed at an exclusive clientele. It made its name as a show-case for Swedish arts and crafts, writing design history when the textiles department, Textil-kammaren, opened in 1937. The manager was the textile artist Astrid Sampe who commissioned leading contemporary artists and designers to supply work. Olle Baertling, Arne Jacobsen, Alvar Aalto and Viola Gråsten all contributed patterns. Sampe also introduced new fabric printing techniques.

Today at NK you can find almost everything from perfume, clothing and sporting equipment to glass, silver and porcelain, but above all, the store is, as its founder Josef Sachs once described it, a commercial and cultural theatre.

Kungsträdgården ❷

Map 3 B1. ⊤ Kungsträdgården. 🚌 2, 47, 55, 62, 65, 69, 76.

THE "KING'S GARDEN" is a popular meeting place for Stockholmers where there is something for everyone going on all year round. This open urban space is bordered by treelined promenades, with a modern fountain in the middle. At the Strömgatan end there is a square named after Karl XII with J P Molin's statue of the warrior king, unveiled in 1868, at its centre. In Kungsträd-gården itself there is a statue of Karl XIII (1809–18) by Erik Göthe. During the summer, the park is the venue for food festivals, concerts, dancing and street theatre. In winter, the skating rink attracts children and grown-ups alike. Also to be seen is Molin's foun-tain, made from gypsum in 1866 and cast in bronze. It is the city's oldest park, starting as the royal kitchen garden in the 15th century. During Erik XIV's reign in the 16th century, it was trans-formed into a formal Renaissance garden. Queen Kristina built a stone summer house here in the 17th century, which stands at Västra Träd-gårdsgatan 2, by the cobble-stoned Lantmäteribacken.

Molin's fountain

Jacobs Kyrka ❸

Jakobs Torg 5. **Map** 3 B1. ☎ 08-723 30 38. ⊤ Kungsträdgården. 🚌 2, 55, 62, 65, 76. ◻ 11am–3pm daily, Thu also 5.30–6.30pm. ✝ 12.10pm Mon–Fri, 11am Sun. In Eng 6pm Sun. **Concerts** 3pm Sat. 📷 by appointment. ♿

IN MEDIEVAL TIMES there was a small chapel where Kungsträdgården now lies. Dedicated to St Jacob, the patron saint of wayfarers, the chapel and another modest-sized church were pulled down by King Gustav Vasa in the 16th century. His son, Johan III, wanted to provide two new churches in Norra Malmen, as the area was then called, and work to build the churches of St Jacob and St Klara (see p68) started in 1580. St Jacob's was consec-rated first, in 1643. It has been restored several times since then, in some cases rather clumsily. However, several valuable items have been preserved, including a baptis-mal font from 1634 and some church silver, as well as porches by the stonemasons Henrik Blom and Hans Hebel.

The organ's façade was created by the architect Carl Hårleman and the large paint-ing on the west wall of the southern nave is by Fredrik Westin, Sweden's most dis-tinguished historical painter of the early 19th century.

Altar in Jacobs Kyrka, dating in part from the 17th century

Kungliga Operan ❹

Gustav Adolfs Torg. **Map** 3 B1. ☎ 08-791 43 00. ⊤ Kungsträdgården. 🚌 43, 62, 65. **Ticket Office** ◻ 12–6pm Mon–Fri, 12–3pm Sat. 📷 by appointment. ♿ ▣ ☎ Ⓦ www.operan.se

OPERA HAS BEEN staged in Sweden since 18 January 1773, when a performance took place at Bollhuset at Slottsbacken. Kungliga Operan (The Royal Opera House) on Gustav Adolfs Torg was inaugurated on 30 September 1782, but by the late 19th century it had become a fire hazard. The architect Axel Anderberg was commissioned to design a new opera house which was

View of Kungsträdgården, towards Hamngatan

The splendid golden foyer at Kungliga Operan

given to the State in 1898 by a consortium founded by the financier K A Wallenberg.

The colouring of the building in late-Renaissance style is in keeping with the Royal Palace and Parliament building, and some details of the architecture are common to all three. The beautiful staircase with ceiling paintings by Axel Jungstedt was inspired by the Paris Opera. The same artist's portrait of Oscar II hangs in the 28-m (92-ft) long golden foyer, where Carl Larsson was responsible for the decorative paintings. The wings at either side of the stage have been retained, as has the width of the proscenium arch (11.4 m/37 ft). Also saved was J T Sergel's group of angels, holding the national coat of arms, above the stage. An angel in Vicke Andrén's ceiling painting is holding a sketch of the Opera House.

Gold ceiling in
Kungliga Operan

Dansmuseet **❺**

Gustav Adolfs Torg 22–24. **Map** 3 B1.
📞 08-441 76 50. 🚇 Kungsträdgården. 🚌 43, 62, 65.
🕐 11am–4pm Tue–Fri, noon–4pm
Sat & Sun. 📷 ♿ 💻 🎦 🚻
🌐 www.dansmuseet.se

IN 1999 THE Dance Museum moved into new premises on Gustav Adolfs Torg, in a former bank building opposite the Norrbro bridge. The

museum was originally established in Paris in 1953 by the Swedish aristocrat Rolf de Maré (1888–1964). He was a noted art collector and founder of the renowned avantgarde company Les Ballets Suédois. The collection features all aspects of dance – costumes and masks, scenery sketches, art and posters, books and documents – and includes an archive on popular dance. Apart from the exhibition hall, there is also a data bank – the Rolf de Maré Study Centre – which contains video facilities, a library and archives. The museum shop stocks Sweden's largest collection of dance videos for sale.

Medelhavs-museet **❻**

Fredsgatan 2. **Map** 3 B1.
📞 08-519 553 80. 🚇 Kungsträdgården. 🚌 43, 62, 65. 🕐 11am–
8pm Tue, 11am–4pm Wed–Fri, noon–
5pm Sat & Sun. 📷 ♿ 💻 🎦 🚻
🌐 www.medelhavsmuseet.se

GODS AND PEOPLE from prehistoric cultures around the Mediterranean rub shoulders in Medelhavsmuseet (the Museum of Mediterranean and Near East Antiquities). Its many treasures include a large group of terracotta figures discovered by archaeologists on Cyprus in the 1930s. There is an extensive display covering

ancient Egypt, with bronze weapons, tools and some remarkable mummies. Greek and Islamic culture, Roman and Etruscan art are all represented and complemented by temporary exhibitions.

Medelhavsmuseet is housed in a former bank, built in the 17th century for Gustav Horn, a general in the Thirty Years War. The stairwell, dating from 1905, and the peristyles and colonnade around the upper part of the hall are worth a visit in themselves.

Arvfurstens Palats **❼**

Gustav Adolfs Torg 1. **Map** 3 B1.
🚇 Kungsträdgården. 🚌 43, 62, 65.
🚫 to the public.

OPPOSITE THE Royal Opera House, on the other side of Gustav Adolfs Torg, stands Arvfurstens Palats (Prince's Palace), built for Gustav III's sister Sofia Albertina and completed in 1794. She commissioned the architect Erik Palmstedt to carry out the work. He was a pupil of Carl Fredrik Adelcrantz, designer of the original opera house.

The palace and its decor are shining examples of the Gustavian style, thanks to the contributions of artists and craftsmen such as Louis Masreliez and Georg Haupt and their pupils Gustaf Adolf Ditzinger, J T Sergel and Gottlieb Iwersson. In 1906 the building was taken over by the Swedish Foreign Office.

Nearby is the elegant Sagerska Palatset (1894) in French Renaissance style, which is used by the prime minister as an official residence.

Arvfurstens Palats (1794), now the Swedish Foreign Office

Edvin Öhrström's obelisk in Sergels Torg, with Kulturhuset to the left

Klara Kyrka **8**

Klara Östra Kyrkogata. **Map** 1 C4.
(08-723 30 31. **T** T-centralen.
= 47, 52, 59, 65. **O** 10am–5pm
daily. **Concert** 6pm Sat. **†** 8am Thu,
11am Sun, 2pm Sun (Swahili). **& &**

THE CONVENT OF St Klara
stood on the site of the
present church and cemetery
until 1527, when it was pulled
down on the orders of Gustav
Vasa. Later, his son Johan III
commissioned a new church,
completed in 1590.
   The church was ravaged by
fire in 1751. Its reconstruction
was planned by two of the
period's most outstanding
architects, Carl Hårleman and
later Carl Fredrik Adelcrantz.
The pulpit was made in 1753
to Hårleman's design, and J T
Sergel *(see p81)* created the
angelic figures in the northern
gallery. A pair of identical
angels adorns the exquisite
chancel, based on the
sculptor's gypsum originals.
   In the 1880s, the 116-m
(380-ft) tower was added. The
20th-century church artist, Olle
Hjortzberg, created the paintings in the vault in 1904.

Interior of Klara Kyrka with
decoration by Olle Hjortzberg

Kulturhuset and Stadsteatern **9**

Sergels Torg 3. **Map** 1 C4. **Kulturhuset**
(08-508 315 08. **Stadsteatern**
(08-506 202 00. **T** T-centralen.
= 47, 52, 59, 69. **O** 11am–6pm
Tue–Fri, 11am–4pm Sat–Sun.
▨ some areas. **& ¶ ▯ ▯**
W www.kulturhuset.stockholm.se

THE DISTINCTIVE GLASS façade
of Kulturhuset (Cultural
Centre) fronts the southern
side of Sergels Torg. The
winning entry in a Nordic
architectural competition,
Kulturhuset has become a
symbol of Swedish Modern-
ism. It was designed by Peter
Celsing and opened in 1974.
   Refurbished to meet the
needs of the new millennium,
the complex contains three
galleries which mount
regularly changing exhib-
itions. In the auditorium, a
varied programme of music,
dance, drama and lectures is

presented. The centre known
as "Kilen" stages an art form
which is a cross between
drama, stand-up comedy,
installation art and dance.
   In the Children's Room,
youngsters can read books,
draw pictures, listen to stories
or watch films. "Lava" focuses
on youth culture nationwide.
There is a library for fans of
strip cartoons and reading
rooms providing international
newspapers and magazines.
   Among the shops here is
Designtorget, selling items of
Swedish design, and an art
bookshop, Konst-ig. There are
two cafés: Café Panorama
serves snacks, and Café Access
is for surfing the Internet.
   Kulturhuset also houses
Stadsteatern (City Theatre),
whose main auditorium
opened in 1990. This part of
the building was formerly
occupied by Parliament while
its chamber on Helgeandsholmen was being rebuilt *(see
p61)*. The theatre was
designed by architects Lars
Fahlsten and Per Ahrbom and
contains six stages of varying
size and style under one roof.

Konserthuset **10**

Hötorget. **Map** 1 C4.
(08-786 02 00. **T** Hötorget. **=** 1,
52, 56. **Ticket Office** **O** 11am–6pm
Mon–Fri, 11am–3pm Sat, and 2 hours
before a concert. **▯ & ▯ ▯**
W www.konserthuset.se

A NORDIC VERSION of a Greek
temple, Konserthuset
(the Concert Hall) is a masterpiece of the architect Ivar
Tengbom (1878–1968) and is

CITY'S TRANSFORMATION

During the 20th century Stockholm's population grew from
250,000 to more than 1.6 million. By the 1920s it was obvious that the old heart of the city
would not meet the future needs
of business, public administration
and the growth in traffic. In 1951
a controversial 30-year ongoing
programme to transform the
lower Norrmalm city centre was
launched. Slums on 335 of the 600
sites were pulled down and 78
new buildings were built. Two-
thirds of the area's buildings were
added during this period.

**The first steps towards a
new Hötorg City, 1958**

The *Orpheus* sculpture group by Carl Milles at Konserthuset

THE NOBEL PRIZES

Alfred Nobel (1833–96) was an outstanding chemist and inventor. He left his fortune to endow the prestigious Nobel Prizes – consisting of a monetary award and a medal – which have been presented every December since 1901. The ceremony takes place in Konserthuset, where prizes are awarded for physics, chemistry, physiology or medicine, and literature. Since 1969 the Bank of Sweden has given a prize for economic sciences in Nobel's memory. The Nobel Peace Prize is presented in Oslo on the same day. In 1901 each prize was worth 150,000 kr; in 2003 the figure was 10 million kr.

The Nobel Medal, awarded annually

an outstanding example of the 1920s' Neo-Classical style. Tengbom's tradition has been carried on by his son Anders (b. 1911), who was in charge of its renovation in 1970–71, and his grandson Svante (b. 1942), who had a similar task in 1993–6.

Constructed in 1923–6, the main hall has undergone major reconstruction and modernization to overcome acoustical problems. Its interior is very simple in contrast to the Grünewald Hall, by the artist Isaac Grünewald (1889–1946), which is in the more lavish style of an Italian Renaissance palace. The four marble statues in the main foyer are by Carl Milles, creator of the *Orpheus* sculpture group outside.

The Concert Hall is the home of the Swedish Royal Philharmonic Orchestra, which gives some 70 concerts every year, and international star soloists perform regularly. It is also the venue for the Nobel Prize presentations.

Strindbergsmuseet Blå Tornet ⓫

Drottninggatan 85. **Map** 1 C3.
📞 08-411 53 54. 🚇 Rådmansgatan.
🚌 52, 65. ⏰ noon–7pm Tue, noon–4pm Wed–Sun; Jun–Aug: noon–4pm Tue–Sun. 📷 2.30pm Thu, 1pm Sat & Sun. 👤 📷 🅰
🌐 www.strindbergsmuseet.se

THE WORLD-FAMOUS dramatist August Strindberg (1849–1912) lived at 24 different addresses in Stockholm over the years. He moved to the last of these in 1908, and gave it the name Blå Tornet (the Blue Tower). By then he had gained international recognition.

The apartment, now the Strindbergsmuseet, was newly built with central heating, toilet and lift, but lacked a kitchen. Instead he relied on Falkner's Pension, in the same building, for food and other services. On his last few birthdays the great man would stand on his balcony and watch his admirers stage a torchlight procession in his honour.

Opened in 1973, the museum shows the author's home with his bedroom and dining room and his study as it was on his death, as well as 3,000 books, photographic archives, press cuttings and posters. In the adjoining premises, a permanent exhibition portrays Strindberg as author, theatrical director, artist and photographer. Temporary exhibitions and other activities are often held here.

Strindberg's desk and writing materials in his study

Adolf Fredriks Kyrka ⓬

Holländargatan 14. **Map** 1 C3.
📞 08-20 70 76. 🚇 Hötorget. 🚌 52. ⏰ 1–7pm Mon, 10am–4pm Tue–Sat, 10am–4pm Sun.
Concert 12.15 Tue. 📷 7pm Mon, 12.15pm Wed & Thu, 11am Sun.
📷 by appointment. 👤 📷 🅰

KING ADOLF FREDRIK laid the foundation stone of this church in 1768 on the site of an earlier chapel dedicated to St Olof. Designed by Carl Fredrik Adelcrantz, in Neo-Classical style with traces of Rococo, the church has been built in the shape of a Greek cross and has a central dome.

The interior has undergone a number of changes, but both the altar and pulpit have remained intact. The sculptor Johan Tobias Sergel created the altarpiece and the memorial to the French philosopher Descartes who died in Stockholm in 1650. The paintings in the dome were added in 1899–1900 by Julius Kronberg. More recent acquisitions include altar silverware by Sigurd Persson.

The cemetery is the resting place of the assassinated Prime Minister Olof Palme (1927–86). J T Sergel is also buried here.

Memorial to Descartes

Armémuseum, with the dome of Hedvig Eleonora Kyrka in the background

Kungliga Biblioteket ⑬

Humlegården. **Map** 2 D3.
☎ 08-463 40 00. Ⓣ Östermalmstorg. 🚌 1, 2, 55, 56, 91, 96.
🕐 9am–8pm Mon–Thu, 9am–7pm
Fri, 10am–5pm Sat; mid-Jun–mid-
Aug: 9am–6pm Mon–Thu, 9am–5pm
Fri, 11am–3pm Sat. 🎫 by appointment. ♿ 🖥 🅆 www.kb.se

THIS IS SWEDEN'S national
library and an autonomous
Government department in its
own right. Ever since 1661,
when there were only nine
printing presses in Sweden,
copies of every piece of
printed matter have had to
be lodged with Kungliga
Biblioteket (Royal Library).
Since 1993 this requirement
has also applied to electronic
documents. As there are now
some 3,000 printers and publishers in Sweden the volume
of material is expanding
rapidly. The stock of books is
increasing at the rate of 35,000
volumes a year.

The imposing original
building, dating from 1865–
78, had to be expanded in the
1920s, and again in the 1990s.

The library is in a beautiful
setting in Humlegården,
created by Gustav II Adolf in
1619 to grow hops for the
royal household. Ever since
the 18th century, the park
has been a favourite
recreation area for
Stockholmers.

**The 13th-century "Devil's Bible"
in Kungliga Biblioteket**

Armémuseum ⑭

Riddargatan 13. **Map** 2 E4.
☎ 08-788 95 60. Ⓣ Östermalmstorg.
🚌 62. 🕐 11am–8pm Tue, 11am–
4pm Wed–Sun. 🎫 📷 ♿ 🚻
🅆 www.armemuseum.org

THE OLD ARMOURY on
Artillerigården has been
the home of the Armémuseum
(Royal Army Museum) since
1879. During the 1990s, the
250-year-old building and its
displays underwent extensive
renovation to create one of
the capital's best-planned and
most interesting museums.

Dramatic life-size settings
have been made to portray
Sweden's history of war and
defence, showing not only
what happened in battle but
how the lives of the women
and children at home were
affected. Diaries, intelligence
manuals, rifles, flags and even
cutlery add a note of reality.

Processions for royal visits
start from the museum and
during the summer guards-
men march from here to the
Royal Palace at 11.45am daily
for the changing of the guard.

Musikmuseet ⑮

Sibyllegatan 2. **Map** 2 E4.
☎ 08-519 554 90. Ⓣ Östermalmstorg. 🚌 47, 62, 69, 76. 🕐
11am–4pm Tue–Fri, noon–4pm
Sat–Sun. 🎫 📷 ∅ ♿ 🖥 🍴 🚻
🅆 www.stockholm.music.museum.se

AFTER BEING HOUSED on nine
different sites, the Museum
of Music finally moved into
this former royal bakery in
1979. It is the capital's oldest
preserved industrial building,
right in the city centre. Bread
was baked here for military
personnel in Stockholm from
1640 right up to 1958. Today

the museum's collection
includes about 6,000 instruments, and it also holds
Sweden's national musical
archive. With 20,000
manuscripts, it is a gold
mine for anyone interes-
ted in Swedish folk
music. The archive is
open to visitors by
appointment.There is
a regular programme
of temporary
exhibitions.

**A so-called *hummel*
instrument once
owned by the trouba-
dour C M Bellman**

Hovstallet ⑯

Väpnargatan 1. **Map** 2 E4. ☎ 08-
402 61 06. Ⓣ Östermalmstorg. 🚌
47, 62, 69, 76. 🕐 for guided tours.
● May–Jun. 🎫 2pm Sat & Sun;
Jul–Aug: 2pm Mon–Fri. 📷

THE ROYAL MEWS looks after
transport for the Royal
Family and Royal Household.
It maintains about 40 carriages,
a dozen cars, carriage horses,
and a few horses used for
riding. The royal horses are
Swedish half-breeds.

There are many treasures
among the carriages, such as
the glass-panelled State Coach
known as a "Berliner". It was
built in Sweden at the Adolf
Freyschuss carriage works
and made its debut at Oscar
II's silver jubilee in 1897. It
is still used today on ceremonial occasions.

Incoming foreign ambassa-
dors travel to the Royal Palace
for their formal audience with
the monarch in Karl XV's
coupé. Open carriages from
the mid-19th century drawn
by two horses are normally
used for processions.

INGMAR BERGMAN

The playwright and producer Ingmar Bergman was born at Östermalm in 1918. His long series of masterly films have

made him world-famous, but he started his career in the theatre. From 1963–6 he was Director of Kungliga Dramatiska Teatern, where he is still a guest producer. His breakthrough as a film producer came with *Smiles of the Summer Night* (1955), and *The Seventh Seal* (1957) was a cinematic milestone. *Fanny and Alexander* (1982) was his last major film, since when he has written screenplays and published his autobiography, *Magic Lantern*.

Ingmar Bergman at a press conference, 1998

The Hallwylska Palatset courtyard, seen through the gateway arch

Kungliga Dramatiska Teatern ⑰

Nybroplan. **Map** 2 E4. ℂ 08-667 06 80. Ⓣ Östermalmstorg. 🚌 47, 62, 69, 76. **Ticket Office** ⏰ noon–7pm Tue–Sat, noon–4pm Sun (except Jun–Aug). 🎫 🚫 ♿ 🎭 Ⓦ www.dramaten.se

WHEN PLANS WERE drawn up in the early 20th century to build the present Kungliga Dramatiska Teatern (Royal Dramatic Theatre) at Nybroplan, the State refused to give financial aid, so it was funded by lotteries instead. The results exceeded all expectations, giving the architect Fredrik Lilljekvist generous resources which he used to the full.

The new theatre, known as Dramaten, took six years to build and opened in 1908. The design was lavish, both in the choice of materials and in the contributions by leading Swedish artists.

The Jugendstil façade, inspired by Viennese archi-

tecture, is in expensive white marble. Christian Ericsson created the powerful relief frieze, Carl Milles the centre section and John Börjesson the bronze statues *Poetry* and *Drama*. These are complemented in the foyer by *Tragedy* and *Comedy* by Börjesson and Theodor Lundberg respectively.

The ceiling in the foyer is by Carl Larsson, while the upper lobby's back wall was painted by Oscar Björk, and the auditorium's ceiling and stage lintel by Julius Kronberg. Gustav Cederström provided the central painting in the marble foyer.

When Gustav III founded the Royal Dramatic Theatre in 1788 it performed in a building on Slottsbacken. The colour scheme there – blue, white and gold – was chosen for the new venue, but was changed to "theatre red" in the 1930s.

The original colours were reinstated in 1988.

Hallwylska Palatset ⑱

Hamngatan 4. **Map** 2 D4. ℂ 08-519 555 99. Ⓣ Östermalmstorg. 🚌 46, 47, 55, 62, 69, 76. 🎫 noon– 3pm every hour Tue–Sun, also 6pm Wed, 1pm Sun (Eng). 26 Jun–15 Aug: 11am–4pm daily every hour, also 6pm Wed, in Eng 1pm daily. 🎭 🚫 🎭 Ⓦ www.hallwylskamuseet.se

THE IMPRESSIVE façade of Hamngatan 4 is nothing in comparison with what is concealed behind the heavy gates. The Hallwyl Palace was built from 1892–7 as a residence for the immensely wealthy Count and Countess Walther and Wilhelmina von Hallwyl. When the Countess died in 1930 the State was left a fantastic gift: an unbelievably ornate palace whose chatelaine had amassed a priceless collection of *objets d'art* over many decades. Eight years later the doors opened on a new museum with 67,000 catalogued items.

Wilhelmina left nothing to chance. The architect Isak Gustav Clason (1856–1930) had no worries about cost and nor did the decorative painter and artistic adviser Julius Kronberg. Every detail had to be perfect. A typical example is the billiards room which has gilt-leather wallpaper and walnut panelling, with billiard balls sculpted into the marble fireplace.

The paintings in the gallery, mostly 16th- and 17th-century Flemish, were bought over a period of only two years.

Kungliga Dramatiska Teatern's Jugendstil façade in white marble

BLASIEHOLMEN & SKEPPSHOLMEN

OPPOSITE THE Royal Palace on the eastern side of the Norrström channel lies Blasieholmen, a natural springboard to the islands of Skeppsholmen and Kastellholmen.

Several elegant palaces were built at Blasieholmen during Sweden's era as a great power in the 17th and early 18th centuries. But the area's present appearance was acquired in the period between the mid-19th century, when buildings such as Nationalmuseum were erected, and just before World War I. In the early 1900s, stately residences such as Bååtska Palatset became overshadowed by smart hotels, opulent bank buildings and entertainment venues. Blasieholmen is also the place for auction houses, art galleries, antiques shops and second-hand bookshops. And the quayside is the departure point for sightseeing and archipelago boats.

Porthole in wooden boat

Skeppsholmen is reached by a wrought-iron bridge with old wooden boats moored next to it. In the middle of the 17th century the island became the base for the Swedish Navy and many of its old buildings were designed as barracks and stores. Today they house some of the city's major museums and cultural institutions, juxtaposed with the avant-garde construction of the Moderna Museet.

SIGHTS AT A GLANCE

Museums
Arkitekturmuseet ❸
Moderna Museet pp78–9 ❷
Nationalmuseum pp80–81 ❼
Östasiatiska Museet ❶

Islands and Squares
Blasieholmstorg ❾
Kastellholmen ❻
Raoul Wallenbergs Torg ⓬

Synagogues
Synagogan ❿

Hotels and Restaurants
af Chapman ❹
Berns' Salonger ⓫
Grand Hôtel ❽

Concert Halls
Nybrokajen 11 ⓭

Public Buildings
Kungliga Konsthogskolan ❺

KEY

▦	Street-by-Street map See pp74–5
🚌	Bus stop
⛴	Ferry landing point
Ⓣ	Tunnelbana station
🅿	Parking

0 metres 250
0 yards 250

◁ **Skeppsholmsbron, linking Blasieholmen and Skeppsholmen, with the ship _af Chapman_ in the background**

Street-by-Street: Skeppsholmen

SKEPPSHOLMEN HAS LONG SINCE lost its importance as a naval base and has been transformed into a centre for culture. Many of the naval buildings have been restored and traditional wooden boats are moored here, but pride of place now goes to the exciting Moderna Museet. The island is ideal for a full-day visit, with its location between the waters of Strömmen and Nybroviken acting as a breathing space in the centre of Stockholm. The attractive buildings, the richly wooded English-style park and the view towards Skeppsbron and Strandvägen also make Skeppsholmen a pleasant place for those who would just prefer to have a quiet stroll.

Teater Galeasen is Stockholm's avant-garde theatre for new Swedish and international drama.

Blasie-holmen

Skepps-holmsbron (bridge)

★ **Östasiatiska Museet**
This belt plaquette in Ordos style from the 1st or 2nd century BC is part of a remarkable collection of arts and crafts from China, Japan, Korea and India, from the Stone Age to the 19th century ❶

Skeppsholmen Church (1824–42) in well-preserved Empire style.

Salute battery (see p76)

Admiralty House

Paradise (1963), a sculpture group by Jean Tinguely and Niki de Saint Phalle for Montreal's World Exposition, has stood outside the site of the Moderna Museet since 1972.

SVENKSUNDSVÄGEN

ÖSTRA BROBÄNKEN

Youth Hostel

Swedish Society of Crafts & Design

af Chapman
Built in 1888, the full-rigged former freighter and school ship has served as a popular youth hostel since 1949. Skeppsholmen Church (left) and the Admiralty House (1647–50, rebuilt 1844–6) are in the background ❹

Kungliga Konsthögskolan
The first part of the Royal College of Fine Arts was completed in the 1770s, but it acquired its present appearance in the mid-1990s. This cast-iron boar stands at the entrance ❺

Loading crane built in 1751 – the oldest of its type in Sweden.

The festival area on the quayside below the Moderna Museet is the venue for the popular International Jazz & Blues Festival, which takes place for a week in July each year.

LOCATOR MAP
See Street Finder map 4

Arkitekturmuseet

The Museum of Architecture highlights thousands of years of building, with a collection of models showing masterpieces worldwide, including this model of the Stockholm City Library by Asplund ❸

ÖSTRA BROBÄNKEN

SVENSKSUNDSV.

LÅNGA RADEN

AMIRALSVÄGEN

SÖDRA BROBÄNKEN

Kastellholmen

★ **Moderna Museet**
Designed by Rafael Moneo, the museum was opened in 1998 when Stockholm was Cultural Capital of Europe. It has an exciting collection of modern art, and fine views across the water ❷

Monument commemorating the battle at Svensksund in 1790 (see p40)

KEY

– – – Suggested route

| 0 metres | 100 |
| 0 yards | 100 |

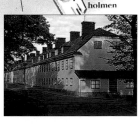

Långa Raden is used by the State Board of Culture, and also for exhibitions and as homes. The buildings, dating from about 1700, originally accommodated King Karl XII's bodyguard.

STAR SIGHTS

★ **Moderna Museet**

★ **Östasiatiska Museet**

Arkitekturmuseet, housed in the Neo-Classical former naval drill hall

Östasiatiska Museet ●

Tyghusplan. **Map** 4 D2. ▮ 08-519 557 70. Ⓣ Kungsträdgården. 🚌 65. 🚢 Djurgårdsfärja. ◯ noon– 8pm Tue, noon–5pm Wed–Sun. ▮ 2pm Sun in Eng by appointment. ✗ ♿ ▯ ⓦ www.ostasiatiska.se

Iᴛ ɪs ɴᴏᴛ ᴜɴᴜsᴜᴀʟ for Western capitals to have a museum devoted to art and archaeology from China, Japan, Korea and India. But it is not every Museum of Far Eastern Antiquities that, like Östasiatiska Museet, can claim one of the world's foremost collections of Chinese art outside Asia.

On a visit to the Yellow River valley in China in the early 1920s, the Swedish geologist Johan Gunnar Andersson discovered hitherto unknown dwellings and graves containing objects dating from the New Stone Age.

He was allowed to take a selection of items back to Sweden, and these formed the basis for the museum, founded in 1926. A key figure in its development was the then Crown Prince, later to become King Gustav VI Adolf,

who was both interested in and knowledgeable about archaeology. Later, he bequeathed to the museum his own large collection of ancient Chinese arts and crafts.

The museum has been on Skeppsholmen since 1963, when it was moved into a restored house which had been built in 1699–1700 as a depot for Karl XII's bodyguard.

Moderna Museet ●

See pp78–9.

Arkitekturmuseet ●

Exercisplan. **Map** 4 E3. ▮ 08-587 270 00. Ⓣ Kungsträdgården. 🚌 65. 🚢 Djurgårdsfärja. ◯ 10am–8pm Tue–Wed, 10am– 6pm Thu–Sun. ▮ 2pm Sat & Sun (in Eng: summer only). ✗ ♿ ▯ 🖥 ▯ ⓦ www.arkitekturmuseet.se

Tʜᴇ sᴡᴇᴅɪsʜ Museum of Architecture shares an entrance hall and restaurant with the new Moderna Museet. It has also reclaimed

its earlier home, a one-time naval drill hall.

In the permanent exhibition, more than 100 architectural models guide visitors through the history of Swedish building. They include the oldest and simplest of wooden houses to the highly sophisticated construction techniques and innovative styles of the present day.

It is fascinating to move from an almost 2,000-year-old longhouse to a modern supermarket, interspersed with examples of architecture in Gothenburg from the 17th century to the 1930s and the new Årsta bridge situated to the south of Stockholm.

Models of historic architectural works worldwide, from 2000 BC up to the present day, are also on show.

The museum offers an ambitious programme – albeit only in Swedish – alongside the permanent and temporary exhibitions, including lectures, study days, city walks, guided tours, school visits and family events on Sunday afternoons, which involve model-building.

Chinese Bodhisattva in limestone (c.530), Östasiatiska Museet

Tʜᴇ Sᴋᴇᴘᴘsʜᴏʟᴍᴇɴ Cᴀɴɴᴏɴs

A salute battery of four 57-mm rapid-fire cannons is sited on Skeppsholmen and is still in use. Salutes are fired to mark national and royal special occasions at 12 noon on weekdays and 1pm at weekends: 28 January – the King's name day; 30 April – the King's birthday; 6 June – Sweden's National Day; 14 July – Crown Princess Victoria's birthday; 8 August – the Queen's name day; 23 December – the Queen's birthday.

The salute battery on Skeppsholmen

af Chapman ❹

Västra Brobänken. **Map** 4 D3.
📞 00 463 22 66. 🚇 Kungsträdgården. 🚌 65. ⛴ Djurgårdsfärja. 🏨
🛏 See **Where to Stay** p281.

THE SAILING SHIP *af Chapman* is one of Sweden's most attractive and unusual youth hostels. The ship has 136 beds, and there are a further 152 beds in the hostel building facing the gangway.

Visitors staying in more conventional accommodation can still go on board and enjoy *af Chapman*'s special atmosphere. The three-masted ship was built in 1888 at the English port of Whitehaven and used as a freight vessel. She came to Sweden in 1915 and saw service as a sail training ship until 1934. The City of Stockholm bought the vessel after World War II and she has been berthed here since 1949. She is named after Fredrik Henrik af Chapman, a master shipbuilder who was born in Gothenburg in 1721.

Kungliga Konsthögskolan ❺

Flaggmansvägen 1. **Map** 4 E3. 📞 08-614 40 00. 🚇 Kungsträdgården. 🚌 65. ⛴ Djurgårdsfärja. ◯ to the public for special events. ♿ 🛏

A STROLL AROUND Skeppsholmen provides an opportunity to have a closer look at the beautifully restored 18th-century naval barracks which now houses Kungliga Konsthögskolan (the Royal College of Fine Arts). At the entrance there are two statues depicting a lion and a boar. "In like a lion and out like a pig" is an old saying among the lecturers and the 200 or so students at this college, still rich in tradition.

The college started out in 1735 as an academy for painting and sculpture for the decorators working on Tessin's new Royal Palace. Gustav III granted it a royal charter in 1773. Before it moved here in 1995, the college was located on Fredsgatan as part of Konstakademien, although since 1978 it had been run independently with departments for painting, sculpture, graphics, computing and video, as well as offering courses for architects.

The college is not normally open to the public, apart from an "open house" once a year. Then visitors can enjoy the beautiful interiors, especially the vaulted 18th-century cellars.

The medieval-style castle on Kastellholmen, built in 1846–8

Kastellholmen ❻

Map 4 F4. 🚇 Kungsträdgården. 🚌 65. ⛴ Djurgårdsfärja.

RIGHT IN THE middle of Stockholm, Kastellholmen is a typical archipelago island with granite rocks and steep cliffs. From Skeppsholmen it is reached by a bridge built in 1880. Every morning since 1640 a sailor has hoisted the three-tailed Swedish war flag at the castle. Whenever a visiting naval vessel arrives, the battery's four cannons fire a welcoming salute from the castle terrace.

The charming brick pavilion by the bridge was built in 1882 for the Royal Skating Club, which used the water between the two islands when it froze.

Nationalmuseum ❼

See pp80–81.

Grand Hôtel ❽

Södra Blasieholmshamnen 8. **Map** 3 C1. 📞 08-679 35 00. 🚇 Kungsträdgården. 🚌 2, 55, 62, 65, 76. See **Where to Stay** p281 and **Where to Eat** p294.

OSCAR II'S head chef, Régis Cadier, founded the Grand Hôtel, Sweden's only five-star hotel, in 1874. Since 1901, the hotel has accommodated the Nobel Prize winners each year.

Traditional Swedish delicacies are served in an abundant *smörgåsbord* in the elegant Grands Veranda. There is also a stylish gourmet restaurant, Franska Matsalen. The Cadier Bar is named after the hotel's founder.

The hotel has 19 banqueting and conference suites, the best known of which is the lofty *Vinterträdgården* (Winter Garden) which can accommodate 800 people. The *Spegelsalen* (Hall of Mirrors) is a copy of the hall at Versailles and was where the Nobel Prize banquet was held until 1929, when it became too big and was moved to City Hall *(see p100).*

Grand Hôtel on Blasieholmen, Sweden's only five-star hotel

Moderna Museet ②

THE MUSEUM OF Modern Art is an airy building, designed by the Catalan architect Rafael Moneo in 1998. The museum has a top-class collection of international and Swedish modern art, as well as photography and film. Built partly underground, the complex includes a cinema and auditorium; the photographic library is the most comprehensive collection of its type in northern Europe and there is also a collection of video art and art documentaries. A wide choice of books on art, photography, film and architecture can be found in the bookshop and the Restaurant MM Mat has attractive views over the water.

Breakfast Outdoors (1962)
This sculpture group by Picasso, executed in sandblasted concrete by Carl Nesjar, stands in the museum garden near the entrance.

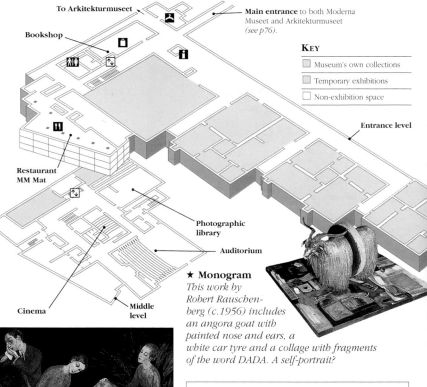

To Arkitekturmuseet

Main entrance to both Moderna Museet and Arkitekturmuseet *(see p76).*

Bookshop

KEY

☐ Museum's own collections

☐ Temporary exhibitions

☐ Non-exhibition space

Entrance level

Restaurant MM Mat

Photographic library

Auditorium

Cinema

Middle level

★ **Monogram**
This work by Robert Rauschenberg (c.1956) includes an angora goat with painted nose and ears, a white car tyre and a collage with fragments of the word DADA. A self-portrait?

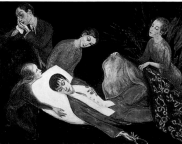

★ **The Dying Dandy** (1918)
The cosmopolitan artist Nils Dardel (1888–1943) produced this Expressionistic painting when he was about to marry. It can be interpreted as a farewell to his misspent youth.

RAFAEL MONEO

Rafael Moneo (b. 1937) is one of the leading contemporary architects. As a young architect, Moneo took part in the project to build the Sydney Opera House. His flair for adapting building design to sensitive surroundings was recognized in 1989 when his was chosen out of 211 entries as the winner of the competition to design the new Moderna Museet.

Moderna Museet's northern façade

VISITORS' CHECKLIST

Exercisplan. **Map** 4 E3.
☎ 08-519 552 00.
🚇 Kungsträdgården. 🚌 65.
🚢 Djurgårdsfärja. ⏰ 10am–
8pm Tue–Wed, 10am–6pm
Thu–Sun. ⬤ 24–25, 31 Dec,
1 Jan and some holidays.
📷 Eng: July–Sep. 🎟 free 1st
Tue each month 5–8pm.
∅ ♿ 🚻 🛗
ⓦ www.modernamuseet.se

GALLERY GUIDE

*The large room on the entrance
level is used for temporary
exhibitions. Three rooms on
the same level have an alternat-
ing selection of collections
from the eras 1900–45, 1946–
70 and 1971 to the present
day. The middle level has an
auditorium, cinema and
photographic library. Another
entrance is at the lowest level.*

★ **The Child's Brain** (1914)
*The surrealist Giorgio de
Chirico gave his work the
title* The Ghost, *but in the
irrational spirit of the movement Louis Aragon renamed
it in a pamphlet about the
artist's 1927 retrospective.*

STAR FEATURES

★ **The Dying Dandy
by Dardel**

★ **Monogram
by Rauschenberg**

★ **The Child's Brain
by de Chirico**

Blasieholmstorg ⑨

Map 3 C1. 🚇 Kungsträdgården.
🚌 2, 55, 62, 65, 76.

TWO OF THE city's oldest
palaces are located in this
square, flanked by two bronze
horses. The palace at No. 8
was built in the mid-17th
century by Field Marshal
Gustaf Horn. It was rebuilt
100 years later, when it
acquired the character of an
18th-century French palace.
Foreign ambassadors and
ministers lodged here when
they visited the
capital, so it
became known
as the Ministers'
Palace. Later it
became a base for
overseas admin-
istration and soon
earned its present
name of Utrikes-
ministerhotellet
(Foreign Ministry
Hotel). Parts of the
building are now used as
offices by the Musical Academy
and the Swedish Institute.

**Bronze horse on
Blasieholmstorg**

Bååtska Palatset stands
nearby at No. 6. Its exterior
dates from 1669 and was
designed by Tessin the Elder.
In 1876–7 it was partly rebuilt
by F W Scholander for the
Freemasons, who still have
their lodge here.

Another interesting complex
of buildings can be found on
the square at No. 10. The
façade which faces on to
Nybrokajen, along the water's
edge, is an attractive example
of the Neo-Renaissance style
of the 1870s and 1880s.

Synagogan ⑩

Warendorfsgatan 3. **Map** 3 C1.
☎ 08-87 858 00. 🚇 Kungsträdgården. 🚌 2, 55, 62, 65, 76.
🎟 all year 9.15am Fri; Jun–Aug:
6.30pm Fri; Hebrew and partly
English. 📷 summer and by
appointment. ♿

IT TOOK MOST OF THE 1860s
to build the Conservative
Jewish community's syna-
gogue on land reclaimed from
the sea. When it was inaugurated in 1870, the building
was standing on 1,300 piles

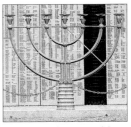

**Monument to the victims of the
Holocaust during World War II**

which had been driven down
to a depth of 15 m (50 ft). It
is built in what the architect,
F W Scholander, called
"ancient Eastern style". The
synagogue can be
visited on guided
tours during the
summer. Alongside
is the congre-
gation's assembly
room and library.
Outside is a
monument erected
in 1998 in memory
of 8,000 victims
of the Holocaust whose
relations had been rescued
and taken to Sweden during
World War II.

There is also an Orthodox
synagogue in the city centre,
reached through the Jewish
Centre (Judiska Centret) on
Nybrogatan at No. 19.

Berns' Salonger ⑪

Berzelii Park. **Map** 2 D4. ☎ 08-566
322 00. 🚇 Kungsträdgården,
Östermalmstorg. 🚌 2, 47, 55, 62,
65, 69, 76. ♿ *Where to Eat p294.*

THIS HAS BEEN one of Stockholm's most legendary
restaurants and entertainment
venues since 1863. Both
salons, with their stately
galleries, magnificent crystal
chandeliers and elegant
mirrors, were restored to their
original splendour by the
British designer and restaur-
ateur Terence Conran to mark
the new millennium.

The new-look Berns' is one
of Stockholm's biggest
restaurants with seating for
400 diners. The gallery level,
with its beautifully decorated
dining rooms, was made
famous by August Strindberg's
novel *The Red Room* (1879).

Nationalmuseum ❼

THE NATIONAL MUSEUM is a landmark on the southern side of Blasieholmen. The location by the Strömmen channel inspired the 19th-century German architect August Stüler to design a building in the Venetian and Florentine Renaissance styles.

Completed in 1866, the museum houses Sweden's largest art collection, with some 16,000 classic paintings and sculptures. Drawings and graphics from the 15th century up to the early 20th century bring the total up to 500,000. The applied art and design section has works spanning five centuries, including a 500-year-old tapestry, porcelain and examples of work by master furniture-makers, such as Georg Haupt. Space is also devoted to the development of modern Swedish design (*see pp22-3*), 1900–2000.

The Love Lesson (1716–17)
Antoine Watteau's speciality was the so-called fêtes galantes, *depicting young couples in playful mood.*

★ **The Conspiracy of the Batavians under Claudius Civilis** (1661–2)
Originally intended for Amsterdam, Rembrandt depicts the Batavians' conspiracy against the Romans, symbolizing the Dutch liberation campaign against Spain.

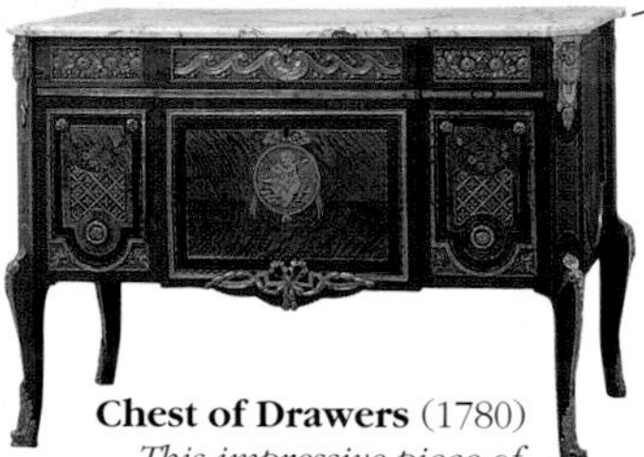

Level 2

Chest of Drawers (1780)
This impressive piece of furniture was created by Georg Haupt, who was one of the foremost Swedish cabinet-makers of the 18th century.

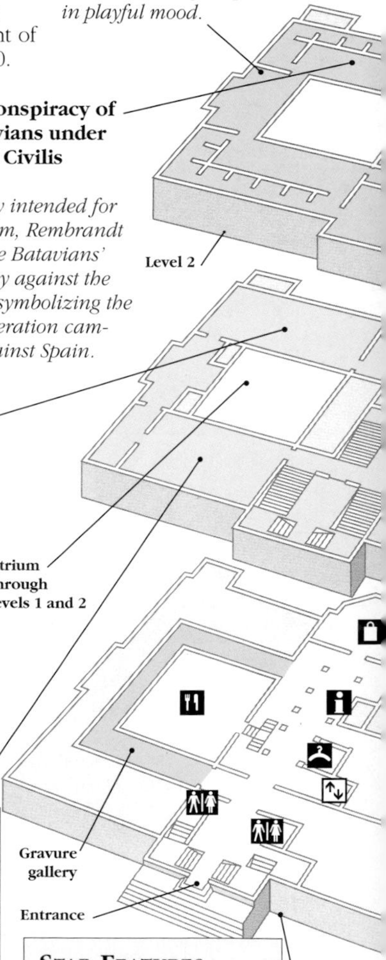

Atrium through levels 1 and 2

Gravure gallery

Entrance

David and Bathsheba (1490)
This tapestry from Brussels is created in the decorative medieval style, with pomegranates, faces and hands forming an exquisite work.

Entry for wheel-chairs

STAR FEATURES

★ **The Lady with the Veil by Roslin**

★ **The Conspiracy of the Batavians by Rembrandt**

★ The Lady with the Veil
Alexander Roslin's elegant portrait (1769) is often considered to be a glamorized symbol of 18th-century Sweden.

The Upper Staircase
At the back is Carl Larsson's monumental mural The Entry of King Gustav Vasa of Sweden in Stockholm 1523. *On the opposite wall is his* Midwinter Sacrifice.

The Faun (1774)
Johan Tobias Sergel was the foremost sculptor of the Gustavian era. This piece is regarded as his most triumphant work.

Level 1

Auditorium

Entrance
level

KEY

☐ Painting and sculpture

☐ Applied art and design

☐ Temporary exhibitions

☐ Non-exhibition space

☐ No admission

GALLERY GUIDE

Level 2 is devoted to painting and sculpture. The accent is on Swedish 18th- to early 20th-century art, but the 17th-century Dutch and Flemish, and 18th-century French schools are also represented. Exhibits may change. Level 1 shows mainly Swedish applied art and design, particularly furniture, porcelain, silver and glass from the 15th century up to modern Swedish design. To the left of the main entrance is the Gravure Gallery with temporary exhibitions of graphics etc.

Raoul Wallenbergs Torg ⓬

Map 2 E4. 🚇 Östermalmstorg.
🚌 2,47, 55, 62, 65, 69, 76.

THIS SQUARE IS dedicated to Raoul Wallenberg (1912–unknown), who during World War II worked as a diplomat at the Swedish Embassy in Budapest. By using Swedish "protective passports" and safe houses throughout the city he helped a large number of Hungarian Jews to escape deportation to the Nazi concentration camps.

In 1945, when Budapest was liberated, Wallenberg was imprisoned by the Soviet Union and according to Russian sources he died in Moscow's Lubianka prison in 1947. His fate has never been satisfactorily explained despite strenuous efforts by the Swedes to seek the truth.

The small square adjoins Berzelii Park and Nybroplan and faces the Nybrokajen waterfront. The definitive design of the square has been hotly debated because it is set in an architecturally sensitive area, but great efforts have been made to ensure that it remains a worthy memorial to Raoul Wallenberg.

Nybrokajen 11 ⓭

Nybrokajen 11. **Map** 3 C1. 🛈 08-407 16 00. 🚇 Kungsträdgården, Östermalmstorg. 🚌 47, 62, 69, 76 🚢 Djurgårdsfärja. 🕐 for concerts (phone for details). ♿ 🌐 www.nybrokajen11.rikskonserter.se

CONSTRUCTED IN the 1870s, this building facing the waters of Nybroviken once housed the Musical Academy. Its concert hall, opened in 1878, was the first in the country, and was used to present the inaugural Nobel Prize in 1901. Designed in Neo-Renaissance style with cast-iron pillars, the hall has a royal box and galleries, and can seat up to 600 people.

It is run by the state musical organization, Rikskonserter, and is a popular venue for chamber and choral concerts, jazz and folk music.

MALMARNA & FURTHER AFIELD

As STOCKHOLM grew, the heart of the city, Gamla Stan, became cramped and building spread out to the surrounding areas, known as "Malmarna" (the "ore hills"). Parts of these now make up present-day Stockholm.

Södermalm came into the ownership of the city in 1436. Much of Stockholm's old charm can still be found in the areas around Fjällgatan, Mosebacke and Maria-berget. To the north, the Norrmalm area expanded rapidly and became known as Stockholm's northern sub-urb in the 17th century. The once-rural Östermalm was transformed in

Old tram at Djurgården

the late 19th century into an affluent residential area with grand, wide boulevards, con-trasting with the 1930s Functionalist style of the adjoining Gärdet district.

To the west is Kungsholmen, the centre for local govern-ment, with distinguished build-ings such as Stadshuset (the City Hall) and Rådhuset (the Law Court). Nationalstadsparken (the National City Park), a green area of ecological and cultural interest sur-rounding the city and reaching into its central districts, offers lovely walking routes and many of the city's foremost museums.

SIGHTS AT A GLANCE

Biologiska Museet **5**
Drottningholm (pp106–9) **36**
Etnografiska Museet **11**
Fjällgatan (p104) **32**
Globen **34**
Gröna Lund **7**
Hagaparken **19**
Historiska Museet (pp84–5) **1**
Judiska Museet **23**
Junibacken **3**

Kaknästornet **14**
Karlbergs Slott **22**
Katarina Kyrka **31**
Katarinahissen **30**
Långholmen **28**
Millesgården **16**
Naturhistoriska Riksmuseet **18**
Nordiska Museet (pp88–9) **4**
Observatoriemuseet **24**
Sjöhistoriska Museet **13**

Skansen **8**
Skogskyrkogården **35**
Stadion **17**
Stadsbiblioteket **25**
Stadshuset (pp100–1) **26**
Stockholm Archipelago (pp110–11) **37**
Stockholms Stads-Museum **29**
Strandvägen **2**
Tekniska Museet **12**

Tessinparken & Nedre Gärdet **15**
Thielska Galleriet **10**
Ulriksdal **20**
Waldemarsudde **9**
Vasamuseet (pp90–91) **6**
Vin- & Sprithistoriska Museet **21**
Vita Bergen **33**
Västerbron **27**

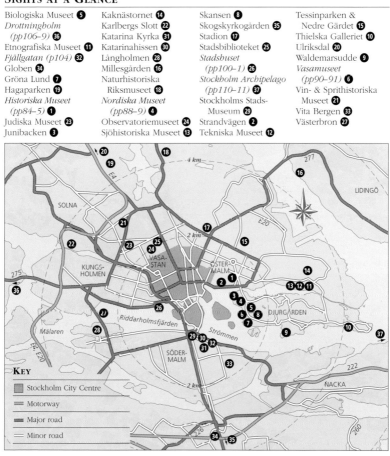

KEY

- ▨ Stockholm City Centre
- ━ Motorway
- ━ Major road
- ─ Minor road

◁ **Stadshuset with Norr Mälarstrand on Kungsholmen and the Västerbron bridge in the background**

Historiska Museet ●

THE MUSEUM OF NATIONAL ANTIQUITIES, Historiska Museet, was opened in 1943. It was designed by Bengt Romare and Georg Sherman. Bror Marklund (1907–77) was responsible for the decoration around the entrance and the richly detailed bronze gateways depicting events in early Swedish history. The museum originally made its name with its exhibits from the Viking era, as well as its outstanding collections from the early Middle Ages. Contemporary church textiles are also on show. Many of Historiska Museet's gold treasures have been gathered together to form one of Stockholm's most remarkable sights, Guldrummet (the Gold Room).

Upper floor

Exhibitions showing the mass migrations and the Wendic era.

Bronze Age Find
This Bronze Age artifact, thought to be a percussion instrument, was discovered in a bog in southern Sweden in 1847.

Courtyard

★ **The Alunda Elk**
This 21-cm (8-inch) stone axe, discovered in 1920 at Alunda in central Sweden, resembles an elk's head. It is a ceremonial axe, probably made in Finland or Karelia in around 2000 BC.

Rosen-gården

Ground floor

The Bäckaskog Woman
The 155-cm (5-ft) tall Bäcka-skog woman lived around 5000 BC. She died at the age of 40–50 and was buried sitting in a cramped pit.

STAR FEATURES

★ **The Alunda Elk**

★ **Maria from Viklau**

★ **The Gold Room**

The Viking Era
This eventful era is reflected in a department whose exhibits include a Viking sword with artistic embellish-ments, and ornaments in the shape of Nordic animals.

The Skog Tapestry
This once hung in the wooden church at Skog in northern Sweden. It is one of the museum's oldest textile treasures.

Baroque Hall

Stairs descending to the Gold Room

Main entrance

★ **Maria from Viklau**
This Madonna figure without child is the best-preserved example from Sweden's early medieval period. The colourful wooden sculpture is richly gilded.

VISITORS' CHECKLIST

Narvavägen 13–17. **Map** 2 F4.
08-519 556 00. 44, 56.
Karlaplan. mid-Sep–mid-May: 11am–5pm Tue–Sun, also 5–8pm Thur; mid-May–mid-Sep: 11am–5pm daily.
24, 25 & 31 Dec and some holidays.
www.historiska.se

GALLERY GUIDE
The exhibitions are divided chronologically on two floors with the prehistoric section on the ground floor and the Middle Ages on the upper floor, where there is also a Baroque Hall. In the basement, reached by a staircase from the entrance hall, is the Gold Room with stunning gold and silver objects.

KEY

- Prehistoric Era
- Middle Ages and Baroque
- Temporary exhibitions
- Non-exhibition space

★ **THE GOLD ROOM**
Since the early 1990s the museum's many priceless gold artifacts have been on show in Guldrummet (the Gold Room), a 700-sq m (7,500-sq ft) underground vault built with 250 tons of reinforced concrete to ensure security. The room is in two circular sections. The inner section houses the main collection, with 50 kg (110 lb) of gold treasures and 250 kg (550 lb) of silver from the Bronze Age to the Middle Ages.

The Elisabeth Reliquary was originally a drinking goblet which was mounted with gold and precious stones in the 11th century. In about 1230 a silver cover was added to enclose the skull of St Elisabeth. Sweden seized it in Wurzburg in 1631, as a trophy in the Thirty Years War.

The Gold Collars were found between 1827 and 1864; the three-ringed collar in a stone quarry in eastern Sweden, the five-ringed in a ditch on the island of Öland, and the seven ringed hanging on a spike in a barn.

The underground Gold Room in Historiska Museet

Strandvägen with its stately houses and boats along the quayside

Strandvägen ❷

Map 4 E1. 🚌 47, 69, 76.
Ⓣ Östermalmstorg, Karlaplan. 🚋 7.

In the early 1900s Stockholm's 10 richest citizens – seven of whom were wholesale merchants – lived in palatial new houses along Strandvägen. Before 1897, when a major exhibition was held just across the water on Djurgården, this muddy, hilly stretch known as Ladugårdslands Strandgata aspired to becoming "a street, the like of which will not be found anywhere else in Europe". It was a long process. Even after all the grand buildings had been completed, the wooden quay erected in the 1860s was something of an eyesore. It was still used up to the 1940s by boats bringing firewood from the archipelago islands.

Nevertheless, the renamed Strandvägen, with its three rows of lime trees, soon became the elegant boulevard envisaged and, then as now, it was a popular place for a stroll, to admire the elegant façades, watch the boats and to see and be seen.

The financiers behind this and other housing projects in the early 1900s were wealthy and could call on the best architects, including I G Clason (1856–1930). Clason was influenced by Italian and French Renaissance styles for his work on No. 19–21 (Thaveniuska Huset) and No. 29–35 (Bünszowska Huset), where he designed gateways made of ships' timbers. No. 55 (Von Rosenska Palatset) is also by Clason.

Junibacken ❸

Galärvarvsvägen. **Map** 4 F1.
🕿 08-587 230 00. 🚌 44, 47. 🚋 7.
⛴ Djurgårdsfärja. ◷ 10am–5pm Tue–Fri, 9am–6pm Sat & Sun; July: 9am–7pm daily. 🈂 ♿ 🚻 🖥 🚹
☒ www.junibacken.se

They are all here – Pippi Longstocking, Mardie, Karlsson on the Roof, Emil, Nils Karlsson Pyssling, Ronja the robber's daughter, the Lionheart Brothers and many more favourite characters

A colourful scene from one of Astrid Lindgren's stories

from Astrid Lindgren's children's books. In accordance with the popular novelist's wishes, visitors can also meet the creations of other Swedish children's authors. When she heard about Staffan Götesam's project for a children's cultural centre she was adamant it should not be just an Astrid Lindgren museum.

Nevertheless Junibacken is still something of a tribute to the much-loved author. It was officially opened by the Royal Family in the summer of 1996 and has become one of the city's most popular tourist attractions. A mini-train takes visitors from a mock-up of the station at Vimmerby (the author's home town) to meet some of her characters, finishing with a visit to Pippi's home in Villekulla Cottage, where children can play in the different rooms.

There is also a well-stocked children's bookshop and a restaurant.

WOODEN BOATS ALONG STRANDVÄGEN

Until the 1940s sailing vessels used to carry firewood from Roslagen on the Baltic coast to the quayside at Strandvägen. This trade had lost its importance by the 1950s, and boating enthusiasts started buying up these old vessels. Some were renovated and sailed to the Caribbean, others became illegal drinking or gambling clubs on Strandvägen. New harbour regulations led to the formation of two associations to administer the boats. The wooden boats moored here today are owned by people who want to preserve a piece of cultural heritage. Every boat has a sign describing its history.

Old wooden boats along the Strandvägen quay

ASTRID LINDGREN AND PIPPI LONGSTOCKING

Astrid Lindgren has written around 100 children's books which have been translated into 74 languages, making her one of the world's most-read children's authors. Publishers turned down her first book about Pippi Longstocking, but she went on to win a children's book competition two years later, in 1945. Her headstrong and tough character Pippi soon won the hearts of children worldwide.

Astrid Lindgren (1907–2002)

Born on 14 November 1907 in Vimmerby in southern Sweden, Astrid stopped writing books at 85, but her characters live on at Junibacken.

Nordiska Museet ❹

See pp88–9.

Biologiska Museet ❺

Lejonslätten. 📞 *08-442 82 15.* 🚌 *44, 47.* 🚋 *7.* ⏰ *Apr–Oct: 11am–4pm daily; Nov–Mar: noon–3 pm Tue–Sun.* 🎫 *by appointment.* ♿ 🅿 🌐 *www.biologiskamuseet.com*

THE NATIONAL ROMANTIC influences of the late 19th century inspired the architect Agi Lindegren when he was commissioned to design Biologiska Museet (Museum of Biology) in the 1890s. He based his plans on the simple lines of the medieval Norwegian stave churches.

The man behind the museum was the zoologist, hunter and conservationist Gustaf Kolthoff (1845–1913). In 1892, he persuaded the industrialist C F Liljevalch – who later financed the nearby art gallery – to form a company with the aim "to develop and maintain a biological museum to include all the Scandinavian mammals and birds as stuffed specimens in natural surroundings". Within a few months of opening in autumn 1893, Gustaf Kolthoff had delivered a couple of thousand stuffed animals, as well as birds' nests, young and eggs, to the museum. Many of the creatures are

shown against a diorama background, with about 300 species of Scandinavian birds and land mammals in their respective biotypes. Kolthoff's friend, the artist Bruno Liljefors, was responsible for the paintings.

Since 1970 the Museum of Biology has belonged to the Skansen Foundation. During the 1990s it underwent extensive renovation and was reopened on 13 November 1993 – exactly 100 years after its original inauguration.

Vasamuseet ❻

See pp90–91.

Gröna Lund ❼

Lilla Allmänna Gränd 9. 📞 *08-587 501 00.* 🚌 *44, 47.* 🚋 *7.* 🚢 *Djurgårdsfärja.* ⏰ *mid-Apr–mid-Sep: opening hours vary.* ♿ ♿ 🍴 📷 🅿 🌐 *www.gronalund.com*

A TAVERN CALLED Gröna Lund (Green Grove) existed on this site in the 18th century, and it was one of the haunts

Biologiska Museet's wooden façade, inspired by Nordic medieval design

Gröna Lund funfair seen from Kastellholmen

of the renowned troubadour Carl Michael Bellman *(see p93).*

Jakob Schultheis used the tavern's name for the modest-sized funfair which he opened here in 1883 with a two-level horse-drawn roundabout as the main attraction. Today Gröna Lund is Sweden's oldest amusement park.

The 130-day season, starting on 1 May, is short but hectic. Gröna Lund draws about 10,000 visitors a day to its attractions, which include a thrilling roller-coaster, ferris wheel and haunted house. The latest addition to the park's attractions is the free-fall "Power Tower", an 80-m (262-ft) high tower from which visitors drop at a frightening speed.

The park also has restaurants and cafés, three stages, a cabaret restaurant, a theatre and beautiful gardens.

Nearby is Liljevalchs Konsthall, a gallery featuring collections of Swedish, Nordic and international art. It also holds temporary exhibitions, including the annual Spring Salon.

Nordiska Museet ❹

RESEMBLING AN EXTRAVAGANT Renaissance castle, Nordiska Museet portrays everyday life in Sweden from the 1520s to the present day. It was created by Artur Hazelius (1833–1901), who was also the founder of Skansen *(see p92)*. In 1872, he started to collect objects which would remind future generations of the old Nordic farming culture.

The present museum, designed by Isak Gustav Clason, was opened in 1907. Today it has more than 1.5 million exhibits, with everything from luxury clothing and priceless jewellery to everyday items, furniture and children's toys, and replicas of period homes.

Doll's Houses
The doll's houses show typical homes from the 17th century to modern times. This example illustrates one from 1860.

Level 3

Corridor to staircase

Level 2 (Main Hall)

Ground floor

State Bedchamber from Ulvsunda Castle
At the end of the 17th century, the lord of the manor at Ulvsunda accommodated prominent guests in this prestigious bedchamber.

STAR FEATURES

★ **Table Settings**

★ **Strindberg Collection**

★ **Main Hall**

Obelisk with the inscription: "The day may dawn when not even all our gold is enough to form a picture of a bygone era."

Equestrian statue of Karl X Gustav

Main entrance

GALLERY GUIDE
The museum has four floors. From the entrance, stairs lead up to the temporary exhibitions in the Main Hall on Level 2. On the ground level is a section covering the Sami People and Culture. Floor 3 has the Strindberg Collection, Doll's Houses, Table Settings, Traditions and the Fashion and Textile Galleries. On the fourth floor are sections on Folk Art, Interiors, Swedish Homes and Small Objects.

★ **Table Settings**
In the mid-17th century, table settings were a feast for the eyes. A swan is the centrepiece at this meal.

The Proposal
This painting, in the Interiors section, is by Knut Ekwall (1843–1912) and depicts a town flat in the 1880s. The room is heavily decorated with objets d'art, *ornaments and textiles.*

Bridal Crown
It used to be a tradition of the church to lend a crown like this to brides as a symbol of innocence.

Level 4

Children's Playworld

★ Strindberg Collection
This picture, Snowstorm at Sea *(1894), by the writer August Strindberg (see p69), is among the museum's collection of 16 of his paintings.*

KEY

☐	Folk art
☐	Small Objects 1700–1900
☐	Swedish Homes, Interiors
☐	Table Settings, Traditions
☐	Strindberg Collection
☐	Fashion Gallery
☐	Doll's Houses
☐	Textile Gallery
☐	The Sami People
☐	Temporary exhibitions
☐	Non-exhibition space

★ Main Hall
As visitors enter this huge hall, they are greeted by a monumental statue of King Gustav Vasa. It was made in painted and gilded oak by Carl Milles in 1924.

Entrance with access for pushchairs, prams and wheelchairs

Vasamuseet ❻

AFTER A MAIDEN VOYAGE of just 1,300 m (1,422 yd) in calm weather, the warship *Vasa* capsized in Stockholm's harbour on 10 August 1628. About 50 people went down with what was supposed to be the pride of the navy, only 100 m (109 yd) off the southern tip of Djurgården. Guns were all that were salvaged from the vessel in the 17th century and it was not until 1956 that a marine archaeologist's persistent search led to the rediscovery of *Vasa*. A complex operation began to salvage the wreck, followed by a 17-year conservation programme. The city's most popular museum opened in 1990, less than a nautical mile from the scene of the disaster.

Gun-port Lion
More than 200 carved ornaments and 500 sculpted figures decorate Vasa.

★ Lion Figurehead
King Gustav II Adolf, who commissioned Vasa, *was known as the Lion of the North. So a springing lion was the obvious choice for the figurehead. It is 4 m (13 ft) long and weighs 450 kg (990 lb).*

To the restaurant

Museum shop

Information desk

Entrance

Emperor Titus
Carvings of 20 Roman emperors stand on parade on Vasa.

Bronze Cannon
More than 50 of Vasa's *64 original cannons were salvaged in the 17th century. Three 11-kg (24-lb) bronze cannons are on display in the museum.*

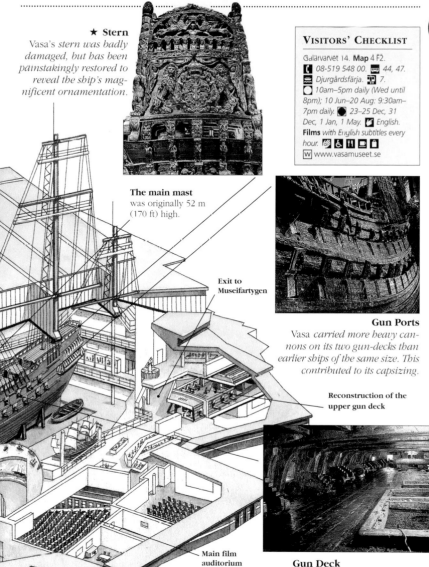

★ **Stern**
Vasa's *stern was badly damaged, but has been painstakingly restored to reveal the ship's magnificent ornamentation.*

The main mast
was originally 52 m (170 ft) high.

Exit to Museifartygen

Gun Ports
Vasa *carried more heavy cannons on its two gun-decks than earlier ships of the same size. This contributed to its capsizing.*

Reconstruction of the upper gun deck

Main film auditorium

Gun Deck
Visitors cannot board the ship, but there is a full-size replica of the upper gun deck with carved wooden dummies of sailors, which gives a good idea of conditions on board.

THE SALVAGE OPERATION

The marine archaeologist Anders Franzén had been looking for *Vasa* for many years. On 25 August 1956 his patience was rewarded when he brought up a piece of blackened oak on his plumb line. From the autumn of 1957, it took divers two years to clear space beneath the hull for the lifting cables. The first lift using six cables was a success, after which *Vasa* was raised in 16 stages into shallow water. Plugs were inserted into holes left by rusted iron bolts, then the final lift began and on 4 May 1961 *Vasa* was towed into dry dock.

Vasa **in dry dock after being salvaged in 1961**

STAR FEATURES

★ **Lion Figurehead**

★ **Stern**

Hornborgastugan, a 19th-century timber cottage at Skansen

Skansen ❽

Djurgårdsslätten 49. 📞 08-442 80 00.
🚌 44, 47. 🚋 7. ⛴ Djurgårdsfärja.
🕐 daily Oct–Apr: 10am–4pm; May:
10am–8pm; Jun–Aug: 10am–10pm;
Sep: 10am–5pm. ⬛ Jun–Aug.
⬤ 24 Dec. 🎨 ♿ 🎁 🍴 🎁
Seglora Kyrka 🚩 call for details.
🌐 www.skansen.se

THE WORLD'S FIRST open-air
museum, Skansen was
established in 1891 to
show an increasingly
industrialized society
how people once
lived. It comprises
around 150 houses
and farm buildings
from all over
Sweden. But it is
not just a museum,
Skansen also plays an
important role in nurturing the
country's folklore and
traditions. Sweden's National
Day, Walpurgis Night, Midsummer, Christmas and New
Year's Eve celebrations take
place here *(see pp26–9)*.

In the Town Quarter,
complete with 19th-century
wooden town houses, glassblowers, bookbinders and
other craftspeople demons-
trate their skills. The 300-year-
old Älvros farmhouse, from
the Härjedalen region,
represents rural life with an
intriguing collection of everyday tools. At the other end of
the scale, Skogaholms
Herrgård *(see p18)*, a Carolian
manor from 1680, shows how
the wealthy lived. The shingle-
roofed Seglora Church (1729)
is popular for weddings.

Nordic animals such as elk,
wolves and bears, can be
seen in the zoo, and exotic
snakes in the aquarium.

**Brown bear
at Skansen**

Waldemarsudde ❾

Prins Eugens Väg 6.
📞 08-545 837 00. 🚌 47. 🚋 7.
🕐 11am–5pm Tue–Sun, 11am–8pm
Thu. 🎨 🖼 ♿ 🍴 🎁 🎁
🌐 www.waldemarsudde.com

PRINCE EUGEN'S Waldemar-
sudde, which passed into
State ownership after his death
in 1947, is one of Sweden's
most visited art galleries.
The prince was trained as a
military officer, but
became a successful
artist and was one
of the leading land-
scape painters of
his generation. He
produced mon-
umental paintings
for several of the city's
important buildings,
including Kungliga Operan,
Kungliga Dramatiska Teatern

and Rådhuset. Among his
own works hanging in
Waldemarsudde, his former
palace, are three of his most
prized paintings: *Spring*
(1891), *The Old Castle* (1893)
and *The Cloud* (1896).

Together with works by his
contemporaries, the gallery
holds an impressive collection
of early 20th-century Swedish
art. Oscar Björck, Carl Fredrik
Hill, Richard Bergh, Nils
Kreuger, Eugène Jansson,
Bruno Liljefors and Anders
Zorn are all featured.

Prince Eugen was a
generous patron to the next
generation – the group known
as "The Young Ones" – so
works by younger artists,
including Isaac Grünewald,
Einar Jolin, Sigrid Hjertén and
Leander Engström are also in
the collection. Sculptors of the
same era are well represented,
particularly Per Hasselberg,
whose works can be seen in
both the gallery and the park.

Prince Eugen and his
architect, Ferdinand Boberg,
drew up the sketches for the
palace, completed in 1905.
The same architect was called
in later to design the gallery,
which was finished in 1913.
This now includes parts of the
collection of some 2,000
works, as well as the Prince's
own paintings.

The guest apartments remain
largely unchanged, and the

Prince Eugen's Waldemarsudde, seen from the water

Hornsgatan (1902) by Eugène Jansson, in Thielska Galleriet

two upper floors with the Prince's studio at the top are used for temporary exhibitions. The buildings are surrounded by beautiful gardens.

Thielska Galleriet ⓾

Sjötullsbacken 6–8.
📞 08 662 58 04. 🚌 69.
🕐 noon–4pm Mon–Sat, 1–4pm Sun.
📷 by appointment. 🖼️ 💻

WHEN THE magnificent apartments of the banker Ernest Thiel (1860–1947) on Strandvägen started to overflow with his comprehensive collection of Nordic art from the late 19th and early 20th centuries, he commissioned the architect Ferdinand Boberg to design a dignified villa on Djurgården.

However, during World War I Thiel lost most of his fortune. His collection was bought by the State, which opened Thielska Galleriet in his villa in 1926.

Thiel was regarded as something of a rebel in the banking world. He was particularly fond of works by painters belonging to the Artists' Union, which had been formed in 1886 to counter the influence of the traditionalist Konstakademien (Royal Academy of the Arts).

There are paintings by all the major Swedish artists who formed an artists' colony at Grèz-sur-Loing, south of Paris, including Carl Larsson, Bruno

Liljefors, Karl Nordström and August Strindberg.

In additon, the gallery features works by Eugène Jansson, Anders Zorn and Prince Eugen, as well as wooden figures by Axel Petersson and sculptures by Christian Eriksson. Thiel also acquired pieces by foreign artists, not least his good friend Edvard Munch.

Etnografiska Museet ⓫

Djurgårdsbrunnsvägen 34.
📞 08-519 550 00. 🚌 69. 🕐 11am–5pm daily. 📷 🖼️ ♿ 🍴 💻 🏪
🌐 www.etnografiska.se

THE NATIONAL MUSEUM of Ethnography is a showcase for the collections brought home to Sweden by enterprising travellers and

scientists from the 18th century to the present day. All are arranged in imaginative displays designed to provide a better understanding of the unknown or unfamiliar from around the world.

Another aspect of the museum's work is to reflect the multicultural influences on Sweden brought about by the large-scale immigration into the country during the late 20th century.

The explorer Sven Hedin (1865–1952), who was the last Swede to be ennobled (in 1902), contributed many exhibits to the museum, including Buddha figures and Chinese costumes, as well as Mongolian temple tents donated by leaders of the Kalmuck people in western China to King Gustav V.

Another section of interest shows masks and totem poles from western Canada.

A Japanese tea house was opened in 1990, which is a work of art in itself. Here, visitors to the museum can take part in traditional tea ceremonies during the summer.

Religious mask from British Columbia

The museum runs an extensive educational programme. It has published an international magazine, *Ethnos*, every year since 1936 and maintains a comprehensive reference library.

The "Babajan" restaurant offers a taste of foods from all over the world, and provides an impressive list of beers from far and near.

AN IMMORTAL TROUBADOUR

Carl Michael Bellman (1740–95) was a much-loved troubadour. Gustav III gave him a job as secretary of a lottery, but he was best known around Stockholm's many taverns – particularly on Djurgården. His works about the drunken watchmaker Jean Fredman and his contemporaries (*Fredman's Epistles* and *Fredman's Songs*) have never lost their popularity and form part of Sweden's musical heritage. A bust of Bellman was unveiled on Djurgården in 1829 in the presence of Queen Desideria.

Bust of Bellman by J N Byström (1829)

Kaknästornet with the buildings of Sjöhistoriska Museet, Tekniska Museet and Folkens Museum Etnografiska in the foreground

Tekniska Museet ⓬

Museivägen 7. 📞 08-450 56 00. 🚌 69. 🕐 10am–5pm Mon–Tue, Thu–Fri, 10am–8pm Wed, 11am–5pm Sat & Sun. 📷 by appointment. 🔶 🔶 🔶 🍴 🖥 🅦 www.tekniskamuseet.se

T HE MUSEUM OF Science and Technology contains a wealth of exhibits connected with Sweden's technical and industrial history. It also houses the science centre, Teknorama, with hands-on experiments designed for children and young people.

The machinery hall features the country's oldest preserved steam engine. Built in 1832, it was used in a coal mine in southern Sweden. The locomotive "Lotta" is here, along with the classic model T-Ford and early Swedish cars from Volvo, Scania and Saab. Swinging from above is Sweden's first commercial aircraft, built in 1924. There is another rarity – the scientist Emanuel Swedenborg's model of a "flying machine" (1716).

The museum also has sections on electric power, computing, technology in the home, and the Swedish forestry, mining, iron and steel industries.

Tekniska Museet's machinery hall with historic aircraft

Sjöhistoriska Museet ⓭

Djurgårdsbrunnsvägen 24. 📞 08-519 549 00. 🚌 69. 🕐 10am–5pm Tue–Sun; spring and autumn also 10am–8.30pm Tue. 📷 🔶 🔶 🔶 🅦 www.sjohistoriska.nu

T HE NATIONAL MARITIME Museum focuses on shipping, shipbuilding and naval defence. It is housed in an attractive building, designed by the architect Ragnar Östberg in 1938, in a beautiful location by the calm waters of Djurgårds-brunnsviken.

There are some 100,000 exhibits, including more than 1,500 model ships. The oldest Swedish model is a reproduction of the "Cathedral ship" from the early 1600s. The model collection comprises every conceivable type of ship from small coasters and Viking longboats to oil tankers, coal vessels, dinghies, full-riggers and submarines. A series of models on a scale of 1:200 shows the development of ships in Scandinavia since the Iron Age.

Life-size settings provide a good idea of life on board the various ships. Among them are the exquisite original cabin and elegant stern from the royal schooner *Amphion.* Designed by the leading shipbuilder F H af Chapman and built at the Djurgården shipyard, *Amphion* was Gustav III's flagship in the

Figurehead, about 1850

1788–90 war with Russia. Contrasting with this is the cramped forecastle from the schooner *Hoppet,* where four crew members ate, slept and spent their time off watch.

The museum has some notable examples of ship decoration from the late 17th century. They include part of the national coat of arms recovered by divers in the 1920s from the stern of the *Riksäpplet,* which sank at Dalarö in 1676. A large relief portrayal of Karl XI on horseback from the stern of *Carolus XI* – an 82-cannon ship launched from the shipyard in 1678 – is also on show. It is thought that the relief was removed some years later when the ship was renamed *Sverige.* There are many fine figureheads in the collection, including one depicting Amphion, the son of Zeus, playing his lyre, which adorned the schooner of the same name.

Linked to the museum is the Swedish Marine Archaeology Archive, containing an extensive collection of maritime documents and photographs. There is a special children's section with a workshop which is open on Sundays and in school holidays.

On the gable facing Djurgårdsbrunnsviken is *The Sailor,* a monument to the victims of naval warfare by Nils Sjögren.

Kaknästornet ⓮

Ladugårdsgärdet. 📞 08-667 21 05. 🚌 69. 🕐 May–Aug: 9am–10pm daily; Sep–Apr: 10am– 9pm daily. 📷 by appointment. 🔶 🔶 🍴 🖥 🅦

A NCHORED BY 72 steel poles, driven 8 m (26 ft) into the rock, the 34-storey Kaknästornet soars to a height of 155 m (508 ft). The tower, designed by the architects Bengt Lindroos and Hans Borgström, was opened in 1967. It was erected as a

centre for the country's television and radio broadcasting and also contains technical equipment to conduct conferences by satellite between European cities. Five dishes to the left of the tower – the largest of which has a diameter of 13 m (43 ft) – relay signals to and from satellites. The main hall containing the transmitters and receivers has been blasted out of the rock below the dishes.

The observation points on levels 30 and 31 provide a spectacular view of the city, and the restaurant on the 28th floor has panoramic windows. It is reached by two lifts, travelling at 18 km/h (11 mph). There is a tourist information office at the entrance, selling souvenirs, maps and the Stockholm Card (see p321). Decorative features include a wall relief by Walter Bengtsson, which was inspired by the tower's daunting technology.

Millesgården, home of the sculptor Carl Milles in the early 20th century

between 1932 and 1937, have their own gardens and blend in such a way that they give the impression of being part of the park itself.

The earliest houses, nearest to Valhallavägen, still show signs of 1920s Classicism, although Gärdet's real hallmark is Functionalism (see p24). The lower white houses along Askrikegatan, marking the northern boundary of the park, are Functionalist in style and noticeably different from other buildings in Gärdet. Some 60 different architects were involved in designing the Gärdet development, including Sture Frölén.

A granite statue of a woman with a suitcase, Housewife's Holiday, stands in the part of Tessin Park adjoining Valhallavägen. It was made by Olof Thorwald Ohlsson in the 1970s. At the other end of the park is a colourful concrete statue, The Egg, by Egon Möller-Nielsen.

Functionalist style, Tessinparken

Tessinparken & Nedre Gärdet ⓯

Map 3 F2. Ⓣ Karlaplan, Gärdet.
🚌 1, 4, 62, 72.

Three generations of the Tessin family of architects (see p24) have given their name to this park which opened at Lower Gärdet in 1931. Tessinparken runs from north to south and is attractively designed with lawns, play areas, paths and ponds. The adjoining houses, built

Millesgården ⓰

Herserudsvägen 32, Lidingö.
Ⓣ Ropsten, then bus 203 or 207, or train to Torsvik. 📞 08-446 75 90.
🕐 mid-May–Aug: 10am–5pm daily; Sep–mid-May: noon–5pm Thur–Sun.
📅 by appointment. ♿ 🎫 🍴 🛍
🌐 www.millesgarden.se

Carl Milles (1875–1955) was one of the 20th century's greatest Swedish sculptors and the best known internationally. From 1931 he lived for 20 years in the USA, where he became a prolific monumental sculptor with works such as the Meeting of the Waters fountain in St Louis and the Resurrection fountain in the National Memorial Park outside Washington DC. In Stockholm visitors can see 15 of his public works, including the Orpheus fountain in front of Konserthuset (see p69).

In 1906 Milles purchased land on the island of Lidingö on which he built a house, completed in 1908. He lived here with his wife until 1931, and also after his return from the USA. In 1936 he and his wife donated the property to the people of Sweden. Millesgården extends over a series of terraces filled with sculptures and includes Milles' studios with originals and replicas of his work. There is a magnificent garden – a work of art in itself – and a fine view over the water.

Tessinparken, surrounded by Functionalist-style housing dating from the late 1930s

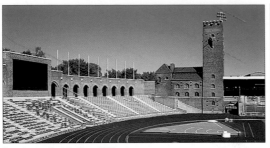

Running track at Stadion, 1912

Stadion ⑰

Lidingövägen 1–3. **Map** 2 E2.
[08-508 260 00. [T] Stadion.
📧 4, 55, 72, 73. ◯ mid-Apr–mid-
Oct. 🎫 during events. ♿ 🔲

A NEW MAIN ARENA was built
for the 1912 Olympic
Games in Stockholm, the
towers of which have become
a familiar landmark on the
capital's skyline. The architect
of Stadion, Torben Grut
(1871–1945), followed the
National Romantic influences
of the day. The complex is
richly decorated. The clock
tower has two
figures by Carl
Fagerberg, *Ask
and Embla*, the
counterparts of
Adam and Eve in
Nordic mythology.
There are also busts of
Victor Balck, the man
behind the 1912
Olympics, and
P H Ling, the
father of Swedish
gymnastics.

Four notable sculptures
were added in the 1930s. The
painter and gymnast Bruno
Liljefors created *Play* at the
main entrance, Carl Eldh
made *The Runners*, and Carl
Fagerberg provided *Relay
Runners* and *The Shot-Putter*.

Stadion has continued to be
an important venue for
athletics events. The European Athletics Championships
were held here in 1958, and
an international athletics gala
is staged every summer. In
1990 it hosted the World
Equestrian Championships.

The arena is also the venue
for ice hockey and bandy (a
type of hockey) champion-
ship events.

Naturhistoriska Riksmuseet ⑱

5 km (3 miles) N of city centre along
road 264. [08-519 540 00.
[T] Universitetet. 📧 40, 540.
◯ 10am–7pm Tue–Sun; Jun–Jul: also
10am–7pm Mon. 🎫 by appointment.
🎫 ♿ 🏛 🔲 🍴 [w] www.nrm.se

C OMPLETED IN 1916, the vast
Naturhistoriska Riks-
museet (Natural History
Museum) was designed by
Axel Anderberg and decorated by Carl Fagerberg. The
museum is a venerable
institution, founded in
1739 by Carl von
Linné *(see p128)* as
part of Vetenskaps-
akademien (the
Academy of
Science). It is one
of the 10 largest
museums of its
kind in the world.
Over the centuries,
the number of
exhibits has risen
to 17 million.

**Polar bear, Natur-
historiska Riksmuseet**

During the 1990s it was
modernized and there are
both permanent and
temporary exhibitions on a
wide range of themes from
dinosaurs and sea creatures to
the "Marvels of the Human
Body". The hugely popular
Cosmonova opened at the
same time. Both a planet-
arium and an IMAX cinema,
its screen is 25 times the size
of a conventional one. The
Vega Monument was erected
in front of the museum in 1930
to mark the 50th anniversary
of explorer Adolf Erik
Nordenskiöld's return from
the first voyage through the
Northeast Passage in his ship
Vega. Designed by Ivar Johnsson, it is an obelisk in granite
topped with a copper ship.

Hagaparken ⑲

4 km (2.5 miles) N of city centre, along
E4. 📧 515. **Haga Parkmuseum**
[08-27 42 52. ◯ Jun–Aug:
11am–5pm Tue–Sun. **Gustav III's
Paviljong** [08-402 61 30. 🎫 every
hour Jun–Aug: noon–3pm Tue–Sun.
Fjärils- & Fågelhuset [08-730 39
81. ◯ Apr–Sep: 10am–4pm Tue–Fri,
11am–5.30pm Sat & Sun; Oct–Apr:
10am–3pm Tue–Fri, 11am–4pm Sat &
Sun. ● 24, 25 & 31 Dec. 🔲 🍴 in
Koppartälten and Fjärils- & Fågelhuset
and Café Vasaslätten.

K ING GUSTAV VASA decided to
create a royal park in the
popular Haga area in the mid-
18th century. The king's
vision was realized by the
architect of the moment,
Fredrik Magnus Piper. The
result was an English-style
park with some very unusual
buildings, including the
Chinese Pagoda and the
Roman battle tent,
Koppartälten. A royal palace
inspired by Versailles in
France was also planned, but
construction came to a halt
after the king's death and it
remained unfinished.

Gustav III's Pavilion, a
Gustavian masterpiece
designed by Olof
Tempelman, with an
interior by Louis
Masreliéz, is the park's
greatest architectural
attraction, while
Fjärils- & Fågelhuset

Hagaparken's Roman battle tent, designed by Louis Jean Desprez (1790)

has exotic butterflies and birds flying freely around a tropical greenhouse.

Haga Slott, built in 1802–04 for Gustav IV Adolf, was the childhood home of the present monarch, Carl XVI Gustaf, and his sisters. Now it is used for government receptions and to accommodate visiting heads of state.

Hagaparken is very popular with Stockholmers, who come all year round. The park is part of Ekoparken, an oasis of nature and culture close to the city centre *(see box)*.

Exotic butterflies in the greenhouses at Hagaparken

Ulriksdal 20

7 km (4 miles) N of Stockholm.
08-402 61 30. 503. **Palace**
Jun–Aug: noon–4pm Tue–Sun.
Jun–Aug: noon, 1pm, 2pm & 3pm. **Orangery** Jun–Aug: noon–4pm Tue–Sun.
w www.royalcourt.se

SITUATED ON a headland in the bay of Edsviken, Ulriksdal's attractive buildings and leafy surroundings are well worth a visit. At the entrance to the grounds is one of Stockholm's best-known restaurants, Ulriksdals Wärdshus *(see p296)*.

The original palace was built in the 1640s and designed by Hans Jakob Kristler in German/Dutch Renaissance style. The owner, Marshal of the Realm Jakob de la Gardie, named the palace Jakobsdal. It was bought in 1669 by the Dowager Queen Hedvig Eleonora. Fifteen years later, she donated the palace to her grandson Ulrik as a christening gift, and it was renamed Ulriksdal.

Around this time the architect Tessin the Elder *(see p24)* suggested some rebuilding

Ulriksdal with its magnificent 18th-century Baroque exterior

work, but only a few of his proposals saw the light of day. However, the stucco work by Carlo Carove in the southern wing can be seen. In the 18th century the palace acquired its Baroque exterior.

After being a popular place for festivities in the time of Gustav III (1746–92), it began to lose its glamour. Interest was revived under Karl XV (1826–72), and furnishings and handicrafts many hundreds of years old are on show in his rooms.

The park was laid out in the mid-17th century. It has 300-year-old lime trees, as well as one of Europe's most northerly beechwoods. Carl Milles's two sculptures of wild

boars stand by the pool in front of the palace. A stream is crossed by a footbridge, which is supported by Per Lundgren's *Moors Dragging the Nets*.

More art can be seen in the orangery, designed by Tessin the Elder in the 1660s and rebuilt in 1705. It now houses a sculpture museum.

The palace chapel, a popular place for weddings, was designed by F W Scholander and built in 1865 in Dutch Neo-Renaissance style. The riding school, built in 1671, was converted into a theatre by Carl Härleman and C F Adelcrantz in the 1750s. Performances are staged in the theatre every summer.

EKOPARKEN – THE NATIONAL CITY PARK

Ekoparken – the world's first National City Park – was established by the Swedish Parliament in 1995. Its creation has enabled the capital to safeguard the ecology of its "green lung", a 27-sq km (10 5-sq miles) area for recreation and outdoor activities.

The park threads through Stockholm's central districts, including Skeppsholmen and the southern part of Djurgården, and continues northwest to northern Djurgården, Hagaparken, Brunnsviken and Ulriksdal. It also encompasses the tiny islands of Fjäderholmarna *(see p110)*. Much of the park was a royal hunting ground as early as the 16th century, scattered with beautiful palaces and other sights.

Haga Forum, at the southern entrance to Hagaparken, provides pleanty of information about Ekoparken.

There are also boat tours on Brunnsviken, with stops at some of the sights. For further details, telephone 08-587 140 40.

Breeding herons at Isbladskärret, part of Ekoparken's rich bird-life

Karlbergs Slott, a palace dating from the 1630s – now one of Sweden's military academies

Vin- & Sprithistoriska Museet ㉑

Dalagatan 100. **Map** 1 A1.
📞 08-744 70 70. Ⓣ Odenplan.
🚌 65, 69. ⏱ 10am–7pm Tue,
10am– 4pm Wed–Fri, noon–4pm Sat
& Sun. 🅿️ 🦽 📷 🏠 🖥️ 🛗
Ⓦ www.vinosprithistoriska.se

SWEDISH PUNSCH and schnapps
are the themes of Vin- &
Sprithistoriska (Wine and
Spirits Historical Museum),
located in a former wine
warehouse. The building was
designed by
Cyrillus Johansson
and completed in
1923, but as the
trade of wine in
barrels decreased,
the warehouse
began to be used
for other pur-
poses until
1967, when the first exhibition
was staged.

**Schnapps label, Vin- &
Sprithistoriska Museet**

Today's museum dates from
1989. It shows how a wine
shop would have looked
around 1900. From the same
era is a typical southern
Swedish distillery in which
potatoes were used to make
schnapps. There is also a
collection of spices added to
schnapps and liqueurs, and
50,000 labels are on show.

Visitors can listen to some
200 "schnapps songs" via a
computer, which also has the
texts of 2,000 drinking songs.

Karlbergs Slott ㉒

Karlsbergs Slottsväg. 📞 08-562 813
01. 🚌 42, 72 to Karlberg station,
then 15-min walk. 📷 groups only, by
appointment.

ADMIRAL KARL Karlsson
Gyllenhielm started to
build Karlbergs Slott in the
1630s, during the Thirty Years
War. From 1670 the palace
was extended and rebuilt by
Magnus Gabriel de la Gardie,
with Jean de la Vallée as his
architect. When Karlberg became royal property in 1688,
it was one of
Sweden's most
majestic palaces.
It was where the
"hero King" Karl
XII (1682–1718)
grew up, and it
was here that he
lay in state after
his death at the
Battle of Fredrikshald *(see
p35)*. In 1792 the architect
C C Gjörwell converted the
property into the Royal
War Academy, which later
became the Karlberg
Military School, and since
1999 it has been the site
for one of the country's
military academies.

The interior decorations
include Carl Carove's
magnificent stucco-work
which can be seen in the
grand hall. The palace
church has been
renovated several times,
but the 17th-century lanterns
are original. De la Gardie's
wood-panelled "rarities room"
is now the sacristy, but once
it housed his collection
of valuables.

Judiska Museet ㉓

Hälsingegatan 2. **Map** 1 A2. 📞 08-
31 01 43. Ⓣ Odenplan. 🚌 2, 4,
47, 72. ⏱ noon–4pm Mon–Fri &
Sun. 📷 in English by appointment.
🎦 🦽 🖥️ 🛗

IN 1774 AARON ISAAC became
the first Jewish immigrant
to settle in Stockholm and
practise his religion. Today,
half of Sweden's Jewish
population of around 18,000
live in the Stockholm area.
Judiska Museet depicts the
history of the Swedish Jews
from Isaac's time to the
present day. It focuses on
Judaism as a religion, its inte-
gration into Swedish society
and the Holocaust. A

**An eight-stemmed *chanuki*
(candlestick) at Judiska Museet**

comprehensive collection of pictures and other items provide an insight into Jewish life in Sweden with its traditions and customs. The beautiful *Torah* (the five books of Moses), the bridal canopy, and the collection of eight-stemmed *chanukis* (candlesticks) are just some of the museum's treasured spiritual artifacts.

The old observatory (1748–53) at the top of the Observatory hill

Observatorie-museet ㉔

Drottninggatan 120. **Map** 1 B2.
📞 08-545 483 90. 🚇 *Odenplan.*
🚌 52. ✅ *Oct–Mar: 6pm Tue includes telescope observation if sky is clear; in Eng by appointment.* 🔲 🚻 ♿
🌐 www.observatoriet.kva.se

A NUMBER OF institutions connected with science and education can be found on and around the hill of Brunkeberg. The oldest is the former observatory designed by Carl Hårleman for the Royal Scientific Academy and opened in 1753. In 1931, astronomical research was moved to Saltsjöbaden in the Stockholm archipelago and replaced by Observatorie-museet (the Observatory Museum). Here visitors can see the observation room with its instruments, the two median rooms, the weather room and the instrument workshop. There is a splendid view of Stockholm from the museum's dome and in good weather it is possible to view the stars.

The grove which surrounds the old observatory began to take shape in the 18th century. It is an idyllic enclosed area, first opened to the public in

the 20th century. On top of Brunkeberg is Sigrid Fridman's statue *The Centaur.*

A park stretches down to Sveavägen, where a pond is fed by a stream running down the hillside. The statue *Dancing Youth* is by Ivar Johnsson. At the southern entrance of the park is Nils Möllerberg's sculpture *Youth.*

Stadsbiblioteket ㉕

Sveavägen 73. **Map** 1 B2.
📞 08-508 311 00. 🚇 *Rådmans-gatan.* 🚌 2, 4, 42, 52, 53, 72.
🕐 *10am–8.30pm Mon–Thu, 10am–6pm Fri, noon–4pm Sat & Sun; Jun–Aug: 11am–7pm Mon–Thu, 11am–5pm Fri.* ♿ 🔲 ♿

G UNNAR ASPLUND'S master-piece, Stadsbiblioteket (City Library), is one of the capital's most architecturally important buildings. Asplund,

the champion of the Functionalist style prevalent in the 1930s, designed a public library which was dominated by Classical ideals. It was opened in 1928.

Internally, the furnishings and many of the light fittings were designed by Asplund himself. The work of Swedish artists is well represented: in the entrance hall are Ivar Johnsson's stucco reliefs with themes from Homer's *Iliad*; the sparkling mural painting in the children's section, *John Blund*, is by Nils Dardel; and the depiction of the stars in the heavens by Ulf Munthe. The door lintels, door handles and drinking fountains are by Nils Sjögren. Hilding Linnqvist was responsible for the giant-sized tapestry, and also for four mural paintings using ancient fresco techniques.

The library lends more than a million books every year.

Stadsbiblioteket, in Neo-Classical style, designed by Gunnar Asplund

Stadshuset 26

PROBABLY SWEDEN'S BIGGEST architectural project of the 20th century, the City Hall was completed in 1923 and has become a symbol of Stockholm. It was designed by Ragnar Östberg (1866–1945), the leading architect of the Swedish National Romantic style, and displays influences of both the Nordic Gothic and Northern Italian schools. Several leading Swedish artists contributed to the rich interior design. The building contains the Council Chamber and 250 offices for city administrative staff. The annual Nobel Prize festivities take place in the Blue Hall.

Engel-brekt

★ The Golden Room
The Byzantine-inspired wall mosaics by Einar Forseth (1892–1988) have 19 million fragments of gold leaf. The theme of the northern wall is Queen of Lake Mälaren.

Norra Trapptornet, crowned by a sun.

Stairway to the gallery

★ The Blue Hall
The banqueting room is made from handmade bricks. The name is from the initial plan to paint the bricks blue, but the architect changed his mind.

★ The Prince's Gallery
A fresco, The City on the Water, *in the Prince's Gallery, was painted by Prince Eugen (see p92), who donated it to the City Hall.*

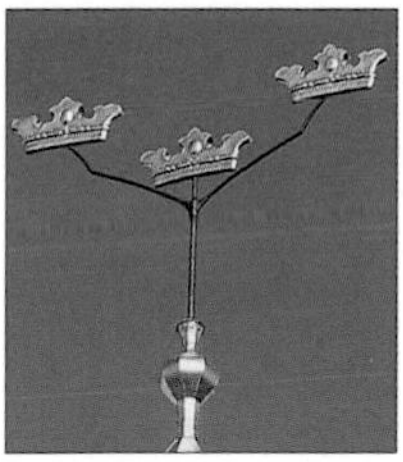

Three Crowns
Sweden's heraldic symbol, Tre Kronor, dating from the 14th century, tops the 106-m (348-ft) tower.

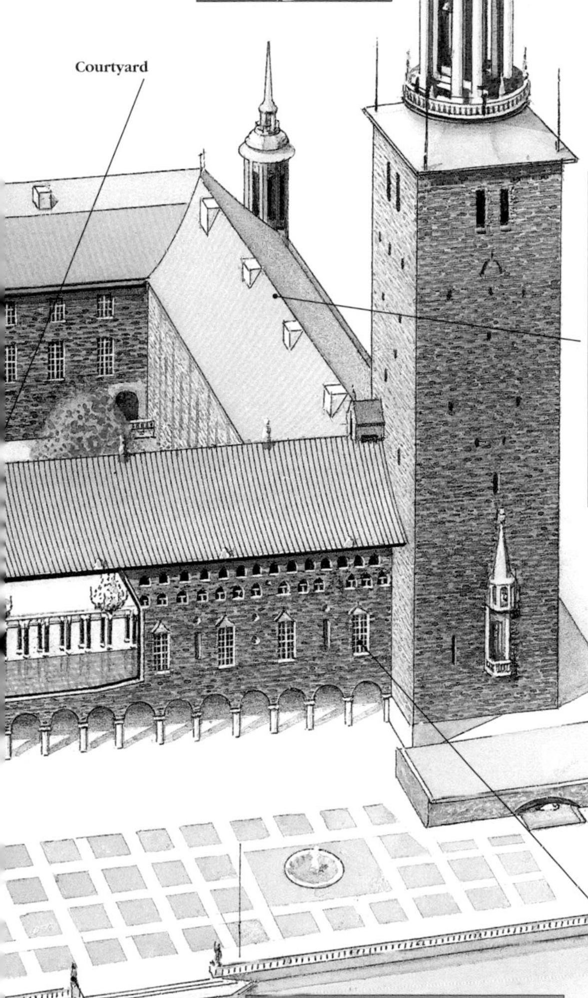

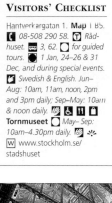

Courtyard
Marriage room

Visitors' Checklist

Hantverkargatan 1. **Map** 1 B5. *08-508 290 58.* *Rådhuset.* *3, 62.* *for guided tours.* *1 Jan, 24–26 & 31 Dec, and during special events.* *Swedish & English. Jun–Aug: 10am, 11am, noon, 2pm and 3pm daily; Sep–May: 10am & noon daily.*
Tornmuseet *May–Sep: 10am–4.30pm daily.*
www.stockholm.se/stadshuset

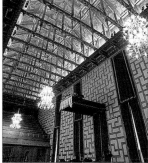

The Council Chamber
Stockholm's 101 councillors meet in this magnificent chamber, which contains furnishings designed by Carl Malmsten.

Engelbrekt the Freedom Fighter
by Christian Eriksson (1858–1935)

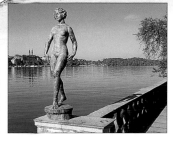

The Dance
The steps leading to Riddarfjärden are flanked by two statues by Carl Eldh. Dansen *is the figure of a woman,* Sången *(The Song) of a man.*

Star Features

- ★ **The Golden Room**
- ★ **The Blue Hall**
- ★ **The Prince's Gallery**

Västerbron bridge, opened in 1935, linking Kungsholmen with Södermalm across Lake Mälaren

Västerbron ②

🚌 4, 40, 74.

AS STOCKHOLM expanded and car-use increased in the 1920s, it became necessary to build an additional bridge between the northern and southern shores of Lake Mälaren. German experts dominated the architectural competition launched in 1930, but their plans were implemented by Swedish architects and engineers and Västerbron bridge was completed in 1935.

The attractive design blends well with the landscape. The bridge is built in two spans of 168 m (551 ft) and 204 m (669 ft) with a vertical clearance of 26 m (85 ft). There are footpaths and cycle lanes on each side and a walk to the centre of Västerbron is rewarded with a magnificent view of central Stockholm.

Exercise yard in the former royal prison on Långholmen

Långholmen ②

🚇 Hornstull, then 3 min walk.
🚌 66. 🅿

BELOW THE MAJESTIC Väster-bron bridge is the island of Långholmen, which is linked to Södermalm by two bridges. Långholmen is best known for the various prisons which have been located here since 1724. During the 20th century it was the site of the largest prison in Sweden, housing 620 inmates. The prison closed in 1975, since when the island has become a popular recreational area.

The prison buildings have been demolished, but the former royal jail dating from 1835 remains. The one-time cells now form both a hotel and a prison museum. There is also a youth hostel and an excellent restaurant, as well as a museum to the poet C M Bellman *(see p93)* with a café in the gardens which run down towards Riddarfjärden.

Långholmen's park has an open-air theatre, and offers excellent swimming both from the beaches and the rocks.

Stockholms Stadsmuseum ②

Ryssgården. **Map** 3 B5.
📞 08-508 316 00. 🚇 *Slussen.* 🚌 2, 3, 43, 53, 55, 76. ◷ *11am–5pm Tue–Sun (Sep–May: also 5–9pm Thu; Jun–Aug: also 5–7pm Thu).* 🎫 🚫
♿ 🅿 🛍 🖾
🖵 www.stadsmuseum.stockholm.se

HEMMED IN between the traffic roundabouts of Slussen and the steep hill up to Mosebacke Torg is Stockholms Stadsmuseum (City Museum). It is housed in a late-17th-century building originally designed by Tessin the Elder as Södra Stadshuset (Southern City Hall). After a fire, it was completed by Tessin the Younger in 1685. It has been used for various purposes over the centuries, including law courts and dungeons, schools and city-hall cellars, theatres and churches, until in the 1930s it became the city museum.

The museum documents the history of Stockholm. The city's main stages of development are described in a slide-show and a series of four permanent exhibitions. The first starts with the Stockholm Bloodbath of 1520 *(see p58)* and continues through the 17th century. The eventful 18th century is illustrated with exhibits that include the Lohe Treasure – 20 kg (44 lb) of silver discovered in Gamla Stan in 1937. The other sections depict industrialization in the 19th century and the tremendous growth in the 20th century with the emergence of a new city centre and new suburbs.

The library has a large picture archive and a reference room where visitors can find out virtually anything they want to know about Stockholm. There are children's activities, concerts and lectures.

The 18th-century Lohe Treasure at Stockholms Stadsmuseum

Katarinahissen ③⓪

Stadsgården. **Map** 3 C5.
🚇 *Slussen.* 🚌 *2, 3, 43, 53, 55, 76.*
🕐 *7.30am–10pm Mon–Sat,
10am–10pm Sun.* ♿ 🍴 ⚱

KATARINAHISSEN IS THE oldest of Stockholm's "high-rise" attractions. The 38-m (125-ft) high lift was opened to the public in March 1883 and is still a prominent silhouette on the Söder skyline. The first Swedish neon sign was erected here in 1909 – a legendary advertisement for Stomatol toothpaste. Since the 1930s, the sign has been placed on a nearby rooftop.

The original lift was driven by steam, but it switched to electricity in 1915.

In the 1930s it was replaced by a new lift when the Cooperative Association (KF) built its large office complex at Slussen. In its first year of operation, the lift was used

Stomatol sign, Katarinahissen

by more than a million passengers, but its record year was 1945, when it carried a total of 1.8 million people between Slussen and Mosebacke Torg.

At the top there is a bar and a gourmet restaurant, Gondolen. The views from here are spectacular.

Katarina Kyrka (1695) after its extensive restoration due to a devastating fire in 1990

Katarina Kyrka ③①

Högbergsgatan 13. 📞 *08-743 68 40.*
🚇 *Slussen, Medborgarplatsen.*
🚌 *2, 3, 53, 76.*
🕐 *Apr–Sep: 11am–5pm Mon–Fri,
10am–5pm Sat & Sun.* 🎫 *Jun–Aug:
12.30pm; other times by appointment.*
✝ *12.30pm Tue & Thu (organ
music), noon Wed.* ♿ 📷 📱

THE BUILDINGS surrounding the hilltop on Katarina-berget date partly from the 18th century, although there have been churches on the site since the late 14th century. The most impressive of all the buildings is the 17th-century Katarina Kyrka,

designed by one of the era's greatest architects, Jean de la Vallée (1620–96). King Karl X Gustaf was also deeply involved in the project, and specified that the church should have a central nave with the altar and pulpit positioned right in the middle. Construction began in 1656 and the church was finally completed in 1695. In 1723 it was badly damaged by fire, along with large parts of the surrounding area, but it was restored over the next couple of decades.

Major restoration was carried out in the 20th century, and a new copper roof was added in 1988. Then two years later, on the night of 16 May 1990, there was another fire and the interior and virtually all its fittings were destroyed. Only the outer walls survived.

The architectural practice of Ove Hidemark was commissioned to design a new church which, as far as possible, was to be a faithful reconstruction of the original.

In order to carry out such a detailed reconstruction, the architects resorted to the use of 17th-century building techniques. Experts and craftsmen skilfully joined heavy timbering on to the central dome in the traditional way, and the church's central arch was rebuilt with bricks specially made in 17th-century style.

In 1995, Katarina Kyrka was reconsecrated and, in the eyes of many people, looked more beautiful than ever. The altar was sited exactly where it was originally planned.

The reconstruction cost 270 million kronor, of which 145 million kronor was covered by insurance. The remainder was raised through public donations.

Katarinahissen with Stockholms Stadsmuseum in the background

Fjällgatan ㉜

Street light

P ER ANDERS FOGELSTRÖM (1917–98), probably Söder's best-known author,
wrote: "Fjällgatan must be the city's most
beautiful street. It's an old-fashioned
narrow street which runs along the hilltop
with well-maintained cobblestones ... and
with street lights jutting out from the
houses. Then the street opens up and
gives a fantastic view of the city and the water..."
This area offers an experience of the authentic
Söder and its unique atmosphere.

The Heights of Söder
*With its 300-year-old houses and
terraced gardens, the Söder hilltop
stands like a giant stage-set
behind Stadsgården harbour.*

Fjällgatan
*Most of the houses were built along
this picturesque street after a devastating fire in 1723. No. 34 is said
to be the area's oldest.*

Viewpoint with
magnificent vista
across the city.

Café

| 0 metres | 100 |
| 0 yards | 100 |

FJÄLLGATAN

Katarina Vägen

Stigberget

STIGBERGSGATAN

Norwegian Church

Mamsell Josabeth's Steps
were named after
Josabeth Sjöbert
(1812–82),
a local painter.

Tjärhovsplan

Sista Styverns Trappor
*This alley of steps was
once known as
Mikaelsgränd after
a 17th-century exe-
cutioner. Later it was
named after the
inn on the harbour,
Sista Styvern ("The
Last Penny").*

Söder Cottages
*Typical well-preserved
cottages can be found
along Stigbergsgatan.
One of them is No. 17,
the house of the block-
maker Olof Krok
during the 1730s.*

KEY

– – – Suggested route

Vita Bergen ③

Södermalm. 🚌 *2, 3, 55, 66, 76.*

Today famous for its popular open-air theatre performances, this park is also an opportunity to see houses originally built for workers at Söder's harbours and factories. They were simple homes, often with a small garden and surrounded by a fence. In 1736 the building of new wooden houses was forbidden because of the fire risk, but slum districts, as this was then, were exempted.

Around 1900, when Sofia Kyrka was built, the area was turned into a leafy hillside park with allotment-garden cottages to the east. The park has a bronze statue, *Elsa Borg*, by Astri Bergman Taube (1972), wife of the great troubadour Evert Taube *(see p60)*.

Globen ③

3 km (2 miles) S of Stockholm.
🚇 *Globen.* 📞 *08-725 10 00.*
🕐 *during events.* 🎟 *by appt.* ♿
🍴 🛈 🛍 🌐 *www.globen.se*

In 1989 Stockholm acquired a new symbol in the shape of the indoor arena Globen. The spherical building has given the southern part of the city a radically new silhouette.

Globen offers a wide programme, ranging from international sports events to top artists and famous personalities such as Nelson Mandela.

Designed by Berg Architects, it has a circumference of 690 m (2,260 ft) and a height of 85 m (279 ft). There are 13-sq m (140-sq ft) viewing screens.

The silhouette of Globen arena dominating the surrounding area

Chapel of the Holy Cross by Gunnar Asplund at Skogskyrkogården

Skogskyrko-gården ⑲

6 km (3.5 miles) S of Stockholm.
📞 *08-508 301 93.* 🚇 *Skogskyrko-gården.* 📅 *May–Sep: 5pm Mon.*
♿ 🛍

Nature and architecture have combined to give the Skogskyrkogården Cemetery a place on the UNESCO World Heritage list. The cemetery is the creation of architects Gunnar Asplund *(see p99)* and Sigurd Lewerentz, winners of a design competition for the site in 1914. It is set amid pinewoods which provide a sombre framework for the various chapels and crematorium, all of which are important examples of Sweden's National Romantic and Functionalist styles.

Asplund's first work, Skogskapellet (Woodland Chapel),

Epitaph to Gunnar Asplund

featuring a steep shingled roof, was opened at the same time as the cemetery in 1920. It was decorated by Carl Milles and contains an an altar painting by Gunnar Torhamn. This was followed five years later by Uppståndelsekapellet (the Resurrection Chapel), designed by Lewerentz.

In 1940 Asplund's last masterpiece, Skogskrematoriet (Woodland Crematorium), was completed, along with its three chapels representing Faith, Hope and the Holy Cross. John Lundqvist's *The Resurrection* stands in the pillared hall of Heliga Korsets Kapell, the largest of the chapels, where there is also a mural painted by Sven Erixson. Adjoining the chapel is Asplund's black granite cross. The Hill of Meditation lies to the west. Skogskyrko-gården is the final resting place of Greta Garbo.

GRETA GARBO

The legendary Greta Garbo, one of the 20th century's outstanding film stars, was born in 1905 in a humble part of Södermalm. At the age of 17 she joined the theatre academy of Dramaten and made her film debut in *Peter the Tramp*. Her breakthrough came in 1924 in Mauritz Stiller's film of Selma Lagerlöf's book *The Atonement of Gösta Berling*. The following year she moved to Hollywood, where she soon became the reigning star. Garbo appeared in 24 films, including *Anna Karenina* (1935) and *Camille* (1936). She never married and lived a solitary life until her death in 1990. Her ashes were interred at the Skogskyrkogården Cemetery in 1999.

Garbo in *As You Desire Me* (1932)

Drottningholm 🄴

THE UNIQUE BAROQUE and Rococo environment of Drottningholm – its palace, theatre, park and Chinese Pavilion – have been perfectly preserved. This royal palace emerged in its present form towards the end of the 17th century, and was one of the most lavish buildings of its era. Contemporary Italian and French architecture inspired Tessin the Elder (1615–81) in his design, which was also intended to glorify royal power. The project was completed by Tessin the Younger, while architects such as Carl Hårleman and Jean Eric Rehn finished the interiors. The Royal Family uses parts of the palace as their private residence. Drottningholm was designated a UNESCO World Heritage Site in 1991.

Baroque Garden
The bronze statue of Hercules (1680s) by the Dutch Renaissance sculptor Adrian de Vries adorns the parterre in the palace's Baroque Gardens.

**Upper South
Bodyguard Room**
This ante-room to the State Room, used for ceremonial occasions, was decorated with stucco works by Giovanni and Carlo Carove, and ceiling paintings by Johan Sylvius.

**Apartments of
the Royal Family**

STAR FEATURES

★ **Staircase**

★ **Queen Lovisa
Ulrika's Library**

★ **Queen Hedvig Eleo-
nora's State Bedroom**

Writing Table by Georg Haupt
Standing in the Queen's Room is this masterpiece (1770) commissioned by King Adolf Fredrik as a gift to Queen Lovisa Ulrika. Textiles for the walls and furnishings date from the 1970s.

★ **Queen Lovisa Ulrika's Library**
The Queen commissioned Jean Eric Rehn (1717–93) to decorate this splendid library, which illustrates her influence on art and science in Sweden in the 18th century.

VISITORS' CHECKLIST

10 km (6 miles) W of Stockholm.
🚇 *Brommaplan, then bus 177, 301, 323.* 🚤 *May–Sep.*
Palace 📞 *08-402 62 80.*
🕐 *May–Aug: 10am– 4.30pm daily; Sep: noon–3.30pm daily; Oct–Apr: noon–3.30pm Sat & Sun.* ● *public hols* 📷 🎥 🚫
🏠 **Chinese Pavilion** 🕐 *May–Sep.* 📷 🎥 🚫 **Theatre Museum** 🕐 *May–Sep.* 📷 🎥
🌐 *www.royalcourt.se*

The Palace Church in the northern cupola was completed by Hårleman in the 1720s.

★ **Queen Hedvig Eleonora's State Bedroom**
Morning receptions ("levées") were held in this lavish Baroque room designed by Tessin the Elder. It took about 15 years for Sweden's foremost artists and craftsmen to decorate the room, which was completed in 1683.

Entrance

★ **Staircase**
Trompe-l'oeil paintings by Johan Sylvius adorn the walls, giving the impression that the already spacious interior stretches further into the palace.

Exploring Drottningholm

THE PALACE OF DROTTNINGHOLM IS complemented by the Court Theatre (Slottsteatern), the world's oldest theatre still in active use, the Theatre Museum (Teatermuseum) and the elegant Chinese Pavilion (Kina Slott). The complex is situated on the shores of Lake Mälaren, surrounded by Baroque and Rococo gardens, and lush English-style parkland. In summer there are jousting tournaments, the theatre stages opera and ballet, and the church is used for High Mass and concerts.

Karl XI's gallery at Drottningholm, featuring the victory at Lund, 1667

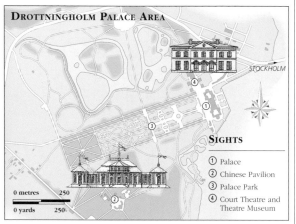

DROTTNINGHOLM PALACE AREA

STOCKHOLM

0 metres 250
0 yards 250

SIGHTS

1. Palace
2. Chinese Pavilion
3. Palace Park
4. Court Theatre and Theatre Museum

THE PALACE APARTMENTS

THE FIRST THING that meets the eye on entering the apartments is a Baroque corridor with a view that frames part of the gardens in all their splendour. The central part of the palace is dominated by the staircase, crowned by a lantern with ceiling paintings by Ehrenstrahl. There are examples of Baroque stucco work by Giovanni and Carlo Carove. Marble statues of the nine muses and their protector, Apollo, are placed at the corners of the balustrades.

The Green Salon is reached from the lower vestibule via the Lower Northern Bodyguard Room. This is the beginning of the main ceremonial suite, which continues with Karl X's Gallery where paintings illustrate his major military exploit, the crossing of the iced-over Store Bælt (Great Belt) by the Swedish army in

Medallion symbolizing life and death

1658. Queen Hedvig Eleonora (1636–1715) held audiences in the Ehrenstrahl Salon, named after the artist whose paintings dominate the walls. More prominent guests were received in the State Bedroom which later in Queen Lovisa Ulrika's time was in fact used for sleeping. Her Meissen porcelain can be seen in the Blue Cabinet; the Library has her collection of more than 2,000 books. Behind the Upper Northern Bodyguard Room, with a ceiling by Johan Sylvius, is a Gustavian drawing room with a bureau by Johan Niklas Eckstein. In 1777, following Gustav III's assumption of power, the Blue Salon was decorated in the Neo-Classical style.

The Chinese Salon was used as a private bedroom by King Adolf Fredrik. It is directly above the Queen's State Bedroom and there is a hidden staircase linking the two floors. The "bureau"

opposite the tiled stove is also a sofa bed. The Oscar Room was refurbished by Oscar I (1799–1859) and is adorned by a tapestry dating from the 1630s. After the General's Room, Karl XI's Gallery commemorating the victory at Lund (1667), and the Golden Salon, comes the Queen's Salon. Just as the adjoining State Room has portraits of all the European monarchs, the portraits in the Queen's Salon are of European queens. This floor finishes with the Upper South Bodyguard Room, an ante-room to the State Room and lavishly decorated by the Carove stucco artists and the ceiling painter Johan Sylvius.

THE CHINESE PAVILION

ON HER 33RD birthday in 1753 Queen Lovisa Ulrika was given a Chinese pavilion by her husband, King Adolf Fredrik. It had been manufactured in Stockholm and the previous night it was shipped to Drottningholm and assembled a short distance from the palace. It had to be taken down after 10 years because rot had set in, and was

The Chinese Pavilion, an extravaganza in blue and gold

replaced by the Chinese Pavilion (Kina Slott) which is still one of the major attractions at Drottningholm. The polished-tile building was designed by D F Adelcrantz (1716–96).

At this time there was great European interest in all things Chinese. In 1733 the newly formed East India Company made its first journey to China. After Lovisa Ulrika's death in 1782 this interest waned, but it was rekindled in the 1840s. The Chinese Pavilion is a mixture of what was considered 250 years ago to be typical Chinese style along with artifacts from China and Japan. Efforts have been made to restore the interior to its original state with the help of a 1777 inventory.

Four smaller pavilions belong to the building. In the northeastern pavilion the king had his lathe and a carpenter's bench. Alongside is the Confidencen pavilion, where meals were taken if he wished to be left undisturbed. The food was prepared in the basement, the floor opened and the dining table hauled up. The adjoining Turkish-style "watch tent" was built as a barracks for Gustav III's dragoons. It now houses a museum about the estate.

Tiled stove in a cabinet in the Chinese Pavilion

sculptor Adrian de Vries (1560–1626) were war trophies from Prague in 1648 and from Fredriksborg Castle in Denmark in 1659.

The avenues of chestnut trees were laid out when the Chinese Pavilion was completed, as well as the Rococo-inspired garden area – a cross between the formal main garden and the freer composition of the English park. The English park has natural paths and a stream with small islands, along with trees and bushes at "natural" irregular intervals. Gustav III is reputed to have been responsible for its design and also planned several buildings. Not all his plans were realized, but he added four statues which he had bought during his travels in Italy.

The first 300 of a total of 846 lime trees were planted in the avenues flanking the Baroque garden as early as 1684.

THE COURT THEATRE AND THEATRE MUSEUM

THE DESIGNER OF the Chinese Pavilion, Carl Fredrik Adelcrantz, was also responsible for the Drottningholm Court Theatre (Slottsteatern), which dates from 1766. The theatre was commissioned by Queen

The magnificent 18th-century stage in the Drottningholm Court Theatre

Lovisa Ulrika, but Adelcrantz did not have the same resources as the architects of the palace itself. This simple wooden building with a plaster façade is now the world's oldest theatre still preserved in its original condition. The interior and fittings are master-pieces of simple functionality. The pilasters, for example, are made from gypsum and the supports from papier mâché. The scenery, with its wooden hand-driven machinery, is still in working order.

After Gustav III's death in 1792 the theatre fell into disuse until the 1920s, when the machinery ropes were replaced, electric lighting was installed, and the original wings were refurbished.

The scenery is adapted to 18th-century plays. It can be changed in just a few seconds with the help of up to 30 scene-shifters. The sound effects are simple but authentic: a wooden box filled with stones creates realistic thunder, a wooden cylinder covered in tent cloth produces a howling wind. Every summer there are about 30 performances, mainly opera and ballet from the 18th century. The theatre is open daily for visitors to the palace.

A Theatre Museum and shop are housed in Duke Carl's pavilion, built in the 1780s. The museum focuses on 18th-century theatre, with decoration sketches, paintings, scenery models and costumes. A *Commedia dell'arte* room contains paintings by Pehr Hilleström and sketches for Gustav III's dramatic productions by Louis Jean Desprez.

THE PALACE PARK

THE PALACE's three gardens are each of a completely different character but still combine to provide a unified whole. The symmetrical formal garden started to take shape in 1640. The garden was designed to stimulate all senses with sights, sounds and smells. It starts by the palace terrace with its "embroidery" parterre and continues as far as the Hercules statue. The water parterre is situated on slightly higher ground and is broken up with waterfalls and topiaries. The sculptures, mainly carved by the Flemish

Court Theatre stage machinery dating from 1766

The Stockholm Archipelago ⑰

E XTENDING 80 KM (50 MILES) EAST from the sheltered
waters of Stockholm to the open sea, the archipelago
encompasses tens of thousands of islands of all shapes
and sizes, some inhabited, others not. Many of the inner
archipelago's larger islands, such as Värmdö, Ingarö and
Ljusterö, are linked to the mainland by bridges and car
ferries, making them in parts little more than city suburbs.
But the majority of the archipelago islands, with their
traditional wooden houses, cosy hotels and youth
hostels, and summer sailing regattas, can be reached by
an extensive network of scheduled ferries departing from
Stockholm, Vaxholm, Stavsnäs and Dalarö.

Huvudskär in Stockholm's outer archipelago

ARCHIPELAGO HIGHLIGHTS

① Fjäderholmarna
② Vaxholm
③ Grinda
④ Finnhamn
⑤ Möja
⑥ Sandhamn
⑦ Utö

Vaxholm Fortress, strategically
sited on the approach to Vaxholm

🔆 Fjäderholmarna

6 km (4 miles) E of Stockholm. 🚌 53.
🛥 May–Sep from Nybrokajen and
Slussen. **Baltic Aquarium** 【 08-718
40 55. ☐ May–mid-Sep. 📷 phone
to book: 08-715 80 65. ☐ 🔢 📷

With the inclusion of the
Fjäderholmarna islands in
Ekoparken (see p97), the city's
"green lung" has acquired a
small part of the archipelago.
The main island, Stora
Fjäderholmen, is only 25
minutes by boat from
Nybrokajen or Slussen.

There was an inn here as
long ago as the 17th century,
conveniently sited for
islanders on their way to the
city to sell their wares. Today
there is an attractive harbour,
restaurants, an art gallery and
museums devoted to boating
and angling, as well as the
Baltic Aquarium. Local handicrafts include
metalwork,
weaving, wood-
carving and glass-
making. The
other three
islands have a
rich birdlife and
one, Libertas, has
Sweden's last
remaining
gas-powered
lighthouse.

🏰 Vaxholm

25 km (16 miles) NE of Stockholm.
【 08-541 314 80. 🚌 670. 🛥 from
Strömkajen and Nybrokajen. **Vaxholm
Fortress** and **Vaxholm Fortress
Museum** 【 08-541 721 56/57. ☐
mid-Jun–Sep: 11.30am–5.30pm daily.

The archipelago's main community, Vaxholm, is easily
reached by boat from
Stockholm on a delightful
one-hour journey through the
archipelago. Vaxholm Fortress,
on the nearby island of
Vaxholmen, guards this busy
port. First fortified in 1548 by
Gustav Vasa, the more recent
19th-century citadel houses a
military museum.

Two of Stockholm's best-
known architects have left
their mark on Vaxholm. The
law courts were given their
present appearance in 1925
by Cyrillus Johansson, and

The Fjäderholmarna islands, a popular summer
excursion just 25 minutes by boat from the city

the hotel on the headland, by
Erik Lallerstedt (1899), has
Jugendstil ornamentation.

The wooden buildings and
shops around the square and
along Hamngatan provide a
pleasant stroll.

🔆 Grinda

30 km (19 miles) E of Stockholm.
【 08-542 490 72. 🚌 670 from
Östra station to Vaxholm, then boat.
🛥 from Strömkajen and Nybrokajen.
☐ 🔢 (summer only).

Grinda is a leafy island,
typical of the inner archipelago, about one and a half
hours by boat from the city. It
has some excellent beaches
and rocks for swimming, as
well as good fishing. The
architect Ernst Stenhammar,
who designed the Grand
Hôtel in Stockholm (see p77),
built a large Jugendstil villa
here, which is now a pub and

Sandhamn, the yachting centre in Stockholm's outer archipelago

restaurant with guest rooms. There are chalets to rent, a campsite and a youth hostel in a former barracks. Boats and bicycles can be hired.

Finnhamn

40 km (25 miles) NE of Stockholm. 08-542 462 12. from Strömkajen and Nybrokajen.

Finnish ships used to moor at Finnhamn on their way to and from Stockholm. This attractive group of islands lies two and a half hours by boat from Stockholm at the point where the softer scenery of the inner archipelago gives way to the harsher landscape of the outer islands. As on Grinda, the main island has a wooden villa designed by Ernst Stenhammar (1912). Today it is the largest youth hostel in the archipelago. There is a restaurant, chalets to rent and a campsite. Smaller islands nearby are accessible by rowing boat.

Möja

50 km (31 miles) E of Stockholm. 08-571 640 53. 670 to Vaxholm, then boat. from Strömkajen and Nybrokajen.

Fishing and strawberry-growing were the mainstays of this idyllic corner of the archipelago. Now there are few Möja strawberry growers and only one professional fisherman among the island's 300 inhabitants. Instead, picturesque harbours attract the sailing fraternity in particular. Nature reserves on and around Möja shelter a rich abundance of wildlife. Services on the island are good in the summer, with cottages, boats and kayaks for hire, and guest houses.

Sandhamn

50 km (31 miles) E of Stockholm. 08-571 530 00. 433, 434 from Slussen to Stavsnäs, then boat. from Strömkajen and Nybrokajen.

Over the past 200 years Sandhamn has been a meeting point for sailors. The Royal Swedish Yacht Club is based in Seglarrestaurangen (Sailors' Restaurant), and every year the world's yachting elite arrive to take part in the Round Gotland Race.

Sandhamn is a pretty village with narrow alleys and houses adorned with decorative carvings. There are shops, crafts centres and a swimming pool. About 100 people live here permanently. The Customs House, built in 1752, is a listed heritage building and former home of poet and artist Elias Sehlstedt (1808–74).

Camping is not permitted, but hotel, bed-and-breakfast and chalet accommodation are available and there are great sandy beaches.

Utö

50 km (31 miles) SE of Stockholm. 08-501 574 10. in summer, from Strömkajen. www.utoturistbyra.se

No other island in the archipelago has as rich a history as Utö, which was inhabited before the Viking era. In the 12th century the islanders started to mine iron ore, and this activity continued until 1879. Their story is told in the Mining Museum adjoining the hotel. Today's holiday homes along Lurgatan were built as miners' cottages in the 18th century. A windmill, built in 1791, provides an unrivalled view of the island.

Utö is one of the best seaside resorts in the Stockholm area, and is ideal for a weekend or full-day excursion.

Hotel, youth hostel, camping, chalet and bed-and-breakfast accommodation are available. Bicycles, rowing boats and canoes can be hired. The bakery is renowned for its delicious "Utölimpa" bread.

> **VISITORS' CHECKLIST**
>
> SL traffic information in Eng, 08-600 10 00. Strömma Kanalbolaget, 08-587 140 00; Vaxholmsbolaget, 08-679 58 30. Vaxholm: Archipelago fair (mid-Aug). Sandhamn: Round Gotland Yacht Race (1st week in Jul), Sandhamn Regatta (3rd week in July), Vaxholm: Archipelago Boat Day (1st Wed in Jun). www.stockholmtown.com

EXCURSIONS BY STEAMBOAT

Traditional steamboats are a familiar feature on the waters around Stockholm. Both in the archipelago and on Lake Mälaren visitors can still enjoy the tranquil atmosphere of a steamboat voyage. One of the veterans, *SS Blidösund*, built in 1911, is operated by voluntary organizations and serves mostly the northern archipelago. Some routes, for example Stockholm–Mariefred, are operated partly or completely by steamers. Most of the other passenger boats from the early 20th century have been fitted with oil-fired engines, but still provide a nostalgic journey back in time.

SS Blidösund, one of the oldest in Stockholm's fleet of steamboats

STOCKHOLM STREET FINDER

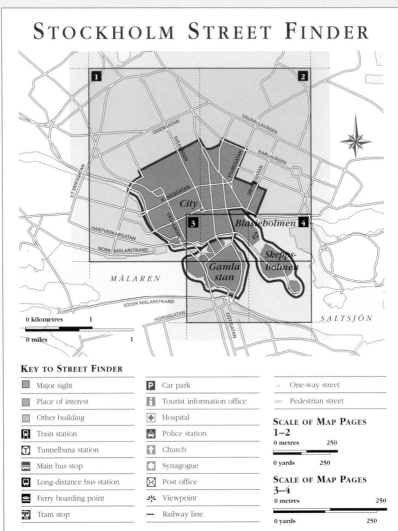

KEY TO STREET FINDER

▨ Major sight	P Car park	– One-way street
▨ Place of interest	ℹ Tourist information office	▬ Pedestrian street
▢ Other building	✛ Hospital	**SCALE OF MAP PAGES 1–2**
▣ Train station	🚓 Police station	0 metres — 250
Ⓣ Tunnelbana station	✛ Church	0 yards — 250
🚌 Main bus stop	✡ Synagogue	**SCALE OF MAP PAGES 3–4**
▣ Long-distance bus station	⊠ Post office	0 metres — 250
⛴ Ferry boarding point	☼ Viewpoint	0 yards — 250
🚋 Tram stop	— Railway line	

A

Adolf Fredriks Kyrkogata	1 C3
Akademigränd	1 C5, 3 A1
Ankargränd	3 B3
Apelbergsgatan	1 C4
Arkivgatan	3 A2
Armfeltsgatan	2 F1
Arsenalsgatan	3 C1
Artillerigatan	2 F2
Atlasgatan	1 A3
Atlasmuren	1 A3

B

Baggensgatan	3 C3
Baldersgatan	2 D2
Banérgatan	2 F4
Barnhusbron	1 B4
Barnhusgatan	1 B4
Bastugatan	3 A5
Bedoirsgränd	3 B3
Bellmansgatan	3 A5
Bergsgatan	1 A5
Beridarebanan	3 A1
Biblioteksgatan	2 D4
Bigarråvägen	1 C1
Birger Jarls Torg	3 A3

Birger Jarlsgatan	1 C2, 2 D3
Blasieholms-gatan	2 E5, 4C1
Blasieholmstorg	2 D5, 3 C1
Blecktornsgränd	3 A5
Blekholmsterrassen	1 B4
Bo Bergmans gata	2 F2
Bolinders plan	1 B5
Bollhusgränd	3 C3
Bragevägen	1 C2
Brahegatan	2 E2
Bredgränd	3 C3
Brinellvägen	2 D1
Brunkebergsgatan	3 A1
Brunkebergstorg	3 A1
Brunnsgatan	2 D3
Brunnsgränd	3 C3
Bryggargatan	1 C4
Brännkyrkagatan	3 A5
Bältgatan	2 F3

C

Cardellgatan	2 E3
Carl-Gustaf Lindstedts gata	1 A4
Cederdalsgatan	1 B1
Celsiusgatan	1 A4
Centralbron	1 C5, 3 B4

D

Dalagatan	1 A2
Danderydsgatan	2 D2
Danderydsplan	2 D2
Dannemoragatan	1 A1
David Bagares gata	2 D3
Didrik Ficks gränd	3 B3
Drakens gränd	3 C3
Drottning Kristinas väg	2 D1
Drottning Sofias väg	2 E1
Drottninggatan	1 C3, 3 A1
Drottninghusgränd	2 D3
Döbelnsgatan	1 C2

E

Engelbrekts Kyrkogata	2 D2
Engelbrektsgatan	2 D2
Engelbrektsplan	2 D3
Erik Dahlbergsallén	2 F3
Erik Dahlbergsgatan	2 F2
Eriksbergsgatan	2 D3
Eriksbergsplan	2 D3
Evert Taubes Terrass	3 A3
Exercisplan	4 E3

F

Ferkens gränd	3 C3

Finska Kyrkogränd	3 C3
Fiskargränd	3 C5
Fiskartorpsvägen	2 E1
Flaggmansvägen	4 E3
Fleminggatan	1 A4
Floragatan	2 E2
Fredsgatan	2 D5, 3 B1
Frejgatan	1 A2
Friggagatan	2 D2
Fryxellsgatan	1 C2
Funckens Gränd	3 B4

G

Gaffelgränd	3 C3
Gambrinusgatan	1 A3
Gamla Brogatan	1 C4
Garvar Lundins gränd	1 A5
Garvargatan	1 A5
Glasbruksgatan	3 C5
Grev Magnigatan	2 F4
Grev Turegatan	2 E2
Grevgatan	2 F3
Grevgränd	3 C1
Grubbens gata	1 A4
Grubbensringen	1 A4
Guldfjärdplan	3 B4

Guldfjärdsplan	3 B4
Guldgränd	3 B5
Gumshornsgatan	2 F4
Gustav Adolfs Torg	2 D5, 3 B1
Gyldéngatan	1 B2
Gymnasiegränd	3 A3
Gånggränd	3 B3
Gästrikegatan	1 A2
Gävlegatan	1 A2
Göran Hälsinges gränd	3 B3
Götgatan	3 B5

H

Hagagatan	1 B1
Hammargatan	2 D2
Hamngatan	2 D4
Hantverkargatan	1 A5
Hedinsgatan	2 F2
Heimdalsgatan	1 B2
Helga Lekamens gränd	3 B3
Herkulesgatan	1 C5, 3 A1
Hjärnegatan	1 A4
Holländargatan	1 C3
Holmamiralens Torg	4 E3
Hornsgatan	3 B5
Hovslagargatan	2 E5, 4 D1
Humlegårdsgatan	2 D3
Hälsingegatan	1 A1
Högvaktsterrassen	3 B2
Hökens gata	3 C5
Hötorget	1 C4

I

Idungatan	1 B1
Ignatiigränd	3 B3
Ingemargatan	1 C1
Iversonsgatan	2 D3

J

Jakob Westinsgatan	1 A5
Jakobs Torg	2 D1, 3 B1
Jakobsbergsgatan	2 D4
Jakobsgatan	1 C5, 3 A1
Jarlaplan	1 C2
Johannesgatan	2 D3
Johannesgränd	3 C3
John Ericssonsgatan	1 A5
Jungfrugatan	2 E3
Jutas Backe	2 D3
Järntorget	3 C4
Järntorgsgatan	3 C4

K

Kallskärsgatan	2 F2
Kammakargatan	1 B3
Kanslikajen	3 B2
Kaplansbacken	1 B5
Kaptensgatan	2 E4
Karduansmakargatan	3 A1
Karl Johans Torg	3 C4
Karl XII:s Torg	2 D5, 3 C1
Karlaplan	2 F3
Karlavägen	1 C2
Karlbergsvägen	1 A2
Kastellbacken	4 E4
Kastellholmsbron	4 E4
Kastellholmskajen	4 E4
Katarinavägen	4 D5
Kindstugränd	3 C3
Klappjaktsvägen	2 E1
Klara Norra Kyrkogata	1 C4
Klara Södra Kyrkogata	3 A1
Klara Tvärgränd	3 A1
Klara Östra Kyrkogata	3 A1
Klarabergsgatan	1 C4
Klarabergsviadukten	1 B5
Klarastrandsleden	1 B5
Klevgränd	3 C5
Klockgjutargränd	3 B2
Kocksgränd	3 B1
Kolmatargränd	3 B3
Kommendörsgatan	2 E2
Kornhamn	3 B4
Kråkgränd	3 C3
Kungsbro Strand	1 B5
Kungsbron	1 B4
Kungsgatan	1 B4
Kungsholms Hamnplan	1 A5
Kungsholms Kyrkoplan	1 B5
Kungsholms Strand	1 A4
Kungsholmsgatan	1 A4
Kungsholmstorg	1 A5
Kungsklippan	1 A5
Kungstensgatan	1 B3
Kungsträdgården	1 D4, 3 B1
Kungsträdgårdsgatan	3 C1

Kåkbrinken	3 B3
Källargränd	3 B3
Köpmanbrinken	3 C3
Köpmangatan	3 B3
Köpmantorget	3 C3
Körsbärsvägen	1 C1

L

Lantmäteribacken	3 B1
Lejonbacken	2 D5, 3 B2
Lejonstedts gränd	3 B4
Lidingövägen	2 F1
Lill-Jans Plan	2 D2
Lilla Hoparegränd	3 C3
Lilla Nygatan	3 B3
Lindstedtsvägen	2 D1
Linnégatan	2 D3
Lodgatan	1 C2
Logårdstrappan	2 D5, 3 C2
Lokstallsgatan	1 A3
Luntmakargatan	1 C3
Lützengatan	2 F3
Lästmakargatan	2 D4
Löjtnantsgatan	2 E2

M

Majorsgatan	2 E3
Malmskillnadsgatan	2 D4
Malmtorgsgatan	2 D5, 3 B1
Maria Trappgränd	3 A5
Mariaberget	3 A4
Mariagatan	3 B5
Mariagränd	3 B5
Mariatorget	3 A5
Markvardsgatan	1 C2
Mosebacke Torg	3 C5
Munkbrogatan	3 B3
Munkbrohamnen	3 A3
Munkbroleden	3 B4
Munkbron	3 B3
Museikajen	2 E5, 4 D2
Myntgatan	3 B2
Mynttorget	3 B2
Målargatan	1 C4
Mårten Trotzigs Gränd	3 C4
Mälartorget	3 B4
Mäster Samuelsgatan	1 C4

N

Narvavägen	2 F3
Norr Mälarstrand	1 B5
Norra Agnegatan	1 A4
Norra Bankogränd	3 C4
Norra Bantorget	1 B4
Norra Brobänken	2 E5, 4 D2
Norra Dryckesgränd	3 C4
Norra Järnvägsbron	3 A2
Norra Riddarholmshamnen	3 A2
Norra Stationsgatan	1 A1
Norrbro	3 B2
Norrlandsgatan	2 D4
Norrmalmstorg	2 D4
Norrtull	1 A1
Norrtullsgatan	1 B2
Nybergsgatan	2 E3
Nybrogatan	2 E2
Nybrokajen	2 E5, 4 D1
Nybroplan	2 E4
Nygränd	3 C3
Näckströmsgatan	2 D4

O

Observatoriegatan	1 B3
Odengatan	1 A3
Odenplan	1 B2
Olof Palmes gata	1 C4
Olofsgatan	1 C3
Ordenstrappan	2 D2
Osquars Backe	2 D1
Oxtorgsgatan	2 D4

P

P O Hallmans gata	1 A4
Packhusgränd	3 C3
Parmmätargatan	1 B5
Peder Fredags gränd	3 C3
Pelikansgränd	3 C3
Peter Myndes Backe	3 B5
Pilgatan	1 A5
Pipersgatan	1 A4
Planterhagsvägen	2 E1
Polhems tvärgränd	1 A4
Polhemsgatan	1 A4
Pryssgränd	3 A4
Prästgatan	3 B3

R

Regeringsgatan	2 D3, 3 B1
Rehnsgatan	1 C2
Riddargatan	2 E4
Riddarholmsbron	3 A5
Riddarhusgränd	3 A2
Riddarhuskajen	3 A2
Riddarhustorget	3 A3
Riksbron	2 D5, 3 A2
Riksplan	2 D5, 3 B2
Rimbogatan	2 D3
Rosengatan	1 C3
Roslagsgatan	1 C1
Roslagstull	1 B1
Runebergsgatan	2 D3
Runebergsplan	2 D2
Rådhusgränd	3 A2
Rådmansgatan	1 B3
Räntmästartrappan	3 C4
Rödabergsbrinken	1 A2
Rödbodgatan	3 A2
Rödbodtorget	3 A2

S

Saltmätargatan	1 C3
Saltsjörampen	3 C4
Salviigränd	3 B2
Samuel Owens gata	1 B5
Sandelsgatan	2 F2
Sankt Eriksgatan	1 A1
Sankt Eriksplan	1 A3
Sankt Paulsgatan	3 B5
Scheelegatan	1 A4
Schering Rosenhanes gränd	3 A3
Schönfeldts gränd	3 B3
Sergelgatan	1 C4
Sergels torg	1 C4
Sibyllegatan	2 E3
Sigtunagatan	1 A2
Själagårdsgränd	3 C3
Sjöbergsplan	3 B4
Skaraborgsgatan	4 D2, 3 B5
Skeppar Karls gränd	3 C3
Skeppar Olofs gränd	3 C3
Skeppargatan	2 F2
Skeppsbrokajen	3 C3
Skeppsbron	3 C3
Skeppsholmsbron	4 D2
Skomakargatan	3 B3
Skottgränd	3 C3
Skräddargränd	3 B3
Sköldungagatan	2 D2
Slottsbacken	3 C2
Slottskajen	2 D5, 3 B2
Slupskjulsvägen	4 E2
Slussen	3 C4
Slussplan	3 C4
Slussterrassen	3 C4
Slöjdgatan	1 C4
Smala gränd	2 D3
Smålandsgatan	2 D4
Snickarbacken	2 D3
Solgränd	3 B3
Spektens gränd	3 B3
Stadsgårdshamnen	4 F5
Stadsgårdsleden	4 D5
Stadshusbron	1 C5
Staffan Sasses gränd	3 C3
Stallbron	2 D5, 3 B2
Stallgatan	2 E5, 3 C1
Starrängsvägen	2 F2
Stenbastugränd	3 B3
Stenbocksgatan	2 D2
Stickelbärsvägen	1 C1
Stora Gråmunkegränd	3 B3
Stora Hoparegränd	3 C3
Stora Nygatan	3 B3
Storgatan	2 F4
Storkyrkobrinken	3 B3
Stortorget	3 B3
Storängsvägen	2 F1
Strandvägen	2 E4
Strindbergsgatan	2 F2
Strömbron	2 D5, 3 C2
Strömgatan	2 D5, 3 A2
Strömkajen	2 D5, 3 C1
Strömparterren	2 D5, 3 B2
Strömsborgsbron	3 A2
Sturegatan	2 E3
Stureplan	2 D4
Styrmansgatan	2 F4
Surbrunnsgatan	1 C2
Svartensgatan	3 C5
Svartmangatan	3 B3
Sveaplan	1 B1
Sveavägen	1 B2

Sven Vintappares gränd	3 B3
Svensksundsvägen	4 D3
Söder Mälarstrand	3 A4
Södermalmstorg	3 B5
Södra Agnegatan	1 A5
Södra Bankogränd	3 C4
Södra Benickebrinken	3 C3
Södra Blasieholmshamnen	2 E5, 3 C2
Södra Brobänken	4 E3
Södra Dryckesgränd	3 C4
Södra Järnvägsbron	3 B4
Södra Riddarholms hamnen	3 A3

T

Tavastgatan	3 A5
Teatergatan	2 E5, 3 C1
Tegelbacken	1 C5, 3 A2
Tegnérgatan	1 B3
Teknikringen	2 D1
Teknologgatan	1 B3
Telegrafgränd	3 C3
Terminalslingan	1 B4
Torgdragargränd	3 B4
Torsgatan	1 A3
Torsgränd	1 A3
Torstenssonsgatan	2 F4
Tre Liljor	1 A1
Triewaldsgränd	3 C4
Tryckerigatan	3 A3
Trädgårdsgatan	3 B3
Trädgårdstvärgränd	3 C3
Träskportsvägen	2 D1
Trångsund	3 B3
Tulegatan	1 C2
Tullgränd	3 C4
Tunnelgatan	1 C3
Tyghusplan	4 D2
Tyrgatan	2 D2
Tyska Brinken	3 B3
Tyska Brunnsplan	3 C3
Tyska Skolgränd	3 C3
Tyska Stallplan	3 C3
Tyskbagargatan	2 E3
Tysta gatan	2 F3

U

Ugglegränd	3 A5
Uggleviksgatan	2 D2
Upplandsgatan	1 A1
Urvädersgränd	3 C5

V–W

Valhallavägen	2 E2
Vanadisplan	1 A2
Vanadisvägen	1 A2
Vasabron	1 C5, 3 A2
Vasagatan	1 B4
Vattugatan	1 C5, 3 A1
Vegagatan	1 B2
Vidargatan	1 B2
Villagatan	2 D2
Vapnargatan	2 E4
Värtavägen	2 F3
Västerlånggatan	3 B3
Västeråsgatan	1 A1
Västmannagatan	1 A1
Västra Brobänken	4 D3
Västra Trädgårdsgatan	2 D4, 3 B1
Völundsgatan	1 A3
Wahrendorffsgatan	3 C1
Wallingatan	1 B3
Wargentinsgatan	1 A4
Wittstocksgatan	2 F3
Wrangelska backen	3 A3

Y

Ynglingagatan	1 B1
Yxsmedsgränd	3 B3

Å

Ångströmsgatan	1 A4

Ö

Örlogsvägen	4 E4
Österlånggatan	3 C3
Östermalmsgatan	2 D2
Östermalmstorg	2 E4
Östra Järnvägsvägen	4 E2
Östra Järnvägsvägen	1 B4
Östra Slussgatan	3 C5
Överskärargränd	3 B3

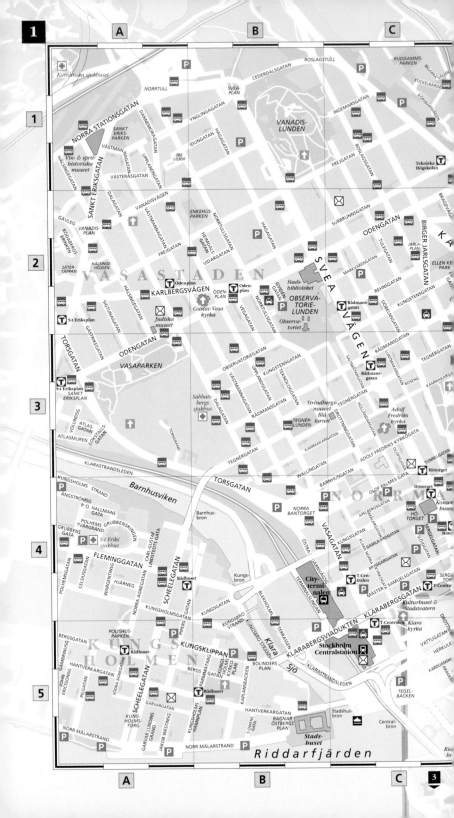

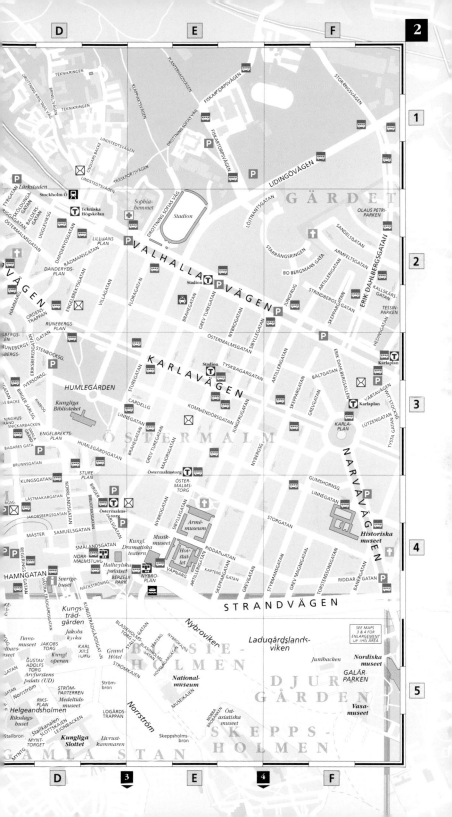

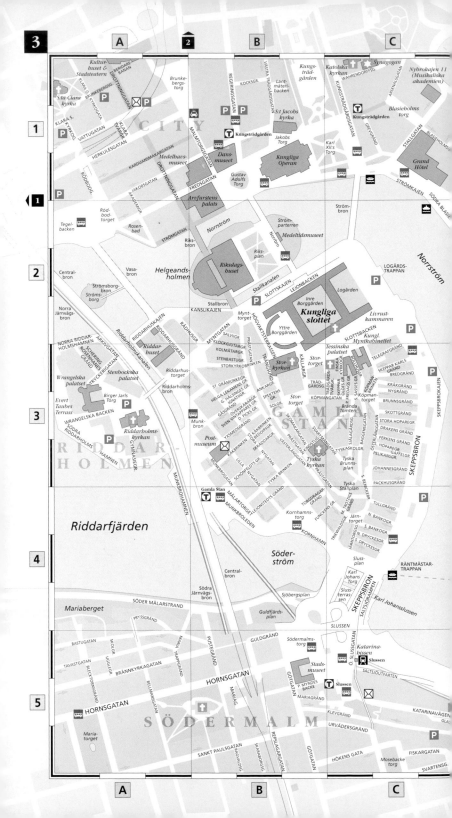

SWEDEN
AREA BY AREA

EASTERN SVEALAND 122-139
EASTERN GÖTALAND 140-157
GOTLAND 158-169
SOUTHERN GÖTALAND 170-189
GOTHENBURG 190-205
WESTERN GÖTALAND 206-227
WESTERN SVEALAND 228-245
SOUTHERN NORRLAND 246-261
NORTHERN NORRLAND 262-275

Sweden at a Glance

SWEDEN IS A LONG COUNTRY, traditionally divided into Norrland, Svealand and Götaland. In Norrland the landscape is characterized by its proximity to the Arctic, with mountains in the west, rivers running east towards the coast, and an interior of forest or marshland. With the exception of the larger towns along the coast, the area is sparsely populated. In Svealand the countryside is hilly, with lakes and rivers interspersed with farmland. Island archipelagos lie offshore. The population is concentrated in Mälardalen, centring on Stockholm. Götaland, comprising the southern part of the country, offers the most variation with differing landscapes and a high urban and rural population.

The Mountains of Härjedalen *are a haven for outdoor activities in both summer and winter (see pp260–61).*

The Fryken Lakes *in Värmland are edged by superb manor houses such as Rottneros, whose park overlooking Mellanfryken contains an outstanding collection of statues, including Carl Milles' Nike (see p232).*

Fiskebäckskil, *with its red fishermen's huts and white wooden houses, is typical of the coastal villages of Bohuslän (see p215).*

Götaplatsen, *Gothenburg's finest square, features Carl Milles' statue Poseidon with Konstmuseet in the background (see p200).*

Österlen, *on the southwestern coast of Skåne, is characterized by rolling agricultural land and the half-timbered farmhouses typical of the area (see p183).*

WESTERN SVEALAND *(See pp228–ℇ)*

WESTERN GÖTALAND *(See pp206–27)*

GOTHENBURG *(See pp190–205)*

SOUTHERN GÖTALAND *(See pp170–ℇ)*

KATTEGATT

NORTHERN
NORRLAND
(See pp262–75)

The Ice Hotel in Jukkasjärvi is an extra-ordinary creation built entirely of ice and snow. It melts in the spring sunshine each year and is recreated in October (see p272).

SOUTHERN
NORRLAND
See pp246–61)

Uppsala, the seat of Sweden's archbishop, has a High Gothic cathedral founded in 1455 – although parts of it date from the 13th century – and the oldest university in the Nordic countries, established in 1477 (see pp128–9).

GULF OF BOTHNIA

EASTERN
SVEALAND
e pp122–39)

STOCKHOLM
(See pp44–117)

BALTIC SEA

Visby, "the town of roses and ruins", with its medieval perimeter wall and half-timbered houses, is a UNESCO World Heritage Site (see pp164–7).

EASTERN
ÖTALAND
e pp140–57)

GOTLAND
(See p158–69)

The Kingdom of Crystal is the part of Småland known for its glassware, both artistic and practical. The plate, Amber, was designed by Göran Wärf at Kosta Glasbruk in 2003 (see pp152–3).

0 kilometres   200

0 miles   100

EASTERN SVEALAND

THE WATERWAYS *of Lake Mälaren and the vast archipelago extending to the Baltic both divide and unite the provinces of Uppland, Södermanland and Västmanland. This is a land of verdant islands and glittering bays, splendid castles and little wooden towns, and a cultural heritage that predates the Vikings. With Stockholm at the centre, the region is home to one-third of Sweden's population.*

This area was the cradle of ancient Svea, as can be seen in the rock carvings, burial mounds and standing stones in the shapes of ships that dot the landscape. It was from the town of Birka on Lake Mälaren and from Roslagen in Uppland that the Vikings headed east on plundering raids and trading missions around Europe and beyond *(see p31)*. The centre of the ancient pagan Æsir cult in Uppsala held out against Christianity until the 12th century. Many beautiful, small medieval churches testify to the fact that Christianity finally dominated. They are richly decorated with paintings depicting biblical scenes for the benefit of the local congregations. Uppsala itself became a cathedral city and the seat of the archbishop in 1258.

The many castles and fortresses which guard the waterways are an eye-catching sight. Several of these date back to the Middle Ages, but the most important, such as Skokloster, are the result of the great wealth which flooded into the country after Sweden's victories in the various European wars of the 17th century *(see pp35–7)*. Shipping brought further prosperity to the region, with centres such as Arboga lying on the iron route between Bergslagen, Stockholm and the Uppland harbours. There are well-preserved ironworks in all three provinces, including Engelsbergs Bruk, a UNESCO World Heritage Site.

The extensive archipelago straddles the coasts of Uppland and Södermanland, and Lake Mälaren itself is so full of islands that the archipelago appears to continue uninterrupted.

All the architectural sights and natural attractions of Eastern Svealand are best enjoyed at a slow pace by bicycle or boat, or on foot.

The flat skerries of the outer archipelago

◁ Gripsholms Slott at Mariefred on Lake Mälaren, established by Gustav Vasa in 1540

Exploring Eastern Svealand

T HIS, THE HEARTLAND OF SWEDEN, offers as many tempting treats as the most well-stocked Swedish *smörgåsbord*. Whether travelling by car, bus, train, bicycle or on foot, visitors will enjoy frequent glimpses of lakes and bays, as water is a constant presence. This makes travelling by boat an unbeatable way of discovering Eastern Svealand's history and culture and enjoying the area's natural beauty. There are hundreds of canoe trails, and canoes and boats can be hired all over the region. For walkers, Sörmlandsleden, Upplandsleden and Bruksleden in Västmanland offer more than 1,500 km (940 miles) of stunning trails.

Botanist Carl von Linné's Hammarby, outside Uppsala *(see p129)*

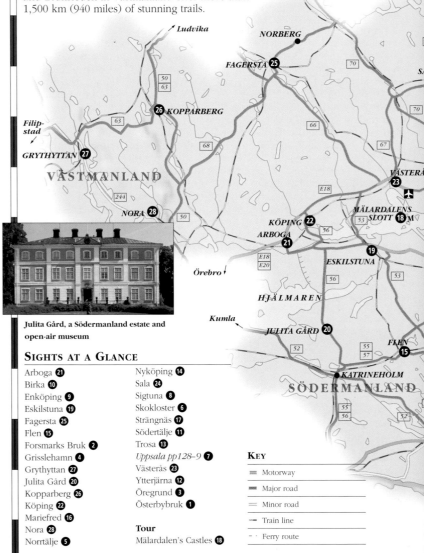

Julita Gård, a Södermanland estate and open-air museum

SIGHTS AT A GLANCE

Arboga **21**
Birka **10**
Enköping **9**
Eskilstuna **19**
Fagersta **25**
Flen **15**
Forsmarks Bruk **2**
Grisslehamn **4**
Grythyttan **27**
Julita Gård **20**
Kopparberg **26**
Köping **22**
Mariefred **16**
Nora **28**
Norrtälje **5**

Nyköping **14**
Sala **24**
Sigtuna **8**
Skokloster **6**
Strängnäs **17**
Södertälje **11**
Trosa **13**
Uppsala pp128–9 **7**
Västerås **23**
Ytterjärna **12**
Öregrund **3**
Österbybruk **1**

Tour
Mälardalen's Castles **18**

KEY

≡	Motorway
▬	Major road
=	Minor road
--	Train line
- ·	Ferry route

Map labels: Ludvika · NORBERG · FAGERSTA **25** · FILIPSTAD · 50 63 · **26** KOPPARBERG · 70 · 66 · 70 · 67 · GRYTHYTTAN **27** · 63 · 68 · VÄSTMANLAND · E18 · VÄSTERÅS **23** · 244 · NORA **28** · 50 · KÖPING **22** · MÄLARDALENS SLOTT **18** · 53 · ARBOGA **21** · 36 · **19** · E18 E20 · ESKILSTUNA · 56 · 53 · Örebro · HJÄLMAREN · 56 · Kumla · JULITA GÅRD **20** · 52 · 55 57 · FLEN **15** · KATRINEHOLM · SÖDERMANLAND · 55 56 · 52

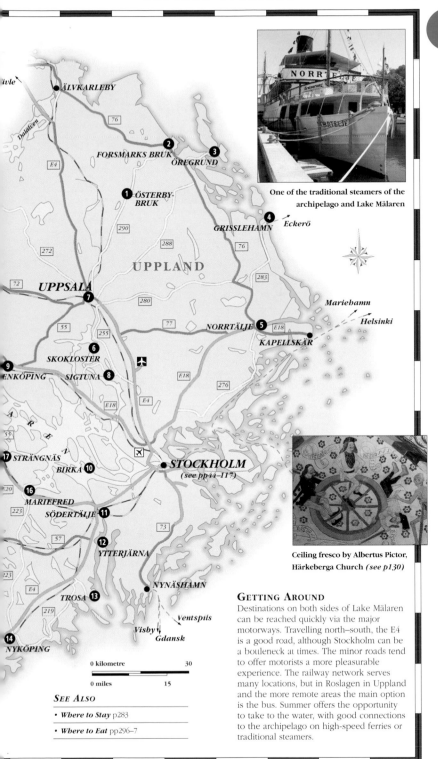

One of the traditional steamers of the archipelago and Lake Mälaren

ÄLVKARLEBY

ivle

76

FORSMARKS BRUK ②

③ **ÖREGRUND**

E4

① **ÖSTERBY-BRUK**

290

④ **GRISSLEHAMN** *Eckerö*

288

272

UPPLAND

76

283

72 **UPPSALA** ⑦

280

Mariehamn

Helsinki

55

255

77

NORRTÄLJE ⑤ E18

KAPELLSKÄR

SKOKLOSTER ⑥

⑨ **ENKÖPING** **SIGTUNA** ⑧

E18

276

E4

⑰ **STRÄNGNÄS**

55

BIRKA ⑩

● **STOCKHOLM**
(*see pp44–117*)

⑯

MARIEFRED

220

223

SÖDERTÄLJE ⑪

57

⑫ **YTTERJÄRNA**

73

NYNÄSHAMN

223

TROSA ⑬

E4

219

⑭ **NYKÖPING**

Ventspils

Visby
Gdansk

Ceiling fresco by Albertus Pictor, Härkeberga Church (*see p130*)

0 kilometre		30
0 miles		15

SEE ALSO

- *Where to Stay* p283
- *Where to Eat* pp296–7

GETTING AROUND

Destinations on both sides of Lake Mälaren can be reached quickly via the major motorways. Travelling north–south, the E4 is a good road, although Stockholm can be a bottleneck at times. The minor roads tend to offer motorists a more pleasurable experience. The railway network serves many locations, but in Roslagen in Uppland and the more remote areas the main option is the bus. Summer offers the opportunity to take to the water, with good connections to the archipelago on high-speed ferries or traditional steamers.

Österbybruk's English gardens with estate offices and clock tower

Österbybruk **1**

Uppland. 🏘 *2,100.* 🚏 *1 Jun–31 Aug: Ånghammaren 0295-214 92.* 🚌 *823 from Uppsala.* 🔲 🚻 **Vallonsmedjan** ◯ *Jun–Aug: 11am–5pm Sat & Sun.* 🔲 *by appointment, 0295-200 72.* **Liljeforsateljén** ◯ *May–mid-Jun, mid-Aug–Sep: noon–4pm Sat & Sun; mid-Jun–mid-Aug: noon–5pm daily.* 🎪 *Hurdy-Gurdy Festival (weekend before Midsummer), Fire Festival (2nd weekend Aug).*

IRON PLAYED a key role in the region and nowhere is this more apparent than at Österbybruk. It is the area's oldest ironworks, dating back to the 15th century, but things only really took off when Dutchman Louis de Geer bought the foundry in 1643. With the help of migrant Walloon blacksmiths, he developed the iron industry so crucial to Sweden's position as a great power.

As the world's only fully preserved Walloon forge, the 15th-century **Vallonsmedjan** uses puppets, sound and light to recreate life in the hammer mills. Around it are charming 18th- and 19th-century streets.

The 18th-century manor house was home to wildlife painter Bruno Liljefors in the early 20th century. In summer, his popular animal paintings are exhibited in **Liljefors-ateljén** in the gardens.

Dannemora Gruva was the mine on which local iron-working was built. Gaping opencast pits such as Storrymningen are relics of an industry that has gone on here since the Middle Ages. Above the mine is the building in which

Mårten Triewald built Sweden's first steam engine in 1726.

🏭 Dannemora Gruva
2 km (1 mile) west of Österbybruk. 📞 *0295-214 92.* ◯ *Jun–Sep: daily.* 🔲 🖥

Forsmarks Bruk **2**

Uppland. 🚌 *from Uppsala.* 🚏 *next to Brukscaféet, Jun–Aug: 0173-500 15.* 🔲 *mid-Jun–mid-Aug: 10am, noon, 2pm Mon–Fri, noon, 2pm Sat & Sun.* 🔲 🚻 🔲 🖥 🛗

THE HISTORIC ironworks of Forsmarks Bruk retains its well-preserved streets with their beautiful, whitewashed rows of houses and a manor house built in 1767–74. The manor is set in extensive English-style gardens.

The nuclear power station of **Forsmarks Kärnkraftverk** lies on the coast, 3 km (2 miles) from the ironworks. It provides one-seventh of Sweden's electricity. Guided tours include such features as the vast biotest lake where the environmental impact of the cooling water is studied.

Louis de Geer's Walloon ironworks empire also included the impressively preserved **Lövstabruk**.

🏛 Forsmarks Kärnkraftverk
3 km (2 miles) north of Forsmark. 🚏 *0173-812 68.* ◯ *Mon–Fri.* 🔲 *mid-May–mid-Aug: tours from Forsmarks Bruk; other times by appointment.* 🛗
🏭 Lövstabruk
16 km (10 miles) north from Forsmark. 🚏 *summer: 0173-500 15.* ◯ *summer: daily (manor).* 🔲 🛗 🔲 🚻

Öregrund **3**

Uppland. 🏘 *1,600.* 🚌 *639 from Stockholm.* 🚏 *Jun–Aug: Harbour Office 0173–305 55; all year round: Östhammar Tourist Office, Rådhus-gatan 6, Östhammar, 0173–178 50.* 🔲 🎣 *Fishing Festival (1st Sat in Jul), Roslagsloppet speedboat race (3rd weekend in Aug).* 🕸 *www.onab.net/turism*

THE TWIN TOWNS of Öregrund and Östhammar are closely linked geographically and historically. At the end of the 15th century, the citizens of Östhammar founded Öregrund in order to obtain a better harbour. Seafaring and iron-exporting became vital to the town. In 1719, Öregrund was burned by the Russians, but the wooden buildings were rebuilt according to a town plan from 1744. The Town Hall is from 1829. At the end of the 19th century, the sleepy area became a seaside resort and continues to attract visitors to this day.

The Öregrund and Östhammar region is home to many well-preserved old ironworking communities, including **Harg** and **Gimo**. Built in 1763–70, Gimo Manor was the first in Sweden to be designed in Gustavian style by Jean Eric Rehn.

Outside Gimo lies **Skäfthammars Kyrka**, a medieval church particularly renowned for its lectern, which was built for the Gimo smiths.

🔐 Skäfthammars Kyrka
Gimo, 16 km (10 miles) southeast of Östhammar. 📞 *0173-419 94.* ◯ *call for info.*

Öregrund Church's shingle-clad, free-standing bell tower (1719)

Albert Engström's studio on the granite cliffs outside Grisslehamn

Grisslehamn ❹

Uppland. 🏛 4,700. 🚌 🛈 *Inner Harbour 0175-331 02.* 🎭 🎏
Postrodden boat race to Åland (Jun).

THE CHOPPY Åland Sea constantly batters the red granite cliffs of northern Väddö at Grisslehamn. This is the closest point in Sweden to Finland and the reason for the town's existence. Today's ferry crossing to Eckerö takes only two hours, but things were much tougher in the 17th and 18th centuries when this was the main link with the eastern outposts of the Swedish empire. Until 1876, the post was rowed across the water by local fishermen in open boats. To commemorate the "post rowers", a race is held across the Åland Sea every year in similar boats.

Today, apart from those making the ferry crossing, the sleepy fishing port of Grisslehamn attracts Väddö's many holidaymakers. Delicious fresh fish can be bought from the red sheds on the harbourside.

In 1900, painter and writer Albert Engström (d. 1940) moved to Grisslehamn. He became much loved for his priceless characters such as the tramp, Kolingen, and the Roslagen figure, Österman. Engström's studio on the coast is now a museum. On the harbour is the **Albert Engströmsmuseet**, a reconstruction of his home containing Engström's art and memorabilia.

🏛 **Albert Engströmsmuseet**
Next to ferry terminal. 📞 *0175-331 02.*
🕐 *May–Sep.* 🎭 📞

Norrtälje ❺

Uppland. 🏛 16,400. 🚌 *610 from Stockholm.* 🛈 *Danskes Gränd 4, 0176-719 90.* 🎭 🎏 *Norrtälje Jazz Festival (late Jun/early Jul).*
🌐 *www.norrtalje.se*

AN IDYLLIC town, built of wood, Norrtälje is the natural hub of Roslagen, the area which covers large parts of the Uppland coast. Norrtälje received its town charter from Gustav II Adolf in 1622, when an important armaments factory was established here. In the second half of the 19th century, the town became a seaside resort, not least due to the health-giving properties of the mud found in Norrtälje Bay.

Thousands of summer residents from Stockholm still head for Norrtälje. The town centre and the buildings along the Norrtäljeån river retain their 18th-century features. The church was built in 1726 and the Town Hall dates from 1792. Attractions include **Roslagsmuseet** in the old armaments factory, focusing on seafaring and coastal life. **Pythagoras** is an unusual museum in a former diesel engine factory and one of Sweden's best preserved industrial relics.

Viking ship in Norrtälje

🏛 **Roslagsmuseet**
Hantverkargatan 23. 📞 *0176-576 30.*
🕐 *Mon–Fri; May–Aug: also Sat.* 🎭 📞
🏛 **Pythagoras**
Verkstadsgatan 6. 📞 *0176-100 50.*
🕐 *mid-Jun–mid-Aug: Mon–Fri.* 🎭 📞

Skokloster ❻

Uppland. 📞 *018-38 60 77.* 🚉 *SJ train from Stockholm to Bålsta, then bus 894.* 🚌 *from Stockholm and Uppsala.* 🕐 *30 min before first tour.*
🎟 *Apr–Oct: 1pm Mon–Fri (Sep: also 3pm), noon, 1pm, 2pm, 3pm Sat & Sun; May–Aug: noon, 1pm, 2pm, 3pm daily (mid-Jun–mid-Aug also 4pm). Eng tours 10 min past the hour except Apr & Oct Mon–Fri.* 🎭 📞 🍴 📞 🎏
Skokloster Pageant (last week in Jul).

ONE OF THE BEST preserved Baroque castles in Europe, Skokloster, on Lake Mälaren, contains a unique collection of furniture, art, weapons, textiles and books. Construction was started in 1654 for army commander Carl Gustav Wrangel, who accumulated incredible treasures during the Thirty Years War (1618–48). This magnificent building was a way for Wrangel to show off his success, but he only ever lived here for a few weeks. Time seems to have stood still at the castle: the Banquet Hall, for example, remains incomplete, with all the tools lying where the craftsmen left them. The most sumptuous rooms are the armoury and library.

Next to the castle is the **Skokloster Motormuseum** with its fine collection of veteran cars and aeroplanes.

🏛 **Skokloster Motormuseum**
📞 *018-38 61 86.* 🕐 *Apr–Sep: daily.*
🎭 📞

The Baroque Skokloster Castle, beautifully situated on Lake Mälaren

Uppsala ⑦

THE CITY OF LEARNING on the idyllic Fyrisån river long remained a small town despite becoming the seat of the archbishop in 1258, having the first university in Scandinavia in 1477 and being the venue for parliaments and coronations. Scientists such as Carl von Linné and Anders Celsius gained the university worldwide glory, but as late as 1800 the town had only 4,000 inhabitants. It wasn't until 20th-century industrialization and the expansion in education that Uppsala grew into Sweden's fourth largest city. The Gothic cathedral, castle, historic university buildings, botanical gardens and ancient Gamla (Old) Uppsala make this one of Sweden's foremost sights.

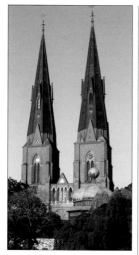

The cathedral's twin spires, restored in the 19th century

🏛 Domkyrkan

Domkyrkoplan 2. ☏ 018-18 72 01. ⏱ daily. 📷 ♿ 🛈 daily. **Skattkammaren** ⏱ daily. 📷

The first sight on approaching Uppsala is the 119-m (390-ft) high twin spires of the largest cathedral in the Nordic region. The building, with its impressive, colonnaded Gothic nave, was consecrated in 1435. Many monarchs have been crowned here and kings Gustav Vasa and Johann III, as well as botanist Carl von Linné and theosophist Emanuel Swedenborg (1688–1772), are buried here. The High Altar contains the remains of St Erik, patron saint of Sweden, in a golden shrine.

The cathedral treasury, Skattkammaren, in the north tower has a superb collection of textiles and silver.

🏛 Gustavianum

Akademigatan 3. ☏ 018-471 75 71. ⏱ Tue–Sun. ● public holidays. 📷 Sat & Sun (also Eng). 📷

Sweden's oldest university building takes its name from Gustav II Adolf who, in 1620, donated a number of medieval buildings from which this one was created. The unusual dome was built in 1662 for Olof Rudbeck's Theatrum Anatomicum. This is an amphitheatre with standing room for 200 spectators – students and paying members of the public – who would gather here to watch dissections of executed criminals. The room which visitors see today is largely a faithful reconstruction.

The Gustavianum mounts exhibitions connected with the work of the university since its foundation in 1477. One of the gems on show is the Augsburg Art Cabinet from the early 17th century. It is a kind of universal museum showing the world view of the time in miniature. Various archaeological collections from Egypt and the Classical world are also on display.

🏛 Universitetshuset

St Olofsgatan/Övre Slottsgatan. ☏ 018-471 57 30. ⏱ Mon–Fri and for events. ♿

The university's imposing main building was constructed in 1887 in Neo-Renaissance style. It contains an attractive auditorium and is home to part of the university's art collection.

🏛 Carolina Rediviva

Dag Hammarskjölds Väg 1. ☏ 018-471 39 00. ⏱ Mon–Sat (mid-May–mid-Sep also Sun). ● public holidays. 📷 mid-May–mid-Sep. ♿

In 1841, the 200-year-old university library moved into this specially designed building which houses 5 million printed books and 4 km (2 miles) of shelving holding handwritten manuscripts. Rarities include the Silver Bible from the 6th century and Olaus Magnus's *Carta Marina* (1539).

🏛 Uppsala Slott

Slottsbacken. ☏ 727 24 85. ⏱ for guided tours. 📷 phone for info. **Konstmuseet** ⏱ Tue–Sun. 🖥 🏛

Standing on a glacial ridge, this Vasa castle competes with the cathedral for domination of the city. Established as a fortress in 1549, it was added to several times, but never finished. A disastrous city fire in 1702 destroyed much of the castle and restoration work was started by Carl Hårleman. The castle now houses Uppsala's art museum and the governor's residence.

CARL VON LINNÉ

"God created, Linné organized," goes the saying about Swedish king of plants. It is thanks to Linné's groundbreaking *Systema Naturae*, first published in 1735, that the

world has the familiar system of binomial nomenclature, giving all plants and animals two Latin names. In 1741, Linné, also known as Linnaeus, became professor of medicine at Uppsala and his spirit has suffused the city ever since. At his country house in Hammarby, Linné tutored students. It was not unknown for him to greet them dressed only in his nightshirt, for the morning's nature walk. According to Linné "nature does not wait for powder and wigs".

Bust of Carl von Linné, 1707–78

Burial mounds next to Gamla Uppsala church and Disagården

VISITORS' CHECKLIST

Uppland 124,000. 25 km
(16 miles) south of the centre.
Kungsgatan. Fyristorg 8,
018-727 48 00.
Vaksala market (Sat).
Walpurgis Night celebrations
(30 Apr), Fyris Festival (early Jun),
Culture Night (2nd Sat in Sep).
www.uppsalatourism.se

🌿 Botaniska Trädgården

Villavägen 8. 018-471 28 38.
daily. public holidays.
greenhouse.

The botanical gardens have had an educational function since the end of the 18th century. They hold more than 130,000 plants, many exotic, in a beautiful setting that includes several greenhouses, one of which is tropical. The first garden was established on the banks of the Fyrisån river by Olof Rudbeck in 1655. In 1741, Carl von Linné took it over and made it one of the leading gardens of its time. Lovingly restored, it is now known as the Linné garden. After a donation from Gustav III in the late 18th century, teaching was switched to the castle garden, where the Linneanum, housing the orangery, opened in 1807.

🏛 Gamla Uppsala

Route 290 or E4, 5 km north of the centre. **Disagården** 018-16 91 00. mid-May–Aug: daily.
Sun.

Gamla Uppsala is like a time capsule. Royal burial mounds rise up from the plain as they have done for 1,500 years. This was a centre for worshipping the Norse gods long into the 11th century, with a temple which, according to Adam of Bremen's description from 1070, was clad entirely in gold and contained images of Odin, Thor and Frey. Every nine years, a bloody festival was celebrated with men, stallions and dogs sacrificed in the trees around the temple. In the early 12th century, the heathen temple gave way to a Christian church, then a cathedral. But in 1273, the seat of the diocese moved to Uppsala and the cathedral became a parish church of which only small parts remain. Nearby is Disagården, an open-air museum focusing on the life of local farmers in the 19th century.

🏛 Linné's Hammarby

13 km (8 miles) southeast of Uppsala.
018-32 60 94. May–Sep:
Gardens daily. Museum Tue–Sun.
Whitsun, Midsummer's Eve.
Linné bought Hammarby farm in 1758, because he thought the air in Uppsala was bad for his health. The estate was his rural retreat, where he was able to cultivate plants that could not tolerate the moist soil in the botanical gardens. The farm is now owned by the state and run by Uppsala University.

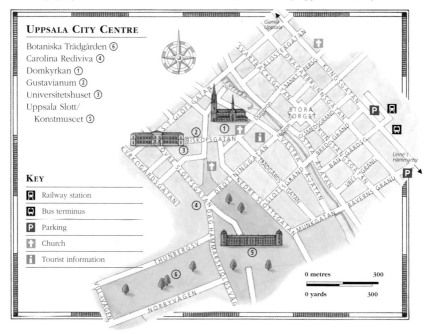

UPPSALA CITY CENTRE

Botaniska Trädgården ⑥
Carolina Rediviva ④
Domkyrkan ①
Gustavianum ②
Universitetshuset ③
Uppsala Slott/
    Konstmuscet ⑤

KEY

🚉 Railway station
🚌 Bus terminus
🅿 Parking
✝ Church
ℹ Tourist information

0 metres   300
0 yards   300

Steninge Slott near Sigtuna, one of the best examples of a 17th-century Carolian country house

Sigtuna ⑧

Uppland. 🏛 7,700. 🚶 🚉 to Märsta
C, then bus. 🚌 ⛴ 🛈 Stora Gatan
33, 08-594 806 50. 🎭 Medieval
Festival (Sat & Sun after Midsummer),
Sigtuna Meeting (last Sat & Sun in
Aug). 🖥 www.sigtuna.se

SWEDEN'S SECOND OLDEST town
after Birka was founded in
980 and soon became a centre
of Christianity. Ruins of three
of the original seven churches
in medieval Sigtuna, St Per,
St Lars and St Olof, still
remain. The attractive main
street, Stora Gatan, is lined
with colourful wooden
buildings and follows the
original route. Still in use today
is the 13th-century church of
St Maria, with its medieval
paintings. It is the oldest brick-
built church in Mälardalen.
    Sigtuna has Sweden's smal-
lest town hall, built in 1744,
and Lundströmska Gården, an
early 20th-century home
furnished in the style of the
period. There are around 150
11th-century rune stones in
the surrounding region.
    The area is also well-
endowed with stately homes.
These include Skokloster (see
p127) and the royal palace of
Rosersberg, with some of
Europe's best-kept interiors
from the period 1795–1825.
    East of Sigtuna is Steninge
Slott, architect Tessin the
Younger's Italianate Baroque
masterpiece built in the 1690s.
The attractive gardens contain
a monument to Count Axel
von Fersen, renowned not
least for his romance with the
French queen Marie
Antoinette, and a cultural
centre and art gallery.

♠ Rosersbergs Slott
15 km (9 miles) from Sigtuna. 📞 08-
590 350 39. 🕒 Mid-May–Aug: daily
for guided tours. 🖼

♠ Steninge Slott
7 km (4 miles) east of Sigtuna. 📞 08-
592 595 00. Palace 🕒 May–Aug daily.
Cultural Centre 🕒 daily. 🖼 🍴

Enköping ⑨

Uppland. 🏛 19,200. 🚉 🚌 🛈
Kungsgatan 42, 0171-250 40.
🖥 www.enkoping.se

THIS CENTRALLY located
town on Lake Mälaren
calls itself Sweden's "nearest
town". Another
name is
"Horseradish
Town" from the vegetable
production which made the
town known in the 19th
century. And Enköping
remains a city of greenery
with its inviting parks.
    Enköping was granted a
town charter in 1300. It was
a spiritual centre with three
churches and a mon-
astery. Of these, only   Triumphal
the largely remodelled   cross, Härke-
Vårfrukyrkan remains.   berga Kyrka
    Northeast of the
town, the medieval church of
Härkeberga is a real gem. At
the end of the 15th century, its
star chamber was decorated
by the master painter Albertus
Pictor with colourful
representations of biblical
stories (see p125).

⛪ Härkeberga Kyrka
10 km (6 miles) northeast of Enköping.
🕒 Mar–Sep daily.

Birka ⑩

Uppland. ⛴ from Stockholm and
Södertälje during summer season.
Birkamuseet 📞 08-560 514 45.
🕒 May–Sep: 10am–5pm daily. 🖼

THE TRADING POST of Birka
on the island of Björkö in
Lake Mälaren was established
in the 8th century and is
thought to be the oldest town
in Scandinavia. The founder
was the Svea king, who
had his royal residence on
nearby Adelsö.
    About 100 years
later, Birka is
described by a
writer as having "many
rich merchants and an
abundance of all types of
goods and a great deal of
money and valuables". It
was thought to have had
1,000 inhabitants, including
craftsmen of every kind,
whose products
attracted merchants
from distant countries.
The town was planned
on uncomplicated
lines. People lived in modest
houses which stood in rows
overlooking the long jetties.
At these lay the ships which
took the Vikings out on
trading missions and war
expeditions. In 830 the arrival
of a monk named Ansgar
marked the start of Sweden's
conversion to Christianity. But
Birka's moment of greatness
soon passed. In the 10th

Iron Age burial ground at Birka on the island of Björkö in Lake Mälaren

century, the town was abandoned in favour of Sigtuna, on the nearby mainland.

Today, Djurkö is a green island with meadows and juniper-covered slopes. It has a fascinating museum and ongoing archaeological digs. The museum shows how Birka would have looked in its heyday, along with some of the finds. Visitors can also share in the day's discoveries when digs are in progress.

In summer, services are held in the Ansgar Chapel. There is a harbour, restaurant, and good places to swim.

Testing the laws of nature at Tom Tits Experiment, Södertälje

Södertälje ⓫

Södermanland. 🏯 63,300. ⛴ 🚗 🚌
🛈 Saltsjögatan 2, 08-550 227 00.
🎫 Broloppet race (3rd Sat in Aug).
🌐 www.sodertaljeturism.com

GOOD COMMUNICATIONS are the key to the economic success of Södertälje, one of Sweden's oldest towns. In the 9th century, a rise in land levels rendered the sound between the Baltic Sea and Lake Mälaren unnavigable and so Tälje became a reloading point. The small town flourished in the Middle Ages but fires, war and plague almost eradicated it in the 17th and 18th centuries. Fortunes improved with the construction of the canal in 1819, and with the arrival of the railway in 1860 industrialization took off. The town grew quickly. Today, major companies such as vehicle-maker Scania and pharmaceuticals giant AstraZeneca form the basis of a booming commercial life.

Södertälje's history is the focus of **Torekällbergets Museum**, an open-air museum with animals, historic buildings and a craft quarter. **Marcus Wallenberg-hallen**

Neat wooden houses lining the harbour canal in Trosa

contains a large collection of veteran vehicles from Scania's 100-year production history.

At **Tom Tits Experiment**, inquisitive children are free to discover for themselves how the laws of nature work through experiments with sound, light, air and water.

🏛 **Torekällbergets Museum**
📞 08-550 214 22. 🕐 Tue–Sun. 🖥 🚻
🏛 **Marcus Wallenberg-hallen**
📞 08-553 825 00. 🕐 Mon–Fri. ⦿ public holidays.
🏛 **Tom Tits Experiment**
Storgatan 33. 📞 08-522 525 00. 🕐 daily. ⦿ 24/12–1/1. 🅿 🖥 🚻 🅿 ♿

Ytterjärna ⓬

Södermanland. 🚉 to Järna, then bus.
🛈 Kulturhuset, 08-554 302 00.
🕐 May–Aug: 9am–4pm daily, Sep–Apr: 9am–4pm Mon–Fri.
⦿ public holidays. 🅿 ♿ 🖥 🚻

SINCE THE 1960s, Ytterjärna has become the centre for Swedish anthroposophists, followers of the teachings of Austrian philosopher Rudolf Steiner (1861–1925). Anthroposophists focus on the development of the whole human being, particularly in the fields of art, music, farming and medicine. There are a number of Steiner organizations here, including schools, the Vidarkliniken hospital, biodynamic farms and market gardens. The Kulturhuset is renowned as a centre for art, music and theatre, and for the building's audacious design by architect Erik Asmussen, with its intertwined dialogue of colour and shape inside and out.

Trosa ⓭

Södermanland. 🏯 4,200. 🚉 to Vagnhärad or Södertälje, then bus.
🛈 Torget 1, 0156-522 22. ♿
🎫 Trosa Market (2nd Sat in Jul).
🎫 Dance at the harbour (Wed in Jul–1st week in Aug).

KNOWN AS THE END of the World, idyllic Trosa is something of a geographical dead end if you are not venturing into the wonderful Trosa archipelago beyond. Like so many coastal towns, it was burned to the ground by the Russians in 1719, although the church dating from 1711 was spared. Pretty groups of red wooden buildings can be found mainly in Kåkstan, where Garvaregården is an arts and crafts museum. The main square, with its miniature town hall and market, is a focal point for the town.

Nearby, **Tullgarns Slott** was the favourite summer residence of Gustav V (1858–1950). The beautiful 18th-century palace has magnificent interiors and English-style gardens.

♣ **Tullgarns Slott**
On E4, 10 km (6 miles) north of Trosa.
📞 08-551 720 11. 🕐 mid-May–Aug: daily, Sep–Sat & Sun. 🅿 🅿

Kulturhuset by Erik Asmussen, in the anthroposophists' Ytterjärna

Nyköpingshus, site of the fatal Nyköping Banquet in 1317

Nyköping ⑭

Södermanland. 🏛 27,200. 🚶 🚌 🚆
ℹ️ Stadshuset, Stora Torget, 0155-24
82 00. 🚢 🎭 Nyköping Banquet
(Tue–Sun in Jul). 🔳 www.nykoping.se

SÖDERMANLAND'S county town
is probably best-known for
the notorious Nyköping
Banquet in 1317. King Birger
invited the Dukes Erik and
Valdemar to a banquet at
which the disputes between
the brothers were to be
resolved. Instead, Birger had
the dukes thrown into
Nyköpinghus's dungeon,
where they were left to die.
The story was retold in summer
in a colourful pageant at the
castle. A fire in 1665 destroyed
the original castle and only
the tower remains. In the
adjoining county governor's
residence, the **Sörmlands
Museum** contains a lively mix
of historical exhibitions.

A pleasant way to see the
sights in the summer is to take
the Tuffis tourist train which
departs from Stora Torget. On
the coast north of the town,
Nynäs Slott is also worth a visit.

🏛 **Sörmlands Museum**
Nyköpingshus. 📞 0155-24 57 00.
⏰ mid-May–mid-Aug: daily, other
times: Tue–Sun. 🎭 🎫 🏠

Flen ⑮

Södermanland. 🏛 6,200. 🚆 🚌 ℹ️
Sveavägen 1, 0157-190 23; Malm-
köping (summer) 0157-194 44. 🍴
Malma Market (last Sat & Sun in Jul).
🎭 Flen Festival (2nd weekend in Jun).

ONE OF THE YOUNGEST towns
in Sweden, Flen only
gained its town charter in
1949. It is the surrounding area

with the same name which
offers the attractions.

ENVIRONS: On Lake
Valdemaren, just east of the
town, lies Stenhammar's
beautiful castle, renowned as
the residence of Prince
Vilhelm in the early 1900s.
The castle is now used by
Carl XVI Gustav and is not
open to the public. Northeast
of Flen is the prime minister's
summer residence, **Harpsund**,
where the gardens are open
to visitors. The old
regimental town of
Malmköping has
Malmahed, a
former military
site, now a
museum and
nature centre.
There are
several military
museums, as well
as **Museispårvägen**,
displaying veteran trams and
other public transport vehicles.
Visitors can enjoy a short tram
ride through the countryside.

🏛 **Museispårvägen**
Malmköping, 17 km (11 miles) north
of Flen, road 55. 📞 0157-204 30.
⏰ 2nd Sat May–1st Sun Sep: Sat,
Sun & public holidays, 4th week
Jun–1st week Aug: daily. 🎭

**Volvo taxi (1950),
Museispårvägen**

Mariefred ⑯

Södermanland. 🏛 4,700. 🚆 🚌
ℹ️ Rådhuset, 0159-297 90. 🚢
🎭 Steam Day (1st Sat & Sun in Jun),
Medieval Festival (3rd Sat & Sun in
Jul). 🔳 www.strangnas.se

THE TOWN OF Mariefred
should ideally be
approached from the water to
get the best view of the
splendid **Gripsholms Slott**.
The first fortress on this site
was built in the 1380s by the
Lord High Chancellor, Bo
Jonsson Grip, who gave the
castle its name. Work on the
present building, initiated by
Gustav Vasa, started in 1537,
but extensive alterations were
made by Gustav III in the late
18th century. It was during
this period that the National
Portrait Gallery was set up. It
now contains 4,000 portraits,
representing the celebrities of
the past 500 years.

Gripsholms Slott has a
number of well-preserved
interiors from various
periods, with
highlights including
Gustav III's theatre
and the White
Salon. The town
of Mariefred,
which grew up
in the shadow of
the castle, derives
its name from a
medieval Carthusian
monastery. An inn has stood
on the site of the monastery
since the early 17th century.

The peaceful old streets of
Mariefred with their delightful
wooden buildings are a
pleasure to stroll around. Art
enthusiasts should head for
Grafikens Hus on a hill
leading up to the former royal
farm, where stables and

Mariefred Town Hall (1784), site of the town's tourist office

◁ **Strömsholms Slott, the centre of Sweden's equestrian sport** (see p136)

haylofts have been converted into attractive galleries.

One of the best ways to visit Mariefred is by boat. The 1903 steamer *S/S Mariefred* plies the three-and-a-half-hour voyage from Stockholm. There is a Railway Museum in the town and **ÖSLJ**, the Östra Södermanlands Järnväg museum society, operates narrow-gauge steam trains from the harbour on a 20-minute trip to Läggesta.

🔱 **Gripsholms Slott**
1 km (half a mile) south of the centre.
🔲 0159-101 94. ⭕ mid-May–mid-Sep: daily; other times: Sat & Sun.
⚫ 21 Dec–1 Jan. 🎫 ✅ 🅿️ 🚻
🏛 **ÖSLJ**
500 m (546 yd) west of the centre.
🔲 0159-210 00. ⭕ 1 May–Sep: Sat & Sun; Midsummer–1st week in Aug also Mon–Fri. 🎫 🅿️

Bedchamber of Duke Karl (Karl IX, 1550–1611), Gripsholms Slott

Strängnäs **17**

Södermanland. 👥 15,000. 🚉 🚌
ℹ️ Grassagården, 0152-296 94 (summer), otherwise 0159-297 90.
🎪 Strängnäs market (2nd Sat in Oct).
🌐 www.strangnas.se

A S KEEPER OF THE KEYS of the Kingdom, Strängnäs was an important centre in the Middle Ages. It was mentioned as an episcopal see as early as 1120 and is dominated by the imposing tower of its Gothic cathedral, **Domkyrkan**, completed in 1280. It was here that Gustav Vasa was chosen as king on 6 June 1523, the date which was to become Sweden's National Day. Quaint wooden buildings surround the cathedral. To its east is Roggeborgen, the bishop's palace from the 1480s.

Strängnäs Municipality includes the largest island in

Red-painted, 18th-century wooden buildings in central Strängnäs

Lake Mälaren, **Selaön**. There are more rune stones here than in any other part of Södermanland, indicating that this was an ancient cultural centre. Selaön is also the location of the former summer residence of the Strängnäs bishops, Tynnelsö Slott, which was transformed by Karl IX in the 17th century into a Renaissance palace.

The newly renovated Mälsåkers Palace dating from the 17th century is another of Selaön's attractions.

⛪ **Domkyrkan**
Stora Torget. 🔲 0152-245 00. ⭕ daily.
🎫 by appointment. ✝️ Wed & Sun.

Mälardalen's Castles **18**

See pp136–7.

Eskilstuna **19**

Södermanland. 👥 80,000. 🚉 🚌
ℹ️ Rademachergatan 50, 016-10 70 00 (also Torshälla).
🌐 www. maranadsforing.eskilstuna.se

T HE TOWN IS NAMED after St Eskil, the Englishman who became Svealand's first Christian bishop and built his

A panda, one of many exotic animals at Eskilstuna's Parken Zoo

church on the riverbank along Eskilstunaån at the end of the 10th century. During Sweden's Age of Greatness in the 17th century, Eskilstuna flourished after Karl X Gustav gave master smith Reinhold Rademacher a 20-year monopoly on the manufacture of items such as cannons, knives and scissors. Rademachergatan still has a few forges kept as they were in the 1650s, where visitors can try their hand at being a blacksmith.

Today's modern industrial town and centre of learning features more than 200 items of public art, including Carl Milles's *Hand of God* (see p95) in Stadsparken.

Parken Zoo is one of Sweden's leading zoos, as well as a popular amusement park with a heated outdoor pool. The entrance is guarded by the Phantom, whose Skull Cave is a magnet for youngsters and comic fans alike.

ENVIRONS: North of Eskilstuna is **Torshälla**, a small town of cobbled streets and well-kept wooden houses. The magnificent 12th-century church dominates the old quarter. Northeast of Torshälla is **Sunbyholms Slott** (see p136) from where a 10-minute walk leads to **Sigurdsristningen**, Sweden's finest rock carving.

🦓 **Parken Zoo**
1 km (half a mile) west of the centre. 🔲 016-100 100. **Zoo** ⭕ Easter week, May–mid-Sep: daily; mid-Sep–Oct: Sat & Sun. **Amusement Park** ⭕ May: Sat & Sun; Jun–mid-Aug: daily; mid-Aug–mid-Sep: Fri–Sun. 🎫 🎫
♿ 🅿️ 🍴 🚻

A Tour of Mälardalen's Castles ⑱

THERE ARE MORE THAN 100 sturdy castles, opulent palaces and ravishing country houses around Lake Mälaren. Often strategically located near Iron Age and Viking settlements, they highlight the significance of this extensive waterway. Wik's 15th-century castle and the Vasa kings' solid, 16th-century fortress of Gripsholm show how long the need for defences lasted. From the mid-17th century, the grand palaces of Sweden's Age of Greatness, such as Skokloster, predominated, as manifestations of their owners' wealth and power. Many have excellent museums.

Engsö ⑤
The medieval castle was reworked in French Rococo style in the 1740s. It has many beautiful interiors from various periods and a major art collection. The castle grounds are a nature reserve full of wildlife.

Grönsöö ④
The grand manor from the early 17th century stands guard high above Lake Mälaren. It is still occupied by the von Ehrenheim family, and its grounds represent 400 years of garden history.

Tidö ⑥
Lord Chancellor Axel Oxenstierna's country house, built in 1642, is a fine example of a Baroque manor. It is noted for its handsome state apartment and 43 inlaid wooden doors. A museum displays 30,000 antique toys.

Strömsholm ⑦
Equestrianism dates from the 16th century at Strömsholm, with its beautiful pastureland and bridle paths. The palace was built in the 1670s in Carolian Baroque style.

KEY

▬ Suggested route

= Other roads

♣ Other castles open to the public

TIPS FOR DRIVERS

This tour, taking in the ten suggested palaces, involves a trip of more than 500 km (300 miles), lasting three days, despite the generally good roads. An option is to select a group of palaces close to each other. For more information, see
Ⓦ www.malarslott.nu
Ⓒ Mälarslott, 016-48 06 80.

Gripsholm ⑧
Gustav Vasa's brick Renaissance castle *(see p134)*, started in 1540, is a symbol of Swedish independence. Visitors have access to 60 rooms from various periods, the highlight of which is Gustav III's theatre, and the National Portrait Gallery.

Map labels: LUDVIKA, SALA, Västerås, Hallsta-hammar, Köping, Strömsholm ⑦, Engsö ⑤, Tidö ⑥, MÄLAREN, Grönsöö ④, Sundbyholm, Fiholm, Enköping, Mälsåker, Arboga, Eskilstuna, E18, E20, Mariefred, Gripsholm

0 kilometres   15

0 miles

Wik ③

This 15th-century castle is Svealand's best-preserved late-medieval fortress. With its solid walls and moat, Wik was considered impregnable. It was remodelled in 1656–60. Today, Wik is a hotel and conference centre.

Skokloster ②

Field Marshal Carl Gustaf Wrangel's 17th-century showpiece contains treasures from his campaigns, as well as exceptional collections of art, furniture, weapons and books. It also has a motor museum (see p127).

Steninge ①

Built in the 1690s, the palace was designed by Nicodemus Tessin the Younger in the style of an Italian villa (see p130).

Drottningholm ⑩

This royal palace, built in the 17th century, was one of the most lavish undertakings in Sweden. With its theatre, gardens and Chinese Pavilion, Drottningholm is a UNESCO World Heritage Site (see pp106–9).

Sturehof ⑨

This stylish 18th-century country house in Botkyrka was designed by C F Adelcrantz for Gustav III's finance minister, Johan Liljekrantz, who owned the renowned Marieberg porcelain factory. The building houses a collection of the factory's famously stunning tiled stoves.

Julita Gård ⑳

Södermanland. 📞 0150-48 75 00.
🚌 🚌 Mälarbanan to Eskilstuna, then bus 404, 405. ⬜ May–Sep daily.

THIS EXTENSIVE Södermanland estate on Lake Öljaren is said to be the world's largest open-air museum. It was created in the first half of the 20th century by the romantic Lieutenant Arthur Bäckström and in 1941 was donated to Stockholm's Nordiska Museet. Julita is a working estate farm with parks and gardens, and an 18th-century manor house built on the site of a medieval Cistercian monastery.

The estate has a collection of buildings reflecting rural life in Södermanland. Threatened national species of cow, pig, sheep, hen and duck are cared for at the Swedish agricultural museum. There is also a dairy museum. Children are welcome to pop into the house of the much-loved children's literary character, Pettson, and his cat Findus.

Julita Gård's buildings representing rural life in Södermanland

Arboga ㉑

Västmanland. 👥 11,000 ✈ 🚌 🚌
🚢 ℹ 🎭 Medieval Festival (Aug).

RED-PAINTED iron warehouses, Ladbron quay and the railway line recall Arboga's great age as the chief shipping port for iron from Bergslagen. Fahlströmska Gården is a typical 16th-century warehouse with a huge loft.

Arboga was an important town in medieval times and the site of Sweden's first parliament in 1435. Churches from the period include the hospital chapel on Stortorget, which has been preserved as a town hall. The 14th-century **Heliga Trefaldighets Kyrka** on Järntorget has a splendid Baroque pulpit by Burchardt Precht.

Anundshögen, the 7th-century burial mound of King Bröt-Anund, with a stone ship in the foreground

Köping ②

Västmanland. 🏠 18,100. 🚆 🚌 🛈
Barnhemsgatan 2, 0221-256 55.
🎉 Köpingsyran Festival (28–30 May).

THE PORT OF KÖPING on Lake Mälaren has been a vital link for transporting products to and from the mines and forests of Bergslagen since medieval times. The city burned down in 1889, but buildings to the west of the river were saved, including the 17th-century **Nyströmska Gården**, a joiner's yard where it is possible to see how the town's special tilt-top table was made. Other attractions include the motor museum, **Bil och Teknikhistoriska Samlingarna**.

East of Köping is the 11th-century church of Munktorp.

🏛 **Bil och Teknikhistoriska Samlingarna**
Glasgatan 19. 📞 0221-206 00. ◻
May–Sep: daily. Pre-booked groups all year round. ◯ Midsummer. 📷 🖥 🎁

Västerås ㉓

Västmanland. 🏃 104,000. 🚆 🚌
🚢 🛈 Stora Gatan 40, 021-10 38 30.
🎉 Arosfestivalen (16–19 Jun), Power meet (9–11 Jul).

STRATEGICALLY SITUATED at the point where the Svartån river runs into Lake Mälaren, the county town of Västerås has been an important trading centre since Viking times. Construction of the castle and cathedral began in the 13th century and in 1527 Parliament was convened here. The cathedral, **Domkyrkan**, contains the sarcophagus of Erik XIV (r.1561–69), the unfortunate king who was allegedly poisoned by his

brother Johan III, by pea soup laced with arsenic.

Around the cathedral lies the town's old centre of learning, where Johannes Rudbeckius opened Sweden's first upper secondary school in 1623.

In the 17th and 18th centuries Västerås became a major port for the Bergslagen region. Today it is an industrial centre and headquarters of the engineering giant Asea-Brown-Boveri (ABB).

To the east of the town lies the 7th-century Anundshögen mound where Bröt-Anund, the king who settled Bergslagen, is said to be buried. Standing stones in the shapes of ships 50 m (164 ft) long can be seen around the mound. The area was an important Viking meeting place.

Northwest of the town is **Skultuna Messingsbruk**, Europe's oldest active brassworks, founded in 1607 and renowned for its cannons and stylish candlesticks.

🚪 **Domkyrkan**
Västra Kyrkogatan 6. 📞 021-81 46 11. ◯ daily. 📷

🏛 **Skultuna Messingsbruk**
16 km (10 miles) NW of Västerås.
📞 021-783 01. ◯ Tue–Sun 10am–4pm. 🚗 tel for info. 🖥 🎁

Sala ㉔

Västmanland. 🏃 12,100. 🚆 🚌
🛈 Norrbygatan 12, 0224-552 02.
🎉 Autumn market (last Fri & Sat in Sep). 🌐 www.sala.se/turism

DURING THE 16th century, the silver mine in Sala was one of the richest in the world; 200,000 kg (440,000 lb) were mined up to 1570, providing valuable funds for the state coffers. The former

Silvergruvan mine is open to the public down to a level of 60 m (200 ft). There are beautiful walks around the old pits and canals, and silver treasure hunts are organized in the mine for children.

Aguélimuseet showcases the work of Sala's own artist, Orientalist Ivan Aguéli (1869–1917), and other Modernists.

🏛 **Silvergruvan**
Drottning Christinas Väg. 📞 0224-131 45. ◯ Sat–Sun noon–4pm, call to book other times. 📷 🚗 🖥
🖥 🍴

🏛 **Aguélimuseet**
Norra Esplanaden 7. 📞 0224-138 20. ◯ Wed–Sat 11am–4pm. 📷 🚗 🎁

Hauling plant at the Sala silver mine, in use until 1908

Fagersta ㉕

Västmanland. 🏃 11,000. 🚆
🛈 Norbergsvag 19, 0223-131 00.
🎉 Spring Festival (21–23 May), Autumn Festival (27–28 Aug).

IRON-WORKING has shaped Fagersta since the outset. In Dunshammer, just south of the town, Iron Age blast furnaces show how iron used to be extracted from bog ore. Today Fagersta is home to metal-manufacturing and stainless steel industries.

At the UNESCO World Heritage Site of **Engelsbergs Bruk**, the historic blast furnace and ironworks have been preserved in working

order and give a remarkable impression of how the site operated between the 17th and 19th centuries.

Oljeön, the world's oldest preserved oil refinery (1875–1902), lies 1.5 km (1 mile) from the ironworks.

Running through Fagersta is the 200-year-old Strömsholm canal from Lake Mälaren to Smedjebacken in Dalarna. It was a vital transport link for the Bergslagen foundries. Twenty-six locks, six of them in Fagersta, raise boats a total of 100 m (330 ft). Passenger ferries operate on the canal.

⛏ Engelsbergs Bruk.
15 km (10 miles) E of Fagersta.
(0223-131 00. ◯ 2nd week in May–Midsummer: Sat & Sun; 4th week in Jun–mid-Aug: daily; 3rd week in Aug–Sep: Sat & Sun. ▨ ▨ ▤ ▥

The mansion at the Engelsberg ironworks, dating from the 1740s

Kopparberg ㉖

Västmanland. ∰ 3,300. ▨ to Örebro, then bus. ▯ Gruvstugutorget, 0580-805 55. ▨ Gold panning competitions (1st weekend in Jul). ▨ www.ljusnarsberg.se

THE DISCOVERY OF copper in the early 17th century attracted miners from Falun, who brought with them the name of their old mine and called the place Nya Kopparberget (New Copper Hill). The 2.5-km (2-mile) path, Kopparstigen, provides a good view of the many mine buildings. Along the way is **Kopparbergs Miljömuseer**, a complex including a goldsmiths' museum, postal museum and 1880s photography studio. The 17th-century courthouse and unusually large and impressive wooden church from 1635 are also worth looking at.

⛏ Kopparbergs Miljömuseer
Gruvstugutorget. **(** 0580-805 55. ◯ Jun–Aug: daily. ▤

Grythyttan ㉗

Västmanland. ∰ 900. **(** 0591-340 60. ▨ to Örebro, then bus. ▯▯

A LOCAL VEIN of silver brought prosperity and town status to Grythyttan in 1649, but when the silver ran out 33 years later, the town charter was withdrawn. In recent years, Grythyttan has awakened from its long slumber and reinvented itself as a gastronomic centre.

It all started when the inn, built in 1640, was given a new lease of life in the 1970s, thanks to inspired innkeeper Carl Jan Granqvist. Now, in addition to Grythyttan's wooden houses and red-painted church, there is a catering college centred on **Måltidens Hus i Norden**. It occupies Sweden's spectacular pavilion built for EXPO 1992 in Seville. A varied range of activities offers something for everyone interested in food and cooking, alongside exhibitions and a cookery book museum.

South of Grythyttan lies **Loka Brunn**, a classic

Grythyttan's inn with its beautifully renovated 17th-century interior

Swedish spa founded in the 1720s. The site has state-of-the-art facilities, but the old spa, with its gardens and spring, has been preserved in the Swedish spa museum. You can sample the spring water and view the restored bathhouse, pharmacy, clinic and royal kitchen built in 1761.

🏛 Måltidens Hus i Norden
Sörälgsvägen 4. **(** 0591-340 60. ◯ end of Jun–mid-Aug: daily; other times: Mon–Fri. ▨ ▨ exhibition. ▤ ▥ ▯▯
⛏ Loka Brunn
15 km (9 miles) S of Grythyttan. **(** 0591-631 00. ◯ daily. ▨ ▨ museum. ▤ ▯▯ ▦ ▧

Nora ㉘

Västmanland. ∰ 6,400. ▨ to Örebro, then bus. ▯ Station House on Norasjön side, 0587-811 20. ▨ Nora Western Festival (1st weekend in Jun), Nora Festival (2nd week in Jun), Nora-marken fair (4th weekend in Aug).

THIS IDYLLIC wooden town is an ideal place to stroll around, with its cobbled streets and charming shops, many in 18th-century buildings. **Göthlinska Gården** (1793) is an interesting museum furnished in the style of a middle-class family home from around 1900.

The highlight of the Nora mining area's monuments is **Pershyttan**, 3 km (2 miles) west of the centre, where the charcoal blast furnace dates from 1856. In summer, a steam train operates from Nora on the Nora Bergslags Veteranjärnväg, Sweden's first normal-gauge railway. Nora's train sheds house historic steam trains, diesel engines and carriages.

Kopparberg's old mining community, now an idyllic wooden village

EASTERN GÖTALAND

THE THREE PROVINCES OF *Östergötland, Småland and Öland, which make up Eastern Götaland, each retain their own distinctive character. Östergötland is the agricultural heart of Sweden, Småland is the centre of glassmaking and Öland attracts sun seekers and nature lovers. They are all popular tourist areas typified by their little red cottages and historical sights, quiet lakes and great coastlines.*

In north Östergötland, the major towns of Norrköping and Linköping are almost part of Greater Stockholm. Once beyond the steep hills of Kolmården, which form the northern border, flat agricultural land extends as far as the eye can see. Besides being the granary of Sweden, this is historical soil – it was here that the royal Folkung dynasty had its roots and it was here that Birgitta Gudmarsson (St Bridget) advised the political and religious leaders of the 14th century.

The hills north of Gränna and the ruins of Brahehus castle mark the beginning of Småland. For a long time Småland formed the border with Denmark and it was from this region that Nils Dacke led a peasants' revolt in the 16th century. The land is poorer and stonier than Östergötland with small farms and crofters. Mass emigration drained the area of thousands of people during the famine of the 19th century. However, Småland has had its success stories: it is the ideal location for one of its major industries, glassworking, which relies on timber and water. The landscape has also been immortalized in the books of Astrid Lindgren, who was born in the province and turned the place where she grew up into a playground for her popular children's characters, Emil and Pippi Longstocking.

The region's archipelago is a favourite with boat-lovers, stretching south from the Sankta Annas islands in Östergötland through the Kalmarsund between Småland and Öland. Thanks to Ölandsbron bridge, the long narrow island of Öland is easily accessible. Holiday-makers are drawn to its sandy beaches, while botanists head for the Alvar plain and ornithologists for Ottenby bird station.

The crew of a sailing boat preparing to pass through the lock at Berg on the Göta Canal

◁ The ruins of Brahehus castle with views over Lake Vättern and the island of Visingö

Exploring Eastern Götaland

THIS IS TOO BIG AN AREA to explore in just a few days, but by leaving the major roads and heading cross-country it is possible to have a taste of the different provinces. In the north, the tourist route between Väderstad and Alvastra is a quiet road which leads to several of Östergötland's main sights. Cycling is the perfect way to get around, and cruising in comfort on the Göta Canal *(see pp146–7)* offers an unforgettable experience. For a tour of the Kingdom of Crystal *(see p152)* a car is almost essential, but otherwise Småland has countless canoeing routes, lakes for swimming and sights along small forested roads ideally explored by bike.

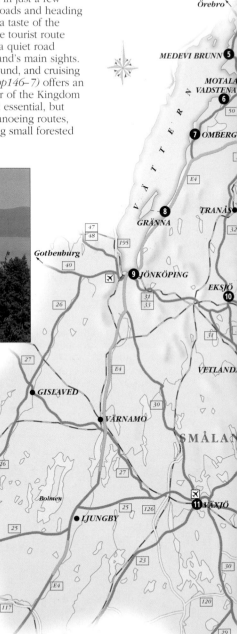

The mythical Omberg on Lake Vättern seen from Brahehus castle *(see p150)*

KEY

▬	Motorway
▬	Major road
═	Minor road
➤	Railway line
- -	Ferry route

GETTING AROUND

The main artery for traffic in this part of the country is the E4 which passes west of Växjö, via the cities of Norrköping, Linköping and Jönköping, on its way south towards Helsingborg. The E22 runs along the coast, leaving the E4 at Norrköping and continuing via Västervik and Kalmar to Malmö. The larger towns, both on the coast and inland, can be reached by train, but local buses or a car will be needed to visit places in the countryside. There are domestic flights to all major cities.

SEE ALSO

• **Where to Stay** pp283–4

• **Where to Eat** pp297–8

Alvastra Monastery, founded by French
Cistercians in 1143

Grazing land on Öland with some of the island's
400 preserved windmills in the background

SIGHTS AT A GLANCE

Blå Jungfrun 🔟6️⃣
Borgholm 🔟9️⃣
Byxelkrok 2️⃣0️⃣
Eketorps Borg 2️⃣3️⃣
Eksjö 🔟0️⃣
Färjestaden 🔟8️⃣
Gränna 8️⃣
Göta Canal pp148–9 4️⃣
Jönköping 9️⃣
Kalmar 🔟7️⃣
Kolmårdens Djurpark 1️⃣
Linköping 3️⃣
Medevi Brunn 5️⃣
Norrköping 2️⃣
Omberg 7️⃣
Oskarshamn 🔟5️⃣
Stora Alvaret 2️⃣2️⃣
Vadstena 6️⃣
Vimmerby 🔟3️⃣
Västervik 🔟4️⃣
Växjö 🔟1️⃣
Ölands Museum 2️⃣1️⃣
Öland's Southern Cape 2️⃣4️⃣

Tour
Kingdom of Crystal 🔟2️⃣

Lion on the prowl in the Safari Park at Kolmårdens Djurpark

Kolmårdens Djurpark ❶

Östergötland. Junction from E4, 12 km (7 miles) N of Norrköping. 🚌
🚌 ℹ️ 011-24 90 00. ⏰ May–Jun, 2nd–last week in Aug: 10am–5pm daily; Jul–first week in Aug: 9am–6pm daily; Sep: 10am–5pm Sat–Sun.
🏞️🔲🍴🛍️♿🚻
W️ www.kolmarden.com

IN 1962 THE IDEA was mooted to turn Kolmården's forests into a recreational area and zoo. Three years later the park opened, but this is no ordinary zoo. The animal enclosures are large and attractively landscaped.

There is a drive-through Safari Park which brings visitors close to the creatures of the savannah who live here alongside Nordic species such as brown bears and wolves.

A Dolphinarium offers spectacular shows with trained dolphins. Snakes and crocodiles inhabit the outdoor Tropicarium, while the Aparium is designed so that the apes can be viewed indoors and out.

There is a cable-car ride around the park providing a bird's-eye view of the grounds.

Norrköping ❷

Östergötland. E4. 👥 8,300. 🚌
🚌 ℹ️ Dalsgatan 9, 011-15 50 00.
📷 Norrköping International Horse Show (4th week in May), National Day Festival (first week in Jun).
W️ www.destination.norrkoping.se

IN THE 17TH CENTURY the skills of entrepreneur Louis de Geer, combined with water power from the Motala Ström

river system, transformed Norrköping into Sweden's first industrial town. Norrköping and neighbouring Linköping make up Sweden's fourth largest urban region.

Although Norrköping is an industrial town, the mix of old and new buildings, parks and trams make it an attractive place to visit. On a small island in Motala Ström sits **Arbetets Museum** (Museum of Labour), in an old spinning mill known as Strykjärnet (the Iron).

ENVIRONS: The area has a long history of habitation – around 1,650 carvings, some dating back to 1000 BC, can be seen at **Himmelstalund** on the edge of town.

About 10 km (6 miles) south of Norrköping on the E4 is the 17th-century **Löfstad Slott** with its beautiful English-style park. The castle remains as it was in 1926 on the death of the owner, Emelie Piper.

🏛️ Arbetets Museum
Laxholmen. ☎️ 011-18 98 00.
⏰ daily. 🔲🚻● public holidays.
🏛️ Löfstad Slott
10 km (6 miles) S of Norrköping.
☎️ 011-33 50 67. ⏰ Jun–Aug: daily; May: Sat, Sun, public holidays; Apr, Sep, Oct: Sun; Nov–Mar: phone for info. 🔲🖥️🍴

Strykjärnet (the Iron) in Norrköping, housing Arbetets Museum

Linköping ❸

Östergötland. E4. 👥 94,000. 🚌
🚌 ❌ ℹ️ Klostergatan 68, 013-20 68 35. 📷 Ekenäs Castle Tournament (Whitsun), Summer Festival (2nd week in Jul), Handicraft Festival and Folk Festival (4th week in Aug).
W️ www.linkoping.se

THE COUNTY capital and cathedral city of Linköping lies in the middle of the Östgöta plain. First populated 3,000 years ago, it is now Sweden's fifth largest city, and is known for its university and high-tech industry.

Construction of the **Domkyrkan** (Cathedral) started in the mid-13th century. The interior contains superb medieval stone carvings. The Renaissance altarpiece is by the Dutch painter M J Van Heemskerck (1498–1574).

The old town open-air museum, **Gamla Linköping**, is a collection of 80 buildings from the city and surrounding area. This charming setting, complete with picturesque wooden buildings, cobbled streets and gardens, is a window on a past way of life.

Malmen, site of Sweden's first military flying school (1911), is now home to the **Flygvapenmuseum** (Swedish Air Force Museum). Exhibits include examples of Swedish military aircraft and other items from aviation history.

ENVIRONS: Kaga Kyrka, one of the region's best-preserved medieval churches, is located on the Svartån river south of Linköping. Dating from the 12th century, its walls are decorated with frescoes.

On Erlången lake, 10 km (6 miles) southeast of the centre, lies the castle of **Sturefors**, renowned for its 18th-century interiors and beautiful grounds. The castle is a private residence, but parts of the grounds are open to the public.

🏛️ Domkyrkan
St Persgatan. ☎️ 013-20 50 50, 20 50 57. ⏰ daily. 📷 phone for info.
♿🚻
🏛️ Gamla Linköping
2 km (3 miles) west of the centre.
☎️ 013-12 11 10. ⏰ daily.
🚌🚻🍴

🏛 **Flygvapenmuseum**
4 km (3 miles) west of the centre.
📞 013-28 35 67. ⏰ Sep–May:
Tue–Sun; Jun–Aug: daily. 🖼
📷 phone for details. 📖 📷

Göta Canal ❹

See pp146–7.

Medevi Brunn ❺

Östergötland. Road 50. 🚉 🚌
🛈 0141-911 00. 🎺 Grötlunken
marching band processions (Jun/Jul).

I N THE 17TH-CENTURY the
scientist and doctor Urban
Hjärne analyzed water from
the Medevi spring and
declared it to be "superior to
other medication". Thus
began the transformation of
Medevi Brunn into a health
spa. Today, the season at
Medevi starts at Midsummer
and lasts for six weeks, during
which time the traditional
brass sextet Brunnsorkester
performs daily concerts.

South of Medevi, on the
edge of Lake Vättern, lies
Övralid, the former home of
poet and Nobel laureate
Verner von Heidenstam
(1859–1940). Designed by
Heidenstam himself, the
house has stunning views
across the lake.

🏛 **Övralid**
10 km (6 miles) N of Motala, Road 50.
📞 0141-22 05 56, 22 00 36.
⏰ 15 May–31 Aug: daily. 🖼
📷 10am–5pm on the hour. 📖

**Medevi Brunn, the first health spa
in the Nordic countries**

Vadstena Slott, built in 1545 for protection against the Danes

Vadstena ❻

Östergötland. Road 50. 🏘 5,700.
🚉 🚌 🛈 Castle, 0143-315 71.
🎭 St Bridget Festival (3rd week in
May), Vadstena Academy Opera
performances (Jul).

S ITUATED ON Lake Vättern,
Vadstena is dominated by
the abbey, which dates back
to the 14th century and St
Bridget, and the mid-16th-cen-
tury castle of the Vasa kings.
Cobbled streets, wooden
buildings and glorious gardens
add to the town's character.
The stately **Vadstena Slott**
was built in 1545 as a fortress
against the Danes and is
surrounded by a moat. As well
as being a museum, the castle
also houses the county record
office and hosts opera, theatre
performances and concerts.
The abbey area encompasses
the original abbey, Vadstena
Kloster, established in 1384

and dissolved after the
Reformation in 1595, and
Vadstena Klosterkyrka
(1430). This abbey church
houses the relics of St Bridget
and a life-like wooden
sculpture of the saint. It is also
the site of the recently founded
convent Pax Mariae, home to
around ten Brigittine nuns.

ENVIRONS: Less than 20 km
(12 miles) south of Vadstena
towards Skänninge is **Bjälbo
Kyrka**, a late-12th-century
church. Bjälbo is said to be
the birthplace of the founder
of Stockholm, Birger Jarl.

🏛 **Vadstena Slott**
100 m (110 yd) SW of the centre.
📞 0143-315 71. ⏰ First 2 weeks in
May, mid-Sep–Apr: Mon–Fri; mid-
May–mid-Sep daily. 📷 Jun–Aug.
📖 🖼
🔔 **Vadstena Klosterkyrka**
⏰ daily. 📞 0143-315 70, 0143-298
50. 🔔 Sun. 📷 Jun–Aug. ♿

ST BRIDGET, SWEDEN'S PATRON SAINT

At the age of only 13, Bridget (c.1303–73) was married to
local dignitary Ulf Gudmarsson. She became lady of the
manor in Ulvåsa in Östergötland and the mother of eight
children. Even as a child, she had religious visions and as
an adult made pilgrimages to Santiago de Compostela in
Spain in 1341–2, Rome in 1349
and Jerusalem in 1372–3.
Some of her visions also had
political themes and Bridget
became influential in the political arena. In 1370 she gained
the Pope's permission to found
a monastic order, the Brigittine
Order. The first nuns were
ordained in 1384. Bridget died
on returning to Rome following
her pilgrimage to Jerusalem. Her
remains were taken to Vadstena
in 1374. Canonized in 1391,
Bridget is the patron saint of
Sweden, and in 1999 became
the patron saint of Europe.

**Sculpture of St Bridget in
Vadstena Klosterkyrka**

Göta Canal ❹

OPENED IN 1832, the Göta Canal provided a vital link for transporting timber and iron between Stockholm and Gothenburg. But it was another 100 years before leisure traffic took off on the waterway. Today in summer, the canal bustles with small craft and passenger boats and it is possible to cruise the entire length on the classic *M/S Diana* (1931), *Wilhelm Tham* (1912) and *Juno* (1874). Other boats take passengers along shorter stretches and there are numerous special packages available, such as combining cycling holidays with canal trips. There are guest marinas offering services along the entire length of the canal. Motala is regarded as the "capital" of the canal, and the man behind its construction, Baltzar von Platen (1766–1830), is buried here.

Building the Canal
Karl XIV Johan inspects construction near Berg in Östergötland with Crown Prince Oscar. Baltzar von Platen is standing bareheaded to the left of the king.

Sjötorp on Lake Vänern marks the end point of the canal in Västergötland.

Karlsborgs Fästning (see p221), towers above the canal.

Lock-keeper
The majority of lock gates along the stretch of canal which lies in Västergötland are still worked by hand by friendly and patient lock-keepers.

Borensberg
The long-established Göta Hotell is an idyllic summer spot on the canal. Built in 1894, it offers food and accommodation to passers-by.

KEY

▨▨	Motorway
▨▨	Other road
▨▨▨	Canal

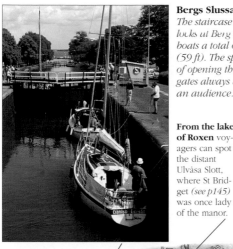

Bergs Slussar
The staircase of seven locks at Berg raises boats a total of 18 m (59 ft). The spectacle of opening the lock gates always attracts an audience.

VISITORS' CHECKLIST

Östergötland and Västergötland.
🚇 AB Göta Kanalbolag in Motala, 0141-20 20 50. 🚌 🚤 ⛴
🎿 Nostalgic Canal Race (early Jul), Göta Kanalrännet Skating Race (early Jan), Sweden Action Games (mid-Jun). 🆆 www.gotakanal.se

From the lake of Roxen voyagers can spot the distant Ulvåsa Slott, where St Bridget (see p145) was once lady of the manor.

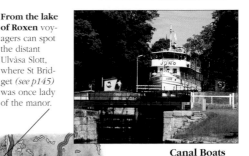

Canal Boats
From May to August traditional white boats such as M/S Juno ply the canal. Built in 1874, Juno is one of the oldest boats afloat with sleeping accommodation still in use.

Mem is the first lock in the canal system on the journey west.

CLIMBING FROM THE BALTIC TO LAKE VÄNERN

"The Blue Band of Sweden" as the Göta Canal is known, is the high point of Swedish engineering history. It took 58,000 men, mainly soldiers, and 22 years to build a waterway across Sweden from the Baltic Sea to join the already completed Trollhättan Canal (see p217), and provide a route through to the Kattegatt. The problem was not simply digging the canal, but coping with a difference in height of around 92 m (301 ft). Completing this mammoth project took more than just spades and advantage was taken of the latest technological innovations – dredgers, hoists, cranes, pile drivers, mortar mills and optical instruments. Most of the machinery was imported from England, but as the project grew, and with it the need for mechanical equipment, Baltzar von Platen eventually took the initiative to set up a factory in Motala where the mechanical equipment could be made or modified. The canal has 58 locks between Mem on the Baltic and Sjötorp on Lake Vänern.

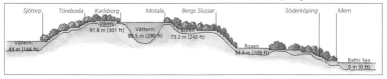

From Mem the canal begins its climb to reach the highest point between Lakes Vättern and Vänern

View over Lake Vättern from Hjässan, the highest point of Omberg

Omberg ❼

Östergötland. 20 km (12 miles) S of Vadstena. 🔲 🎐 *Naturum, Stocklycke, 0144-332 45.* 🔲 *May– Aug: 11am–5pm daily; Apr, Sep & Oct: noon–4pm daily.* 🗹 🔲 🇼 www.e.lst.se/omberg

R ISING MOUNTAIN-LIKE from the wide Östgöta plains is Omberg. Its highest point is 175 m (574 ft) above Lake Vättern. It is the legendary home of Queen Omma, whose name means "steam" and indeed the fog that often surrounds the hill gives it a mythical quality. Orchid marshes, beech woodlands and ancient forest flourish on the limestone-rich rock. Walking trails cross the area. To the south lies author Ellen Key's home, **Strand**, and the nature reserves of Bokskogen and Stora Lund. On the plains southeast of Omberg is the ruin of **Alvastra Kloster** where St Bridget *(see p145)* once stayed.

To the east, Omberg slopes down to Lake **Tåkern**, barely 1 m (3 ft) deep and favoured by flocks of geese and cranes in spring and autumn. The **Rökstenen** at Röks Kyrka is a large 9th-century runestone.

🏛 **Strand**
1 km (half a mile) W of Ödeshög. 🇨
0144-330 30. 🔲 *15 Apr–Midsummer, mid-Aug–mid-Sep: Tue–Sun.* 🗹

Gränna ❽

Småland. E4. 🏘 *2,600.* 🔲
🎐 *Brahegatan 38, 0390-410 10.*
🎪 *Andrée Festival (2nd week in Jul), County Festival (3rd week in Jul).*
🇼 www.grm.se/turistinfo

G RÄNNA WAS AT its height in the 17th century in the days of Count Per Brahe, who founded the town and whose

plan is still evident today. On the square in the centre of town, **Gränna Museum** has fascinating tales to tell of the tragic expedition to the North Pole headed by the town's famous son Salomon August Andrée in the hot-air balloon *Örnen.* Inspired by Andrée, Gränna has become a centre for balloon flights. The town is also known for its *polkagris* (peppermint rock), an ideal souvenir. The red and white sweet originated in 1859 when widow Amalia Eriksson started a rock factory in the town.

Along the beautiful stretch of the E4 beside Lake Vättern, just north of Gränna, lies the ruined **Brahehus** castle, built for Count Per Brahe in the 1640s. On a clear day Brahehus offers magnificent views over Vättern towards Västergötland on the other side of the lake and **Visingsö**. This flat island can be reached by boat from Gränna. It is the largest island in Lake Vättern, 14 km (9 miles) long and 3 km (2 miles) wide with a population of 800. In the 12th and 13th

Polka-gris

centuries the island was the seat of Sweden's first kings, including Magnus Ladulås. Per Brahe built the castle, Visingsborgs Slott, now a ruin, and a church on the island in the 17th century. The boat trip from Gränna takes about 25 minutes and the service is frequent in the summer months.

🏛 **Grenna Museum**
Brahegatan 38–40. 🇨 *0390-410 15.*
🔲 *daily.* ◐ *24, 25, 31 Dec, 1 Jan.*
🗹 🔲 🎨 🇨

Jönköping ❾

Småland. E4. 🏘 *81,400.* 🔲 🔲 🚶
🎐 *Railway station, 036-10 50 50.*
🎪 *Jönköping Market (end of May), Kalajs Carnival (May/Jun).*
🇼 www.jonkoping.se

K ING MAGNUS Ladulås granted Jönköping its charter in 1284, by which time the town was already an important trading centre. For a long time Småland formed Sweden's southern border with Denmark, but when the Danes invaded in 1612 the people set fire to their town and fled to Visingsö.

In the 19th century Jönköping became synonymous with matchstick production; the Lundström brothers opened their first factory here in the 1840s. In the old part of town, **Tändsticksmuseet** (the Match Museum) is set in a former match factory (1848). The historic Västra Storgatan 37 houses **Viktor Rydbergs**

The ruins of Brahehus Castle on Lake Vättern looking towards Visingsö

◁ Kapelludden on the east of Öland, and the 13th-century ruins of St Bridget's chapel

Museum. Local history comes under the spotlight at **Jönköpings Läns Museum**. The museum also has a display of work by the local artist John Bauer *(see p21)*, as well as contemporary art.

ENVIRONS: Just outside Jönköping, **Hakarps Kyrka** is famous for its paintings by Edvard Orm. **Taberg**, a hill south of Jönköping, is known as "the Alps of Småland". It has a café at its peak, 343 m (1,125 ft) above sea level. The countryside is stunning, with extensive views over Lake Vättern. Sights include a mine and an industrial museum and there are hiking trails and overnight accommodation.

🏛 **Tändsticksmuseet**
Tändsticksgränd 27. 📞 *036-10 55 43.* ⭕ *daily.* ● *public holidays & eves of public holidays.* 📷 🎥 🎬 🛗

🏛 **Jönköpings Läns Museum**
Dag Hammarskjölds Plats 2. 📞 *036-30 18 00.* ⭕ *Tue–Sun.* 📷 🎥 🛗

Eksjö ❿

Småland. Road 32/33. 🚶 *16,000.*
🚆 🚌 🏨 *Norra Storgatan 29, 0381-361 70.* 🎪 *Ränneslättsloppet Motocross Race (4th week in Oct), Hussar Festival (last Sun in Jun).* 🌐 *www.eksjo.se*

THE SMALL TOWN of Eksjö, in the highlands of southern Sweden, is the country's most genuine wooden town. It has a long military tradition. This was border country until the 17th century and Eksjö was burned down by its own people in conjunction with a Danish retreat. In the 1560s Erik XIV drew up a new town plan for Eksjö, which largely remains today. Gamla Stan (the Old Town) escaped the fire and its buildings remain intact and have been sympathetically renovated.

ENVIRONS: About 13 km (8 miles) east of Eksjö, the **Skurugata** nature reserve encompasses an impressive canyon in porphyritic rock, 800 m (2,625 ft) long and 35 m (115 ft) deep. From Eksjö to the neighbouring town of **Nässjö** is just over 20 km (12

miles). Nässjö owes its existence to the coming of the railway in the 1860s. At that time the village had 57 inhabitants; today it has nearly 30,000 and the railway companies Statens Järnvägar and Banverket are still the main employers. Sights in Nässjö include **Järnvägsmuseum** (the Railway Museum) and Hembygdsparken with its collection of 18th-and 19th-century buildings.

🏛 **Järnvägsmuseum**
Brogatan 10, Nässjö. 📞 *0380-722 07.* ⭕ *15 Jun–13 Aug: Wed, Sat–Sun.*

Växjö ⓫

Småland. Road 25/30. 🚶 *52,000.*
🚆 🚌 🏨 🏨 *Norra Järnvägsgatan 3, 0470-414 10.* 🎪 *Karl-Oskar Festival (first week in Aug), Children's Festival (early June).* 🌐 *www.vaxjo.se*

A BISHOPRIC as early as the 12th century, Växjö was granted its town charter by King Magnus Erikson in 1342. For some time the town lay on the border with Denmark and it was from here that Nils Dacke led his peasant revolt against the Danes in the 16th century. Devastating fires, the most recent in 1843, destroyed the town, which has since been rebuilt. The cathedral dates originally from the end of the 12th century, but has

The twin steeples of Växjö's 12th-century cathedral

been remodelled over the centuries. It contains an altar-piece in glass and wood made in 2002 by the glass artist Bertil Vallien.

Smålands Museum, with Sveriges Glasmuseum (Glass Museum), depicts the history of the county of Kronoberg and the development of the glassworks. Next to it is **Utvandrarnas Hus**, which focuses on the mass emigration in the 19th century.

🏛 **Smålands Museum**
Södra Järnvägsgatan 2. 📞 *0470-70 42 00.* ⭕ *Jun–Aug: daily; Sep–May: Tue–Sun.* ● *public holidays.*

🏛 **Utvandrarnas Hus**
Vilhelm Mobergs Gata 4. 📞 *0470-201 20.* ⭕ *Sep–Apr: Tue–Sat; May–Aug: daily.* 🎥 📷 🛗 🖥 ♿

EMIGRATION TO AMERICA

Disillusioned by poverty, religious intolerance and political discontent, many Swedes in the late 1860s dreamed of a better life in North America. Famine in Sweden, combined with the end of the Civil War in the fast expanding USA, prompted around 100,000 Swedes to emigrate in 1868–71, the majority from southern Sweden, particularly the barren lands of Småland. Another major wave followed in the 1880s when 350,000 people left Sweden.

Nobel Prize-winner Vilhelm Moberg's epic trilogy *The Emigrants* describes the tough life Swedish emigrants faced in their new land.

Emigration to the USA tailed off with the Depression of the 1930s, but by then 1.2 million Swedes had already left their homeland.

Emigrants on the Way to Gothenburg, Geskel Saloman (1821–1902)

A Tour through the Kingdom of Crystal ⑫

Växjö, "GATEWAY TO THE KINGDOM OF CRYSTAL", is an
ideal starting point for a tour of at least nine of
the famous glassworks set in the beautiful countryside between Växjö and Nybro. Access to timber
and water accounts for the concentration of glassworks in this area of Småland, where forest, lakes
and waterways dominate the landscape. The
glassworks are mostly only 20–30 km (12–20 miles)
apart, and many have shops offering discounted
items and displays of the designers' latest creations.

Bergdala ①
Bergdala's signature is
blue-edged glass, but
designers are pushing
the boundaries when it
comes to colour and
shape. The temperature
of the smelting oven is
a constant 1,150° C
(2,102° F).

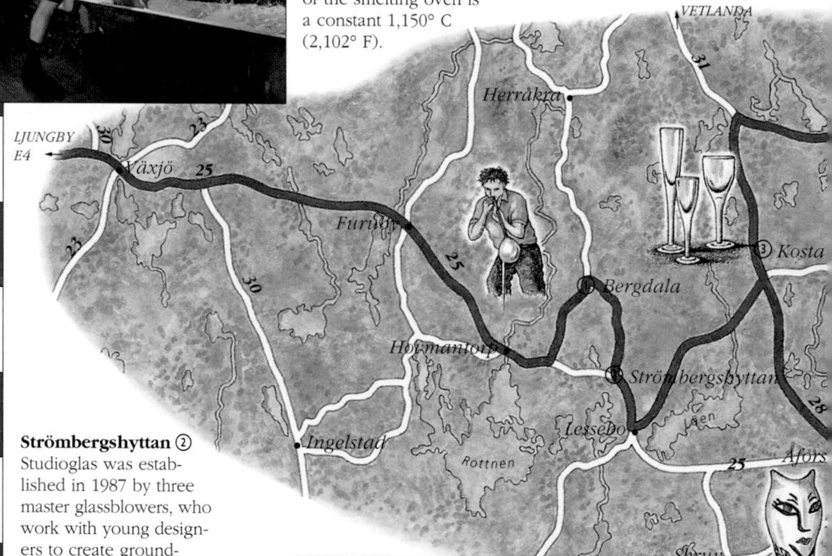

Kosta ③
The oldest glassworks, Kosta
(1742), like Boda and Åfors,
has attracted some of Sweden's
foremost contemporary
designers. Shown here is the
entrance to the original office.

Strömbergshyttan ②
Studioglas was estab-
lished in 1987 by three
master glassblowers, who
work with young design-
ers to create ground-
breaking works of art.

KEY

■ Suggested route

＝ Other roads

Åfors ④
The trio Bertil Vallien, Ulrica Hydman-
Vallien and Gunnel Sahlin work for the
glassworks in Fina Stugan, one of the
most exciting galleries in the area. Glass
eggs are by Ulrica Hydman-Vallien.

TIPS FOR DRIVERS

Length: Växjö–Nybro, road 25,
approx. 85 km (53 miles). Well
signposted.
Places to eat: Many glassworks
have a café/restaurant and some
of the larger ones serve herring
dishes at special herring evenings.

Map labels: VETLANDA, Herråkra, LJUNGBY E4, Växjö, 25, Furuby, Kosta, Bergdala, Hovmantorp, Strömbergshyttan, Ingelstad, Lessebo, Röttnen, Åfors, Skruv

0 kilometres   10

0 miles   5

Orrefors ⑧

The glassworks was founded in 1898 and has become the flagship of Swedish glass-making, producing functional, decorative items and *objets d'art*. The work of Orrefors over the years is on show in its museum.

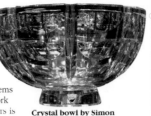

Crystal bowl by Simon Gate (1883–1945)

Målerås ⑨

The employees bought this glassworks from Kosta in 1981. It is famous for its crystal animal reliefs by glass artist and master etcher Mats Jonasson.

Pukeberg ⑦
The glassworks was founded in 1871. Extensive production in this beautiful old setting has mainly been focused on lighting and domestic glassware using traditional methods.

(Map of Eastern Götaland area showing: Målerås, Hälleberga, Orrefors, Hermanstorp, Boda, Örsjö, Nybro, Pukeberg, KALMAR, Johansfors, Emmaboda, KARLSKRONA, with roads 31, 25, 120)

Johansfors ⑤

This glassworks is known as the Eden of the Kingdom of Crystal, symbolized by Christopher Ramsey's *Astrakhan Apple*. Glass-blowing is demonstrated daily and there is a museum.

Boda ⑥
Skilled designers at Boda have made Swedish glass world famous over the years. Kjell Engman is taking this tradition further, here with a piece made in 2003.

Vimmerby ⑬

Småland. Road 33/34. 🏠 8,000. 🚌
🚗 ✕ ℹ Västra Tullportsgatan 3, 0492-310 10. 🎭 Stora Tabberaset local festival (first weekend in Aug), Holiday Race (2nd week in Jul).

THE SMALL TOWN of Vimmerby began as a marketplace on the "King's Road" between Stockholm and Kalmar. It was strategic-ally important and constantly fought over by the Danes, who burned it to the ground on many occasions. Few old buildings remain, but along Storgatan there is the austere Neo-Classical-style Rådhuset (Town Hall) from the 1820s. Like the houses of Tenngjutar-gården and Grankvistgården, it is one of Vimmerby's historical monuments.

For many years Vimmerby has been associated with Astrid Lindgren *(see p87)*, who was born in Näs and set many of her popular children's books in this area. All her beloved characters can be encountered in **Astrid Lindgrens Värld** (Astrid Lindgren's World). The park also includes the Astrid Lindgren Centre with an exhibition about the author.

ENVIRONS: Norra Kvill National Park, 20 km (12 miles) northwest of Vimmerby, is an area of virgin forest in the highlands of Småland containing pine trees over 350 years old. The park slopes down to a small lake, Stora Idegölen, with waterlilies and bogbean.

🎡 **Astrid Lindgrens Värld**
Fabriksgatan. 📞 0492-798 00.
🕐 15 May– end of Aug: daily. 📷 🎫
♿ 🏠 🛍 🍴 🌐 www.alv.se

Miniature house in Astrid Lindgrens Värld, Vimmerby

Picturesque red cottages on Båtsmansgränd in Västervik

Västervik ⑭

Småland. E22. 🏛 21,000. 🚗 🚆 ✖
🛈 Strömsholmen, 0490-889 00.
📅 Song Festival (first week in Jul).
🌐 www.vastervik.se/turist

STRATEGICALLY SITED at the mouth of Gamlebyviken Bay, Västervik was the subject of frequent Danish attacks, despite protection from the once mighty fortress of Stegeholm. The last attack in 1677 destroyed the town. Rebuilt, it became a major seafaring centre. The area known as Gamla Norr contains the oldest preserved houses in Västervik, including Aspagården and the former poor-house, Cederflychtska Huset. **Kulbackens Museum** outlines the history of the town. Part of the museum is in the open air with animals and traditional buildings. The railway line was closed in 1984, but train enthusiasts have reopened the 70-km (43-mile) stretch from Västervik to Hultfred, to preserve it as part of Sweden's industrial heritage.

The annual Folk Festival first took place in 1966 and has since grown to become a major event. It is held in the ruins of Stegeholm fortress. **Lunds By**, just outside Västervik, is the oldest and best preserved village in the region, comprising eight small red cottages around a square. This charming place was chosen as a location to film Astrid Lindgren's book *The Bullerby Children*.

🏛 **Västerviks Museum**
Kulbacken. 📞 0490-211 77.
🕐 May–Aug: daily; Sep–Apr:
Mon–Fri. 🅿 📷 🖥 🎦

Oskarshamn ⑮

Småland. E22. 🏛 17,100. 🚆 🚆
🛈 Hantverksgatan 18, 0491-881 88.
📅 Oskarshamn Harbour Festival (mid-Jul). 🌐 www.oskarshamn.se/turistbyra

KING OSKAR I gave his name to this town, previously known as Döderhultsvik, which gained its charter in 1856. It grew up around the harbour and today is still an important place with a lively seafaring industry. The old areas of Besväret and Fnyket have wooden 19th-century houses and are ideal for exploring on foot. There are great views over the water and the island Blå Jungfrun from Långa Soffan, an extraordinarily long 72-m (79-yd) bench built close to the harbour in 1867.

Oskarshamn has several museums. On show at **Döderhultarmuseet** are the original wooden figures by sculptor Axel Petersson, also known as "Döderhultarn", together with a description of his life in late-19th-century Småland. **Oskarshamns Sjöfartsmuseum** (Maritime Museum) has a superb collection of local maritime history.

An expressive carved wooden figure by "Döderhultarn" Axel Petersson (1865–1925)

ENVIRONS: Stensjö By is a cultural museum showing how a village looked in the 18th century, with meadows, arable land and animals. Just under 40 km (25 miles) west of Oskarshamn at Högsby there is the **Aboda Klint** nature reserve and a permanent exhibition about film star Greta Garbo, whose mother came from here. Children and adults enjoy the toy museum, **Nostalgia**, in Fågelfors, where visitors can see but not touch 2,000 toys from the past.

🏛 **Döderhultarmuseet**
Hantverksgatan 18. 📞 0491-880 40.
🕐 Tue–Sun. 📷 pre-book. 🅿 🖥
🎦 ♿
🏛 **Oskarshamns Sjöfartsmuseum**
Hantverksgatan 18. 📞 0491-880 45.
🕐 Tue–Sun. 📷 pre-book. 🅿 🖥
🎦 ♿
🏛 **Nostalgia**
Bruksgatan 43, Fågelfors, 40 km (25 miles) W of Oskarshamn. 📞 070-304 18 63. 🕐 end Jun–first week in Sep: Tue–Sun. 🎦

Blå Jungfrun ⑯

Småland. 20 km (12 miles) E of Oskarshamn. 🚢 from Oskarshamn & Byxelkrok. 🛈 Oskarshamn Tourist Office, 0491-881 88.

IN THE NORTHERN part of Kalmarsund, the sound separating the mainland from the island of Öland, the national park Blå Jungfrun (the Blue Maiden) encompasses an island about 800 m (875 yd) in diameter and the waters surrounding it. Blå Jungfrun's highest point is 86 m (282 ft) above sea level, making it easily visible from the mainland and from Öland.

According to legend, the island is the site of Blåkulla, home of the witches, and is the subject of many a dark tale. Carl von Linné *(see p24)* described it as "horrible". Others have found it romantic, including the poet Verner von Heidenstam, who was married here in 1896. The island is mainly bare pink granite, polished smooth by ice and

Medieval Kalmar Slott, a beautifully preserved castle rebuilt in Renaissance style in the 16th century

water, with deciduous forest in the south and a population of black guillemots. It is unlikely that it was inhabited, although a stone labyrinth was built here and there are caves. Boats run from Oskars-hamn or Byxelkrok *(see p156)* to Blå Jungfrun, once a day, weather permitting. The journey takes 90 minutes from Oskarshamn with a three-and-a-half-hour stay on the island.

Kalmar **⑰**

Småland. E22. 👥 *34,000.* 🚉 🚌 ⛴
ℹ️ *Ölandskajen 9, 0480 41 77 00.*
🎭 *Kalmar Market (3rd week in Jul), Medieval Market in Salvestaden (3rd week in Jul).* W *www.kalmar.se*

FOUNDED IN THE 12th century, Kalmar's key position on Kalmarsund made it a flourishing trading post as well as a target for Danish attack. To prevent the latter, **Kalmar Slott** was built in 1200 and it was here in the castle that the Kalmar Union was formed in 1397, binding the Scandinavian kingdoms for 130 years *(see p33).* In 1523 Gustav Vasa gained control of Kalmar and fortified the town.

Today, the magnificent Renaissance castle has been restored and contains furnished apartments and exhibitions. With its twisting streets and 17th and 18th-century buildings, the area around the castle, Gamla Stan (Old Town), is made for walking. Next to the castle is **Kalmar Konstmuseum** (Art Museum) showing Swedish art.

The Italian Baroque **Domkyrkan** (cathedral) on the island of Kvarnholmen dates from the second half of the 17th century and was

designed by Tessin the Elder *(see p24)*. In front of it is the square Stortorget, restored to its original austere appearance. Kvarnholmen is also home to **Kalmar Läns Museum** with the man-of-war *Kronan* and out on "Kattrumpan" **Kalmar Sjöfartsmuseum**, featuring 5,000 maritime exhibits.

ENVIRONS: Ölandsbron, the bridge across Kalmarsund, opened in 1972 and provided a major boost for tourism to Öland. The bridge is 6,072 m (19,921 ft) long, 13 m (43 ft) wide and a sight in its own right. Nearly 35 km (22 miles) north of Kalmar on the coast is the idyllic village of **Pataholm**, a shipbuilding and seafaring community dating from the Middle Ages, with well-preserved historic buildings and cobbled streets.

🏰 **Kalmar Slott**
Kungsgatan 1. 📞 *0480 45 14 90*
🕐 *Apr–Sep: daily; other times: 2nd weekend in the month.* 🎫 🎧 🚻
🏛 **Kalmar Konstmuseum**
Slottsvägen 1D. 📞 *0480-42 62 82.*
🕐 *daily.* ● *24, 25 & 31 Dec.*
🎫 *pre-book.* 🎧 🚻
🏛 **Kalmar Läns Museum**
Skeppsbrogatan 51. 📞 *0480-45 13 00.* 🕐 *daily.* ● *24, 25 & 31Dec, 1 Jan, 1 May.* 🎫 *pre-book.* 🎧 🚻 🚻

Färjestaden **⑱**

Öland. Road 136. 👥 *4,500.* 🚌 ℹ️
Träffpunkt Öland, 0485-56 06 00.
🎭 *Victoria Day (14 Jul).*

THE ÖLANDSBRON Bridge connects Färjestaden on Öland with the mainland. Since the bridge's arrival in the 1970s, Färjestaden has more or less become a suburb of Kalmar. The first

turning to the north in Färjestaden leads to **Ölands Djurpark**, a popular destination for families. The zoo has 200 species of animals, a water world and amusement park, circus and theatre performances.

Beijershamn, south of Färjestaden, is an interesting reed-covered birdwatching area with wetland and archipelago species. Not far from here is **Karlevistenen**, a remarkable 11th-century runestone dedicated to a hero named Sibbe the Wise.

Vickleby village street, on road 136 to the south, is the epitome of idyllic Öland. Next to the church is Capellagården School of Craft and Design, founded by furniture designer Carl Malmsten in the 1950s and currently a centre for various design-related courses. The school exhibits and sells students' work.

East of Färjestaden, in the forest, is the Iron Age fort of **Gråborg** with the medieval ruins of St Knut's chapel just outside it.

🐾 **Ölands Djurpark**
3 km (2 miles) N of Färjestaden.
📞 *0485-392 22, info 0485-308 73.*
🕐 *mid-May–Sep: daily.* 🎫 📷 🚻

A gigantic clown at the entrance to Ölands Djurpark

Solliden, the king's summer residence, whose park is open to the public

Borgholm ⑲

Öland. Road 136. 🏛 *3,200.* 🚻
ℹ *Sandgatan 25, 0485-890 00.*
🎭 *Borgholm Festival 1 Jul, Victoria Day 14 Jul.*

IN SUMMER Borgholm town centre bustles with shoppers and boats fill the guest harbour. Borgholm became a seaside resort at the end of the 19th century and some of the older buildings still have their ornamented wooden verandas where gentlemen enjoyed their coffee and punsch at the beginning of the last century.

Dominating the town is **Borgholms Slottsruin**, a vast ruined medieval castle with an eventful past. There is a museum inside. Guides recount the history of the ruins and offer special tours for children in summer. Also in summer, the castle stage is a popular venue for concerts.

ENVIRONS: Just south of the centre lies **Sollidens Slott**, the summer residence of the Swedish royal family, completed in 1906. On 14 July each year, the birthday of Crown Princess Victoria is celebrated here with various events. Exhibitions are held in the pavilion and there is a palace gift shop.

Störlinge Kvarnrad, a row of seven windmills on the eastern coast road, is just a sample of the 400 windmills still standing on the island. There are around 150 km (93 miles) of beaches around Borgholm, two of the best being Köpingsvik and Böda.

🏛 **Borgholms Slottsruin**
1 km (half a mile) S of Borgholm.
📞 *0485-123 33.* ⭘ *Apr–Sep: daily; Oct–Mar: by app.* 🎫 🚻 ♿ 🎦 📷 🍴
🎪 **Solliden**
1.5 km (1 mile) S of Borgholm.
📞 *0485-153 56.* ⭘ *mid-May–mid-Sep: daily.* 🎫 🚻 ♿ 🎦 📷

Byxelkrok ⑳

Öland. Road 136. 🏛 *200.* 🚻
ℹ *Tourist Information Skeftekärr, 0485-221 11.*

ALMOST AT THE northernmost end of Öland's west coast on Kalmarsund is the popular old fishing village of Byxelkrok. Boats to Blå Jungfrun *(see p154)* depart from here. About 5 km (3 miles) to the north is **Neptuni Åkrar**, an area of ridged stones resembling ploughed fields with several ancient monuments, including the Iron Age stone ship Forgalla-skeppet.

Löttorp, the largest town in northern Öland, is home to a paradise for car-mad children – **Lådbilslandet** (Boxcar Country), Glabo Gocart. Here youngsters can race round the 6-km (4-mile) course in

The island Blå Jungfrun *(see p154)* seen from Byxelkrok harbour

motorized vehicles, attend driving school or enjoy the playground.

Böda, 10 km (6 miles) north of Löttorp, has wonderful sandy beaches. It is also the site of **Skäftekärr Järnåldersby**, a reconstructed Iron Age village. Complete with goods, animals, houses and people, it provides a fascinating insight into Iron Age life. The village also has an arboretum featuring a collection of *Thuja occidentalis* planted in the late 19th century.

🏛 **Lådbilslandet**
40 km (25 miles) N of Borgholm.
📞 *0485-203 35.* ⭘ *mid-Jun–mid Aug: daily.* 🎫 🎦 📷
🏛 **Skäftekärr Järnåldersby**
50 km (31 miles) N of Borgholm.
📞 *0485-221 11.* ⭘ *2nd week in Jun–mid-Aug: daily. 1 May–first week in Jun, third–first week in Oct: Fri–Sun; Wed & Thu: pre-book.* 🎫 📷 🎦 🚻

Ölands Museum ㉑

Öland. 20 km (12 miles) NE of Färjestaden. 🚌 🚻 📞 *0485-56 10 22.* ⭘ *May–Aug: 10am–5.30pm daily.* 🎫 🎦 🚻

HIMMELSBERGA, in the centre of the island, is home to Ölands Museum, an open-air museum of art and cultural history. It centres around a well-preserved linear village with 18th- and 19th-century farms. The interiors of the houses show how life was once lived, and pigs, chickens and sheep are kept in the grounds. A shop sells crafts and books about Öland. Next to the museum is a gallery showing work by local artists.

South of Himmelsberga, **Gärdslösa Kyrka** is one of the most interesting churches on Öland. It dates from the mid-13th century and has excellent limestone murals, a beautiful votive ship and a 17th-century pulpit.

The fort of **Ismantorps Borg** in Långlöt has been dated to the 5th century. Archaeological finds

show that it was probably an important marketplace and cult site. It is encircled by a wall up to 6 m (19 ft) thick and 3 m (10 ft) high with nine gates.

Öland's best preserved row of windmills can be seen in Lerkaka, just to the south of Himmelsberga. The interesting **Lerkaka Linmuseum** shows how linen is made.

🏛 **Lerkaka Linmuseum**
25 km (16 miles) NE of Färjestaden.
📞 0485-56 20 90.
🕐 Midsummer–mid-Aug: daily.

Stora Alvaret ㉒

Öland. 🚌 🚻 Ölands Turist, 0485-56 06 00.

T HE EXTRAORDINARY lime- stone plain of Stora Alvaret dominates southern Öland. Here, the bedrock is around 400 million years old and is covered in a thin layer of soil that was used from prehistoric times as grazing land. In the year 2000 the area was declared a UNESCO World Heritage Site.

In spring the ground is covered in pasque flowers (*Pulsatilla pratensis*). The dominant species include meadow oat-grass (*Helictotrichon pratense*), sheep's fescue (*Festuca ovina*) and a moss species, *kalkbackmossa* (*Homalothecium lutescens*). Juniper bushes are common and lichen inches over bare rock.

The extreme climate has created almost desert-like conditions to which the flora and fauna have had to adapt. Mountain and Mediterranean plants grow here as well as a unique species of rock-rose (*Helianthemum oelandicum*). The island is a resting place for cranes, but conditions on the plain are so harsh that only a few birds, such as the skylark and wheatear, have succeeded in adapting to the environment.

Eketorps Borg ㉓

Öland. 🚌 🚻 0485-66 20 00. 🕐 May–Aug: daily; first three weekends in Sep. 🌑 Midsummer's Eve. 🎭 Iron Age Festival (first week in Aug). 🌐 www.kalmarlansmuseum.se/eketorp

T HE ONLY ONE of Öland's ancient forts to have been completely excavated, Eketorps Borg was built in three stages. It originated in the 4th century to protect the population and was later converted into a fortified farming village with military functions, but was abandoned in the 7th century. It was thrust into use again at the end of the 12th century in the war between the royal houses of Erik and Sverker.

The fort has been partly reconstructed to show how people lived and worked in the Iron Age. In the museum the numerous artifacts uncovered on the site are on display, including jewellery and weapons.

Around 10 km (6 miles) north of Eketorp lies **Seby Gravfält** with no fewer than 285 visible ancient monuments in the form of different kinds of burial sites, mainly dating from the Iron Age.

Långe Jan at Öland's Southern Cape, Sweden's tallest lighthouse

Öland's Southern Cape ㉔

Öland. 🚌 🚻 Ottenby Naturum, 0485-66 12 00 (Easter–Oct: daily). 🎫

I N THE MID-16TH CENTURY the area around Öland's southern cape became a royal hunting ground and even today descendants of the fallow deer introduced by Johan III in 1569 can be spotted. The northern boundary of his land is marked by Karl X's wall, built in the 1650s to prevent local people and their animals from entering the grounds. To the south, Sweden's oldest and tallest lighthouse, **Långe Jan**, stands to attention, 41.6 m (136 ft) high, and offers amazing views.

Look out for hedgehogs, a threatened species

At the southernmost tip of the island is a nature reserve, Ottenby Naturum, and **Ottenby Fågelstation** (the bird station). Ornithologists come here to study migratory birds close up and conduct research. The station has several bird-related exhibitions and offers guided tours around the nature reserve.

🦅 **Ottenby Fågelstation**
Öland's Southern Cape. 📞 0485-66 12 00. 🕐 Easter–Oct: daily.
🎫 Set guided bird tours Jul–first week in Aug. 🌐 🖥

The mighty walls of Eketorps Borg, a partly reconstructed Iron Age fort

GOTLAND

·····································

S WEDEN'S LARGEST ISLAND, *Gotland is a popular holiday destination, favoured for its mild climate, sandy beaches, distinctive landscape and beautiful walled town of Visby. It is known as the "Pearl of the Baltic". The island's strategic position made it an important trading centre especially in the Middle Ages. Gotland celebrates its heritage with enthusiasm in the annual Visby Medieval Week.*

In geological terms, Gotland is fairly old. It consists of layers of rocks which were deposited in a tropical sea during the Silurian period around 400 million years ago. Fossils can still be found washed up along the shore. At the northern and southernmost tips of the island, the limestone comes to the surface and plant life is sparse. In the centre of the island forest dominates. The high limestone cliffs with their large bird population are broken by sandy beaches beloved by sun-worshippers, and standing offshore are numerous extraordinary sea stacks, known as *raukar*.

The long, warm autumns and mild winters allow trees such as walnut and apricot to survive in sheltered spots. No less than 35 different orchids can be found on the island and the flower meadows which blossom at Midsummer are typical of Gotland. The island's fauna lacks the large mammals of the mainland. The odd fallow deer is probably an escapee from an enclosure, but there is a herd of *russ*, Gotland's little wild ponies, as well as foxes and wild rabbits.

A wealth of archaeological finds have been uncovered on the island, from the ship burials of the Bronze Age to the silver treasure of the Viking period. More than 90 medieval churches dot the landscape and the museums have numerous artifacts from the Hanseatic period and the Danish King Valdemar Atterdag's capture of Visby in 1361. Visby itself is a UNESCO World Heritage Site.

Gotlanders have their own dialect, *Gutamål*, and their own traditions. These are especially reflected in the games of the annual Gotland Olympics and in the Medieval Week in Visby *(see p27)*, a 21st-century recreation of the Middle Ages with tournaments, jesters and fair maidens.

Hoburgen in southern Gotland, a 35-m (115-ft) high limestone cliff containing red "Hoburg" marble

◁ **Domkyrkan Sta Maria dating from 1225, the only one of Visby's ancient churches which is not in ruins**

Exploring Gotland

A VISIT TO GOTLAND naturally begins in Visby, where the ferry terminal and airport are located. To experience this unusual part of Sweden it is best to strike out into the countryside and discover the exceptional landscape with its distinctive flora, long sandy beaches, curious limestone sea stacks and multitude of medieval churches. Hiring a bike and cycling round Gotland is a popular way of seeing the island. There are almost no hills and car-free country lanes constantly lead to new hideaways. There is plenty of bed-and-breakfast accommodation and the island has many good campsites for those with tents or caravans. Bookings should be made well in advance for the month of July.

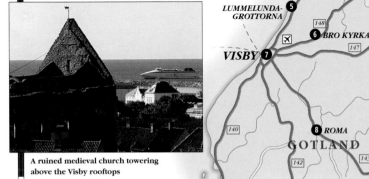

A ruined medieval church towering above the Visby rooftops

SIGHTS AT A GLANCE

Bro Kyrka **6**
Bunge **2**
Fårö **1**
Fröjel Kyrka **11**
Gotska Sandön **15**
Hoburgen **14**
Karlsöarna **12**
Ljugarn **9**
Lojsta **10**
Lummelundagrottorna **5**
Petes **13**
Roma **8**
Slite **3**
Tingstäde **4**
Visby pp164–7 **7**

KEY

— Major road
= Minor road
· · Ferry route

(Map of Gotland)

TINGSTÄDE **4**
LUMMELUNDA-
GROTTORNA **5**
SLITE **3**
BRO KYRKA **6**
VISBY **7**
ROMA **8**
GOTLAND
KLINTEHAMN
LJUGARN **9**
FRÖJEL
KYRKA **11**
LOJSTA **10**
KARLSÖARNA **12**
HEMSE
PETES **13**
BURGSVIK
HOBURGEN **14**

149
147
148
147
146
140
142
143
143
140
141
144
140
142

0 kilometres
0 miles   10

SEE ALSO

• *Where to Stay* pp284–5
• *Where to Eat* p298

Sheep grazing in front of a typical Gotland farmhouse, today a tempting renovation project for incomers from the mainland

GETTING AROUND

The most common way to get to Gotland is by ferry or fast catamaran, either from Nynäshamn or Oskarshamn. In summer there are several crossings a day to Visby. Another option is to arrive by air on one of the daily flights from Stockholm, Norrköping or Nyköping. On Gotland, the only means of public transport is the bus. Services outside Visby are infrequent with perhaps just one morning and one afternoon bus, making a car or a bike a necessity for getting around. Bicycles can be hired at the ferry terminal and elsewhere around the island.

One of Gotland's many long sandy beaches attracting hundreds of thousands of visitors to the island every summer

Fårö ❶

Gotland. 👥 600. 🚌 🛈 Mar–Sep: at Fårö church 0498-22 40 22; Oct–Feb: Visby Tourist Office, 0498-20 17 00. 🎭 Lamb festival (last Sat in Sep).

A SUMMER PARADISE for visitors from the mainland and further afield, Fårö appears exotic even to a Gotlander from the main island. Lying at the northern tip of Gotland, the little island of Fårö has a language and traditions all of its own. During the summer car ferries shuttle back and forth on the 15-minute trip from Fårösund to Broa. At other times of year the service is more limited.

Sparse, low pine forest and moorland with swamp and marshland cover the island. There are sheep everywhere. Off the main road between Broa and Fårö lighthouse there are plenty of cattle grids, which prevent the sheep from straying.

Off the northwest coast are the spectacular limestone stacks, known as *raukar*, of Langhammars and Diger-huvud. The sand dune of Ullahau is at the northern end of the island, and Sudersand's long sandy beach is popular with holiday-makers. The easternmost cape of Holmudden is topped by the 30-m (98-ft) high lighthouse, Fårö Fyr. Roughly in the centre of the island, **Fårö Kyrka** offers stunning views over the inlet of Kyrkviken. The church contains votive paintings dating from 1618 and 1767, depicting seal hunters miraculously being rescued from the sea.

🛈 Fårö Kyrka

5 km (3 miles) N of Broa. 📞 0498-22 10 74. 🕐 Jun–Aug: daily; Sep–May: Sat & Sun. 🚻 🛂 by appointment.

"The coffee pot", an eroded limestone stack on Fårö's coast

Bunge ❷

Gotland. Road 148. 🏠 *900.* 🚌
ℹ️ *Fårösund, 0498-22 11 12.*
🎪 *Tournament (first week in Jul).*

THE VILLAGE of Bunge is renowned for its 14th-century church **Bunge Kyrka**, built in Gothic style. Its tower was constructed in the 13th century to defend an earlier church – holes from pikes and arrows in the north wall bear witness to past battles.

Inside are beautiful limestone paintings dating from around 1400, which are thought to depict the Teutonic Knights fighting the Vitalien brothers, pirates of Mecklenburg who occupied Gotland in the 1390s. In the chancel is a poor box in limestone signed by stone-mason Lafrans Botvidarson. Like the font, it dates from the 13th century.

8th-century picture stone, Bungemuseet

Next to the church is **Bungemuseet**, one of Sweden's largest rural museums. It was created in 1917 by Bunge schoolteacher Theodor Erlandsson, who wanted to show how the people of Gotland used to live. In the fields next to the school he gathered together cottages, buildings and cultural objects from different parts of Gotland covering the 17th, 18th and 19th centuries as well as four carved stones from the 8th century. The museum hosts many events in the summer, including medieval tournaments, markets and handicraft festivals. In Snäckerssstugan cottage, with the date 1700 carved into the gable, visitors can enjoy a cup of coffee and attempt to make out the Gotland proverbs painted on the ceiling.

Just north of Bunge is the busy **Fårösund**, one of the larger towns in northern Gotland with around 1,000 inhabitants. For many years the area was dominated by the military and countless young men were drilled here in defence of the island. Since the coastal artillery unit was disbanded in 2000 with the loss of many jobs, the area risks going into decline.

🏛 **Bunge Kyrka**
60 km (37 miles) N of Visby.
📞 *0498-22 10 74 (Tue & Fri).* ⏰ *mid-May–Aug: daily.* 🏛 *every other Sun.*
🏛 **Bungemuseet**
2 km (1 mile) E of Bunge. 📞 *0498-22 10 18.* ⏰ *15 May–15 Aug: daily.*
📷 *ring for appointment.* 🎫🏠🖥

Slite ❸

Gotland. Road 147 🏠 *1,600.* 🚌
⛴ ℹ️ *Square, 0498-22 24 63 (May–Aug).* 🏌️ *Golf round Gotland (2nd week in May).*

OCCUPYING A stunning setting in a bay facing its own archipelago is the town of Slite. It is the second largest community in Gotland. Slite had a long and troubled history from the

Majestic limestone stack at Kyllaj, Slite Bay

Viking period onwards, and development only really took off in the late 19th century with an upturn in seafaring. Today the town is dominated by a cement factory.

In summer, the fine sandy beaches, harbour, tennis courts, stunning stone stacks and lime kiln attract holiday-makers. The islands offshore are perfect for short trips, including Enholmen with Karlsvärd fortress, which dates from 1853–6.

ENVIRONS: On the opposite side of the bay is Hellvi, with the delightful old harbour of **Kyllaj** complete with lime kilns. The quiet beach is in a beautiful setting overlooking weathered sea stacks. Strandridaregården, the 18th-century coastguard's house, now belongs to Bungemuseet.

Northwest of Slite is **Lärbro Kyrka**, a mid-13th century church with an 11th-century watch tower next to it. In the churchyard are buried 44 of the former prisoners of war who came from the German concentration camps to the hospital at Lärbro in 1945.

St Olofsholm, nearby, is dedicated to Olav the Holy who visited Gotland in 1029 to convert the island to Christianity. In medieval times it was a place of pilgrimage. This is also the site of Ytterholmen's large group of limestone stacks and a glorious pebble beach.

🏛 **Lärbro Kyrka**
10 km (6 miles) N of Slite. 📞 *0498-22 51 25.* ⏰ *15 May–30 Sep: daily.* 🏛 *every other Sun.* 🎫🖥🏠♿

Buildings at Bungemuseet with thatched roofs of Gotland sedge

Tingstäde ❹

23 km (14 miles) N of Visby. 🚗 280.
🚌 🏨 *Bunge Tourist Office, Fårösund
(May–Aug) 0498-22 11 22.*
🌿 *Nature trail with lady's slipper in
flower (early Jun).*

H ALFWAY BETWEEN Visby and
Fårösund on road 148
lies Tingstäde, a community
best-known for its sea rescue
radio station and its marsh.
The church dating from the
13th and 14th centuries has
one of the highest towers on
the island.

Tingstäde marsh is, in fact,
a shallow lake and popular,
child-friendly bathing spot.
Submerged in the centre of
the lake is Bulverket, a
10th–11th-century fortress
surrounded by a palisade of
1,500 stakes.

Lummelunda-grottorna ❺

Road 149, 13 km (8 miles) N of Visby.
🚌 🏨 *11 May- 15 Sep: 0498-27 30
50, other times ring to book.*
📷 *obligatory. Cave adventure must
be pre-booked.* ♿ 🎧 🚻 🏨

I N 1948 TWO local school-
boys discovered an
opening in the ground in
Martebo marsh and crawled
in. They had chanced upon
the entrance to a giant network of caves and passage-
ways, now Gotland's main
tourist attraction. Today the
entrance is at Lummelundas
Bruk. Exploration of the caves
continues, but the part which
is open for viewing provides
a fantastic show of stalactites
and stalagmites, magic
mirrors of water and spine-
tinglingly tight openings. The

geological museum,
Silurum, is located at
the entrance.

Immediately to the
south of the caves is
Krusmyntagården, a
herb garden designed
in traditional monastic
style with wonderful
views over the sea.

🌿 **Krusmyntagården**
Road 149, 10 km (6 miles) N
of Visby. 🏨 *0498-29 69 00.*
⏰ *Jun–Aug: daily.* 🚻 🏨

Bro Kyrka ❻

Road 148, 11 km (7 miles) NE of
Visby. 🚌 🏨 *0498-27 27 55,
070-25 92 070.* ⏰ *Apr–Oct: 8.30am–
7pm daily.* ✝ *every other Sun.*

T RADITION HAS IT that Bro
Kyrka is built over a votive
well and in medieval times it
was a famous votive church,
particularly among sailors. The
building dates from the 13th
and 14th centuries. Inside, the
prayer chamber contains
5th-century picture stones.

About 1 km (half a mile)
north of Bro Kyrka, on road
148, are two picture stones
known as "Bro Stajnkällingar".
According to legend, two
elderly women were turned to
stone for arguing on the way
to the Christmas Mass.

From Bro, a turning leads to
Fole church on road 147, and
a short detour takes you to
Vatlings Gård. The estate has
Gotland's best-preserved
medieval stone house outside
Visby and is well worth a visit.

🏛 **Vatlings Gård**
Road 147, 18 km 18 km (11 miles)
E of Visby.
⏰ *daily.* 🏨 *0498-29 27 00.*

Roma Kungsgård, built in 1733 using
materials from Roma Kloster

Visby ❼

See pp164–7.

Roma ❽

18 km (11 miles) SE of Visby. 🚌
🏨 *Roma Kungsgård: 0498-500 57,
501 23.* ⏰ *Jun–Aug: daily.*

C ISTERCIAN MONKS from
Nydala monastery in
Småland founded **Roma
Kloster** in 1164. The
monastery was built on the
pattern of the French mother
monastery and became a
religious centre for the entire
Baltic region. The three-aisle
church in the Fontenay style
was completed in the 13th
century. The monastery was
abandoned during the
Reformation in 1530 and
ended up in the ownership of
the Danish crown as a royal
manor under Visborg Castle.

When Gotland came under
Swedish rule in 1645, the
monastery was practically in
ruins. The county governor
used materials from the site to
build his residence, **Roma
Kungsgård**, in 1733. Only
the church remained intact,
and that was used as a stable.
In 1822, Roma Kungsgård was
rented to the crown and
served as an army store.

The ruins of Roma
monastery are a popular
tourist attraction. Even today
they bear witness to the
monks' skill in construction
techniques. The beautiful
vaulted ceilings are reminiscent of Roman aqueducts.

In the summer, Romateatern
performs Shakespearian plays
on an open-air stage set
among the ruins.

A painting on wood in Bro Kyrka showing Adam and Eve in paradise

Street-by-Street: Visby ⑦

Sign for Gamla Apoteket

A TOWN OF ROSES and ruins, the walled city of Visby is a UNESCO World Heritage Site as well as a popular party town in summer, when it fills up with holiday-makers from the mainland. Its cobbled streets are lined with pictur-esque cottages, haunting medieval ruins and a multitude of cafés and bars. Away from the busy, more touristy parts of Strandgatan, Stora Torget and around the pleasure boat harbour, the evocative ambience recalls the town's medieval history *(see p167)*. This is also evident from the imposing town wall and its many towers, including Kruttornet (the Gunpowder Tower), which offers great views.

Konstmuseet
Visby Town Wall *by Hanna Pauli (1864–1940) is on display in the Museum of Art.*

★ Gotlands Fornsal
The Historical Museum is devoted to Got-land's past from ancient times to modern day. The Science Centre and Natural History Museum are in the same building.

Burmeisterska Huset
Hans Burmeister, a wealthy merchant from Lübeck, built this house in the 17th century. It is one of the best-preserved examples of its kind in Visby.

Visby town wall has 19 towers and gates, including Kruttornet (Gun-powder Tower).

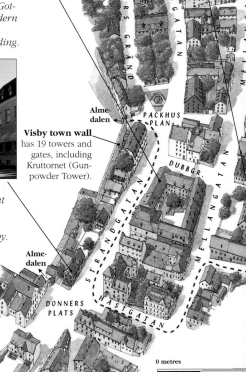

Krut-tornet

RIGA GRÄND

LYBSKA GR.

BIRGERS GRÄND

STRANDGATAN

MELLANGATAN

Alme-dalen

PACKHUS PLAN

DUBBGR.

Alme-dalen

STRANDGATAN

MELLANGATAN

DONNERS PLATS

HÄSTGATAN

KEY

‑ ‑ ‑ Suggested route

STAR SIGHTS

★ **Domkyrkan Sta Maria**

★ **Gotlands Fornsal**

0 metres

0 yards   100

Kapitelhusgården
In this leafy medieval courtyard setting, the public can try their hand at medieval crafts. During the summer, it can become busy, especially during Medieval Week.

Botaniska Trädgården

St Drotten, the sister church to St Lars.

VISITORS' CHECKLIST

Gotland. 🚗 22,000. 🚌 🚢 ✈
🏛 🛈 *Gotlands Turistförening, Hamngatan 4, 0498-20 17 00.*
🎭 *Midsummer Week (Jun), Medieval Week (first week in Aug), Gotland Chamber Music Festival (Jul), Visby Festival (first Sat in Oct), Gotland Grand National (first weekend in Nov).*
🌐 *www.gotland.info*

ST DROTTENS GATA

SKOLGATAN

S:T HANSGATAN

P:KYRKOGATAN

S:T KYRKOGATAN

STORA TORGET

★ **Domkyrkan Sta Maria**
Completed in 1225, the cathedral was the church of the German merchants. It is the only one of Visby's 17 medieval churches which is not in ruins.

St Lars, also known as the church of Sta Anna after the mother of the Virgin Mary.

Söderport

Around Stora Torget
Entertainment focuses on the main square, Stora Torget. Gutekällaren, with a summer terrace on the square, is one of the many restaurants and bars here.

Ruins of Sta Karin (St Catherine's) Church
Franciscan monks built the church and monastery of Sta Karin in 1233. Dominicans rebuilt it in the 14th century. But in 1525 was destroyed by an army from Lübeck.

Exploring Visby

WITHIN THE WALLS, Visby is relatively small and all the sights are within easy walking distance. The main streets run north to south: Strandgatan with historic sights and nightlife spots, St Hansgatan with its many churches, and Adelsgatan, the shopping street leading from Söderport (South Gate) to Stora Torget, the main square. North of here are quieter residential streets and alleyways, making for a lovely stroll. Near Norderport (North Gate) it is possible to climb up on the ramparts and admire the magnificent wall.

VISBY TOWN CENTRE

◼ Street-by-Street: Visby,
see pp164–5

Medieval vaulted street in Visby, a UNESCO World Heritage Site

The Heart of the Town

The medieval inner town of Visby is shaped by its mighty town wall, almost 3.5 km (2 miles) in length. Construction of the wall began at the end of the 13th century. It was originally 5.5 m (18 ft) high and designed to protect against attack from the sea. On the inland side, the wall was surrounded by a deep moat. Within the ramparts, narrow cobbled streets are lined with tightly-packed houses, wealthy merchants' homes and the ruins of historic churches. UNESCO described the town as the "best fortified commercial city in northern Europe" and declared it a World Heritage Site in 1995.

Just outside the wall is Almedalen, the former site of the Hanseatic harbour. Today the area is a park. South of Almedalen is Visby marina, which throngs with boats, especially during Medieval Week in August.

🚩 Around Stora Torget

At the heart of Visby lies Stora Torget (Big Square) from which the roads to the town gates radiate. This is still a focal point for visitors to Visby, despite the development of a modern town centre outside Österport, and there is a lively market here in summer. Several medieval houses surround the square, including the restaurants of Gutekällaren, with its characteristic stepped gable, and Munkkällaren, with its deep vaulted cellars and inner courtyard.

The ruins of the church of Sta Karin (St Catherine), dating from the 1230s, form a dramatic backdrop on the southern side of Stora Torget. In the cloisters there is a permanent exhibition on Visby's medieval churches. In the shadow of the ruins is Rosengård, a café where generations have ordered coffee and delicious pastries.

🏛 Gotlands Fornsal

Strandgatan 14. 📞 0498-29 27 00.
🕐 15 May–14 Sep: daily; 15 Sep–14 May: Tue–Sun. 🈺 💳 📷 🛆 🔳 ♿
Gotland's long history going back to prehistoric times has made this collection one of Sweden's richest regional museums. It is housed in a

former royal distillery, built in the 1770s.

The Hall of Picture Stones contains an impressive array of carved stones from the 5th–11th centuries, some of which feature runic inscriptions. Next door, the Gravkammaren (Grave Room) shows burial customs from ancient times to the Vikings. Several skeletons are on display, including the 8,000-years-old Stenkyrkamannen (Stenkyrka Man). One of the most remarkable sights is the collection of Viking silver treasure – no fewer than 700 items have been recovered from sites around the island.

Church art is well represented. The museum holds the original, Gothic Öja Madonna (Öja church in southern Gotland has to make do with a copy). A large gallery displays medieval furniture, as well as collections from later periods, including shops and toys.

Picture stones from the 5th–11th centuries in Gotlands Fornsal

Visby's medieval town wall, approximately 3.5 km (2 miles) long and up to 5.5 m (18 ft) high

⚑ Ruins of St Nicolai

St Nicolaigatan. 🛈 *Visby Tourist Office 0498-20 17 00.*

The ruins of St Nicolai are all that remains of a Dominican monastery founded in Visby in 1228. The Black Friars expanded it and built a Gothic cathedral which they dedicated to the patron saint of sailors and merchants, St Nicholas. When the people of Lübeck stormed Visby in 1525 much of the cathedral was destroyed.

Between 1929 and 1990 a pageant, *Petrus de Dacia,* was performed here every summer. This Gotlander was a famous mystic and author, and prior of the Dominican monastery at the end of the 13th century. Today, musical and theatrical events are staged in the ruins and the Gotland Chamber Music Festival is held here each summer. The audience sit protected by wind and weather by the remaining part of the roof.

⚑ Ruins of Helge And

Helge Ands Plan. 🛈 *Gotlands Länsmuseum 0498-29 27 00.*

Helgeandstiftelserna was a religious order founded during the early 13th century to take care of the poor and the sick. The ruin of Helge And (Church of the Holy Spirit) is one of Visby's most remarkable church ruins and dates from this period. The octagonal building has two floors opening onto a choir. Two large staircases lead up to the first floor. It was designed in this way to allow patients from the hospital to reach the church via a passage from the upper floor. Today the ruins are used for cultural events and are open to visitors during the summer.

✿ Botaniska Trädgården

Kärleksporten. 🛈 *0498-21 83 87.* ⏰ *24 hrs daily.* ⚫ *Nights in Medieval Week.*

Gotland's Botanical Garden was founded in 1856 by the Badande Wännerna (Society of the Bathing Friends), a gentlemen's club formed in 1814 to work for the benefit of the public. The society also established Gotland's first school and set up its first bank. To reach the garden, follow the promenade along the shore from the harbour and go through Kärleksporten (Gate of Love) in the north-west corner of the town wall.

Inside the gate, the lush park offers a spice-scented herb garden and a pretty rose garden (at its peak Jul–Aug). There are also many plants and trees exotic to the Nordic countries, such as walnut, mulberry and ginkgo. In its midst stand the ivy-clad ruins of St Olof's church and there is a water-lily pond and a small pavilion making an ideal resting place.

VISBY'S EARLY HISTORY

Archaeological finds, including Roman, Arabic and Russian coins, show that Gotland had a lively foreign trade already in Viking times. At the end of the 12th century, trade with Germany took off and the Hanseatic League was formed – a mercantile and political association between German merchants and towns around the North Sea and the Baltic. The League was centred on Visby and the town enjoyed a boom in the 13th century with people coming from all around to settle here. Towards the end of the century a trading-political power struggle on Gotland led to internal strife and the gradual decline of Visby. Poor harvests and the Black Death contributed to the decline, as did the introduction of large ships capable of travelling longer distances. In 1361 Visby was captured by Valdemar Atterdag and Gotland succumbed to Danish rule. Then in 1525 Visby was plundered by its rival Hanseatic town, Lübeck, and buildings were destroyed or abandoned.

Valdemar Atterdag pillaging Visby in 1361

The small community of Ljugarn with typical Gotland limestone houses close to the sea

had rebuilt and decorated in Empire style. Today there is a hotel and youth hostel here, but the manor house itself is a private home.

⚡ Gotlands Djurpark
48 km (30 miles) SE of Visby. 📞 0498-49 35 00. ⏰ late May–Aug: daily. 🖼 🖵 🛈

Ljugarn ❾

40 km (25 miles) SW of Visby.
🏃 295. 🖵 🛈 Visby Tourist Office, 0498-20 17 00. 🏐 Beach volleyball cup (3rd week in Jul).

THIS CHEERFUL resort was Gotland's first and makes a good centre for touring the southeast of the island. There was a harbour here long before Russian forces raided Ljugarn on their way to laying waste to the east coast of Sweden in 1714–18. By 1900, the small community, with its long sandy beach, limestone sea stacks and guesthouse, had become a popular bathing place.

In Alskog, just outside Ljugarn, among fields of Bronze and Iron Age relics, is **Gotlands Djurpark**, a zoo of non-Nordic animals such as camels, zebras and kangaroos.

South of Ljugarn is the 13th–14th century **Lau Kyrka**. One of Gotland's largest churches, it has a triumphal crucifix from the 13th century.

Northwest of Ljugarn, **Torsburgen** fortress was built in the 3rd or 4th century and is one of the largest of its kind in Scandinavia. It is protected by naturally steep slopes and a wall 7 m (23 ft) high and up to 24 m (79 ft) wide. To reach it, take the forest road from the 146 towards Östergarn, 2 km (1 mile) east of Kräklingbo church.

The idyllic **Katthammars-vik**, north of Ljugarn, was once a flourishing port and limeworks. In the early 1800s lime baron Axel Hägg bought Katthamra manor, which he

Lojsta ❿

15 km (9 miles) S of Visby.
🏃 120. 🖵 🛈 Visby Tourist Office, 0498-20 17 00. 🏇 Gotland pony judging (4th week in Jul).

LIKE SO MANY of Gotland's churches, **Lojsta Kyrka** dates from the mid-13th century. The choir and the nave have ornamental paint-ings and the figures above the triumphal arch are by the master known as "Egypticus" in the mid-14th century.

On **Lojsta Hed**, an area of forest and heath north of the church, lives a herd of semi-wild Gotland ponies *(russ)*, the stubborn little horse native to the island. The animals are owned by local farmers and by Gotlands Läns Hushållningssällskap. Several annual events are organized, such as the release of the stallion in early June, and the high point of the year, the Gotland pony judging at the end of July.

About 2.5 km (2 miles) from Lojsta towards Etelhem is a large building with a sedge roof, **Lojstahallen**. This is an excellent recon-struction of a late-Iron Age hall building. Next to it is a medieval fortress, Lojsta Slott.

Fröjel Kyrka ⓫

40 km (25 miles) S of Visby. 🚗
📞 0498-24 00 05, 070-51 71 38. ⏰ May–Aug: 8am–8pm daily; 1 Sep–15 Sep: 8am–7pm daily, other times ring. 🛈 every other Sun. 🖼 🖵 🛵

IN A STUNNING LOCATION, high up overlooking the sea, is the saddle-roof church of Fröjel Kyrka, built in the 12th and 13th centuries. Inside is an impressive triumphal crucifix by the craftsman who created the rood screen of Öja church. The churchyard has an ancient maze which shows that the site was used long before the arrival of Christianity.

North of the church lies the magnificent **Gannarve Skeppssättning** (Gannarve Ship Barrow). This has been dated to the late Bronze Age (1000–300 BC) and is 30 m (98 ft) long and 5 m (16 ft) wide.

The splendid Gannarve Bronze Age stone ship barrow

Karlsöarna ⓬

Gotland. **Stora Karlsö** 🚢 from Klinte-hamn. 🛈 Visby Tourist Office, 0498-20 17 00. 🖼 🖵 ⓫ Lilla Karlsö 🚢 from Djupvik. 🛈 0498-48 52 48, summer: 0498-24 11 39. 🖼

MANY MYTHS have been spun around Stora and Lilla Karlsö, the rocky islands 6.5 km (4 miles) off the west coast of Gotland.

Stora Karlsö covers 2.5 sq km (1 sq mile) and is a nature reserve with steep cliffs, caves such as "Stora Förvar",

Bird islands Lilla Karlsön (left) and Stora Karlsön seen from Gotland

moorland, leafy groves, and rare flowers and birds. Here, between the bare rocks in May and June, the orchids *Adam och Eva (Dactylorhiza sambucina)* and *Sankt Pers nycklar (Orchis mascula)* form carpets of blooms. Sea birds such as auks, gulls and eider duck can be seen. Razorbills lay their eggs among the stones on the beach, while guillemots prefer the shelves of the steep cliffs.

A guided tour takes a couple of hours and is included in the price of the boat crossing. There is also a museum in Norderhamn.

Like Stora Karlsö, **Lilla Karlsö** is also a nature reserve. The island has been grazed by sheep since the Bronze Age. It is home to guillemots, razorbills, cormorants and gulls. Eider duck, little terns, Sandwich terns and velvet scoters nest on the flat land. The Swedish Society for Nature Conservation organizes guided tours. There is a youth hostel on the island – book in advance.

Petes Museigård, typical 18th- and 19th-century Gotland houses

Petes **⑬**

Gotland. 🚗 🚹 *Länsmuseet på Gotland, 0498-29 27 00.* ⏰ *Mid-Jun–Aug: 11am–5pm, daily.*

T O THE SOUTHWEST of Gotland, just before Hablingbo church on coastal road 140, there is a turning to the seaside community of Petes. Here, the well-preserved houses show Gotland's architecture from the 18th and 19th centuries.

For younger visitors, **Barnens Petes** displays classic toys such as stilts, hobby horses, hoops, wooden rifles and wooden dolls.

The unbroken sandy beaches of Gotska Sandön

Hoburgen **⑭**

80 km (50 miles) S of Visby. 🚌

F AR TO THE SOUTH lies Hoburgen, a 35-m (115-ft) high steep cliff of fossil-rich limestone with seams of the local red Hoburgen marble. On the clifftop is a lighthouse built in 1846. From here it is 176 km (97 miles) to the northernmost lighthouse on the island of Fårö.

Below the lighthouse is Sweden's most famous sea stack, Hoburgsgubben (the Old Man of Hoburg), guarding the caves of Skattkammaren (the Treasure Chamber) and Sängkammaren (the Bed Chamber).

Hoburgen is a favourite spot for ornithologists who come to study the multitude of birds which swoop over Gotland's southernmost outpost all year round. In summer there is a restaurant nearby.

Profile of Hoburgsgubben, the "Old Man of Hoburg"

Gotska Sandön **⑮**

🚹 *Visby Tourist Office, 0498-20 17 00; booking: 0498-24 04 50.* 🚢 *from Nynäshamn and Fårösund.*

J UST 40 KM (25 MILES) north of Fårö lies the most isolated island in the Baltic, Gotska Sandön. It is one of Sweden's national parks and features a unique landscape of deserted, constantly changing sandy beaches and dunes, pine forests and a rich flora. There are migratory birds, unusual beetles, but only one mammal, the hare. The island became a national park in 1909.

Gotska Sandön has been inhabited since the dawn of civilization, although the population has never been large. Colonies of grey seals led seal hunters to settle on the island and the dangerous waters offshore attracted wreck plunderers. In the 17th and 18th centuries sheep were grazed here and later crops were grown. As recently as the 1950s a few lighthouse keepers and their families (and one female teacher) lived here, but now the lighthouse is automated and the only permanent resident is a caretaker.

There is no harbour and regular boat traffic from Fårö or Nynäshamn is infrequent and dependent on the weather. It is possible to camp or stay in a shared sleeping hut or cottage. Accommodation must be booked before arrival.

SOUTHERN GÖTALAND

S WEDEN'S TWO SOUTHERNMOST PROVINCES, *Skåne and Blekinge,* *together form Southern Götaland, with the country's third* *largest city, Malmö, as the region's main town and gateway to* *Europe. The gentle, undulating landscape retains its Danish atmos-* *phere from times past. Castles and medieval and Viking sites abound,* *and the historic naval port of Karlskrona is a* UNESCO *World Heritage Site.*

The province of Skåne has an undeserved reputation for being completely flat, but apart from the plain of Söderslätt the countryside is surprisingly hilly with the rocky ridges of Söderåsen, Linderödsåsen and Romeleåsen dividing the region. To the northwest, the area is bounded by the imposing Hallandsåsen ridge.

The province of Blekinge, crisscrossed by rivers and lakes, is known as the Garden of Sweden. It has its own island archipelago with sheltered harbours beloved by sailors. North, towards the border with Småland, the slightly wild forest landscape predominates.

Throughout Southern Götaland the Danish influence prior to 1645 *(see p35)* is still evident, not least in the architecture, which differs greatly from elsewhere in Sweden. A common sight in rural Skåne is the traditional, often half-timbered farmhouse with a thatched roof, built around a cobbled courtyard. Castles and manor houses, in many cases built by the Danish nobility, are a feature of the countryside. In the coastal communities, former fishing huts are today cherished by their summer residents.

Southern Götaland differs from the rest of Sweden in atmosphere, too. The people of Skåne are known for being relaxed and for loving good food – and in large quantities – something which has lent this part of the country its inn culture, which has its equivalent in the Danish *kroen* just across Öresund.

Having been sparring partners in the long-distant past, Sweden and Denmark have recently been linked by the Öresund Bridge from Malmö to Copehhagen. Both sides of the sound are now collaborating over the creation of a visionary new Swedish-Danish region, Örestad.

Ales Stenar, a stone ship on Skåne's south coast, thought to be a late Viking grave or cult site

◁ Traditional thatched-roof farmhouse in Östarp, built in 1811 and set around a courtyard

Exploring Southern Götaland

As well as arable fields and willow windbreaks, this southernmost part of Sweden has its share of gently rolling hills, forests and lakes. The region is ideal for cycling through the country from village to village, discovering manor houses and castles along the way, walking through nature reserves or along the Skåneleden trail, canoeing, fishing, swimming in the many small lakes and rivers, driving, or sailing along the coast and putting into shore at fishing harbours on tiny islands. Towns such as Lund and Malmö offer a wealth of history, best discovered on foot, Karlskrona is renowned for its naval port and maritime past, and Trelleborg has a reconstructed Viking fortress.

Spiral beech trees in Trollskogen forest, Torna Hällestad

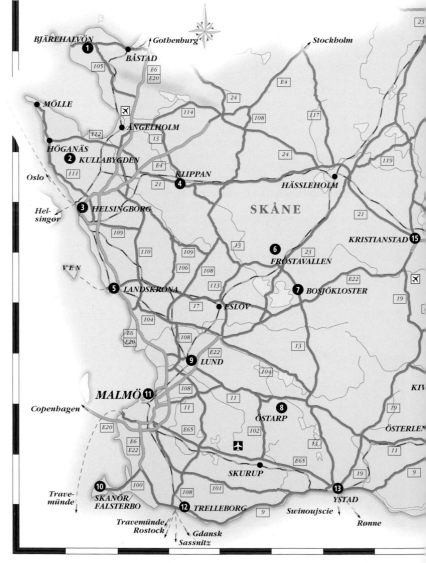

SIGHTS AT A GLANCE

Bjärehalvön **1**
Bosjökloster **7**
Frostavallen **6**
Helsingborg **3**
Karlshamn **17**
Karlskrona pp188–9 **20**
Klippan **4**
Kristianopel **19**
Kristianstad **15**
Kullabygden **2**
Landskrona **5**

Lund **9**
Malmö pp178–81 **11**
Ronneby **18**
Skanör/Falsterbo **10**
Sölvesborg **16**
Trelleborg **12**
Ystad **13**
Östarp **8**

Tour
Österlen **14**

0 kilometres   30

0 miles   20

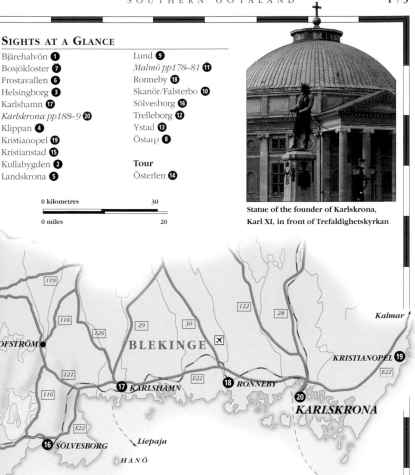

**Statue of the founder of Karlskrona,
Karl XI, in front of Trefaldighetskyrkan**

119
116   *122*   *28*   Kalmar
126   *29*   *30*
OFSTRÖM   BLEKINGE ✖   KRISTIANOPEL **19**
121   *E22*   *E22*
116   **17** KARLSHAMN   **18** RONNEBY
E22   **20**
16 SÖLVESBORG   \ Liepaja   KARLSKRONA
⌂ HANÖ

**The 8-km (5-mile) long Öresund Bridge, completed in 2000,
linking Sweden with Denmark and Continental Europe**

RISHAMN

US
Gdynia

KEY

━━━ Motorway

━━━ Major road

═══ Minor road

┄┄ Railway line

- - Ferry route

GETTING AROUND

The E20 motorway across the
Öresund Bridge from Continental
Europe joins the E6, E22 and E65
south of Malmö and continues north
to Helsingborg where it meets the
E4 to Stockholm. The region has
several airports and there are train
connections to the large towns. Local
commuter trains serve districts around
the major cities. Ferries from Germany
operate to Trelleborg and Ystad and
there are frequent ferries from
Denmark to Helsingborg.

SEE ALSO

• *Where to Stay* pp285–6

• *Where to Eat* pp298–9

Hovs Hallar, a nature reserve on the bay of Laholmsbukten

Bjärehalvön ●

Skåne. Road 105. 🅿 🅿 🆇 🅷
*Båstad Tourist Office 0431-750 45,
Torekov Tourist Office 0431-36 31 80.*
🎼 *Båstad Chamber Music Festival (4th
week in Jun), Båstad tennis (Jun/Jul).*
🆆 *www.bastad.se*

SEVERAL POPULAR resorts surround the peninsula of Bjärehalvön, between the bays of Skälderviken and Laholmsbukten. The medieval town of **Båstad** is now best known for hosting the annual Swedish Open tennis tournament, but it also has beautiful old houses and glorious beaches. Just over 10 km (6 miles) to the west is the old fishing village of **Torekov**. Boat trips run from Torekov to the nature reserve **Hallands Väderö**, a remnant of the Hallandsåsen ridge now left 3 km (2 miles) out to sea. Of special note is the alder marsh.

On the northern cape of the peninsula is **Hovs Hallar**, a geologically interesting area with dramatic rocks and caves. The area is a nature reserve popular with birdwatchers and walkers. Hovs Hallar is the westernmost end of the Hallandsåsen ridge, which forms the border between the Bjärehalvön peninsula and Halland *(see p207)*. With its meadows and varied flora, the ridge is ideal for walking.

West of Båstad along the coast is **Norrvikens Trädgårdar**, a paradise for garden lovers created by architect Rudolf Abelin in the early 20th century. There are

Fruit trees in blossom at
Norrvikens Trädgårdar gardens

several different gardens, including a Baroque garden and a Japanese garden.

The town of **Ängelholm**, nestling between the Bjärehalvön and Kullahalvön peninsulas at the end of the bay of Skälderviken, has a sandy beach 6 km (4 miles) long. Historically, Ängelholm was known for its pottery industry and today clay cuckoos, the town's symbol, are made here.

🌿 **Norrvikens Trädgårdar**
5 km (3 miles) W of Båstad.
🅲 *0431-36 90 40.* 🕐 *May–Aug: daily.* 🄯 🄯 🄯

Kullabygden ❷

Skåne. Road 111/112. 🅿 🅿 🅷 *Centralgatan 20, Höganäs, 042-33 77 74.*
🎼 *Music in Kullabygden (2nd week in Jul), Kulla Market in Jonstorp (first week in Jul).*

THE BEAUTIFUL Kullen Peninsula has been inhabited since the Iron and Bronze Ages. Today, the pretty medieval fishing villages of Arild, Mölle, Höganäs and Viken have become popular seaside resorts. Höganäs is best known for its ceramics.

Just outside Arild lies **Brunnby Kyrka**, parts of which are 12th-century. The church contains impressive ceiling paintings. **Krapperups Slott**, north of Höganäs, dates from the mid-16th century; the castle houses an art gallery and museum.

🏛 **Krapperups Slott**
7 km (4 miles) N of Höganäs. 🅲 *042-34 41 90.* **Castle** 🕐 *by appointment.*
Gallery & museum 🕐 *late-Apr–May:
Fri–Sun; Jun–Jul: daily; Aug: Tue–Sun;
selected days in Dec.* 🄯 🄯 🄯

Helsingborg ❸

Skåne. E4. 🚶 *88,000.* 🆇 🅿 🅿 🛥
🅷 *Stortorget/Södra Storgatan 1, 042-10 43 50.* 🎼 *Helsingborg Festival
(3rd week in Jul), Horse Festival (last
weekend in Jul).*
🆆 *www.helsingborgsguiden.com*

KNOWN AS THE "Pearl of the Sound", Helsingborg is a lively town, spectacularly

TYCHO BRAHE

Astronomer Tycho Brahe was born in Skåne in 1546 into a Danish noble family. At the age of 13 he was sent to university in Copenhagen to study philosophy and went on to study at several German universities. Inspired by an eclipse of the sun in 1560, he took up astronomy. He believed that the old methods of measurement to determine the position of the planets were not sufficiently exact and designed a new system. In 1572 he observed a new bright star in the constellation Cassiopeia. His discoveries in astronomy paved the way for a new view of the universe. In recognition, the Danish king granted Brahe the island of Ven, where he had an observatory built *(see p175)* which became the finest in Europe. Following a difference of opinion with the Danish court, Brahe went into exile and settled in Prague where he died in Prague in 1601.

**Statue of Tycho Brahe in
St Ibbs Kyrka on Ven island**

located on the shores of the Öresund within sight of the Danish coast. The town's strategic position at the narrowest point of the sound led to a stormy history, and the 34-m (111-ft) tower **Kärnan** is all that remains of its 12th-century fortress. The brick tower of the town hall (1897) also features on the skyline. It was designed by architect Alfred Hellerström and contains glass paintings by Gustav Cederström, which are well worth a look.

Jacob Hansen's half-timbered house, built in 1641, is the oldest house in Helsingborg. The new **Dunkers Kultur-hus**, by Danish architect Kim Utzon, encompasses a museum, art gallery and theatre under one roof.

The open-air **Fredriksdal Friluftsmuseum** displays historical buildings from the region and has a botanical garden containing the wild plants of Skåne.

ENVIRONS: Ramlösa Brunn, 5 km (3 miles) southeast of Helsingborg, is known for its spring water, discovered in the late 19th century and now on offer in the Water Pavilion.

The castle of **Sofiero** was bequeathed to Helsingborg municipality by Gustav VI Adolf. The park is particularly famous for its Royal Gardens containing more than 300 varieties of rhododendron.

Kärnan
Slottshagen. ☎ 042-10 59 91. ☐ Apr–Oct: daily. ☑ ☐

Helsingborg's recently renovated tower, Kärnan

Tycho Brahe's underground observatory on the island of Ven

Dunkers Kulturhus
Kungsgatan 11. ☎ 042-10 74 00. ☐ Tue–Sun. ☑ ☐ ☑
Fredriksdals Frilufts-museum
Hävertgatan 1. ☎ 042-10 45 00. ☐ daily. ☑ ☐ ☑
Sofiero
Sofierovägen, 5 km (3 miles) N of the centre. ☎ 042-13 74 00. **Parken** ☐ Apr– Sep: daily. ☑ ☑ **Slottet** ☐ Jun–Aug: guided tours only. ☑ ☑

Klippan ●

Skåne. Road 21. ☒ 8,000. ☐ ☐ ☐ Storgatan 46, 0435-282 00. ☑ Åby Market (3rd Tue–Wed in Jun), Ljungbyhed old-time market (3rd Fri–Sat in Aug).

LOCATED ON the Söderåsen ridge, 30 km (19 miles) east of Helsingborg, Klippan is known for having Sweden's oldest operating paper mill, built in the 16th century.

There are many churches in the area worth a visit. Today only the sacristy remains of **Herrevadskloster**, a former Cistercian monastery founded in the 12th century. This has been restored and is used as a chapel. Art exhibitions are held here in the summer.

Söderåsen National Park offers leafy forests, dramatic screes, babbling brooks and breathtaking views from Kopparhatten and Hjort-språnget. The Skåneleden trail runs through the park.

The 17th-century mansion **Vrams Gunnarstorp**, 10 km (6 miles) west of Klippan, is built in the Dutch Renaissance style. The stunning park with its acclaimed hornbeam avenue is open to the public.

Herrevadskloster
10 km (6 miles) E of Klippan, road 13. ☎ 0435-44 19 90. **Museum** ☐ daily. ☑ pre-book. ☐ ☐ ☑ ☐

Landskrona ●

Skåne. ☒ 27,000. ☐ ☐ ☐ Storgatan 36, 0418-47 30 00. ☑ Vallåkraträffen Customized Car Festival (mid-Aug), Gardening Festival (Aug).

THE SHIPBUILDING town of Landskrona was granted its charter in the 15th century. In 1549, the Danish king Christian III built the Citadel as protection against the Swedes. This substantial fortress surrounded by a moat dominates the town. Most of the sights can be found in the area around it, including **Landskrona Museum**, with its local history collection, and Konsthallen (Art Gallery) surrounded by a sculpture park.

ENVIRONS: In the sound between Sweden and Denmark lies the island of **Ven**, where Tycho Brahe set up his underground observatory, Stjärneborg, in the 1580s. The Tycho Brahe Museum features multimedia shows about the observatory.

There is a ruined castle on Ven, Uraniborg, and at the highest point of the island stands the medieval church of St Ibb. Steep Backafallen is the place for the most spectacular views.

The island can be reached by regular ferries from Landskrona all year round and by fishing boat from Råå during the summer.

Landskrona Museum
Slottsgatan. ☎ 0418-47 31 20. ☐ noon–5pm daily. ● Easter Saturday, Saturday before Whitsun, Midsummer Eve, 24, 25 & 31 Dec.
Ven
In Öresund 7 km (4 miles) W of Landskrona. ☒ from Landskrona. ☎ 0418-47 30 00, 0418-724 20. **Tycho Brahe Museum** ☐ 11 Apr–30 Sep: daily. ☑ pre-book. ☑ ☐ ☑ ☐

Bosjökloster, originally an 11th-century Benedictine convent

Frostavallen ❻

Skåne. 3 km (2 miles) N of Höör on road 21. 🚌 to Höör. 🚌 ℹ Höör Tourist Office, 0413-275 75.

THE BEAUTIFUL countryside around Höör in central Skåne offers something for everyone, from hiking, canoeing and swimming to fishing from the shore or by boat on Vaxsjön lake. The availability of restaurants, cafés, hotels, cottages and campsites makes Frostavallen ideal for a day trip or a longer stay. There are playgrounds and all kinds of leisure equipment are available for hire.

Nearby is **Skånes Djurpark**, a zoo specializing in Nordic animals, which makes a popular excursion for children. It has more than 1,000 wild and domesticated Nordic animals. Watch lynx being fed or enjoy a pony ride.

A very different kind of experience is offered at **Höörs Stenåldersby**, where visitors can see for themselves what life was like in a Stone Age village. Flint-knapping and bow-making can be tried.

🐾 **Skånes Djurpark**
Frostavallen. 📞 0413-55 30 60. 🕐 daily. 📷 💳 🎁 🖵 summertime. ♿
🏛 **Höörs Stenåldersby**
Next to Skånes Djurpark. 📞 0413-55 32 70. 🕐 Jul by appointment.

Bosjökloster ❼

Skåne. Road 13. 📞 0413-250 48. 🚌 🕐 May–Sep: 10am–6pm. 📷 📷 🖵 🍴 **Park** 🕐 May–Oct: 8am–8pm; other times: 10am–5pm. 🎣 Hunting and Fishing Festival (last weekend in Aug).

ON A PENINSULA between the lakes of Östra and Västra Ringsjön lies one of Sweden's most remarkable houses. Bosjökloster was built around 1080 as a convent and soon became one of the wealthiest in Skåne. Rich families paid a great deal to secure a place for their daughters, often donating goods and land. This all came to an end with the Danish Reformation in 1536 and its possessions were transferred into private ownership.

In 1875–9 Bosjökloster was reconstructed to a design by architect Helgo Zettervall and became the prime example of his skill for renovating Swedish manors and palaces.

In the early 20th century the property was bought by Count Philip Bonde and today it is owned by his grandson.

The family opened the house to the public in 1962 and is now it is one of the most popular stately homes in Skåne with parks and gardens, a restaurant, café, mini-zoo, boats for hire and fishing, too. The park features a 1,000-year-old oak tree. The oldest room in the house, Stensalen, is devoted to exhibitions of arts and crafts.

Östarp ❽

Skåne. Near road 11. 🚌 **Kulturens Östarp** 📞 046-804 07. 🕐 15 Apr–30 Sep: 11am–5pm Tue–Sun; 1 Oct–14 Apr: noon–5pm Tue–Sun. 📷 🖵 🍴 🎣 Medieval Festival (2nd weekend in Jun). 🖵 www.kulturen.com

IN THE MIDDLE AGES the town of Östarp was owned by a monastery. But it fell to the crown during the Reformation in the 16th century and was subsequently destroyed to make way for a manor house, which itself burned down. All that remained of the town was Östarps Gamlegård, built in 1812. This farmhouse was bought in 1923 by Kulturen in Lund, and today forms the centrepiece of the open-air Kulturens Östarp. It is a living museum using horses rather than machinery to farm the land. There is an excellent inn.

The countryside around Östarp is dotted with castles and stately homes, and Lake Vombsjön is a paradise for birdwatchers and fishermen alike. On the eastern shore of the lake is **Övedskloster**, a beautiful 18th-century manor house set in an elegant park. The property has been owned by the Ramel family since 1753. The main house, "Stora huset", is one of the most stunning Rococo-style houses in Sweden. It was designed by Carl Hårleman (see p24) and completed in 1776. The park, modelled on Versailles, is open to the public in the summer. Surrounding the

The 18th-century windmill at Kulturens Östarp museum

Old buildings of Lund preserved by the open-air museum of Kulturen

estate is a village of fine half-timbered houses.

🏛 Övedskloster

Road 11 from Lund towards Sjöbo.
🔲 046-630 63. ⭕ daily (park only).
📷 Horse trials (early Sep).

Lund ❾

Skåne. E 22. 🏠 60,000. ✈ Sturup.
🔲 🔲 🔲 Kyrkogatan 11, 046-35 50
40. 📷 Walpurgis Night (30 Apr
& 1 May), Cultural Evening (3rd Sat
in Sep).

FOUNDED BY King Sven
Tveskägg more than 1,000
years ago, the university town
of Lund was once Denmark's
capital. In the Middle Ages it
was a religious, political and
cultural centre and site of a
cathedral, **Lund Domkyrka**,
which was consecrated in
1145. Over the centuries it
has been rebuilt, most recently
by Helgo Zettervall, 1860–80.
Look out for the 14th-century
astronomical clock and a
sculpture in the crypt of the
giant Finn supporting the
cathedral's vaulting.

Lund University was established in 1666, in the grounds
of the bishop's palace,
Lundagård. A new main
building was completed in
1882, and now the university
is the second largest seat of
learning in Sweden with
around 40,000 students.

In the heart of the partly
medieval city centre lies
Kulturen, an open-air
museum with perfectly
preserved streets, cottages
and town houses. Kulturen

also has extensive historical
collections. The 14th-century
chapel of Laurentiikapellet, in
central Lund, is thought to
have been the library of the
monastery of St Laurence.

Of Lund's many museums,
Historiska Museet, containing
Domkyrkomuseet, is one of
Sweden's largest museums
of archaeology, and
includes an exhibition
devoted to the history of
the cathedral. **Lunds
Konsthall,** designed by
Klas Anshelm and
opened in 1957, displays
contemporary art.

ENVIRONS: The spring
flowers are magnificent
at **Dalby Söderskog,** a
national park 10 km (6
miles) southeast of Lund,
where there is a forest of
elm, ash and oak trees.
Gårdstånga Kyrka,
10 km (6 miles) north
of Lund, is a 12th-
century Romanesque
church. The impressive
carvings inside were crafted
by local woodcarver Jacob
Kremberg in the 17th century.

Giant Finn in
the cathedral

🔒 Lunds Domkyrka

Kyrkogatan. 🔲 046-35 87 00.
⭕ daily. 📷 🔒 ♿

🏛 Kulturen

Tegnerplatsen. 🔲 046-35 04 00.
⭕ May–Sep: daily, Oct–Apr:
Tue–Sun. 📷 🔒 🏠 🖥 ♿
🏛 Historiska Museet

Krafts Torg 1. 🔲 046-222 79 44.
⭕ Tue–Fri. 📷 📷
🏛 Lunds Konsthall

Mårtenstorget 3. 🔲 046-35 52 95.
⭕ Tue–Sun. 📷 📷 Thu & Sun. 🏠 ♿

Skanör/Falsterbo ❿

Skåne. Road 100. 🏠 7,000. ✈
Sturur. 🔲 🔲 Östra Hamnplan 2,
040-42 54 54. 📷 Falsterbo Horse
Show (first weekend in Jul),
Sandcastle Competition (last Sat in
Jul). 🔲 www.vellinge.se/turism

TODAY THE TWIN towns at the
far end of Skåne's south-
western cape are idyllic
seaside resorts, but they owe
their development to the
lucrative herring industry in
the Middle Ages.

Sights include the ruins of
the 14th-century fort
of **Falsterbohus,**
Falsterbo Museum
with its local history
collection, and **Falsterbo
Konsthall,** an art gallery
in the old railway station.
On the headland is
Falsterbo Lighthouse,
built in 1793. It is now a
historical monument
although it is still in
working order. Skanör
Town Hall dates from
1777 and the church is
13th-century.

Bärnstensmuseet,
the Amber Museum
in Höllviken, near the
Viking earthworks of
Kämpinge Vall, is worth
visiting to see both the amber
and archaeological finds.

🏛 Bärnstensmuseet

Kämpinge, 10 km (6 miles) E of
Falsterbo. 🔲 🔲 040-45 45 04.
⭕ Tue–Sun. 📷 📷

The low, single-storey houses in the small town of Skanör

Malmö ⑪

SWEDEN'S GATEWAY TO EUROPE, Malmö is the country's third largest city. It was founded in the mid-13th century. Under Danish rule from 1397 to 1523, Malmö was an important town, but once it was returned to Sweden its position waned until an upturn in its fortunes at the end of the 18th century. Today, thanks largely to the Öresund Bridge and associated development, Malmö is once more in the spotlight. The city has a lively, distinctly European atmosphere and has become a centre for contemporary art and design. The old town is centred on Stortorget with its historic Town Hall and governor's residence.

Stortorget with Residenset (left) and Rådhuset (right)

⊞ Rådhuset

Stortorget. ● *to the public.*
◪ *by special arrangement, phone 040-34 12 00.*

The centre of Malmö is the square Stortorget, laid out in the 1530s by the town's mayor Jörgen Kock. Stortorget is dominated by Rådhuset, the town hall, originally built in Renaissance Dutch style in 1546. Only the cellar remains of the medieval building, which had a stepped roof and served both as a prison and an inn. In the 1860s architect Helgo Zettervall carried out extensive renovation work, giving the town hall a completely new look. A number of changes were, in fact, made in the cellars, too (including the removal of the prisoners). The inn is still standing today and is one of the most popular bars in Malmö.

⊞ Jörgen Kocks Hus

Stortorget. ● *to the public.*
Stortorget also contains Jörgen Kocks Hus, a large six-storey building with a stepped gable roof, constructed in 1525. Jörgen Kock, appointed mint-master for Denmark in 1518, moved the work of the mint

to his house in Malmö. Four years later he was elected mayor of the city and became one of the most powerful men in Malmö. He was involved in the rebellion over the Danish succession and was captured and sentenced to death, but escaped and was reinstated as mayor of Malmö in 1540.

⊞ Residenset

Stortorget. ● *to the public.*
In the mid-18th century the two buildings Kungshuset and Gyllenpalmska Huset were combined to form the new governor's residence. Around 100 years later the building was given a new façade by architect F W Scholander, to which Helgo Zettervall adapted his extensive redesign of the town hall. Today the building is the home of the county governor.

⬥ St Petri Kyrka

Göran Olsgatan 1. ◖ *040-35 90 56.*
○ *daily.* ⬥ ◪ *by appointment, phone 040-35 90 49 to book.* ⬥
In a street behind Stortorget is Malmö's cathedral, St Petri Kyrka. Built in the early 12th century, the church was modelled on St Mary's in

Lübeck and is made from red brick. The high tower, constructed in the late 19th century after two 15th-century towers collapsed, is a prominent landmark on the Malmö skyline. Originally the church contained beautiful limestone paintings, but these were removed during renovation in the mid-19th century. Only the paintings in Krämar-kapellet (the Tradesman's Chapel) are preserved in their medieval state.

The cathedral is full of treasures from the 16th and 17th centuries when Malmö's prosperity was at its height. The magnificent 15-m (49-ft) high altar in Renaissance style is beautifully ornamented, painted and gilded. The pulpit dating from 1599 is in sandstone and black limestone. Later additions include the organ front, a masterpiece created to a design approved by Gustav III in 1785. The original medieval organ is said to be the oldest working organ in the world and is now in Malmö Museum.

⯊ Vagnmuseum

Drottningtorget. ◖ *040-34 44 59.*
○ *Jun–Aug: Fri & Sun; Sep–May: Fri.*
◪ ◪ *by appointment.*
In Drottningtorget square, Vagnmuseum (the Carriage Museum) is housed in the 19th-century hussars' riding school. The museum contains a superior collection of horse-drawn carriages, from the elegant to the everyday, fire engines and bicycles.

Vagnmuseum is part of Malmö Museer and is covered by the joint entrance ticket.

The hussars' riding school containing the Vagnmuseum

**Rooseum art gallery occupying
an old power station**

🏛 Rooseum

Gasverksgatan 22. **(** 040-12 17 16.
◯ Wed–Sun. ● some public
holidays. 🎟 free admission Fri.
📷 Wed–Sat. 🖥 ⚙

Rooseum was founded in
1988 by the Swedish art
collector and financier Fredrik
Roos as a showcase for
contemporary art. Its exhibitions are often at the cutting

edge of modern art, such as
the artist Surasi Kuslwong's
installation *No Conclusion –
Time is the Answer*.

The gallery occupies a
former power station built in
1900. It was imaginatively
converted by architect Jan
Holmgren to provide three
galleries on three floors
centred around the former
steam turbine hall.
Renovation work in 2001
added a microcinema and a
public auditorium showing
alternative and underground
films. There is a good café.

🏛 Malmö Konsthall

St Johannesgatan 7. **(** 040-34 12
93. ◯ daily. ● Midsummer Eve,
Midsummer, 24, 25 & 31 Dec.
🖥 🅿 ⚙ daily. ⚙

The Art Hall mounts around
ten exhibitions a year, with an
international focus spanning
the entire spectrum from
modern classics to experi-
mental art. The sculptures of

VISITORS' CHECKLIST

Skåne. E6/E22. 🏠 267,000.
✈ 30 km (19 miles) E of centre. 🚉
Skeppsbron. 🚌 Skeppsbron 10.
ℹ Central station, 040-34 12 00;
Skånegården (E 20, 1 km/half a mile
E of Öresund Bridge), 040-34 12 00.
🎭 Malmö Festival (Aug), Flower
Festival (mid-Jun), Winterland
(Dec–Jan). 🌐 www.malmo.se

Tony Cragg and an instal-
lation by Peter Greenaway
have featured among the
shows. A cornerstone of the
gallery's permanent collection
is the bequest to the city by
private donors Jules and
Karin Shyl. During the 20th
century they collected more
than 100 works, including
drawings by contemporary
artists Per Kirkeby, Richard
Serra and Miroslav Balka.

The Konsthall was designed
by architect Klas Anshelm and
opened in 1975.

CENTRAL MALMÖ

Jörgen Kocks Hus ②
Kommendanthuset ⑩
Malmö Konsthall ⑦
Malmöhus/
   Malmö Museum ⑨
Residenset ③
Rooseum ⑥

Rådhuset ①
St Petri Kyrka ④
Stadsbiblioteket ⑧
Teknikens och Sjöfartens
   Hus ⑪
Vagnmuseum ⑤

KEY

🚉	Railway station
🚌	Bus terminal
🅿	Parking
✝	Church
ℹ	Tourist information

0 metres   500

0 yards   500

Exploring Malmö

THE CENTRE OF MALMÖ, where most of the sights are located, is compact and easy to explore on foot. Start at Västra Hamnen, near the fortress of Malmöhus, and walk towards the centre, in the direction of the tower of St Petri Kyrka on Stortorget. Lilla Torg and Möllevångs-torget are lively market squares, and the beautiful parks, such as Slottsparken or Pildammsparken, are a delight to wander through. While the centre retains its old-town atmosphere, futuristic projects are taking shape on the outskirts as part of the visionary new Öresund region.

Malmöhus fortress, built in 1537 and now the home of Malmö Museum

⛲ Stadsbiblioteket

Kung Oscars Väg. 📞 040-660 85 00.
🕐 May–Aug: Mon–Sat; Sep–Apr: daily. ⬤ public holidays.
🖼 🖥 ♿

The City Library moved into the "castle" on Kung Oscars Väg in 1946, but even by the 1960s there was talk of expansion. Finally, in 1999, the new state-of-the-art library opened. The architect, Henning Larsen, renovated and extended the old building, introducing large, modern glass panels. He also created the bright and airy Calendar of Light hall.
The library is fitted with the latest modern technology. Electronic, telephone and data connections can be accessed throughout the building and

The spacious Calendar of Light hall in Malmö's award-winning new library

visitors can consult the library's databases, internet and CD-ROM network on 40 computers. The people of Malmö are regular users: eight out of ten residents have visited it, borrowing an estimated 1,500,000 items a year.

🏛 Malmöhus/Malmö Museum

Malmöhusvägen. 📞 040-34 44 37.
🕐 daily. ⬤ 24, 25 & 31 Dec, 1 Jan, Midsummer Eve, Midsummer. 🖼
🖼 by appointment. 🖥 🏠 ♿ partly.
Originally built by Erik of Pomerania in 1434, the fortress of Malmöhus was largely destroyed by war. It was rebuilt by Christian III in 1537. Today it is the oldest preserved Renaissance castle in the Nordic region. Originally, it was a fortified royal manor and mint. After the 17th century the fortress was reinforced with bastions, but it fell into disrepair and through most of the 18th and 19th centuries served as a prison. The solid brick fort is surrounded by a deep moat. Extensive restoration work was carried out in 1932, after which

Malmö Museum moved into the building. The museum's collections cover archaeology, ethnography, the history of art and handicrafts, and zoology.
Stadsmuseet (the City Museum) illustrates the history of Malmö and surrounding Skåne with tools, weapons and domestic objects. It contains models, a large textiles collection and an ethnographical collection.
Some of the rooms in the fortress can also be seen. Another popular attraction is the 18th-century tower with its 7.5-m (25-ft) thick walls and original cannons.
Malmö Museer runs Teknikens och Sjöfartens Hus, Kommendanthuset, Ebbas Hus, Vagnmuseet and Malmö Konstmuseum, which can all be visited on a single ticket.

🏛 Kommendanthuset

Malmöhusvägen. 📞 040-34 44 39.
🕐 daily. ⬤ 24, 25 & 31 Dec, 1 Jan, Midsummer Eve, Midsummer. 🖼 🖋
by appointment. 🖥 🏠 ♿
In the latter part of the 18th century the storage buildings in the Malmöhus courtyard had fallen into disrepair and Gustav III ordered the construction of a new armoury. It was built outside the fortress in the Banér bastion and was completed in 1794. By 1814 the fortress's military days were over and it had become a prison. Kommendanthuset (the Governor's House) became the quarters first for the prison's doctor and priest and later the prison governor.
In the 20th century the city of Malmö took over the building, restored it to its original appearance, and incorporated it into Malmö Museer. Its collections feature military history and the history of weaponry. Temporary exhibitions are also held here.

🏛 Teknikens och Sjöfartens Hus

Malmöhusvägen. 📞 040-34 44 38.
🕐 daily. ⬤ 24, 25 & 31 Dec, I Jan, Midsummer Eve, Midsummer. 🖼
🖋 by appointment. 🖥 🏠 ♿
The Museum of Technology and Seafaring is also part of Malmö Museer. Its exhibits cover virtually everything to do with technological

The 8-km (5-mile) long Öresund Bridge between Sweden and Denmark, carrying a motorway and railway line

development and seafaring, as well as the history of roadbuilding and aviation, engines, and steam engines in particular. Among the exhibits is the delta-winged fighter plane J35 Draken from the 1960s. The technically curious can satisfy their urge to experiment in the *kunskaps-tivoli* interactive test lab.

The museum also covers the industrial and seafaring history of Skåne. Here, the star exhibits include the *U3* submarine and the steam launch *Schebo*. For those who have never been in a sub-marine, it is an opportunity not to be missed. The shipbuilding and shipping industry and the development of the ports from the 17th century onwards are highlighted, as is ferry traffic, so vital to Skåne. Temporary exhibitions are also held.

Limhamn

5 km (3 miles) SW of the centre.
Malmö Tourist Office, 040-34 12 00.
On the southern edge of Malmö lies Limhamn, a shipping port for lime since the 16th century. Today Limhamn-Bunkeflo is one of the ten districts which make up the city of Malmö.

One of Limhamn's sights is the early-19th century small, blue Soldat-torpet (soldier's house), which shows how a soldier used to live. The cottage was inhabited until 1956. Limhamn Museum Society runs the museum and various events, especially at Midsummer and Christmas.

The Öresund Bridge

E20. 6 km (3 miles) SW of the centre.
The idea of a bridge between Sweden and Denmark had been discussed for more than 100 years, but it was not until 1991 that both countries agreed on how and where this dream could be realized.

Opened in July 2000, the Öresund Bridge is an 8-km (5-mile) long link between Lernacken in Sweden, southwest of Malmö, and the 4-km (2.5-mile) long Danish artificial island of Peberholm, south of Saltholm. The high-est part of the bridge rests on four pylons each 204 m (670 ft) tall and the roadway is around 30 m (100 ft) wide. The E20 runs along the upper level of the bridge and the railway along the lower level. It is said to be the longest cable-stayed bridge to carry both a railway and a motorway.

On the west side of Peber-holm the link plunges into a 4-km (2.5-mile) long tunnel leading to Copenhagen's international airport, Kastrup. Today the journey by train from Malmö to Copenhagen takes 35 minutes. By 2009 the link will be augmented by a railway tunnel to central Malmö, which will further shorten the journey.

THE ÖRESUND REGION

As part of the EU's vision for a Europe without borders, the Öresund Region project aims to integrate southern Skåne in Sweden with the area around Copenhagen in Denmark, allowing people to cross from one country to another without restrictions. The construction of the Öresund Bridge and tunnel has brought with it enormous benefits for the city of Malmö. It has made the region considerably more attractive to business, the new suburb of Brostaden (Bridge City) has sprung up, cultural exchanges between the two countries are easier and the improved communications have brought more visitors. Architect Santiago Calatrava's Turning Torso housing, due for com-pletion in 2005, is an incredibly bold creation that can be seen as an expression of the region's faith in the future. But the joy is not absolute – there are still many problems to be resolved if the region is to acheive its goal and bring its 3.5 million inhabitants closer together.

The Turning Torso building soaring 190 m (623 ft) high

Trelleborgen, a reconstructed Viking fortress

Trelleborg ⑫

Skåne. E22. 🏠 24,850. 🚃 🚌 ⛴
ℹ️ Hamngatan 9, 0410-533 20.
🎭 Smygehuk Jazz Festival (mid-Jul),
Michaelmas Market.
🌐 www.trelleborg.se

THE CENTREPIECE of modern-day Trelleborg is
Trelleborgen, a remarkable re-creation of a Viking fortress. It is based on the original fortress, thought to have been built by King Harald Blue Tooth in the 10th century and excavated 1,000 years later. The reconstruction opened in 1995.

The town was at its most prosperous in the Middle Ages when German merchants came to trade salt for herring. Some of the old Skåne houses still remain in the quarter around Gamla Torg (Old Square) and in Kloster-gränden, where the ruins of a 13th-century Franciscan monastery still stand. The monastery itself was closed during the Reformation, but its garden is a recreated oasis with a herb, hop and pleasure garden. Stadsparken, the town park with a gorgeous rose garden, is well worth a visit.

Among the other sights is **Trelleborgs Museum**, focusing on local history, **Sjöfartsmuseet** (the Sea-faring Museum) and **Axel Ebbehallen**, which has a large collection of sculptures by Skåne artist Axel Ebbe.

ENVIRONS: A short distance west of Trelleborg lies the village of Skegrie and beside the E6 is **Skegriedösen**, a Stone Age burial mound. The rectangular grave chamber is formed from four stone blocks with a giant pointed block as a roof, surrounded by 17 footstones. This type of Stone Age burial site is only found in southern and western Sweden.

∩ Trelleborgen
Bryggaregatan. 📞 0410-460 77.
🕐 daily. 🅿 🏠 🍴
🏛 Trelleborgs Museum
Östergatan 1. 📞 0410-530 50.
🕐 Tue–Sun. 🅿 🛗 🏠 🍴
🏛 Axel Ebbehallen
Hesekillgatan 1. 📞 0410-530 56.
🕐 Jun–Aug: Tue–Sun. 🅿 🛗 🍴

Ystad ⑬

Skåne. E65. 🏠 16,850. 🚃 🚌 ⛴
ℹ️ St Knuts Torg, 0411-57 76 81.
🎭 Ystad Festival (last weekend in Jul). 🌐 www.visitystad.com

IN YSTAD THE IMPACT of Danish rule and contact with the German Hanseatic League is apparent and the medieval church and monastery communities have also left their mark on the town. Among the many old build-

Apoteksgården, one of Ystad's many fine half-timbered houses

ings is the 13th-century **Sta Mariakyrkan**, where every night the watchman in the tower declares that all is well by blowing his horn. In **Karl XII's Hus** on Stora Väster-gatan the warrior king is said to have spent the night in 1715 following his return from Turkey (see p35).

Ystad has a number of museums, including **Ystads Konstmuseum** (Art Museum), **Ystads Hantverksmuseum** (Handicraft Museum) and a military museum. There is a fine theatre on the harbour-side, the home of the Ystad opera company.

ENVIRONS: High above the fishing community of Kåseberga lies the stone ship **Ales Stenar**. The 67-m (220-ft) monument comprises 58 stones and was probably created by the Vikings as a grave or a cult site.

Bollerups Borg, 20 km (12 miles) east of Ystad, is a 13th-century fortress which has been rebuilt several times. The fort is owned by an agricultural college, but is open to the public.

Sandhammaren is best known for its sandy beaches, but in the past was feared by sailors as new reefs were constantly forming around the cape. The lighthouse dates from 1862.

Svaneholm is one of the few Skåne castles which is open to the public. Built on an island in Lake Svanesjön, it was originally a fortress, but was converted into a Baroque castle with magnificent interiors around 1700.

Valleberga Kyrka lies 17 km (11 miles) east of Ystad and is the only round church in Skåne. It has a 12th-century font by Majestatis.

🏛 Ystads Konstmuseum
St Knuts Torg. 📞 0411-577 285. 🕐
Tue–Sun. 🌑 public holidays. 🅿 🏠 🍴
∩ Ales Stenar
Kåseberga. Road 9, 15 km (9 miles) E of Ystad. 📞 0411-57 76 81. 🕐 daily.
⛪ Svaneholm
Skurup on E65, 20 km NW of Ystad.
📞 0411-400 12. 🕐 Apr–Jun & Aug: Tue–Sun; Jul: daily; Sep: Wed–Sun; Oct: Sat–Sun; Nov–Mar: by appointment 🅿 🍴 🍴

A Tour of Österlen ⓮

THE NAME ÖSTERLEN means "the land to the east" and refers to the southeast corner of Skåne from Ravlunda south to Ystad and west to the Linderödsåsen ridge. The land is the most fertile in Sweden and across the rolling plains are many of the country's most treasured ancient monuments, grandest castles and forts and oldest churches. Along the coast, idyllic fishing villages are dotted like pearls on a string and the entire region has become a haven for painters and writers.

Apple orchard in spring, Kivik

Kivik ②

Kivik is best known for its annual market and apple orchards, but it is also a charming fishing village with winding streets and half-timbered houses.

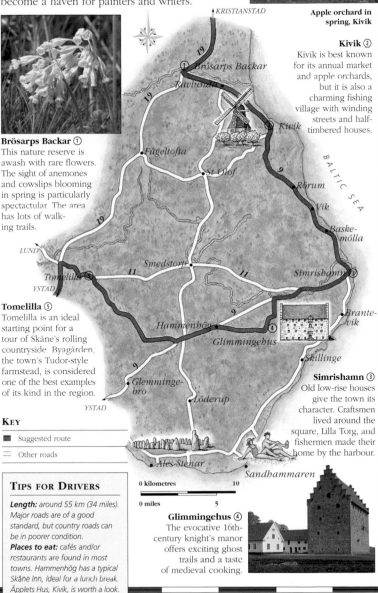

Brösarps Backar ①

This nature reserve is awash with rare flowers. The sight of anemones and cowslips blooming in spring is particularly spectacular. The area has lots of walking trails.

Tomelilla ⑤

Tomelilla is an ideal starting point for a tour of Skåne's rolling countryside. Byagården, the town's Tudor-style farmstead, is considered one of the best examples of its kind in the region.

Simrishamn ③

Old low-rise houses give the town its character. Craftsmen lived around the square, Lilla Torg, and fishermen made their home by the harbour.

KEY

■ Suggested route

= Other roads

Map labels: KRISTIANSTAD, Brösarps Backar ①, Ravlunda, Kivik, Fågeltofta, St Olof, Rörum, Vik, Baske-mölla, BALTIC SEA, LUND, Smedstorp, Simrishamn ③, Tomelilla ⑤, YSTAD, Hammenhög, Brante-vik, Glimmingehus ④, Skillinge, Glemminge-bro, Löderup, YSTAD, Ales Stenar, Sandhammaren

TIPS FOR DRIVERS

Length: around 55 km (34 miles). Major roads are of a good standard, but country roads can be in poorer condition.
Places to eat: cafés and/or restaurants are found in most towns. Hammenhög has a typical Skåne Inn, ideal for a lunch break. Äpplets Hus, Kivik, is worth a look.

0 kilometres   10
0 miles   5

Glimmingehus ④

The evocative 16th-century knight's manor offers exciting ghost trails and a taste of medieval cooking.

Heliga Trefaldighetskyrkan, a Renaissance church, Kristianstad

Kristianstad 🕥

Skåne. E22. 👥 31,600. ✈ 🚌 🚉
🛈 Stora Torg, 044-12 19 88.
🎭 Christianstad Festival (10 days in Jul). 🌐 www.kristianstad.se

THE DANISH KING Christian IV built the town of Kristianstad in the early 17th century and the original street layout with two gates can still be seen today. The town's main sight is **Heliga Trefaldighets-kyrkan** (the Church of the Holy Trinity) from the same period, an excellent example of Renaissance architecture. A more recent attraction is the eco-museum **Vattenriket**, a 35-km (22-mile) stretch of wetlands on the Helgeån river. It is best seen on a guided river tour. Fishing permits can be bought at the tourist office.

ENVIRONS: About 15 km (9 miles) to the northeast is **Bäckaskog Slott**, a former monastery dating from the 13th century, which was rented by the Swedish royal family during the 19th century. The castle is set in beautiful parkland with a herb garden. **Rinkaby Kyrka** lies halfway between Kristianstad and Åhus. The 13th-century church

contains paintings from the 15th century depicting the seasons and farming life.

Among the most idiosyncratic objects to be seen at the castle of **Trolle-Ljungby**, 10 km (6 miles) east of Kristianstad, are the Ljungby drinking horn and pipe, which feature in a local legend. On Wednesdays and Saturdays in summer they are exhibited in a window facing the courtyard.

The park of **Wanås Slott**, 20 km (12 miles) northwest of Kristianstad, is a setting for international contemporary art.

Åhus, 14 km (9 miles) southeast of Kristianstad, is a coastal community with half-timbered houses and sandy beaches. There are 20 golf courses in a 50-km (30-mile) radius.

🏞 Vattenriket
🛈 Kristianstads Tourist Office, 044-12 19 88. ⏱ daily. 🎫 🚻 (some parts)
🌐 www.vattenriket.kristianstad.se

🏰 Bäckaskog Slott
Fjälkinge, 15 km (9 miles) NE of Kristianstad. 📞 044-532 20.
⏱ Apr–Sep: daily. 🎫 🚻 🍴 🚻

🏰 Trolle-Ljungby
Fjälkinge, 10 km (6 miles) NE of Kristianstad. 📞 044-550 43. ⏱ (park & courtyard only) Jun–Sep: Wed & Sat.

Sölvesborg 🕦

Blekinge. E22. 👥 16,500. 🚌 🚉 🛈
Repslagaregatan 1, 0456-100 88. 🎭
Nogersund Harbour Festival (early Jul).
🌐 www.solvesborg.se

IN THE MIDDLE AGES, Sölvesborg, on the cape of Listerlandet, was an important trading centre protected by a castle. The town has a Danish feel to it and still retains its medieval charm. In a former granary and distillery, **Sölvesborgs Museum** traces the history of Lister. The town's oldest building is St **Nicolai Kyrka**, a church

with parts dating from the 13th century.

ENVIRONS: West of Sölvesborg and at the far end of the cape lies the old town of **Hällevik** with its traditional wooden houses, fishing harbour, smokery and guest harbour. It also has a great little fishing museum and is well worth a visit.

Ferries run from Nogersund to the island of **Hanö** in Hanöbukten bay. It's an attractive place and a popular destination for sailors. The island served as an English naval base in the Napoleonic Wars in the early 19th century and there is a graveyard here for British seamen.

🏛 Sölvesborgs Museum
Skeppsbrogatan. 📞 0456-161 57.
⏱ May–Aug: daily; Sep–Apr: by arrangement.

Karlshamn 🕗

Blekinge. E22. 👥 18,900. ✈ 🚌 🚉
🛈 Ronnebygatan 1, 0454-812 13
🎭 Baltic Festival (2nd week in Jul).

THE TOWN OF Karlshamn was founded in 1664. It was planned as a naval base and **Kastellet**, on the island of Frisholmen, was built to defend it. However, the naval port role went to Karlskrona (*see pp188–9*) and Karlshamn became a trading centre with a reputation for the production of punsch. A reconstruction of Punschfabriken, the factory which produced the delectable "Flaggpunsch" (*see p293*), forms part of **Karlshamns Museum**. Next to the punsch factory is **Karlshamns Konsthall** (Art Gallery).

Other places of interest include **Skottsbergska Gården**, a merchant's house built in 1763 where both the living

Kastellet on the island of Frisholmen, Karlshamn

◁ **A carpet of white and yellow anemones on a spring day in Stenshuvud National Park**

quarters and tobacco shop
can be seen as they were in
the 18th century. **Asschierska
Huset** on Stortorget was
Karlshamn's first town hall.
The celebrated **Mörrumsån**
salmon fishing river runs
through the municipality.

ENVIRONS: Around 15 km
(9 miles) east of Karlshamn
is **Eriksbergs Vilt- och
Naturpark**, one of the
largest wildlife and nature
sanctuaries in Europe and
home to golden eagles.
    Tjärö, in the idyllic Blekinge
archipelago, is a 15-minute
boat trip away.

Renovated spa pavilions at Brunnsparken in Ronneby

🏛 **Karlshamns Museum**
Vinkelgatan 8. ☎ 0454-148 68.
🕒 mid-Jun–mid-Aug: Tue–Sun. 🎫 ♿

Ronneby ⑱

Blekinge. E22. 🏠 11,900. ✈ 🚆 🚌
🛈 Västra Torggatan 1, 0457-188 50.
🎭 Tosia Bonnadan Festival (2nd week
in Jul). 🌐 www.ronneby.se

FOUNDED IN THE 13th century,
Ronneby did not become
Swedish until 1658. Prior to
that, it was the main town of
Blekinge and a busy trading
centre. In 1564, during the
Seven Years War with the
Danes, it was overrun by the
army of Erik XIV and burned.
About 3,000 inhabitants – the
majority of the population –

were slaughtered in what became known as the Ronneby
Bloodbath. In the early 19th
century the town gained a
new lease of life thanks to the
Kockums foundry and enamel
works in Kallinge and the
Ronneby Brunn spa.
    There are a few old
buildings in Bergslagen and
around Brunnskällan, and the
beautiful 18th-century spa
park has been restored.

ENVIRONS: Just east of Ronneby
is the 13th-century church
Edestads Kyrka, which once
served as a defensive fort. A
remarkable 4-m (13-ft) high,
8th-century runestone,
Björketorpsstenen, lies 7 km
(4 miles) east of the town.
The text inscribed on the
stone is a curse.
    Hjortsberga Grave Field
on the Johannishus ridge
contains 120 ancient burial
mounds. About 12 km (7

miles) northeast of Ronneby
is **Johannishus Åsar**, a
nature reserve set in beautiful
pasture land.

Kristianopel ⑲

Blekinge. E22. 🏠 1,500. 🚆 🚌
🛈 Stortorget 2, 0455-30 34 90. 🎭
Medieval Market (4th week in Aug).

ENJOYING A beautiful location
on a peninsula in
Kalmarsund, the little fortified
town of Kristianopel has
become a popular summer
haunt with a guest harbour
and tourist facilities. It was
built by the Danish King
Christian IV and gained its
town charter in 1600. At the
Peace of Roskilde in 1658 it
became Swedish. Garden
lovers head for **Rosengården**,
a private garden filled with
more than 500 different
varieties of old roses.

ENVIRONS: Brömsebro lies
8 km (5 miles) north of
Kristianopel, just inland from
the coast. Here on the border
between Blekinge and
Småland is where peace with
Denmark was declared in
1645, when Jämtland, Härjedalen and Gotland once more
became Swedish provinces.
The negotiations were held
on an islet in Brömsebäcken
river and a commemorative
stone was raised here in 1915.
At the mouth of the river are
the ruins of Brömsehus, a
fortress which was captured
in 1436 by Swedish rebel
hero Engelbrekt *(see p33)*.

♣ **Rosengården**
☎ 0455-36 62 36. 🕒 mid-May–
mid-Sep: daily; other times: by
appointment. 🚻

SALMON FISHING IN MÖRRUMSÅN

Every year the salmon fishing in the Mörrumsån river
attracts enthusiasts from all over the world. Fishing here
dates back to the 13th century when the king held all the
rights. The river flows through a beautiful landscape from
Lake Vrången in the north to
the sea at Elleholm via the
lakes of Helgasjön and Åsnen.
    A fishing permit is required
and these cost between 300
and 500 kr per day. During the
2003 season 1,160 salmon
were caught here, the record
catch weighing in at 17.98 kg
(39.6 lbs).
    Laxens Hus (Salmon World)
in Mörrum gathers together
everything to do with fishing
and mounts a variety of exhibitions on, for example, the
animal life of the river, and the
history of the sport.

**Fly-fishing for salmon in
Mörrumsån**

Karlskrona ⑳

Karl XI, the town's founder

T HE NAVAL TOWN OF KARLSKRONA is built over several islands in the Blekinge archipelago. Granted a town charter in 1680, it was planned by Erik Dahlbergh and is said to have been inspired by both Versailles and Rome. It centres around the two squares, Stortorget on the island of Trossö, and Amiralitetstorget. The decision to locate Sweden's main naval base in Karlskrona was taken because in winter the fleet was often ice-bound in Stockholm, and an ice-free port was needed further south. Karlskrona has a number of outstanding sights from Sweden's Age of Greatness *(see pp36–7)*. In 1998 the town was declared a UNESCO World Heritage Site on account of its naval architecture.

Fredrikskyrkan on Stortorget, designed by Tessin the Younger in Baroque style, 1744

🏛 Grevagården/Blekinge Museum
Fisktorget 2. 📞 0455-30 49 60.
🕐 mid-Jun–mid-Aug: daily; rest of the year: Tue–Sun. 🌐 some public holidays. 🍴🔲🚻📷🏛

Grevagården on Fisktorget is the main building of Blekinge Museum. The building dates from the early 18th century and was the home of Admiral-General Hans Wachtmeister – the café is set in what was once his kitchen and store room. The museum focuses on the history of Blekinge and Karlskrona's heyday. There is a small Baroque garden reached via a double staircase flanked by two yew trees, believed to date from 1704. Outside on the square stands the statue of the *Fisherwoman* by Erik Höglund.

🏛 Stortorget
The imposing square – said to be the largest in northern Europe – is flanked, in the Baroque tradition, by two impressive churches, both designed by the architect Nicodemus Tessin the Younger.

Fredrikskyrkan is a large basilica consecrated in 1744, but characterized by the 17th-century taste for Baroque lines. The southern tower has 35 bells which ring three times a day. The other church, Heliga Trefaldighets-kyrkan (Holy Trinity), is also known as the German Church after Admiral-General Hans Wachtmeister who inspired it and is buried in the crypt. It was completed in 1709. After a fire in 1790 the church was rebuilt with a lower dome than its predecessor.

The town hall, completed in 1798, has been rebuilt several times. Today it serves as the seat of Karlskrona district court.

Vattenborgen, the now protected water tower, was built in 1863 to supply Trossö with fresh water. It was replaced by a water tower outside the town in 1939.

🏛 Marinmuseum
Stumholmen. 📞 0455-539 02.
🕐 Jun–Aug: daily; Sep–May: Tue–Sun. 🍴🚻📷🏛♿🔲
🌐 www.marinmuseum.se

The fascinating naval museum, opened in 1997, stands on the harbour on Stumholmen, an island which for almost 300 years has been part of the main base of the Swedish navy. The museum was founded originally in 1752 by King Adolf Fredrik to collect and document naval objects in what was known as Modellkammaren (the Model Room).

Marinmuseum covers every imaginable aspect of maritime activity. It holds a particularly impressive collection of figureheads, weapons and uniforms. From an under-water glass corridor it is possible to see the wreck of an 18th-century ship lying on the bottom of the sea.

One of the world's smallest full-rigged ships, *Jarramas*, a training ship for naval ratings, is moored on the quay outside the museum, along with the minesweeper *Bremön* and the torpedo boat *T38*. The Sloop and Long-Boat Shed contains an exhibition of working boats and often allows visitors the opportunity to see how old wooden boats are restored.

Marinmuseum, showcase for Karlskrona's naval heritage

🏛 Gamla Örlogsvarvet
Högvakten, Amiralitetstorget 1.
📞 0455-30 34 91. 🕐 Jun–Aug: daily. 📷🚻 compulsory.

The Karlskrona shipyard, founded in 1679, became over time one of the country's foremost military shipyards, a position it still holds today. Fortifications and buildings were constructed to build, equip and repair warships. Additional buildings went up on the islands of Lindholmen,

The "Old Man" Rosenbom poor-box outside Amiralitetskyrkan

Söderstjärna and Stumholmen. The only way to see this vast naval harbour and its many 18th-century buildings and workshops is to take a guided tour. Among the most interesting sights in Gamla Örlogsvarvet are the 300-m (984-ft) long Rope Walk, where the rigging for the fleet was manufactured, the Wasa Shed and Polhem Dock on Lindholmen and Five-finger Dock and the Old Mast Crane in the western part of the shipyard. It is the existence of buildings such as these, and the fact that Karlskrona is such a well-preserved example of a late-17th-century planned naval base, that has earned the town World Heritage Site status. Karlskrona was a model for other naval bases throughout Europe in the 18th century.

Close to the entrance to the old shipyard, Högvakten, is Amiralitetskyrkan (the Admiralty church). Consecrated in 1685, it is Sweden's largest wooden church. In front of the church is a replica of the Gubben "Old Man" Rosenbom poor-box.

Today's high-tech shipyard, Karlskronavarvet, run by Kockums, is not open to the public, but new vessels can often be seen along the quay.

🚂 Skärfva Herrgård
5 km (3 miles) W of centre, E 22. ☎ 0455-490 03. ○ daily (park). ◨ ✗
In 1785 the ship designer Fredrik Henrik af Chapman built a summer house on the shore between Karlskrona and Nättraby. The building is an unusual mix of a traditional Blekinge cottage open to the roof space and other architectural styles, including an entrance reminiscent of a Doric temple in front of an octagonal cupola crowned with a lantern.

Inside, several rooms are preserved in their original state, including af Chapman's workroom in the form of a ship's cabin. The house is set in an English-style park with a temple-like summer house.

The surroundings are part of Skärfva Nature Reserve which protects the flora and fauna of the manor house estate.

During the summer boats run daily from Karlskrona to Skärfva.

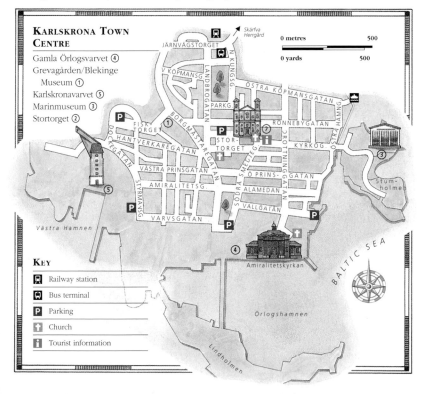

KARLSKRONA TOWN CENTRE

Gamla Örlogsvarvet ④
Grevagården/Blekinge Museum ①
Karlskronavarvet ⑤
Marinmuseum ③
Stortorget ②

0 metres   500
0 yards   500

KEY

🚉 Railway station
🚌 Bus terminal
🅿 Parking
✝ Church
🛈 Tourist information

GOTHENBURG

THE PEOPLE OF GOTHENBURG *have nicknamed their city "the face of Sweden". This maritime metropolis has for centuries been one of Sweden's gateways to the outside world. Historically, the Göta Älv river was the country's only outlet to the west, as can be seen by the remains of fortresses and earthworks that once protected it. Gothenburg is still Sweden's most important port and holds fast to its maritime past.*

With its great harbour and seafaring traditions, it is perhaps only natural that Sweden's second largest city is also its most outward looking. Visitors are always welcome and it is not for nothing that the entertainment on offer and the atmosphere have led to Gothenburg being called "Little London".

Today's Gothenburg (Göteborg in Swedish) was preceded by four earlier towns along the Göta Älv river. These were pawns in a period of constant conflict between Sweden and Denmark. The first town was built by Dutch settlers on the island of Hisingen in the early 17th century. It was hardly established before Gustav II Adolf decided in 1619 that it should be moved to the area where the suburbs of Vallgraven and Nordstaden now stand. The inhabitants still came from Holland and the grid of canals is reminiscent of Amsterdam. Gothenburg's 17th-century incarnation was as a fortified town created by the architect and field marshal Erik Dahlbergh. The 18th century saw Gothenburg become even more cosmopolitan thanks to German, English and Scottish immigration. With the advent of steam power, the shipping industry flourished in the mid-19th century, and the city became a prominent shipbuilding centre. The shipyards have mostly gone, but Gothenburg is still a major industrial city and home of the car manufacturer Volvo.

This vibrant little metropolis of 500,000 people (famous for their particular wittiness) is ideal for sightseeing, and is peppered with green spaces, such as the Botanical Gardens and the amusement park, Liseberg. It is a good starting point for excursions to the west coast islands with their pretty fishing villages and smooth rocks for bathing.

Gothenburg's Botanical Gardens, a green oasis not far from the centre of the city

◁ An old windjammer, the barque *Viking*, at Lilla Bommen in Gothenburg's inner harbour

Exploring Gothenburg

A GOOD QUICK WAY to get an overview of Gothenburg is to see the city from one of the many excellent observation points such as GötheborgsUtkiken, Sjömanstornet or LisebergsTornet. The central parts of the town lie south of the Göta Älv river, but it is easy to cross to the large island of Hisingen by ferry, or by car via the Götaälvbron or Älvsborgsbron bridges, or the Tingstad tunnel. Gothenburg has retained its excellent tram network which provides an ideal way to tour the town, especially on the vintage carriages of the Ringlinjen line. Paddan's white tour boats *(see p205)* operate trips along the 17th-century canals and out into the lively harbour.

Feskekörka fish market reflecting in the water of the Rosenlund Canal

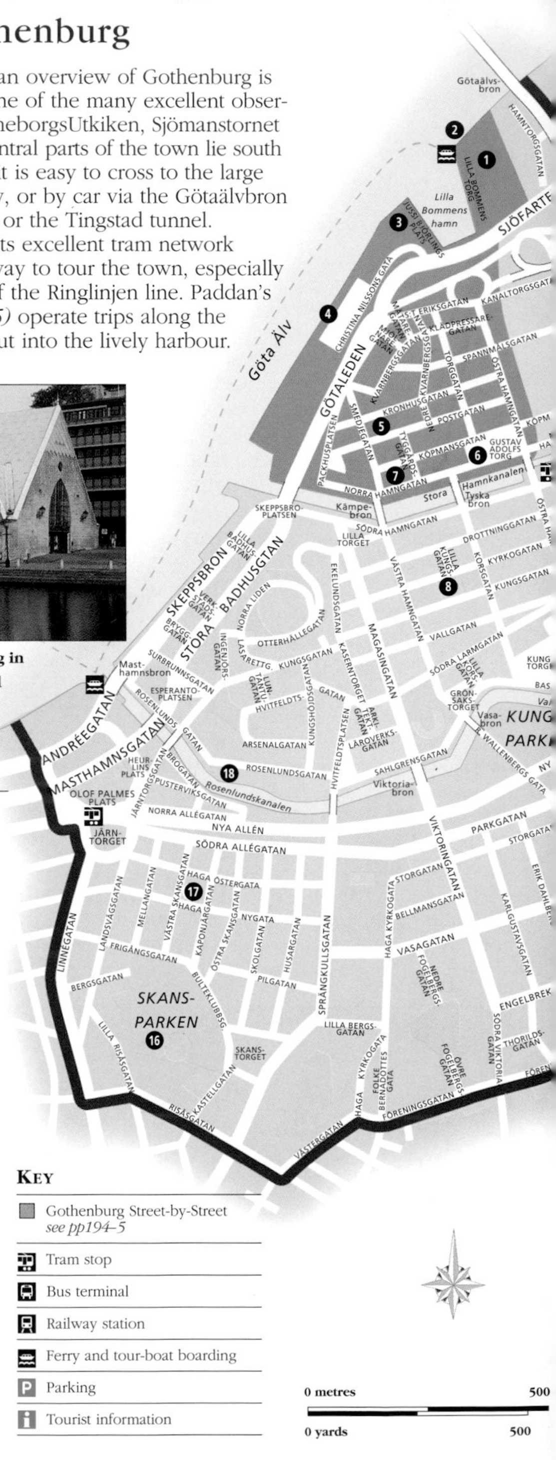

SIGHTS AT A GLANCE

Barken Viking ❷
Botaniska Trädgården ㉒
Domkyrkan ❽
Feskekörka ⑱
Gamla Haga ⑰
Gathenhielmska Huset ⑳
Gustav Adolfs Torg ❻
Götaplatsen ⑮
Göteborgs Maritima
  Centrum ❹
Göteborgs Stadsmuseum ❼
GöteborgsOperan ❸
GötheborgsUtkiken ❶
The Harbour ㉓
Kronhuset ❺
Liseberg ⑭
Nya Älvsborgs Fästning ㉔
Röhsska Museet ⑪
Skansen Kronan ⑯
Sjöfartsmuseet and
  Akvariet ⑲
Slottsskogen and Natur-
  historiska Museet ㉑
Trädgårdsföreningen ❾
Ullevi ⑩
Universeum ⑫
Världskulturmuseet ⑬

KEY

▢ Gothenburg Street-by-Street
  see pp194–5

🚋 Tram stop

🚌 Bus terminal

🚉 Railway station

⛴ Ferry and tour-boat boarding

🅿 Parking

ℹ Tourist information

| 0 metres | 500 |
| 0 yards | 500 |

GETTING TO GOTHENBURG

The sea has always been the key to Gothenburg and ferries run daily from Norway, Denmark, Germany and the UK. Fast trains whisk travellers from Stockholm or Malmö in three hours. A well-developed commuter train network and express bus lines ease regional trips. The E6 along the west coast and the E20 from Stockholm meet at the Göta Älv river. Landvetter international airport is Sweden's second largest airport with direct flights to many domestic and international destinations.

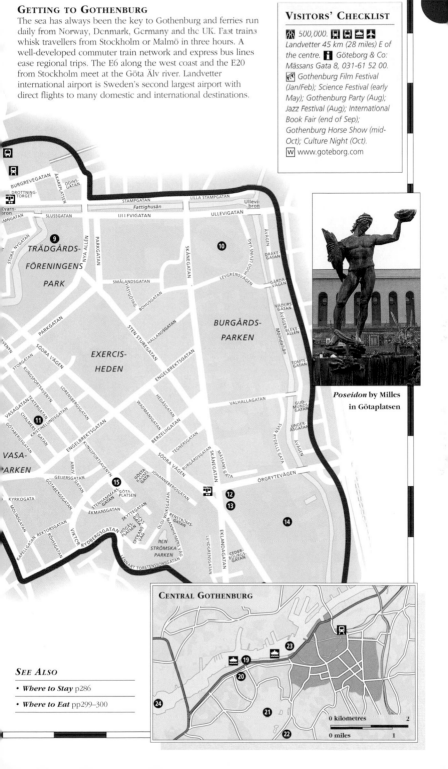

Poseidon by Milles
in Götaplatsen

SEE ALSO

• **Where to Stay** p286

• **Where to Eat** pp299–300

CENTRAL GOTHENBURG

0 kilometres   2

0 miles   1

Street-by-Street: Västra Nordstan

THIS PART OF GOTHENBURG is the pulse of the
seafaring city, encapsulating almost 400 years of
history. On the quayside along the Göta Älv river the
maritime world is ever present, with museum ships at
anchor and the constant to-ing and fro-ing of boats
and ferries. Spectacular new buildings, such as
GöteborgsOperan and GötheborgsUtkiken, contrast
with the city's historic monuments. These include the
East India Company building on Stora Hamnkanalen, a
reminder of the Dutch influence on Gothenburg's
design, and Kronhuset, the city's oldest secular
building. Shoppers should head for nearby Östra
Nordstan and its department stores and galleries.

GöteborgsOperan
*Generous donations
enabled the building of the
long-awaited Opera House,
which opened in 1994* ❸

★ Göteborgs Maritima Centrum
*In the harbour is one of the world's largest
floating ship museums. Both the destroyer
Småland, launched 1952 (in the background), and the submarine Nordkaparen, 1962, can be boarded.* ❹

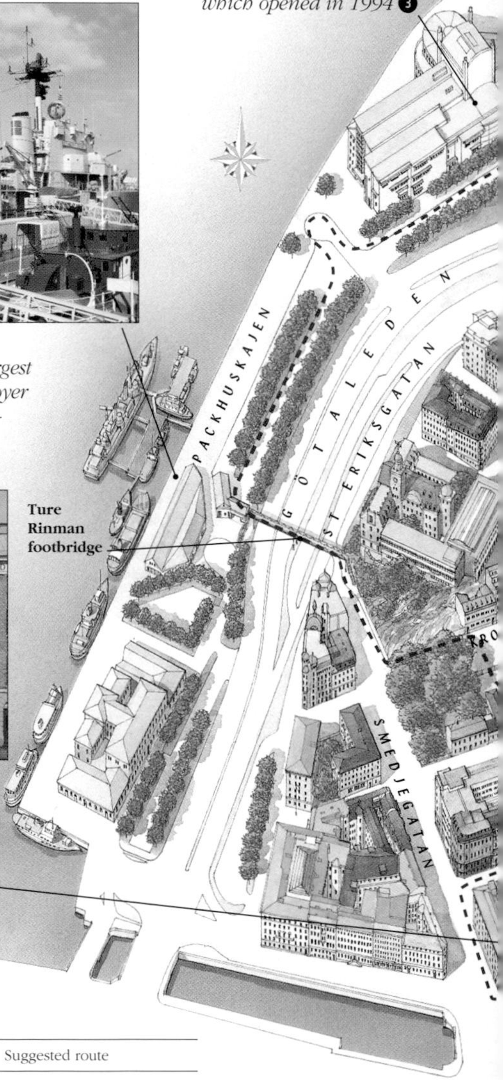

Göteborgs Stadsmuseum
*The former East India Company's
classical 18th-century headquarters
building is now the setting for
Göteborgs Stadsmuseum* ❼

**Ture
Rinman
footbridge**

PACKHUSKAJEN

GÖTALEDEN

STERIKSGATAN

SMEDJEGATAN

STAR SIGHTS

**★ Göteborgs Maritima
Centrum**

★ Barken Viking

KEY

- - - Suggested route

GötheborgsUtkiken

The top of the striped skyscraper provides an excellent view over the river and the bustling harbour below ❶

LOCATOR MAP
See map pp192–3

Lilla
Bommen
marina

Torsten
Henrikssons
footbridge

Nordstan
shopping-
mall

★ Barken Viking
After a lifetime on the high seas, the 1906 barque, Viking, lies at anchor in the harbour. It now serves as a restaurant and hotel ❷

Gustav Adolfs Torg
"The town shall be here," pointed King Gustav II Adolf, as depicted by Bengt Erland Fogelberg's statue (1854). The anniversary of the king's death at the Battle of Lützen on 6 November 1632 is commemorated in the square every year ❻

Kronhuset and Kronhusbodarna
Next to the 17th-century Kronhuset, the Kronhusbodarna sheds are now occupied by craft-workers and restaurants ❺

0 metres   200

0 yards   200

GötheborgsUtkiken (the"Lipstick"), and the sailing ship *Viking*

Götheborgs-Utkiken **❶**

Lilla Bommen 2. **【** *031-15 61 47.* **🚊** *5, 10.* **🚌** *40, 41, 52, 85, 140.* ◯ *mid-May–mid-Aug: 10am–4pm daily; other times: 11am–4pm Mon–Fri.* 🖵 🏷️

THE CHEEKY RED and white GötheborgsUtkiken office building has dominated the Lilla Bommen harbour area since 1989. Architects Ralph Erskine and Heikki Särg's daring design was soon christened the "Lipstick" by Gothenburg wits. Standing 86 m (282 ft) above sea level, it offers incredible views over the harbour and the city centre from the top floor.

Barken Viking **❷**

Gullbergskajen. **【** *031-63 58 00.* **🚊** *5, 10.* **🚌** *40, 41, 52, 85, 140.* ◯ *daily.* ● *22–31 Dec.* 🍴 summer. 🍴 🏷️ *limited access.*

ONE OF THE WORLD'S few preserved four-masted barques from the great age of sail is permanently moored in Gothenburg. The *Viking* was built in 1906 by the Copenhagen shipyard Burmeister & Wain. She sailed the wheat route to Australia and shipped guano from Chile in South America. A fast and beautiful vessel, she logged a record speed of 15.5 knots in 1909. Her days as a merchant ship ended in 1948. In 1950 she

became a training centre for sailors and chefs.

Today, the *Viking* is an unusual setting for an hotel and conference centre. In summer the 97 m (318 ft) deck becomes a popular harbourside café, restaurant and bar, with a very lively, bustling atmosphere.

Göteborgs-Operan **❸**

Christina Nilssons Gata. **【** *031-13 13 00.* **🚊** *5, 10.* **🚌** *40, 41, 52, 80, 85, 140.* ◯ *mid Aug–Jun: in conjunction with performances; other times: phone for info.* ● *24, 25, 31 Dec, 1 May, Good Friday.* 📷 ♿ 🎫 *book.* 🖵 🍴 📷 ⓦ *www.opera.se.*

THE 1994 OPENING of the impressive Opera House reflected in the water of the Göta Älv river had been eagerly anticipated by western Sweden's music lovers. This is shown by the vast donation wall listing the names of the 6,000 people who helped to fund the new building.

The theatre is designed on a grand scale in every sense. The octagonal auditorium has the capacity for an audience of 1,300, all able to enjoy the excellent acoustics. The main stage covering 500 sq m (5,380 sq ft) is complemented by a further four equally large

The striking exterior of the riverside GöteborgsOperan, the city's main venue for opera, musicals and ballet

areas for storing sets. Using advanced technology, it is possible to switch quickly between productions, thus enabling the Opera House to stage a repertoire of opera, musicals and ballet.

Architect Jan Izikowitz was inspired by Gothenburg's harbourside location, the aim of his design being for the "building to be possessed by a lightness which encourages thoughts to soar like seagulls' wings over the mighty river landscape".

Gustav Adolfs Torg flanked on its north side by Börsen, built in 1859

The destroyer *Småland*, 1952, in Göteborgs Maritima Centrum

Göteborgs Maritima Centrum ➍

Packhuskajen 8. 📞 *031-10 59 50.* 🚊 *5,10.* 🚌 *40, 41, 52, 85, 140.* 🕐 *May–Aug: 10am–6pm daily; Nov: 10am–4pm Fri–Sun; other times: 10am–4pm daily.* 🅿️ 🔗

A s the city's new port facilities moved further out towards the sea, Gothenburg's inner harbour became denuded of ships. Fortunately, the situation was rectified in 1987 when Göteborgs Maritima Centrum was set up on the harbour. The museum now has 18 vessels at anchor, comprising what is said to be the world's largest floating ship museum.

Vessels include the destroyer *Småland*, built in 1952 at Eriksbergs shipyard on the other side of the river, the submarine *Nordkaparen* (1962), and the monitor *Sölve* (1875), as well as lightships, fireboats and tugs.

Kronhuset ➎

Postgatan 6–8. 🚊 *1, 3, 4, 5, 6, 7, 9, 10, 11.* 🚌 *40, 41, 50, 52, 58, 60, 85, 86, 91, 140, 771.* 🔗 🅿️ ♿

A GRAND BRICK building in Dutch style, Kronhuset was constructed in 1643–55 and is Gothenburg's oldest preserved secular building. This part of town was originally a storage area for the artillery. The ground floor of Kronhuset was converted into a chamber for the parliament of 1660.

Today, the building is used for concerts and exhibitions. The second floor is devoted to an exhibition illustrating Gothenburg in Sweden's Age of Greatness *(see pp36–7)*.

Around the square are Kronhusbodarna (the Kronhus sheds), which create a

Mid-17th century Kronhuset, one of Gothenburg's oldest buildings

pleasant setting for crafts people, an old-fashioned country store and glassworks.

Gustav Adolfs Torg ➏

🚊 *1, 3, 4, 5, 6, 7, 9, 10, 11.* 🚌 *40, 41, 50, 52, 58, 60, 85, 86, 91, 140, 771.* **Rådhuset** 🕐 *8am–4.30pm daily.* ♿ *public holidays.* **Stadshuset** ♿ *to the public.* **Börsen** ♿ *to the public.*

G OTHENBURG'S founder, Gustav II Adolf, gave his name to the city's central square. Since 1854 Bengt Erland Fogelberg's statue of the "hero king" has gazed imperiously over the square and Rådhuset (the Town Hall), Börsen (the Stock Exchange) and Stadshuset (the City Hall).

On 6 November, the date on which the king died at the Battle of Lützen in 1632, schoolchildren parade in his honour here and a special marzipan cake is made in the shape of the king's head.

Rådhuset, closest to Norra Hamngatan, was designed by Nicodemus Tessin the Elder *(see p24)* and completed in 1673. It has a Functionalist extension designed in 1937 by Gunnar Asplund *(see p99)*.

The 18th-century **Stadshuset** and Wenngrenska Villa on the north side of the square are used by the city administration. **Börsen**, designed by P J Ekman in 1849, is the city's main venue for receptions and council meetings.

Ostindiska Huset (East India House) housing Göteborgs Stadsmuseum

Göteborgs Stadsmuseum **7**

Norra Hamngatan 12. **C** 031-61 27 70. **T** 1–11. **E** 40, 41, 50, 52, 58, 60, 85, 86, 91, 140, 771. **O** Sep–Apr: 10am–5pm Tue–Sun, 10am–8pm Wed; May–Aug: 10am–5pm daily. pre-book.

THE CITY MUSEUM is aptly located in the historic Ostindiska Huset (East India House). The building, designed by Bengt Wilhelm Carlberg and Carl Hårleman, was constructed in 1747–62 as management premises, auction rooms and a ware-house for the East India

Chinese plate in the collection of Göteborgs Stadsmuseum

Company. When trading ceased in the early 19th century the building became a natural history museum, and in 1861 the City Museum was founded.

The permanent exhibitions show the early history of Western Sweden and the importance of the Göta Älv river as a route to Europe from the Viking period onwards. Displays focus on the history of the first inhabitants of Gothenburg and the industrialization and social upheavals of the 20th century. The work of the East India Company and its trade in exotic goods such as Chinese porcelain, silk and lacquer work, is also featured.

Domkyrkan **8**

Västra Hamngatan. **C** 031-731 61 50. **T** 1, 2, 6, 9, 11. **E** 60. **O** daily. pre-book. summer. daily.

GOTHENBURG'S cathedral, Gustavi Domkyrka, was designed by C W Carlberg in Neo-Classical style in 1815–25. It stands on the ruins of its two predecessors, which were both destroyed by fire.

In front of the cathedral in Domkyrkoplan is one of the city's preserved watering places: from the late 18th century water was transported here in hollowed-out oak logs from the well of Gustafs Källa to the south of the city.

Gustavi Domkyrka's impressive gilded altar-piece

Trädgårds-föreningen **9**

Slussgatan. **C** 031-365 58 58. **T** 1, 3–9, 11, 13, 14. **E** 25, 28, 29, 34, 58, 60, 61, 514. **Park** **O** May–Aug: 7am–9pm daily, Sep–Apr: 7am–7.30pm. **Palm House** **C** 031-41 57 73. Sep–Apr: 10am–4pm daily; May–Aug: 10am–5pm daily. 24, 25 & 31 Dec.

GOTHENBURG HAS many parks, but Trädgårds-föreningen is in a class of its own. In 1842 work began to transform a marshland south of Vallgraven into beautiful parkland for the benefit of the city's residents.

The flora of five continents are represented in the magnificent Palmhuset (Palm House) built in 1878. The building is filled with flowering camellias, giant bamboo, exotic orchids and plenty of palm trees.

Vattenhuset (the Water House) is carpeted by the twisting roots of mangrove trees and the 2-m (6-ft) wide petals of the giant water-lily.

The Rosarium is not to be missed, especially by rose lovers. It has become a leading world collection with more than 2,000 varieties.

There are cafés in the park and Trägår'n, a restaurant and

THE EAST INDIA COMPANY

Attracted by goods such as tea, silk and porcelain, Sweden was one of the countries which invested in trade with China in the 18th century and Gothenburg became a natural centre for this highly lucrative industry. The Swedish East India Company received its charter in 1731 and operated for 82 years, based in Ostindiska Huset (see above). In total, 132 expeditions were made to China in 38 different ships. In recent years interest in the work of the Company has resulted in the building of the East Indiaman *Götheborg*. This exact replica of the ship, which sank off Nya Älvsborgs Fästning (see p205) on its homeward voyage 250 years ago, was built at the Terra Nova shipyard in Eriksberg. In 2005 the ship set out to sail the traditional trade route to Canton.

The East Indiaman *Wasa* at Nya Älvsborgs Fästning

Trädgårdsföreningen's Palmhuset, containing plants and trees from five continents in various climatic zones

nightclub which has been entertaining pleasure-seeking locals since the 19th century. It is now housed in a new building with a large open-air terrace for partying.

Ullevi ❿

Skånegatan. 🕿 031- 81 10 20. ╦ 1, 3, 6. ▦ 51, 60. ◯ during events. 🔒 ♿

SWEDEN'S LARGEST sporting arena, Ullevi, opened for the 1958 football World Cup and over the years has hosted numerous international events. Architect Fritz Jaenecke's elegant wave-shaped ellipse has been renovated and modernized several times. The arena seats 43,000 spectators for sporting events and can accommodate an audience of 60,000 for concerts.

On the other side of Skånegatan, in front of Gamla Ullevi football stadium, is a statue of Gunnar Gren (1920–91), one of Sweden's greatest-ever footballers.

Röhsska Muscet ⓫

Vasagatan 37–39. 🕿 031-61 38 50. ╦ 3, 4, 5, 7, 10. ▦ 40, 41, 58, 140. ◯ noon–9pm Tue, noon–5pm Wed–Sun. ● Good Friday. 🎟 🖊 pre-book. 🖥 🎦 ♿ w www.designmuseum.se

THE COUNTRY'S leading museum of applied art and design, Röhsska Museet contains a marvellous collection of 20th-century Nordic domestic and decorative items. Other parts of the museum are devoted to European applied art, and antiquities from the ancient world, Japan and China. A

mere fraction of the total of 50,000 objects can be displayed at any one time. Specialist temporary exhibitions are also mounted.

The museum was founded with donations from financiers Wilhelm and August Röhss. It opened in 1916 as the Röhss Museum of Handicrafts in the beautiful brick building designed by architect Carl Westman.

Next to the museum is the University College for Arts and Crafts Design.

Chinese sculpture, Röhsska Museet

Universeum ⓬

Korsvägen. 🕿 031-335 64 50. ╦ 4 5, 6, 7, 8, 13, 14. ▦ 50, 51, 52, 61, 761, 771. ◯ Jan–Apr & mid-Aug– Dec: 11am–6pm Tue, Thu–Sun, 11am–8pm Wed; May–Jun & 1st week in Nov: 10am–6pm Mon–Fri (to 8pm Wed), 11am–6pm Sat–Sun; Jul–mid-Aug: 9am–7pm daily. 🖥 🍴 🎟 ♿ w www.universeum.se

ALONG THE Mölndalsån river, not far from Kungsports-avenyn, spreads an area containing several of Gothenburg's major sights

Universeum, designed by Gert Wingårdh and built in 2001

and venues, including Liseberg (see p200), Ullevi and Scandinavium sporting arenas and the conference centre Svenska Mässan.

The Universeum science centre is the latest addition. Opened in 2001, the environmentally friendly building was designed by Gothenburg architect Gert Wingårdh and voted Sweden's best contemporary building in the same year. The centre aims to stimulate the interest of children and young people in science and technology. Here, they can come face-to-face with exotic creatures such as sting-rays and anacondas, study galaxies and moon buggies and conduct ingenious experiments.

Världskultur-museet ⓭

Södra Vägen 54. 🕿 031-63 27 30. ╦ 4, 5, 6, 7, 8, 13, 14. ▦ 50, 51, 52, 61. ◯ noon–5pm Tue, Sat–Sun, noon–9pm Wed–Fri. 🎟 🖥 🍴 🖊 ♿ w www.varldskulturmuseet.se

DESIGNED by the London-based architects Cécile Brisac and Edgar Gonzalez, the icecube-like Världskultur-museet is a new museum of world cultures, completed in 2005. The exhibitions, like the building, are far from traditional; they are intended to surprise, provoke and question stereotyped attitudes towards culture and subculture, and are complemented by a programme of concerts, films, dance and poetry.

Konstmuseet on Götaplatsen, the city's main square, with Carl Milles' statue of Poseidon in the foreground

Liseberg ⑭

Örgrytevägen 1. 🚋 5 🚌 50, 61. 📞 031-400 100. ⏱ *last week in Apr–last week in Sep: opening times vary.* ⬚ 🅿 🛒 ♿ 🍴 ⅲ www.liseberg.se

THE PEOPLE OF Gothenburg are rightly proud of their amusement park which attracts huge numbers of visitors. Apart from the latest rides, this is the place for dancing and entertainment, shows and theatre performances. It is also a beautiful green park where garden design has always played a major role.

The park's history began in the 18th century when financier Johan Anders Lamberg bought the land and built the first magnificent house, Landeriet, in 1753. He had two passions in life –

Flower Girl by
**Gerhard Henning in
Liseberg park**

gardening and his wife Lisa, after whom the new house on the hill was named, Liseberg.

The City of Gothenburg bought the site for the Gothenburg Exhibition in 1923 and founded the amusement park with the installation of an impressive wooden roller-coaster. Other rides followed, attracting 140 million visitors over the past 80 years. In 2003, a new roller-coaster, named after the Norse god "Balder", opened. Also built out of wood, Balder is the biggest roller-coaster in the Nordic countries. It reaches a speed of 90 km/h (56 mph) from a top height of 36 m (118 ft). "Kanonen", opened in 2004, offers another extreme experience, with its rapid acceleration, sharp loops and turns and 360-degree rotation.

Liseberg's main stage and venue for shows, bands, acrobats and more

Götaplatsen ⑮

🚋 4, 5. 🚌 40, 41, 58. **Konstmuseet** 📞 031-61 29 80. ⏱ 11am–6pm Tue, Thu, Fri; 11am–9pm Wed; 11am–5pm Fri, Sun & public holidays. ⬚ 24, 25 & 31 Dec, Good Friday, 1 May, Midsummer. ⬚ ♿ 🅿 ⬚ **Konsthallen** 📞 031-61 50 40. ⏱ as Konstmuseet. ⬚ ♿ 🅿 ⬚ **Konserthuset** ⬚ for concerts. 📞 031-726 53 10. **Stadsteatern** 📞 031-61 50 55. ⏱ for performances.

THE FOCAL POINT of the city is Götaplatsen, the square at the southwestern end of Kungsportsavenyn. Here Gothenburg's bastions of culture, Konstmuseet (the Art Museum), Konsthallen (the Art Hall), Konserthuset (the Concert Hall), Stadsteatern (the City Theatre) and Stadsbiblioteket (the City Library) sit in state. In the centre of this grand square, the water plays around Carl Milles' giant statue *Poseidon*, which has become the symbol of Gothenburg.

Götaplatsen was built for the city's 300th anniversary and the Gothenburg Exhibition in 1923, which is why many of the buildings were exhibition premises from the start. Wide steps lead up from the southeastern side of the square to **Konstmuseet**, designed by Sigfrid Ericson, which became a museum in 1925. It contains a rich collection of Nordic art, with key works by Carl Larsson, Ernst Josephson and the Gothenburg Colourists. The

Danish golden age, Dutch and Flemish painting and French Modernists are also represented. Pride of place is taken by Furstenbergska Galleriet, a copy of the gallery which the great patron of the arts had in his private palace in the late 19th century. The neighbouring **Konsthallen** shows temporary exhibitions. The bronze lion on the façade is by Palle Pernevi.

Konserthuset on the south-western side of the square was designed by Nils Einar Eriksson and opened in 1935. The foyer is decorated with murals by Prince Eugen (*Grove of Memories*) and Otte Sköld (*Folk Song*) as well as a large tapestry by Sven X-et Erixson (*Melodies in the Square*).

Stadsteatern, built in 1934, reopened in 2002 after extensive renovation to highlight the best of Carl Bergsten's elegant 1930's architecture.

Skansen Kronan fortress (1687) on guard high above Gothenburg

Skansen Kronan ⑯

Skansberget. 🚋 6. 🚌 80, 760, 764, 765. 📞 0705-20 88 08. ⏰ Tue noon–2pm, Sat–Sun noon–3pm. ● public holidays. 🎫 🛒 pre-book. ♿ limited access.

TOPPED BY A GOLDEN crown, the octagonal Skansen Kronan fortress dates from Sweden's Age of Greatness (*see pp36–7*). It sits enthroned on the peak of Skansberget. Like its counterpart Skansen Lejonet, near the station area, Kronan is one of the most striking survivors of Erik Dahlbergh's fortifications. It was built in 1687 to protect the city from attack from the south.

The fortress is now a military museum displaying uniforms and weapons. It is surrounded by Skansberget, a leafy park offering excellent views from the top, up steep steps.

Walkers and shoppers in Gamla Haga with its pleasant wooden houses

Gamla Haga ⑰

🚋 1, 3, 6, 9, 11. 🚌 80, 85, 760, 764, 765.

THE FORMER working-class area of the city south of Vallgraven is one of the few places to experience old Gothenburg. The cobbled streets, courtyards and wooden houses of Gamla Haga are home to craftspeople and lined with small shops, cafés and restaurants.

Haga was Gothenburg's first suburb as early as the 17th century and was mainly populated by harbour workers. During the industrialization of the 19th century a shanty town grew up here and tenements filled with people thronging in from the countryside to seek work.

In the 1960s and 70s Haga was fast becoming a slum and threatened with demolition. Widespread public opposition to the plans ensured that important parts were saved and the houses renovated. Some of the *landshövdingehusen* ("county governor's houses") typical of the area can be seen. These were built in the 1880s, when rules set in 1854 banning wooden houses in the centre more than two storeys high were circumvented – with the governor's approval. Providing the building had a ground floor in brick, as these do, it could have two wooden floors above and not constitute a fire risk.

Feskekörka ⑱

Rosenlundsgatan. 🚋 3, 6, 9, 11. 🚌 80, 85, 760, 764, 765. ⏰ 9am–5pm Tue–Thu; 9am–6pm Fri; 11am–2pm Sat. ● public holidays. 🖥 🍴 ♿

IT IS EASY TO SEE why the wits of Gothenburg nicknamed the fish market Feskekörka (the fish church). Victor von Gegerfelt borrowed from Gothic church architecture when he designed this market hall in 1874, incorporating a steeply pitched roof and large oriel windows.

The catch from the North Sea is brought here directly, guaranteeing the freshest mackerel and the most delicious shellfish. These days there is more to the market than simply selling fish over the counter – the hall provides a colourful setting for restaurant tables at which seafood specialities can be sampled.

Feskekörka fish market, a paradise for lovers of fish and seafood

Sjöfartsmuseet and Akvariet ⑲

Karl Johansgatan 1–3. 📞 031-61 29 00. 🚋 3, 9 and 11. ⏰ Sep–Apr: 9am–4pm Tue, Thu & Fri, 9am–9pm Wed; 11am–5pm Sat, Sun & public holidays; May–Aug: 10am–5pm daily. ● Good Friday, 1 May, Midsummer's Eve, Midsummer. 🏷️ 🎟️ phone for info. ♿ 🎁 🖥️
Sjömanstornet 📞 0731-81 56 00. ⏰ groups only, phone for info. 🏷️ 🌐 www.sjofartsmuseum.goteborg.se

Gathenhielmska Huset, once the home of Privateer Captain Lars Gathenhielm

THE MARITIME history of Gothenburg and Bohuslän is the subject of Sjöfartsmuseet (the Maritime Museum). Set up in 1933, it was funded by the Broström shipping family and is situated on Stigberget, high above the Göta Älv river.

The work of Sweden's largest port, changes in the shipbuilding industry over the centuries and the history of Gothenburg's many shipping lines come under the spotlight. Fishing from the medieval herring period to today also features prominently.

Akvariet (the Aquarium) is dedicated to the marine life of the west coast. Here, it is possible to see how crabs, starfish and sea anemones live 40 m (130 ft) below the surface.

Gamla Varvsparken contains various busts including one of the shipbuilder F H af Chapman (1721–1808) (see p77).

Sjömanstornet tower outside the museum is topped by Ivar Johansson's bronze sculpture *Woman by the Sea*, 1933, in memory of the sailors from western Sweden who died in World War I.

The sculpture *Woman by the Sea* topping the "sailors' tower"

Gathenhielmska Huset ⑳

Allmänna Vägen. 🚋 3, 9, 11. ● to the public apart from the café. 🖥️

THE WESTERN side of the Stigberget hill was formerly the site of the Amiralitetsvarvet shipyard and it was here in the early 1700s that Privateer Captain Lars Gathenhielm was granted land by Karl XII. His widow built a two-storey manor house here in 1740. It is one of Sweden's best examples of a Carolian wooden house designed to imitate stone.

Next to the house is an open-air museum of small wooden houses showing what a suburb looked like in 1800.

Slottsskogen and Naturhistoriska Museet ㉑

Linnéplatsen. 🚌 80, 51, 52, 760, 764, 765. 🚋 1, 6. **Naturhistoriska museet** 📞 031-775 24 00. ⏰ Sep–Apr: 9am–4pm Tue–Fri, 11am–5pm Sat–Sun; (Feb–Mar: to 9pm Wed); May–Aug: 11am–5pm daily; 2 May–13 Jun: 9am–5pm Mon–Fri. ● Good Friday. 🏷️ 🎟️ phone to book. 🎁 🖥️ ♿ 🌐 www.gnm.se

SINCE THE 1870s, Slottsskogen has been one of the city's finest green spaces. Criss-crossed by paths, it features dazzling planting, ponds, a zoo and various activities. In spring the azalea valley is ablaze with colour. In 1999, what was then the world's longest border, with over 90,000 flowering bulbs, was created. There are a number of old cottages from western Sweden to be seen in the park. Areas for sport and outdoor activities include Slottsskogsvallen.

Gothenburg's oldest museum, **Naturhistoriska Museet** (the Museum of Natural History), lies in the northern part of the park. Dating from 1833, it moved to Slottsskogen in 1923. Its vast collection of more than 10 million exhibits includes animals from all around the world.

The most famous of its stuffed animals is Malmska Valen, a blue whale measuring more than 16 m (52 ft) long, which was beached in Askimviken in 1865. It was stuffed and mounted on a treetrunk. The upper jaw opens, and inside the whale there is a room with benches and wall hangings where it is said coffee used to be served. Now the whale is only open for visits on special occasions.

Botaniska Trädgården ㉒

Carl Skottsbergs Gata 22 A. 📞 031-741 11 11. 🚌 58. 🚋 1, 7, 8. ⏰ 9am–sunset daily. 🏷️ voluntary. ♿ 🎁 🖥️ 🌐 www.goteborg.se/botaniska

COVERING 1,750,000 sq m (432 acres) and containing 16,000 species, Gothenburg's Botanical Garden is one of the largest of its kind in Europe. Just under a fifth of the area is gardens while the remainder forms a nature reserve partly consisting of primeval forest.

The gardens began to be designed in 1916 and have been expanded continually ever since. The Rhododendron Valley offers a rich tapestry

◁ Gamla Haga's "county governor's buildings" with a stone ground floor and two wooden storeys above

of dazzling flowers in late spring each year.

The Rock Garden, in a former quarry, contains 5,000 alpine plants from around the world. In early summer the Japanese Glade with its scented magnolias is a delight while autumn sees an oriental riot of colour.

Large greenhouses shelter the plants from the sometimes bitter climate. The controlled environments within recreate a variety of conditions from desert to steaming rain forest. In the tropical house, bamboo and banana plants stretch more than 10 m (33 ft) up to the ceiling and there are 1,500 orchids in the most amazing colours and shapes.

Botaniska Trädgården, a blossoming oasis in the city

The Harbour ㉓

N of the centre between Götaälvbron and Älvsborgsbron bridges. 🚢 to Lilla Bommen, 74, 75. 🚢 Paddan sight-seeing boat from Kungsportsbron, up to 4 times an hour.

SEAFARING HAS BEEN of immense importance to Gothenburg and the harbour and shipyard have long dominated the area of the city along the Göta Älv river. Now the shipbuilding industry is a

Eriksbergs shipyard with Sjömanstornet and Älvsborgsbron bridge

shadow of its former self and apart from ferry traffic, the major shipping activities have moved down to the mouth of the river. Yet, although there is little loading and unloading to be seen in the centre of the city these days, three times more goods are shipped today than in the 1960s.

The inner harbour and shipyard area bordered by the imposing **Älvsborgsbron** bridge have been transformed to provide housing, offices and centres for research and education. Nevertheless, the pulse of seafaring can still be experienced either on a regular ferry from Lilla Bommen to **Eriksbergsvarvet** shipyard, or on the white flat-bottomed **Paddan Boats** which run from Kungs-portsbron bridge via 17th-century Vallgraven down the river to Storhamnen. The round trip takes about 50 minutes.

GöteborgsOperan is best viewed from the water *(see p196)*, as are **Barken Viking** *(see p196)* and **Göteborgs Maritima Centrum** *(see p197)*. **Terra Nova** at the

Eriksbergs shipyard on Hisingen is the home port of the spectacular East Indiaman *Götheborg (see p198)*. Tours also operate around the island of Hisingen and the outer harbour, and to the Gothenburg archipelago. The **Fishing Harbour** holds an auction every weekday at 7am.

Nya Älvsborgs Fästning ㉔

8 km (3 miles) W of the centre.
📞 031-15 81 51. 🚢 from Lilla Bommen. ◻ May– Aug. 🖼 🍴 🛒

IN 1660 A NEW fortress on Kyrkogårdsholmen, at the mouth of the Göta Älv river, replaced the dilapidated, centrally located Älvsborg castle to defend Sweden's precious gateway to the North Sea. It was besieged by the Danes in 1717 and 1719, but never captured. In the late 18th century it became a prison which closed in 1869.

Today the fortress is a popular tourist destination in summer; it even has a wedding chapel.

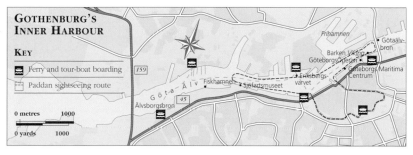

GOTHENBURG'S INNER HARBOUR

KEY

🚢 Ferry and tour-boat boarding

⛺ Paddan sightseeing route

| 0 metres | 1000 |
| 0 yards | 1000 |

Frihamnen
Götaälv-bron
Barken Viking
GöteborgsOperan
Göteborgs Maritima Centrum
Eriksbergs-varvet
Fiskhamnen
Sjöfartsmuseet
Göta Älv
Älvsborgsbron

WESTERN GÖTALAND

SPANNING FOUR PROVINCES – Dalsland, Bohuslän, Västergötland and Halland – this attractive and immensely diverse part of Sweden borders Norway to the west, touches on the great forests in the north and reaches to Lake Vättern in the east. Sweden's largest lake, Vänern, lies at its heart. The waters of the Kattegat and Skagerrak wash the rocky shores and sandy beaches along the coast.

Dalsland in the northwest of Western Götaland is one of Sweden's smallest provinces and is relatively unknown even among Swedes. The landscape is hilly and it is often said that the border with Norrland starts here with the mountain area of Kroppefjäll as its southwestern outpost. From the plains of agricultural Dalsland this border can be seen rearing up like a dark forest-clad wall to the west, while the blue expanse of Lake Vänern glistens to the east. The area is sparsely populated, but campaigns are in hand to attract Norwegians over the border to swell the numbers.

In the southwest, Dalsland borders Bohuslän, a coastal province where the smooth bare rocks are dotted with brightly-painted little wooden houses. Here fishing and the stone industry have been the backbone of the economy since the Middle Ages, but today tourism is the chief money earner; the population of many coastal communities doubles in summer. Bohuslän's main city is Gothenburg, Sweden's second largest metropolis *(see pp190–205)*.

Västergötland lies between lakes Vänern and Vättern. The area has been inhabited since ancient times and has many prehistoric remains. It was the first region in Sweden to be converted to Christianity and has an abundance of early churches. The country's first Christian king, Olof Skötkonung, is thought to have been baptised at Husaby in 1008 *(see p32)* and two of the medieval royal dynasties had their roots in Västergötland. Some claim that this was indeed the cradle of Sweden.

Halland, the coastal region south of Gothenburg, is also a summer paradise, with its long sandy beaches. There are several towns for shopping and some of southern Sweden's most interesting castles and manor houses.

Gunnebo, a wealthy merchant's 18th-century manor house near Gothenburg, now a museum

◁ Tjärnö in Bohuslän, a typical west-coast settlement with fishermen's huts, boats and lobster pots

Exploring Western Götaland

D RIVING IS ONE OF THE BEST ways to explore Western Götaland and experience Dalsand's landscape of lakes, mountain plateaus and rural flatlands, and still have time to spend on the sandy beaches of Halland in the south. Boat trips are a popular way of seeing the small islands and fishing hamlets off the coast of Bohuslän, while the scenery around lakes Vänern and Vättern can be enjoyed from aboard a ferry. Between the lakes, the great forest of Tiveden offers opportunities for hiking. The region as a whole is one in which the ancient past is always present, especially at the UNESCO World Heritage Site of Tanum, where Bronze Age people carved pictures in the rock.

The former lighthouse-keeper's cottage on the approach to Marstrand, now an exclusive summer residence

GETTING AROUND

For drivers, two major roads cross through Western Götaland: the E20, which comes from the northeast via Örebro across the plains to Gothenburg on the west coast, and the E6, which follows the coast northwards towards Norway. Road 45 from Värmland runs south through Dalsland. There are bus and train links between the large towns and populated areas. Regular ferries operate to the majority of inhabited islands along the coast.

Tylösand outside Halmstad, one of the many glorious, long sandy beaches of Halland

KEY

▬	Motorway
▬	Major road
═	Minor road
⌐	Railway line
˙ ˙	Ferry route

SEE ALSO

- *Where to Stay* pp286–7
- *Where to Eat* pp300–1

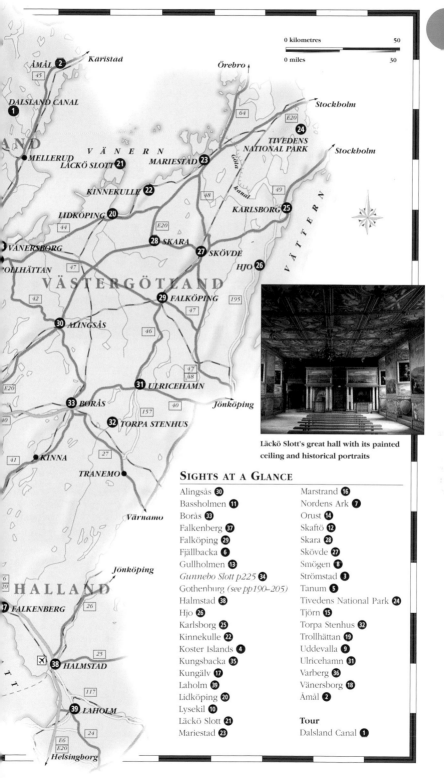

0 kilometres 50

0 miles 30

Läckö Slott's great hall with its painted ceiling and historical portraits

SIGHTS AT A GLANCE

Alingsås 30
Bassholmen 11
Borås 33
Falkenberg 37
Falköping 29
Fjällbacka 6
Gullholmen 13
Gunnebo Slott p225 34
Gothenburg (see pp190–205)
Halmstad 38
Hjo 26
Karlsborg 25
Kinnekulle 22
Koster Islands 4
Kungsbacka 35
Kungälv 17
Laholm 39
Lidköping 20
Lysekil 10
Läckö Slott 21
Mariestad 23

Marstrand 16
Nordens Ark 7
Orust 14
Skaftö 12
Skara 28
Skövde 27
Smögen 8
Strömstad 3
Tanum 5
Tivedens National Park 24
Tjörn 15
Torpa Stenhus 32
Trollhättan 19
Uddevalla 9
Ulricehamn 31
Varberg 36
Vänersborg 18
Åmål 2

Tour
Dalsland Canal 1

A Tour on the Dalsland Canal ❶

FROM BENGTSFORS THE DALSLAND CANAL carves its way
south towards Köpmannebro on Lake Vänern,
passing through 19 locks and dropping 45 m (148 ft)
to the lake. The scenery varies from beautiful, almost
untouched countryside to modern communities, from
old ironworks to historic manor houses. The
spectacular aqueduct at Håverud is formed from a
series of steel plates joined by 33,000 rivets. Both a
rail and a road bridge traverse the deep gorge. The
canal was designed by Nils Ericsson in the 1860s.

**One of the canal's 19 locks
making navigation possible**

Baldersnäs Herrgård ②
The manor house stands on a promontory in Lake Laxsjö, on the Dalsland
Canal. It is set in a romantic park with
paths, caves and artificial islands.

Bengtsfors ①
The canal trip begins or
ends here. Don't miss
Gammelgården open-air
museum with its wooden
cottages and storehouses.

KEY

▬	Suggested route by car
--	Route by boat
=	Other roads
—	Railway line

TIPS FOR THE TRIP

Length: 5½ hours by boat.
Boat route: from Bengtsfors to
Köpmannabro or reverse. The
boat stops at several points along
the way. Return by bus or train,
around 1 hour.

**Högsbyn Rock
Carvings ③**
Pictures of ships,
people and
footprints carved
in stone 3,000
years ago can be
reached by special
boat from Håverud,
or by car.

**Håverud
Aqueduct ④**
A solution to the
problem of crossing a
gorge and a 9-m
(30-ft) high waterfall
was to build four
locks and a long steel
aqueduct over the
waterfall, followed
by another lock.

0 kilometres   5

0 miles   3

Hotell Skagerack on the harbourfront in Strömstad

Åmål ❷

Dalsland. Road 45. 🏠 *9,400*. 🚉
🚉 ✗ *Karlstad*. ⛴ 🛈 *Marinan,
Hamngatan 1, 0532-170 98.* 🎭 *Åmål
Blues Festival (second week in Jul).*
🖥 *www.dalsland.se*

D ALSLANDS ONLY TOWN, Åmål,
was founded in 1643.
Thanks to its strategic location
on Lake Vänern, Åmål soon
became an important market
place, controlling timber
exports to Norway and later
acting as a transit port for
timber and iron to Gothenburg.
After several fires in the 17th
century and a major fire in
1901, a new town was built
on the north side of the
Åmålsån river. Little remains
of the original buildings apart
from a few 18th-century
houses around the town park,
Plantaget. The local history
museum, **Åmåls Hembygds-
museum**, whose three floors
house a dentist's clinic and a
flat furnished in 1920s style,
can be found in Snarhögs-
gården. The Railway Museum
is located in former engine
sheds at Åmål Östra.

At **Forsbacka** on the
Åmålsån river, 7 km (4 miles)
from Åmål towards
Bengtsfors, a mechanical
hammer for producing iron
bars was built at the end of
the 17th century. It was used
until the end of the 19th
century. Today the 18th-
century house at Forsbacka
ironworks is a hotel and the
old buildings are protected. A
golf course is on the land.

🏛 Åmåls Hembygds-
museum
Hamngatan 4. 🎟 *0532-158 20.*
🔓 *mid-Jun–Aug: daily.* 🎫 🚻 *partly.*

Strömstad ❸

Bohuslän. E6. 🏠 *6,000*. 🚉 🚉
🚢 *from Sandefjord, Norway*. ⛴
🛈 *Norra Hamnen, 0526-623 30.*
🎭 *Strömstad Festival (2nd Sat in Jul).
Summer music (Jul), Man Must
Dance (last weekend in Jul).*

W HEN STRÖMSTAD became
Swedish in 1658 it was
just a small fishing village,
but by 1676 it had become a
town, acting as a strategic
counter to the Norwegian
towns of Halden and
Fredrikstad. In the mid-19th
century sea-bathing
became the fashion and
ever since, Strömstad,
with its glorious island
archipelago and many
hours of sunshine, has
been one of Sweden's
major holiday resorts.

After a fire in the
1870s Strömstad was
rebuilt. Today it is a
modern town and its
proximity to Norway is
evident from the
number of Norwegian
cars and boats.

The **Strömstads Museum**
focuses on local history, while
Friluftsmuseet Fiskartorpet
is an open-air museum

featuring fishermen's cottages
and fishing tackle.

The harbour with bars and
shops is in the centre of the
town and boats from here
serve the islands, including
Kosteröarna. Seal safaris
operate to waters around the
Ursholmarna islands south of
Sydkoster. The nature
reserves on Rossö and Saltö
can be reached by car.

🏛 Strömstad Museum
Södra Hamngatan 22. 🎟 *0526-102
75.* 🔓 *Mon–Sat.* ⬤ *public holidays.*
🏛 Friluftsmuseet
Fiskartorpet
Karlsgatan 45. 🎟 *0526-617 53.*
🔓 *summer: daily.* 🚻

Koster Islands ❹

Bohuslän. 🏠 *300*. 🚢 *from Strömstad.*
⛴ 🛈 *Strömstad Tourist, 0526-623
30.* 🎭 *Rowing race (2nd Sun in Aug).*

T HE ISLANDS OF Koster are
renowned for their beauty
and their flora. Together they
form a nature reserve. These
are the westernmost
Swedish islands to be
inhabited: Nordkoster
has a permanent
population of around 40
people. Sydkoster is the
largest island in the
group. It is greener than
Nordkoster and is best
explored by bike. In
contrast, Nordkoster is
much more barren and
can easily be explored
on foot.

The highlights of
the Koster Islands'
calendar include the annual
rowing race across the sound
between the islands in August
and the lobster festival in
the autumn.

**Boiled Koster
lobster**

Made for sunbathing, the polished granite rocks on Nordkoster

Tanum ❺

Bohuslän. E6. 🏠 *12,000.* 🚊 🚌
ℹ️ *Tourist Office, Tanumshede, 0525-
183 80.* Ⓦ *www.tanumturist.se*

THE MUNICIPALITY of Tanum has an extraordinary 525 km (326 miles) of coastline indented with fjords and bays. It stretches from Gerlesborg in the south to Galtö in the north, and is sheltered by a mass of islets and skerries offshore. Inland, farms nestle between rocky outcrops.

Above all, Tanum is renowned for its Bronze Age rock carvings, with the earliest dating from around 1000 BC. Indeed, the concentration of these pictorial images and their contribution to the understanding of Bronze Age culture is such that they were designated a UNESCO World Heritage Site in 1994. Subjects include human life, animals, boats and weapons carved onto smooth rock.

The largest carving, covering 200 sq m (2,150 sq ft), can be seen at Vitlycke. **Vitlycke Museum** is well worth a visit for a fascinating insight into this form of rock art. The museum contains exhibitions and a reconstructed Bronze Age farm. Guided tours by night, when carvings that are

Fjällbacka's painted wooden houses in the shadow of Vetteberget

not visible by day emerge in the light of a torch, are especially enthralling for any age group.

Around the region, carvings featuring hunting scenes can be seen at **Fossum**, east of Tanumshede; **Tegneby** has images of ships; and at **Asberget** scenes containing animals, ploughs and axes can be found.

🏛 Vitlycke Museum

3 km (2 miles) S of Tanumshede. 📞
0525-209 50. ◯ *Apr–Sep: daily.* 🏛
🔌 🖥 🍴 🎁 🛒 *by arrangement.* ♿

BRONZE AGE ROCK CARVINGS

The rock carvings at Tanum represent a high point in the artistic language of pictures and symbols used by Bronze Age people more than 3,000 years ago. Images reflect daily life and hardships, battles won and lost, weapons and hunting scenes. Mating scenes, fertility symbols and the afterlife are also common. The importance of the sea is reflected in the proliferation of ships and fishing scenes. It is thought that the rock paintings were primarily of ritual significance, but the depiction of animals could have acted as a calendar to show when various creatures could be hunted. Hands and feet as motifs are thought to be associated with a godly being too holy to have his whole body depicted.

Bronze Age warrior in a state of sexual arousal, Tanum

Rock carvings can be found all over the world, with the oldest dating from 20,000 BC. Those in Sweden are younger, since it wasn't completely free of ice until 6,500 BC. The carvings at Tanum date from 1000–500 BC.

Fjällbacka ❻

Bohuslän. E6/road 163. 🏠 *850.*
🚌 *to Tanum, then bus.* 🚌 ℹ️ *Torget,
0525-321 20.* 🎣 *Mackerel Fishing
World Championships (last Sat
in Aug).*

ON THE COAST between Strömstad and Uddevalla lies the picturesque village of Fjällbacka. There has been a settlement here since the 17th century and like many other villages along this coast the community made a living from herring fishing and seafaring. Today, holiday-makers come for the swimming and boating.

Attractive low-rise wooden houses and shops line the narrow streets, but it is the harbour which is the heart of the community. This is where the fishing huts, bars and tourist services are located. Fjällbacka has a stunning

Bust of actress Ingrid Bergman (1915–82) in Fjällbacka

location with islands offshore and the 70-m (230-ft) high mountain, Vetteberget, creating a precipitous backdrop to the village centre and square known as Ingrid Bergmans Torg. Actress Ingrid Bergman spent many summers in Fjällbacka and after her death her name was given to the square and a bust made by Gudmar Olovson (1983).

Vetteberget is divided by a huge gorge, known as Kungsklyfta, named after King Oscar II who visited Fjällbacka in 1887 and had his name carved at the entrance to the chasm. This dramatic setting was also used as a location for the film of Astrid Lindgren's children's book *Ronja Rövardotter* (Ronja the Robber's Daughter).

Nordens Ark

Bohuslän. Road 17, 20 km (12 miles) N of Smögen. 🚌 🚆 0523-795 90. ◯ Apr–mid-Jun daily: 10am–5pm; mid-Jun–mid-Aug: 10am–7pm; mid-Aug–Oct: 10am–5pm; Nov–Mar: 10am–4pm. ♿ 🅿 🚻
Ⓦ www.nordensark.se

THE NATURE PARK and ZOO, Nordens Ark, caters specifically for endangered species. Located in Åby Säteri, it contains animals from every corner of the world, including ancient Swedish breeds such as Gotland sheep and mountain cows, Nordic wild

Panda family among the many endangered species at Nordens Ark

animals such as wolves and wolverine, and exotic species such as the Amur leopard and a variety of parrots. Many of the creatures are part of special programmes to protect them from extinction.

To see the animals at close quarters, follow the 3-km (2-mile) walk around the park – and bring binoculars to spot the wide variety of birds. The route takes you between the enclosures via wooden bridges and along gravel paths. Admission in the summer includes a guided tour. The breeding and quarantine areas are not open to the public.

Nordens Ark is a particularly enjoyable outing for families as there are special children's activities throughout the park. Youngsters can find out how animals adapt in relation to their food, enemies and the

environment by being active themselves, trying things out and playing – even adults find these activities entertaining.

Overnight accommodation is also available.

Smögen ❽

Bohuslän. E6/Road 174. 👥 1,500. 🚌 from Gothenburg. ♿ ⓘ Sotenäs Tourist Office, Kungshamn, 0523-66 55 50. 🎏 Herring and Shellfish Festival (3rd weekend in Jul), Tradjazz (first weekend in Aug).
Ⓦ www.sotenasturism.se

ONE OF SWEDEN'S largest fishing communities, Smögen today is a delightful holiday resort with shrimp trawlers and the daily fish auction providing popular entertainment. Commerce is particularly lively along the wooden quayside.

Ferries operate to the island of Hållö, a nature reserve south of Smögen where there is a lighthouse, **Hållö Fyr**, which has guided seafarers since 1842.

The **Sotenkanalen** links Smögen and Hunnebostrand. Built in the 1930s, the canal is 6 km (4 miles) long and a popular tourist route. **Hunnebostrand** is a typical west coast holiday destination and home to Svenska Hummerakademien (the Swedish Lobster Academy). The village's development was based on stonemasonry.

Wooden houses lining the quays of Smögen's well-protected harbour

Uddevalla ❾

Bohuslän. E6, road 44. 🏛 *36,000.*
🚉 🚌 ☒ *Trollhättan.*
ℹ️ *Kungstorget, 0522-997 20.*
🎭 *Motocross World Championships
(first weekend in Jul), West Coast
Dance Festival (mid-Jul), Fjord Festival
(last weekend in Jul).*
ⓦ *www.uddevallaforum.se*

THE TOWN OF Uddevalla was famous for shipbuilding on a grand scale until the 1970s when an economic crisis forced the closure of its shipyard. Uddevalla's history dates from 1496 when it gained its town charter. Its strategic location helped trade to flourish, but also left it open to attack. It became Swedish in the Peace of Roskilde in 1658, as the statues of Karl X Gustav and Erik Dahlbergh in front of the town hall testify.

Among the town's attractions, the collections at **Bohusläns Museum** focus on the cultural and natural heritage of the region. The museum is by the harbour, near **Konstgalleriet**, a gallery for contemporary art. **Sveriges Sjömanshusmuseum** concentrates on the history of seafaring. **Bohusläns Försvarsmuseum** (Defence Museum) has a soldier's cottage among its exhibits.

ENVIRONS: For nature lovers the unusual shellbanks and museum devoted to them, **Skalbanksmuseet**, are not to be missed. The museum is in Kuröd, outside Uddevalla.

The old church of **Bokenäs** is originally from the 12th century. The tower and the church's restored ceiling paintings date from the 18th century. The church is on

Ornate carving on the façade of Restaurang Havsbadet, Lysekil

road 161, 23 km (14 miles) west of Uddevalla.

🏛 **Bohusläns Museum**
Museigatan 1. 📞 *0522-65 65 00.*
🕐 *Jun–Aug: daily; Sep–May: Sat & Sun.* 🎫 *by arrangement.* 🚻 🍴 ♿

🏛 **Skalbanksmuseet**
5 km (3 miles) E of Uddevalla. 📞 *0522-997 20.* 🕐 *Jun–Aug: daily; May & Sep: Sat & Sun.* ♿

Lysekil ❿

Bohuslän. E6/road 162. 🏛 *7,300.*
🚉 *to Uddevalla, then bus.* 🚌 🚢 *from Fiskebäckskil.* ℹ️ *Södra Hamngatan 6, 0523-130 50.* 🎭 *Hot Bulb Engine Festival (3rd weekend in Jul).*
ⓦ *www.lysekil.se*

WHEN LYSEKIL gained its town charter in 1903 the town was already an established seaside resort. Buildings in the old part of Lysekil, Gamlestan, are more than 200 years old. A walk along Strandgatan reveals the charm of this old quarter.

The 19th-century sea-bathing area has been beautifully restored. There is a cold bath house, Oscars Festsal, and the Nordic-style Curmanska Villas. The rest of the town is dominated by the large, Neo-Gothic granite church dating from 1901.

Lysekil lies at the far end of the Stångenäset peninsula, with Gullmarsfjorden – Sweden's only real "fjord" in a Norwegian sense – to the south and Brofjorden to the north, and here the sea has always played a major role. The

town's aquarium, **Havets Hus**, is devoted to the marine and plant life found off the Bohuslän coast. Around 100 different species of fish can be viewed in their natural habitats. There is a walk-through aquarium and a multi-media centre. The town's fishing traditions can also be experienced at the Hot Bulb Engine Festival.

🏛 **Havets Hus**
Strandvägen 9. 📞 *0523-196 71.*
🕐 *Feb–Sep: daily.*
🎫 ♿

Bassholmen ⓫

Bohuslän. Road 161 towards Fiskebäckskil. 🚌 *to Källeviken, then 2 km (1 mile) walk and boat.* 🚢 *from Uddevalla Tue–Sat.* 🏛 ℹ️ *Uddevalla Tourist Office, 0522-997 20.*
Youth Hostel 📞 *0522-65 13 08.*

THE NATURE RESERVE on the island of Bassholmen, between Orust and Skaftö, is one of the highlights of the Bohuslän archipelago. The landscape is one of narrow valleys, leafy meadows and pine forest, with grazing horses and sheep. It is a particularly attractive area for walking. In the centre of the island an old farm stands amid parkland and trees. The former farm building, with its many courtyards, is now a youth hostel.

Bassholmen is also home to a number of traditional shipbuilder's yards, which come under the care of the Föreningen Allmoge Båtar, a society which works to preserve and renovate the traditional wooden boats of

Bohusläns Museum in Uddevalla with a display of old working boats

Bohuslän. Many of these boats can be seen in the museum.

Every summer boating enthusiasts converge on the island for a nostalgic feast to study the craftsmanship involved in greater detail and experience the life of a boatman at the end of the 19th century.

There is a guest jetty in the former shipyard for visiting craft. In summer boats run to Bassholmen from Uddevalla.

Grundsund harbour, edged with original fishermen's huts

Fiskebäckskil, a summer paradise on Skaftö in Gullmarsfjorden

Skaftö ⑫

Bohuslän. Road 161 towards Fiskebäckskil. 🚌 from Uddevalla. ℹ *Lysekil Tourist Office, 0523-130 50.*

THE BEST WAY TO see the island of Skaftö is to walk or cycle around it. The scenery varies between fertile agricultural land, pine forests and bare hills. Skaftö's potatoes and strawberries are justifiably famous. In the centre of the island is Gunnesbo, a favourite spot for children where pony rides and a mini-zoo can be found.

In the far south on the slopes running down towards the sea lies **Rågårdsvik**, a small community overlooking the wide Ellösefjorden and the village of Ellöse, site of the internationally successful Hallberg Rassy shipyard. Rågårdsvik Pensionat provides excellent west-coast cuisine.

Between Skaftölandet and Orust are the winding, narrow Malö straits, made famous by the songs of troubadour Evert Taube, while the beautiful Snäckedjupet separates Skaftö

from the mainland. **Fiskebäckskil** in Gullmarsfjorden is a seafaring community established at the end of the 19th century, featuring a captain's house, richly decorated wooden cottages and romantic gardens. It is also the site of Kristineberg Marine Research Station.

The village of **Grundsund** dates from the 17th century. A canal runs through it past the closely packed red fishermen's huts on the lively quayside, so typical of the west coast. The small wooden church, built in 1799, is well worth a look. Delicious fresh seafood is served in the harbourside inn.

Weathervane, Fiskebäckskil

Gullholmen ⑬

Bohuslän. 🚶 150. 🚌 from Tuvesvik, Orust. ℹ *Henåns Tourist Office, 0304-311 40.* 🌐 *www.bastkusten.se*

DATING FROM 1585, Gullholmen is one of the oldest fishing communities in Bohuslän. In the mid-19th century one of Sweden's early canning factories was set up here. Line fishing on the Dogger Bank in the North Sea

produced good catches and in 1910 Gullholmen had a fishing fleet of more than 50 cutters. As the fishing industry declined, so did the population and summer residents have taken over many of the houses. Gullholmen is a typical west-coast summer paradise.

Sights include the church, inaugurated in 1799, and the pilot's lookout which was dismantled in 1916, but is now being rebuilt. **Skepparhuset**, a late 19th-century captain's home with original interiors, is well worth a look. South of Gullholmen, as if thrown out to sea, lies the completely barren **Käringön**. The island is so bare that in the past earth for its small churchyard had to be transported from Orust. The charming tightly-packed houses are almost entirely used by summer visitors and in the season the popular guest harbour is bursting with life. A fishing cottage houses a small museum. The island can be reached by boat from Hällevikstrand on Orust.

🏛 **Skepparhuset**
📞 *0304-570 70.* ⏰ *3rd week of Jun–first week of Aug: Tue & Sun. Other times by arrangement.*

Sailing past the picturesque houses of Gullholmen

Mollösund, a typical fishing village on Orust

Orust ⑭

Bohuslän. 🏘 15,100. 🚍 from Stenungsund. 🚏 Henån Tourist Office, Strandvägen 3, 0304-311 40. 🎫 Taube Festival on Flatön (mid-Jul), Boatyard open days (last weekend in Aug). 🖳 www.bastkusten.se

O NE OF SWEDEN'S largest islands, Orust's fortunes over the centuries have been tied to the rise and fall of herring fishing. On the southwest coast, the village of **Mollösund** dates from the 16th century when herring fishing was at its height. A decline in stocks brought poverty, but with the herring's reappearance in the 1750s the population increased, inns opened and refineries for making train oil from herring developed. The bare rocks of Bohuslän are a reminder of this time; the train oil refineries needed lots of wood and the coastline was practically deforested.

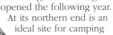

Fishing net float

Most homes had a fisherman's hut on the harbour and even today the houses and huts are closely packed together. There is a strong smell of stockfish hanging out to dry to produce *Lutfisk* for the Swedish Christmas table.

Today Orust is a centre for the manufacture of superior leisure boats. Half the boats exported from Sweden come from here. The boatyards display their craft in the "Öppna Varv" open days.

Tjörn ⑮

Bohuslän. 🏘 15,000. 🚍 from Stenungsund. 🚏 Skärhamn Tourist Office, 0304-67 10 40. 🎫 Round Tjörn Yacht Race (3rd Sat in Aug). 🖳 www.bastkusten.se

T HE MUNICIPALITY of Tjörn comprises six inhabited islands. Fishing, boat-building and small businesses are the cornerstones of the economy and in summer the population doubles with the arrival of holidaymakers.

Opened in 1960, the **Tjörn Bridges** offer fantastic views over land and water. Tjörnbroleden, the road linking the islands of Tjörn and Orust to the mainland at Stenungsund, crosses the bridges of Stenungsöbron, Källosundsbron and Tjörnbron over Askeröfjorden. In 1980 Tjörnbron collapsed when a ship collided with it in thick fog; a new bridge opened the following year. At its northern end is an ideal site for camping with great views.

Skärhamn, on the west side of Tjörn, is the island's main town. It has a guest harbour, restaurants and hotel. Sights include **Sjöfarts-museum** (the Seafaring Museum), Smedja Volund smithy and the popular **Nordiska Akvarellmuseet** (Nordic Watercolour Museum), a stunning building

Tjörn Bridge, 664 m (726 yd) long, and 45 m (147 ft) high

hosting exhibitions and courses for amateur painters.

Pilane Gravfält, a burial site with more than 100 Iron Age mounds, stone circles, rings and standing stones, is on northwest Tjörn. Take the road towards Kyrkesund, turn left to Hällene and after 1 km (half a mile) there is a car park.

🏛 **Nordiska Akvarellmuseet**
Skärhamn. Södra Hamnen. 📞 0304-60 00 80. 🕐 Jun–Sep: daily; Oct–Apr: Tue–Sun. ● some public holidays. 🎫
🖳 🍴 🛍 🚻

The Watercolour Museum, Tjörn, resting on piles in the water

Marstrand ⑯

Bohuslän. Road 168. 🏘 1,400. 🚍 🚢 ⛴ 🚏 Hamngatan, 0303-600 87. 🎫 Fortress Re-enactments, Swedish Match Cup (2nd week in Jul), Marstrand Regatta (4th week in Jul). 🖳 www. kungalv.se

S UN, SAILING and the smell of the sea are what Marstrand is all about. The little town of pastel-coloured wooden houses has its roots in the herring boom of the mid-16th century, which attracted fortune-hunters. But it really took off in the mid-19th century as a fashionable seaside resort. Marstrand built its baths and society arrived.

The town is crowned by the impressive **Carlstens Fästning**, a fortress built in 1666–73 and redesigned in the 1680s by architect Erik Dahlbergh. At one time it was a notorious prison. Tours provide a glimpse into the life and times of the fortress and its inmates in the 18th century. Plays are staged here and feasts held during the summer.

Northwards into the wide waters of Marstrandsfjorden is the rocky island of **Åstol,** almost entirely covered by

characteristic white houses and fishing huts. The island can be reached by a 10-minute ferry ride from Rönnäng on Tjörn.

🍴 Carlstens Fästning
[0303-602 65. ◯ daily. 📷 🎫 🅿
🚹 partly.

Kungälv ⑰

Bohuslän. E6. 🏠 20,500. 🚂 to Ytterby then bus. 🚌 🛥 Landvetter.
🏨 Ytterbyvägen 2, 0303-23 92 00.
📷 Medieval Festival (mid-Jul).
🌐 www. kungalv.se

STRATEGICALLY located between the Nordre Älv and Göta Älv rivers, Kungälv occupies the site of the 10th-century Viking settlement of Kongahälla. It is dominated by the ruins of **Bohus Fästning**, a fortress built by the Norwegian King Håkon Magnusson in 1308. Constructed first in wood and later in stone, the fortress was at the frontline in the constant wars between Sweden, Norway and Denmark. At the Peace of Roskilde in 1658 it became Swedish, but it went on to be besieged no less than 14 times without being captured.

In 1678, 900 Swedish defenders faced 9,000 Norwegians and 7,000 German mercenaries, but still the castle didn't fall. In the 18th century it became a prison and in 1789 all the towers were destroyed apart from the main one known as "Fars Hatt" (Father's Hat).

Kungälv church, situated in the market square, dates from 1679.

🍴 Bohus Fästning
[0303-23 92 00. ◯ May–Sep: daily. ⬤ Midsummer's Eve. 📷
🎫 by arrangement.

Bohus Fästning, the impregnable 14th-century fortress at Kungälv

Vänersborg ⑱

Västergötland. Road 45. 🏠 4,700.
🚂 🚌 ✕ 🏨 Railway Station, 0521-27 14 00. 📷 Rockadfestival (end Jul). Christmas market (Dec).
🌐 www.vanersborg.se

IN THE SOUTHERNMOST bay of Lake Vänern lies Vänersborg, otherwise known as "Little Paris" after the poems of Birger Sjöberg (1885–1929). A statue of the local poet's muse, Frida, can be seen in the beautiful Skräckleparken on the lake shore, and a reconstruction of his home is in **Vänersborgs Museum**.. Other museums focus on medical history, dolls and sport.

The town was founded in 1644 and its Neo-Classical church completed in 1784.

ENVIRONS: Just over 5 km (3 miles) east of the town, the steeply-sided hills of Halleberg and Hunneberg rise up over the landscape. The hillside forests are a nature reserve featuring a large elk population, which is the focus of an annual royal hunt.

On top of Hunneberg is **Kungajaktmuseet Älgens Berg** where the "king of the forest" is presented in interactive displays. The intricacies of elk hunting are explained and visitors can try their hand at shooting an elk themselves, virtually of course.

🏛 Vänersborgs Museum
[0521-26 41 00. ◯ May–Aug: daily; other times: Mon–Fri. 🅿 🚹
🏛 Kungajaktmuseet Älgens Berg
Hunneberg. On road 44.
[0521-27 79 91. ◯ Jun–Sep: daily; other times: Tue–Sun.
⬤ eves of public holidays. 📷
🎫 by appointment. 🅿 🖥 🍴 🚹

Staircase of locks on the Troll-hättan Canal, rising 32 m (105 ft)

Trollhättan ⑲

Västergötland. Road 45. 🏠 44,000.
🚂 🚌 ✕ 🛥 🏨 Innovatum, Åkersjö-vägen 10, 0520-48 84 72.
📷 Fallens Dagar (3rd weekend in Jul).
🌐 www.trollhattan.se

THE OPENING of the Trollhättan Canal in 1800, linking Lake Vänern and the North Sea, marked the birth of Trollhättan as an industrial town. Today, Trollhättan successfully combines high-tech industries such as SAAB and Volvo Aero with a burgeoning film industry that has earned the town its local nickname, "Trollywood".

The town's main sight is the waterfall area where four locks regulate the once wild 32-m (105-ft) high falls. In summer the sluices are opened several times a week to let the mass of water rush freely down river.

The technology centre **Innovatum Kunskapens Hus** (IKH) features multi-media exhibits on the history and development of Troll-hättan. From the centre, a cable car transports visitors 30 m (98 ft) above the canal to the opposite bank. A short walk leads to the Canal Museum.

🏛 Innovatum (IKH)
Åkersjövägen 10. **[** 0520-48 84 80.
◯ mid-Jun–mid-Aug: daily; other times Tue–Sun.
📷 🅿 🖥 🍴 🚹

Lidköping ⓴

Västergötland. Road 44. 🏠 24,500.
☒ 🚌 🚊 🛈 *Stationshuset, Bangatan
3, 0510-77 05 00.* 🎭 *Arnspelen
Pageant (2nd & 3rd weeks in Jul),
GladJazz Festival (4th weekend in Jul).*
🖥 www.lidkoping.se

THE TOWN OF Lidköping lies
at the heart of the area of
Västergötland that is considered to be the cradle of the
Svea Kingdom. Like so many
of Sweden's wooden towns,
Lidköping suffered a devastating fire in 1849, though
some of the 17th-century
buildings around the square
of Limtorget survived.

The Lidan river divides the
town into old and new, and
the two main squares (1446
and 1671 respectively) face
each other across the water.
Nya Stadens Torg (New Town
Square) is the site of a former
hunting lodge, which the
founder of the new town,
Magnus Gabriel de la Gardie,
brought here to serve as a
town hall.

Lidköping is known for the
Rörstrands Porcelain Factory
and **Rörstrands Museum**
attracts visitors in search of
bargain dinner services or
simply to enjoy the show-
pieces in the museum.
Vänermuseet with the
Paleo Geology Centre is an
interactive science museum.

Läckö Slott, a splendid castle on the shore of Lake Vänern

ENVIRONS: Husaby, 10 km (6
miles) east of Lidköping,
encapsulates Swedish history.
It was here at Husaby well
that King Olof Skötkonung
was baptised by the English
monk Sigfrid in 1008. A 12th-
century church now stands at
the site. **Gösslunda Kyrka**,
just west of the town, also
dates from the 12th century.
Outside is a rune stone that
was originally part of the
church wall.

Jan Guillou's popular novels
about the fictional knight Arn
have attracted unexpected
attention to the Lidköping
region. Guided coach tours
are organised in summer.

🏛 **Rörstrands Museum**
Fabriksgatan 4. 📞 *0510-823 48.*
◯ *daily.* ● *some public holidays.*
🚻 🖳 🍴
🏛 **Vänermuseet**
10 min walk from the centre. 📞 *0510-
77 00 65.* ◯ *Jun–Aug: daily; Sep–May:
Tue–Sun.* ● *some public holidays.*
🚶 *by arrangement.* 🖼 🖳 🍴 🚻

Läckö Slott ㉑

Västergötland. 20 km (12 miles) N of
Lidköping. 🚌 *from Lidköping.*
📞 *0510-103 20.* ◯ *May–Sep:
11am–6pm daily.* 🖼 🚶 🖳 🚻 ⛪
🎭 *Medieval Market 3rd week in Jun.*
🖥 www.lackoslott.se

JAKOB DE LA GARDIE was the
first to make his mark on
Läckö Slott after it was
assigned to him in 1615. In
2001 Läckö was named the
most beautiful castle in

Sweden. It is surrounded by
water on three sides. Originally built in the 13th century
by Bishop Brynolf Algotsson,
it became the seat of the
bishops of Skara. Count Jakob
and his son, Magnus de la
Gardie, embarked on
remodelling the castle in the
17th century. But in 1681
Läckö was claimed by Karl XI
in his recovery of crown
lands from the nobility and its
contents were scattered.

Restoration work in the
20th century has revealed
more than 200 rooms,
including the richly decorated
apartment of Princess Marie
Euphrosyne, wife of Marcus
de la Gardie, and the King's
Hall with its paintings of the
Thirty Years' War.

Läckö is the setting for art
exhibitions and summer
opera performances are held
in the courtyard. The garden
is also open to the public.

Kinnekulle ㉒

Västergötland. Road 44. 🛈 *Götene-
Lidköping Tourist Office, Bangatan 3,
Lidköping, 0510-77 05 00.*

THE 306-M (1,000-ft) high
plateau of Kinnekulle,
known as "the flowering
mountain", rises from the
Västergötland landscape,
providing habitats for wild
flowers, deciduous woods,
pine forests, meadows and
pastures. It is topped with bare
limestone and a 20-m (66-ft)
high lookout tower. Those not

Rörstrand ceramic stove, now in
the porcelain factory museum

◁ Sailing boats mooring for the night at Marstrand in Bohuslän

up to the climb can enjoy the views from the restaurant at Högkullen. Limestone has been quarried here since the 12th century. In summer demonstrations at the remaining quarry show how the work used to be carried out.

The area is peppered with ancient Stone Age and Bronze Age sites.

Forshems Kyrka, just to the east, dates from the 12th century and is known for its stone reliefs. The churchyard of the 12th-century church at **Kinne-Vedum,** 2 km (1 mile) north of Götene, has several lily stones, typical of this area.

Mariestad ㉓

Västergötland. E20. 🎯 15,000. 🚐
🚐 ✕ Lidköping. 🚢 🛈 Hamnplan,
0501-100 01. 🏊 Göta Canal Swim
(4th week in Jul).
🌐 www.vastsverige.com

DUKE KARL founded the pretty town of Mariestad in 1583, naming it after his wife, Maria of Pfalz. He built the cathedral and lavishly decorated it in the Baroque style. It is well worth exploring the interesting little streets surrounding the cathedral, lined with buildings from the 18th and 19th centuries.

In 1660 Mariestad became the county town of Skaraborg. The former royal manor of Marieholm, on an island where the River Tidan flows into Lake Vänern, was the governor's residence. It now houses **Vadsmo Museum** and **Mariestads Industrimuseum** (Industrial Museum).

Mariestad's location on Lake Vänern and the River Tidan makes it an idyllic summer town. The Göta Canal *(see pp146–7)* runs through it and

Kanalmuseet (the Canal Museum) is located in Sjötorp just north of the town.

Those keen on rural life should head for **Klockarbolet** in Odensåker, a reconstructed village dating from the 17th and 18th centuries.

🏛 Vadsbo Museum and Mariestads Industrimuseum
Marieholm. 🎯 0501-632 14.
◯ Sep–May: Sat & Sun; Jun–Aug:
Tue–Sun. 🏠 🗟 🖾 🛈 🖾 🕭
🏛 Kanalmuseet
Sjötorp, off road Rv 26. 🎯 0501-512
01. ◯ Mid-Jun–mid-Aug: daily. 🗟

Tivedens National Park ㉔

Västergötland. Road 49. 🚐 from
Karlsborg. 🛈 Karlsborgs Tourist
Office, 0505-173 50.

ON THE BORDER between Närke and Västergötland lies Tiveden national park, an untouched area of rugged wilderness. It was established in 1983 to protect the remaining primeval forest and lakes, of which Fagertärn is the original habitat of the large red water-lily *(see p17)*.

The area is very hilly and demanding for walkers. There is a visitor centre at Stenkälla with information on trails, parking and things to see inside the park.

Giant Ice Age boulders, some up to 10 m (33 ft) high, litter the forest around **Trollkyrka,** the hill east of the road by the visitor centre. The mountain's name is thought to be derived from the fact that the site was used by local people who came here to worship after the ban in 1726 on holding religious services outside churches.

Karlsborgs Fästning, a 19th-century wartime hideaway

Karlsborg ㉕

Västergötland. Road 49. 🎯 4,700.
🚐 🚐 🚢 🛈 Karlsborgs Tourist
Office, Ankarvägen 2, 0505-173 50.
Fortress ◯ mid-May–Aug: 10am–5pm
daily; other times 10am–3pm Mon–
Fri. 🏠 🗟 Eng by appointment 🚐

IN 1819 KING Karl XIV Johan decided that a fortress should be built at Vanäs on the shore of Lake Vättern. It was named Karlsborg and was to act as an emergency capital in the event of war; a place of safety for the royal family, the national bank and the government. The 90 years it took to build meant that by the time it was finally finished the fortress was out of date and it never had any real significance. Today, however, it is a major tourist attraction. The "town" enclosed within the 3-km (2-mile) long walls is best viewed on one of the guided tours that run daily in the summer. Action fans can watch *Fästningsäventyret,* an adventure depicting life in the fortress in the 1860s complete with stunt men and special effects.

Outside the fortress, the Göta Canal wends its way towards Lake Vänern, passing **Forsviks Bruk,** which offers an interesting glimpse into Sweden's industrial heritage, with a blacksmith's forge, sawmill and working flour mill.

🏛 Forsviks Bruk
8 km (5 miles) north of the centre.
🎯 Karlsborgs Tourist Office, 0505-
173 50. ◯ Jun–Aug: daily. 🗟

Marieholm, the former governor's residence in Mariestad

Hjo's wooden buildings, awarded the Europa Nostra medal in 1990

Hjo 26

Västergötland. Road 193/194.
🏃 6,000. 🚌 to Skövde then bus.
⛴ 🛈 Floragatan 1, 0503-352 55.
🎪 Craft Fair (2nd weekend in Jul),
Round Vättern cycle race (3rd
weekend in Jun). ⊡ www.hjo.se

MENTION HJO and Swedes
immediately think of the
exquisite little wooden
houses dating from the end of
the 19th century with their
ornately carved verandas. Hjo
is a delightful town to visit.
On the shore of Lake Vättern
is Stadsparken, a park created
when Hjo Spa was founded
in the late 19th century. Villa
Svea, one of the former spa
buildings in the park, houses
Hjo Stadsmuseum (the
Town Museum). It is worth a
look for its remarkable
calendar clock *Hjouret*, and
recreated rooms from the
heyday of the spa. The park
also contains Fjärilsmuseum
(the Butterfly Museum) and
Vätternakvarium, an aquarium.
   Just like the town, the
harbour has medieval origins,
but the present one was built
in the mid-19th century after
the construction of the Göta
Canal. In summer, the *Lok-
Hjo-Motivet* train takes guided
tours (daily except Monday)
through the town starting from
the harbour. The steamer *S/S
Trafik* (1892) runs Sunday
tours to Visingö, and jazz
cruises to Vadstena across
the lake.
   The Hjoån river valley,
stretching from Lake Vättern
to Mullsjön lake 4 km (2.5
miles) west of Hjo has several
spectacular waterfalls.

🏛 **Hjo Stadsmuseum**
Villa Svea, Stadsparken. 📞 0503-351
15. ◯ May–Aug. ♿ partly.

Skövde 27

Västergötland. Road 48/49.
🏃 32,500 🚌 🚇 🛈 Sandtorget,
0500-44 66 88. 🎪 Food Festival (last
weekend in Aug), Skövde Film Festival
(mid-Oct).

THE MODERN industrial town
of Skövde celebrated its
600th anniversary in 2001.
Skövde has been destroyed
by fire several times, but after
a devastating fire in 1715 little
remained other than a single
17th-century house,
Helénsgården. Today the
house is part of Skövde
Stadsmuseum (the Town
Museum), along with Gamla
Rådhuset (the Old Town Hall),
1776, and the neighbouring
Gamla Kanslihuset (the Old
Government Building), 1915.
The museum also holds exhibitions in Hertig Johans Torg.
   Kulturhuset, designed by
Hans-Erland Heineman in
1964, houses the
library, art museum
and an art gallery
exhibiting Swedish
modern art. The
library contains Siri
Derkert's relief *The
Mustard Tree*. In the
square in front of
Kulturhuset are the
sculptures *Monument
of an Axeman* by Eric
Grate (1965) and *La
Mano* by Liss Eriksson.
The latter was raised
in 1986 in memory of
murdered Prime
Minister Olof Palme.

ENVIRONS: Rising to
the west of Skövde is
the 300-m (984-ft)
high **Billingen**
plateau, with views
stretching as far as
Lake Vättern. The area

is a popular recreation spot
with hiking trails, holiday
cottages and campsites. The
exclusive Billingehus Hotel
contains a sports museum.
   West of Skövde, on road 49,
is the 12th-century church
Våmbs Kyrka. The church
was restored to its original
appearance in the 1940s. On
the same road, slightly nearer
to Skövde, is **Varnhems
Klosterkyrka**, a 13th-century
three-aisle basilica.

🏛 **Helénsgården**
Helénsparken. 📞 0500-49 80 69.
◯ summer. 🎫 📷 by arrangement.
🏛 **Kulturhuset**
Trädgårdsgatan. 📞 0500-49 85 60.
Konsthallen & Konstmuseet ◯ Sep–
May: Tue–Sun; Jun–Aug: Tue–Sat.
● eves of public holidays. 🖥 🔧

Skara 28

Västergötland. E20. 🏃 10,700. 🚌
🚇 🛈 Bladska Huset, Skolgatan 1,
0511-32580. 🎪 Naturum Crane
Dance (end Mar–Apr).

TRADITIONALLY an important
seat of learning and a
bishopric, Skara is one of
Sweden's oldest towns. The
11th-century cathedral lies at
its heart, surrounded by a
network of streets following a
pattern set out in the Middle
Ages. On Stora Torget stands
Krönikebrunnen, a well which

The nave of Skara's Gothic cathedral,
founded in the 12th century

on its exterior chronicles important events in the history of Skara and of Sweden. **Stadsparken** is the site of Västergötlands Museum with its local history collection, and Fornbyn, an open-air museum complete with cottages and animals showing how people lived in the past.

ENVIRONS: Axvall, 10 km (6 miles) from Skara on road 49, is the location for the children's favourite spot, **Skara Sommarland**, a large amusement park with a water park, campsite and holiday cottages.

Around 20 km (12 miles) east of Skara, Lake **Hornborgasjön** is a popular resting place for birds, especially dancing cranes in April–May. There is an observation tower and two information centres.

🛶 **Skara Sommarland**
Axvall, road 49 towards Skövde.
📞 *0511-70 300.* 🕐 *29 May–22 Aug.* 📷

🦌 **Hornborgasjön**
Naturum Hornborgasjön, road 189.
📞 *0515-72 70 63.* 🕐 *daily in season.*

Falköping ㉙

Västergötland. Road 46. 🚶 *15,400.*
🚉 ℹ️ *Odengatan 24, 0515-77 70 50.* 🌐 *www.falkoping.nu*

BETWEEN THE HILLS of Mösseberget and Ålleberg lies the old town of Falköping. Of particular interest are the 12th-century church, St Olofs Kyrka, the medieval wooden houses and the town square, Stora Torget, with Ivar Tengbom's statue *Venus Rising from the Waves* (1931). **Falbygdens Museum** describes the local history.

ENVIRONS: **Ekornavallen**, 15 km (9 miles) north of Falköping, is an important historic burial site from the Stone, Iron and Bronze Ages.

Dalénmuseet in Stenstorp uses sound-and-light shows to illustrate the life and work of the 1912 Nobel laureate Gustaf Dalén, an innovator in the field of lighting technology and inventor of the AGA oven.

Gökhems Kyrka, west of the town, is a small Romanesque apse church without a tower. It dates from the early 12th century. Inside, limestone paintings depict *The Creation*.

Gudhems Klosterruin and **Klostermuseum** north of the town are the ruins of a convent founded in 1160. Today it is a museum. **Karleby**, to the east, is one of three villages along a road which probably existed in the Stone Age. Each farm had its burial site and there are 13 passage tumuli here, including one with a burial chamber 17 m (56 ft) long.

🏛 **Falbygdens Museum**
St Olofsgatan 23. 📞 *0515-850 50.*
🕐 *Tue–Fri & Sun.* 🌑 *some public holidays.*

🏛 **Dalénmuseet**
Stenstorp, 10 km (6 miles) N of centre.
📞 *0500-45 71 65.* 🕐 *Mar–Sep: Tue–Sun, Jul also Mon; Oct–Nov: Sat & Sun* 🌑 *Dec–Feb, Midsummer Eve.* 📷

Alingsås ㉚

Västergötland. E20. 🚶 *25,000.*
🚉 🚉 *Stora Torget 1, 0322-61 62 00.*
🎉 *Potato Festival (3rd weekend in Jun); Ljus i Alingsås (Oct).*
🌐 *www.alingsas.se*

JONAS ALSTRÖMER and the textile industry have, between them, left their mark on Alingsås. In the early 18th century, Ahlströmer founded his textile factory and on the proceeds he built **Nolhaga Slott**, a manor which today

Skulls of Stone Age inhabitants from the Falköping area in Falbygdens Museum

has a zoo and bird park. **Alingsås Museum** is housed in the 1730s Ahlströmerska Magazinet. The newly opened **Alingsås Kulturhus** contains an art gallery and library.

ENVIRONS: **Gräfsnäs Slottsruin and Park** is a ruined castle and park on Lake Anten, 20 km (12 miles) north of Alingsås. An exhibition describes its history. On the road towards Gothenburg lies **Nääs Slott**, a 17th-century castle with an impressive 19th-century interior. Here, the handicraft tradition of western Sweden is cultivated through events and exhibitions. The Midsummer celebrations here are fantastic.

🏛 **Alingsås Museum**
Lilla Torget 1. 📞 *0322-61 65 96.*
🕐 *Tue–Sat.*

🏛 **Alingsås Kulturhus**
Sa Ringgtan 3. 📞 *0322-61 65 98.*
🕐 *Wed–Mon.* 🌑 *some public holidays.* ♿

🏰 **Nääs Slott**
Floda, E20, 30 km (19 miles) N of Gothenburg. 📞 *0302-318 39.*
🕐 *May–mid-Jun: Sat, Sun & public holidays; mid-Jun–mid-Aug: daily; mid-Aug–Sep: Sat, Sun & public holidays.* 📷📷📷

Nolhaga Slott, home of the textile magnate Jonas Ahlströmer, 1727

Ulricehamn Town Hall, 1799, housing the town's tourist office

Ulricehamn ③

Västergötland. Road 40. 👥 9,100.
🚇 🏢 🛈 Rådhuset, 0321-271 75.
🎪 Kärringrallyt (all year round: Thu).
[W] www.ulricehamnsturistbyra.se

THE TOWN OF Ulricehamn occupies a beautiful setting on Lake Åsunden in an area rich in historic monuments. Originally known as Bogesund, there has been a settlement here since the 14th century. The old coaching road across Västergötland to Halland ran through the town along Storgatan. The local history museum, Ulricehamns Museum, is located in an 1868 schoolhouse, while **Ulricehamns Konst- och Östasiatiska Museum**, with its fine collection of Chinese ceramics, is in the old railway station.

Textile enterprises dominate the local economy and in Gällstad the knitwear factories south of the town open their gates to bargain hunters every Thursday afternoon for what is known as *Kärringrallyt* (the "old women's race").

ENVIRONS: Bystad, a farmstead 30 km (19 miles) south of Ulricehamn, has one of Sweden's oldest animal traps, a pit measuring about 5 m (16 ft) in diameter and more than 3.5 m (11 ft) deep.

Along the road between Ulricehamn and Mullsjö lies **Näs Gård**. The manor's six

historic red-painted buildings date from the 17th, 18th and 19th centuries and now form a regional cultural centre and art gallery. Concerts and other cultural events are held here.
Södra Vings Kyrka is a medieval gem of a church, dating in part from the 12th century. The artistic decoration is unusually lavish and includes 15th-century limestone paintings in the nave. The stately lectern was carved in Rococo style in 1748.

🏛 **Ulricehamns Konst- och Östasiatiska Museum**
Järnvägstorget. [0321-150 90.
◯ Jan–Dec: Sun. 📷 🎥 by arrangement. 🍴 🛗

Torpa Stenhus ③

Västergötland. 26 km (16 miles) N of Borås. 🛈 Borås Tourist Office, 033-35 70 90. ◯ May–mid-Sep: 11am–5pm. 🎥 Eng 11am; eve in Eng: phone Tourist Office in advance. 🛗

Painting of Saturn at Torpa Stenhus

STANDING ON A promontory at the southern end of Lake Åsunden is the medieval castle Torpa Stenhus. It belonged to the Stenbock family and from the 14th–mid-17th century was an important stronghold for defence against the Danes. The evening guided tour includes thrilling ghost stories from the castle's past. Theatre performances, known as *Torpaspelen*, are staged here in summer.

Borås ③

Västergötland. Road 40. 👥 62,000.
🚉 🚇 🏢 🛈 Hallbergsplatsen 1,
033-35 70 90. 🎪 Culture Night (first week in May), Harvest Festival (first week in Sep). [W] www.boras.se.

IN 1620 KING Gustav II Adolf decided that the textile pedlars of the Knallebygden area should have a town of

their own and Borås was founded. Textile factories still line the Viskan river, which winds through the town, although the industry has lost ground in recent years.

Borås is a green town with beautiful parks: Stadsparken in the centre is popular, as is Ramnaparken where the open-air Borås Museum is located. Also in the town centre is **Borås Djurpark**, a zoo with more than 80 species from all corners of the world. Large enclosures and attractive grounds make this zoo a pleasant family park.

ENVIRONS: On the road between Borås and Alingsås lies **Hedareds Kapell**, Sweden's only preserved stave church. Apart from its windows and shingled roof, the little, wooden 16th-century church remains as it was when it was built, complete with original 16th-century paintings.

Textilmuseet (the Textile Museum) is a living museum housed in a late-19th-century spinning shed. The history of the textile industry is brought to life with recreated scenes and art and textile exhibitions.

🦁 **Borås Djurpark**
Boråsparken, bus line 2 from Södra parken. [033-35 32 70. ◯ May–mid-Sep: daily; Oct & Apr: Sat & Sun; school holidays: daily 📷 🛗 🛈
🏛 **Textilmuseet**
Druverforsvägen 8, road 40.
[033-35 89 50. ◯ Tue–Sun.
◯ some public holidays. 📷 🎥 by arrangement. 🛗 🛈

Pink flamingo, one of the many exotic species at Borås Djurpark

Gunnebo Slott ❹

In the 1780s, JOHN HALL, one of the richest men in Sweden at the time, commissioned city architect Carl Wilhelm Carlberg of Gothenburg to design a summer villa and park at Gunnebo. On completion in 1796, Carlberg had created one of the most beautiful and stylistically pure examples of Neo-Classical Swedish architecture. Hall is said to have paid the bill with 38 barrels of gold, but that included everything: the interiors, servants' quarters, orangery, park, kitchen gardens and greenhouse. An adjoining farm made the estate virtually self-sufficient.

VISITORS' CHECKLIST

15 km (9 miles) SE of Gothenburg. E6/E20, then Gunnebogatan. [] 031-334 16 00. **Mansion** [] (tours only) Oct–Apr: Sun & public holidays: noon, 1pm; May–mid-Jun & Sep: Sat, Sun & public hols noon, 1pm, 2pm. [] [] **Garden** [] all year. [] Jun–Sep: Sun & public hols 2pm. [] [] 24, 31 Dec, Midsummer's Eve. [W] www.gunneboslott.se

The Salon
Three magnificent French windows let in the sunlight, which is reflected on the beautiful parquet floor.

Northern Façade
Ionian columns frame the sheltered terrace which opens onto the garden with its neatly clipped trees.

The frieze on the southern gable is made from lead painted to imitate marble.

Oval vestibule

The staircase leads to the park with its parterres and gravel paths.

The entrance is through the cellar, the starting point for tours.

Ceramic Stoves
The interior design, including exquisite ceramic stoves, is by Carlberg who adopted the light Gustavian style which pervades the entire house.

Park and Gardens
The French-inspired formal garden surrounding the house was also designed by Carlberg, as was the English park, which makes an ideal setting for a walk.

Varberg Fästning, a fortress on the shores of the Kattegat housing a local history museum

Kungsbacka 🄌

Halland. E6/E20. 🏃 *17,200*. 🚊 🚌
ℹ️ *Storgatan 41, 0300-83 45 95.* 🎭
*Kungsbacka Chamber Music Festival
(first weekend in Aug).*
🅆 *www.kungsbacka.se*

ALTHOUGH KUNGSBACKA was an important trading centre in the 13th century, almost nothing remains of the old wooden town. All but two of the houses were destroyed in a devastating fire in 1846. The two survivors are the red cottage in Norra Torggatan and the mayor's house at Östergatan 10. The pretty pastel-painted wooden houses that replaced the old at the end of the 19th century can be seen around the square. Today, Kungsbacka is almost a southern suburb of Gothenburg.

ENVIRONS: Around 10 km (6 miles) outside Kungsbacka at Rydet is **Mårtagården**, a typical 18th-century sea captain's house. The house is open to the public in the summer.

Tjolöholms Slott, one of Sweden's more unusual buildings, lies 15 km (9 miles) south of Kungsbacka. This magnificent English Tudor-style mansion was built for a Scottish merchant and completed in 1904. It contained state-of-the-art features such as vacuum cleaners, showers and

Tjolöholms Slott, an eccentric English Tudor-style mansion with Art Nouveau interiors

hot-air heating. The house is surrounded by beautiful parkland and also has a wagon museum.

🚂 Tjolöholms Slott
10 km (6 miles) S of the centre, E6/E20 to Fjärås exit, then road 939. 📞 *0300-83 45 95.* 🕐 *May–Aug: daily; Sep: Sat & Sun; Oct: Sun.* **Park** 🕐 *daily.* 🎫

Varberg 🄍

Halland. E6/E20. 🏃 *25,000*. 🚊 🚌
🚢 *from Grenå.* ℹ️ *Brunnsparken, 0340-887 70.* 🎭 *Wheels & Wings motor exhibition (mid-Jul).*
🅆 *www.turist.varberg.se*

THE COASTAL TOWN of Varberg has, since the 19th century, been famous for its bathing, whether the cold curative baths fashionable of the period or swimming from the rocks and sandy beaches. The town was founded in the 13th century, but little from that time remains after several fires.

The harbour area is worth a look and, in particular, **Kallbadhuset**, the renovated cold bath house in Moorish style with separate sections for men and women. The oriental touch is repeated in **Societetshuset**, built in the 1880s when the town's popularity as a spa was at its height. Today it houses a café, restaurant, pub and disco, playground and mini-golf. On summer evenings concerts are held on the stage in the park.

Guarding the approach from the sea is the mighty Varbergs Fästning. Most of the fortress was built in the 17th century with parts dating from the 13th century. Today it houses a museum,

Länsmuseet Varbergs Fästning, focusing on the history of Halland. The museum's biggest attraction is the 14th-century Bocksten Man whose body was discovered in a bog still dressed in a complete outfit from the Middle Ages. The notorious bullet which killed King Karl XII in 1718 is also on show. An outpost of the museum is Båtmuseet, the boat museum in Galtabäck, 10 km (6 miles) south of Varberg, displaying traditional boats and models.

🏛 Länsmuseet Varbergs Fästning
Varbergs Fästning. 📞 *0340-185 20.*
🕐 *daily.* 🎫 *by arrangement.*

Falkenberg 🄎

Halland. E6/E20. 🏃 *18,600*. 🚊 🚌
ℹ️ *Holgersgatan 11, 0346-88 61 00.*
🎭 *Song festival (first week in Jul).*
🅆 *www.falkenbergsturist.se*

A TOWN WITH medieval roots, Falkenberg stands at the mouth of the River Ätran. The oldest areas of the town still have their wooden buildings, including St Laurentii Kyrka (St Laurence's church), parts of which date from the 14th century.

The pottery **Törngrens Krukmakeri** (1789) is still in operation, run by the seventh generation of potters.
Falkenbergs Museum is housed in a half-timbered granary at Söderbron. The grain dryer is a lofty landmark in the old town. The museum features a faithful reproduction of an apartment from the 1950s and the café has a working jukebox.

Falkenberg has several interesting smaller museums, including **Falkenbergs Hembygdsmuseum** (Rural

Museum) in St Lars Kyrkogata, a rural museum with a section on salmon fishing. The **Fotomuseet Olympia** in Sandgatan is housed in the town's first cinema (1912) and displays cameras and photos.

ENVIRONS: North of the town is **Morups Tånge**, known for its 28-m (91-ft) high granite lighthouse built in the mid-19th century. The beach below is a nature reserve, a wetland area of international interest and a home for waders.

🏺 **Törngrens Krukmakeri**
Krukmakaregatan 4. 📞 0346-103 54
🕐 daily. 🏠 Nygatan 34.
🏛 **Falkenbergs Museum**
Skepparesträtet 2. 📞 0346-88 61 25.
🕐 Sep–May: Tue, Fri & Sun; Jun–Aug: Tue–Sun. 🅿

Fly-fishing in the salmon-rich River Ätran in Falkenberg

Halmstad 🕸

Halland. E6/E20. 🏃 53,500. 🚆 🚌
✈ 🚢 from Grenå. 🚹 Tourist Office, Halmstad Slott, 035-13 23 20.
📅 Street Theatre Festival (Aug).
🌐 www.halmstad.se

A T THE POINT where the River Nissan flows into Laholmsbukten bay lies Halmstad. In the Middle Ages it was the largest town on the west coast. Today, the medieval inner city with its half-timbered architecture is classified as being of national interest. Kirsten Munk's house on Storgatan is an exceptional 17th-century building in greenglazed Dutch brick. Local craftsmen can be seen at work in **Fattighuset**, Lilla Torg, a former poorhouse dated 1859.

Several modern artists have left their mark on the town and Carl Milles' fountain

The former training ship *Najaden* against a backdrop of Halmstad Slott

Europa and the Bull in Stora Torg and Picasso's *Woman's Head*, which stands between the bridges over the river Nissan, are easily encountered on a stroll.

Halmstad Slott, a 17th-century castle, was built by the Danish King Christian IV. The former training ship *Najaden* is moored on the quayside in front of the castle.

Länsmuseet (the County Museum) has a wide collection of art and cultural history, including painted furniture and tapestries.

Tropikcenter in Strandgatan is exciting for children with more than 100 species of tropical animals set in their natural habitats. Another hit for children is **Miniland**, a park with models of famous Swedish buildings on a scale of 1:25 and several kids' play attractions such as a BMX track and motorized lorries.

ENVIRONS: To the north, the popular summer resorts of Tylösand, Haverdal and Frösakull spread out along the coast. **Simlångsdalen**, around 20 km (12 miles) from Halmstad on road 25, has several natural attractions including Danska Fall in the River Assman, a 36-m (118-ft) high waterfall.

🏺 **Fattighuset**
Lilla Torg. 📞 035-21 15
15. 🕐 daily. 🅿
✴ **Tropikcenter**
Strandgatan. 📞 035-12 33
33. 🕐 daily. 🎫 🅿
🏵 **Miniland**
Ga Tylösandsvägen 1. 📞
035-10 84 60. 🕐 May–first
week of Sep: daily. 🎫 🚹

Laholm 🕸

Halland. Road 24. 🏃 5,600. 🚆 🚌
🚹 Rådhuset, Stortorget, 0430-154
50. 📅 Waterfall Day (2nd Sun in Aug), Salmon Festival (3rd Sun in Aug).

H ALLAND'S OLDEST and smallest town, Laholm is primarily associated with the long sandy beaches around the bay of Laholmsbukten. Mellbystrand, on the bay 6 km (4 miles) to the west of the town, throngs with holiday makers in summer. The River Lagan also attracts visitors for the salmon fishing.

Laholm itself is characterized by its winding streets and low houses, reminiscent of Danish rule before 1645. Of the buildings around the square, the 200-year-old **Rådhuset** (Town Hall) is particularly beautiful. Open year round, it houses the Tourist Office, Laholms Teckningsmuseum (the Drawing Museum), a small exhibition on the history of the town and a cell from the time when the building served as a police station. On the western gable there is an automaton symbolizing the meeting in Laholm in 1278 between the Swedish King Magnus Ladulås and Danish King Erik Klipping.

Laholm's tidy rows of houses bearing the hallmarks of the town's Danish past

WESTERN SVEALAND

V ÄRMLAND, NÄRKE AND DALARNA, *with their rich rural heritage, colourful folk costumes, red-painted wooden houses and pastoral scenes, attracted visitors long before the onset of tourism. Stretching from the flatlands of Närke to the mountains of Dalarna, this region is known for its annual ski race and Midsummer festivities, as well as its industrial heritage based on mining and forestry.*

Large expanses of water dominate all three provinces. Southern Värmland encompasses the huge Lake Vänern, which is also the end of the line for the arterial Klarälven river. The beautiful Fryken lakes provided inspiration for one of the province's well-known authors, Selma Lagerlöf *(see p233)*. Her home, Mårbacka, was in this region where so many of her adventures are set. There is plenty of scope for outdoor activities in Värmland, including boating, canoeing, rafting on the Klarälven river and fishing. The forests have exciting trails where walkers are unlucky if they don't see an elk, and on wildlife safaris there is even the chance of glimpsing one of the big four predators – bear, wolf, lynx or wolverine.

Närke, one of Sweden's smallest provinces, is sandwiched between two large lakes, Hjälmaren and Vättern. The centre of the province is dominated by the fertile Närke flatlands, encircled by forest, including the once infamous haunt of bandits, Tiveden, in the south. Örebro, Western Svealand's largest metropolis and Närke's county town, has all the charm of a small town.

Dalarna has the beautiful Siljan lake and the Dalälven river with its arms stretching into the mountains. The province offers more contrasts than most – from the gentle farmland around Siljan to the mountainous north. Every March, these are linked by the Vasaloppet race *(see p245)*, when some 10,000 skiers head from Sälen down to Mora. Midsummer celebrations on Siljan are emblematic of Dalarna. Villages compete to see who has the most stylish maypole, the most accomplished musicians and the best folk dancers.

Rustic interior of Gammelgården in Mora, Dalarna

◁ **Stora Kils church on Nedre Fryken lake, Värmland**

Exploring Western Svealand

FERTILE AGRICULTURAL LAND spreads out around the major lakes, Vänern, Vättern, Hjälmaren and Siljan, and along the river valleys, giving way to a predominantly forested landscape. The region provides ample opportunities for nature lovers, with its abundance of wildlife, and for anglers, who will easily find a good catch. The mountains in Dalarna are the setting for some of the country's most popular ski resorts, walking trails and national parks. Motorists have many attractive small roads to choose from, while the Fryksdalsbanan and Inlandsbanan railway lines guarantee spectacular sights from the train window and leisurely boat trips provide glorious views from the water.

Author and Nobel laureate Selma Lagerlöf's Mårbacka, one of Värmland's many stately homes

GETTING AROUND

Passing through Örebro and Karlstad, the E18 motorway crossing from Stockholm to Oslo is the main artery for traffic to this region. Travelling up into Värmland and Dalarna, the roads follow the river valleys, where the local population is also concentrated. Rail links are good to the southern parts of the provinces, but the northern areas can only be reached by car or bus. Between towns and popular tourist areas the bus services are quite frequent, but they can be patchy in rural areas. In summer, boats ply the major lakes of Vänern, Hjälmaren and Siljan.

KEY

▬	Motorway
▬	Major road
▬	Minor road
▬	Railway line

SEE ALSO

- **Where to Stay** pp287–8
- **Where to Eat** pp301–2

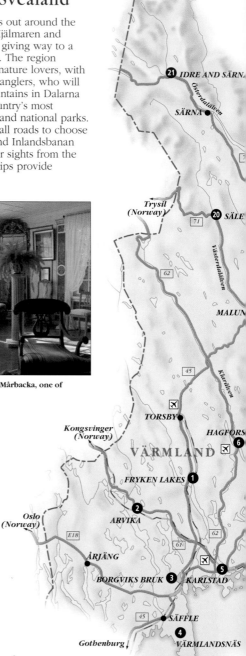

㉑ IDRE AND SÄRN.

Österdalälven

SÄRNA ●

Trysil (Norway)

⑳ SÄLE

71

Västerdalälven

62

MALUN

45

Klarälven

TORSBY ●

Kongsvinger (Norway)

HAGFORS
⑥

VÄRMLAND

FRYKEN LAKES ①

②

Oslo (Norway)

ARVIKA

E18

62

61

ÄRJÄNG

⑤

BORGVIKS BRUK ③   KARLSTAD

45

SÄFFLE

Gothenburg   VÄRMLANDSNÄS ④

VÄNERN

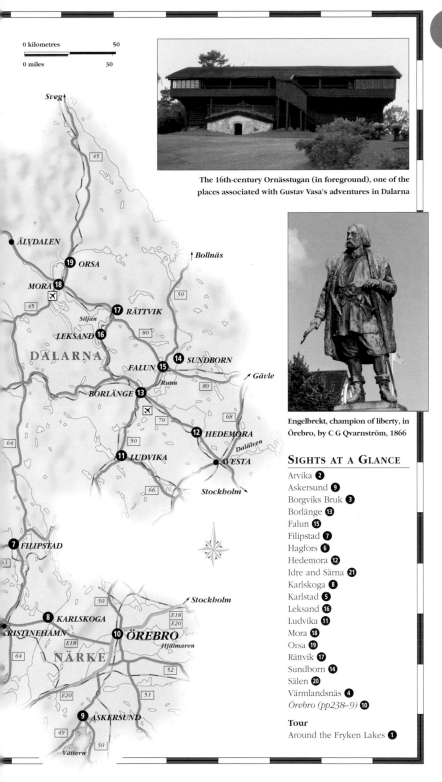

The 16th-century Ornässtugan (in foreground), one of the places associated with Gustav Vasa's adventures in Dalarna

Engelbrekt, champion of liberty, in Örebro, by C G Qvarnström, 1866

SIGHTS AT A GLANCE

Arvika **2**
Askersund **9**
Borgviks Bruk **3**
Borlänge **13**
Falun **15**
Filipstad **7**
Hagfors **6**
Hedemora **12**
Idre and Särna **21**
Karlskoga **8**
Karlstad **5**
Leksand **16**
Ludvika **11**
Mora **18**
Orsa **19**
Rättvik **17**
Sundborn **14**
Sälen **20**
Värmlandsnäs **4**
Örebro (pp238–9) **10**

Tour
Around the Fryken Lakes **1**

A Tour around the Fryken Lakes ❶

Author SELMA LAGERLÖF called the Fryken lakes the "smiling leaves", and it is the natural surroundings, the glittering waters, the flowering meadows and the dark forests on the horizon that strike visitors most. The author's spirit is a constant presence, and no more so than at the Rottneros estate, which is Ekeby in *Gösta Berling's Saga*, and the author's home, Mårbacka, across the water. The best ways to experience the lakes are aboard the vintage steamer *Freja af Fryken*, or by bicycle or car from Sunne, the main centre of the area.

View across Övre Fryken from Tossebergsklätten

Sahlströmska Gården ①
The home of artist siblings Sahlström in Utterbyn features mementoes of some of the early 20th century's most colourful Swedish artists.

Sunne ②
The regional centre of the Fryksdal valley, Sunne is beautifully situated on the water between Övre Fryken and Mellanfryken. Heritage centres and a host of events in summer, including the Fryksdal Dance, reflect the area's rich folk traditions.

Mårbacka ④
Nobel laureate Selma Lagerlöf's home has been kept just as it was on her death in 1940. Exhibitions linked to the author's work are held in the summer.

Rottneros ③
The estate has magnificent gardens and a large sculpture collection. For children, there is Nils Holgersson's Adventure Park.

KEY

▬ Suggested route

= Other roads

— Fryksdalsbanan railway line

S/S Freja av Fryken ⑤
In 1896, the queen of the Fryken lakes capsized; 98 years later she was salvaged from the lake bed and now sails from the port of Kil, powered by her original 1868 engine.

TIPS FOR THE TRIP

Length: 75 km (47 miles) by road.
Stopping-off point: Tosseberg, 20 km (12 miles) north of Sunne on the road to Torsby.
Other routes: train, Kil–Torsby on Fryksdalsbanan, "Sweden's most beautiful railway". Boat trips: S/S Freja av Fryken (tel: 0554-475 90).

0 kilometres   8

0 miles   5

Arvika ②

Värmland. Road 61. 🚂 14,000.
🚊 🚌 ☒ ⛴ ℹ Storgatan 22,
0570-817 90. 🎵 Arvika Festival (mid-
Jul), Harbour Festival (Jun).
ⓦ www.arvika.se

THE PEOPLE OF Värmland are known for their wit and ability to tell funny stories, particularly in Jösse, where Arvika is the main town. It is situated on a hill above the bay of Kyrkviken, which is linked to the lake of Glafs-fjorden by a narrow strait.

Arvika Fordonsmuseum, centrally located next to the fire station, has an exciting collection of veteran vehicles, including hundreds of cars, motorcycles and carriages.

The area has long been home to craftworkers and artists, as can be seen in the **Rackstadmuseet** in Taserud just outside the town. This is where sculptor Christian Eriksson set up his studio, Oppstuhage, in the mid-1890s. For many years it was a magnet for artists attracted by the pristine Värmland country-side, such as the painter Gustaf Fjaestad, renowned for his winter scenes.

Klässbols Linneväveri, 20 km (12 miles) south of Arvika, is the Nordic region's only damask weaving mill and a rewarding destination for those who want to see how the linen tablecloths for the Nobel Prize banquets, or fabric for the Royal Family, are made.

A 1903 Humber in Arvika Fordonsmuseum

🏛 **Arvika Fordonsmuseum**
Thermiavägen 2. 📞 0570-803 90.
⭕ Sep–May: Sat–Sun; Jun–Aug:
daily. Group bookings: by appoint-
ment. 🖵 🏠 🛒 ♿
🏛 **Rackstadmuseet**
Sandgrundsudden. 📞 054-14 31 00.
⭕ Oct–Mar: Thu, Sat, Sun; May
& Sep: Tue–Sun; Jun–Aug: daily;
other times by appointment. 🖵 🏠
🏨 **Klässbols Linneväveri**
Damastvägen 5. 20 km (16 miles) S of
Arvika. 📞 0570-46 01 85. ⭕ Oct–
Apr: Mon–Fri & Sat; May–Sep: daily.
🛒 only pre-booked. 🖵 🏠 ♿

Borgviks Bruk ③

Värmland. 35 km (22 miles) W of
Karlstad. Road 45. 🚂 400. 🅿
Borgvik Byggnadsvård 📞 0555-
743 80, winter: 054-14 31 00.
⭕ Jun–Aug.

THE IRONWORKS IN Borgvik operated from 1600 to 1925. The foundry ruins and works buildings along with the striking manor and 18th-

century church make Borgvik one of the leading monu-ments to a bygone industrial age in Värmland. Near Västra Smedbyn is **von Echstedtska Gården**. This impressive 1760s' Carolian manor is known for its murals. Even the privy has burlesque and, to say the least, educational paintings.

🏨 **von Echstedtska Gården**
Västra Smedbyn. 20 km (12 miles) NW
of Säffle. 📞 0533-630 74. ⭕ Jun–
Aug. 🎵 🛒 only pre-booked. 🖵 🏠

Värmlandsnäs ④

Värmland. 5 km (2 miles) S of Säffle.

JUTTING OUT INTO Lake Vänern is a large peninsula noted for its excellent agricultural land and the medieval churches of **Botilsäter** and **Millesvik**.

From the southernmost tip in Ekenäs it is possible to head out to **Lurö**, Sweden's largest inland archipelago. This is the ideal spot to enjoy countryside well off the beaten track. The boat trip to the main island of Lurö takes an hour.

Perfect bathing spots along the shore at Värmlandsnäs

SELMA LAGERLÖF

In 1909, Selma Lagerlöf (1858–1940) became the first woman to receive the Nobel prize for literature. And despite the passing of a century since she wrote her first masterpiece, interest in the author's captivating adventures continues unabated. Numerous film and TV versions of her works have been produced, including *The Treasure*, *Thy Soul Shall Bear Witness!*, *The Emperor of Portugallia* and *Jerusalem*. When she made her debut in 1891 with the imaginative novel *Gösta Berling's Saga*, she put the Värmland countryside around the Fryken lakes and the family estate of Mårbacka on the literary map. Even more remarkable was the success of *The Wonderful Adventures of Nils*. The tale of the tiny boy's epic journey with wild geese was translated around the world.

Selma Lagerlöf, sculpture by Carl Eldh, Rottneros

The Almen quarter, a heritage centre in Karlstad on the Klarälven river

Karlstad ❺

Värmland. E18. 🏠 57,000. ✈ 🚂
🚌 ℹ Norra Strandgatan, 054-29 84
00. 📷 Harbour Festival (Jul/Aug),
Round Vänern Race (Jul/Aug),
Swedish Rally (1st weekend in Feb).
w www.karlstad.se

THE PHRASE "Sola i Karlsta"
(Enjoy the sun in Karlstad)
has been used to attract visitors
to the Värmland metropolis.
Yet the truth is that this is no
sunnier a place than any other
in the province. It was, in fact,
a jovial hostess at the town's
inn who brought sunshine into
people's lives in the early 19th
century – her statue now
stands outside the Stadshotell.
But Karlstad has plenty of
other attractions. It was built
on the delta formed by the
Klarälven river before it flows
into Lake Vänern, and was a
market town in medieval
times. It received its charter in
1584 along with its name from
the then king, Karl IX.
   Karlstad has been devastated
by fire on many occasions,
most recently in 1865. The
Almen quarter on Västra
Älvgrenen is a heritage centre
comprising traditional wooden
houses which survived the
blaze. Thanks to its large
garden, another survivor was
the bishop's palace, built in
1781. The cathedral was less
fortunate, having to have its
exterior rebuilt along with
its tower. Parts of the early
18th-century interior were
preserved. A well-known
feature of the town is the 12-
arched Östra Bron bridge,
built in 1811. A good insight
into Värmland's history and

folk culture can be gained at
Värmlands Museum down
by the river. The museum also
runs the beautifully situated
Alsters Herrgård, 8 km (5
miles) east of Karlstad, birthplace of poet Gustaf Fröding
in 1860. The manor is a
memorial to him and
other local poets.
   The open-air
museum in **Marie-
bergsskogen** has
several historic
buildings, including a
sauna and smoking
hut built by Finnish
immigrants to the
manor of Marieberg.
In the grounds lies
Värmlands Naturum,
featuring the flora and fauna
of the province.

**Gustaf Fröding
(1860–1911)**

🏛 **Värmlands Museum**
Sandgrundsudden. 400 m (440 yd) N
of the centre. 📞 054-14 31 00.
⭘ Tue–Sun. 📷 ✉ 🔌 🍴 🛍 ♿
🏛 **Alsters Herrgård**
8 km (5 miles) E of Karlstad. 📞 054-
83 40 81. ⭘ May–Aug: daily;
Sep–Dec & Feb–Apr: one weekend a
month. 📷 ✉ 📷 🔌

Hagfors ❻

Värmland. Road 62. 🏠 6,500.
🚌 ℹ Folkets Väg 1, 0563-156 50.
📷 Swedish Rally (early Feb),
Klarhelgen Festival (early Jul),
Klarälvsmässan Fair (3rd week in Aug).

IN THE HEART OF Värmland on
the Klarälven river lies
Hagfors, which has long been
a centre for the steel and
forestry industries. Today,
steel is still manufactured in
Uddeholm just to the west of
the town.
   Hagfors is a good starting
point for trips up the Klarälven
valley and out into the forest.
Various places upriver offer raft
trips, which provide the opportunity to spend a few relaxing
days drifting at 1–2 knots,
watching the world go by.
Ekshärad, 20 km (12 miles)
north of Hagfors, has a
red shingled church
built in 1686 with
superb views of the
river. The church-
yard is known for
around 300 iron
crosses with "leaves"
which play in
the wind.
   South of the
town is the
Rovdjurscenter,
which specializes in
the big four predators: lynx,
bear, wolf and wolverine. In
addition to its permanent
exhibits, the centre offers
guided tours of the habitats
of these animals.

🦌 **Rovdjurscenter,
Ekshärad**
25 km (16 miles) NW of Hagfors.
📞 0563-54 05 90. ⭘ 19 May–
17 Sep: daily. 📷 ✉ 🔌 🛍 ♿

Alsters Herrgård, near Karlstad, birthplace of poet Gustaf Fröding

Filipstad ❼

Varmland. Road 63. 🚶 6,500. 🚘 🚉
ℹ️ *Stora Torget 3 D, 0590-613 54.*
🎪 *Oxhälja Market (1st week in Sep).*

KARL IX FOUNDED Filipstad in 1611, naming it after his son Karl Filip. Mining, ironworking and blacksmithing were the mainstay of the town, but today it is known for a very different type of industry – it is home to the world's largest crispbread bakery, owned by Wasabröd. Guided tours of the factory show how this very Swedish product is made.

Two of the town's great sons have contrasting memorials. A life-size sculpture by K G Bejemark of the popular poet and songwriter Nils Ferlin (1898–1961) in top hat and tails has been placed on a park bench. Next to Daglösen lake stands inventor John Ericsson's imposing mausoleum. He was a locomotive and warship pioneer and inventor of the screw propeller. Two *Monitor*-type cannons stand next to the monument.

John Ericsson grew up along with his equally illustrious brother Nils in the mining community of **Långban**, 20 km (12 miles) north of Filipstad. Here an entire community built around iron has been

Alfred Nobel's laboratory in the Nobelmuseet, as it was when he died

preserved, including a foundry, now renovated, gaming house and pithead buildings. Mineral hunters investigating the slag heaps of Långban have unearthed an exceptionally diverse collection of no less than 312 minerals.

🚇 Långban
20 km (12 miles) N of Filipstad.
📞 *0590-221 81.* ⭕ *Jun–Aug: daily.*
🖼️ 🚻 🅿️

Poet Nils Ferlin on his park bench in Filipstad

Karlskoga ❽

Värmland. E18. 🚶 29,000. 🚘
ℹ️ *Kyrkbacken 9, 0586-614 74.*
🎪 *Swedish Touring Car Championship (end May & mid-Aug); Beach Festival (end Jul).*

IRON ORE has been mined and processed in this area since the 13th century, but it was not until Alfred Nobel *(see p69)* bought the Bofors ironworks and cannon factory in 1894 that the foundation was laid for Karlskoga's expansion. During the 20th century, Bofors grew to become one of the world's leading arms manufacturers.

The **Nobelmuseet** in Björkborns manor, Nobel's last home, shows developments at Bofors and offers an insight into the life of the inventor. Nobel's laboratory is just as he left it when he died. The stable where he kept his Russian stallions is now an industrial museum displaying the history of the ironworks.

Karlskoga's only preserved blast furnace can be found at **Granbergsdals Hytta**, 10 km (6 miles) north of the town.

At the end of the Ice Age water poured out from a lake at **Sveafallen** near Degerfors, 15 km (9 miles) south of Karlskoga. The landscape it created can be seen in the Domedagsdalen (Doomsday valley) and from walking trails through the nature reserve.

Kristinehamn is an idyllic town 25 km (16 miles) west of Karlskoga. Its claim to fame is Picasso's 15-m (50-ft) high sculpture of a Native American head to the south of the town.

🏛️ Nobelmuseet
2 km (1 mile) N of the centre.
📞 *0586-834 94.* ⭕ *Jun–Aug: daily; other times: phone to book.* 🅿️ 🚹

THE INVENTOR JOHN ERICSSON

The multi-talented Swedish-American inventor John Ericsson (1803–89) was born in Långban, Värmland, where his father was mine captain. At the age of 13, he was employed in the construction of the Göta Canal *(see p146)*, together with his brother, Nils (1802–70), the father of the Swedish railway. He wrestled with the development of a steam engine and in his early twenties went to England to exploit his invention. He constructed a groundbreaking engine (1829) which, in

John Ericsson's mausoleum

the locomotive *Novelty*, took part in the Manchester-Liverpool race and was narrowly beaten by George Stephenson's *Rocket*. In the USA, Ericsson designed the frigate *Princeton*, and fitted his newly created screw propeller. In competition, the ship claimed victory over the fastest paddle-steamer of the day, the *Great Western*. Ericsson's ultimate triumph came in the American Civil War with the design of the armour-plated warship *Monitor*, with a rotating cannon tower. She overcame the Southern States' *Merrimac* in 1862.

Stjärnsunds Slott, home of Gustaf, the 19th-century "singing prince"

Askersund ⑨

Närke. 👤 4,000. 🚉 🚌 🛈 Rådhuset, 0583-810 00. 🎿 Trad Jazz
Festival (2nd week in Jun), Golf Week
(2nd week in Jul), All Car and Bike
Meet (end of Jul).

ON THE NORTH SHORE of Lake
Vättern lies Askersund,
the main town of southern
Närke, offering easy access to
the forests of Tiveden and
islands on the lake. Askersund
received a mention in a Papal
letter dated 1314. A devastating
fire struck the town in 1776,
but many wooden buildings
constructed since then have
been preserved.

The brick-built church,
Landskyrkan, designed by
Jean de la Vallé in 1670,
survived the fire. It is one of
the most splendid religious
buildings from Sweden's Age
of Greatness (see pp36–7),
with its magnificent Baroque
pulpit and altar-piece. The
Oxenstierna-Soopska chapel
designed by Erik Dahlbergh
contains a tin sarcophagus.

ENVIRONS: Lake Vättern's northern archipelago comprises
around 50 islands, most of
which are a nature reserve.
The islands can be reached by
boat from Askersund. Plying
the route is the *S/S Motala
Express*, which entered service
in 1895 and is known as "the
prisoner of Vättern" as she is
too large to leave the lake via
the Göta Canal.

Stjärnsunds Slott 4 km (2
miles) south of Askersund was
the home of the "singing
prince" Gustaf (1827–52), the
song-writing son of Oscar I.
Built in the early 19th century,
it was so lavishly decorated
that today it is considered to

contain Sweden's finest mid-
19th-century interiors.

🏛 Stjärnsunds Slott
4 km (2 miles) S of Askersund.
📞 0583-100 04. ◷ 1 May–31 Aug:
daily; other times by appointment. 🎫
🎟 obligatory. 💻

Örebro ⑩

See pp238–9.

Ludvika ⑪

Dalarna. Road 50. 👤 14,000. 🚉 🚌
✖ 🛈 Fredsgatan 10, 0240-860 50.
🎿 Dan Andersson Week (last week in
Jul), Dragon Boat Festival (May/Jun),
Ludvika Festival (1st week in Jul).
🌐 www.ludvika.se

THE WESTERN part of Bergslagen has foundries, mines
and mining magnates' estates
around every corner. The
industry has also left its mark
on the main town, Ludvika.
**Ludvika Gammelgård och
Gruvmuseum** offers a good
impression of mining as it was
in bygone times and more can
be seen out and about in the
surrounding countryside.

ENVIRONS: For many years
Grängesberg, 16 km (10
miles) southwest of Ludvika,

was central Sweden's largest
iron ore mine. It was closed
in 1989. Ore deposits extended beneath the settlement,
and in places buildings had to
be abandoned to allow mining
to continue. The ore was
taken by railway to Oxelö-
sund on the Baltic coast.
**Grängesbergs Lok-
museum** (the Locomotive
Museum) contains the world's
only operational steam
turbine locomotive.

Skattlösberg 35 km (22
miles) northwest of Ludvika,
is where Dan Andersson,
"poet of the forests", was born
in 1888. It is typical of the
villages created by immigrant
Finns in the 17th and 18th
centuries. **Luossastugan**,
where Andersson used to
write, is now a memorial to
the much loved poet.

🏛 Ludvika Gammelgård
och Gruvmuseum
Ludvika. 📞 0240-100 19.
◷ 16 Jun–17 Aug: daily; 1–15 Jun
& 18–31 Aug: Mon–Fri. 🎫 🎟 💻
🏛 Grängesbergs
Lokmuseum
Grängesberg. 📞 0240-204 93.
◷ 10 Jun–10 Jul: daily. ● Midsummer's Eve. 🎫 🎟 💻 🛗
🏛 Luossastugan
Skattlösberg. 📞 0240-860 50.
◷ 15 May–Aug: daily. 🎫 🎟

Hedemora ⑫

Dalarna. Road 70. 👤 16,000. 🚉 🚌
🛈 Långgatan 1, 0225-343 48.
🎿 Daldansen Dance Festival (last week
in Jul), Hedemora Market (mid-May).

THIS SMALL DALARNA town is
the oldest in the province
with a charter dating from
1459. The 13th-century church
and the pharmacy built in 1779
are among the few buildings
which survived a major fire in

Hedemora, Dalarna's oldest town, granted a town charter in 1459

1849. Another survivor is **Theaterladan** from the 1820s. It was built by a theatre-loving merchant above a granary. Performances take place here in the spirit of the early 19th century and the grain has made way for a museum.

ENVIRONS: Husbyringen, north of Hedemora, is the location for a 60-km (37-mile) circular tour, taking in the countryside and local culture. There are mining centres en route, such as Silvhyttå and Långshyttan. Kloster has the ruins of an abbey. The star feature is Stjärnsund's 18th-century mining settlement, where the father of Swedish mechanics, Christopher Polhem, worked. **Polhemsmuseet** exhibits the work of this inventive genius, including the Stjärnsund clock and ingenious Polhem lock.

Christopher Polhem (1661–1751)

▦ Theaterladan
Gussarvsgatan 10. **[** 0225-151 15. **○** 15 May–Sep. **✆** phone for tour. **⛪** Polhemsmuseet
Stjärnsund, 15 km (9 miles) S of Hede-mora. **[** 0225-800 90, winter 0225-80131. **○** Jun: Sat–Sun; Jul–Aug: daily. **▨ ✆** pre-book. **🅿 🚻 ♿**

Borlänge ⓭

Dalarna. Road 50. **▦** 45,000. **🚃**
🚌 ℹ Sveagatan 1, 0243-25 74 90.
🎿 Darlekarlia Cup (early Jul); Festival salute (1st week in Sep).
ⓦ www.borlange.com

DALARNA'S SECOND largest town, Borlänge came to prominence in the 1870s when the Domnarvets Jern-verk ironworks was estab-lished and several railway lines came together here. But it only received its town charter in 1944. In recent years it has gained a university college to add to its iron and paper industries. **Jussi Björlingmuseet** celebrates the town's greatest son, the internationally renowned tenor Jussi Björling (1911–60). All his recordings can be enjoyed here.

Carl Larssongården, a place of pilgrimage for interior designers

ENVIRONS: Stora Tuna, 4 km (2 miles) southeast of Borlänge, is the traditional centre of the flatlands. The medieval church was built at the end of the 15th century with the aim of becoming Dalarna's cathedral, but the province never became a diocese. Its treasures include a 15th-century crucifix.

At **Ornässtugan**, it is said that in the 16th century the future king, Gustav Vasa, fled ignominiously from Danish knights via the privy.

⛪ Jussi Björlingmuseet
Borganäsvägen 25. **[** 0243- 742 40.
○ Sep–May: Tue–Fri; Jun–Aug: daily.
● 1 & 6 Jan, Easter, Ascension Day, Midsummer, 24 & 31 Dec. **✆ 🚻 ♿**
⛪ Ornässtugan
8 km (5 miles) NE of Borlänge.
[0243-22 30 72, 745 49. **○** Jun–Aug: daily; May, Sep pre-booking. **▨**
✆ obligatory. **🅿 🚻**

Sundborn ⓮

Dalarna. 12 km (7 miles) NE of Falun.
▦ 800. **🚃 🚌 🚻** 023-600 53.

SITUATED IN THE village of Sundborn is **Carl Larsson-gården**, Lilla Hyttnäs, home of the artist Carl Larsson (1853–1919). The interior, containing wooden furniture and trad-itional Swedish textiles, along with influences from the Arts and Crafts movement and Art Nouveau, has been carefully preserved. Sundborn's shingled wooden church, built in 1755, features paintings by Larsson (1905) and the graveyard contains the artist's family plot.

Nearby, **Stora Hyttnäs** manor is a complete home from the start of the last cen-tury with an interesting textile collection and garden.

⛪ Carl Larssongården
[023-600 53. **○** May–Sep: daily; Oct–Apr: Tue. **▨ ✆ 🅿 🚻 ♿** limited access.

CARL AND KARIN LARSSON

Through his book *A Home* (1899), the interior design of artist Carl Larsson and particularly his wife, Karin, as expressed in their house in Sundborn, attracted attention worldwide. The couple had lived around Europe before settling with their children in a wooden farmhouse in Sundborn. Here they were able to develop their ideas for home interiors, producing a decorative scheme in traditional rural Swedish style using rustic furniture, home-woven textiles and colourful country patterns combined with a touch of the Arts and Crafts and Art Nouveau movements. This was in strong contrast to the stifled, bourgeois tastes which prevailed at the end of the 19th century. The joy and happiness in the Larsson home can be traced in every brushstroke and line of his book illustrations, which perhaps explains why Carl and Karin's Swedish idyll continues to inspire interior designers *(see pp22–3)*.

Karin and Kersti by Carl Larsson

Örebro ⓾

THERE HAS BEEN A TOWN on this site for 750 years, but in 1854 a major fire destroyed the centre of Örebro. This gave scope for a new, more spacious layout on both sides of the Svartån river and elegant buildings coupled with the castle and St Nicolai Kyrka created a particularly fine townscape. A local newspaper described it as "a magnificent 19th-century salon, extravagantly furnished with buildings which proclaim growth and success". But there is also a greener side to Örebro with the promenade that follows the Svartån river to the delights of Wadköping and Karlslund. The river can be explored on foot, by bicycle or in a rowing boat. The free salmon fishing should not be missed.

Örebro Slott on the Svartån river, now the county governor's residence

🏰 Örebro Slott
Kansligatan. **(** 019-21 21 21.
◯ Sep–May: Sat–Sun; Jun–Aug: daily.
🖊 obligatory. 🔲 🍴 🏠 🚻 limited
access. **Northwest Tower** ◯ daily,
admission free.
Örebro Slott has dominated the town since Örebro received its charter in the 13th century. In 1347, King Magnus Eriksson gathered the great and the good at Örebro House, as the castle was then called, to adopt a common law for Sweden. At the end of the 16th century, King Karl IX remodelled the castle to create a Renaissance palace. Today's appearance, however, with its mighty round towers, is the result of major rebuilding in the 1890s.

The castle has been the scene of a number of historical events, including the adoption of the first Swedish Parliament Act in 1617 and the election of the French Marshal Jean-Baptiste Bernadotte as heir to the Swedish throne in 1810. Now it is the official residence of the county governor and also houses Örebro Tourist Office. An exhibition in the Northwest Tower highlights the castle's history.

🏛 Örebro Läns Museum
Engelbrektsgatan 3. **(** 019-602 87 00. ◯ daily. ⚫ public holidays
🖊 phone to book. 🔲 🚻
With its roots in the 1850s, the county museum is Sweden's oldest, although the main collection of more than 100,000 objects from across the county is on show in a 1960s' building in Slottsparken. A permanent exhibition focuses on farming since the Stone Age. The museum's most valuable artifacts, including the Viking silver from Eketorp (see p157), are housed in the Treasury. The museum also runs **Landstings-museet** in north Örebro, which is set in an 18th-century hospital building and covers healthcare and mental health through the centuries.

🏰 Rådhuset
Stora Torget. ⚫ closed to the public.
Built in 1858–63, the magnificent Neo-Gothic Town Hall was something of a showpiece in its time. King Karl XV didn't think the castle-like building befitted a provincial town, calling it: "...sparkling wine not weak beer!" Today only a fraction of Örebro's administration fits into the Town Hall, although it remains the seat of the Municipal Executive Board. When the clock chimes, automatons from Örebro's history appear, such as reformer Olaus Petri (see p53).

⛪ St Nicolai Kyrka
Nikolaigatan 8. **(** 019-20 95 30.
◯ daily. 🖊 phone for info.
🚻 🏠 Sun.
The church on Stortorget has origins from the 13th century, but has been restyled many times. The north and south entrances are from the original church and were carved from Närke limestone. The rest is an example of English-inspired Neo-Gothic style, with the tower added at the end of the 19th century.

🏛 Wadköping
On the Svartån river, 1 km (half a mile) from the centre. **(** Tourist Office, 019-21 21 21. ◯ daily.
The beautiful promenade along the Svartån river through Stadsparken leads to the idyllic wooden houses of Wadköping. This is a cultural centre to which old buildings have been moved to make way for the modern town. It is a vibrant community with craftworkers and small shops, and many people live here. The oldest building is the early 16th-century Kungs-stugan (King's Cabin), named after its use by the then Duke

Wadköping, an open-air museum with traditional wooden houses

Karl on his visits to Örebro in the 1580s. His bedchamber has murals painted by his personal artist. Other buildings include Hamiltonska Huset (1844), moved here from the south of the town, where it was the grandest building of its era, and Cajsa Warg's Hus (17th century), the childhood home of the well-known cookery writer Casja Warg. In summer there are concerts and theatre performances.

Svampen

Dalbygatan 3. 019-611 37 35. May–Aug: daily; Sep–Apr: Sat–Sun.

The mushroom-shaped water tower, which offers a superb view of the town, the flatlands of Närke and Lake Hjälmaren, has become a symbol of Örebro. Since its opening in 1958, 8 million visitors have enjoyed the panorama from a height of 55 m (180 ft). Its construction has set something of a trend – there is a copy in Riyadh in Saudi Arabia.

The tower contains the science centre **Aqua Nova**, where the public has the opportunity to conduct practical experiments with water in all its forms.

Karlslunds Herrgård

5 km (3 miles) W of Örebro. Diedens Allé 11. 019-27 07 88. by appointment. pre-book.

Owned by Örebro town, the royal estate of Karlslunds Herregård dates from the 16th century and brings together nature and culture in perfect harmony. The Gustavian manor house, built in 1804–1809, incorporates wings from the 18th century.

The estate was once a self-sufficient community with around 80 buildings. Craftspeople and artists work here and there are several museums and shops, as well

Karlslunds Herrgård's Gustavian manor house dating from 1804–1809

as nature trails. Carlslunds Kraftstation, built in 1897, is the country's oldest working power station. There is a restored mill housing technological exhibits and an experiment workshop. In the dairy, a museum shows the harsh life of the agricultural labourer in the early 20th century.

Originally, the gardens at Karlslund were remarkably grand and over the past 30 years work has been ongoing to restore them to their former glory, partly in the form of an ecopark.

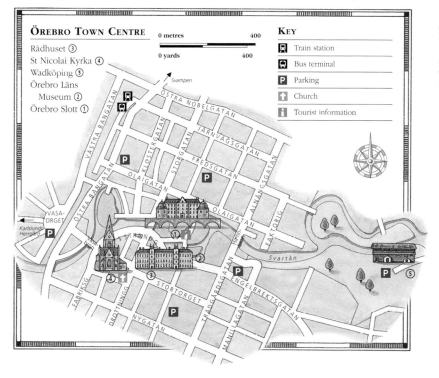

ÖREBRO TOWN CENTRE

Rådhuset ③
St Nicolai Kyrka ④
Wadköping ⑤
Örebro Läns Museum ②
Örebro Slott ①

0 metres 400
0 yards 400

KEY

- Train station
- Bus terminal
- Parking
- Church
- Tourist information

The huge Stora Stöten (Great Pit) in the old Falu copper mine outside Falun

Falun ⑮

Dalarna. Road 50. 🏘 35,000. 🚉
🚉 ☒ 🛈 Ttotzgatan 10–12,
023-830 50. 🎻 Falukalaset (start of
Jun), Falun Då – festival at World
Heritage Site (start of Jul), Falun Folk
Festival (mid-Jul).

IT GOES WITHOUT saying that
Falun has had a colourful
impact on Sweden. Wooden
buildings painted in the
distinctive Falu red can be
seen everywhere. The paint
has been made since the 17th
century from powdered ore
containing ferrous sulphate
from the Falu mine, on the
back of which the town was
founded. Stora Kopparberget
(Copper Mountain) was the
country's treasure chest – at
its peak, two-thirds of the
world's copper was mined
here. The entire area, including Stora Stöten (the Great
Pit, formed by a collapse in
1687), Falun's historic
buildings and industrial
remains, outlying settlements
and the **Gruvmuseet** (the
Mining Museum), was
designated as UNESCO World
Heritage Site in 2001.
    Dalarnas Museum gives a
broad insight into the cultural
history of Dalarna with
extensive collections of folk
costumes, local paintings and
traditional craftwork.

🏛 Gruvmuseet
1 km (half a mile) S of the centre.
🚪 023-78 20 30. ☐ Oct–Apr: Sat,
Sun; May–Sep: daily. ● 1 Jan, Good
Friday, Midsummer, 24 & 25 Dec.
🏞 🚪 🖳 🎭 🖪
🏛 Dalarnas Museum
🚪 023-76 55 00. ☐ daily. ● Good
Friday, Midsummer, 24 & 25 Dec.
🏞 🚪 🖳 🖳

Leksand ⑯

Dalarna. Road 70. 🏘 15,500. 🚉 🚉
🛈 Norsgatan, 0247-79 61 30.
🎻 Music on Siljan Lake (Jul), Rowing
race in church boats (1st Sun Jul),
Himlaspelet Pageant (Jul).
🌐 www.siljan.se

THE LANDSCAPE around Siljan
lake is especially beautiful,
but the Leksand area is the
most striking. One of the best
times to see the lake is during
the annual rowing race in
church boats in early July.
    Another annual event is
Himlaspelet, one of Sweden's
oldest rural pageants. First
performed in 1941, Rune
Lindström's play about a path
which leads to heaven depicts
the witch trials of the 1670s.
    The onion dome of Lek-
sand's 18th-century Baroque
church can be seen from far
and wide. Parts of the church
date from the 13th century.

**ENVIRONS: Karlfeldtsgården –
Sångs i Sjugare** was the
summer retreat of author and
Nobel prize-winner Erik Axel
Karlfeldt (1864–1931). It lies

The folk sculpture *Dalecarlian
Couple* **in Leksand**

on Opplimen lake just north
of Leksand. Here it is possible
to follow in the footsteps of
the author's heroine, who
came wandering over the
meadows of Sjugare. Also
worth a visit is the garden on
the poet's estate.
    Younger visitors to Leksand
will be attracted by **Äventyret
Sommarland**, comprising
three amusement parks on the
banks of Siljan lake: Waterland,
Motorland and Summerland.
    Insjön, 8 km (5 miles) south
of Leksand was the birthplace
in 1899 of the Swedish mail
order business run by Åhlén &
Holms. The mail order
tradition lives on with Clas
Ohlson, whose store attracts
so many DIY enthusiasts that
Insjön has become Dalarna's
most visited tourist destination.

🏛 Karlfeldtsgården – Sångs
i Sjugare
7 km (4 miles) N of the centre. Road
Rv 70. 🚪 0247-600 28. ☐ Jun–Jul:
Tue, Thu & Sat. 🎭
🎡 Äventyret Sommarland
🚪 0247-13375. ☐ May–Aug daily.
● Midsummer's Eve. 🎭
🚪 🖳 🖪

Rättvik ⑰

Dalarna. Road 70. 🏘 4,500. 🚉 🚉
🛈 Stationshuset, 0248-79 72 10.
🎻 Music on Siljan Lake (Jul), Classic
Car Week (late Jul).

NO ONE CAN FAIL TO notice
Rättvik's landmark, Lång-
bryggan pier. After docking at
the pier on the *M/S Gustaf
Wasa*, passengers have a 628-
m (690-yd) walk to reach the
mainland. The pier with all its
fine carpentry was built in
1895 to allow steam boats to

moor near the shallow shore. Rättvik also has a medieval church, beautifully situated on a promontory surrounded by former church stables – the oldest dating from the 1470s.

ENVIRONS: A search for older Dalarna buildings, rural communities and paintings will be rewarded at **Gammelstan** in Norrboda, 35 km (22 miles) north of Rättvik. The village street is lined with old buildings, some of which date back to the 17th century.

Tällberg, 12 km (7 miles) south on the shore of Lake Siljan, has many preserved timber houses in the classic Dalarna style. It is also known for its top-class hotels and guest houses, including the renowned Åkerblads *(see p288)* with its excellent restaurant. At the top of the village, Holens Gammelgård features workshops selling traditional handicrafts.

At **Dalhalla**, 7 km (4 miles) north of Rättvik, a limestone quarry has been converted into an auditorium. The quarry forms an amphitheatre with unique acoustics which have been praised by the world's top opera singers. Concerts are held in summer, and Dalhalla can also be toured in the day. The area was formed 360 million years ago when a meteor landed here, creating a crater which encompasses the whole of the Siljan region.

Dalhalla
7 km (4 miles) NW of the centre. Road 70. **[** 0248-79 79 50. **○** for performances and tours. 📷 ▣ 🍴 🚻 🛗

Mora ❶⑧

Dalarna. Road 70. 🏛 11,000. ▣ ▣ ☒ ⓗ *Siljan Tourism Mora, Stationsvägen, 0250-59 20 20.* 📷 *Vasaloppet Ski Race (1st Sun in Mar), Stora Daldansen Dance Festival (3rd week in May).*

THE MUNICIPALITY of Mora and the town itself – beautifully situated between Orsasjön and Siljan lakes – offers a wide range of

Bedroom in Zorngården, Anders Zorn's home and studio

attractions. Mora is particularly associated with King Gustav Vasa (1496–1560) and artist Anders Zorn (1860–1920). Gustav Vasa's travels in Dalarna in 1520 to mobilize local men against the Danish occupation have left many traces. Near Mora, the Utmeland monument (1860) shows several romanticized paintings chronicling Gustav's adventures. It was built over the cellar where he is said to have hidden from Danish scouts. The annual Vasaloppet ski race *(see p245)* is another memorial to the king. At the finishing line in Mora stands Anders Zorn's statue of Gustav Vasa and the nearby **Vasaloppsmuseet** recounts the history of the famous ski race.

Zorn's statue of Gustav Vasa in Mora

Anders Zorn became known internationally not least for his portraits of plump, naked local women. He was genuinely interested in peasant culture and an ardent collector of local handicrafts. In **Zorngården**, which he built himself, he revelled in a world of National Romanticism. On the estate there are a number of older buildings which have been moved here, such as the 12th-century bakehouse which was used as a studio. The nearby Zornmuseet displays Zorn's own art and private collections.

ENVIRONS: Nusnäs, 8 km (5 miles) south of Mora, is where the national symbol of Sweden, the Dala horse, is manufactured. Originally a 19th-century toy, the horses

are carved with a knife and colourfully decorated. It is possible to watch them being made on weekdays.

On the island of **Sollerön** on Lake Siljan is the boatyard where the traditional church boats used on church outings and rowing races between the lakeside villages are made. There is also a pretty church dating from 1785.

Tomteland in Gesunda is the home of Father Christmas and his workshop, which is busy all summer making presents for children. The huge park offers various activities, including the witch's school – strictly for youngsters who want to learn about magic and how to help friends and protect the environment.

Vasaloppsmuseet
Vasaloppets Hus. **[** 0250-392 25. **○** *16 Jun–14 Aug: daily; 15 Aug–15 Jun: Mon–Fri.* ● *public holidays.* 📷 📷 🛗 ▣ 🛗

Zorngården
Vasagatan 36. **[** 0250-59 23 10, 0250-59 23 16. **○** *daily.* ● *24 & 25 Dec, Good Friday.* 📷 📷

Tomteland
Gesunda. 12 km (7.5 miles) S of Mora. **[** 0250-287 70. **○** *varies, phone for info.* 📷 ▣

A giant-sized Dala horse, manufactured in Nusnäs

Horse-riding in Dalafjällen, one of the many outdoor activities on offer

Orsa ⑲

Dalarna. Road Rv 45. 🏠 *5,200.* 🚌
🛈 *Dalagatan 1, 0250-55 25 50.*
🎣 *Stone Symposium (Jun), Orsayran Music Festival (Weds in Jul).*

THE ORSA REGION extends from the gentle agricultural landscape around Lake Orsasjön to the desolate lands of Finnmark in the north.

In the past many of the local inhabitants made grindstones as a sideline, a skill which can now be studied at **Slipstensmuseet** in Mässbacken, 12 km (7 miles) northeast of Orsa.

In this part of Sweden animals are still taken to the mountains for summer grazing. Around Djurberga, Fryksås and Hallberg it is possible to see how dairymaids used to live, far from their villages, churning butter and making cheese from the milk of hornless mountain cattle and goats.

In **Våmhus**, on the western side of Orsasjön, two crafts are practised which in the past were a major source of income locally: basket weaving and making jewellery out of hair. The women used to walk as far afield as St Petersburg in Russia, and Germany, to sell their work.

Orsa Grönklitt, 10 km (6 miles) north of Orsa, is the main area for outdoor activities. At Orsa Björnpark (Orsa Bear Park) special paths and ramps allow a close-up view of the bears, wolves, lynx and wolverine which live here in large enclosures.

🏛 **Slipstensmuseet**
Mässbacken. 📞 *0250-55 02 55.*
⭘ *summer.* 📷 🎫 *pre-book.* 🖥 🍴

🎿 Orsa Grönklitt
Grönklitt. 15 km (9 miles) NW of Orsa. 🛈 *0250-462 00.* ⭘ *daily.* 🖥
🍴 🏠 ♿

Sälen ⑳

Dalarna. Road 71. 🏠 *500.* 🚌 🛈
Centrumhuset, 0280-187 00. 🎣
Snowboarding World Cup, Speed Skiing World Cup (May), Vasaloppet Ski Race (first Sun in Mar).

LIKE THE MAJORITY of Dalarna's mountains, Transtrandsfjällen, with Sälen at their heart, are rounded and undulating and less dramatic than the those further to the north. The highest peak, Östra Granfjället, is 949 m (3,114 ft) above sea level. However, the terrain is excellent for both downhill and cross-country skiing and this, combined with its relative proximity to Sweden's cities, has made the area one of the country's leading destinations for winter sports enthusiasts.

Whether it's black runs for advanced skiers, velodrome curves, spines or jumps for snowboarders, or family slopes for children, there is plenty to choose from in Sälen. Around 200 km (124 miles) of trails are marked for cross-country skiers and summer hikers alike.

Sälen is the starting point of the 90-km (56-mile) Vasaloppet ski race to Mora.

Idre and Särna ㉑

Dalarna. Road 70. 🏠 *1,500.* 🚌 🛈
Framgårdsvägen 1, Idre; Särnavägen 6, Särna; 0253-200 00. 🎣 *Mountain Orienteering (4th week in Jun), Mountain Festival (2nd week in Jul), Festival Week (3rd week in Jul).*

NORTHERNMOST Dalarna, with the towns of Idre and Särna, belonged to Norway until 1644 and the local dialects still sound Norwegian. This is a mountainous region and the views from the peaks are impressive. In the Nipfjället mountains it is possible to drive up to a height of 1,000 m (3,280 ft) for a good view of Städjan, a peak 1,131 m (3,710 ft) high. The STF mountain station at **Grövelsjön** on Långfjället, to the north, is an ideal starting point for mountain tours.

Idrefjäll is a modern tourist resort on Idresjön lake with excellent slopes and lifts. Särna has a beautiful wooden church dating from the late 17th century and the rural museum of Buskgården.

Fulufjället National Park contains Sweden's highest waterfall, Njupeskär, with a drop of 90 m (295 ft). The effects of a violent storm in August 1997 can still be seen here when 400 mm (16 in) of rain fell in 24 hours. Streams became torrents and fallen trees dammed the water, ploughing wide furrows through the forest.

The distinctive peak of Städjan in the Nipfjället mountains

◁ Interior of a traditional mountain pasture hut at Balungen in eastern Dalarna

The Vasaloppet Ski Race

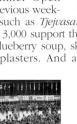

Wreath bearer

THE WORLD'S LONGEST and oldest ski race was first held in 1922 when 136 competitors skied the 90 km (56 miles) from Sälen to Mora. Today more than 14,000 skiers take on the challenge on the first Sunday in March. Many more prefer the calmer Open Track race held the previous weekend or special races such as *Tjejvasan* for women. A staff of 3,000 support the skiers by providing blueberry soup, ski waxing and blister plasters. And all

because in 1520 Gustav Vasa could not get the men of Dalarna to rise up against the Danes. Disheartened, he fled on skis from the Danish troops towards Norway, but when the local men heard about the Stockholm Bloodbath *(see p58)*, they changed their minds and their two best skiers raced to intercept their future king near Sälen.

In summer, a hiking trail follows the course from Berga in Sälen to the finish at Zorn's statue of Gustav Vasa in Mora.

Berga, just south of the village of Sälen, is the starting point for the 14,000 skiers who are let loose in the early dawn in several stages, top skiers first.

Evertsberg lies halfway between Sälen and Mora. Here, as in many places along the route, the competitors fortify themselves with blueberry soup. Those only skiing half the race can leave the track at this point.

The first steep hills are succeeded by flat marshland.

VÄSTERDALÄLVEN
Sälen
Smågan
11 km (7 miles)
Berga
Transtrand
VÄNAN
Mångsbodarna
24 km (15 miles)
Risberg
35 km (22 miles)
Evertsberg
47 km (29 miles)
ÖSTERDALÄLVEN
Oxberg
61 km (38 miles)
Hökberg
70 km (43 miles)
Mora
90 km (56 miles)
Eldris
80 km (50 miles)

| 0 kilometres | 20 |
| 0 miles | 10 |

THE FIRST VASALOPPET

At Christmas 1520 Gustav Vasa fled on skis from Mora towards Norway to escape Danish troops. At Lima, near Sälen, local men caught up with him and persuaded the future king to turn back. Since 1922 almost 750,000 skiers have repeated the achievement, albeit skiing in the opposite direction.

Mora marks the end of the race. The winning time is usually just over four hours, but some entrants can take ten hours. The text on the finishing line reads: "In the footsteps of our forefathers for the victories of tomorrow."

SOUTHERN NORRLAND

THE SIX PROVINCES OF SOUTHERN NORRLAND *cover almost a quarter of the country. The character shifts noticeably from the coast with its industry and fishing to the farming communities up along the river valleys, then westwards through forests to the mountains of Härjedalen and Jämtland. Natural resources such as timber and waterpower have had a visible impact on the region.*

In the Middle Ages, the southeasterly province of Gästrikland belonged to Svealand and its gently rolling landscape is more akin to that of neighbouring Uppland than Norrland. An offshoot of the Bergslagen mining district extends into this area and iron-working formed the basis of today's manufacturing industry. The trading port of Gävle has long been a gateway to Norrland.

The pass between Kölberget and Digerberget in the province of Hälsingland is another gateway to the north, beyond which the mountainous Norrland landscape becomes more evident. Huge wooden mansions stand proud with their ornate porches and exquisitely decorated interiors. These houses are evidence of the successful trade in the green gold of the local forests in a landscape of which 80 per cent is covered with productive woodland.

Exploitation of the forests had an even bigger impact on the provinces of Medelpad and Ångermanland. At the end of the 19th century, the timber barons of Sundsvall and Ådalen made themselves a fortune. Today, processing wood into pulp and paper is still a key industry. The smell of sulphur can be quite striking – or could it be the herring dish *surströmming*, best sampled by those who dare at one of the fishing villages along the High Coast, a UNESCO World Heritage Site *(see p256)*.

The provinces of Jämtland and Härjedalen only became part of Sweden in 1645. There is often talk of the "Republic of Jämtland" among diehard locals who seek self-rule. The mountains stretch out to the west, attracting visitors both to the ski resorts and to the upland areas where the wildlife and countryside can still be enjoyed undisturbed.

A reindeer herd round-up for division according to owner, by use of lassos and ear tags

◁ The mighty Tännforsen Falls on the Åreälven river, with a drop of 26 m (85 ft)

Exploring Southern Norrland

I N THIS REGION OF IMMENSE CONTRASTS, the coastal provinces
of Gästrikland and Hälsingland are home to a colourful
rural culture enlivened with traditional folk music and
dancing. The High Coast, with its dramatic island archipelago accessible by bridges and ferries, is Ångermanland's
contribution to UNESCO's list of World Heritage Sites.
Inland, the mountainous provinces of Jämtland and
Härjedalen offer wide open spaces for skiing and hiking.

One of the best ways to experience Norrland's
varied landscape is to start from the coast and
follow one of the river valleys which cut across
the country. As the roads wind up-river, they
pass through dense forests and on up into
the mountains. Alternatively, the
Inlandsbanan railway provides a more
unusual way of enjoying the
hinterland in comfort *(see p331)*.

The heather and rushing streams of Helag, with
the mountain of Helagsfjället in the distance

GETTING AROUND

The E4 along the coast and the E14
from Sundsvall across the country to
Trondheim in Norway are the main
arteries for motorists. The inland
roads running north-south are of a
generally good standard. The roads
east-west tend to follow the courses
of the rivers. The main railway line
runs north-south. Along the coast, the
railway goes as far north as
Härnösand before heading inland.
The Jämtland mountains can be
reached by train, but in Härjedalen
transport is by car or bus. The
Inlandsbanan railway operates in
summer. Air travel is an option and
the range of domestic flights is good.

KEY

― Motorway

▬ Major road

= Minor road

⁻ Railway line

A wooden mansion in Arbro, Hälsingland, typical
of the area's traditional architecture

SEE ALSO

• *Where to Stay* pp288–9

• *Where to Eat* pp302–3

Map labels:

E6
(Norway)

GÄDDE

JÄMTLAND

Kallsjön

Trondheim
(Norway)

336

340

339

322

ÅRE
16

E14

Annsjön
17
STORLIEN

Indalsälven

321

Stor-
sjön
15

ÖSTERSUND

Sylarna
▲ 1728 m
(5,670 ft)

Helagsfjället
1797 m
Røros
(Norway)
(5,895 ft)

Ljungan

45

18 MOUNTAINS OF
HÄRJEDALEN

84

Ljusnan

HÄRJEDALEN

ÄLV
SVEG **19**

Mora

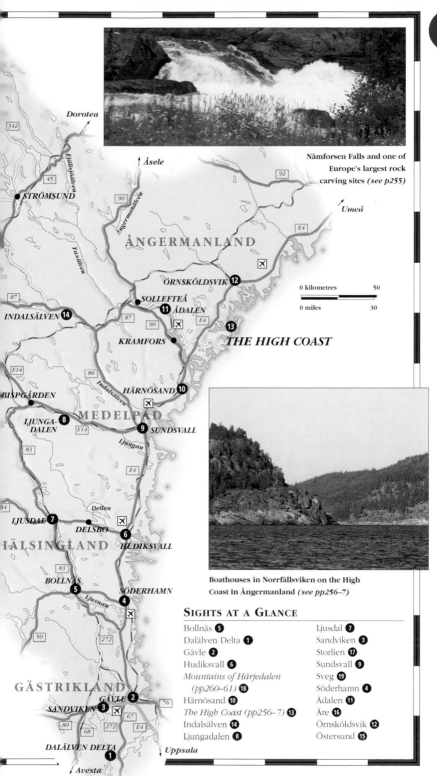

Nämforsen Falls and one of
Europe's largest rock
carving sites *(see p255)*

342
Dorotea
Åsele
92
Fjällsjöälven
45
90
STRÖMSUND
Ångermanälven
Umeå
E4
ÅNGERMANLAND
Faxälven

0 kilometres   50

0 miles   30

ÖRNSKÖLDSVIK 12
SOLLEFTEÅ
87
SOLLEFTEÅ 11 ÅDALEN
INDALSÄLVEN 14
87   90   E4
KRAMFORS   13

THE HIGH COAST

E14   86
Indalsälven
BISPGÅRDEN   HÄRNÖSAND 10
LJUNGA-   MEDELPAD
DALEN 8   E14
83   9 SUNDSVALL
Ljungan
E4

Dellen
LJUSDAL 7
DELSBO
HÄLSINGLAND   6
HUDIKSVALL

83
BOLLNÄS
5
SÖDERHAMN
Ljusnan   4

50   272
E4

GÄSTRIKLAND
GÄVLE 2
SANDVIKEN 3   76
80   67
68   272   E4
DALÄLVEN DELTA
1
Uppsala
Avesta

Boathouses in Norrfällsviken on the High
Coast in Ångermanland *(see pp256–7)*

Sights at a Glance

Bollnäs 5
Dalälven Delta 1
Gävle 2
Hudiksvall 6
*Mountains of Härjedalen
  (pp260–61)* 18
Härnösand 10
The High Coast (pp256–7) 13
Indalsälven 14
Ljungadalen 8

Ljusdal 7
Sandviken 3
Storlien 17
Sundsvall 9
Sveg 19
Söderhamn 4
Ådalen 11
Åre 16
Örnsköldsvik 12
Östersund 15

The Dalälven delta, one of the top ten fishing spots in Sweden

Dalälven Delta ❶

Gästrikland, Uppland. 🛈 *Gysingö Tourist Office, 0291-210 00.* 🎭 *Weir Day in Älvkarleby (first Sun before Midsummer).*

BEFORE THE MIGHTY Dalälven river empties into the bay at Gävle, it forms an expansive delta with hundreds of small islands. The flora and fauna are particularly abundant and the area offers some of the best sport fishing in Sweden.

Least affected by forestry and farming is the area around Färnebofjärden, part of which was declared a national park in 1998. The birdlife is incredibly diverse, with more than 100 breeding species, including several different endangered woodpeckers and owls.

A good place to start exploring the area is Gysinge on road Rv 67, 38 km (24 miles) south of Gävle. The falls between Färnebofjärden and Hedesundafjärden attracted ironworking here at the end of the 17th century. The well-preserved industrial community has a main street dating from the 1770s and a magnificent manor from 1840. Gysinge is also home to **Dalälvarnas Flottnings-museum**, which shows just how important the river once was for timber transportation.

Another important feature of the Dalälven river is hydro-electric power, which manifests itself in **Älvkarleby**, further down-river. The imposing power station, built in 1915, is an attraction in itself, but the most impressive sight is when the water is released at full-flow on Weir Day. Älvkarleby attracts many anglers, who annually land as much as 20 tonnes of salmon and sea trout.

In **Österfärnebo**, Koversta rural heritage centre is an 18th-century village, offering an insight into local rural life.

🏛 Dalälvarnas Flottningsmuseum

Gysinge Bruk. 🚗 *0291-210 00.* ⏰ *mid-May–mid-Aug: daily.* 🅿 ♿

Gävle ❷

Gästrikland. 🚶 *68,000.* 🚆 🚌 🛈 *at the central station, 026-14 74 30.* 🎭 *City Festival (1st week in Aug, Wed–Sat), Country Festival (1st week-end in Aug).*

GÄSTRIKLAND'S main town has been the gateway to Norrland since the Middle Ages. The mouth of the Gävleån river made an ideal port and traders set up base here to conduct business in the north. The harbourside warehouses along Skeppsbron bear witness to this. Gävle remains one of Sweden's larger ports, although operations have moved further out into the bay. A fire in 1869 destroyed the buildings north of the river, with the exception of the town hall built in 1790 and **Heliga Trefaldighets-kyrkan**, a three-aisle Baroque church dating from 1654. As a result, Gävle has attractive 19th-century buildings and broad tree-lined esplanades as protection against fires. The jewel is the splendid theatre on Rådhusesplanaden, built in 1878. The city park, **Boulog-nerskogen**, which features Carl Milles's famous sculpture, *Five Playing Geniuses,* is the most popular of Gävle's parks.

South of the Gävleån river lies **Gävle Slott**, Sweden's northernmost royal fortification, dating from the 16th century. This is also the location of the old town, "Gamla Gefle", with fine streets of wooden houses from the 18th century which have attracted many artists and craftsmen. **Joe Hill Gården** on N Bergsgatan, the birthplace of the Swedish-American union agitator, is now a museum. Other museums include **Länsmuseet Gävleborg** with extensive collections relating to the history of Gästrikland. **Sveriges Järnvägsmuseum** offers a delightful selection of old locomotives and carriages,

The oldest Swedish locomotive (1855) in Sveriges Järnvägsmuseum

from mining titans to neat little narrow-gauge carriages.

Fängelsemuseet is a small but fascinating museum housed in 17th-century prison cells. It gives an insight into prison life at the time.

Furuviksparken attracts families who come to enjoy its Nordic and exotic animals, and live performances, and to swim in a beautiful setting.

🏛 Länsmuseet Gävleborg
S. Strandgatan 20. **📞** 026-65 56 00.
☐ Tue–Sun. ● public holidays. ☐ ☐
🏛 Sveriges Järnvägsmuseum
Rälsgatan 1. **📞** 026-14 46 15.
☐ Jun–Aug: daily; Sep–May: Tue–Sun.
● public holidays. ☐ ☐ ☐
🏛 Fängelsemuseet
Hamiltongatan 1. **📞** 026-65 44 30.
☐ Tue–Thu, Sat–Sun.
● public holidays.
🦌 Furuviksparken
10 km (6 miles) E of the centre. Road
Rv 76. ☐ **📞** 026-17 73 00.
☐ May–Aug: daily; Sep–Apr: by
appointment. ☐ ☐ ☐ ☐

Sandviken ❸

Gästrikland. 🏛 23,000. ☐ ☐
ℹ Folkets Hus, Köpmangatan 5–7,
026-24 13 80 🎷 Bangen Jazz Festival
(end Jun), Chamber Music Festival
(end Jul).

THE TOWN OF Sandviken grew up with the establishment of an ironworks on the shore of Storsjön lake in 1860. The new railway line to Gävle was one of the factors in its location. Using the groundbreaking Bessemer production process, Sandviken soon gained a reputation for its steel. In the 1920s it began making stainless steel and by the 1940s it was the world's leading producer of steel for tools and drill bits.

ENVIRONS: Evidence of Sandviken's ironworking roots can be seen in Högbo. Today the community is a centre for recreation and adventure sports. It is also home to the **Textilmuseet**, an offshoot of Nordiska Museet (see pp88–9), with the country's finest collection of textiles and handicrafts.

Opposite Sandviken, on the southern shores of Storsjön,

lies the medieval church of **Årsunda**, with paintings by the master Eghil. Just south of the church is a Viking burial ground, which inspired the Årsunda Viking centre, offering activities with a Viking slant.

🏛 Textilmuseet
Högbo, 5 km (3 miles) N
of the centre. **📞** 026-21
50 01 ☐ Jul: daily; Aug–Jun:
Tue–Sun. ● some public holidays.
☐ ☐

Söderhamn ❹

Hälsingland. 🏛 12,700. ☐ ☐
ℹ Resecentrum, railway station,
0270-753 53. 🎆 Family fun evenings
at Östra Berget (Thu in Jul), Herring
Games (mid-Aug).

SWEDEN'S AMBITIONS for power and the need for armaments lead to the foundation of Söderhamn in 1620. Hälsingland's weapon makers were brought together from around the region to work in the town. The gun and rifle-making factory, built in 1748, now houses the town museum, **Söderhamns Stadsmuseum**.

Russian attacks in 1721 and four disastrous fires have meant that the only remaining building of significance is **Ulrika Eleonora Kyrka**. The

Part of an old furnace in the town of Sandviken, famous for its steel production

pink cruciform church was designed by Tessin the Younger in 1693. The upside of the fires is that a series of parks now creates a green patchwork around the city. Söderhamn's landmark is the **Oscarsborg** tower, which rises proudly on Östra Berget. Anyone braving the 125 steps is rewarded with a breathtaking view of the town and archipelago.

ENVIRONS: The 10 km (6 miles) of the Söderhamnsfjärden inlet were lined with 11 steam-powered sawmills during the industrial boom of the late 19th century. The industrial museum in Ljusne and **Bergviks Industrimuseum** tell the story. A museum featuring more modern technology is **Söderhamns/ F15 Flygmuseum**, which exhibits military aircraft.

The 13th-century church **Tronö Kyrka**, 17 km (11 miles) northwest of Söderhamn, complete with walls, gates and bell tower, is unusually redolent of the Middle Ages. The archbishop and Nobel prize-winner Nathan Söderblom (1866–1931) was born in the rectory, which now houses his memorabilia.

**🏛 Söderhamns
Stadsmuseum**
Oxtorgsgatan 5. **📞** 0270-157 91.
☐ May–Aug: daily; Sep–Apr: Sat & Sun.
🏛 Bergviks Industrimuseum
15 km (9 miles) west of the centre.
📞 0270-42 32 80. ☐ by
appointment. ☐ ☐ voluntary.
**🏛 Söderhamns/F15 Flyg-
museum**
Flygstaden, 4 km (2 miles) east of
the centre. **📞** 0270-142 84.
☐ Jun–Aug: daily; Sep–Apr: Sun.
☐ ☐ ☐ by appointment.

Oscarsborg lookout tower, offering a superb view of Söderhamn

Kämpen rural heritage centre at a 16th-century farm in Bollnäs

Bollnäs **❺**

Hälsingland. 🏘 *13,000.* 🚃 🚌
ℹ️ *Stadshustorget, 0278-258 80.*
🎭 *Hälsingehambo Polka Festival (1st Sat after 1st Sun in Jul), Flax Week (1st week Aug).*

L OCATED IN the heart of Hälsingland's rich farming land, Bollnäs is the gateway to the valleys of the Voxnan and Ljusnan rivers. The town itself has a semi-modern centre, with some wooden mansions. The church, built in the 1460s, contains ornate medieval sculpture work. In the Classical-style **Bollnäs Museum** (1929), there is a room devoted to Onbacken, an Iron Age settlement just a stone's throw from the museum. Also worth visiting is **Kämpen** rural heritage centre, a 16th-century farm displaying a wealth of local culture. Bollnäs is on the route of the lively Hälsinge-hambo marathon dance from Hårga to Järvsö in early July.

ENVIRONS: Hälsingland was a major flax-growing area in the 18th century, and local land-owners displayed their wealth in lavishly decorated wooden mansions *(see p18).* Some of Hälsingland's finest estates and farms can be seen around Alfta, about 20 km (12 km) into the Voxnadalen valley. Alfta rural heritage centre, **Löka**, in Gundbo, comprises three farm buildings, some with beautiful murals. **Hansers** farm has wall hangings from the 15th century. In **Arbrå**, 16 km (10 miles) north of Bollnäs, there is an 18th-century

wooden mansion on the Hans-Andersgården estate where journalist Willy Maria Lundberg (b.1909) created a centre for the preservation of old buildings. As well as being an attraction in its own right, the manor also has exhibitions and specialist gardens. In summer, the tourist office runs guided tours of Hälsingland's farms and manor houses.

Växbo, east of Bollnäs, has the only flax-spinning works in Sweden, which produces and sells items such as tablecloths and napkins.

Log-floater by Per Nilsson Öst (1972)

🏛 **Bollnäs Museum**
Odengatan 17. 📞 *0278-253 26.* 🕐 *Jun–Aug: Tue–Sun; Sep–May: Tue–Sat.* ⬤ *some public holidays.* 🅿️ ♿

Hudiksvall **❻**

Hälsingland. 🏘 *15,000.* 🚃 🚌 🛳
ℹ️ *Storgatan 33, 0650-191 00.*
🎭 *Delsbo Festival (1st Sun Jul), Music at Dellen (1st week in Jul), Town Festival (last week in Jul).*
🌐 *www.hudiksvall.se/turism*

F ISHING, SEAFARING and trade have been the mainstay of Hudiksvall throughout its 400-

year history. In the late 19th century the timber industry boomed and the town became known for its high living, giving rise to the phrase "Happy Hudik".

Despite attacks by Russian forces in the 18th century and numerous fires, a number of older buildings remain, giving the town charm and character. The Sundskanal in the centre, a canal linking Lillfjärden and Hudiksvalls-fjärden inlets, is lined with red huts and merchants' warehouses from the mid-19th century.

East of the inlet is Fiskarstan (Fishermen's Town), with its partly-preserved wooden houses from the early 19th century. Along Hamngatan there are several fine old merchants' yards featuring the elegant wood-panelled architecture of the time. They have terraces on the water-side and shops on the parallel street of Storgatan. An example is the **Bruns Gård** pharmacy, which has an ornate pharmacy entrance on Storgatan and a winged house on the terraces of Hamngatan.

Dominating the skyline is **St Jakobs Kyrka**, a church built in the 17th and 18th centuries, although its onion dome dates from 1888.

Hälsinglands Museum, in an imposing former bank building, provides a good picture of the colourful history of the area.

ENVIRONS: Hudiksvall municip-ality covers a large area of northern Hälsingland, including **Delsbo** and the beautiful Dellensjö lakes to the west. South of the town is **Iggesund**, with its 400 years of ironworking history, and

Picturesque warehouses and quay on Sundskanalen in Hudiksvall

Torpsjön, a typical lake on the mighty Ljungan river, with Fränsta Kyrka on its shore

Enånger, where the 15th-century church contains exquisite medieval ceiling paintings by Andreas Erici and wooden sculptures by master sculptor Håkon Gullesson.

🏛 **Hälsinglands Museum**
Storgatan 31. ▮ 0650-196 00. ◯ daily. ◐ public holidays & eves of public holidays. ☑ by appointment. ▯ ◔

Ljusdal ⓰

Hälsingland. ▤ ▣ ▮ Turistvägen 29, Järvsö, 0651-403 06. ◪ Hälsingehambo Polka Festival (1st Sat after 1st Sun in July), Butterfly Week (2nd Sun Jul), Bandy World Cup (end Oct).
ⓦ www.ljusdal.se

IN THE HEART OF northwest Hälsingland on the Ljusnan river is Ljusdal. Settlers have long been attracted to this fertile valley and their history is explored at **Ljusdalsbygdens Museum**. Christianity came early to the area; parts of the church of **St Olovs Kyrka** are 12th-century.

The Swedish national sport of bandy – similar to ice hockey – is enormously popular in Ljusdal, where teams of bandy players assemble for three days in October to compete for the World Cup.

ENVIRONS: Opportunities for fishing and walking present themselves at every turn. From **Lassekrog**, 40 km (25 miles) upstream from Ljusdal, those who dare can run the rapids on the Ljusnan river. Lassekrog has been an inn since the 17th century. Here, author Albert Viksten's forest camp is a monument to the foresters of old.

South of Ljusdal, at **Järvsö**, wildlife from the north,

including predators such as bear, wolf, wolverine and lynx and their prey, can be seen at **Järvzoo Djurpark** and the adjacent Rovdjurscentret (Predator Centre). Järvsö village itself is known for having Sweden's largest provincial church; when it was completed in 1838 it had space for 2,400 parishioners. On the opposite bank lies **Stenegård**, a 19th-century trading post, now a centre for arts and crafts, with a theatre in the wooden barn.

Stenegård is also the end point for the annual Hälsingehambo Polka Festival, which starts in Hårga, 65 km (40 miles) to the south.

🏛 **Ljusdalsbygdens Museum**
Museivägen 5, Ljusdal.
▮ 0651-71 16 65. ◯ Tue–Sat.
◐ public holidays. ☑ by appointment. ▯
🦌 **Järvzoo Djurpark**
1 km (half a mile) south of Järvsö centre. ▮ 0651-411 25. ◯ daily.
▧ ☑ by appointment. ▯

Ljusdalsbygdens Museum, in a wooden Hälsingland building

Ljungadalen ⓱

Medelpad. E14. ▮ Sundsvalls Tourist Office, 060-61 04 50.

THE 350-KM (220-mile) Ljungan river rises at Helagsfjällen mountain and flows into the Gulf of Bothnia just south of the town of Sundsvall. In Medelpad, the river forms an often wide valley with a series of lakes. The E14 follows long stretches of the river, offering spectacular views. The great Norrland forests loom on the horizon and the river was an important timber route.

Stöde Kyrkby on Stödesjön lake, 40 km (25 miles) west of Sundsvall, has a long history, which is illustrated at the Huberget rural heritage centre. The church was built in the 1750s, but contains medieval artifacts from an older, now demolished church.

Borgsjö, 40 km (25 miles) further upriver, has a fine Rococo church built in 1768, with a superb wooden bell tower from 1782. Next to the church is Borgsjö rural heritage centre featuring Jämtkrogen Inn, which was relocated here from the Jämtland border.

Ånge, a railway junction 100 km (60 miles) west of Sundsvall, is an ideal starting point for exploring the area. To the west, the countryside of Haverö spreads out around the Havern and Holmsjön lakes, which are good for canoeing. **Haverö Strömmar** is an 8-km (5-mile) stretch of at times wild rapids with three streams where former dams, mills and fishing huts have been preserved. **Alby**, just off route 83, has a restored eel house showing a fishing method used in the 16th century.

The carefully restored Hotell Knaust's marble staircase

Sundsvall ❾

Medelpad. 🏛 *50,000.* 🚉 🚌
✈ *Midlanda.* 🚢 🛈 *Stora Torget,
060-61 04 50.* 🎪 *Sundsvall Street
Festival (1st or 2nd weekend Jul),
Dragonboat Festival (1st week in Aug),
Selånger market (2nd weekend in
Aug).* 🌐 *www.sundsvallturism.com*

THE VIEW FROM Norra and
Södra Stadsberget hills
shows Sundsvall sandwiched
between the mouths of the
Ljungan and Indalsälven
rivers. The sheltered inlets
attracted traders to this spot
in the 6th century, as can be
seen from the Högom burial
ground near Selånger. Alongside Selånger's 12th-century
church lay St Olofs Hamn,
the starting point for
trading missions and
pilgrimages to
Norway's
Nidaros
(Trondheim).
  Sundsvall
was founded in
1624. It took off in
the mid-1800s
with the advent of
the steam-powered sawmill.
Sweden's first such sawmill
was built in 1849 in Tunadal;
when the industry was at its
height there were 19 sawmills
on the island of Alnön alone.
In 1888, fire destroyed large
parts of the town centre. The
railway station survived, and
the attractive wooden
building is now a casino. A
grand "stone town" rose from

**Statues on the roof of
Sundsvall town hall**

the ashes. In Stora Torget
stands the statue of the
founder King Gustav II Adolf.
The square is flanked by the
Town Hall and the **Hirschska
Huset** with its extravagant
pinnacles and towers. A
notable building on Storgatan
is the newly renovated **Hotell
Knaust**, built in 1890, with its
superb marble staircase. The
cultural centre, Kulturmaga-
sinet, near the harbour,
contains the town library and
Sundsvalls Museum. On
Norra Stadsberget lies
Sundsvalls Stadspark,
which has a collection of
buildings from Medelpad, as
well as animal enclosures and
lookout towers. Södra
Stadsberget's outdoor
recreation
centre has
adventure
trails for
children.

ENVIRONS:
Linked to
Sundsvall by the
Alnöbron bridge,
Alnön has many
monuments to the timber
industry. The 13th-century
church is interesting for its
wooden interior and medieval
paintings and sculptures, and
the fishing village of **Spikarna**
is well worth a visit.
  Around 26 km (16 miles)
southeast of Sundsvall lies
Galtström, Medelpad's first
ironworks, built in 1695. The
works have been restored.

🏛 **Sundsvalls Museum**
Kultumagasinet. 📞 060-19 18 03.
◯ Mon–Sat. ● Easter Mon, Whit
Mon, Midsummer's Eve. 🎟 by
appointment. 🖼 🖥 ♿
🏛 **Sundsvalls Stadspark**
Norra Stadsberget. 📞 060-15 40 40.
◯ daily. ● eves of public holidays.
🎟 by appointment. 🖼 (by Stads-
parken). 🖥 🍴 🖼 ♿

Härnösand ❿

Ångermanland. 🏛 *18,000.* 🚉
🚌 🚢 🛈 *Härnösands Municipality,
0611-34 80 00.* 🎪 *Midsummer
celebrations at Murberget,
Härnösandskalaset (Jul), Park Festival
(2nd–3rd week in Jul).*

THE COUNTY TOWN of west-
ern Norrland has a proud
history. It received its town
charter from Johan III in 1585,
became diocesan capital in
1647 and had an upper
secondary school by 1650.
  Härnösand's rich history,
combined with the fact that,
in contrast to other Norrland
coastal towns, it was spared
major fires for almost 300
years, makes it an interesting
place to stroll around. The
Russians plundered
Härnösand in 1721. A new
wooden town replaced the
old and charming districts
such as Östanbäcken and
Norrstan still remain. Standing
out among the many public
buildings are the town hall
from the 1790s on Stora
Torget, the old upper
secondary school and the
county governor's residence.
  At Murbergets Frilufts-
museum, which is part of
**Länsmuseet Västernorr-
land**, 18th-century buildings
have been preserved, including the town hall built in
1727. This large open-air
museum also reflects farming
culture, with crofts and farms,
a blacksmith's and sawmill,
and a Norrland church village.
  Skeppsbron fills with yachts
in July when the town's maritime history is celebrated at
the Härnösandskalaset festival.

🏛 **Länsmuseet
Västernorrland**
Murberget. 📞 0611-886 10.
◯ Tue–Sun. ● 24, 31 Dec, 1 Jan, Eas-
ter Sat. 🎟 by appointment. 🖼 🖥 ♿

Ådalen ⓫

Ångermanland. Road 90.
🚂 from Örnsköldsvik. ℹ️ Kramfors
Tourist Office, 0612-801 20.
🎭 Kramfors Town Festival (weekend
before Midsummer).

AS THE FORESTRY industry
flourished, Ådalen, the
river valley leading to Junsele,
became a hotbed of trade
unionism and earned the
nickname "Red Ådalen". In
1931, the year of the Great
Depression, a most unlikely
event occurred: the military
shot indiscriminately into a
peaceful strikers' march in
Lunde, killing five people.
Lenny Clarhäll's powerful
sculpture depicting the drama
stands on Sandöbron bridge.

Already in the mid-18th
century, Livonian Johan
Kramm set up a water-
powered sawmill on the site
which in 1947 became the
town of Kramfors. Cargo
ships were able to navigate
50 km (31 miles) up the river
and the lower valley became
a magnet for the forestry
industry. The line of factories

One of the many rock carvings in
Nämforsen from around 4000 BC

is now almost entirely
gone. Further up river,
however, there are
numerous power
stations – the Faxälven
tributary is home to 36
alone. Particularly worth
visiting is **Nämforsen**,
where in summer visitors
can view the large power
station and occasionally
see the mighty waterfall
burst into life. The islands
in the falls are an out-
standing site for rock
carvings. From 4000–
2300 BC, hunters carved
out over 2,500 figures.

Örnsköldsvik ⓬

Ångermanland. 🚂 to Sundsvall or
Mellansel, then bus/taxi. 🚌 ✈️
♿ ℹ️ Nygatan 18, 0660-881 00.
🎭 Harbour Festival (1st weekend in
Jul), Dragonboat Festival (mid-Aug).
🌐 www.ornskoldsvik.se/turism

NOLASKOGS is one of the
names by which this part
of northern Ångermanland is
known. It means "north of the
forest" – the wild frontier
forest of Skule (see p256).

Its main town, Örnsköldsvik,
or Ö-vik as it is often called,
was founded in 1842.
Unusually for the time, it was
named after a non-royal
figure, the county governor
Per Abraham Örnsköld. There
are good views of the town
from Varvsberget and from
the top of the ski-jumping
tower on Paradiskullen. Many
of the town's older buildings

Arken, designed by architect
Per Eddi Byggstam, 1991

have been lost to modern
developments. A few exceptions include the delightful
town hall which, thankfully
for Ö-vik's remarkably large
artists' colony, was saved as
an exhibition space. The
beautifully restored junior
secondary school houses
Örnsköldsviks Museum,
which displays the history
of Nolaskogs.

Attractive new architecture
can be seen in the development of the inner harbour,
where **Arken** – a centre for
offices, university buildings
and a library – forms an
exciting backdrop. One of its
glass-roofed courtyards
houses the **Hans Hedbergs
Museum** dedicated to the
Swedish sculptor (see p22).

ENVIRONS: Next to an excav-
ation site in **Gene Fornby**,
5 km (3 miles) south of the
town, a 6th century farm has
been reconstructed, where
people come to live and work
as they did in the Iron Age.

The most striking medieval
church in the area is the
octagonal **Själevads Kyrka**
from 1880, which was voted
Sweden's most beautiful
church in a nationwide poll.

🏛 **Örnsköldsviks Museum**
Läroverksgatan 1. ☎ 0660-886 01.
🔵 Midsummer–Aug: daily; other times:
Tue–Sun. 🌑 public holidays. 🔲 🔳
🏛 **Arken**
Strandgatan 21. ☎ 0660-785 00.
Public areas 🔵 daily. **Hans
Hedbergs Museum** 🔵 ring Tourist
Office 0660-881 00 for info. 🌑 public
holidays. 🔲 🔳

SURSTRÖMMING, A FISHY DELICACY

The coast of Southern Norrland has a speciality which
many Swedes, not only the people of Norrland, consider to
be the ultimate delicacy, although the majority probably
detest it. This treat is fermented herring, known as
surströmming, which, after around eight weeks of
fermenting, is canned. When the can is
opened it produces what is, to say the
least, a characteristic aroma, which
aficionados consider absolutely divine.
The fishing villages along the High Coast
(see pp256–7), such as Ulvöhamn, are the
centre of production, and a market is now
opening up as far afield as Japan. The
fermented herring is eaten reverentially,
almost ritually, in early autumn, accompanied by small
almond-shaped potatoes and chopped onion. It is best
washed down with copious amounts of beer and schnapps.

**Can of
Surströmming**

The High Coast ⑬

SWEDEN'S SPECTACULAR HIGH COAST is best experienced on a light summer evening, when the wooded hills are reflected in the calm waters of the bays, or on the quay in Ulvöhamn during the *surströmming* season *(see p255),* when the peculiar speciality of fermented herring is enjoyed with flat bread, tiny potatoes and schnapps. A boat is ideal for getting around, but the new Höga-kustenbron bridge provides easy access and ferries sail regularly from several ports. The dramatic landscape is the main attraction. Declared a UNESCO World Heritage Site in 2000, it is the result of the land rising 300 m (984 ft) since the ice receded around 9,600 years ago. At that time Skuleberget hill, north of Docksta, was a tiny island.

Skuleskogens National Park
Watched over by Skuleberget hill, the park covers 30 sq km (12 sq miles) of wilderness, with walking trails through magical ancient forest and over the clifftops along the coast.

Ullångersfjärden
Motorists on the E4 rejoin the Gulf of Bothnia at Ullångersfjärden bay which, with its high, sheer cliffs, is almost fjord-like.

Nordingrå
"Fair Nordingrå" was a tourist destination long before the term High Coast was coined. Beautiful roads lined with steep hills pass through stunning scenery.

Högakustenbron
Since 1997, the 1,800-m (6,000-ft) bridge, suspended on 180-m (600-ft) high pylons, has saved travellers the 13-km (8-mile) detour up the Ångermanälven valley to the Sandöbron bridge.

Örnskölds

E4

Norrf

Docksta

Ullånger

Ullånge

Nordingrå

Gaviks

E4

Ångermanälven

Noråfjärden

STORÖ

Härnösand

Skagsudde

The High Coast walking trail stretches 127 km (79 miles) from the mouth of the Ångermanälven to Örnsköldsvik.

VISITORS' CHECKLIST

Ångermanland. E4.
🚹 Örnsköldsvik Tourist Office, 0660-881 00. Kramfors Tourist Office, 0612-801 20. 🚢 from Örnsköldsvik.
Skule National Park Skule Naturum, 0613-401 71.
🎫 Skule Song Festival (1st weekend in Jul).
🌐 www.hogakusten.com

Trysunda
One of the best-preserved villages, Trysunda has a richly-decorated, 17th-century fishermen's chapel. Part of the island is a nature reserve.

Köpmanholmen

Trysunda

N. ULVÖN

MJÄLTÖN

Ulvöhamn

GULF OF BOTHNIA

S. ULVÖN

Ulvöhamn
This is the spiritual home of the herring speciality, surströmming. Norrland's largest fishing fleet made its home in the sheltered harbour lying between Norra and Södra Ulvön. The chapel dates from 1622.

jällom

Norrfällsviken

Omnefjärden

Bönhamn

0 kilometres   10

0 miles   5

Högbonden
The 100-year-old lighthouse on the island of Högbonden warned shipping of the rocky coastline. Today it is a youth hostel, reached by boat from Bönhamn, the most authentic fishing village on the mainland, and the place to savour local specialities such as fresh river salmon, whitefish and, of course, surströmming.

KEY

▬ Major road

═ Minor road

-- Ferry route

- - High Coast walking trail

National Park

Nature Reserve

**Thai monument in Utanede, commemor-
ating the King of Siam's royal visit in 1897**

Indalsälven ⑭

Jämtland/Medelpad. Road 86. 🚉 *to
Sundsvall, then bus.* 🚌 *Ragunda
Tourist Office, 0696-68 20 90.*
🎪 *Vildhussen Festival (1st and 2nd
weeks in Jul).* 🆆 *www.ragunda.se*

THE 430-KM (270-mile) long
Indalsälven river rises in
the mountains of Norway and
flows into Klingerfjärden,
north of Sundsvall. The lower
stretch of the river from
Ragunda in Jämtland includes
Döda Fallet (the Dead Falls)
caused by a disastrous attempt
by Vildhussen (*see box*) to
control the river in 1796.

Döda Fallet is now a nature
reserve where it is possible to
walk around the rocky landscape and see the giant basins
carved out by stones in the
falls. An extraordinary open-
air theatre has been created
next to the falls, where the

stand for an audience
of 420 revolves twice
a minute. A stage in
the round is set
against breathtaking
natural scenery.

Utanede features an
exotic Thai pavilion, the
**King Chulalongkorn
Memorial**, erected in
memory of the King of
Siam's trip along the
river in 1897 as a guest
of King Oscar II. The
decorative elements of
the golden pavilion
were built by Thai
craftsmen and seven
million parts were shipped to
Sweden and assembled. The
interior holds a life-sized
bronze statue of the king.

Among the churches along
the river, **Lidens Kyrka**,
dating from 1510, has the
most attractive location (road
86, 37 km/23 miles northwest
of Sundsvall) and contains
medieval sculptures, with a
Madonna from the 13th
century. Vildhussen is buried
in the cemetery here.

Bergeforsen on the coast
is the last of the river's many
power stations. There is an
aquarium where Baltic fish
such as salmon, sea trout and
eel are raised.

🏛 King Chulalongkorn Memorial

*Utanede. Road 86, 7 km (4 miles)
south of Bispgården.* 📞 *0696-321
06.* ⭕ *mid-May–mid-Sep: daily.* 🏳
📷 *hourly.* 🅿 🖭 ♿ *some facilities.*

Östersund ⑮

Jämtland. 🏔 *44,000.* 🚆 🚌 🛫
ℹ *Rådhusgatan 44, 063-14 40 01.*
🎪 *Storsjöyran Festival (last weekend
in Jul), Armljot Games (Jul).*
🆆 *www.ostersund.se/turist*

ESTABLISHED ON the shores of
Storsjön lake in 1786, the
county town of Östersund lies
opposite Jämtland's ancient
centre of Frösön. Before
coming under Norwegian rule
in 1178, the people of Jämtland had ruled themselves
and would be happy to do so
again if the Republic of
Jämtland movement had its
way. In a fairly lighthearted
manner, the movement
protects local culture – the
highpoint is the Storsjöyran
Festival at the end of July.

The county museum, **Jamtli**,
with its highly praised
Historieland feature, offers an
exciting picture of life around
Storsjön. This time machine
transports visitors to scenes
from the 18th and 19th
centuries, where history can
be felt, heard and even tasted.
The museum's showpiece are
the oldest preserved Viking
Överbogdal tapestries.

A short bridge leads to the
rolling, green island of Frösön.
Its eastern parts are more like
a part of town, but the views
across Storsjön to the peak of
Oviksfjällen inspired the
composer Wilhelm Peterson-
Berger to create his distinctive
home, **Sommarhagen**, in
1914. The house is now a
museum and the rich interior
with decorative paintings by
Paul Jonze is something of a
companion to Carl Larsson's
Sundborn (*see p240*). Every

VILDHUSSEN AND THE DEAD FALLS

A drama which was to have a lasting impact unfolded on 6
June 1796 in Ragunda on the Indalsälven river. Magnus Huss,
known as Vildhussen (Wild Huss), a merchant in Sundsvall,
had been building a log flume to bypass the 38-m (125-ft)
high Storforsen waterfall when an unusually high spring flood
put pressure on the lake above the falls. The log flume burst
and the river forged a new route, emptying the 27-km (17-

**Döda Fallet, Vild-
hussen's creation**

mile) long lake in just four hours and send-
ing so much soil and debris downstream
that it formed Sweden's largest delta at the
river mouth. The Storforsen waterfall had
become Döda Fallet (the Dead Falls). Local
people were sceptical of Huss's scheme
from the start and despite the now navig-
able river and fertile land on the old lake
bed, discontent brewed. A year later Huss
died when his boat capsized. Rumour has
it that the oars had been hidden and his
boat pushed out into the fast-flowing river.

**Old stone fireplace in Jamtli
Museum, Östersund**

summer *Arnljot*, Peterson-Berger's drama about the Viking from 11th-century Frösö, is performed in a field a short distance away.

The 12th-century **Frösö Kyrka** is one of Sweden's most popular churches in which to get married. **Frösö Zoo** has 700 animal species from around the world.

ENVIRONS: Storsjön lake is best explored on a steamer, such as the 1875 *S/S Thomeé*, Sweden's oldest steamer still in regular use. Many enthusiasts try to spot the elusive Storsjö Monster, the so-called sister of Scotland's Loch Ness monster.

Brunflo, 15 km (9 miles) south of Östersund, has an 18th-century church with a 12th-century lookout tower.

🏛 **Jamtli**
Museiplan. 📞 *063-15 01 10.*
⭕ *Jun–Aug: daily; Sep–May: Tue–Sun.*
⚫ *24, 25, 31 Dec.* 🅰 💪 *summer.*
🖥 🍴 🎁 &

🏛 **Sommarhagen**
Frösön, 9 km (6 miles from the centre).
📞 *063-430 41.* ⭕ *End May–end Aug: daily; other times by arrangement.* 💪 *by appointment.* 🖥 🎁
💥 **Frösö Zoo**
3 km (2 miles) south of the centre. 📞
063-51 47 53. ⭕ *2nd week in Jun–3rd week in Aug: daily.* 📷 🖥 🍴 🎁 &

Åre 🔟

Jämtland. E14. 🏃 *1,000.* 🚌 🚍
⊠ *Östersund.* ℹ️ *St Olofs Väg, 0647-177 20.* 📷 *Alpine World Cup (Feb), Country Festival (2nd week in Jul).*

Å RESKUTAN IS Sweden's most visited mountain peak. The cable car lifts passengers from the village of Åre to within 150 m (490 ft) of the summit at 1,420 m (4,658 ft). At this altitude, the skiing season lasts into June. Facilities are plentiful in what has become Sweden's leading ski destination. There are 40 lifts and 100 pistes, some of which are the longest and steepest in the country. Hotels and conference centres rise up into the sky. This is

The 1,700-m (5,600-ft) high Syl, just over a day's walk south of Storlien

in great contrast to how the resort looked at the end of the 19th century with hotels such as Åregården and the Grand. Still here is the Bergbanan run, which has attracted toboganists of all ages. Prominent visitors have included Winston Churchill, who came to hunt elk. Today's range of adventure activities includes scooter safaris, dog sledding, para-skiing, ice-climbing, caving, surfing rapids and mountain biking on Åreskutan.

ENVIRONS: The **Tännforsen** waterfall, 20 km (12 miles) west of Åre, is one of the most impressive in Jämtland, with a drop of 37 m (120 ft).

Narke Sameläger, on an island on Häggsjön lake, has a Sami camp where visitors can learn how to lasso, or taste delicacies such as reindeer heart. On Åreskutan's eastern spur, 10 km (6 miles) from Åre, lies **Fröå Gruva**, where copper was mined from 1752 to 1916. The countryside is beautiful to wander through, with buildings from various eras. At **Huså Bruk**, another centre for copper mining further to the north, is Huså Herrgård, a manor built in 1838.

Skiers resting at a hut on Åreskutan, Sweden's top ski resort

Storlien 🔳

Jämtland. E14. 🚌 🚍 ⊠ *Östersund.*
ℹ️ *Åre Tourist Office, 0647-177 20.*
🅆 *www.storlien.nu*

T HE ARRIVAL OF the railway in Trondheim in the 1880s opened up new opportunities for Storlien, which is located near the border with Norway. It is only 60 km (37 miles) to the Trondheim Fjord, and the broad pass between Stenfjället and Skurdalshöjden allows mild Atlantic winds to sweep through. The healthy air attracted spa guests to a mountain sanatorium, and with the dawn of the 20th century tourists began arriving.

Today, Storlien is one of Sweden's leading ski centres for both cross-country and downhill. It is also a starting point for walks in the Jämtland mountains, such as via the STF stations of Blåhammaren, Storulvån, Sylarna and Vålådalen. The mountains can also be reached from Enafors on the E14 and by train.

Popular with birdwatchers, nearby **Ånnsjön** lake has a bird station and sanctuary. **Handöl**, on the western shore, has been a site for soapstone mining since the late Middle Ages. It was also where the surviving Carolian forces gathered in 1799 after Carl Gustaf Armfelt's catastrophic retreat from Norway. The Carolian monument on the waterfront is a memorial to the 3,700 men who froze to death in the mountains. Today accommodation and better equipment have prompted more and more people to take up the challenge of completing the 75-km (47-mile) long Carolian March.

The Mountains of Härjedalen ⑱

THE TREE LINE IN HÄRJEDALEN is at 900 m (2,950 ft) and even in the forested lowlands in the east there are mountains with bare summits such as Sånfjället and Vemdalsfjällen. But the mightiest mountains loom large in the west towards Norway and the province of Jämtland, with Helagsfjället the highest peak at 1,797 m (5,900 ft). Funäsdalen is the local hub, from where in summer Sweden's highest road runs via the Sami village of Mittådalen and the plateau of Flatruet to Ljungdalen. There are many opportunities for ski-touring and downhill skiing, fishing in summer and hiking along the southern part of the Kungsleden trail.

Helags
STF (see p314) has a mountain station at the base of Helagsfjället, Sweden's highest peak south of the Arctic Circle.

Ramundberget
In the summer, this popular winter sports venue, known for its early snowfalls, is a good starting point for mountain hikes to Helags, Ljungdalen and Fjällnäs.

The road over the Flatruet Plateau is only open in summer.

Röros (Norway)

Fjällnäs ⚡

Tänndalen 84

Ljungdalen

Mittådalen

Bruksvallarna ⚡

Tännäs

Högvålen

Idre

Funäsdalen
This lively town in the Härjedalen mountains has the award-winning Härjedalens Fjällmuseum, which shows how the Sami and upland farmers survived the challenges of past times.

Rogen
The nature reserve around Härjedalen's largest lake system has unusual flora and fauna. It is great for canoeing. The Sami village of Ruvhten offers ice-fishing for grayling and char.

KEY

▬▬	Major road
═══	Minor road
-- --	Walking trail
⚡	Ski resort

Reindeer Pastures
The Sami villages of Mittådalen and Ruvhten (Tännäs) have summer pastures in the western mountains. The winter pastures stretch as far as the forests of Sveg and into Dalarna.

Vemdalsfjällen
This skiers' paradise has a joint lift system for the main resorts: Vemdalskalet, Björnrike, Klövsjö and Storhågna, as well as great facilities for cross-country skiing.

Klövsjö 🎿

Vemdalsskalet 🎿

Storhågna
Ånge

Vemdalen

Björnrike 🎿

Sveg

Sånfjället
Parts of this mountain in the forest were declared a national park in 1909, partly to protect the bear population. Wolves, lynx and wolverine also live here.

Sveg

Skärsjövalen 🎿

Hede

84

Lofsdalen 🎿

0 kilometres   20

0 miles   10

Sveg ⑲

Härjedalen. 🚶 2,700. 🚆 Inlandsbanan (summer), or to Mora or Ljusdal then bus. 🚌 ✈ ℹ Ljusnegatan 1, 0680-107 75. 🎭 Olsmäss Festival (last weekend in Jul), Julisveg Festival (Jul).

HÄRJEDALEN'S central town is Sveg, the gateway to the mountains. The municipality of the same name covers an area larger than many counties, and with just 11,000 inhabitants it has a population density of less than one person per sq km. Forest stretches in every direction. Winding waterways provide opportunities for fishing, canoeing and beaver safaris. The nearest mountain for skiing is a 30-minute drive away.

Around Sveg, small villages such as Duvberg, Ytterberg, Överberg and Äggen are well-preserved, with 18th-century features. **Gammel-Remsgården**, 15 km (9 miles) north of Sveg, is a typical early-18th-century Härjedalen manor house with richly decorated interiors. About 15 km (9 miles) east of Sveg lies the village of **Älvros**, whose church has a beautifully painted bell tower.

Lillhärdal, 30 km (19 miles) south of Sveg, is said to have been founded in the 9th century by the Viking Härjulf Hornbrytare. Bildhöst has one of the last working crofts, complete with cattle and milkmaids, while Hamre Skans is a timbered fortification from the 18th century.

Älvros church near Sveg, with a free-standing, painted bell tower

NORTHERN NORRLAND

TRETCHING FROM THE POPULATED BALTIC *coast through wild forests and marshes to the open expanses of the mountains, Northern Norrland is a vast, almost untouched region. The biting chill and eternal darkness of the long northern winter are compensated for by summer's midnight sun, when nature seizes its short window of opportunity to flourish and the reindeer are moved to new pastures.*

The three provinces of Västerbotten, Norrbotten and Lappland make up Sweden's most northerly region. Västerbotten, on the Gulf of Bothnia, is the most southerly. Its coast and river valleys had booming settlements for many centuries. But today commercial activity is concentrated in towns such as Umeå, with its university and youthful population, and Skellefteå, known as the "Town of Gold" because of its proximity to two of Europe's largest gold deposits. Inland, the wilderness takes hold with vast tracts of forest and marsh. After a journey between Lycksele and Sorsele, Carl von Linné wrote: "A priest could never make Hell sound worse than this." But with modern transport, today's traveller can look forward to outdoor adventures and wildlife in this unspoilt landscape.

North of Västerbotten, Norrbotten's coastline harbours features of rural culture such as the church village in Gammelstad, a UNESCO World Heritage Site. The Norrbotten archipelago is renowned for being the sunniest place in the country and its beach resorts lure holiday-makers. The border with Finland lies along the Torne river, but here the phrase "two countries, one people" is the most applicable.

Lappland borders Norway in the west and Finland in the northeast, but for the Sami (Lapp) people their land extends beyond official boundaries, across the mountains and forests and down to the coast, where their thriving culture of reindeer herding, hunting and fishing prevail. Known as Laponia, this area is also a UNESCO World Heritage Site. National parks such as Sarek protect the alpine landscape with its glaciers and waterfalls. The main towns of Kiruna and Gällivare in northern Lappland owe their existence to the mining industry.

Dog sledding in Jukkasjärvi, Lapland

◁ Kaitumsjön Lake, Lapland

Exploring Northern Norrland

AN AREA COVERING MORE THAN one-third of Sweden cannot be explored in a hurry. And things are not made easier by the large areas of wilderness north of the Arctic Circle without roads, in Europe's most sparsely populated region. Despite their northerly latitude, the coastal areas combine a captivating archipelago landscape with rich cultural sights. Spectacular roads lead up into the mountains with romantic names such as "Saga Vägen" (the Saga Highway) and "Blå Vägen" (the Blue Highway). Skiers are tempted by the record-length season, while for hikers, the northernmost section of the 440-km (275-mile) long Kungsleden trail *(see p274)* between Abisko and Hemavan crosses the mountainous UNESCO World Heritage Site of Laponia.

Lake Saggat seen from the Kvikkjokk road in northwestern Lappland

GETTING AROUND

Flying is the most comfortable means of transport. Around a dozen airports offer scheduled flights. Only a few trains travel on the Vännäs–Luleå line and the Malmbanan line running Luleå– Kiruna–Riksgränsen. The Inlandsbanan line through Lappland from Gällivare provides a summer tourist route. The major roads E4, E10 and E12 (the Blue Highway) are of a high standard, but road conditions are variable elsewhere. Bus services between the main towns are usually good, but almost non-existent in the wilder areas. Ferries operate across some mountain lakes in summer, saving time for hikers.

KEY

━ Major road

═ Minor road

⚊⚊ Railway line

- ∙ Ferry route

Narvik (Norway)

ABIS

Kebnek
2104

Akkajaure

Stora Lu

Sarektjåkkå
2090 m

KUNGSLEDEN ⑱

Bodø (Norway)

KVIKKJOKK●

Lilla Luleäl

Piteälven

LAPPLAN

Skellefteälven

Mo i Rana (Norway)

95

Horn-
avan

ARJEPLOG ⑰

●AMMARNÄS

✕●HEMAVAN

Vindelälven

Stor
ava

E12

Umeälven

●STORUMAN
✕

●VILHELMINA
✕

45   90

ÅSELE

92

SEE ALSO

- **Where to Stay** p289

- **Where to Eat** p303

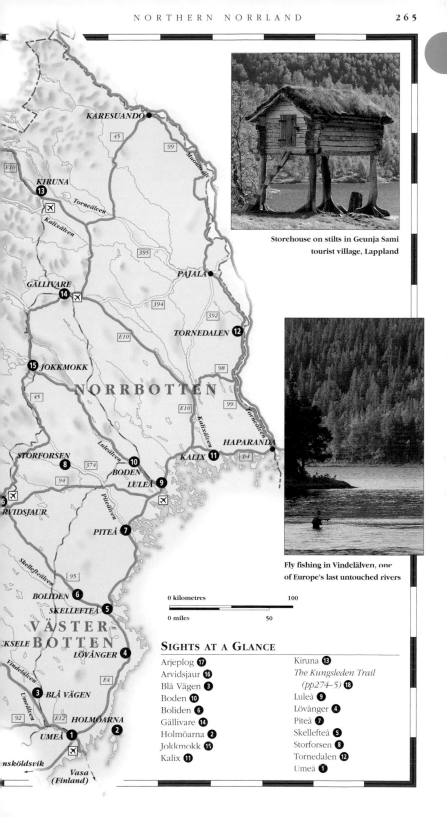

**Storehouse on stilts in Geunja Sami
tourist village, Lappland**

**Fly fishing in Vindelälven, one
of Europe's last untouched rivers**

SIGHTS AT A GLANCE

Arjeplog **17**

Arvidsjaur **16**

Blå Vägen **3**

Boden **10**

Boliden **6**

Gällivare **14**

Holmöarna **2**

Jokkmokk **15**

Kalix **11**

Kiruna **13**

The Kungsleden Trail
  (pp274–5) **18**

Luleå **9**

Lövånger **4**

Piteå **7**

Skellefteå **5**

Storforsen **8**

Tornedalen **12**

Umeå **1**

Birch avenue in Umeå, with the Town Hall in the background

Umeå ❶

Västerbotten. 🏛 71,000. 🚉 🚌 ⊠ 🛥 from Vasa, Finland. 🛈 Renmarkstorget 15, 090-16 16 16. 🎿 Int. Chamber Music Festival (2nd week in Jun), Film Festival (2nd weekend in Sep). Ⓦ www.visitumea.se

WITH 3,000 BIRCH trees lining the streets, it is not surprising that Umeå is known as "The City of Birches". After a major fire in 1888, a new city was built with broad, tree-lined esplanades and parks to prevent fires spreading. Post-fire buildings of interest include the **Scharinska villa** on Storgatan, designed by Ragnar Östberg, and **Moritska Gården**, Umeå's grandest residence for a local timber baron. The city's Neo-Gothic church was completed in 1894.

Umeå dates back to the 16th century and became a county town in 1622. It was an important trading and administrative centre. The opening of a new university in 1965 prompted an expansion that transformed Umeå into a city – Norrland's only one. With 30,000 students and lecturers, it is very much a

young persons' place (average age 36), which is reflected in the wide range of entertainment on offer.

In Gammlia, a 10-minute walk from the centre, the **Västerbottens Museum** is one of Sweden's most rewarding county museums, focusing on the history of Umeå and Västerbotten. It includes Svenska Skidmuseet, which covers the history of skiing, and the fishing and maritime museum Fiske- och Sjöfartsmuseet. In the summer, the open-air museum **Gammlia Friluftsmuseum** shows off its historic farm buildings, complete with pets, and there are activities for children.

Gammlia is also the location of **Bildmuseet**, a museum for contemporary visual arts.

🏛 **Västerbottens Museum**
Gammlia. 🕿 090-17 18 00. 🚌 ◯ mid-May–mid-Aug: daily; other times: Tue–Sun. ◯ 24, 31 Dec. 🚌
🚌 ♿ **Gammlia Friluftsmuseum** ◯ mid-May–mid-Aug: daily. ♿
🏛 **Bildmuseet**
Gammlia. 🕿 090-786 52 27. ◯ mid-Jun–mid-Aug: daily; other times: Tue–Sun. 🎨 by appointment. 🚌 🎨 ♿

Holmöarna ❷

Västerbotten. 🏛 90. 🚌 to Norrfjärden 30 km (19 miles) N of Umeå, then ferry. 🛈 Umeå Tourist Office, 090-16 16 16. 🎿 Holmö Folk Festival (last weekend in July).

A 45-MINUTE FREE ferry trip from Norrfjärden leads to the Holmö archipelago. There are four main islands – Holmön, Grossgrundet, Angesön and Holmögadd – and several smaller ones. The majority of the group forms part of Sweden's largest archipelago nature reserve. It is an area of exciting geological formations and extensive fields of rubble stones. The forest and shorelines provide habitats for 130 species of birds and a variety of flora.

The islands have been inhabited since the 14th century and **Holmöns Båtmuseum** focuses on the lives of the local fishermen, seal hunters and farmers.

The archipelago is ideal for cycling, bathing and fishing.

🏛 **Holmöns Båtmuseum**
At the ferry quay. 🕿 090-552 20 (summer). ◯ mid-Jun–mid-Aug: daily.
🎨 🎨

Encountering a reindeer on the Blue Highway

Blå Vägen ❸

Västerbotten, Lappland. E12. 🚌 🛈 Umeå Tourist Office, 090-16 16 16.

FROM LAKE ONEGA in Russia to Träna on Norway's Atlantic coast, the Blå Vägen (Blue Highway, E12) stretches 1,700 km (1,050 miles). The Swedish section follows the Umeälven river from Umeå through the towns of Lycksele, Storuman and

---

SWEDEN'S 200-YEAR PEACE

Infantryman, model, 1807

Sweden has enjoyed almost 200 years of peace. The last battles on Swedish soil took place in Sävar and Ratan north of Umeå in August 1809. Russian troops had been plundering the coast and a Swedish expeditionary force landed at the port of Ratan to attack the Russians from the rear. The troops marched south towards Sävar and clashed with the Russians on 19 August. The Swedes were defeated and withdrew to Ratan, where another battle was fought the next day. This time the Swedish troops stood their ground, but 1,000 men died in the conflict. A memorial in Sävar honours the fallen. As a result of the war, Finland was lost to Russia.

Hemavan. Klabböle, near Umeå, is the site of the river's first power station, built in 1899. It now houses the museum of **Umeå Energicentrum**, and is well worth a visit. Children enjoy the "Playing with Energy" exhibit and trying to balance on logs like a log driver. **Stornorrfors**, 6 km (4 miles) upstream, is one of Europe's largest hydroelectric power stations. The immense turbine hall, 90 m (295 ft) underground, is open to the public.

At **Vännäs**, 26 km (16 miles) from Umeå, the unspoilt Vindelälven river joins the Umeälven, and a detour can be made to the mighty **Mårdsele falls** to ride the rapids or fish for salmon, salmon trout and grayling.

Lycksele, the only town in southern Lappland, lies 123 km (76 miles) from Umeå. The local zoo, **Lycksele Djurpark**, specializes in Nordic wildlife.

🏛 **Umeå Energicentrum**
10 km (6 miles) W of Umeå. ☎ 090-480 28. ◯ 2nd week in Jun–3rd week in Aug: daily. 🎫 ▭
🦌 **Lycksele Djurpark**
Brännbergsvägen. ☎ 0950-167 10. ◯ 3rd week in May–Aug: daily. 🚱
🅿 🍴 🎫 🏠 ♿

Lövånger ❹

Västerbotten. E4. 🏠 2,400. 🚊 🚹 Lövånger Tourist Office, 0913-104 80.

THE CHURCH village at Lövånger is one of the largest in the country with 117 cabins. It dates from the Middle Ages, although the oldest surviving cabin is from 1746. The village was built to accommodate churchgoers from remote outlying areas during church festivals. A number of cabins have been restored and are let to visitors. The 16th-century granite church of St Anne is decorated with medieval sculptures.

Sockenmuseet, just north of the church, illustrates how the people of Lövånger lived in the 19th century.

🏛 **Sockenmuseet**
☎ 0913-100 40. ◯ odd weeks: Thu–Fri; even weeks: Tue–Wed. 🎫

The church village in Lövånger with accommodation for churchgoers

Skellefteå ❺

Västerbotten. E4. 🏠 34,800. 🚊 to Bastuträsk, then bus. 🚊 🚌 🚹 Trädgårdsgatan 7, 0910-73 60 20. 🎪 Skellefteå Festival (4th weekend in Jun). 🅆 www.skelleftea.se/English

NORTHERN VÄSTERBOTTEN had to wait until 1845 for its first town, but there had long been a marketplace alongside Skellefteå church. In order to accommodate the large congregation, an impressive Neo-Classical cruciform church was built in 1800 on the site of a 15th-century church. Worshippers came from far afield, staying in Bonnstan, Skellefteå's church village built in the mid-19th century.

It was with the boom in the mining industry in the 1920s that Skellefteå's development took off, fuelled by the huge smelting plant at the mouth of the Skellefteälven river.

The town's green lung is the Nordanå Kulturcentrum, a park stretching along the northern bank of the river. It houses an art gallery, **Skellefteå Museum** and historic buildings.

🏛 **Skellefteå Museum**
1.5 km (1 mile) W of the centre. ☎ 0910-73 55 10. ◯ daily. ◯ some public holidays. 🚱 🅿 🍴 🏠 ♿

Boliden ❻

Västerbotten. E4/road 95. 🚊 🚌 Skellefteå, then bus. 🚹 Skellefteå Tourist Office, 0910-73 60 20. 🎪 Geology Festival (end Aug/early Sep).

THE KINGDOM of Gold is the name given to Skellefteå's ore field which, with Boliden

at its heart, stretches from Bottenviken through northern Västerbotten towards the mountains of Lappland. Europe's two largest gold deposits are mined here, in addition to zinc, copper, silver and tungsten.

Bergrum Boliden, in the old mining office, traces the history of the formation of the sulphide ores more than 4,600 million years ago to their extraction today.

In World War II, the world's longest cable car system was constructed to transport the ore 96 km (60 miles) from the mines in Kristineberg. It is possible to travel along a 13-km (8-mile) long stretch from Örträsk to Mensträsk, swinging over the beautiful countryside at a sedate 10 km/h (6 mph).

🏛 **Bergrum Boliden**
1 km (half a mile) NW of the centre. ☎ 0910-58 00 60. ◯ May–Aug: daily; other times by appointment. 🚱 🅿 🎫 🏠 ♿

The Kristineberg cable car system, once used to transport ore

Piteå's sandy beach, and Sweden's best chance of sun

Piteå ❼

Norrbotten. E4. 🚶 22,000. 🚍
✈ Kallax. 🚍 ⛴ ♁ Sundsgatan 41,
0911-933 90. 🎭 Piteå Dances and
Smiles Festival (last week Jul).
🖥 www.pitea.se

ORIGINALLY SITUATED next to
Öjebyn, Piteå was moved
after a fire to the mouth of the
Piteälven river. The new town
was burned by the Russians in
1721 and rebuilt. Picturesque
wooden buildings from the
19th century can be found on
the square of Rådhustorget,
where the attractive Town Hall
dates from 1830. But it is the
coast that is the main attraction.
The **"Nordic Riviera"** offers
extensive sandy beaches and
Sweden's best chance of sun.
If the weather turns, there is
an indoor fun pool.
   Öjebyn has a 15th-century
church and a well-preserved
church village.

ENVIRONS: **Jävre**, off the E4
south of Piteå, has traces of
Norrbotten's first settlers from
the Bronze Age. The archaeology trail takes in graves, sacri-
ficial stones and labyrinths.

Storforsen ❽

Norrbotten. 80 km (50 miles) NW of
Piteå, road 374. 🚍 ♁ Storforsen
Turism, 0929-72100. 🍴
🖥 www.storforsen.com

EUROPE'S MIGHTIEST untamed
stretch of whitewater can
be found on the Piteälven
river, 40 km (25 miles) north
of Älvsbyn. The rapids drop
82 m (270 ft) over 5 km

(3 miles), at speeds of over
800 cubic metres (176,000
gallons) per second. Efforts to
channel the rapids into a
single course created Döda
Fallet (the Dead Falls), where
giant basins can be seen. Log
floating has ceased, but a visit
to the **Skogs- och Flottningsmuseet** will reveal how things
looked when Storforsen's
huge log jams were formed.

🏛 Skogs- och
Flottningsmuseet
Storforsen. 📞 0929-721 00. ⏰ May-
Aug: daily. 🎟 📷 obligatory. 🚻 🍴

**Storforsen in the Piteälven river, a
vast expanse of whitewater rapids**

Luleå ❾

Norrbotten. E4. 🚶 45,000. ✈ 🚍
🚍 ⛴ ♁ Kulturcentrum Ebeneser,
Storgatan 43 B, 0920-29 35 00.
🎭 Luleå Party (first week in Aug).
🖥 www.lulea.se

THE COUNTY TOWN of Luleå is
surrounded by water as
the Luleälven river flows into
glittering bays with a lush
archipelago beyond. A good
harbour was the reason for
the town's location here in
the mid-17th century, when
the original site upstream
became too shallow.
   The church village,
Gammelstads Kyrkstad, and

its church, Nederluleå Kyrka,
form a unique monument to
the old trading centre and in
1996 were designated a UNESCO
World Heritage Site. The 15th-
century granite building with
its perimeter wall is upper
Norrland's largest medieval
church. The white steeple
towers over a group of 408
small red cabins. This is
where churchgoers from
remote villages would stay
overnight and stable their
horses. The church's star vaulting is decorated with paintings
from the Albert Pictor school
of the 1480s. The magnificent
altar-screen from Antwerp
dates from 1520.
   The cathedral in the new
Luleå was built in 1893.
Norrbottens Museum
concentrates on the history
of Luleå and Norrbotten.
   The ore-loading harbour
and SSAB's steelworks are the
cornerstones of Luleå. They
also influence the science
museum, **Teknikens Hus**,
where technical experiments
can be attempted, such as
drilling in a mine and
launching a space rocket.

ENVIRONS: **Luleå archipelago**,
comprising more than 700
islands and islets, is a
favourite place for boat
owners. Ferries provide
access to places of interest,
such as the fishing villages on
Rödkallen and Brändöskär.

♁ Gammelstads Kyrkstad
10 km (6 miles) NW of the centre. 🚍
📞 0920-29 35 81. ⏰ 2nd week in
Jun–mid-Aug: daily; other times:
Tue–Thu. 🎟 📷 🍴 🚻 ⚕ ♿
🏛 Norrbottens Museum
Storgatan 2. 📞 0920-24 35 00.
⏰ Tue–Sun. ⚫ public holidays. 🚻
📷 ♿
🏛 Teknikens Hus
University district, 5 km (3 miles) N of
the centre. 📞 0920-49 22 01.
⏰ Tue–Sun. 🎟 🚻 🍴 ⚕ ♿

**Norrbottens Museum with a Sami
summer tent and hut**

Boden ⑩

Norrbotten. 35 km NW of Luleå, Road 97. Kallax. Kungsgatan 40, 0921-624 10. *Kanonfestdagen Festival (end Jul), Harvest Festival (Aug).* www.boden.se

ITS STRATEGIC LOCATION on the Luleälven river, at the intersection of two main train lines, has made Boden a centre for Sweden's northerly defences. It became the country's largest garrison town at the beginning of the last century and countless young men from across the country have completed their military service here. Five artillery forts circled the town. The nuclear bunker deep in the rock was top secret until only a few years ago. Now **Rödbergsfortet** is a national monument open to the public who can experience life in the fort and even stay in rooms carved out of the rock.

The central Björknäs area is also worth a visit for its open-air heated swimming pool and to see historic Norrbotten farms.

About 3 km (2 miles) north of the centre, a Wild West ranch has been built which offers a taste of pioneering life in the 19th century.

Cannon from Boden fort

Rödbergsfortet

5 km (3 miles) W of the centre. 070-366 31 62. *3rd week in Jun–1st week in Aug; other times by appointment.* *limited access.*

Kalix ⑪

Norrbotten. E4, 50 km (31 miles) W of Haparanda. Kallax. *Töre Tourist Office, 0923-64 10 60.* *Grayling Day (end Jul), National River Festival (mid-Aug).* www.kalix.se

THE KALIX AREA to the north of the Gulf of Bothnia has been inhabited since Stone Age times. **Nederkalix** became a parish in the 15th century, but its church has had a turbulent history, with devastating fires and plundering by the Russians. During the 1809 war, it served as a stable for Russian horses. Englundsgården Cultural Heritage Centre is a good example of Norrland's beautiful wooden architecture.

Kalixälven river, one of Europe's few entirely unregulated large rivers

ENVIRONS: The **Kalixälven** is one of Sweden's few unregulated rivers, ensuring good catches of salmon trout and salmon. The archipelago offers pike and whitefish and the opportunity for seine fishing. Of the islands which can be reached by tour boat, Malören has a timber chapel dating from 1769, an old lighthouse and a pilot station.

Tornedalen ⑫

Norrbotten. Road 99. *Haparanda-Tornio Tourist Office, 0922-120 10.* *Whitefish Festival in Kukkola (last weekend in Jul), Pajala Market (end Jun).*

THE TORNE RIVER and its tributary, Muonio, form the border with Finland, but culturally the areas along both shores are united. Place names are in Finnish, and many of the inhabitants speak a local form of Finnish.

Haparanda, at the mouth of the river, was created as a border town when Torneå became part of Finland in the peace treaty of 1809. A bridge links the sister towns and they share a tourist office.

The disproportionately large train station, which has both normal and Russian wider gauge tracks, is a legacy from its time as a Russian border town.

Fishing is an important part of life on the Torne. Whitefish has been caught in the Kukkola rapids 15 km (9 miles) upstream since the 13th century, using large nets fixed to piers. The best fishing is to be had in late July, when the whitefish festival is held.

Övertorneå, 70 km (43 miles) north of Haparanda, is a fertile horticultural area. The long light summer nights help berries, fruit and vegetables to develop an exceptional flavour. There is a church dating from the 17th century and a good view from the top of the mountain, Luppioberget, where Father Christmas is said to live.

Pajala is the centre of northern Tornedalen. The area is popular for fishing and wilderness camps and it is possible to shoot the rapids on the Torne and Tärendö rivers. The latter is a 50-km (31-mile) long natural link between the Torne and Kalix rivers. **Laestadius Pörte** and museum attract Laestadian Lutherans on a pilgrimage to the simple cabin of the revivalist preacher and botanist Lars Levi Laestadius (1800–61).

Laestadius Pörte

Pajala. 0978-120 55. *May–Aug: daily.*

Octagonal church in Övertorneå, the Tornedalen valley's main town

Strikingly shaped church in Kiruna, inspired by a Sami hut

Kiruna ⑱

Lappland. E10. 🏛 19,100. 🚉 🚌 ✈
ℹ Folkets Hus, Lars Janssonsgatan
17, 0980-188 80. 🎿 Snow Festival
(last weekend in Jan), Kiruna Festival
(4th weekend in Jun).
ⓦ www.lappland.se

I N TERMS OF AREA, Kiruna is one of the world's largest municipalities. It is the site of Sweden's highest mountain, Kebnekaise, 2,111 m (6,925 ft), from where, on a clear day, one can see one-eleventh of the country. For 50 days in summer the sun never sets, and for 20 winter days it never rises. But even in the dark and cold, the people make the best of things. In January they hold a snow festival which is renowned for its ice sculpture competition.

Kiruna's development is due largely to the local iron ore deposits. In 1899 the first ore train rolled out from the mine on the newly laid railway line to Luleå. Ten years later, Kiruna had grown to a town of 7,000 inhabitants. Older buildings include the church, a gift of the mining company LKAB in 1912, whose shape was inspired by a Sami hut, and which is richly decorated by artists of the time, including Prince Eugen, Christian Eriksson and Ossian Elgström.

The Kirunavaara mine is open to visitors for guided tours. **LKAB InfoMine** lies 540 m (1,772 ft) below ground and paints a vivid picture of the development of mining in the region. Shiitake mushrooms are grown in some of the mine's disused tunnels.

ENVIRONS: The space centre **Esrange**, 40 km (25 miles) east of Kiruna has, since the first rocket was launched in 1966, been a vital link in the European space programme. Guided tours can be arranged.

The former Sami village of **Jukkasjärvi**, 17 km (11 miles) east of Kiruna, has Lappland's oldest chapel, dating from 1607. It houses Bror Hjorth's altar-screen in wood depicting the charismatic 19th-century preacher Lars Levi Laestadius' missionary work among the Sami and Swedish pioneers.

Jukkasjärvi has achieved renown more recently through the **Icehotel**. In November every year, a 5,000 sq m (53,820 sq ft) edifice is built out of ice and snow. Drinks are served in the cool Icebar and guests sleep on ice beds, wrapped in furs, even though it is -40°C outside. Spectacular ice sculptures decorate the building. The Ice Globe Theatre, a copy of the Shakespearean Globe Theatre in London, is also erected every year and performances are given of *Macbeth* in Sami and Verdi's *Falstaff*. At the end of April everything melts away, but in summer ice sculptures are displayed in the Artcenter, and the restaurant is open all year.

Kiruna's vast mountain landscape is traversed by the **Kungsleden** trail *(see p274)*.

Altar-screen by Bror Hjorth, Jukkasjärvi church

🏛 LKAB InfoMine
ℹ Kiruna Tourist Office, 0980-188 80
for bookings. 🔲 daily. 🖼 ⓩ
🏨 Icehotel Jukkasjärvi
40 km (25 miles) E of Kiruna.
🚍 from Kiruna. **ℹ** 0980-668 00.
Icehotel 🔲 Dec–Apr. 🖼 ⓩ 🍴 🏨
Ice Globe Theatre 🎭 Dec–Apr:
daily. Artcentrum 🔲 daily.

Gällivare ⑭

Lappland. E10. 🏛 4,700. ✈ 🚉 🚌
ℹ Centralplan 3, 0970-166 60.
🎿 Winter Market (mid-Mar),
Laponia Festival (first weekend in Jul).
ⓦ www.gellivare.se

T HE TWIN communities of Gällivare and Malmberget grew rapidly from the late-19th century as the mining industry developed. But there was a settlement here long before that time: a chapel was built for the Sami in the 17th century and the Sami church on the Vassaraälven river opened in 1751. The arrival of the railway in 1888 sparked an iron ore rush which can be relived at **Kåkstan** in Malmberget and experienced from 1,000 m (3,280 ft) down in the enormous Aitik open-cast copper mine. **LKAB's Gruvmuseum** focuses on 250 years of mining history.

The Gällivare municipality stretches to the Norwegian border, covering parts of the Laponia UNESCO World Heritage Site *(see p275)*. The Dundret

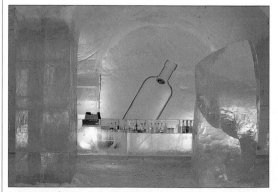

Icebar in the 60-room Icehotel, Jukkasjärvi, a creation of ice and snow

◁ **Kebnekaise massif, Lappland, with Sydtoppen, Sweden's highest peak, in the foreground**

nature reserve has good cross-country skiing facilities. Dug into the rock here, the adventure centre **Boda Borg** runs activities for families.

🏞 Boda Borg
Dundret. 【 0970-660 68. ◯ phone for info. ▨ ▢ ♿

Jokkmokk ⑮

Lappland. Road 97 & 45. 🏃 3,500. ▣ ▣ ⓘ Stortorget 4, 0971-222 50. ▨ Jokkmokk Market (1st Thu–Sat Feb), Music week in Saltoluokta (early Aug). Ⓦ www.turism.jokkmokk.se

T HE TOWN OF Jokkmokk, celebrating its 400th anniversary in 2005, is best-known for its winter market. For a few days in February, snow, darkness and cold give way to light, warmth and sparkling colours, when more than 30,000 people arrive to browse among the 500 market stalls and join in the festivities. The annual reindeer race through the town often causes chaos, but things are even faster at the reindeer race on the frozen Lake Talvatissjön.

The life of the Sami and the pioneering Swedish settlers is depicted in **Ájtte Fjäll- och Samemuseum**. Unfortunately in 1972 the Sami church built in 1753 burned down. The exterior of the new church replicates the original, but it has a modern interior.

ENVIRONS: The municipality includes the magnificent national parks of Padjclanta, Sarek, Stora Sjöfallet and a section of Muddus, which is part of the Laponia UNESCO World Heritage Site (see p275).

Porjus, 40 km (25 miles) north of Jokkmokk, was Sweden's first major hydroelectric power station (1910–15) Its story is related in **Porjus Expo** which has a power station museum 50 m (164 ft) underground.

In Vuollerim, 43 km (26 miles) south of Jokkmokk, Stone Age settlements have been uncovered on the Stora Luleälv river. The museum **Vuollerim 6000 År** gives visitors the chance to experience Stone Age life.

Muddus National Park, part of the Laponia UNESCO World Heritage Site

🏛 Ájtte fjäll- och Samemuseum
Kungsgatan 3. 【 0971-170 70. ◯ Jun–Aug: daily; other times: Mon–Fri. ▨ ◫ ◻ ♿
🏛 Porjus Expo
Porjus. 40 km (25 miles) N of Jokkmokk, road 45. 【 0973-776 00. ◯ Jun–Aug: daily; other times by appointment. ▨ ◪ ◻ 【
🏛 Vuollerim 6000 År
Vuollerim. 42 km (26 miles) SW of Jokkmokk, road 97. 【 0976-101 65. ◯ Jun–Aug: daily; other times: Tue & Wed. ▨ ◪ ◻ ♿

Arvidsjaur ⑯

Lappland. Road 94 & 45. 🏃 4,700. ▣ to Jörn, then bus. ▣ ⊠ ⓘ 0960-175 00. ▨ Arvidsjaur Streetmarket (mid-Jul), Sami Festival (last weekend in Aug).

T HIS COMMUNITY in central Lapland was founded in the early 17th century when King Karl IX set up a church here to bring Christianity to the Sami. **Arvidsjaur's Sami church village** contains 80 huts and log cabins from the 18th century.

Modern-day Arvidsjaur was experiencing a declining population until when in 1980

Traditional huts and log cabins in Arvidsjaur's 18th-century Sami church village

it received a boost with the relocation here of Norrland's dragoon regiment from Umeå. Guided tours provide an insight into their physically demanding military training programme (foreign citizens must book in advance).

In the summer a steam train operates on the Inlandsbanan line to the **Rallarmuseet** in Moskosel, which tells of the pioneers who built the railway.

🏛 Rallarmuseet
Moskosel, 40 km (25 miles) N of Arvidsjaur, road Rv 45. 【 0960-175 00. ◯ mid-Jun–mid-Aug: daily. ▢ ♿ limited access.

Arjeplog ⑰

Lappland. Road 95. 🏃 4,700. ⊠ Arvidsjaur. ▣ ⓘ Torget 1, 0961-222 30. ▨ Mårkan (1st week Mar), Silveryran Festival (Jul). Ⓦ www.arjeploglappland.se

O N THE "Silver Road" between Hornavan and Uddjaur lies Arjeplog, home to the **Silvermuseet**. It was created by the "Lappland doctor" Einar Wallquist, whose home Doktorsgården is open to the public in July. In addition to 16th-century Sami silverwork, the museum looks at the life of the Sami and the pioneering incomers.

The area has much to offer hunting and fishing enthusiasts.

🏛 Silvermuseeet
Torget. 【 Tourist Office, 0961-612 90. ◯ Jun–mid-Aug: daily; other times: Mon–Sat. ▨ ◪ ▢ ♿ limited access.

The Kungsleden Trail ⑱

T HE BEST WAY to experience the magnificence of the
Swedish mountains is to hike along a few stages of
the Kungsleden Trail. In 1900, the Swedish tourism
organisation, Svenska Turistföreningen (STF), drew up
plans for a network of marked walking trails and huts
for overnight stays through the mountains from Lappland
south to Grövelsjön lake in Dalarna. Today, the 440-km
(275-mile) long stretch between Abisko mountain station
on the Malmbanan railway line in the north and
Hemavan in southern Lappland forms the Kungsleden
Trail. The simple huts have given way to mountain
stations and rest cabins which offer hikers shelter in bad
weather and overnight accommodation. Some also have
a ferry service to help people on their way.

**Mountain walkers on the well-
marked Kungsleden Trail**

Sarek
*Perhaps the most spectacular of Sweden's national
parks, Sarek has 200 lofty peaks, more than 100
glaciers, wild waterfalls and valleys such as
Rapadalen. It is home to elk, lynx and wolverine.*

Ammarnäs
*The village is located
in the Vindelfjällen
nature reserve, created
in 1976 and known
for its fauna. Its
200 inhabitants
mostly live off
tourism and
reindeer herding.*

Hemavan is the final point
for the Kungsleden Trail's
northern section. With the
ski town of Tärnaby close
by, it is a mecca for
alpine skiers.

Padjelanta
National Park

Vaisalu
Kutjaure
Kis
Läddejåkka
Arasluo
Stáloluokta
Tuottac
Sårjåsjåure
Staddajåkkå
Tarraluopp
Sámmárlapp
Vajmok
Pieskehaure
Tarrekais
Vuonatjviki
Jakk
Pieljekaise
Adolfström
Báverholmen
Dalovardo
Sjnjultie
Vitnjul
Rávfallsstugan
Skidbäcksstugan
Tärnasjö
Viterskalet
Serve
Ammarnäs
Syter
Aigert
363
Hemavan
E12
Tärnaby

KEY

- - – Kungsleden Trail
- – – Other walking trails
- ▦ Major road
- ═ Minor road
- — Railway line
- ⌂ Mountain stations and cabins

0 kilometres   30

0 miles   20

Riksgränsen is the last station on the Malmbanan line and a skier's paradise with lifts often operating until as late as Midsummer.

VISITORS' CHECKLIST

Lappland. E12 to Hemavan, E10 to Kiruna and Abisko. **i** *Kiruna Tourist Office, 0980-188 80, Abisko Tourist Station, 0980-402 00, Tärnaby Tourist Office, 0954-104 50.* **✕** *Storuman or Kiruna, then bus.* **▯** *to Kiruna and Abisko.* **▯ ▯** *guided tours in some parts.* **W** *www.stfturist.se*

Abisko
Thanks to the E10 and its own train station, the STF tourist facility at Torneträsk in Abisko national park is a natural starting point for mountain walkers.

Nikkaluokta is the end of the road. It is a 19-km (12-mile) walk to the STF mountain station at Kebnekaise; 7 km (4 miles) can be cut by catching the lake ferry

Kebnekaise
Topping the Kebnekaise massif is Sweden's highest peak at 2,111 m (6,925 ft). Below the summit, the STF station in Ladtjodalen, 690 m (2,264 ft), is a good starting point for tackling the range.

Stora Sjöfallet
This area is impressive for the mountains and glaciers of Akka and the primeval pine forests, but the waterfall is dry due to hydro-electric schemes.

LAPONIA WORLD HERITAGE SITE

The mountainous region of Lappland was designated a UNESCO World Heritage Site in 1996. Laponia has been home to the Sami since prehistoric times and provides the ideal conditions for their traditional nomadic reindeer herding, governed by the seasons. It is also Europe's largest single wilderness area, home to brown bears and alpine flora, as well as being geologically important. These factors contributed to its inclusion on UNESCO's list. The region includes the four national parks Padjelanta, Sarek, Stora Sjöfallet and Muddus, as well as the wetlands of Sjaunja with their rich birdlife.

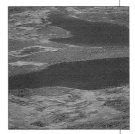

Sjaunja National Park's extensive wetlands

TRAVELLERS' NEEDS

WHERE TO STAY 278-289
WHERE TO EAT 290-303
SHOPPING IN SWEDEN 304-309
ENTERTAINMENT IN SWEDEN 310-313
SPORTS AND OUTDOOR ACTIVITIES 314-317

WHERE TO STAY

SWEDEN HAS THOUSANDS of hotels and guesthouses to suit all tastes and budgets, from small family-run establishments to large luxury hotels. In addition, there are almost 500 youth hostels which offer great value accommodation for all ages and will normally provide breakfast for a small charge. There is also a range of bed-and-breakfast accommodation, some-

Hotel doorman

times advertised by a discreet sign outside saying *"RUM"* ("room"). In the mountains large ski resorts offer both hotels and small cottages to rent. Cottages are also plentiful elsewhere in Sweden, often on sites which also offer camping. Pages 280–9 have details of 125 places to stay throughout the country, covering a wide selection from cosy youth hostels to grand hotels.

The elegant Hotel Diplomat on Stockholm's Strandvägen

CHOOSING A HOTEL

WHEN YOU STAY at a beautifully-located classic hotel, you pay for the privilege. But there are plenty of cheaper options which provide good accommodation and many hotels have a star rating as a guide. There are 500 youth hostels (*"Vandrarhem"*) for the budget traveller and these are normally of a high standard. A self-catering cottage may provide ideal family accommodation at a reasonable price.

The larger hotels cater mainly for business travellers and conference-goers, and are often fully-booked during the week. Most hotels offer attractive weekend packages.

It is highly recommended that you book a room in advance, particularly during the week in cities. Hotels in Stockholm tend to be busy from May to November and, when events or trade fairs are on, it can be hard to find a hotel room in the capital. To

find out when the busiest times are likely to be, check the **Stockholm Visitor Board's** events calendar on the Internet (*see p321*).

HOW TO BOOK

IF YOU DO NOT BOOK a hotel through a travel agent, you can easily make your own reservation on the Internet. One excellent site is **Visit Sweden** (*see p321*), operated by Sveriges Rese-och Turistråd. The site allows you to search for all kinds of accommodation, such as hotels, youth hostels and B&Bs, and provides contact information so you can make a booking. If you find yourself in Stockholm looking for a room, pay a visit to **Hotellcentralen** at the city's Central Station for a friendly booking service which charges a small fee.

HOTEL CHAINS

THERE ARE SEVERAL chains with hotels across Sweden. Many of these have at least one hotel in every major town, although the

The spectacular Icehotel in Jukkasjärvi, built entirely from ice

main focus is on the largest cities. These hotels cater mainly for business travellers, but often offer good deals for tourists off-season and at weekends. All the chains offer central booking facilities, either by phone or online. Of course, you can always contact your chosen hotel direct to make a reservation.

Choice Hotels Scandinavia has around 50 hotels in Sweden in three categories: Comfort, Quality and the premium Clarion.

Elite has centrally-located hotels in Swedish towns, often in classic buildings.

First is a Nordic chain with an environmentally-friendly ethos and hotels in three categories: First Hotel, First Express and First Resort.

Radisson SAS has a number of larger hotels at the higher end of the price range in around ten Swedish cities.

Ramada is an international chain with almost 50 hotels from Malmö in the south to Gällivare in the north.

Rica City Hotels has 20 or so hotels in Sweden, including some in the mountains.

Romantik Hotels has, as its name implies, some particularly romantic hotels.

Scandic Hotels is the leading chain in the Nordic region, with nearly 70 hotels across Sweden.

PRICES AND PAYMENT

PRICES IN THE hotel listing are for the cheapest double room, including breakfast, service and VAT. However, most hotels offer rooms at greatly reduced rates at

◁ **Östermalmshallen, offering an abundance of delicacies in a well-preserved 1880s setting**

The lobby of the pleasant Wisby Hotel on Gotland

weekends and in low season. For cheaper hotels this means a price reduction of 100–300 Kr per night; for medium-priced hotels around 500 Kr and for top hotels up to 1,000 Kr.

Nearly all hotels accept the major credit cards. Larger hotels will also change foreign currency, but the easiest and cheapest way of changing money is to use a bureau de change (see p324).

YOUTH HOSTELS

THERE ARE almost 500 youth hostels in Sweden, of which more than 300 are affiliated to the **Svenska Turistföreningen (STF)**. The flagship is the tall ship *af Chapman*, in Stockholm – floating proof that a youth hostel can be just as spectacular as a top-class hotel. **Sveriges Vandrarhem i Förening (SVIF)** has more than 150 youth hostels throughout the country. Both STF and SVIF are members of the International Youth Hostel Federation (IYHF).

The standard of youth hostels is generally high, particularly at those affiliated to the STF, and they are popular with people of all ages. Expect

The Svenska Turistföreningen (STF) youth hostel in Motala

to pay around 200 Kr per person in a double room; 100 Kr in a larger room or dormitory, with a discount of around 50 Kr for STF members. Prices usually exclude breakfast and bed linen hire.

It is always wise to book ahead, and the simplest way is to phone or e-mail the hostel direct. You can book online for some hostels by visiting the STF or SVIF website. Many youth hostels close in winter.

BED & BREAKFAST

BED & BREAKFASTS can be a good alternative to staying in a hotel or youth hostel. There is usually a reasonable range of B&B accommodation in large towns and close to major roads. You can choose between single or double rooms or an apartment, and breakfast, bed linen and towels are generally provided. Expect to pay 300–500 Kr per person per night at a town B&B; an apartment will cost from 600 Kr per night. In the capital, rooms can be booked through **Bed & Breakfast Service Stockholm** (a small booking fee is charged).

COTTAGES AND CAMPING

SWEDEN'S RIGHT to roam allows freedom to camp in forests and on open land (but not in view of houses on private land), but staying at a campsite will ensure a more comfortable stay. Campsites often offer cottages to rent. Visit the **Sveriges Camping-och Stugförctagares Riks-organisation** website for details. Campsites are graded on a scale of one to five stars.

DIRECTORY

CENTRAL BOOKING

Hotellcentralen
(For reservations in Stockholm.)
Centralstationen, Vasagatan.
☎ 08-789 24 90.
ⓦ www.stockholmtown.com

Göteborg & Co
(For reservations in Gothenborg.)
☎ 020-83 84 85.
ⓦ www.goteborg.com

HOTEL CHAINS

Choice Hotels
☎ 020-666 000.
ⓦ www.choicehotels.se

Elite Hotels
☎ 0771-788 789.
ⓦ www.elite.se

First Hotels
☎ 020-41 11 11.
ⓦ www.firsthotels.com

Radisson SAS
☎ 020-238 238.
ⓦ www.radissonsas.se

Ramada
☎ 0771-777 000.
ⓦ www.ramadasweden.se

Rica Hotels
☎ 08-723 72 72.
ⓦ www.rica.se

Romantik Hotels
ⓦ www.romantikhotels.se

Scandic Hotels
☎ 08-517 516 00.
ⓦ www.scandic-hotels.se

YOUTH HOSTELS

STF
☎ 08-463 22 70.
ⓦ www.stfturist.se

SVIF
☎ 0413-55 34 50.
ⓦ www.svif.se

COTTAGES, CAMPING, BED & BREAKFAST

Sveriges Camping-och Stugföretagare
ⓦ www.camping.se

Bed & Breakfast Service Stockholm
☎ 08-660 55 65.
ⓦ www.bedbreakfast.a.se

Choosing a Hotel

T HE HOTELS LISTED HERE have been selected on the basis of value for money, character and location. The listings start with central Stockholm followed by a selection of hotels area by area throughout Sweden. Many hotels also have a recommended restaurant – for a listing of restaurants, see *pp294–303*. For Stockholm map references, see the Street Finder map, *pp112–17*.

	CREDIT CARDS	CHILDREN'S FACILITIES	PARKING	RESTAURANT	BAR

STOCKHOLM

GAMLA STAN: *Mälardrottningen Hotel & Restaurant*   ⓚⓚ
Riddarholmen, 111 28 Stockholm. **Map** 3 A3. 🄲 08-545 187 80. 𝖥𝖠𝖷 08-24 36 76.
Ⓦ www.malardrottningen.se
Barbara Hutton's former luxury yacht offers elegantly furnished, well-equipped cabins and two excellent seafood restaurants. 🚪 📺 📶 🔒 *Rooms: 60*

| AE DC MC V | ● | ■ | ● | ■ |

GAMLA STAN: *Rica City Hotel Gamla Stan*   ⓚⓚⓚ
Lilla Nygatan 25, 111 28 Stockholm. **Map** 3 B3. 🄲 08-723 72 50.
𝖥𝖠𝖷 08-723 72 59. Ⓦ www.rica.se
Newly refurbished in Gustavian style in a building dating from the 1650s. Conferences accommodated in the historic cellars. 🚪 📺 🍸 📶 🔒 *Rooms: 51*

| AE DC MC V | | ■ | | |

GAMLA STAN: *First Hotel Reisen*   ⓚⓚⓚⓚ
Skeppsbron 12, 111 30 Stockholm. **Map** 3 C3. 🄲 08-22 32 60.
𝖥𝖠𝖷 08-20 15 59. Ⓦ www.firsthotels.se
Old building at Skeppsbron with beautiful views of the water. The 17th-century vaulted cellar houses a sauna suite complete with cold plunge pool. The restaurant serves Swedish specialities. 🚪 📺 🍸 📶 🔒 ♿ *Rooms: 144*

| AE DC MC V | ● | ■ | ● | ■ |

GAMLA STAN: *Victory Hotel & Conference*   ⓚⓚⓚⓚ
Lilla Nygatan 5, 111 28 Stockholm. **Map** 3 B3. 🄲 08-506 400 00.
𝖥𝖠𝖷 08-506 400 10. Ⓦ www.trehotell.se
Exclusive little five-star hotel named after Lord Nelson's flagship *HMS Victory*. Naval antiques and nautical treasures at every turn.
🚪 📺 🍸 📶 🔒 ♿ *Rooms: 49*

| AE DC MC V | ● | ■ | ● | ■ |

CITY: *Comfort Hotel Stockholm*   ⓚⓚ
Kungsbron 1, 111 22 Stockholm. **Map** 1 B4. 🄲 08-566 222 00.
𝖥𝖠𝖷 08-566 224 44. Ⓦ www.choicehotels.se
Modern, good-value business hotel in the World Trade Centre, next to the Arlanda Express terminal. Instead of double rooms, it has combi-rooms, which means that an extra bed folds down from the wall. 🚪 📺 📶 🔒 ♿ *Rooms: 163*

| AE DC MC V | | ■ | | |

CITY: *Crystal Plaza Hotel*   ⓚⓚⓚ
Birger Jarlsgatan 35, 111 45 Stockholm. **Map** 2 D4. 🄲 08-406 88 00.
𝖥𝖠𝖷 08-24 15 11. Ⓦ www.crystalplazahotel.se
Newly refurbished rooms in an 1895 building close to Stureplan. The popular Ming restaurant serves Chinese and Thai food.
🚪 📺 🍸 📶 🔒 🎫 *Rooms: 117*

| AE DC MC V | ● | ■ | ● | ■ |

CITY: *Lydmar*   ⓚⓚⓚⓚ
Sturegatan 10, 114 36 Stockholm. **Map** 3 E4. 🄲 08-566 113 00.
𝖥𝖠𝖷 08-566 113 01. Ⓦ www.lydmar.se
The trendy hotel's status as the in-place is reflected in the uniquely designed rooms and in the bars and restaurants, which regularly host live music and art exhibitions. Centrally located near Stureplan. 🚪 📺 🍸 📶 🔒 *Rooms: 62*

| AE DC MC V | ● | ■ | ● | ■ |

CITY: *Nordic Light Hotel*   ⓚⓚⓚⓚ
Vasaplan, Box 884, 101 37 Stockholm. **Map** 2 D3. 🄲 08-505 630 00.
𝖥𝖠𝖷 08-505 630 40. Ⓦ www.nordiclighthotel.com
Designer hotel next to Central Station. Interiors take their inspiration from the fundamental Nordic element – light.
🚪 📺 🍸 📶 🔒 🎫 ♿ *Rooms: 175*

| AE DC MC V | ● | ■ | ● | ■ |

CITY: *Radisson SAS Royal Viking Hotel*   ⓚⓚⓚⓚ
Vasagatan 1, 101 24 Stockholm. **Map** 1 C4. 🄲 08-506 540 00.
𝖥𝖠𝖷 08-506 540 01. Ⓦ www.radissonsas.se
One of Stockholm's top hotels, with the superb Stockholm Fisk restaurant and dizzying views from the SkyBar. An excellent and convenient location next to Central Station.
🚪 📺 🍸 📶 🔒 🎫 🏊 ♿ *Rooms: 459*

| AE DC MC V | ● | ■ | ● | ■ |

Price categories for a double room per night, including breakfast unless otherwise stated, plus tax and service.

🍴 Youth hostel *(see pp279)*
Ⓚ under 700 Kr
ⓀⓀ 700–1,400 Kr
ⓀⓀⓀ 1,400–2,100 Kr
ⓀⓀⓀⓀ over 2,100 Kr

CHILDREN'S FACILITIES
Cots and highchairs are available and some hotels will also provide a baby-sitting service.
PARKING
Parking is provided by the hotel, either in a private car park or a private garage nearby.
RESTAURANT
The hotel has a restaurant for residents, which also welcomes non-residents – usually only open for evening meals.
BAR
The hotel has a bar that is open to non-residents as well as those staying in the hotel.

CITY: *Scandic Sergel Plaza* ⓀⓀⓀⓀ
Brunkebergstorg 9, 103 27 Stockholm. **Map** 3 A1. ☎ 08-517 263 00.
FAX 508-517 263 11. W www.scandic-hotels.com
In the heart of the city, but still in a quiet spot behind Kulturhuset. Mowitz Restaurang & Bar is a cosy place to meet for a coffee or a bite to eat. 🅿 TV 🍸 🏊 🏋 ♿ *Rooms: 403*

Credit Cards: AE DC MC V

CITY: *Sheraton Stockholm Hotel & Towers* ⓀⓀⓀⓀ
Tegelbacken 6, 101 23 Stockholm. **Map** 1 C5, 3 A2. ☎ 08-412 34 00.
FAX 08-412 34 09. W www.sheraton.com/stockholm
International deluxe hotel with the largest hotel rooms in Stockholm. Centrally located. Many rooms have great views of Riddarfjärden and Stadshuset. Piano bar and two restaurants. 🅿 TV 🍸 🏊 🏋 🍴 ♿ *Rooms: 462*

Credit Cards: AE DC MC V

BLASIEHOLMEN & SKEPPSHOLMEN: *af Chapman & Skeppsholmen (STF)* 🍴
Flaggmansvägen 8, 111 49 Stockholm. **Map** 4 D3. ☎ 08-463 22 66. FAX 08-611 71 55.
W www.stfchapman.com
Perhaps one of the world's most beautiful youth hostels, with beds on board the ship *(see p 77)* or ashore in Hantverkshuset. 🏊 ♿ *Beds: 293*

Credit Cards: AE MC V

BLASIEHOLMEN & SKEPPSHOLMEN: *Grand Hôtel Stockholm* ⓀⓀⓀⓀ
S Blasieholmshamnen, 103 27 Stockholm. **Map** 3 C1. ☎ 08-679 35 00.
FAX 08-611 86 86. W www.grandhotel.se
A grand hotel in the old style in a magnificent location. The Cadier bar and Franska Matsalen restaurant are renowned. 🅿 TV 🍸 🏊 🏋 🍴 ♿ *Rooms: 307*

Credit Cards: AE DC MC V

BLASIEHOLMEN & SKEPPSHOLMEN: *Radisson SAS Strand Hotel* ⓀⓀⓀⓀ
Nybrokajen 9, 103 27 Stockholm. **Map** 3 C1. ☎ 08-506 640 00.
FAX 08-506 640 01. W www.radissonsas.se
First-class hotel overlooking Nybroviken. Fantastic city views from the sauna on the top floor. Strand Restaurant & Lounge serves exclusive but uncomplicated meals. 🅿 TV 🍸 🏊 🏋 🍴 ♿ *Rooms: 152*

Credit Cards: AE DC MC V

DJURGÅRDEN: *Scandic Hotel Hasselbacken* ⓀⓀⓀⓀ
Hazeliusbacken 20, 100 55 Stockholm. ☎ 08-517 343 00. FAX 08-517 343 11.
W www.scandic-hotels.se/hasselbacken
Beautifully restored hotel adjoining Skansen, dating from 1765. Award-winning Hasselbacken restaurant is one of Stockholm's best. Brunch is served at weekends. 🅿 TV 🍸 🏊 🏋 ♿ *Rooms: 112*

Credit Cards: AE DC MC V

ÖSTERMALM: *Hotel Diplomat* ⓀⓀⓀ
Strandvägen 7C, 104 40 Stockholm. **Map** 2 E4. ☎ 08-459 68 00. FAX 08-459 68 20.
W www.diplomathotel.com
Typical Swedish decor with elegant bathrooms in a well-preserved Jugendstil building from 1907. The T/BAR restaurant is popular. 🅿 TV 🍸 🏊 🏋 *Rooms: 128*

Credit Cards: AE DC MC V

VASASTAN: *Clas på Hörnet* ⓀⓀ
Surbrunnsgatan 20, 113 48 Stockholm. **Map** 1 C2. ☎ 08-16 51 30. FAX 08-612 53 15.
W www.claspahornet.com
Romantic inn with 18th-century atmosphere. Rooms dedicated to Swedish celebrities. Excellent Swedish food in the restaurant. 🅿 TV 🍸 🏊 *Rooms: 10*

Credit Cards: AE DC MC V

VASASTAN: *Ramada Hotel Tegnérlunden* ⓀⓀⓀ
Tegnérlunden 8, 113 59 Stockholm. **Map** 1 B3. ☎ 08-545 455 50.
FAX 08-545 455 51. W www.hoteltegnerlunden.com
Hotel with a casual atmosphere in a quiet location near August Strindberg's residence and museum on Drottninggatan. 🅿 TV 🏊 🏋 ♿ *Rooms: 102*

Credit Cards: AE DC MC V

KUNGSHOLMEN: *Elite Palace Hotel* ⓀⓀⓀ
St Eriksgatan 115, 100 31 Stockholm. **Map** 1 A1. ☎ 08-566 217 00.
FAX 08-566 217 01. W www.elite.se
Quiet but accessible location in Vasastan. Family-friendly with modern rooms. Full gym, spa and sauna suite. Pub. 🅿 TV 🏊 🏋 🍴 *Rooms: 216*

Credit Cards: AE DC MC V

For key to symbols see back flap

Price categories for a double room per night, including breakfast unless otherwise stated, plus tax and service.

🡢 Youth hostel *(see pp279)*
Ⓚ under 700 Kr
ⓀⓀ 700–1,400 Kr
ⓀⓀⓀ 1,400–2,100 Kr .
ⓀⓀⓀⓀ over 2,100 Kr

CHILDREN'S FACILITIES
Cots and highchairs are available and some hotels will also provide a baby-sitting service.

PARKING
Parking is provided by the hotel, either in a private car park or a private garage nearby.

RESTAURANT
The hotel has a restaurant for residents, which also welcomes non-residents – usually only open for evening meals.

BAR
The hotel has a bar that is open to non-residents as well as those staying in the hotel.

	CREDIT CARDS	CHILDREN'S FACILITIES	PARKING	RESTAURANT	BAR
KUNGSHOLMEN: *First Hotel Amaranten* ⓀⓀⓀⓀ Kungsholmsgatan 31, 104 20 Stockholm. **Map** 1 A4. **☎** 08-692 52 00. **FAX** 08-652 62 48. ⓦ www.firsthotels.se Newly refurbished full-service hotel near Central Station. Modern Nordic decor using materials such as granite and walnut. Several bars and restaurants. Serves a substantial breakfast. 🛏 📺 🍷 💱 🏋 🍽 ♨ ♿ *Rooms: 423*	AE DC MC V	●	■	●	●
SÖDERMALM: *Columbus Hotel* ⓀⓀⓀ Tjärhovsgatan 11, 116 21 Stockholm. **☎** 08-503 112 00. **FAX** 608-503 112 01. ⓦ www.columbushotell.se Charming hotel in a listed former barracks dating from 1780. All rooms decorated in Gustavian style. Buffet breakfast in the courtyard in summer. 🛏 📺 💱 *Rooms: 40*	AE DC MC V	●	■		●
SÖDERMALM: *Clarion Hotel Stockholm* ⓀⓀⓀⓀ Ringvägen 98, 104 60 Stockhom. **☎** 08-62 10 00. **FAX** 08-462 10 99. ⓦ www.clarionstockholm.com Söder's largest hotel with exciting architecture and stylish decor. Contemporary Nordic art features in the reception, restaurant and bars. 🛏 📺 🍷 💱 🏋 🍽 ♿ *Rooms: 532*	AE DC MC V	●	■		
SÖDERMALM: *Hilton Stockholm Slussen* ⓀⓀⓀⓀ Guldgränd 8, 104 65 Stockholm. **Map** 1 B4. **☎** 08-517 517 00. **FAX** 108-517 517 11. ⓦ www.hilton.com Well-equipped, five-star hotel of modern design with several restaurants and bars. Superb views of Gamla Stan. 🛏 📺 🍷 💱 🏋 🍽 ♨ ♿ *Rooms: 289*	AE DC MC V	●	■		
SÖDERMALM: *Långholmen Hotell & Restaurang* ⓀⓀⓀ 🡢 Kronohäktet, Långholmen, 102 72 Stockholm. **☎** 08-720 85 00. **FAX** 08-720 85 75. ⓦ www.langholmen.com This former prison offers accommodation in modernized cells on a leafy island in the city centre. Excellent restaurant and wine cellars. 🛏 📺 💱 🏋 ♿ *Rooms: 102.* Part of the old prison is a youth hostel. *Beds: 26–125*	AE DC MC V	●	■		
FURTHER AFIELD: *IBIS Hotell Stockholm Hägersten* ⓀⓀ Västertorpsvägen 131, 129 44 Hägersten. **☎** 08-556 323 30. **FAX** 08-97 64 27. ⓦ www.ibishotel.com Good-value hotel of high standard located 8 km (5 miles) south of city centre. Near Stockholm International Fairs. 🛏 📺 💱 🏋 🍽 ♿ *Rooms: 190*	AE DC MC V		■		●
FURTHER AFIELD: *Arlanda Hotellby* ⓀⓀ Bristagatan 22, 190 45 Stockholm-Arlanda. **☎** 08-597 897 00. **FAX** 08-597 898 00. ⓦ www.arlandahotellby.se Comfortable and good-value hotel only 5 min from Arlanda Airport. Transfer to and from the airport 24 hours a day. 🛏 📺 🍷 💱 🏋 🍽 ♿ *Rooms: 148*	AE DC MC V	●	■		●
FURTHER AFIELD: *Foresta Hotell & Konferens* ⓀⓀⓀ Herserudsvägen 22, 181 25 Lidingö. **☎** 08-505 505 00. **FAX** 08-505 505 90. ⓦ www.foresta.se Near Millesgården *(see p 95)* on the suburban island of Lidingö. Rooms are decorated in light natural materials. 🛏 📺 🍷 💱 🏋 🍽 ♿ *Rooms: 95*	AE DC MC V	●	■	●	●
STOCKHOLM ARCHIPELAGO: *Finnhamns Vandrarhem* 🡢 Finnhamns Brygga, 130 25 Ingmarsö. **☎** 08-542 462 12. **FAX** 08-542 461 33. ⓦ www.finnhamn.nu Housed in a grand old merchant's villa, a 10-min walk from the steamer quay. Open all year round. 💱 *Beds: 89*	AE MC V	●		●	
STOCKHOLM ARCHIPELAGO: *Sandhamn Hotell & Konferens* ⓀⓀⓀ Box 124, 130 39 Sandhamn. **☎** 08-574 704 00. **FAX** 08-574 504 50. Newly-built hotel next to the Seglar Restaurangen, a restaurant dating from 1897 which is a popular meeting place, particularly during regattas. 🛏 📺 💱 🍽 ♨ ♿ *Rooms: 81*	AE DC MC V	●		●	■

EASTERN SVEALAND

ESKILSTUNA: *Sundhbyholms Slott* ⓀⓀ
635 08 Eskilstuna. ☎ 016-42 84 00. FAX 016-965 78. Ⓦ www.sundbyholms-slott.se
Just under 10 km (6 miles) north of Eskilstuna, this splendid palace is beautifully
located in the beech woods on the banks of Lake Mälaren. 🛏 📺 💱 🛅 *Rooms:* 99

	AE	●	■	●	■
DC				
MC				
V				

NORRTÄLJE: *Pensionat Granparken* ⓀⓀ
Gjuterivägen 10, 761 40 Norrtälje. ☎ 0176-103 54. FAX 0176-125 02.
Ⓦ www.pensionatgranparken.se
Charming family-owned guest house with a 100-year history. Quiet location
within walking distance of the centre. Restaurant with several pleasant dining
rooms, all decorated in different styles. 🛏 📺 💱 🍽 *Rooms:* 16

AE	●	■	●	■
DC				
MC				
V				

NYKÖPING: *Park Inn Nyköping* ⓀⓀ
Brunnsgatan 33, 611 26 Nyköping. ☎ 0155-29 35 00. FAX 0155-29 35 09.
Ⓦ www.rezidorparkinn.com
Good-value, family-friendly hotel in a convenient location for Kolmårdens
Djurpark *(see p144)* and Skavsta Airport 🛏 📺 🍷 💱 🛅 🖼 *Rooms:* 98

AE	●	■	●	■
DC				
MC				
V				

NYNÄSHAMN: *Skärgårdshotellet* ⓀⓀ
Kaptensgatan 2, 149 31 Nynäshamn. ☎ 08-520 111 20. FAX 08 520 105 77
Located above the harbour, far enough from the centre to enjoy a sense of
the archipelago. Many rooms have sea views and a balcony.
🛏 📺 💱 🖼 *Rooms:* 75

AE	●	■		■
DC				
MC				
V				

SIGTUNA: *Sigtuna Stadshotell* ⓀⓀⓀⓀ
Stora Nygatan 3, 193 30 Sigtuna. ☎ 08-592 501 00. FAX 08-592 515 87.
Small designer hotel in the heart of Sweden's oldest town. One of the few hotels
with five stars under the Swedish classification system. Classic Scandinavian
interiors, mainly using natural materials. 🛏 📺 🍷 💱 🛅 *Rooms:* 27

AE	●	■	●	■
DC				
MC				
V				

SÖDERTÄLJE: *Best Western Hotell Skogshöjd* ⓀⓀⓀ
Täppgatan 15, 151 21 Södertälje. ☎ 08-550 926 00. FAX 08-550 926 60.
Well-equipped large hotel with a focus on conferences. Very comfortable
rooms, plus pool and fitness suite.
🛏 📺 🍷 💱 🛅 🖼 🔳 🖼 *Rooms:* 225

AE	●	■	●	■
DC				
MC				
V				

UPPSALA: *Hotel Uppsala* ⓀⓀ ⌗
Kungsgatan 27, 753 21 Uppsala. ☎ 018-480 50 00. FAX 018-480 50 50.
Ⓦ www.profilhotels.se
Uppsala's largest hotel, newly refurbished and centrally located. Also, there is a
STF youth hostel. 🛏 📺 💱 🛅 🖼 *Rooms:* 213

AE	●	■	●	■
DC				
MC				
V				

UPPSALA: *Radisson SAS Hotel Gillet* ⓀⓀⓀ
Dragarbrunnsgatan 23, 753 20 Uppsala. ☎ 018-68 18 00. FAX 018-68 18 18.
Ⓦ www.radissonsas.se
Full-service hotel with a 200-year history in the heart of the city. Two restaurants
offering international and Scandinavian dishes. 🛏 📺 💱 🛅 🖼 🔳 🖼 *Rooms:* 160

AE		■		■
DC				
MC				
V				

VÄSTERÅS: *Elite Stadshotellet Västerås* ⓀⓀ
Stora torget, 721 03 Västerås. ☎ 021-10 28 00. FAX 021-10 28 10. Ⓦ www.elite.se
High-class, central hotel in a beautiful Jugendstil building. Stadskällaren restaurant
has an interior from the end of the 19th century. 🛏 📺 💱 🛅 🖼 *Rooms:* 137

AE	●	■	●	■
DC				
MC				
V				

EASTERN GÖTALAND

GLASRIKET: *STF Ljuders Vandrarhem* ⌗
Grimsnäs Herrgård, 360 53 Skruv. ☎ & FAX 0478-204 00.
A manor house in a natural rural setting in the heart of Småland's Kingdom
of Crystal *(see p152)*. 💱 *Beds:* 64

| MC | ● | ■ |
| V | | |

JÖNKÖPING: *Elite Stora Hotellet* ⓀⓀⓀ
Norra Flaggstångsgatan 7, 51 12 Jönköping. ☎ 036-10 00 00. FAX 036-215 50 25.
Ⓦ www.elite.se
Beautiful 19th-century building on the southern shore of Lake Vättern. Furnished
in Gustavian style. 🛏 📺 💱 🛅 🖼 *Rooms:* 135

AE	●	■	●	■
DC				
MC				
V				

KALMAR: *Slottshotellet* ⓀⓀⓀ
Slottsvägen 7, 392 33 Kalmar. ☎ 0480-882 60. FAX 0480-882 66. Ⓦ www.slottshotellet.se
A little oasis opposite Kalmar castle. The buildings have been sympathetically
renovated, retaining their old charm. Individually designed rooms with wood
floors, antique furniture and tiled stoves. 🛏 📺 💱 🛅 *Rooms:* 44

AE	●	■	●	■
DC				
MC				
V				

Price categories for a double room per night, including breakfast unless otherwise stated, plus tax and service.
⌁ Youth hostel (*see pp279*)
Ⓚ under 700 Kr
ⓀⓀ 700–1,400 Kr
ⓀⓀⓀ 1,400–2,100 Kr
ⓀⓀⓀⓀ over 2,100 Kr

CHILDREN'S FACILITIES
Cots and highchairs are available and some hotels will also provide a baby-sitting service.
PARKING
Parking is provided by the hotel, either in a private car park or a private garage nearby.
RESTAURANT
The hotel has a restaurant for residents, which also welcomes non-residents – usually only open for evening meals.
BAR
The hotel has a bar that is open to non-residents as well as those staying in the hotel.

	CREDIT CARDS	CHILDREN'S FACILITIES	PARKING	RESTAURANT	BAR
LINKÖPING: *Hotell du Nord* ⓀⓀ Repslagaregatan 5, 581 22 Linköping. 📞 013-12 98 95. FAX 013-14 52 91. 🆆 www.hotelldunord.se An unusual little hotel with a personal atmosphere. Pleasant location in its own gardens, close to the train station and Stångån river. �GTV⚡ *Rooms: 28*	AE DC MC V	●	■		
LINKÖPING: *Scandic Frimurarehotellet* ⓀⓀⓀ St Larsgatan 14, 582 24 Linköping. 📞 013-495 30 00. FAX 013-495 30 11. 🆆 www.scandic-hotels.se/frimurarehotellet This classic hotel, which conjures up images of a bygone era, stands right on the town's main street. The Alberts Hall pub serves international food and drink. 🚄TV🚄TV▣⚡▣▣▣ *Rooms: 84*	AE DC MC V	●	■	●	■
NORRKÖPING: *Elite Grand Hotel Norrköping* ⓀⓀⓀ Tyska Torget 2, 600 24 Norrköping. 📞 011-36 41 00. FAX 011-36 41 01. Grand building dating from 1906 in a peaceful location on the Motala Ström river within walking distance of the train station. There is a basement spa and in the summer a special playroom for children. 🚄TV⚡▣ *Rooms: 206*	AE DC MC V	●	■		
NÄSSJÖ: *Hotell Högland* ⓀⓀ Esplanaden 4, 571 23 Nässjö. 📞 0380-131 00. FAX 0380-101 25. The hotel stands next to the train station. Well-equipped rooms and a good relaxation suite with a spa pool and solarium. 🚄TV▣⚡▣ *Rooms: 104*	AE DC MC V	●			
OSKARSHAMN: *Ramada Hotel Corallen* ⓀⓀ Gröndalsgatan 35, 572 35 Oskarshamn. 📞 0491-76 81 81. FAX 0491-76 81 80. 🆆 www.hotelcorallen.se This modern hotel is situated on the harbour with a superb view of the Baltic Sea and the Blå Jungfrun island (*see p 154*). 🚄TV⚡▣▣▣ *Rooms: 74*	AE DC MC V		■		
VADSTENA: *Vadstena Klosterhotel* ⓀⓀⓀ Klosterområdet, 592 30 Vadstena. 📞 0143-315 30. FAX 0143-136 48. 🆆 www.klosterhotel.se Newly refurbished hotel in the former abbey in Vadstena which was planned by St Bridget. 🚄TV⚡▣▣ *Rooms: 68*	AE DC MC V	●	■	●	●
VÄSTERVIK: *Best Western Västerviks Stadshotell* ⓀⓀⓀ Storgatan 3, 593 30 Västervik. 📞 0490-820 00. FAX 0490-820 01. 🆆 www.stadshotellet.nu Next to the harbour and the sea, but still centrally located on Västervik's main street. Newly built with an eye on the past, the exterior is a replica of the former town hotel. 🚄TV⚡▣▣ *Rooms: 101*	AE DC MC V	●		●	●
VÄXJÖ: *Elite Stadshotellet Växjö* ⓀⓀ Kungsgatan 6, 351 04 Växjö. 📞 0470-134 00. FAX 0470-448 37. 🆆 www.elite.se This grand, traditional hotel lies in the town centre. The restaurant serves internationally inspired food with a nod to Småland cuisine. 🚄⚡▣▣ *Rooms: 132*	AE DC MC V	●	■		
ÖLAND: *Hotell Borgholm* ⓀⓀ Trädgårdsgatan 15-19, 387 31 Borgholm. 📞 0485-770 60. FAX 0485-124 66. Charming small-town hotel reopening in 2005 after extensive renovations following a fire. 🚄TV⚡ *Rooms: 135*	AE DC MC V			●	■

GOTLAND

	CREDIT CARDS	CHILDREN'S FACILITIES	PARKING	RESTAURANT	BAR
VISBY: *Hotell Gute & Breda Blick* ⓀⓀ Mellangatan 29, 621 56 Visby. 📞 0498-20 22 60. FAX 0498-20 22 62. 🆆 www.hotellgute.se Hotel with old-fashioned charm and a central location. Most rooms have broadband access. Sauna and solarium. 🚄TV⚡ *Rooms: 43*	AE DC MC V	●			

VISBY: *Hotell St Clemens* (Kr)(Kr)
Smedjegatan 3, 621 55 Visby. [0498-21 90 00. FAX 0498-27 94 43.
[W] www.clemenshotell.se
The five buildings of the hotel are linked by gardens alongside the ruins of
the medieval church of St Clemens. 🛏 TV 🍸 🏊 🅿 🚻 *Rooms:* 30

	AE	●	■		
	DC				
	MC				
	V				

VISBY: *Wisby Hotell* (Kr)(Kr)(Kr)
Strandgatan 6, 621 24 Visby. [0498-25 75 00. FAX 0498-25 75 50.
Like the town, the hotel is a mix of medieval and contemporary. 🛏 TV 🍸 🏊
🅿 🏊 🚻 *Rooms:* 134

	AE	●	■	●	■
	DC				
	MC				
	V				

KLINTEHAMN: *Pensionat Warfsholm* (Kr)(Kr) 🌊
620 20 Klintehamn. [0498-24 00 10. FAX 0498-24 14 11. [W] www.warfsholm.se
Charming guest house, set on its own peninsula, 30 km (19 miles) south of
Visby. Also cottage and youth hostel accommodation. TV 🏊 *Rooms:* 20. *Beds:* 90

	AE	●	■		
	DC				
	MC				
	V				

SOUTHERN GÖTALAND

HELSINGBORG: *Radisson SAS Grand Hotell, Helsingborg* (Kr)(Kr)(Kr)
Stortorget 8-12, 251 11 Helsingborg. [042-38 04 00. FAX 042-38 04 04.
[W] www.radissonsas.se
First-class, newly refurbished hotel, centrally located next to the harbour and
station. The restaurant serves Scandinavian cuisine. 🛏 TV 🍸 🏊 🅿 🚻 *Rooms:* 117

	AE	●		■	
	DC				
	MC				
	V				

KARLSKRONA: *First Hotel Statt* (Kr)(Kr)(Kr)
Ronnebygatan 37-39, 371 33 Karlskrona. [0455-555 50. FAX 0455-169 09.
[W] www.firsthotels.se
Elegantly designed hotel and banqueting hall from the early 20th century. Popular
pub with a range of beers and whiskies. 🛏 TV 🏊 🅿 🚻 🚻 *Rooms:* 107

	AE	●	■		
	DC				
	MC				
	V				

KRISTIANSTAD: *Quality Hotel Grand* (Kr)(Kr)(Kr)
Västra Storgatan 15, 291 21 Kristianstad. [044-28 48 00. FAX 044-28 48 10.
[W] www.choicehotels.se
The town's largest hotel, located opposite the church of Heliga Trefaldighets.
Restaurant, nightclub, relaxation suite with sauna. 🛏 TV 🍸 🏊 🅿 🚻 *Rooms:* 148

	AE	●	■		
	DC				
	MC				
	V				

LANDSKRONA: *Hotel Öresund* (Kr)(Kr)
Kungsgatan 15, 261 31 Landskrona. [0418-47 40 00. FAX 0418-47 40 10.
[W] www.hoteloresund.se
Privately run classic hotel, dating back to the 18th century in a leafy town
location. Three restaurants. 🛏 TV 🏊 🅿 🚻 🚻 *Rooms:* 130

	AE	●	■		
	DC				
	MC				
	V				

LUND: *Grand Hotel* (Kr)(Kr)(Kr)
Bantorget 1, 221 04 Lund. [046-280 61 00. FAX 046-280 61 50. [W] www.grandilund.se
Built at the end of the 19th century in French Renaissance style. Individually
designed rooms. 🛏 TV 🍸 🏊 🅿 🚻 🚻 *Rooms:* 84

	AE	●	■		
	DC				
	MC				
	V				

MALMÖ: *Hotell Plaza* (Kr)(Kr)
Kasinogatan 6, 200 10 Malmö. [040-33 05 50. FAX 040-33 05 51.
[W] www.hotel-plaza.com
Small, friendly hotel in central Malmö in a quiet location off Södra
Förstadsgatan, the city's main pedestrianized street. 🛏 TV 🏊 *Rooms:* 48

	AE	●	■		■
	DC				
	MC				
	V				

MALMÖ: *Best Western Premier Mäster Johan* (Kr)(Kr)(Kr)
Mäster Johansgatan 13, 211 21 Malmö. [040-664 64 00. FAX 040-664 64 01.
[W] www.masterjohan.se
Modern, award-winning hotel, named best individual business hotel. Newly
built in a traditional style in the heart of the city. 🛏 TV 🏊 🅿 🚻 🚻 *Rooms:* 69

	AE	●	■		
	DC				
	MC				
	V				

MALMÖ: *Elite Hotel Savoy* (Kr)(Kr)(Kr)
Norra Vallgatan 62. Box 880, 201 80 Malmö. [040-664 48 00.
FAX 040-664 48 50. [W] www.savoy.elite.se
This modern and historically interesting hotel lies in the heart of Malmö within
walking distance of the Central Station. 🛏 TV 🍸 🏊 🅿 *Rooms:* 109

	AE	●	■		
	DC				
	MC				
	V				

MALMÖ: *Hilton Malmö City* (Kr)(Kr)(Kr)
Triangeln 2, 200 10 Malmö. [040-693 47 00. FAX 040-693 47 11. [W] www.hilton.com
The 20-storey building dominates the shopping district around Triangeln
Square. Full service and fantastic views. 🛏 TV 🍸 🏊 🅿 🚻 🚻 *Rooms:* 216

	AE	●	■	●	■
	DC				
	MC				
	V				

SKANÖR: *Hotell Gässlingen* (Kr)(Kr)(Kr)
Rådhustorget 6, 239 30 Skanör. [040-45 91 00. FAX 040-45 91 13.
A picturesque exterior in traditional regional style hides the very modern
interior of this special hotel. Beautiful countryside close to the sea and
beaches. 🛏 TV 🏊 🅿 🚻 🏊 *Rooms:* 26

	AE	●	■		■
	DC				
	MC				
	V				

<table>
<tr><td>

Price categories for a double room per night, including breakfast unless otherwise stated, plus tax and service.

☞ Youth hostel *(see pp279)*
Ⓚ under 700 Kr
ⓀⓀ 700–1,400 Kr
ⓀⓀⓀ 1,400–2,100 Kr
ⓀⓀⓀⓀ over 2,100 Kr

</td><td>

CHILDREN'S FACILITIES
Cots and highchairs are available and some hotels will also provide a baby-sitting service.
PARKING
Parking is provided by the hotel, either in a private car park or a private garage nearby.
RESTAURANT
The hotel has a restaurant for residents, which also welcomes non-residents – usually only open for evening meals.
BAR
The hotel has a bar that is open to non-residents as well as those staying in the hotel.

</td></tr>
</table>

	CREDIT CARDS	CHILDREN'S FACILITIES	PARKING	RESTAURANT	BAR

YSTAD: *Hotell Continental*   ⓀⓀ
Hamngatan 13, 271 43 Ystad. 【 *0411-137 00.* FAX *0411-125 70.*
W *www.hotelcontinental-ystad.se*
In the heart of Ystad, this hotel was opened in 1829. Thoughtfully refurbished with grand interiors and light rooms. ⌨ TV ⛵ ☷ & *Rooms: 52*

| AE DC MC V | ● | ▪ | ● | ▪ |

GOTHENBURG

CENTRE: *Hotel Vasa*   ⓀⓀ
Viktoriag. 6, 411 25 Gothenburg. 【 *031-17 36 30.* FAX *031-711 95 97.* W *www.hotelvasa.se*
Newly refurbished family-run hotel in the middle of Vasastaden. In summer the breakfast buffet is set up in the inner courtyard. ⌨ TV ⛵ ☷ *Rooms: 50*

| AE DC MC V | ● | ▪ | | |

CENTRE: *Eggers Hotell & Restaurang*   ⓀⓀⓀ
Drottningtorget. Box 323, 401 25 Gothenburg. 【 *031-33 34 44.* FAX *031-15 42 43.*
W *www.hoteleggers.se*
A listed building in the heart of the city, with early-20th-century character. Located a stone's throw from the train station. ⌨ TV ⛵ ☷ *Rooms: 67*

| AE DC MC V | ● | ▪ | ● | ▪ |

CENTRE: *Hotel Gothia Towers*   ⓀⓀⓀ
Mässans gata 24. Box 5184, 402 26 Gothenburg. 【 *031-750 88 10.*
FAX *031-750 88 82.* W *www.gothiatowers.com*
Gothenburg's tallest hotel (23 floors) is situated opposite Liseberg amusement park and the Swedish Exhibition Centre. ⌨ TV Ⓨ ⛵ ☷ 📺 & *Rooms: 704*

| AE DC MC V | ● | ▪ | ● | ▪ |

CENTRE: *Elite Plaza Hotel*   ⓀⓀⓀⓀ
Västra Hamng. 3, 404 22 Gothenburg. 【 *031-720 40 00.* FAX *031-720 40 10.*
W *www.elite.se*
New five-star hotel in a palatial old building dating from 1889. Exquisitely refurbished, with well-preserved original features combined with modern art and design. ⌨ TV Ⓨ ⛵ ☷ 📺 & *Rooms: 143*

| AE DC MC V | ● | ▪ | ● | ▪ |

CENTRE: *Radisson SAS Park Avenue Hotel*   ⓀⓀⓀ
Kungsportsavenyn 36-38. Box 53233, 400 16 Gothenburg. 【 *031-758 40 00.*
FAX *031-758 40 01.* W *www.radissonsas.se*
Luxury modern hotel near Götaplatsen with tastefully decorated rooms, plus conference and banqueting facilities. ⌨ TV Ⓨ ☷ 📺 & *Rooms: 318*

| AE DC MC V | ● | ▪ | ● | ▪ |

FURTHER AFIELD: *Mölndal/Torrekulla Turiststation*   ☞
428 35 Kållered. 【 *031-795 14 95.* FAX *031-795 51 40.* @ *info@torrekulla.stfturist.se*
Picturesque, child-friendly location in Sandsjöbacka nature reserve, 10 min by car south of the centre. Outdoor activities nearby, such as swimming. ⛵ & *Beds: 132*

| MC V | ● | ▪ | | |

WESTERN GÖTALAND

BORÅS: *Ramada Hotell Vävaren*   ⓀⓀ
Allégatan 21, 503 32 Borås. 【 *033-10 00 20.* FAX *033-41 18 82.*
W *www.hotel-vavaren.se*
Well-equipped, central hotel with a friendly atmosphere.
⌨ TV Ⓨ ⛵ ☷ 📺 & *Rooms: 97*

| AE DC MC V | ● | ▪ | ● | ▪ |

FALKENBERG: *Grand Hotel Falkenberg*   ⓀⓀ
Hotellgatan 1, 311 31 Falkenberg. 【 *0346-144 50.* FAX *0346-144 59.*
Built in 1931, this central hotel is Falkenberg's entertainment hub with dance music and nightclub. Set beside the pretty Ätran river.
⌨ TV Ⓨ ⛵ ☷ & *Rooms: 70*

| AE DC MC V | ● | ▪ | ● | ▪ |

FJÄLLBACKA: *Stora Hotellet Fjällbacka*   ⓀⓀⓀ
Galärbacken 3, 450 71 Fjällbacka. 【 *0525-310 03.* FAX *0525-310 93.*
Charming little hotel with a marine theme inspired by Klassen, a sea captain who set up the hotel in the late 19th century. The rooms are named after people and places from the captain's travels on the high seas and decorated accordingly. ⌨ TV Ⓨ ⛵ *Rooms: 23*

| AE DC MC V | ● | ▪ | ● | ▪ |

HALMSTAD: *Grand Hotel Halmstad* ⓚⓚⓚ
Stationsgatan 44, 302 45 Halmstad. 🕿 035-280 81 00. ꜰᴀx 035-280 81 10.
Dating from 1905, the hotel offers a good standard and is located in the middle
of town, near the train station, shopping and restaurants.
🛏 📺 💱 🗝 ♿ *Rooms: 108*

	AE	●		●	■
	DC				
	MC				
	V				

LIDKÖPING: *Best Western Stadt Lidköping* ⓚⓚ
Gamla Stadens Torg 1, 531 02 Lidköping. 🕿 0510-220 85. ꜰᴀx 0510-215 32.
ⓦ www.stadtlidkoping.se
Business and leisure hotel, beautifully situated on the Lidan river in the old
town centre. 🛏 📺 💱 🗝 ♿ *Rooms: 67*

	AE	●		●	■
	DC				
	MC				
	V				

MARSTRAND: *Båtellet* ✑
Kungsplan, 440 30 Marstrand. 🕿 0303-600 10. ꜰᴀx 0303-606 07.
@ marstrandsvarmbadhus@telia.com
The wonderful 19th-century spa house has a restaurant and a youth hostel with
self-catering facilities. 💱 🍴 ♿ *Beds: 113*

	MC	●		●	■
	V				
	DC				

SKÖVDE: *Scandic Hotel Billingen* ⓚⓚⓚ
Trädgårdsgatan 10, 541 30 Skövde. 🕿 0500-74 50 00. ꜰᴀx 0500-74 50 11.
ⓦ www.scandic hotels.se
Lovely old hotel from the late 19th century with fine architecture and a grand
function suite. 🛏 📺 💱 🗝 🍴 ♿ *Rooms: 107*

	AE	●	■	●	■
	DC				
	MC				
	V				

SMÖGEN: *Hotell Smögens Havsbad* ⓚⓚ
Hotellgatan 26, 450 43 Smögen. 🕿 0523-66 84 50. ꜰᴀx 0523-66 84 55.
Part listed building and part newly-built hotel in light natural materials
overlooking the water. The restaurant specializes in fish and seafood.
🛏 📺 🍸 💱 ♿ *Rooms: 76*

	AE	●	■	●	■
	DC				
	MC				
	V				

STRÖMSTAD: *Laholmen Hotell* ⓚⓚⓚ
452 30 Strömstad. 🕿 0526-197 00. ꜰᴀx 0526-100 36.
Situated on a promontory in the harbour. Most rooms have superb views across
Kosterfjorden. The restaurant offers seafood delicacies. 🛏 📺 💱 🗝 ♿
Rooms: 152

	AE	●	■	●	■
	DC				
	MC				
	V				

TROLLHÄTTAN: *Albert Kök – Hotel och Konferens* ⓚⓚ
Strömsberg, 461 57 Trollhättan. 🕿 0520-129 90. ꜰᴀx 0520-133 11.
ⓦ www.alberthotell.com
The main building from 1856 stands on a hill with wonderful views down the
slope to the town. Top class restaurant. 🛏 📺 🍸 💱 🗝 ♿ *Rooms: 28*

	AF	●	■	●	■
	DC				
	MC				
	V				

VARBERG: *Best Western Varbergs Stadshotell & Asia Spa* ⓚⓚ
Kungsgatan 24–26, 432 41 Varberg. 🕿 0340-69 01 00. ꜰᴀx 0340-69 01 01.
ⓦ www.varbergsstadshotell.com
Attractive early-20th-century decor, offering comfort and a good standard of
technology. Award-winning restaurant and an oriental-style spa.
🛏 📺 🍸 💱 🗝 ♿ *Rooms: 125*

	AE	●	■	●	■
	DC				
	MC				
	V				

ÅMÅL: *Åmåls Studshotell* ⓚⓚ
Kungsgatan 9, Box 2, 662 21 Åmål. 🕿 0532-616 10. ꜰᴀx 0532-616 19.
Charming, well-renovated town hotel from 1904. In summer food and drink
are served outside in the hotel garden. 🛏 📺 🍸 💱 🗝 ♿ *Rooms: 29*

	AE	●	■	●	■
	DC				
	MC				
	V				

WESTERN SVEALAND

BORLÄNGE: *Scandic Hotell Borlänge* ⓚⓚⓚ
Stationsgatan 21, 784 35 Borlänge. 🕿 0243-79 90 00. ꜰᴀx 0243-79 90 11.
ⓦ www.scandic-hotels.se
Family-friendly hotel in the heart of Borlänge. Restaurant with good Swedish
fare. 🛏 📺 💱 🗝 🍴 ♿ *Rooms: 113*

	AE	●		●	■
	DC				
	MC				
	V				

FALUN: *First Hotel Grand Falun* ⓚⓚ
Trotzgatan 9-11, 791 71 Falun. 🕿 023-79 48 80. ꜰᴀx 023-141 43.
ⓦ www.firsthotels.com
In central Falun, handy for shopping and entertainment. The same
building has a spa and fitness centre. The restaurant is a popular spot.
🛏 📺 💱 🗝 🍴 🍴 ♿ *Rooms: 151*

	AE	●	■	●	■
	DC				
	MC				
	V				

KARLSTAD: *Elite Stadshotellet Karlstad* ⓚⓚ
Kungsgatan 22, Box 317, 651 08 Karlstad. 🕿 054-29 30 00. ꜰᴀx 054-29 30 31.
@ stadshotellet.karlstad@elite.se
Centrally located on the Klarälven river. Traditional atmosphere, individually
decorated rooms and a grand function suite. 🛏 📺 💱 🗝 🍴 🍴 ♿ *Rooms: 139*

	AE	●	■	●	■
	DC				
	MC				
	V				

<table>
<tr><td colspan="2">

Price categories for a double room per night, including breakfast unless otherwise stated, plus tax and service.

◇ Youth hostel *(see pp279)*
Ⓚ under 700 Kr
ⓀⓀ 700–1,400 Kr
ⓀⓀⓀ 1,400–2,100 Kr
ⓀⓀⓀⓀ over 2,100 Kr

</td><td colspan="3">

CHILDREN'S FACILITIES
Cots and highchairs are available and some hotels will also provide a baby-sitting service.
PARKING
Parking is provided by the hotel, either in a private car park or a private garage nearby.
RESTAURANT
The hotel has a restaurant for residents, which also welcomes non-residents – usually only open for evening meals.
BAR
The hotel has a bar that is open to non-residents as well as those staying in the hotel.

</td></tr>
</table>

	CREDIT CARDS	CHILDREN'S FACILITIES	PARKING	RESTAURANT	BAR
MORA: *First Hotel Mora* ⓀⓀ Strandgatan 12, 792 30 Mora. ☎ 0250-59 26 50. FAX 0250-189 81. 🔲 www.firsthotels.se Fully refurbished town hotel from the 1830s, right in the centre. Good spa. 🛏 TV ⚡ 🛎 🍴 🎿 ♿ *Rooms: 141*	AE DC MC V	●	■	●	■
SUNNE: *Quality Hotel & Spa Selma Lagerlöf* ⓀⓀ Box 500, 686 28 Sunne. ☎ 0565-166 00. FAX 0565-166 20. 🔲 www.selmaspa.se Hotel and spa on Fryken lake, 60 km (37 miles) north of Karlstad. Cosy setting and good food. 🛏 TV 🍷 🛎 🍴 🏊 ♿ *Rooms: 340*	AE DC MC V	●	■	●	■
SÄLEN: *Sälens Högfjällshotell* ⓀⓀⓀ 780 67 Sälen. ☎ 0280-870 00. FAX 0280-211 61. 🔲 www.salen-hotell.se Next to the Högfjället/Lindvallen lift system. In addition to hotel rooms, it has a number of self-catering apartments. Activities include skiing and snow-scooter safaris. There is a spa, after-ski and nightclub. 🛏 TV ⚡ 🛎 *Rooms: 106*	AE DC MC V	●	■	●	■
TÄLLBERG: *Åkerblads Hotell* ⓀⓀ Sjögattu 2, 793 70 Tällberg. ☎ 0247-508 00. FAX 0247-506 52. Pretty, romantic country house dating back to medieval times on Lake Siljan. Many suites and mini-suites. Excellent food. 🛏 TV ⚡ 🏊 ♿ *Rooms: 69*	AE DC MC V	●	■	●	■
ÖREBRO: *Elite Stora Hotellet* ⓀⓀⓀ Drottninggatan 1, 701 45 Örebro. ☎ 019-15 69 00. FAX 019-15 69 50. 🔲 www.elite.se Beautifully situated next to the castle in a mid-19th century building. Slottskällaren restaurant is set in the 14th-century vaults. 🛏 TV ⚡ 🛎 *Rooms: 132*	AE DC MC V	●	■	●	■

SOUTHERN NORRLAND

	CREDIT CARDS	CHILDREN'S FACILITIES	PARKING	RESTAURANT	BAR
GÄVLE: *Scandic Grand Hotel Central* ⓀⓀⓀ Nygatan 45, 803 20 Gävle. ☎ 026-495 84 00. FAX 026-495 84 11. 🔲 www.scandic-hotels.se/grandcentral Large business and family hotel in central Gävle. Every child receives a small present at check-in. 🛏 TV ⚡ 🛎 🍴 ♿ *Rooms: 220.*	AE DC MC V	●	■	●	■
HUDIKSVALL: *First Hotel Statt Hudiksvall* ⓀⓀⓀ Storgatan 36, Box 55, 824 22 Hudiksvall. ☎ 0650-150 60. FAX 0650-960 95. 🔲 www.firsthotels.se Well-equipped hotel in a splendid building in the middle of town. The dance restaurant is the hub of the town's nightlife. 🛏 TV ⚡ 🛎 🍴 🏊 ♿ *Rooms: 106*	AE DC MC V	●	■	●	■
HÄRNÖSAND: *First Hotel Stadt Härnösand* ⓀⓀⓀ Skeppsbron 9, 871 30 Härnösand. ☎ 0611-55 44 40. FAX 0611-55 44 47. 🔲 www.firsthotels.se A late-20th century hotel in a central location with fine views of the canal and harbour. 🛏 TV ⚡ 🛎 ♿ *Rooms: 95*	AE DC MC V	●	■	●	■
HIGH COAST: *Hotell Höga Kusten* ⓀⓀ Hornöberget, 872 94 Sandöverken. ☎ 0613-72 22 70. FAX 0613-72 22 79. 🔲 www.hotellhoga-kusten.se A modern hotel at the base of one of the world's longest suspension bridges. It has a superb view across the Ångermanälven river. 🛏 TV ⚡ 🛎 ♿ *Rooms: 28*	AE DC MC V	●	■	●	■
SUNDSVALL: *STF Vandrarhem Sundsvall* ◇ Norra Stadsberget, 856 40 Sundsvall. ☎ & FAX 060-61 21 19. 🔲 www.stfturist.se Pretty, quiet and leafy location, 20-min walk from the centre. Several double rooms with shower and TV. ⚡ ♿ *Beds: 137*	MC V	●	■		
SUNDSVALL: *Elite Hotel Knaust* ⓀⓀⓀ Storgatan 13, 851 05 Sundsvall. ☎ 060-608 00 00. FAX 060-608 00 10. 🔲 www.elite.se Classic hotel dating from 1891, known for its magnificent staircase. Decor is a combination of old tradition and modern design. 🛏 TV 🍷 ⚡ 🛎 🍴 *Rooms: 94*	AE DC MC V	●	■	●	■

SÖDERHAMN: *First Hotel Statt Söderhamn*   (Ki)(Ki)(Ki)
Oxtorgsgatan 17, 826 22 Söderhamn. **(** *0270-735 70.* **FAX** *0270-135 24.*
[W] www.firsthotels.se
Newly refurbished, first-class hotel, next to the town hall. 🔜 TV 💱 🔋 📶 ♿ *Rooms: 70*

AF	●	■		■	
DC					
MC					
V					

UMEÅ: *Royal Hotel Umeå*   (Ki)(Ki)
Skolgatan 62, Vasaplan, 903 29 Umeå. **(** *090-10 07 30.* **FAX** *090-10 07 39.*
[W] www.royalhotelumea.com
Film is the theme of this central Umeå hotel, which has its own cinema and is decorated with portraits of Hollywood stars. 🔜 TV 💱 🔋 📶 ≋ *Rooms: 68*

AE	●	■		■	
DC					
MC					
V					

ÅRE: *Hotel Diplomat Åregården*   (Ki)(Ki)
Box 6, 890 13 Åre. **(** *0647-178 00.* **FAX** *0647-179 60.* [W] www.diplomathotel.com
A National Romantic-style building on Åre Torg. Classic hotel accommodation with full service. Open only during the skiing season. 🔜 TV 💱 🔋 ≋ *Rooms: 54*

AE	●	■		■	
DC					
MC					
V					

ÖRNSKÖLDSVIK: *First Hotel Statt*   (Ki)(Ki)
Lasarettgatan 2, 891 21 Örnsköldsvik. **(** *0660-26 55 90.* **FAX** *0660-837 91.*
[W] www.firsthotels.se
First-class hotel in the middle of town. Modern creature comforts in a building with old-fashioned charm. 🔜 TV 💱 🔋 ♿ *Rooms: 115*

AE	●	■		■	
DC					
MC					
V					

ÖSTERSUND: *Ramada Plaza Hotel Östersund*   (Ki)(Ki)(Ki)
Kyrkgatan 70, 831 21 Östersund. **(** *063-57 57 00.* **FAX** *063-57 57 11.*
Family-friendly business hotel with an Internet-linked TV in every room. Several restaurants and bars. 🔜 TV 📶 💱 🔋 📶 ♿ *Rooms: 126*

AE	●	■		■	
DC					
MC					
V					

NORTHERN NORRLAND

ABISKO: *STF Abisko Turiststation*   (Ki)(Ki)
981 07 Abisko. **(** *0980-402 00.* **FAX** *0980-401 40.* [W] www.stfabisko.com
Choose between hotel, youth hostel-type accommodation, or self-catering cottages. Hotel offers buffet-style breakfast, lunch and dinner. Open all year, but with full service only during March and April. 💱 ♿ *Beds: 300*

AE	●	■		■	
MC					
V					

HAPARANDA: *Haparanda Stadshotell*   (Ki)(Ki)(Ki)
Torget 7, 953 31 Haparanda. **(** *0922-614 90.* **FAX** *0922-102 23.*
[W] www.haparandastadshotell.se
Classic hotel in a splendid late-19th-century building. The Viltkällaren restaurant specializes in using local ingredients. 🔜 TV 💱 🔋 ♿ *Rooms: 89*

AE	●	■		■	
DC					
MC					
V					

JUKKASJÄRVI: *Icehotel*   (Ki)(Ki)(Ki)(Ki)
981 91 Jukkasjärvi. **(** *0980-668 00.* **FAX** *0980-668 90.*
[W] www.icehotel.com
The world's first ice hotel and a major tourist attraction in its own right *(see p272).* Open mid-Dec to early May. 💱 *Rooms: 66*

AE		■		■	
DC					
MC					
V					

KIRUNA: *Scandic Hotel Ferrooms*   (Ki)(Ki)(Ki)
Lars Janssonsgatan 15, 981 31 Kiruna. **(** *0980-39 86 00.* **FAX** *0980-39 86 11.*
[W] www.scandic-hotels.com/ferrooms
Family-friendly hotel of a high standard. One restaurant offering traditional Swedish fare and one for Norrland specialities. 🔜 TV 💱 🔋 📶 ♿ *Rooms: 171*

AE	●	■		■	
DC					
MC					
V					

LULEÅ: *Elite Stadshotellet Luleå*   (Ki)(Ki)(Ki)
Storgatan 15, 971 28 Luleå. **(** *0920-670 00.* **FAX** *0920-670 92.* [W] www.elite.se
Elegant modern hotel in central Luleå, but with a 100-year history. Grand ballroom, fine restaurant and pub. 🔜 TV 📶 💱 🔋 ♿ *Rooms: 135*

AE	●	■		■	
DC					
MC					
V					

LYCKSELE: *Hotell Lappland*   (Ki)(Ki)(Ki)
Korpberget 1, Box 34, 921 21 Lycksele. **(** *0950-370 00.* **FAX** *0950-375 15.*
[W] www.hotelllappland.se
Conference hotel, exhibition centre and the world's largest Sami tent. A selection of fun activities is organised for guests. 🔜 TV 💱 🔋 📶 ♿ *Rooms: 201*

AE	●	■		■	
DC					
MC					
V					

PITEÅ: *Pite Havsbad*   (Ki)(Ki)
Box 815, 941 28 Piteå. **(** *0911-327 00.* **FAX** *0911-327 99.* [W] www.pite-havsbad.se
Huge hotel on the "Norrland Riviera". Pool and many outdoor activities. In addition to traditional hotel accommodation, there are also cottages and a campsite. 🔜 TV 💱 🔋 📶 ≋ ♿ *Rooms: 394*

AE	●	■	●	■	
DC					
MC					
V					

SKELLEFTEÅ: *First Hotel Statt Skellefteå*   (Ki)(Ki)
Stationsg. 8, 931 31 Skellefteå. **(** *0910-141 40.* **FAX** *0910-71 10 65.* [W] www.firsthotels.se
Modern, central, full-service hotel dating from 1863. The current building is a typically functional design from the 1950s. 🔜 TV 💱 🔋 📶 ♿ *Rooms: 87*

AE	●	■	●	■	
DC					
MC					
V					

For key to symbols see back flap

WHERE TO EAT

SWEDEN IS ONE OF Europe's liveliest and most varied countries for eating out. Swedish cuisine has won many international awards in recent years, and a number of restaurants have been awarded Michelin stars. Many of the best restaurants are relatively small and informal as a number of top chefs have opened their own establishments. Various ethnic styles of cooking are often combined to create

Swedish hot dog

innovative and delicious dishes in what is called "cross-over" cuisine. Traditional Swedish dishes are frequently served at lunchtime and are excellent value for money. There are also plenty of fast-food outlets, pubs, Chinese restaurants, pizzerias and kebab houses offering inexpensive food. Hot-dog stands, providing filling snacks, can be found practically everywhere.

WHERE TO EAT

SWEDEN HAS a very wide range of restaurants. The majority are found in the larger cities and towns, but there are a number of good places to eat in the smaller towns. Restaurants and cafés can be found in the larger department stores and shopping malls, as well as at most museums. Along the coast and inland there are many friendly restaurants that open just for summer. Larger towns often have market halls with excellent restaurants and cafés, but they are not open in the evening for dinner.

Open sandwiches with a variety of fillings can be bought at cafés and cake shops, which often serve inexpensive hot dishes at lunchtime as well.

Outdoor cafés spring up on many streets and squares with the arrival of summer, and also in parks and green areas such as Djurgården in Stockholm and Kungsportsavenyn in Gothenburg.

TYPES OF RESTAURANT

FASHIONABLE restaurants usually attract a young clientele, and the trendiest places sometimes have a rather stark decor and extremely high noise levels. If you are looking for somewhere quieter, which also has good service, it is often best to choose an established restaurant. There are many specialist restaurants serving cuisine from abroad, or "cross-over" cooking, which is a combination of styles.

Most restaurants charge roughly the same prices, regardless of quality. If you are looking for somewhere cheaper to eat, there are pizzerias, pubs, kebab houses, sushi bars, fast food chains and cafés to choose from.

Those with a sweet tooth shouldn't miss a visit to one

Inn sign, Gamla Stan

of the many modern cafés or traditional cake shops which offer delicious Danish pastries, cinnamon buns, cakes and gateaux.

There are few bars as such and the best can be found at the most popular restaurants. Dress is usually informal, even at the more elegant restaurants. Ties are not required but shorts are not acceptable. Most restaurants have a no-smoking section and Government legislation is proposing a total ban on smoking in restaurants.

OPENING TIMES

THE MAJORITY OF restaurants open for lunch at 11.30am and close at around 10pm. Dinner is served from 6pm or even earlier. A number of restaurants are closed on Sundays or Mondays. Smaller restaurants may close for their annual holiday during July.

Prices for lunch are often extremely reasonable, even at the more elegant establishments, so lunchtime is an ideal opportunity to enjoy an inexpensive meal at a pleasant restaurant. *Dagens lunch* (Lunch of the Day) is generally not served after 2pm, even if the restaurant is open in the afternoon.

A number of restaurants and pubs serve food right up to midnight or even later, particularly those which provide entertainment, music

Magnificent interior of Café Opera in Stockholm

Outdoor café in Riddarhustorget in Gamla Stan, Stockholm

or a disco. Anyone still hungry during the night can find hot-dog kiosks which stay open very late, sometimes even round the clock.

VEGETARIAN FOOD

INTEREST IN vegetarian food is increasing in Sweden, and this is reflected by the fact that excellent vegetarian cuisine is now served at most restaurants. There are also several completely vegetarian restaurants in the major cities.

BOOKING A TABLE

RESERVATIONS should be made for evening meals, but many restaurants do not accept bookings for lunch. If you want to be sure of a table at midday, it is best to arrive at the restaurant before 11.30am or after 1pm, by which time most of the lunch-time clientele will have left.

CHILDREN

ALL CHILDREN are welcome in restaurants without exception. They will usually be offered a special children's menu, or half portions from the normal menu. Almost all restaurants have highchairs.

PRICES

PRICES OF MEALS in Sweden are very similar. At most places hot dishes cost from about 100 kr, or 200 kr or more at expensive restaurants. Lunch prices are around 60–70 kr, and that often includes a non-alcoholic drink and coffee. However, the

price of beer, wine and other alcoholic drinks can vary considerably. It generally follows that the more expensive the restaurant, the higher the price of the wine. The house wine is usually the cheapest, with a bottle normally costing from 150 kr. Beer is cheaper in pubs than in restaurants. Tap water is free of charge, and Sweden's drinking water is of excellent quality.

Tips are always included in the price, but if you want to reward good service you can round up the bill. If the restaurant has a manned cloakroom, the normal price is 10 kr per person. A number of restaurants do not allow guests to take outdoor clothing into the dining room. Credit cards are accepted in virtually every restaurant.

READING THE MENU

DINNER AT A Swedish restaurant usually includes a starter (förrätt), hot main course (varmrätt) and dessert (efterrätt). Most offer one or more fixed-price meals with a choice of two or three dishes at a lower price than the à la carte menu. It is perfectly acceptable to have just a starter or main course. At lunchtime most people order only one course. The meal is nearly always served on the plate, but the more elegant restaurants often have dessert or

cheese trolleys. Many restaurants have menus in English; if they don't, the waiters and waitresses are usually familiar with English and will be pleased to explain the menu to you.

Some restaurants serve a typical Swedish smörgåsbord, usually on Sundays. Some specialize in a fish or shellfish buffet. During December a Julbord is usually available. This is similar to the normal smörgåsbord, but with a lavish buffet selection of traditional seasonal dishes. You can eat as much as you like at a fixed price, but drinks are not included.

WHAT TO DRINK

WINE AND BEER are the normal accompaniments to a meal, as well as mineral water. The wine list often features wine from countries outside Europe, along with a house wine. Vintage wines are usually not available at medium-price restaurants.

Many pubs and restaurants offer a wide selection of beers, often with one or more on draught. A few small Swedish breweries make an excellent non-filtered beer. Beer is graded into three classes, with Class I the weakest.

Herring or "home-cooking" is usually washed down with beer, sometimes accompanied by one of the many different flavoured schnapps.

Spirits and wines are more expensive in Swedish restaurants than in most other countries because of the high duty on alcohol and the State retail alcohol monopoly.

Grythyttan, a gastronomic haven with a well-stocked wine cellar which also offers tastings

What to Eat in Sweden

Crisp-
bread

SWEDEN OFFERS some very special gastronomic ingredients such as elk, reindeer, bleak roe, shellfish and local fish. Thanks to strict regulations, Sweden's food is among the purest in Europe. Salmon can be caught in the heart of Stockholm, and zander, pike, Baltic herring and perch in the archipelago. Char is fished in Lake Vättern and freshwater crayfish are plentiful in lakes and rivers in autumn. Varieties of mushrooms, and lingonberries, blueberries and cloudberries all grow wild.

Cheese
Swedish cheese goes well with herring, such as cheese spiced with cumin (left) or the nutty Västerbotten cheese (right).

Pickled herring, chopped onion and sour cream.

"Gubbröra" (anchovies, beetroot, onion, capers, egg yolk).

Pickled herring

Herring marinated in mustard

"Jansson's temptation", a gratin of anchovies, potatoes, sliced onion and double cream.

Böckling, smoked herring.

Bleak roe with chopped onion and sour cream.

Herring, fried and pickled in vinegar and chopped onion.

SMÖRGÅSBORD

This typically Swedish buffet has a variety of dishes, but often starts with a selection of herring *(sill)* prepared in different ways. Cold dishes come next, then hot dishes and desserts. Diners help themselves and change plates between courses.

Shellfish Soup
Fresh shellfish such as oysters, mussels, lobster, shrimps and prawns come from Sweden's west coast.

Gravad Lax
Salmon marinated for two days in sugar, salt and dill, is served with a cold sweet and sour mustard sauce and dill.

Quiche with Salad
Many cafés serve inexpensive lunches with, for example, a quiche filled with shellfish, ham, cheese or vegetables.

PEAS WITH PORK

Traditionally served on Thursdays, this national dish is yellow pea soup with lightly salted meat or sausage accompanied by mustard. Hot punsch is served on festive occasions. It is followed by pancakes with jam.

Mustard

Hot punsch

Grilled Salmon
Sweden has a rich variety of fish from the sea and the lakes, and they are prepared in more different ways than in most countries. Salmon is served as a starter as well as a main course. It can be boiled, fried, grilled, poached and served cold, marinated, smoked or salted. Here the grilled salmon is served with a selection of blanched vegetables.

Grilled Zander
Freshly caught zander from the Stockholm archipelago or Lake Mälaren is served with shrimps and grated horseradish.

Swedish Meatballs
Always part of a smörgåsbord, this national dish is also eaten hot with mashed potato, preserved lingonberries and gherkins.

Brisket of Beef
Boiled salted brisket of beef with root vegetables is one of the most common Swedish "home-cooked" dishes.

Reindeer Calf Fillet
Reindeer meat is very tender, lean and delicious. Here it is grilled with chanterelles, black salsify and cranberries.

Cheesecake and Cloudberries
A traditional dessert made with eggs and almonds, served here with cloudberries from the north or the archipelago.

Rosehip Soup
This can be eaten hot or cold, with whipped cream or ice cream. Served here with vanilla parfait and almond biscuits.

Hot Chocolate and Cinnamon Buns
A bun is popular with hot chocolate or coffee.

DRINKS

Sweden imports a huge variety of wine from all over the world, but people usually drink beer or schnapps with herring or a *smörgåsbord*. Punsch (a sweet arak spirit) is often served with coffee, or hot with pea soup. Swedish vodka is popular worldwide, but there are also some 60 types of local schnapps flavoured with different herbs and spices. Swedish beer is enjoying a renaissance, with products such as non-filtered beer, light ale and blueberry beer being produced at new small breweries.

Mineral water　　**Non-filtered beer**　　**Akvavit schnapps**　　**Swedish punsch**

Choosing a Restaurant

THIS LISTING COVERS some 120 restaurants in all price categories selected for their good value, excellent food and/or location. The restaurants, bars and cafés are listed alphabetically, area by area, starting with those in central Stockholm. For map references in Stockholm, see the Street Finder map, *pp112–17*. The key to the symbols is on the back flap.

	CREDIT CARDS	OPEN LUNCH-TIME	OPEN LATE	FIXED-PRICE MENU	GOOD WINE LIST

STOCKHOLM

GAMLA STAN: *Den Gyldene Freden*   ⓚⓚⓚ
Österlånggatan 51, 103 17 Stockholm. **Map** 3 C3. 🕻 *08-24 97 60.*
An artists' restaurant with a long tradition. Swedish/French cuisine, as well as modestly priced traditional Swedish fare. 🖶 🔆 Ⅴ Ⓨ
AE DC MC V — Open Late ■, Good Wine List ■

GAMLA STAN: *Pontus in the Greenhouse*   ⓚⓚⓚⓚ
Österlånggatan 17, 111 31 Stockholm. **Map** 4 C3. 🕻 *08-545 273 00.*
One of Stockholm's virtuoso young chefs creates culinary masterpieces with prices to match. Affluent clientele and comfortable location on first floor. Pleasant bistro with lower prices at street level. 🖶 🔆 Ⅴ Ⓨ
AE DC MC V — Open Lunch-Time ●, Open Late ■, Fixed-Price Menu ●, Good Wine List ■

CITY: *Bistro Jarl*   ⓚⓚ
Birger Jarlsgatan 7, 111 45 Stockholm. **Map** 2 D4. 🕻 *08-611 76 30.*
Small, luxurious restaurant, a favourite spot for sophisticated city folk. Mediterranean and Swedish dishes. The city's only champagne bar. 🖶 Ⓨ
AE DC MC V — Open Lunch-Time ●, Open Late ■

CITY: *Prinsen*   ⓚⓚⓚ
Mäster Samuelsgatan 4, 111 44 Stockholm. **Map** 2 D4. 🕻 *08-611 13 31.*
Hundred year-old restaurant with a noisy, arty clientele. The menu is traditional with a modern twist. Swedish and Continental dishes. 🖶 🔆
AE DC MC V — Open Lunch-Time ●, Open Late ■, Good Wine List ■

CITY: *Restaurangen*   ⓚⓚⓚ
Oxtorgsgatan 14, 111 57 Stockholm. **Map** 2 D4. 🕻 *08-22 09 52.*
Choose five dishes at a fixed price and try various wines as well. Beautifully presented food and stylish decor. ♿ 🖶 Ⅴ Ⓨ
AE DC MC V — Open Lunch-Time ●, Open Late ■, Good Wine List ■

CITY: *Fredsgatan 12*   ⓚⓚⓚⓚ
Fredsgatan 12, 111 52 Stockholm. **Map** 2 D5. 🕻 *08-24 80 52.*
Star chef Melker Andersson offers a gastronomic experience with his "world cooking", combining the cuisines of many countries. Austere modern decor and trendy clientele. ♿ 🖶 🔆 Ⅴ Ⓨ
AE DC MC V — Open Lunch-Time ●, Open Late ■, Fixed-Price Menu ●, Good Wine List ■

CITY: *Operakällaren*   ⓚⓚⓚⓚ
Operahuset, Karl XII's Torg, 111 86 Stockholm. **Map** 2 D5, 3 B1. 🕻 *08-676 58 01.*
The capital's classic temple of gastronomy. The chefs are young and creative, the dining room with its lavish 19th-century ceiling paintings and the Jugendstil bar are attractions in themselves. Café Opera has lower prices and a famous afternoon cake buffet. One Michelin star.
♿ 🖶 🔆 Ⅴ Ⓨ
AE DC MC V — Good Wine List ■

BLASIEHOLMEN & SKEPPSHOLMEN: *Berns' Salonger*   ⓚⓚⓚ
Näckströmsgatan 8, Berzelii Park, 103 27 Stockholm. **Map** 2 D4. 🕻 *08-566 322 22.*
Sir Terence Conran designed this spacious new restaurant in a building rich in tradition. The restaurant, seating 248, focuses on seafood. The Bar & Grill can seat 110 people. ♿ 🖶 Ⅴ Ⓨ
AE DC MC V — Open Lunch-Time ●, Open Late ■, Good Wine List ■

BLASIEHOLMEN & SKEPPSHOLMEN: *Grands Veranda*   ⓚⓚⓚⓚ
Södra Blasieholmshamnen 8, 103 27 Stockholm. **Map** 3 C1. 🕻 *08-679 35 86.*
A popular meeting place with views over Strömmen, Gamla Stan and the Royal Palace. Hotel guests, locals and tourists enjoy breakfast, lunch and dinner here every day of the year. ♿ 🖶 🔆 Ⅴ Ⓨ
AE DC MC V — Open Lunch-Time ●, Open Late ■, Fixed-Price Menu ●, Good Wine List ■

ÖSTERMALM: *Ett Litet Hak*   ⓚⓚⓚ
Grev Turegatan 15, 114 46 Stockholm. **Map** 2 D4. 🕻 *08-660 13 09.*
Atmospheric local bar with trendy Continental food and considerate staff.
🖶 Ⅴ Ⓨ
AE DC MC V — Open Lunch-Time ●, Open Late ■

ÖSTERMALM: *Halv Grek Plus Turk*   ⓚⓚⓚ
Jungfrugatan 33, 114 44 Stockholm. **Map** 2 E3. 🕻 *08-665 94 22.*
Excellent tasty food and a friendly atmosphere. Choose from a variety of hot and cold Greek and Turkish dishes. ♿ 🖶 Ⅴ Ⓨ
AE DC MC V — Open Late ■, Good Wine List ■

	Average prices explanation			

Average prices for a three-course meal for one, half a bottle of house wine and unavoidable charges such as service and cover:

- (Kr) under 300 Kr
- (Kr)(Kr) 300–400 Kr
- (Kr)(Kr)(Kr) 400–500 Kr
- (Kr)(Kr)(Kr)(Kr) over 500 Kr

OPEN LUNCH-TIME
These restaurants are open for lunch and usually serve inexpensive meals.

OPEN LATE
Restaurants which remain open with their full menu after 10pm.

FIXED-PRICE MENU
A fixed-price menu is available for lunch, dinner or both, usually with three courses.

GOOD WINE LIST
Restaurant has a wide choice of good wines, or a more specialized range.

	Credit Cards	Open Lunch-time	Open Late	Fixed-price Menu	Good Wine List
ÖSTERMALM: *Brasserie Godot* (Kr)(Kr) Grev Turegatan 36, 114 38 Stockholm. **Map** 2 E3. 08-660 06 14. Fashionable restaurant offering classic French and Swedish cuisine. Highlights include duck-thigh confit with orange sauce. Good value. & V Y	AE DC MC V		■		■
ÖSTERMALM: *Paul & Norbert* (Kr)(Kr)(Kr)(Kr) Strandvägen 9, 114 56 Stockholm. **Map** 2 E4. 08-663 81 83 A gastronomic jewel for gourmets. Elegant, discreet and modern decor, superb service and delicious seasonal food. V	AE DC MC V	●		●	■
ÖSTERMALM: *Villa Källhagen* (Kr)(Kr)(Kr) Djurgårdsbrunnsvägen 10, 115 27 Stockholm. 08-665 03 00. One of Stockholm's best restaurants with a beautiful waterfront location. The cuisine is international with the accent on Swedish ingredients. Pleasant outdoor terrace. & V Y	AE DC MC V	●		●	■
DJURGÅRDEN: *Värdshuset Ulla Winbladh* (Kr)(Kr)(Kr) Rosendalsvägen 8, 115 21 Stockholm. 08-663 05 71. Beautifully located restaurant with olde-worlde atmosphere and well-prepared food. Swedish specialities and some more modern dishes. The outdoor café is very popular in the summer. & V Y	AE DC MC V	●	■		■
DJURGÅRDEN: *Restaurant Hasselbacken* (Kr)(Kr)(Kr)(Kr) Hazeliusbacken 20, 100 55 Stockholm. 08-517 343 00. Well-prepared traditional restaurant fare is served in a finely restored 1850s setting. In summer there is an outdoor café. & V Y	AE DC MC V	●			■
KUNGSHOLMEN: *Roppongi* (Kr)(Kr) Hantverkargatan 76c, 113 38 Stockholm. 08-650 17 72. A high-class sushi restaurant offering a range of Japanese delicacies. V	AE DC MC V	●	●		
KUNGSHOLMEN: *Spisa Hos Helena* (Kr)(Kr) Scheelegatan 18, 112 28 Stockholm. **Map** 1 A5. 08-654 49 26. Atmospheric and award-winning eatery where the food is good and the staff welcoming. & V Y	AE DC MC V		●		
VASASTAN: *Rolfs Kök* (Kr)(Kr)(Kr) Tegnérgatan 41, 111 61 Stockholm. **Map** 1 C3. 08-10 16 96. Reliable local spot with stylish interior and great food. Cross-over and Swedish cuisine in perfect harmony. Faithful clientele. & Y	AE DC MC V	●			■
VASASTAN: *Wasahof* (Kr)(Kr)(Kr) Dalagatan 46, 113 24 Stockholm. **Map** 1 A3. 08-32 34 40. Brasserie-style restaurant popular among theatre and opera folk. The speciality is seafood, but Swedish and international dishes are also on the menu. Adjoins an oyster bar. & Y	AE DC MC V		■	●	■
VASASTAN: *Storstad* (Kr)(Kr)(Kr) Odengatan 41, 113 51 Stockholm. **Map** 1 C2. 08-673 38 00. This is where people go if they want to be seen, and the bar is usually packed. Minimalist decor, comfortable seating, imaginative food and courteous staff. & V Y	AE DC MC V		■		■
SÖDER: *Bistro Humlehof* (Kr) Folkungagatan 128, 116 30 Stockholm. 08-641 03 02. Traditional pub food with German and Czech beer on tap. Great atmosphere and caring staff. & Y	AE MC V				
SÖDER: *Östgötakällaren* (Kr)(Kr) Östgötagatan 41, 116 25 Stockholm. 08-643 22 40. Local restaurant serving excellent food at low prices. Fantastic staff. V Y ● Jul	AE DC MC V	●	■		

For key to symbols see back flap

		CREDIT CARDS	OPEN LUNCH-TIME	OPEN LATE	FIXED-PRICE MENU	GOOD WINE LIST

Average prices for a three-course meal for one, half a bottle of house wine and unavoidable charges such as service and cover:

Ⓚ under 300 Kr
ⓀⓀ 300–400 Kr
ⓀⓀⓀ 400–500 Kr
ⓀⓀⓀⓀ over 500 Kr

OPEN LUNCH-TIME
These restaurants are open for lunch and usually serve inexpensive meals.

OPEN LATE
Restaurants which remain open with their full menu after 10pm.

FIXED-PRICE MENU
A fixed-price menu is available for lunch, dinner or both, usually with three courses.

GOOD WINE LIST
Restaurant has a wide choice of good wines, or a more specialized range.

Restaurant	Price	Credit Cards	Open Lunch-time	Open Late	Fixed-price Menu	Good Wine List
SÖDER: *Lo Scudetto* Åsögatan 163, 116 32 Stockholm. 08-640 42 15. Top-class traditional and innovative dishes, cheerful service and football pictures on the walls. 🔧 🔳	ⓀⓀⓀ	AE MC V				■
SÖDER: *Texas Long Horn* Sankt Paulsgatan 4a, 118 46 Stockholm. Map 3 B5. 08-702 06 82. A tiny establishment which serves perfectly grilled juicy steaks at unbeatable prices. Often full with queues for admission. 🔳	ⓀⓀ	AE DC MC V				
FURTHER AFIELD: *Stallmästaregården* Norrtull, 113 47 Stockholm. 08-610 13 00. A 17th-century inn in an idyllic location on Brunnsviken and close to WennerGren Centre. Barbecue, rotisserie and top Swedish dishes. Outdoor terrace. 🔧🔳🔳🔳🔳	ⓀⓀⓀ	AE DC MC V	●		●	■
FURTHER AFIELD: *Edsbacka Krog* Sollentunavägen 220, 191 35 Sollentuna. 08-96 33 00. International cuisine at an inn dating from 1626, with a setting and service to match. Food is based on the best Swedish ingredients, expertly prepared and beautifully presented. Two Michelin stars. 🔧🔳🔳	ⓀⓀⓀⓀ	AE DC MC V			●	■
FURTHER AFIELD: *Ulriksdals Wärdshus* Ulriksdals Slottspark, 170 79 Solna. 08-85 08 15. Legendary inn in a stunning location with beautiful interior. Elegant and ambitious food. According to the *Guinness Book of Records*, it has the world's best wine list. Famous for its excellent *smörgåsbord*. 🔧🔳🔳🔳	ⓀⓀⓀⓀ	AE DC MC V	●	■	●	■
ARCHIPELAGO: *Utö Värdshus* Gruvbryggan, 130 56 Utö. 08-504 203 00. A boat is required to reach this island, either your own or the regular ferry. The restaurant is large and often busy in the summer. Traditional, value-for-money menu. Overnight accommodation. 🔧🔳🔳🔳🔳 ● Jan–Feb	ⓀⓀⓀ	AE DC MC V	●	■		

EASTERN SVEALAND

Restaurant	Price	Credit Cards	Open Lunch-time	Open Late	Fixed-price Menu	Good Wine List
HÖLÖ: *Oaxen Skärgårdskrog* Oaxen, 153 93 Hölö. 08-551 531 05. Archipelago restaurant open in the summer, which has become a popular destination thanks to good food with local ingredients and an emphasis on fish dishes. Reached by own boat or car ferry via Mörkö. 🔳🔳🔳	ⓀⓀⓀⓀ	AE DC MC V			●	■
JÖNÅKER: *Wreta Gestgifveri* Wretas Gård, 610 50 Jönåker. 0155-720 22. Romantic Gustavian dining room with period decor, but modern top-class food. Overnight accommodation. 🔧🔳	ⓀⓀⓀ	AE MC V	●			
NYKÖPING: *Mickes Skafferi* Västra Storgatan 29, 611 32 Nyköping. 0155-26 99 50. Great cooking with Swedish and Continental touches. Outdoor terrace in the summer, but can be difficult to get a table. 🔧🔳	ⓀⓀⓀ	AE DC MC V			●	
SIGTUNA: *Sigtuna Stads Hotell* Stora Nygatan 3, 193 30 Sigtuna. 08-592 501 00. Genuine Swedish cuisine in a modern guise served in the restaurant of this Scandinavian-style designer hotel. 🔧🔳🔳🔳🔳	ⓀⓀⓀⓀ	AE DC MC V	●		●	■
SÖDERTÄLJE: *St Ansgars Källare* Kaplansgatan 1, 151 72 Södertälje. 08-550 325 25 Classic food served in the brick-lined cellar of one of the town's oldest stone houses. One of the better restaurants in Södertälje. 🔳🔳🔳🔳	ⓀⓀⓀ	AE DC MC V				■

TROSA: *Bomans Hotel & Restaurant*   Ⓚ Ⓚ
Östra Hamnplan, 619 30 Trosa. ☎ 0156-525 00.
Menu almost entirely Swedish with some French touches. Even though it may not appear particularly original, the food is excellent and good value for money. Helpful staff. 🅰 ⚡ 🕴 🅈 ⬤ *Christmas and New Year.*

AE ⬤   ⬤ ◼
DC
MC
V

UPPSALA: *Hambers Fisk*   Ⓚ Ⓚ
Fyristorg 8, 753 10 Uppsala. ☎ 018-71 00 50.
Charming combination of delicatessen and restaurant. The delicatessen platter is a safe bet, but otherwise the atmosphere, the staff and the champagne are possibly the biggest attractions. 🅰 ⚡ 🅈

AE   ◼
DC
MC
V

UPPSALA: *Wermlandskällaren*   Ⓚ Ⓚ Ⓚ
Slottsgatan 2, 753 09 Uppsala. ☎ 018-13 22 00.
Traditional restaurant in smart period setting. A great menu, including truffles and foie gras and all that goes with them. ⚡ 🆅 ⬤ *July.*

AE   ◼
DC
MC
V

VÄSTERÅS: *Avenue*   Ⓚ Ⓚ Ⓚ
Kopparbergsvägen 3, 721 09 Västerås. ☎ 021-10 11 90.
Swedish cuisine with French and Italian twists served in a bright open space with lighting designed by Poulsen. Somes tables are in glass booths for undisturbed conversation. 🅰 ⚡ 🅈 ⬤ *6 weeks in summer.*

AE ⬤   ⬤ ◼
DC
MC
V

EASTERN GÖTALAND

BORGHOLM: *Bakfickan, Hotell Borgholm*   Ⓚ Ⓚ
Trädgårdsgatan 15, 387 31 Borgholm. ☎ 0485-770 60.
Small, high-class restaurant, which has developed its own special cuisine based on well-seasoned quality ingredients. It has been renovated after a fire in 2004. 🅰 ⚡ 🅈

AE ⬤   ⬤ ◼
DC
MC
V

JÖNKÖPING: *Svarta Börsen*   Ⓚ Ⓚ Ⓚ
Kyrkogatan 4, 553 16 Jönköping. ☎ 036-71 22 22.
Classic eatery located behind the town hall. Traditional menu highlighting Vättern char, game and lamb. 🅰 ⚡ 🆅 🅈 🎵 ⬤ *6 weeks in summer.*

AE ⬤   ⬤ ◼
DC
MC
V

KALMAR: *Helen & Jörgens*   Ⓚ Ⓚ
Olof Palmes Gata 2, 392 33 Kalmar. ☎ 0480-288 30.
Friendly restaurant with a personal style and a menu that hits the spot; the empahsis is towards Mediterranean cooking. Fresh lobsters from the restaurant's aquarium. 🅰 ⚡ 🕴 🆅 🅈

AE ⬤   ⬤ ◼
DC
MC
V

LINKÖPING: *Stångs Pm & Co*   Ⓚ Ⓚ Ⓚ
Södra Stånggatan 1, 582 73 Linköping. ☎ 013-31 21 00.
Linköping's trendiest place to eat is located in a warehouse by the Stångån river. Ambitious food, often local game. 🅰 ⚡ 🅈 ⬤ *Christmas and New Year.*

AE ⬤   ⬤ ◼
DC
MC
V

MOTALA: *O´Learys Bar & Restaurang*   Ⓚ
Platensgatan 15, 591 35 Motala. ☎ 0141-21 04 00.
Well-cooked, good food. Menu covers everything from hamburgers and salads to chicken and steaks. Sporting events shown on the screen. 🅰 ⚡ 🕴 🆅 🅈

AE
DC
MC
V

NORRKÖPING: *Pappa Grappa Trattoria & Bar*   Ⓚ Ⓚ Ⓚ
Gamla Rådstugegatan 26, 600 46 Norrköping. ☎ 011-18 00 14.
Jolly Italian trattoria in a rustic setting, known for its huge portions and excellent desserts. 🅰 🆅 🅈

AE ◼
DC
MC
V

NÄSSJÖ: *Entré Bar & Restaurang*   Ⓚ Ⓚ
Borgmästargränd 10, 553 20 Jönköping. ☎ 036-16 14 40.
This restaurant in an old wooden building near Storgatan has a sober interior and modern art on the walls. Value-for-money menu with many exotic dishes from all corners of the world. Warm and friendly. 🅰 ⚡ 🆅 🅈 🕴

AE ⬤   ⬤ ◼
DC
MC
V

SÖDERKÖPING: *Stegeborgs Hamnkrog*   Ⓚ
Stegeborg, 614 97 Söderköping. ☎ 0121-420 01.
Archipelago restaurant on a small island. Large outdoor terrace in the summer. Popular and pleasant "local restaurant" with good food to suit every pocket. Open from end of April to mid-September. 🅰 ⚡ 🕴 🆅 🅈

AE ⬤
DC
MC
V

VADSTENA: *Valven*   Ⓚ Ⓚ
Storgatan 18, 592 30 Vadstena. ☎ 0143-123 40.
Centrally located in Vadstena, close to the main square of Stora Torget, and set in the historic building Helgeandshuset. The fried Lake Vättern char with dill potatoes and crayfish sauce is much in demand. ⚡ 🕴 🆅 🅈

AE ⬤   ◼
DC
MC
V

For key to symbols see back flap

		Credit Cards	Open Lunch-Time	Open Late	Fixed-Price Menu	Good Wine List
Average prices for a three-course meal for one, half a bottle of house wine and unavoidable charges such as service and cover: (Kr) under 300 Kr (Kr)(Kr) 300–400 Kr (Kr)(Kr)(Kr) 400–500 Kr (Kr)(Kr)(Kr)(Kr) over 500 Kr	**OPEN LUNCH-TIME** These restaurants are open for lunch and usually serve inexpensive meals. **OPEN LATE** Restaurants which remain open with their full menu after 10pm. **FIXED-PRICE MENU** A fixed-price menu is available for lunch, dinner or both, usually with three courses. **GOOD WINE LIST** Restaurant has a wide choice of good wines, or a more specialized range.					
VÄXJÖ: *Fiskepiren* (Kr)(Kr) Båtsmanstorget 1, 352 30 Växjö. (0470-156 56. Value-for-money fish restaurant in minimalist setting. Pike-perch fillet and shellfish platters are the top items on the menu.		AE DC MC V	●		●	
GOTLAND						
VISBY: *Bakfickan* (Kr)(Kr) Stora Torget 1, 621 56 Visby. (0498-27 18 07. Charming, simple and cosy restaurant with the emphasis on fish and shellfish. The food is simple but good and the wine list mainly features white wines, many by the glass. Busy in the summer.		AE DC MC V	●			■
VISBY: *Donners Brunn Restaurang & Bar* (Kr)(Kr)(Kr) Donners Plats 3, 621 57 Visby. (0498-27 10 90. Well-known restaurant in the heart of Visby serving dishes with a Gotland touch. Welcoming staff. ● *Christmas and New Year.*		AE DC MC V			●	■
SOUTHERN GÖTALAND						
BILLEBERGA: *Farbror Elofs Skafferi* (Kr)(Kr) Kvarnvägen 1, 260 21 Billeberga. (0418-43 11 77. A restaurant with a difference which can get quite chaotic. The dining room is packed with knick-knacks. Seasonal menu; good, well-cooked food.		AE MC V	●	■	●	
BRANTEVIK: *Branteviks Bykrog* (Kr)(Kr)(Kr) Mästergränd 2, 272 38 Brantevik. (0414-220 69. Village restaurant, often full in summer, which can mean a long wait for food. Impressive wine cellar.		AE DC MC V	●		●	■
GENARP: *Häckeberga Slott* (Kr)(Kr)(Kr) 240 13 Genarp. (040-48 04 40. A gastronomic experience in a captivating castle setting. The menu is constantly changing and the chef aims high.		AE DC MC V	●		●	■
HELSINGBORG: *Gastro* (Kr)(Kr)(Kr)(Kr) Södra Storgatan 11-13, 252 23 Helsingborg. (042-24 34 70. The menu offers an interesting and unexpected mix of flavours and ingredients. The wine list and sommelier are just two of the restaurant's highlights.		AE DC MC V	■		●	■
HELSINGBORG: *Niklas* (Kr)(Kr)(Kr)(Kr) Norra Storgatan 16, 252 20 Helsingborg. (042-28 00 50. Commended, elegant restaurant with delicacies such as frogs' legs and foie gras. Impressive and exciting wine cellar.		AE DC MC V			●	■
KARLSKRONA: *PM Pub & Mat* (Kr) Ronnebygatan 46, Kronanhuset, 371 33 Karlskrona. (0455-818 80. Centrally located eatery on Karlskrona's main street with a typical pub menu.		AE MC V	●			
KRISTIANSTAD: *Bar-B-ko* (Kr)(Kr) Tivoligatan 4, 291 31 Kristianstad. (044-21 33 55. A popular, central restaurant with outdoor tables in summer. Barbecued meat, fish and vegetarian options. ● *Christmas and New Year.*		AE DC MC V		■		
KRISTIANSTAD: *Tomarp Gårdshotell* (Kr)(Kr)(Kr) Helmershusvägen 105, 291 94 Kristianstad. (044-931 18. Charming country-hotel restaurant. Menu focuses on hearty home-cooking. Considerate staff.		AE MC V	●		●	
LANDSKRONA: *Akropolis Rådhusrestaurangen* (Kr) Nygatan 2, 261 31 Landskrona. (0418-102 86. Traditional Greek food, including meat and fish, served on a plank.		AE DC MC V	●			

LUND: *&Bar* ⓀⓀ
Mårtenstorget 9, 223 51 Lund. ☎ 046-211 22 88.
Typical restaurant in medium-sized town, with minimalist decor and excellent value for money food. Enthusiastic staff and small, but interesting wine list. 🗲 ▾ ▾
AE DC MC V

LÖDERUP: *Mötesplats Österlen* ⓀⓀⓀⓀ
Örum 52, 276 40 Löderup. ☎ 0411-55 66 88.
Exquisite gourmet restaurant in a renovated former school. Exciting flavours and impressive fresh ingredients, many sourced locally. ♿ 🗲
AE MC V

MALMÖ: *Tempo Bar & Kök* ⓀⓀ
Södra Skolgatan 30a, 214 23 Malmö. ☎ 040-12 60 21.
Value-for-money bar with excellent food and adventurous chefs. Starters the size of a main meal. Great atmosphere and popular with the younger crowd. 🗲 ▾ ♣ ▾
AE MC V

MALMÖ: *1 R.O.K.* ⓀⓀ
St Pauli Kyrkogata 11, 211 49 Malmö. ☎ 040-30 20 24.
Small gourmet restaurant alongside a brasserie. Exciting, innovative cuisine with a touch of the East. ♿ 🗲 ▾ ▾ ● *Christmas and New Year.*
AE DC MC V

MALMÖ: *Lemongrass* ⓀⓀ
Grynbodgatan 9, 211 33 Malmö. ☎ 040-30 69 79.
In-restaurant with a Continental atmosphere and dishes representing various countries and cuisines of Asia. ♿ 🗲 ▾ ▾ ● *4 weeks in summer.*
AE DC MC V

MALMÖ: *Sturehof* ⓀⓀ
Adelsgatan 13, 211 22 Malmö. ☎ 040-12 12 53.
A touch of nostalgia with brown walls and black-and-white service. Traditional food, including herring buffet and steak Rydberg. 🗲 ● *Christmas and New Year.*
AE DC MC V

MALMÖ: *Johan P Saluhallens Fiskrestaurang* ⓀⓀⓀ
Landbygatan 3, 211 34 Malmö. ☎ 040-97 18 18.
Restaurant combined with a fishmonger's and chocolate shop. One of the best fish restaurants in Malmö with a menu featuring eel, herring and shellfish dishes. ♿ 🗲 ▾ ▾
AE DC MC V

MÖLLE: *Maritime* ⓀⓀⓀ
Bökebolsvägen 11, 260 42 Mölle. ☎ 042-36 22 30.
Beautiful dining room overlooking the harbour and Kullaberg. Set menu of three to eight dishes. 🗲 ♣ ▾ ● *Sep–Jun, except to guests who make a booking.*
AE DC MC V

NYHAMNSLÄGE: *Rut På Skäret* ⓀⓀⓀ
Gläntan 6, Skäret, 260 41 Nyhamnsläge. ☎ 042-34 61 88.
Delicacies from Skåne and more modern dishes served in a rustic cottage in the countryside. ♿ 🗲 ▾ ● *Jan–Mar.*
AE DC MC V

TRELLEBORG: *Dannegården* ⓀⓀⓀ
Strandgatan 32, 231 62 Trelleborg. ☎ 0410-481 80.
Restaurant with slightly old-fashioned decor and high-class food. Large range of whisky, Calvados and Armagnac. 🗲 ▾ ▾
AE MC V

YSTAD: *Restaurang Bryggeriet* ⓀⓀ
Långgatan 20, 271 43 Ystad. ☎ 0411-699 99.
Varied menu from around the world. Also a focus on Skåne cuisine with dessert menu featuring *spettkaka*, the local pyramid cake from Nedraby. ♿ 🗲 ▾ ♫ ▾
AE DC MC V

GOTHENBURG

CENTRE: *Mañana* Ⓚ
Lasarettsgatan 6, 411 19 Gothenburg. ☎ 031-711 72 90.
Minimalist modern interior and menu based on the simple ingredients of Mediterranean cuisine. Excellent food and pleasant bistro atmosphere. ♿ 🗲 ▾ ▾
AE MC V

CENTRE: *Fond* ⓀⓀⓀ
Götaplatsen, 412 56 Gothenburg. ☎ 031-81 25 80.
Located on Gothenburg's main square. The restaurant uses purely Swedish ingredients in its dishes and has a good wine list. One Michelin star. ♿ 🗲 ▾ ▾
AE DC MC V

CENTRE: *Trägår'n* ⓀⓀⓀ
Nya Allén, 411 38 Gothenburg. ☎ 031-10 20 80.
There may be a nightclub next door, but this restaurant is peaceful and ambitious. The food is inspired, with Asian influences.
♿ 🗲 ♣ ♫ ▾ ▾
AE DC MC V

Average prices for a three-course meal for one, half a bottle of house wine and unavoidable charges such as service and cover:	
Ⓚ under 300 Kr	
ⓀⓀ 300–400 Kr	
ⓀⓀⓀ 400–500 Kr	
ⓀⓀⓀⓀ over 500 Kr	

OPEN LUNCH-TIME These restaurants are open for lunch and usually serve inexpensive meals.
OPEN LATE Restaurants which remain open with their full menu after 10pm.
FIXED-PRICE MENU A fixed-price menu is available for lunch, dinner or both, usually with three courses.
GOOD WINE LIST Restaurant has a wide choice of good wines, or a more specialized range.

	CREDIT CARDS	OPEN LUNCH-TIME	OPEN LATE	FIXED-PRICE MENU	GOOD WINE LIST
CENTRE: Herr Dahls Mat & Martinis ⓀⓀⓀ Kungstorget 14, 411 10 Gothenburg. 031-13 45 55. Trendy restaurant with a modern menu. Mr Dahl himself is renowned as a member of the Swedish culinary Olympic team. ♿ 🚭 🍸 ● *last week in Jul.*	AE DC MC V	●	■	●	■
CENTRE: Kock & Vin ⓀⓀⓀ Viktoriagatan 12, 411 25 Gothenburg. 031-701 79 79. Restaurant and wine bar. The wine bar serves light small dishes and all wines by the glass. The dining room offers excellent value-for-money food in a congenial setting. ♿ 🚭 🍸	AE DC MC V		■	●	■
CENTRE: 28+ ⓀⓀⓀ Götabergsgatan 28, 411 34 Gothenburg. 031-20 21 61. One of the city's best restaurants with a style all of its own. It also features one of the better wine cellars in town. Professional staff. One Michelin star. ♿ 🚭	AE DC MC V		■		■
CENTRE: Fiskekrogen ⓀⓀⓀⓀ Lilla Torget 1, 411 18 Gothenburg. 031-10 10 05. Famous fish restaurant, renowned for its turbot, and shellfish buffet. Popular for lunches. Large wine cellar with a wide range of champagne. ♿ 🚭 🍸 ● *Jul.*	AE DC MC V	●	■	●	■
CENTRE: Thörnströms Kök ⓀⓀⓀⓀ Teknologgatan 3, 411 32 Gothenburg. 031-16 20 66. Fine dining for an adult clientele. Faultless decor and staff. 🚭 V 🍸 ● *Jul.*	AE DC MC V		■		■
CENTRE: Tvåkanten ⓀⓀⓀⓀ Kungsportsavenyn 27, 411 36 Gothenburg. 031-18 21 15. Relaxed, top-end restaurant with an adult clientele. Food served outdoors in the summer, making for a livelier atmosphere. Good, simple Swedish fare, and great value. ♿ 🚭 V 🍸	AE DC MC V	●	■		■
FURTHER AFIELD: Hos Pelle ⓀⓀⓀ Djupedalsgatan 2, 413 07 Gothenburg. 031-12 10 31. Local restaurant with art exhibitions. Ambitious menu. Professional staff and a great wine list. ♿ 🚭 V 🍸 ● *Jul.*	AE DC MC V		■	●	■
FURTHER AFIELD: Sjömagasinet ⓀⓀⓀ Klippans Kulturreservat, 414 51 Gothenburg. 031-775 59 20. Popular fish restaurant with fried crab, smoked mussels, lobster and other delicious seafood as its biggest sellers. Good wine list. One Michelin star. ♿ 🚭 V ● *Jul.*	AE DC MC V	●		●	■

WESTERN GÖTALAND

	CREDIT CARDS	OPEN LUNCH-TIME	OPEN LATE	FIXED-PRICE MENU	GOOD WINE LIST
BORÅS: Oliven Ⓚ Lilla Brogatan 11, 503 30 Borås. 033-10 10 65. Friendly local restaurant offering a largely Mediterranean menu, with a special emphasis on Greek cuisine. ♿ 🚭 V 🍸	AE MC V	●		●	■
GREBBESTAD: Grebys ⓀⓀ Strandvägen 1, 457 72 Grebbestad. 0525-140 00. Shellfish restaurant in a former jam factory. Great atmosphere and fresh seasonal shellfish. Very busy in the summer, when it can be difficult to get a table. 🚭 🚶 🎵 🍸	AE DC MC V			●	■
HALMSTAD: Akvarell ⓀⓀⓀⓀ Hotell Tylösand, 301 16 Halmstad. 035-305 01. Non-smoking dining room with renovated minimalist design and fantastic views. Exciting menu and great wine list, many served by the glass. ♿ 🚭 🍸	AE DC MC V		■	●	■

KVÄNUM: *Bjertorp Slott* Ⓚ Ⓚ Ⓚ Ⓚ
535 91 Kvänum. 【 0512-203 90.
Grand castle dining room with original fittings. Three-course menus change
daily. Famous for its wine cellar and expert staff who can be relied upon to
recommend the right wine for every meal. 🚫 ⚡ ♜

SKÖVDE: *Husaren* Ⓚ
Sta Helena Gata 10, 541 30 Skövde. 【 0500-41 79 79.
Classic restaurant with good food. Dishes include chicken marinated in soya and
ginger. Live music, usually Fri–Sat. 🚫 ⚡ Ⓥ ♪ Ⓨ

STRÖMSTAD: *Gusto Restaurang* Ⓚ Ⓚ
Norra Hamngatan 9a, 452 31 Strömstad. 【 0526-600 62.
Small town restaurant with limited menu. Emphasis on tapas, but grilled meat
and some fish dishes also served. ⚡ ♜ Ⓥ Ⓨ ● *weekdays Dec–Feb.*

TROLLHÄTTAN: *Aquavit Grill och Bar* Ⓚ Ⓚ
Kungsgatan 24, 461 30 Trollhättan. 【 0520-187 33.
Popular restaurant for business lunches with an emphasis on home-cooking.
Less busy in evenings and at weekends when the menu is more sophisticated.
Wine tastings also arranged. ⚡ ♜ Ⓥ Ⓨ

TROLLHÄTTAN: *Albert Kök* Ⓚ Ⓚ Ⓚ
Strömsberg, 461 57 Trollhättan. 【 0520-129 90.
Seasonal menu using local ingredients. Elegant restaurant with magnificent
views from the terrace. 🚫 ⚡ Ⓥ

UDDEVALLA: *Agassis Restaurang* Ⓚ
Kungsgatan 31, 451 30 Uddevalla. 【 0522-301 55.
Meat, fish and pasta, plus vegetarian dishes. Important sporting events shown
on the wide screen. 🚫 ⚡ ♜ ♪ Ⓥ Ⓨ

VARBERG: *Restaurang Borggården* Ⓚ Ⓚ Ⓚ
Fästningen, 432 44 Varberg. 【 0340-108 66.
Themed medieval or Viking-style banquets set in Varberg's fortress. Open for
lunch in the summer with no need to pre-book. 🚫 ⚡ ♜ ♪

WESTERN SVEALAND

BORLÄNGE: *Ulfshyttans Herrgård* Ⓚ Ⓚ Ⓚ
781 96 Borlänge. 【 0243-25 13 00.
Good food served in a historical manor house. Also spa/relaxation centre and
live music. 🚫 ⚡ ♜ Ⓥ ♪

FALUN: *Mariann's Pub och Restaurang* Ⓚ
Stigaregatan 6, 791 60 Falun. 【 023-201 01.
Classic à la carte and pub menu. Bar, dining room and veranda. In the centre
of town with alfresco dining in the summer. 🚫 ⚡ ♜ Ⓥ Ⓨ

FALUN: *Banken Bar & Brasseri* Ⓚ Ⓚ Ⓚ
Stadshusgränd 2, 791 12 Falun. 【 023-17 19 11.
A varied menu is on offer at this centrally located restaurant.
⚡ Ⓥ Ⓨ

HÄLLEFORS: *Sikfors Herrgård* Ⓚ Ⓚ Ⓚ
Sikfors, 712 93 Hällefors. 【 0591-151 15.
A stylishly decorated 19th-century manor house offering a set three-course
menu with a rural touch. ⚡ ♜ Ⓥ

KARLSTAD: *Glada Ankan* Ⓚ
Kungsgatan 12, 652 24 Karlstad. 【 054-21 05 51.
Restaurant and night club serving Mexican food, soup and pasta. Live music.
🚫 ⚡ ♪ Ⓨ.

KARLSTAD: *Blå Restaurang & Bar* Ⓚ Ⓚ Ⓚ
Kungsgatan 14, 652 24 Karlstad. 【 054-10 18 15.
Elegant restaurant with modern interior and views over the square.
Expert staff and beautifully served food from an interesting, innovative
menu. 🚫 ⚡ Ⓨ

MORA: *Jernet Bar och Matsal* Ⓚ Ⓚ
Strandgatan 6, 792 30 Mora. 【 0250 150 20.
The restaurant is housed in Mora's oldest industrial building dating from the
late 19th century. Dishes include Swedish classics and international cuisine.
🚫 ⚡ ♪ Ⓨ ● *2 weeks in Jan.*

Average prices for a three-course meal for one, half a bottle of house wine and unavoidable charges such as service and cover: ⓚ under 300 Kr ⓚⓚ 300–400 Kr ⓚⓚⓚ 400–500 Kr ⓚⓚⓚⓚ over 500 Kr	**OPEN LUNCH-TIME** These restaurants are open for lunch and usually serve inexpensive meals. **OPEN LATE** Restaurants which remain open with their full menu after 10pm. **FIXED-PRICE MENU** A fixed-price menu is available for lunch, dinner or both, usually with three courses. **GOOD WINE LIST** Restaurant has a wide choice of good wines, or a more specialized range.

Restaurant	CREDIT CARDS	OPEN LUNCH-TIME	OPEN LATE	FIXED-PRICE MENU	GOOD WINE LIST
SÄLEN: *Lammet och Grisen* ⓚⓚⓚ Lindvallen, 780 67 Sälen. (0280-210 90. Satisfying restaurant where guests can eat as much meat as they like and select delicacies from the buffet. ♿ ⚡ 🚶 🍸	AE DC MC V		■	●	■
SÄLEN: *Olarsgården* ⓚⓚⓚ 780 67 Sälen. (0280-210 29. Considered to be the best restaurant in the ski resort with specialities such as elk heart, air-dried capercaillie and venison on the game menu. Large wine list. On Sälfjällstorget, 1 km (half a mile) from Lindvallen. ♿ ⚡ 🚶 🍸	AE DC MC V	●		●	■
SÄLEN: *Onkel Jean* ⓚⓚⓚⓚ Sälens Högfjällshotell, 780 67 Sälen. (0280-870 20. Luxury restaurant at the Högfjällshotellet, complete with white tablecloths and chandeliers. Russian caviar and champagne as well as local ingredients from the mountains feature on the menu. ♿ ⚡ 🅥 🍸	AE DC MC V			●	■
ÖREBRO: *Slottsskänken* ⓚⓚ Örebro Slott, 701 42 Örebro. (019-12 23 39. Good cooking and a delightful atmosphere at Örebro Slott. Dine à la carte with a glass of wine or a beer. ♿ ⚡ 🎵 🍸	MC V	●	■	●	■
ÖREBRO: *Drängen* ⓚⓚⓚ Oskarsvägen 1, 702 14 Örebro. (019-32 32 96. Rustic and friendly cottage setting with Falu red walls and the buzz of guests. The food is simple, uncomplicated, good and value for money, especially the desserts. ♿ ⚡ 🚶 🍸	AE DC MC V	●	■	●	
SOUTHERN NORRLAND					
BRUNFLO: *Mikado* ⓚⓚⓚ Grytan, 834 98 Brunflor. (063-209 08. Remarkably exotic gem of a restaurant in Jämtland. Orders should be placed in advance when a table is booked. Many dishes are fondues and prepared at the table, accompanied by sake, green tea or Japanese beer. ♿ ⚡ 🅥	AE DC MC V		■	●	
GÄVLE: *Skeppet* ⓚⓚⓚ Nygatan 45, 803 11 Gävle. (026-12 99 50. Restaurant in the vaults below the Grand Central Hotell. Relaxed, professional atmosphere with a menu of classic dishes. ⚡	MC V			●	
HUDIKSVALL: *Gretas Krog* ⓚⓚ Västra Tvärkajen, 824 12 Hudiksvall. (0650-966 00. Traditional Swedish à la carte menu served in a wood-pannelled restaurant. Large windows overlook the waterfront and harbour. Outdoor seating in summer. ♿ ⚡ 🚶 🅥 🍸	AE DC MC V	●	■		
SANDVIKEN: *Högbo Bruksbotell* ⓚⓚⓚⓚ Hans Hiertas väg 20, 811 92 Sandviken. (026-24 52 31. Hotel restaurant which has gained a name for its top-class cuisine under Gert Klötzke, a member of the Swedish Culinary Olympic team. The food is really something out of the ordinary and well worth the price. ♿ ⚡ 🅥 🍸	AE DC MC V	●	■	●	■
SUNDSVALL: *Il Barone* ⓚⓚ Kyrkogatan 14, 852 31 Sundsvall. (060-17 66 04. Famously the best restaurant in Sundsvall. Friendly Italian bistro with large portions and reasonable prices. Known for its excellent pasta and long wine list, many by the glass. ⚡ 🅥 🍸	AE DC MC V		■		■
UMEÅ: *Rex Grill och Bar* ⓚⓚ Rådhustorget 1, 903 26 Umeå. (090-12 60 50. This former town hall houses Rex bar, which also has a quieter restaurant. Simple cuisine. ⚡ 🚶 🎵 🅥 🍸	AE DC MC V	●	■	●	■

UMEÅ: *Viktor* (Kr)(Kr)(Kr) AE DC MC V
Vasagatan 11, 902 29 Umeå. ☎ 090-71 11 15.
High quality through and through. Menus change often and ingredients are always fresh. Good wine cellar and friendly setting. ♿ ⚡ 🅥 🍸

ÅRE: *Villa Tottebo* (Kr)(Kr) AE DC MC V
Parkvägen 1, 830 13 Åre. ☎ 0647-506 20.
Unpretentious eatery reminiscent of a local restaurant in Southern Europe. The food is excellent. Star chefs often invited to cook. ♿ ⚡ 🚻 🅥 🍸

ÅRE: *Marmite Matsal* (Kr)(Kr)(Kr)(Kr) AE DC MC V
Årevägen 72, 830 13 Åre. ☎ 0647-502 40.
Small restaurant with big ambitions. Four menus offering exciting tastes: Swedish, French, Spanish and Italian. Great wine list and selection of liqueurs. Expert staff. ♿ ⚡ 🍸

ÖRNSKÖLDSVIK: *Restaurang Mammamia* (Kr)(Kr) AE DC MC V
Storgatan 6, 891 27 Örnsköldsvik. ☎ 0660-147 00.
Traditional Italian restaurant with the focus on pizza and pasta.
♿ ⚡ 🅥 🍸 🎵

ÖSTERSUND: *Innefickan* (Kr)(Kr) AE DC MC V
Postgränd 11, 831 31 Östersund. ☎ 063-12 90 99.
Local ingredients are successfully combined with the flavours of Italy and the Mediterranean and served in a cellar dining room. Welcoming atmosphere.
♿ ⚡ 🅥 🍸

NORTHERN NORRLAND

BODEN: *Pär & Mickes* (Kr)(Kr) MC V
Kungsgatan 20, 961 31 Boden. ☎ 0921-538 35.
Varied menu featuring international dishes and local ingredients.
♿ ⚡ 🅥 🍸

GAMMELSTAD: *Margaretas Wärdshus* (Kr)(Kr) AE DC MC V
Lulevägen 2, 954 33 Gammelstad. ☎ 0920-225 42 90.
Typical Norrbotten restaurant with the emphasis on local cuisine. Try grouse, elk, capercaillie and bear, or smoked reindeer and mountain char, and finish off with cloudberries or Arctic raspberries. ♿ ⚡ ● *Christmas and New Year.*

JUKKASJÄRVI: *Icehotel Restaurang* (Kr)(Kr)(Kr)(Kr) AE DC MC V
981 91 Jukkasjärvi. ☎ 0980-668 84.
This famous restaurant offers gastronomic specialities in the unusual setting of a restaurant built of ice. ♿ ⚡ 🅥 🍸 ● *May–Sep.*

KIRUNA: *3nd Baren & Restaurang Landström* (Kr)(Kr) AE DC MC V
Föreningsgatan 11, 981 32 Kiruna. ☎ 0980-663 80.
Good food in a congenial location in the centre of Kiruna. Many Norrland specialities on the menu. ♿ ⚡ 🍸

LULEÅ: *Nautiska Kompaniet* (Kr)(Kr)(Kr) AE DC MC V
Storgatan 28, 972 32 Luleå. ☎ 0920-22 78 80.
Well-designed à la carte menu based on seasonal ingredients from Norrland.
♿ ⚡ 🍸 ● *July–Sep.*

LYCKSELE: *Restaurang Lorentus* (Kr) AE DC MC V
Verkstadsvägen 11, 921 45 Lycksele. ☎ 0950-107 11.
Swedish traditional cooking, plus pizza, fish, meat and Mexican dishes. Live music some evenings. ♿ ⚡ 🎵 🍸

PITEÅ: *Piteå Stadshotell* (Kr)(Kr) AE DC MC V
Olof Palmes gata 1, 941 33 Piteå. ☎ 0911-23 40 00.
Food from all corners of the world accompanied by cool beer from the cellar.
♿ ⚡ 🎵 🍸

SKELLEFTEÅ: *Restaurang Vitberget* (Kr)(Kr) AE MC V
Mossgatan, 931 70 Skellefteå. ☎ 0910-77 58 00.
The wonderful views across the town of Skellefteå are matched by the star turn on the menu, barbecued meat. Only Swedish ingredients used. ⚡ 🍸

VILHELMINA: *Hotell Wilhelmina* (Kr)(Kr)(Kr) AE DC MC V
Volgsjövägen 16, 912 34 Vilhelmina. ☎ 0940-554 20.
Excellent dinners in a relaxing setting. Many of the ingredients are gathered from the countryside of southern Lapland.
♿ ⚡ 🚻 🅥 🍸

SHOPPING IN SWEDEN

NOWADAYS SWEDEN IS worth visiting for the shopping alone. In all Swedish towns, and even in the big cities, the shops are within easy walking distance of each other. The city centres offer a good range of small, trendy boutiques for fashion and interiors, shops for antiques and curios, luxury international designer outlets and well-stocked department stores. Cameras, mobile phones, furs, children's clothing, toys and Swedish glass and designer goods are cheaper in Sweden than in many other countries. Those looking for a typical Swedish souvenir could buy a Dala horse or a proper Swedish schnapps glass from one of the factories in the Kingdom of Crystal. Although Lapland is a long way north, Sami handicrafts can be bought in most craft shops, including knives with carved bone handles and silverwork. Leather and fur goods are also good value.

Dala horse
(see p306)

OPENING TIMES

MOST SHOPS USUALLY open at 10am and close at 6pm, although many in Stockholm city centre remain open until 7pm. Most shops are open until 2pm on Saturdays, while the major department stores stay open until 5pm. Large stores, shopping malls and some city-centre shops are open on Sundays. Market halls are closed on Sundays and public holidays. Many larger supermarkets are open daily until 8pm.

PAYMENT

ALL THE MAJOR credit cards and traveller's cheques are accepted at most Swedish shops. You may be asked for proof of identity. Some larger shops also accept euros *(see p324)*. Goods can be exchanged if you produce the receipt. Purchases can be made on a sale-or-return basis if this is noted on the receipt.

VALUE ADDED TAX

VALUE ADDED TAX ("moms" in Swedish) is charged on all items except daily newspapers. The VAT rate is 25 per cent; but only 12 per cent on food and 6 per cent on books. VAT is always included in the total price.

TAX-FREE SHOPPING

RESIDENTS OF countries outside the European Union are entitled to a refund of the VAT paid on their purchases. Look for the "Tax-free shopping" sign in shop windows. Keep your receipts and on departure from the EU go to the Global Refund office at the airport or ferry terminal to obtain a 15–18 per cent refund.

Sale-time at an elegant shoe shop in Stockholm

SALES

TWICE A YEAR Sweden's shops and department stores have sales with reduced prices on clothing, shoes and other fashion goods. Sales are indicated by the *rea* sign. The year's first sales period starts after Christmas and continues throughout January. The second sales period lasts from late June to the end of July.

SHOPPING CENTRES AND DEPARTMENT STORES

THE BEST-KNOWN Swedish superstore internationally is **IKEA**, which has 14 outlets across the country from Sundsvall in the north to Malmö in the south, and has become a popular tourist attraction in its own right. It sells not only furniture, but everything else for the home. The textiles section is particularly good, as well as

NK, Stockholm's most exclusive department store

IKEA's home furnishings stores can be found in many parts of Sweden

the kitchenware and china departments.

Another well-known store is the fashion house **H&M** (Hennes & Mauritz), which has branches in many towns. It stocks the latest fashions at low prices. H&M has its own designers and makes clothing for women, men, teenagers and children. The shops also sell accessories, underwear, perfume and cosmetics.

NK (Nordiska Kompaniet) in Stockholm and Gothenburg is Sweden's leading department store, in which many well-known names in fashion and cosmetics have their own outlets. NK is a practical choice for those in a hurry. It stocks everything from Swedish-designed products, jewellery, handicrafts and souvenirs to cameras, films, books and CDs.

Åhléns, which has stores in many towns and cities, offers most items at good prices.

British chain **Debenhams** offers a slightly different range from other department stores.

Åfors glassworks store, Kingdom of Crystal, Småland (see pp152–3)

Almost every large town has its own shopping centre or mall with a standard range of stores such as H&M, Lindex, Kappahl, Twilfit and Dressmann (clothing), Guldfynd (jewellery), Duka (glass and china), Hemtex (textiles), Expert (cameras, stereos, TVs) and Teknik-magasinet (electronics).

In Stockholm, **Gallerian** on Hamngatan is the largest mall and the prices are lower than in the elegant **Sturegallerian** near Stureplan with its many trendy boutiques.

Nordstan, off Brunnsparken in Gothenburg, is a mall with department stores such as Åhléns and specialist shops.

HansaCompagniet in central Malmö is a modern shopping centre.

A few examples of the larger shopping centres around the country include **Kungspassagen** in Umeå, **Forumgallerian** in Uppsala and **Krämaren** in Örebro.

Most towns have local markets selling flowers, fruit, vegetables and sometimes also handicrafts. Smaller places only have an outdoor market once a week, but in Hötorget in Stockholm, trading carries on every day except Sundays.

WINES AND SPIRITS

THE ONLY SHOPS selling alcohol in Sweden are run by Systembolaget, the state monopoly chain. They are open Mon–Fri 10am–6pm and Sat 10am–2pm (except public holiday weekends). The minimum age for buying alcohol at Systembolaget shops is 20 and staff are entitled to ask for proof of age (see also p321).

DIRECTORY

SHOPPING CENTRES & DEPARTMENT STORES

Åhléns
Klarabergsgatan 50, Stockholm.
Map 1 C4.
(08-676 60 00.

Debenhams
Drottninggatan 53, Stockholm.
Map 3 A1.
(08-505 740 00.

Forumgallerian
Bredgränd 6, Uppsala.
Map see p129.
(018-12 19 66.

Gallerian
Hamngatan 37, Stockholm.
Map 2 D4. (08-791 24 45.

HansaCompagniet
Stora Nygatan, Malmö.
Map see p179. (040-770 00.

H&M
Hamngatan 22, Stockholm.
Map 2 D4.
(08-796 54 34.

IKEA
Kungens Kurva, Stockholm.
(020-43 90 50.

Kompassen
Kungsgatan 58–60, Gothenburg.
Map see p192.
(031-13 88 08.

Krämaren
Drottninggatan 29, Örebro.
Map see p239.
(019-12 88 28.

Kungspassagen
Skolgatan 62, Umeå.
(090-10 07 38.

NK
Drottninggatan 39, Gothenburg.
Map see p192.
(031-710 10 00.

NK
Hamngatan 18–20, Stockholm.
Map 2 D4.
(08-762 80 00.

Nordstan
Brunnsparken, Gothenburg.
Map see p192.
(031-700 86 60.

Sturegallerian
Grev Turegatan 9 A, Stockholm.
Map 2 D4. (08-611 46 06.

Triangeln Köpcentrum
Södra Förstadsgatan 41, Malmö.
Map see p179. (040-23 02 06.

What to Buy in Sweden

THE DALA wooden horse must be the most typical Swedish souvenir. But it is facing strong competition from the elk, which has become a symbol for a nation with vast tracts of unspoilt countryside. The Swedes love the great outdoors, so there are plenty of shops selling top-class sporting equipment.

Elk candlestick

Swedish glass and crystal are renowned around the world. Orrefors and Kosta are just two of several glassworks producing both classic and modern glassware. Educational toys in natural materials are a Swedish speciality and so are clogs, which can be found in most shoe shops.

Hand-painted clogs

HANDICRAFTS & DESIGN

Modern Swedish design is a familiar concept worldwide, even for simple everyday items *(see pp22–3)*. Handicrafts have a long tradition in Sweden and contemporary designers often use old crafts such as wrought-iron work, weaving, pottery and woodcarving.

Dala Horse and Cockerel
Originally the brightly painted Dala horses and cockerels were toys carved from left-over fragments of wood. Later the horse became a national symbol, now sold in many variants.

Swedish Glass
Hand-blown sets are made in Småland's glassworks, as well as artistic crystal creations and objects for daily use.

Cheese slicer and knife by Michael Björnstierna

Tray with design by Josef Frank, Svenskt Tenn

Nobel **glass carafe from Orrefors by Gunnar Cyrén**

Traditional schnapps glasses

Objects for the Home
The larger department stores often commission well-known designers for porcelain, glass, textiles and household items which make highly desirable gifts.

Mama, **a humorous clothes hanger**

Crux **rug by Pia Wallén**

Children's Toys
Colourful wooden toys from Brio are worldwide favourites. Educational picture books, games and puzzles are all excellent gifts for children.

OUTDOOR GEAR

Many Swedes enjoy outdoor pursuits such as fishing, hunting, sailing, golf, camping and all types of winter sports, so there are plenty of well-equipped sports shops around. Unique items include Sami handicrafts beautifully made from reindeer horn or skin.

Hand Knits
Caps and gloves with attractive designs, known as lovikka, *are made from a special wool which gives good protection in cold or wet conditions.*

Reindeer Skin Rucksack
Rucksacks have always been popular in Sweden. This exclusive leather model is made in Lapland.

Drinking vessel in carved wood

Sami Handicrafts
A hunting knife with a sheath of reindeer horn, or a kåsa, *a drinking vessel carved in birch, are not only attractive, but useful when out walking in the wild.*

Spinning Reel and Lures
ABU-Garcia makes top-quality fishing tackle, perfect for Sweden's long coastline, countless lakes and rivers with their rich and varied fishing.

SWEDISH DELICACIES

Among the many Swedish goodies are preserves made from wild berries, such as lingonberries (served with meatballs or pancakes) and cloudberries (delicious with whipped cream). Ginger biscuits are for Christmas while crispbread is great year-round, especially with herring.

Lingonberry preserve   **Cloudberry jam**

Pickled Herring
Pickled herring should be enjoyed with new potatoes cooked with dill, chopped chives and sour cream. Versions flavoured with mustard, dill or other herbs or spices are also available.

Swedish schnapps gift-pack miniatures

"Raspberry boat" candy   **Salt liquorice**   **Crispbread**   **Ginger biscuits**

Where to Shop in Sweden

CLOTHING FROM ALL the well-known international fashion houses can be found in Stockholm, Malmö and Gothenburg. If you want something rather different, it is worth seeking out the creations of younger Swedish fashion designers. Swedish interior design is famous for its clean lines, functionalism and the use of pale wood, and the country is a paradise for anyone interested in design. Handicrafts are of a high quality. Leisurewear and sports goods offer excellent value for money.

FASHION

STOCKHOLM'S top places for fashion are in the "golden triangle" bounded by Stureplan, Nybroplan and Norrmalmstorg. Clothing at more moderate prices can be bought in department stores and shopping centres across the country. **GeKås** in Ullared and **Knalleland** in Borås have become popular attractions due to their low prices and large number of stores and factory outlets, not least in the "mail-order town" of Borås, with its weaving and textile traditions.

If you are looking for Swedish designers, **NK** in Stockholm and Gothenburg (see p305) has a good selection of clothing created by younger designers as well as mainstream Swedish brands. Classic men's clothing of high quality is designed by Oscar Jacobsson, while Stenström shirts are sold in department stores and the more elegant menswear boutiques. **Björn Borg** has his own shops selling men's and women's clothing and underwear, perfume and accessories. The designer **Filippa K** produces smart clothing for fashionable women and men.

DESIGN AND INTERIOR DECORATION

STOCKHOLM, Gothenburg and Malmö have a number of interior decoration shops selling the products of young designers and well-known artists. To see the latest on offer, it is worth visiting **DesignTorget**, which has stores in all three cities displaying designers' work. Stockholm's **R.O.O.M** on Kungsholmen and **Asplund** in Östermalm, and **Norrgavel** in Stockholm, Gothenburg, Malmö and Lammhult, are just a few of the shops with the most up-to-the-minute selection of products. **Svenskt Tenn** is Stockholm's oldest shop for interiors, with both new and classic designs. **Nordiska Galleriet** in Stockholm has exclusive modern furniture and decorative items, while **Blås & Knåda** on Hornsgatan displays and sells the largest selection of contemporary Swedish ceramics and glass, both objects of art and items for everyday use. **Nordiska Kristall** on Kungsgatan has a wide choice of Swedish glassware, which can also be found in department stores.

MUSIC AND MULTIMEDIA

MANY SWEDISH POP bands now have an international reputation. Exciting new talents continue to find their way into the charts, and the latest products can often be bought in the large record shops before they become available outside Sweden. Apart from pop and rock, Sweden has a long folk-music tradition, as well as many jazz musicians and opera singers. **MEGA Skivakademien** in Stockholm stocks a wide selection of CDs, as do the large department stores.

SPORT AND LEISURE

THE SWEDES devote a lot of time to outdoor sports and activities. With shops all over the country, **Naturkompaniet** and **Peak Performance** have an exclusive selection of sportswear and equipment. **Stadium** and **Team Sportia** have a varied choice of sports clothing and equipment at attractive prices and are also nationwide. Good equipment and exclusive clothing for hunting and fishing can be bought at **Walter Borg** in central Stockholm. **Löplabbet** countrywide specializes in running and jogging.

SOUVENIRS AND HANDICRAFTS

SCHNAPPS GLASSES, silver jewellery, hand-painted clogs, Sami crafts, hand-knitted garments, candles, Christmas decorations and wrought-iron products can all be bought in department stores and shops specialising in Swedish handicrafts.

At Skansen open-air museum in Stockholm, visitors can shop for handicrafts in attractive little houses.

Nusnäs in Dalarna is the place to buy the original Dala horse, which can be found at **Nils Olsson Hemslöjd AB**.

Yllet in Visby sells hand-spun wool, woollen garments and sheepskin goods.

MARKETS

SMALL LOCAL markets can be found almost everywhere, but a few have become so big that they have attracted international attention.

Jokkmokk's winter market (1st Thu–Sat in Feb) is a major Sami market. The Kivik market (mid-Jul) is like an amusement park. Skänninge market (1st Wed–Thu in Aug) is a classic affair dating back to the Middle Ages. Michaelmas markets are held in central Sweden in autumn.

The bustling flea market in Skärholmen, Stockholm, is the place to find a bargain every day of the week. Entrance fee Sat–Sun, free on other days.

GLASS AND CHINA

MOST DEPARTMENT stores and gift shops sell glass from Swedish manufacturers. Visitors to the Kingdom of Crystal in Småland have a choice of no fewer than 14 glassworks within a radius of a few miles (see pp152–3). At **Orrefors** and **Kosta**, there

are bargains to be had among the everyday glassware and the studio glass. **Reijmyre** in Östergötland is also popular among bargain-hunters. For porcelain, the factory shop at **Rörstrand** offers value for money.

SWEDISH DELICACIES

THE CAPITAL HAS three market halls – **Östermalms-hallen**, **Hötorgshallen** and **Söderhallarna** – which are a

joy to just wander around. Salmon, bleak roe, smoked eel and smoked reindeer meat are all delicious culinary souvenirs. Malmö's **Johan P** and Gothenburg's **Briggen** are also pleasant market halls offering mouth-watering Swedish delicacies.

On the west coast, seafood is a must and whether you are after prawns, crab or autumn's black gold, lobster, it is best purchased at the harbourside when the boats come in. In

the north, game of various kinds is the big attraction and you can often find smoked reindeer and reindeer heart in grocery stores, along with fermented Baltic herring and Norrland cloudberry jam.

Swedish crispbread is another delicacy and the bakery in Leksand has a factory shop. Traditional red and white striped candy rock originates from Gränna, which has a large number of shops selling rock.

DIRECTORY

FASHION

Björn Borg
Sergelgatan 12,
Stockholm. **Map** 1 C4.
08-21 70 40.

Champagne
Fredsgatan 1, Gothenburg.
Map see p92.
031-15 73 71.

Filippa K
Grev Turegatan 18,
Stockholm. **Map** 2 D4.
08-545 888 88.

Ge-Kås i Ullared
Danska Vägen, Halmstad.
0346-375 00.

Imperium
Vallgatan 22, Gothenburg.
Map see p192.
031-711 13 36.

Knalleland
Borås.
033-14 03 35.

MQ
Södra Tullgatan 3, Malmö.
040-12 01 31.
Strömpilsplatsen 1, Umeå.
090-786 36 80.

Olsén Mode
Södergatan 21, Malmö.
Map see p179.
040-12 10 50.

DESIGN AND INTERIORS

Asplund
Sibyllegatan 31,
Stockholm. **Map** 2 E3.
08-662 52 84.

Blås & Knåda
Hornsgatan 36,
Stockholm.
Map 3 A5.
08-642 77 67.

DesignTorget
Kulturhuset,
Sergels Torg 3, Stockholm.
Map 1 C4.
08–508 315 20.
Götgatan 31, Stockholm.
08-462 35 20.
Vallgatan 14, Gothenburg
Map see p192.
031-774 00 17.

House
Humlegårdsgatan 14,
Stockholm.
Map 2 E3.
08-545 853 40.

Nordiska Galleriet
Nybrogatan 11,
Stockholm.
Map 2 E4.
08-442 83 60.

Nordiska Kristall
Kungsgatan 9,
Stockholm.
Map 2 E4.
08-10 43 72.

Norrgavel
Birger Jarlsgatan 27,
Stockholm.
Map 2 D3.
08-545 220 50.
Engelbrektsgatan 20,
Malmö. **Map** see p179.
040-12 22 46.

R.O.O.M
Alströmergatan 20,
Stockholm.
08-692 50 00.

Svenskt Tenn
Strandvägen 5,
Stockholm. **Map** 2 E4.
08-670 16 00.

MUSIC

MEGA Skivakademien
Sergelarkaden 6,
Stockholm.
Map 1 C4.
08-566 157 00.

Skivhuset CDmedia
Lilla Klädpressaregatan 7,
Gothenburg.
031-15 55 05.

SPORT AND LEISURE

Löplabbet
Rundelsgatan 16, Malmö.
040-12 35 70.

Naturkompaniet
Kungsgatan 4A,
Stockholm. **Map** 2 D4.
08-723 15 81.

Peak Performance
Biblioteksgatan 18,
Stockholm.
Map 2 D4.
08-611 34 00.
Södergatan 9,
Malmö.
Map see p179.
040-97 02 20.

Stadium
Fredsgatan 8,
Gothenburg.
Map see p192.
031-711 06 09.

Team Sportia
Bruksgatan 6, Umeå.
090-71 79 70.

Walter Borg
Klara Norra Kyrkogata 26,
Stockholm. **Map** 1 C4.
08-14 38 65.

SOUVENIRS AND HANDICRAFTS

Nils Olsson Hemslöjd AB
Edåkersvägen 17, Nusnäs.
0250-372 00.

Svensk Hemslöjd
Sveavägen 44, Stockholm.
Map 1 C3.
08-23 21 15.

Yllet
St Hansgatan 19, Visby.
0498-21 40 44.

GLASS AND CHINA

Kosta Glasbruk
Kosta. 0478-345 00.

Orrefors Glasbruk
Orrefors. 0481-341 89.

Reijmyre
Reijmyre.
011-871 84.

Rörstrand
Lidköping.
0510-823 46.
Gustavsberg.
08-570 356 55.

SWEDISH DELICACIES

Briggen
Linnéstaden, Gothenburg.
0247-448 20.

Hötorgshallen
Hötorget, Stockholm.
Map 1 C4.

Johan P
Saluhallen, Malmö.

Östermalmshallen
Östermalmstorg,
Stockholm.
Map 2 E4.

ENTERTAINMENT IN SWEDEN

THE RANGE OF CULTURAL events and entertainment in Sweden is large and richly varied. The whole spectrum is covered from outdoor celebrations to mark local customs to top international acts performing in giant arenas. The seasons have an effect on what's on: large city theatres tend to close during the summer and launch their new programmes of plays, opera and dance in late August or early September. Meanwhile, summer reviews, popular comedies and local historical plays are staged across the country. In parks, palace gardens and amusement parks, summer is a particularly eventful time, with artists of every imaginable kind putting on a performance. Added to that are the countless markets, festivals covering film, jazz, music, food, theatre, folklore, and much more besides. Winter brings ski races and skating, indoor fairs and Christmas markets. Nightlife continues all year. There are excellent nightclubs and casinos in the major cities. Jazz clubs and pubs offer a wide range of live music to suit all tastes.

Folk Dancers,
Rättvik

SOURCES OF INFORMATION

A RELIABLE SOURCE of information is **Sveriges Rese- och Turistråd**'s official tourist and events guide on the Internet. This provides listings for everything from music and sport to seasonal events such as Medieval Week in Visby or the Vasaloppet ski race in Dalarna. The site has links to the websites of Stockholm, Gothenburg and Malmö, but also has details of events across the country.

Daily newspapers and free local papers are an excellent source for regional events such as concerts, theatre performances and nightclubs. The tourist information offices and most hotels also have listings and can often help with advice and booking tickets.

BOOKING TICKETS

TICKETS FOR most events can usually be bought at the box office of the theatre or sports arena in question, but to ensure admission it may be more practical to book in advance, with the help either of the hotel or a tourist information office. Another alternative is to use a booking agency, such as **Biljett Direkt**, which, for a small fee, will take telephone bookings for tickets to stage shows, concerts and sports events. At **Box-office** in Stockholm, tickets can be purchased over the counter for various events in Sweden and beyond, and tickets ordered via the event organizer can be collected. Many tickets are also sold via the gaming agent ATG across the country.

Dalhalla's music stage *(see p241)* in a dramatic quarry near Rättvik

MAJOR ARENAS AND CULTURAL CENTRES

IN ADDITION TO the long-established, traditional theatres, many towns and cities have more recently built multi-purpose cultural complexes offering a wide spectrum of public events. Often such centres are home to the local theatre company and orchestra.

The major entertainment and event arenas such as **Globen** in Stockholm and **Scandinavium** in Gothenburg have a huge audience capacity. International rock and pop concerts, charity galas and major sporting events are usually held at these enormous venues.

In the summer, the large outdoor stages, for example at Skansen and Gröna Lund in Stockholm, Liseberg in Gothenburg and Dalhalla, between Rättvik and Mora, attract a wide range of jazz, folk and classical artists alike.

Sea of people at the Philharmonic's annual outdoor concert, Stockholm

THEATRE

Sweden has almost 500 theatres spread across the country. Many are town or county theatres, but there are also private theatres with long traditions and small park and amateur theatres.

Sweden's national theatre is **Kungliga Dramatiska Teatern** *(see p71)*, which has six stages. It regularly mounts international and Swedish classics, including Shakespeare and Strindberg, as well as modern foreign and Swedish works.

Lighter plays and musicals are often performed at **ChinaTeatern** in Stockholm and **Lorensbergsteatern** in Gothenburg. Venues such as **Konsertteatern** in Sundsvall and **Göta Lejon** in Stockholm often stage performances suitable for children and families.

CLASSICAL MUSIC, DANCE AND OPERA

World-class music can be heard at **Berwaldhallen** in Stockholm, the home of Sveriges Radios Symfoniorkester and the Radiokören choir, considered one of the internationally leading a cappella ensembles. **Konserthuset** *(see p68)* is the base of for Kungliga Filharmoniska Orkestern. The season runs from August to May.

Konserthuset in Gothenburg is home to Göteborgs Symfoniker. Norrköping has the **De Geerhallen** venue and Folkets Park in Sundsvall has **Tonhallen**, one of Sweden's best concert halls.

Classical opera and ballet of the highest quality can be seen at **Kungliga Operan** *(see p66)*. Every season at

Sundsvalls Teater, an ambitious, go-ahead regional theatre

GöteborgsOperan, with a wide repertoire of opera and musicals

least three major ballets delight packed houses. This venue also stages traditional performances of most operas in their original language. During the summer, popular opera performances are held at **Drottningholms Slottsteater** *(see p109)*. All the operas staged here are from the 18th century, with an orchestra of the period.

The spectacular modern **GöteborgsOperan** *(see p196)* is an exciting, internationally-renowned venue for opera, ballet and musicals. Norrlandsoperan in Umeå and Malmö Opera och Musikteater are two of the country's other major venues for opera and ballet.

Dansens Hus in Stockholm, which has taken over the National Theatre's former venue, often hosts top-name dance companies from Sweden and abroad.

FOLK MUSIC

Swedish folk music is enjoying a resurgence in popularity. Skansen in Stockholm *(see p92)* is the prime venue, where musicians and folk dancing troupes perform regularly at traditional events. However, there are local folk groups and regional clubs covering practically every corner of the country. The easiest way of finding out where and how to enjoy Swedish folk music is to check at the local tourist information office or in the local press.

There are a few permanent venues for folk music: **Folkmusikhuset** in Stockholm,

Folkmusikkaféet in Gothenburg and **Folkmusikens Hus** in Rättvik are just some of the places offering a wide programme of performances and information about forthcoming events.

CHURCH MUSIC

Many churches in the cities hold organ recitals at lunchtime, for example Jacobs Kyrka in Stockholm *(see p66)*, where visitors can take a breather in a tranquil setting. Storkyrkan *(see p53)* also holds concerts on Saturday and Sunday afternoons in the spring and autumn. The cathedrals of Uppsala Domkyrka *(see p128)* and Västerås Domkyrka *(see p138)* stage organ recitals every Saturday. Many churches also have a concert programme, particularly in conjunction with major religious festivals.

ROCK AND POP

The largest of the venues for rock and pop music are **Globen** in Stockholm and **Scandinavium** in Gothenburg. These attract top international artists, along with the many successful Swedish bands. **Cirkus** in Stockholm is a well-established venue for music and theatre in a beautiful old setting. More modern rock venues include **Munchenbryggeriet** in Stockholm, **Kulturbolaget** in Malmö and **Trädgår'n** in Gothenburg. Around the country there are smaller theatres, students' unions and clubs where groups and artists perform.

Concert in the ruins of Bohus Castle in Kungälv

JAZZ CLUBS

JAZZ HAS ENJOYED a renaissance in recent years and the range on offer increases annually. One venue of repute is **Fasching** in Stockholm, with performances almost daily. Another jazz haunt in the capital is **Stampen**, which attracts a rather more mature audience. Gothenburg has **Nefertiti** and in Malmö there is **Jeriko**. Across the country there are jazz clubs holding concerts once a month or so.

Jazz cruises have become popular in the summer. The Stockholm archipelago is plied by *S/S Blidösund*. Cruises are also organized elsewhere in the country, for instance across Lake Vättern and the Åland Sea, on the Dalälven river and out into the Gothenburg archipelago.

MUSIC PUBS

SWEDISH PUB culture has changed enormously and it is becoming increasingly common to follow the Continental pattern of slipping into a bar or pub for a while after work, having a beer and listening to music.

Many pubs have introduced live music – some have folk singers performing on a regular basis, while others have a DJ. The best way of being sure to hear live music is to scan the local press entertainment *(nöjen)* pages.

In Stockholm, the Irish pub **The Dubliner** offers live Irish music. The popular **Engelen**

bar has live music several days a week. Gothenburg's finest pubs include **Sticky Fingers** and Jameson's pub, and Helsingborg has its own English pub, Charles Dickens, where the clientele can enjoy karaoke, live music, singers, bands and various other forms of entertainment.

There are a number of traditional English and Irish-style pubs spread across the country, usually offering a wide range of beer and spirits and serving a selection of bar snacks.

NIGHTCLUBS, CASINOS AND SHOWS

GENERALLY SPEAKING, nightclubs hold traditional disco nights on Friday and Saturday. During the rest of the week the venue is usually hired by various clubs focusing on different styles of music. Almost all the larger towns and cities have one or two nightclubs, but the quality varies, as does the music on offer. In Stockholm,

the majority and the best of the capital's nightclubs are located around Stureplan. At the rear of the Opera House is **Café Opera**, Stockholm's longest-established nightclub, with an international style. The crowd is usually quite mixed – young, trendy types and older, smartly-dressed folks. **Sturecompagniet** is a large club on several floors. At street level there is also a rock bar. Swedish celebrities and visiting foreign stars mingle at top celeb hangout **Spy Bar**, but it can be difficult to get in on certain nights. Other well-known nightclubs include **Crown** in Malmö and **Gutekällaren** in Visby.

A relative newcomer to the entertainment scene is the state-run casino chain **Casino Cosmopol**, which to date has opened branches in Stockholm, Gothenburg, Malmö and Sundsvall.

A combination of good food and top-flight entertainment is on offer at **Hamburger Börs** in Stockholm, with its shows featuring the best Swedish artists. **Wallmans Salonger**, which can be found in Stockholm and Malmö, offers musical entertainment with dinner served by waiters and waitresses who are, in fact, professional performers.

In Gothenburg, **Rondo** is a classic show venue.

FESTIVALS

COUNTLESS festivals large and small are organized all across Sweden in the summer. Almost every town has its own festival, some with a specific focus, such as folk, jazz or rock.

Among the most renowned of the local festivals are Göteborgskalaset in Gothenburg, Storsjöyran in Östersund and Gatufesten in Sundsvall.

There are numerous music festivals, the largest of which – for example the Hultsfred Festival – attract huge

A traditional folk music festival in Tällberg on Lake Siljan in Dalarna

audiences. Other famous music festivals include the Falun Folk Music Festival, the Sweden Rock Festival in Sölvesborg, the Gotland Chamber Music Festival in Visby, the Stockholm Jazz Festival and the Umeå International Jazz Festival.

The best-known film festivals are the **Gothenburg Film Festival** (Jan/Feb) and the **Stockholm International Film Festival** (Nov), but several other cities and towns hold their own film festivals with a different focus, such as Umeå (Sep).

DIRECTORY

SOURCES OF INFORMATION

Sveriges Rese- och Turistråd
W www.visit-sweden.com
C 08- 789 10 00.

BOOKING TICKETS

Biljett Direkt
W www.ticnet.se
C 077-170 70 70.

Box-office
Palmhuset, Norrmalmstorg, Stockholm. Map 2 D4.
C 08-10 88 00.

ARENAS, CULTURAL CENTRES

Globen
Globentorget 2, Stockholm.
C 077-131 00 00.

Scandinavium
Valhallagatan 1, Gothenburg. C 031-81 10 20.

THEATRE

China Teatern
Berzelii Park 9, Stockholm. Map 2 D4.
C 08-566 323 50.

Göta Lejon
Götgatan 55, Stockholm.
C 08-643 67 00.

Konsertteatern
Köpmangatan 11, Sundsvall. C 060-61 32 62.

Kungliga Dramatiska Teatern
Nybroplan, Stockholm. Map 2 E4. C 08-667 06 80.

Lorensbergsteatern
Lorensbergsparken, Gothenburg. C 031-708 62 00.

CLASSICAL MUSIC, DANCE, OPERA

Berwaldhallen
Dag Hammarskjölds Väg 3, Stockholm.
C 08-784 50 00.

Dansens Hus
Barnhusgatan 12–14, Stockholm. Map 1 C3.
C 08-508 990 90.

De Geerhallen
Dalsgatan 15, Norrköping.
C 011-15 50 30.

Drottningholms Slottsteater
Drottningholms Slott, Lovön, W of Stockholm.
C 08-660 82 25.

GöteborgsOperan
Christina Nilssons Gata, 41, Gothenburg.
C 031-13 13 00.

Konserthuset
Götaplatsen, Gothenburg.
C 031-726 53 00.

Konserthuset
Hötorget, Stockholm.
Map 1 C4.
C 08-786 02 00.

Kungliga Operan
Gustav Adolfs Torg, Stockholm. Map 2 D5.
C 08-791 43 00.

Tonhallen
Fabriksgatan 14, Sundsvall.
C 060-19 88 00.

FOLK MUSIC

Folkmusikens Hus
Dalagatan 7, Rättvik.
C 0248-79 79 50.

Folkmusikhuset
Skeppsholmsgården, Stockholm. Map 2 E5.
C 08-411 99 88.

Folkmusikkaféet
Allégården, Gothenburg.
C 031-701 76 61.

ROCK AND POP

Cirkus
Djurgårdsslätten, Stockholm. C 08-587 987 00.

Kulturbolaget
Bergsgatan 18, Malmö.
C 040 30 20 11.

Münchenbryggeriet
Söder Malarstrand 29, Stockholm.
C 08-658 13 00.

Trädgår'n
Nya Allén, Gothenburg.
C 031-10 20 80.

JAZZ CLUBS

Fasching
Kungsgatan 63, Stockholm. Map 1 B4.
C 08-534 829 60.

Jeriko
Spångatan 38, Malmö.
C 040-611 84 29.

Nefertiti
Hvitfeldtsplatsen 6, Gothenburg.
C 0318-711 15 33.

Stampen
Stora Nygatan 5, Stockholm. Map 3 B4.
C 08-20 57 93.

MUSIC PUBS

Engelen
Kornhamnstorg 59 B, Stockholm. Map 3 B4.
C 08-505 560 00.

Sticky Fingers
Kaserntorget 7, Gothenburg.
C 031-701 07 17.

The Dubliner
Smålandsgatan 8, Stockholm.
Map 2 D4.
C 08-679 97 02.

NIGHTCLUBS, CASINOS, SHOWS

Café Opera
Operahuset, Stockholm.
Map 3 B1.
C 08-676 58 07.

Casino Cosmopol
Kungsgatan 65, Stockholm. Map 1 B4.

C 08-781 88 00.
Packhusplatsen 7, Gothenburg.
C 031-333 55 00.
Slottsgatan 33, Malmö.
C 040-664 18 00.
Casinoparken 1, Sundsvall.
C 060-14 11 00.

Crown
Amiralsgatan 19, Malmö.
C 040-611 80 88.

Gutekällaren
Stora Torget, Visby.
C 0498-21 00 43.

Hamburger Börs
Jakobsgatan 6, Stockholm. Map 2 D5.
C 08-787 85 00.

Rondo
Örgrytevägen 5, Gothenburg. C 031 40 02 00.

Spy Bar
Birger Jarlsgatan 20, Stockholm. Map 2 D3.
C 08-545 037 01.

Sturecompagniet
Sturegatan 4, Stockholm.
Map 2 D3.
C 08- 611 78 00.

Wallmans Salonger
Teatergatan 3, Stockholm.
Map 2 E5.
C 08-505 560 00.
Generalsgatan 1, Malmö.
C 040-749 45.

FESTIVALS

Gothenburg Film Festival
Heurlins Plats 11, Gothenburg.
W www.filmfestival.org
C 031-339 30 00.

Stockholm International Film Festival
Slupskjulsvägen 36, Stockholm. Map 4 E2.
W www.filmfestivalen.se
C 08-677 50 00.

SPORTS AND
OUTDOOR ACTIVITIES

S WEDEN HAS countryside in abundance and the *"allemannsrätt"* (Right to Roam) makes it accessible in a way rarely found elsewhere in the world. No wonder an active outdoor life has become such a staple of the Swedish lifestyle. Constantly rising demand for outdoor activities has led to an increasing range of trails for hiking, canoeing and cycling, and the construction of hundreds of new ski lifts, golf courses and

**Recommended
cycle trail**

guest harbours. There has also been a boom in adventure sports – from challenging hikes in remote mountain regions and sea kayaking in the outer archipelagos to competing in the long-distance Vasaloppet skiing race, the Vansbrosimningen swimming race or the Vätternrundan cycling race, which together make up what is known as the "Swedish Classic". More leisurely pursuits include horse riding and fishing.

GENERAL INFORMATION

I N ADDITION to the tourist information offices, there are a number of organizations to assist outdoors enthusiasts. The state-run **Naturvårdsverket** has an excellent website, which also provides useful information about Sweden's 28 national parks. **Friluftsfrämjandet** is a 100-year-old voluntary organization – the backbone of outdoor life for its many activities and operations.

HIKING TRAILS

A LTHOUGH IT IS possible to pitch a tent almost anywhere, it is often more practical to follow one of the many well-tended hiking trails. There are numerous lowland trails, such as the Skåneleden, which runs south to north through Skåne. Mountain trails

proliferate, the best of which is the renowned Kungsleden stretching 450 km (280 miles) *(see pp274–5).*

Maps of the trails usually provide information about stopping-off points, attractions, accommodation and services along the way.

The most popular mountain areas have marked trails for day trips and longer hikes with overnight accommodation in huts and at mountain stations. For more than 100 years, **Svenska Turistföreningen (STF)** has been the main provider of services in the mountains in summer and winter.

The mountain trails mainly run through road-free land. There are STF mountain stations at strategic locations from Abisko in Lapland to Grövelsjön in Dalarna. Although out in the wilds, these are relatively easy to access and make an excellent

Walking with poles, a popular form of exercise

starting point for hiking tours in the mountains. The stations have hotel-standard accommodation, restaurants, self-catering kitchens, shops and equipment hire.

Along the trails, there are simple huts in which to stay, with a self-catering kitchen and in some cases provisions for sale. Space cannot be booked in advance, but everyone usually gets a roof over their head. In the summer, STF has special hosts to help with tips and advice.

The trails crossing the high mountains can be extremely demanding for the uninitiated. It is important not to be too ambitious and to have appropriate equipment.

Whatever the time of year, the weather changes quickly, so keep up to date with the forecast, which is usually posted at stations and huts. The summer season for mountain hiking is from about mid-June to mid-September.

A hiker en route to the Sylarna mountain station, Jämtland

One of STF's many huts across the mountains

ENDURANCE TESTS

COMPETITIONS for elite ath-letes and fitness enthusiasts alike have become increasingly popular in Sweden, attracting thousands of participants of all levels. Some enter the "Swedish Classic", in which over one year competitors ski the Vasaloppet *(see p245)* or Engelbrektsloppet (60 km/37 miles), cycle the Vätternrundan (300 km/190 miles), swim the Vansbros-imningen (3 km/2 miles) and run the Lidingöloppet (30 km/19 miles). Other events include the Stockholm Marathon *(see p27)* and the O-ringen in orienteering.

SWIMMING

THERE ARE generally no restrictions for anyone wanting to take a dip in lakes, rivers and the sea. However, there is no need to take any risks as there are thousands of public bathing areas where the water quality is checked by the health authorities. Even in the north,

there are plenty of opportunities to swim, for example at Pite Havsbad, where the sunny beaches are known as "The Nordic Riviera" *(see p268)*. In many places, the natural bathing spots are supplemented by water parks and fun pools offering all kinds of watery activities, such as at Skara Sommarland *(see p223)* and Sydpoolen in Södertälje.

Generally, water quality is high in Sweden and even in the cities it is sometimes possible to swim from rocks and beaches. Långholmen in central Stockholm is a favourite spot for a dip. In hot summers, however, poisonous algae sometimes blooms along the coast, so take advice locally on whether swimming is advisable.

Indoor pools are a popular choice. Stockholm has the historic Centralbadet and Sturebadet among others.

The spa and bathing culture has a long tradition in Sweden, particularly in places such as Loka *(see p141)*, with its modern facilities.

CYCLING

PEDAL POWER is a great way to experience towns and countryside alike. The bicycle has enjoyed something of a renaissance in Sweden and Stockholm in particular has invested heavily in cycle paths and special cycle routes.

Cycling holidays have long been popular on islands with little traffic such as Öland and Gotland. However, there are now cycle trails following minor roads and disused railway lines, often marked by green cycle-trail signs. A wide range of cycling packages is available and there are plenty of places to hire bicycles, tandems and trailers.

There are 30 or so regional cycle trails around the country, which require one or more stopovers to complete the distance. They can often be combined with the extensive Sverigeleden national trail which runs 2,590 km (1,600 miles) from Helsingborg in the south to Karesuando in the far north. The trail is well-signposted and special maps are available.

On the easier routes, 97 per cent of which are paved, those who have the time for a really long cycling holiday can experience Sweden's ever-changing landscape. Information about cycling trails is available from **Svenska Cykelsällskapet**.

Another option for those who fancy pedalling is to take a trolley trip on several railway tracks across the country where rail traffic has ceased

A cycling trip on Visingsö in Lake Vättern, offering easy routes, fascinating sights and beautiful countryside

Trekkers heading for Storsylen in the Jämtland mountains

WINTER ACTIVITIES

IT IS NO SURPRISE that Swedish skiers have dominated the World Cup at times, both in downhill and cross-country skiing. In winter, much of the country is covered in snow and there is some great skiing to be had.

There is an extensive network of cross-country skiing trails, many of which are floodlit, a necessity during the long dark evenings. It is also possible to ski on snow-covered golf courses or on iced-over lakes and the frozen waters of the archipelagos. The ice is also ideal for skating, an enjoyable experience on a sunny winter's day. Check the safety information first, as things can quickly turn serious if the ice cracks.

Sweden has hundreds of lifts for downhill skiers, which

Snowboarding and skiing are popular in the Swedish mountains

are listed on the website for the skiing organization **SLAO**. The two largest ski resorts are Åre, 600 km (370 miles) north of Stockholm, and Sälen, just over 400 km (250 miles) north of the capital. Most people on mountain holidays stay in self-catering cottages or apartments. Accommodation must be booked well in advance, particularly during the high season, and usually for complete weeks (Sun–Sun), weekends (Thu–Sun) or short weeks (Sun–Thu). It is easiest to buy lift passes and hire skis or snowboards at the resort.

GOLF

SWEDISH GOLFERS have achieved major successes in recent years, particularly in the ladies' events, with Annika Sörenstam leading the way. This golfing phenomenon is partly due to the ambitious junior programme supported by many of the country's golf clubs. Under the umbrella of the **Svenska Golfförbundet**, there are more than 400 golf courses, an extremely high figure in relation to the population size. Although the climate in parts of the country may be considered unsuitable for golf, the courses offer high quality during the summer. Almost all courses are open

to guest players, but demand is great and it can be difficult to find a suitable teeing-off time in high season at many clubs. Green fees vary from 150 kr on basic courses to more than 500 kr at exclusive city clubs. You must be a member of a golf club to play as a guest on a Swedish course.

HORSE RIDING

HORSE RIDING is a popular sport in Sweden, and there are almost 1,000 riding clubs. There is a wide range of riding available, from trips for beginners on Icelandic ponies to mountain trekking for those with experience. The tourist offices can provide local contacts.

Trekking on Icelandic ponies

BOATING, CANOEING, WHITE-WATER RAFTING

THE LONG coastline, inviting archipelagos and numerous lakes make exploring the country by water particularly rewarding. There are almost 500 classified guest harbours offering good facilities for sailors. The classification is administered by **Svenska Kryssarklubben**, which is also a good source of information about natural harbours and boating in general. All types of craft from simple rowing boats to large motor boats and yachts can be hired from marinas around the country.

Although there are no specific requirements for sailing smaller boats, you will need basic knowledge of boating even for a day trip. As a rule, documented

qualifications equivalent to the Swedish skipper's certificate *"förarintyg"* are required for taking out larger boats.

There are great opportunities for canoeing, with almost 20,000 km (12,500 miles) of trails on inland waters and around the archipelagos. The website for **Kanotleder i Sverige** lists 400 tours in Canadian canoes and kayaks, along with canoeing centres and rental sites across the country. For more advanced canoeists, there are plenty of opportunities to try sea kayaks in the outer archipelagos and white-water canoeing on the Norrland rivers. White-water rides are also possible, heading down the rapids in large rubber rafts or up on jetskis.

HUNTING AND FISHING

SWEDEN HAS more than 300,000 hunters and during the elk hunting season some forest villages are packed. Around 100,000 elks are shot every year. As a guest of land owners and hunting teams, foreign hunters can take part in small game and elk hunts. However, in the latter case, a special elk shooting test is required as well as a hunting permit. Taking your own weapon requires a great deal of bureaucracy, so hiring a weapon is recommended. Details about conditions, hunting times and hunt organizers are available from **Svenska Jägareförbundet**.

A third of all Swedes go fishing at least once a year, and no wonder with access to

Rod fishing, often free along Sweden's lengthy coastline

the most extensive fishing waters in Europe. There are more than 200 species of saltwater fish on the west coast, some of which also venture into the brackish water of the Baltic Sea. Added to this are around 40 species of freshwater fish in the lakes and rivers.

Rod fishing in coastal waters is often free. In other waters, the necessary fishing permit can be purchased locally. The **Sveafiskekortet** permit is a nationwide option offered by Sveaskog, which administers the national forests and land covering a fifth of the country. Sweden's leading and most traditional salmon fishing waters in Blekinge's Mörrum *(see p186)* are also state-owned.

Salmon and sea trout can even be fished in the heart of Stockholm, where Strömmen has unusually clean water for a city of a million people.

Fishing trips by boat are offered widely. **Sportfiskarna** provides information about sport fishing.

Experiencing the Swedish countryside by canoe

DIRECTORY

GENERAL INFORMATION

Friluftsfrämjandet
☎ 08-447 44 40.
@ info@frilufts.se

Naturvårdsverket
☎ 08-698 10 00.
w www.naturvardsverket.se

Svenska Turistföreningen (STF)
☎ 08-463 21 00.
w www.svenskaturistforeningen.se

CYCLING

Svenska Cykelsällskapet
Sweden's cycle trails.
w www.svenska-cykelsallskapet.se

WINTER ACTIVITIES

Skistar
Central reservations for ski resorts of Sälen, Vemdalen and Åre.
w www.skistar.com

SLAO
Swedish ski lifts. @ slao@slao.se

GOLF

Svenska Golfförbundet
☎ 08-622 1500.
@ info@sgf.golf.se

BOATING, CANOEING

Kanotleder i Sverige
Canoe trails and canoe hire.
w www.kanotguiden.com

Marinliv
Boat hire. @ info@marinliv.com

Svenska Kryssarklubben
☎ 08-448 2880. @ info@sxk.se

HUNTING, FISHING

Sportfiskarna
☎ 08-704 44 80.
@ hk@sportfiskarna.se

Sveafiskekortet
☎ 08-704 44 80.
@ info@sveaskog.se

Svenska Jägarförbundet
☎ 0155-24 62 00.
@ info@jagareforbundet.se

SURVIVAL
GUIDE

PRACTICAL INFORMATION 320-327
TRAVEL INFORMATION 328-335

PRACTICAL INFORMATION

SWEDEN IS a country of huge distances – it is as far from Malmö in the south to Treriksröset in the north as it is from Malmö to Rome. So, it is worth planning any trip in advance. The local tourist offices publish useful information on the Internet. All types of accommodation from luxury hotels to bed-and-breakfasts can be booked online. Once you have arrived in Sweden, there are more than

Tourist office symbol

300 authorized tourist information offices nationwide which can provide help. The towns all have modern facilities for the traveller, including banking services and emergency medical care, and the public telephone system is first-class. Customs and border controls now apply mainly to travellers from countries outside the EU. For EU citizens and Norwegians, the entry procedure is relatively straightforward.

TOURIST INFORMATION

SWEDEN HAS a number of tourist offices abroad, run by **Sveriges Rese- och Turistråd**. An overview of what's on offer for tourists and links to all the local tourist offices can be found at www.visit-sweden.com.

Another user-friendly general website is **Svensk TuristGuide** at www.sverige turism.se. Visitors can click on the map to reach regional tourism organizations and obtain detailed information about accommodation, eating out, attractions and events. Brochures and travel tips can also be requested by e-mail or phone.

In addition to the 300 official tourist information offices, information points open in summer, often attached to larger attractions. Offices with the blue and yellow "i" sign usually offer a broader service than those with the green and white "i".

The hub of Stockholm's tourist information is the **Tourist Centre Stockholm** in Sverigehuset.

PASSPORTS AND CUSTOMS

CITIZENS OF virtually all countries can enter Sweden as tourists without a visa. Norwegians and visitors from European countries which have signed the Schengen agreement do not, in principle, need a passport. However, all airlines require passports for passengers flying from countries outside the Nordic region, so it is always wise to carry your passport.

Different customs regulations apply to travellers from the European Union (EU) and those from other countries. Citizens of EU countries can take an unlimited amount of alcohol and tobacco products into Sweden without having to pay tax, provided they are for personal use. Citizens from non-EU countries can take in 1 litre of spirits or 2 litres of fortified wine, including sparkling wine, 2 litres of wine and an unlimited amount of strong beer, 200 cigarettes, or 100 cigarillos, or 50 cigars or 250 g tobacco. But they can only take in goods up to a value of

1,700 Kr in addition to normal travel-related items. To import alcohol, you must be 20 years old, and for tobacco, 18.

Items such as milk, cheese, butter, eggs and potatoes may not be taken into Sweden by private individuals. Norwegians and EU citizens may only take in a maximum of 15 kg (33 lb) of meat or fish. Visitors from some other countries are permitted to bring in 1 kg (2.2 lb) of meat and 1 kg (2.2 lb) of fish, but sometimes a certificate from a recognized exporter is required.

Dogs and cats from EU countries can be taken into Sweden, providing they have a veterinary certificate from the animal's home country. The animal must also have an identification marking, as well as an import permit issued by the Swedish Board of Agriculture (available from Swedish embassies).

Tax-free sales in Sweden are permitted only for travellers with a final destination outside the EU.

Tullverket provides up-to-date information in several languages by telephone and on its website.

OPENING HOURS

MOST MUSEUMS and major sights are open between 10am and 6pm all year, and they often have longer opening hours in the summer. Many museums close on Mondays. Some have extended opening hours one evening in the week. Admission to a number of state-run museums is free of charge. Admission charges for other museums

Tourist information office, Stockholm

◁ **A ferry bringing summer visitors to the isolated Baltic island of Gotska Sandön, north of Gotland**

vary between about 30 and 70 Kr. There is usually a discounted price for children, students and senior citizens. In many places, churches are only open for services, although some have opening hours for visitors.

Stockholm and other cities have special discount cards for tourists. They can be purchased from tourist information offices and many hotels and are valid for one or more days. A family card is usually also available. The card gives free travel on public transport, free or discounted admission to museums and other attractions and events, and may also offer discounts at restaurants and shops.

Discos and nightclubs generally charge an entrance fee of 60–120 kr. Tickets for the theatre, concerts and sporting events can be bought locally, in the cities at special ticket offices, or at the gambling service ATG's outlets via **BiljettDirekt**, www.ticnet.se.

DISABLED VISITORS

I N SWEDEN, public areas have to be accessible for physically or visually disabled people, as well as those suffering from allergies. Sweden is a long away ahead of many other countries in this respect. Wheelchair ramps and spacious toilets for disabled people are fitted in all new buildings.

Disabled car drivers with a disability permit from their home country can park in special areas.

In Stockholm, the Tunnelbana underground network and local trains are adapted for disabled passengers. Buses "kneel" at bus stops to give a reasonable height for passengers to get on or off. Visitors from abroad can

The GöteborgPass, giving free admission to museums

obtain information in English before their stay from **De Handikappades Riksförbund** by telephone or via the Internet. Brochures with information about facilities for disabled visitors at theatres, cinemas, museums and libraries are available from tourist information offices.

ETIQUETTE

B ANS ON SMOKING are increasingly common throughout Sweden. Smoking is generally not permitted in public places, including all local transport and queues at bus stops and railway stations. Restaurants are obliged to provide no-smoking areas.

The Swedes queue patiently, but guard their place jealously. They are usually friendly and pleased to help foreign tourists. The use of first names is the norm and a friendly *"Hej!"* is the common greeting.

Casual clothing is acceptable almost everywhere, including restaurants, particularly in the summer.

Service is always included in restaurant prices, but it is usual to round up the bill by up to 10 per cent for good service.

The logo of Systembolaget, the state-owned liquor store

ALCOHOL

S WEDISH POLICY towards alcohol is restrictive. Wines and spirits can be bought only in the relatively few shops of the state monopoly **Systembolaget**. They are open Monday–Friday 10am–6pm, and Saturday 10am– 2pm. The minimum age for buying alcohol in these shops is 20, and young people may be asked to produce proof of their age. In restaurants, the minimum age for buying alcohol is 18. Most restaurants and pubs stop selling alcohol at 1am, but some bars stay

open till 5am. With a maximum permitted blood alcohol level of only 0.2 per mil, drinking is effectively banned for car drivers.

The Swedish custom of *"skåling"* confounds many visitors. To *"skål"*, look the person in the eye, raise your glass, drink, then repeat the eye contact before putting down your glass. If the glasses are full of schnapps, then Swedes like to sing their special schnapps songs.

Personal Security and Health

Police symbol

SWEDEN IS A SAFE destination compared with most countries in the world. You needn't worry about natural disasters such as earthquakes or hurricanes. Crime does occur, with some cities suffering more than others, but this is rarely a concern for tourists. However, it is important to lock the car and hide valuables when parked. Look out for pickpockets in the summer and avoid the empty, commercial parts of city centres late at night. Sweden has a well-developed network of emergency services which travellers can call on. Rescue services and hospital emergency clinics are highly efficient.

Policeman   Guard

Police car

PROTECTING PROPERTY

ALTHOUGH SWEDEN is a comparatively safe place, tourists can still run into trouble at times. Especially in the summer months, the many popular events attract bag-snatchers and pick-pockets. In the cities and in crowded public areas visitors should be particularly careful to keep an eye on their property, especially handbags and cameras. Avoid using unmanned cloakrooms at restaurants and museums.

Valuables and personal documents should always be locked in the hotel safe. It is equally important not to leave any valuables in your car; ideally, choose a hotel with its own parking facilities.

There is no need to carry large amounts of cash. All major credit and debit cards are accepted in virtually all shops and restaurants, and cash machines are common, at least in larger places. When taking out cash, watch out for conmen who may offer to help, but are actually after your money or card.

PERSONAL SAFETY

THE SWEDISH POLICE are generally extremely helpful and speak good English. Police patrolling on foot or in cars are a routine sight in the cities, and moun-ted police are often in evid-ence at special events. In the suburbs, however, police can be thin on the ground. Out in the country, the police pres-ence is low. Not all towns

Mounted police

have evening and night police patrols and even fewer have open police stations.

In many places, uniformed security guards have taken over the function of the police. They are a common feature in department stores, at train and Tunnelbana stations and as car patrols.

Stockholm, Gothenburg and Malmö are safe to stroll around on foot. Stockholm's Tunnelbana (underground railway) is efficient and comfortable, as well as being safe at most times. CCTV security systems are installed at some stations, squares, department stores and shops.

Beware the strict rules regarding alcohol, drugs and some medications when driving. A driver is guilty of drunk driving with a blood alcohol level of only 0.2 per mil and gross drunk driving (from 1.0 per mil) is punish-able by imprisonment. The possession of drugs is illegal.

Breaking traffic rules, particularly speed limits, may lead to hefty fines.

For some years it has been illegal to buy sexual services in Sweden so it is the buyer, not the prostitute, who is prosecuted. Street prostitutes are now a very rare sight in the inner cities.

LOST PROPERTY

LOST OR STOLEN property should be reported to the nearest police station. A police report will be needed for any insurance claim. In addition to the police lost property offices (Polisens

Hittegodsexpedition), large towns and cities have lost property offices (Hittegodsavdelning) at railway stations, bus stations and airports. They are often only open during the day and not all of them will give information over the phone. There is usually a good chance of recovering lost goods.

Visitors from abroad should contact their embassy or consulate if they lose their passport.

EMERGENCIES

THE EMERGENCY telephone number for police, fire or ambulance is **112**. It can be dialled free of charge from all public telephones, but should be used only in emergencies.

HEALTHCARE

No SPECIAL vaccinations are needed to visit Sweden. Medical assistance is available across the country from doctors and district nurses at the local medical centre open surgeries.

There are duty clinics in the evenings and at weekends, but you must make an appointment by phone. Many hospitals have accident and emergency departments, some of which are privately run. Patients should not report to emergency clinics with minor ailments. First, contact the healthcare information service **Sjukvårdsrådgivningen** for instructions in English. Its staff have up-to-date knowledge about the current situation in the city's hospitals and can assign patients to a suitable hospital or duty doctor. Particularly during the holiday period, it is always advisable to use this central information service, to avoid

unnecessarily long waiting times. For severe toothache, patients can usually receive the help of a local dentist and larger places have special duty dentists.

Citizens of other EU and EEA countries are entitled to emergency medical care at the same low rate as Swedes if they produce form E111 and a valid passport or other form of identification. More extensive treatment costs extra so it is advisable to take out separate medical insurance covering specialist care, hospital expenses and repatriation before travelling.

MEDICINES

IN SWEDEN, medicines are only sold at pharmacies. Medicines for minor ailments are available without a prescription, but many medicines which are available over the counter abroad require a prescription in Sweden. There is also a risk that the medication prescribed at home may not be approved in Sweden. It is best to ensure that you pack sufficient medication for the duration of your trip.

Pharmacy staff are well trained and can give good advice. Unfortunately, pharmacies can be hard to find in the countryside and they are not open on Sundays. A limited number of natural remedies are also sold in health food stores.

Pharmacy sign

OUT AND ABOUT

SWEDEN HAS a varied landscape and climate and it is important to respect the forces of nature. In the mountains, the weather can change very quickly from still and sunny one moment to fog

or a storm the next. If you have the right equipment and follow the rules, a trip in the mountains need not be dangerous. The STF mountain stations offer good advice about safe trails.

Along the coast drowning accidents claim many lives every year. Avoid going out in flimsy craft and boats which are beyond your capabilities. Take advice from local people about the weather.

There is no need to worry about the forest predators – bears, wolves, lynxes and wolverines. They are shy creatures and prefer to avoid people. The same applies to Sweden's only poisonous snake, the adder. However, anyone bitten by a snake should seek medical advice.

Mosquitoes can be a nuisance from June to autumn, especially at dusk, along waterways and in the mountains. Pharmacies stock mosquito repellent. In the archipelagos, there is also a risk of being bitten by ticks, which carry a number of diseases. Ticks should be removed from the skin with tweezers as quickly as possible. If the redness around the bite area persists, consult a doctor.

Ambulance

Banking and Local Currency

SWEDEN HAS RETAINED its own currency, the Swedish krona, rather than adopting the euro. A number of shops in major tourist areas will accept euros, but goods are almost exclusively priced in kronor. Visitors can change currency in banks, but better rates of exchange can often be obtained at bureaux de change in the main towns, which have longer opening hours. Automatic cash machines can be found outside most banks and in shopping centres across the country. Credit and debit cards are accepted virtually everywhere, and the larger stores will take traveller's cheques.

Bankomat, the joint cash-machine system of the business banks

BANKS

THERE ARE plenty of banks in the towns, all providing a good service. Their opening times vary, but the normal hours are 9.30am–3pm. Some banks stay open until 6pm at least once a week. All banks are closed at weekends and on public holidays, as well as the day before a public holiday.

Svenska Kassaservice, which handles the Swedish post office Posten's cash transactions, has almost 1,000 offices around the country. They are agents for certain banks and accept withdrawals on a debit card.

There are nearly 3,000 automatic cash machines throughout the country. They come in two types: Bankomat machines are the joint system of the business banks, while Uttag machines belong to FöreningsSparbanken. Foreign visitors can use all cash machines provided that they have a bank card with a PIN code that is linked to, for example, Visa or MasterCard. Machines usually have instructions in several languages. The charge for withdrawing cash varies according to the type of card.

CURRENCY EXCHANGE

VARIOUS BUREAUX de change chains are represented in Sweden. Generally they provide a better exchange rate than the banks, and in city centres there is always a bureau de change office close by. Changing money in your hotel is the most expensive option. It is worth checking exchange rates and commission charges, because the differences can be significant. Currency can be changed at international airports from 5.30am, and from 7am at city train stations seven days a week.

The head office of Handelsbanken on Kungsträdgårdsgatan, Stockholm

Forex bureau de change, situated in large towns and at airports

CREDIT CARDS

ALL THE WELL-KNOWN credit cards, such as **Visa**, **Diners Club**, **Eurocard** and **MasterCard**, are accepted across Sweden, but not all places accept American Express because of opposition to the relatively high charges which the retailer has to pay.

Cards can be used not just at larger hotels and restaurants, but at nearly all shops and services. If you pay by credit card, most shops will ask you to produce proof of identity. Some shops also offer a cash withdrawal service for small amounts in conjunction with purchases.

Cash machines can be used to make withdrawals using an internationally accepted credit card with a PIN code.

TRAVELLER'S CHEQUES

TRAVELLER'S CHEQUES are one of the safest ways of carrying large amounts of money. They are not accepted in all shops, but can be changed at banks. It is sensible to keep a receipt showing the serial numbers of the cheques in a separate place. When buying cheques in your home country, it is worth checking the procedure if you lose any of your cheques.

CURRENCY

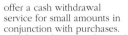

SWEDEN'S CURRENCY is the krona (plural kronor). The krona (abbreviated as SEK or Kr) is divided into 100 öre. The smallest coin is 50 öre and the largest note is 1,000 kronor, which is not used much. If possible, it is advisable not to carry notes of more than 500 Kr.

Although Sweden has not adopted the euro, many shops in tourist areas and border towns will accept payment in euros, but will usually give change in kronor.

20 Kr (Selma Lagerlöf)

Notes
Swedish currency notes are issued in denominations of 20, 50, 100, 500 and 1,000 kronor. They depict famous Swedes, including monarchs, scientists and authors.

50 Kr (Jenny Lind)

100 Kr (Carl von Linné)

500 Kr (King Karl XI)

1000 Kr (King Gustav Vasa)

Coins
Coins are issued in values of 50 öre, and 1, 5 and 10 kronor. The 1 Kr and 10 Kr coins depict Sweden's monarch on the obverse side while the 5 Kr has his monogram on the reverse side. The 50 öre piece incorporates the state "three crowns" symbol.

50 öre   1 krona   5 kronor   10 kronor

Telecommunications, Post and Media

SWEDEN HAS A FIRST-CLASS public telephone system. A top-ranking telecommunications industry and high living standards have placed the Swedes among the world's biggest users of telephones. Although the fixed telephone system is well developed, there are now nearly as many mobile phone users as there are people in the country. With the advent of the 3G system allowing video telephony and advanced data services, the aim is for 99 per cent of the population to have coverage by the end of 2004. Internet use is widespread, with impressive investment in broadband.

A modern Swedish phone kiosk

MAKING A PHONE CALL

SWEDEN IS DIVIDED into 250 dialling code areas. The prefix for international calls from Sweden is 00. Then dial the country code and the phone number without the initial zero of the area code. To dial Sweden from abroad, the country code is 46. For enquiries such as whether your phone will operate in the mountains, call Telia's customer services on 0046 771 99 02 00. For directory enquiries in Sweden, call 118 118. This also provides listings of mobile numbers.

The number of public telephone kiosks has shown a marked decline, as most Swedes have a mobile phone. The remaining public phones are mainly card-operated. They are owned by Telia and are cheapest to use with a Swedish phonecard. These can be bought at newspaper kiosks and in shops, and are available for 50 or 120 units. For a local call, the minimum charge is four units to a landline, with higher charges for calls to mobile phones and international calls. Some credit cards, petrol cards and international phonecards such as Access can be used, but at a higher rate. Instructions on how to use public telephones are also shown in English. It is possible to make reverse-charge (collect) calls within Sweden from all public phones by dialling 2#. The emergency number is 112. Some 020 and 0200 numbers can be called free of charge.

Coin-operated phones are very rare. Should you find one, they also have instructions in English and accept 1 Kr, 5 Kr and 10 Kr coins.

MOBILE PHONES

THE NORDIC countries have long had the analogue NMT network, which was known for its good coverage. Now the digital GSM network has taken over, offering a broader range of mobile services, and good coverage outside the cities.

Next-generation mobile telephony, 3G, was introduced in 2003 and offers even more advanced services. Coverage has so far been poor in many places, but plans are in place to rectify this. Having a mobile phone is a good idea even out in the wilderness, but there is no guarantee that you will be able to call for help when you need it.

In most cases, European visitors can use their GSM and 3G phones in Sweden.

FAX, E-MAIL, INTERNET

THE MAJORITY of hotels, airports, train stations and large shopping centres offer fax, telegram, e-mail and Internet services. There are

USING A CARD TELEPHONE

1 Select instructions in the language of your choice.

2 Lift the receiver.

3 Insert the card and wait for the dialling tone.

4 Dial the number and wait to be connected. If your phonecard credit is running out, you will hear a signal. Press the cardswitch button and insert a new card to continue the call.

5 Remove the card. If you forget, you will hear a signal.

Telephone cards
for 50 units.

Internet cafés dotted around the country. Hotels which focus on business travellers may have computers available for use in your room.

Swedish postage stamps

POST

THE SWEDISH POSTAL service has an almost 400-year history, but many Swedes think the service has deteriorated in recent years. Post offices have been closed and replaced by a few large postal centres, mainly for companies. For the general public, there are small service points, primarily in supermarkets and at petrol stations. They have the advantage of longer opening hours in the evenings and at weekends. The disadvantage is a frequent lack of space and services. Cash transactions have also been split off into a special company with its own offices, Svensk Kassaservice (see p324). Perhaps the best service is provided in the really remote areas by mobile postal workers. Stamps can be

Post office logo

Yellow postbox for national and international, blue for local mail

bought at post offices, Pressbyrån kiosks and tourist information offices. The basic postage for a postcard or letter under 20 g within Sweden is 5 Kr (non-denominated stamp) or 5.50 Kr (denominated stamp); for abroad the postage is 10 Kr. Postboxes are painted blue for local letters and yellow for other domestic and international mail. Collection times are shown on the postbox and sometimes take place in the early afternoon. In large towns there are last-minute postboxes, which are emptied in the evenings.

Most international courier services are represented in the cities and special services are also operated by the Swedish post office, Posten.

TV AND RADIO

MOST HOTELS provide a television in the room with both national and foreign channels. The most frequently used are the Swedish SVT1, SVT2, TV3, TV4 and Channel 5, as well as the international CNN, Sky News, BBC and Eurosport channels. SVT1 and 2 are state-run public-service channels. SVT2 and TV4 broadcast local programmes in the morning and evening, including weather forecasts.

There are also a number of local radio stations, broadcasting mainly international and Swedish music. P6, Stockholm International, has English and German-language programmes on 89.6 MHz.

NEWSPAPERS AND MAGAZINES

MAJOR FOREIGN newspapers and magazines can be bought in the cities, at airports and at other transport hubs. Pressbyrån kiosks, tobacconists, department stores

One of the country's many Pressbyrån kiosks

and some tourist information offices stock a limited selection of foreign publications. See the directory below for a range of newsagents.

TRAVEL INFORMATION

Stockholm Arlanda is the busiest of Sweden's international airports, although a number of other airports have international flights, notably Gothenburg's Landvetter and Sturup, near Malmö, in the south. Since summer 2000, Sweden has been linked with Continental Europe by a bridge over the Öresund Strait to Denmark for road and rail traffic. It is now possible to fly to

Aircraft of Scandinavian Airlines (SAS)

Copenhagen and take a short train journey across the bridge to Malmö. There are still a number of car ferry services operating between Denmark and Sweden, as well as across the Baltic Sea from Finland and the Baltic States, and across the North Sea from Norway and Great Britain. In summer, an increasing number of cruise liners call into Swedish ports. Express buses operate services from cities across Europe.

ARRIVAL BY AIR

MOST MAJOR EUROPEAN cities have direct flights to one of Stockholm's three airports: Arlanda, Skavsta and Bromma. Landvetter near Gothenburg and Sturup outside Malmö also have international traffic. Arlanda is served by around 60 international airlines. It is also possible to fly via Copenhagen in Denmark. The leading Scandinavian airline **SAS** dominates. Other operators include **Lufthansa**, **British Airways** and **Finnair**. **Delta Air Lines** operates from the US to Paris with onward flights to Stockholm via Air France; **American Airlines** flies to the UK with onward connections via British Airways or Finnair.

Arlanda is 40 km (25 miles) north of central Stockholm and is also a hub for Swedish domestic flights and charter services. Bromma, close to the centre, may only be used by environmentally friendly aircraft. Skavsta lies 100 km

Arlanda Express linking Arlanda Airport with central Stockholm

(60 miles) south of Stockholm, near Nyköping. Low-cost airline **Ryanair** flies to Skavsta and Gothenburg, from London Stansted and Glasgow, and also serves Malmö from Stansted and Skavsta from Glasgow.

GETTING FROM AND TO THE AIRPORT

ALL THE INTERNATIONAL airports are served by airport buses to the city centre in conjunction with

arrivals and departure times. Stockholm's Arlanda Airport has a "Flygbussarna" bus service, which operates every five minutes at peak times. Journey time is 45 minutes to the City Terminal at Central Station. An onward journey by taxi can be booked on the bus. The taxi ride into town from the airport is quicker, but more expensive. Most taxi firms have a fixed charge to the city centre. Avoid unauthorized taxis and check the fare before departure. The shortest journey time is by the pricier Arlanda Express train, a 20-minute trip to Central Station. Trains depart every 15 min from the two stations, Arlanda South (serving terminals 2, 3 and 4) and Arlanda North (for terminal 5).

AIR FARES

FARE OPTIONS are many and varied, particularly if you are flexible about departure and arrival dates, or can book well in advance.

Increased competition between the airlines has made it considerably cheaper to fly to Sweden from many European destinations, and now SAS offers low-cost tickets with a no-frills service to meet the competition. It is possible to find return flights from London, Paris or Frankfurt for less than £80. Tour operators often have packages with attractive air fares and accommodation included. Newspaper advertisements and travel companies' websites have details of last-minute deals.

Terminal 5 (International) at Stockholm's Arlanda Airport

Ferry from Finland on the way to its terminal in Stockholm

ARRIVAL BY FERRY

A NUMBER OF FERRY companies operate direct services across the North Sea and the Baltic to Sweden. The large car ferries used on most routes offer plenty of passenger comforts, good food, entertainment and shopping.

From Newcastle in the UK, **DFDS** sails to Gothenburg via Kristiansand in Norway.

Although the new Öresund Bridge has reduced ferry traffic from Denmark, the short Helsingør–Helsingborg hop still has several ferries an hour operated by **Scandlines** and **HH-Ferries**. **Stena Line** has the routes Grenå–Varberg and Fredrikshavn–Gothenburg.

The busiest route in terms of passenger numbers is from Finland with regular crossings from Helsinki, Turku and Mariehamn to Stockholm and Kapellskär. Both **Viking Line** and **Silja Line** have terminals in Stockholm at Stadsgården and Värtahamnen respectively. The crossing takes about 15.5 hours from Helsinki and 11 hours from Turku. Silja also operates ferries between Vaasa in Finland and Umeå in northern Sweden. From Estonia, **Tallink** operates the routes Tallinn– Stockholm and Paldiski– Kapellskär. **Riga Sea Line** operates between Riga in Latvia and Stockholm.

Polferries has the routes Świnoujście–Ystad and Gdańsk–Nynäshamn. **Stena Line** operates the Gdynia–Karlskrona route.

Trelleborg is the major port for traffic from Germany. **TT-Line** goes from Rostock and Travemünde, **Scandlines** from Rostock and Sassnitz. **Stena Line** sails the Kiel–Gothenburg route.

ARRIVAL BY TRAIN OR EXPRESS BUS

T HERE ARE EXCELLENT train links from Continental Europe and Norway and a large network of express bus routes. **Tågplusguiden/ Expressbussguiden** is a good online search service providing an overview of train and long distance bus services.

ARRIVAL BY CAR

M OTORISTS ARRIVING from Denmark can use the spectacular Öresund Bridge between Copenhagen and Malmö *(see p181)*. On the Swedish side, the toll bridge connects with the E4 motorway to Stockholm and the north. Alternatively, there are car ferries.

Car ferries are also the most practical option from Finland and the Baltic States, as driving around the Baltic Sea can take two days.

The borders with Finland and Norway have customs posts which are often unmanned. However, the entry regulations still apply *(see p320)*.

Arrival hall at the Central Station in Stockholm

Getting Around Sweden

FLYING WITHIN SWEDEN has its advantages considering the enormous distances between places, and in many cases the fares are reasonably priced. The high standard of overnight sleeper trains makes long journeys by train a comfortable option. The X2000 Express train running between the major cities often competes well in terms of time and comfort with domestic flights. Elsewhere in the country, buses provide much of the public transport. Travelling by boat offers exciting opportunities to discover Sweden's magnificent archipelagos and waterways.

Skyways, one of many companies offering domestic flights in Sweden

DOMESTIC FLIGHTS

THE VAST LENGTH of Sweden makes domestic flights a convenient option, and deregulation and increased competition in recent years have made prices more reasonable. Of the 47 airports offering scheduled flights, the 19 largest are state-run by **Luftfartsverket**. Its website contains information about the airports, flights and current arrivals and departures.

Stockholm/Arlanda dominates the domestic flight scene, but several companies have chosen to fly from the capital's more centrally located Bromma Airport. Landvetter, outside Gothenburg, and Sturup, outside Malmö, are other major airports.

Flight times are generally short: Stockholm–Gothenburg takes 55 minutes. The longest direct flight, Stockholm–Kiruna, takes 1 hr 50 mins.

SAS is still the leading airline in terms of passenger numbers, but with its 27 destinations, **Skyways** reaches most parts of the country. Other operators include **Malmö Aviation** and **Nordic Airlink**. Tickets can be bought at travel agents or

directly from the airlines. Tickets booked online can generally be paid for with a credit card and collected at the airport. It is worth searching for the lowest prices, particularly if you book a long way in advance. Young people under 26 can buy cheap standby tickets.

Travellers to Malmö could consider flying to Kastrup in Copenhagen, as there is a fast train transfer to central Malmö across the Öresund Bridge.

Larger airports are served by airport buses, which operate in conjunction with arrivals and departures.

SJ logo

Malmbanan line from Kiruna to Narvik in northernmost Norrland

TRAVELLING BY TRAIN

THERE IS A well-developed train network covering parts of Sweden from the Öresund Bridge in the south to Riksgränsen in the north. Stations and services are good by international standards. The trains are run by a number of competing companies. The state-run **SJ** operates most long-distance routes. Other major players include **Connex** and **Tågcompaniet**, which have parts of the lines in Norrland. At county level, train services are run by local train companies in partnership with bus services and in some cases ferry services.

Travel involving different companies and forms of transport is administered by **Samtrafiken**, which is part-owned by each of the transport companies. SJ offers a booking service for Tågplus tickets for English-speaking travellers.

In recent years, airlines have experienced tough competition from the X2000 Express train which links the cities of Copenhagen/ Malmö, Gothenburg, Härnösand and Mora to Stockholm. The journey time is around 5 hours from Malmö and 3 hours from Gothenburg. The trains offer a business class service similar to that of airlines.

InterCity is the main long-distance alternative to the X2000, offering first- and second-class seats. The overnight sleeper trains are recommended for longer journeys such as Gothenburg– Östersund and Connex routes in northern Norrland. The standard is high and you can often have your own compartment with shower, if you wish. Normal compartments contain three berths, but there are also six-berth compartments. Ticket prices vary

considerably depending on the type of train. Discounts are worth searching for.

Tickets can be bought via ATG's outlets around the country and at larger stations. Buying tickets on the train attracts a fee of around 30 kr. Note that seat/berth reservations are necessary for the X2000 and night trains.

The **Inlandsbanan** line operates in summer, offering the opportunity to travel through the Swedish wilderness, forests and mountains. It runs 1,300 km (800 miles) from Kristinehamn on Lake Vänern north to Gällivare in northern Lapland.

TRAVELLING BY BUS

IN MANY PLACES buses are the only public transport available and although services are patchy in rural areas, it is possible to get about. Local timetables are on **Samtrafiken**'s website.

Express buses compete with trains and airlines on longer routes. Journey times are longer, but ticket prices are lower and the buses are modern. See Samtrafiken's Expressbussguiden for routes and times. Some bus companies, such as **Swebus Express**, do not require prebooking. If one bus is full, another one is laid on.

Many express bus companies arrange special excursions in the tourist season. Contact the tourist information offices for information. Trips are also arranged to the southern Fjällen where there is no train line. **Fjällexpressen** is one of the operators running ski buses from Stockholm and Gothenburg.

Abisko's modest station building on the Malmbanan line

TRAVELLING BY BOAT

SWEDEN'S LONG coastline, vast lakes and extensive archipelagos make for busy boat services. In addition to the scheduled services, sightseeing trips and tours are offered in summer, occasionally on classic old steamers.

The Dalsland, Strömsholm and Kinda canals attract some charming boats, but the tourist trail to beat them all is the Göta canal (see pp146–7). Sweden's blue ribbon takes you 611 km (380 miles) in a relaxed three days, negotiating 65 locks, the country's three largest lakes and some of Sweden's most attractive scenery.

Boat services to the Baltic Sea's largest island, Gotland, are run by **Destination Gotland**, with its modern high-speed ferries, which take less than three hours on either of the Nynäshamn–Visby or Oskarshamn–Visby routes. In peak summer season, there are up to eight departures a day. Although the ferries can take 500 cars per trip, it can be difficult to get a place for a car during public holidays and other holiday periods if you have not booked in advance.

DIRECTORY

DOMESTIC FLIGHTS

Luftfartsverket
Airports, timetables, information
w www.lfv.se

SAS
[0770-727 727.
w www.scandinavian.net

Skyways
[08-595 130 50.
w www.skyways.se

Malmö Aviation
[0771-55 00 10.
w www.malmoaviation.se

Nordic Airlink
[0900–108 15 15.
w www.flynordic.com

TRAIN, BUS, BOAT

Samtrafiken
Information and bookings via
Tågplusguiden/Expressbussguiden
[0771-87 87 87
w www.resplus.se

TRAIN TRAVEL

SJ
[0771-75 75 75.
w www.sj.se

Connex
[0771-26 00 00.
w www.connex.se

Tågkompaniet
[0771-444 111.

Inlandsbanan
[0771-53 53 53.
w www.inlandsbanan.se

BUS TRAVEL

Swebus Express
[0200-218 218.
w www.swebusexpress.se

Fjällexpressen
[08-727 90 35.
w www.fjallexpressen.com

BOAT TRAVEL

Destination Gotland
[0771-22 33 00.
w www.destinationgotland.se

Rederi AB Göta Kanal
[031-80 63 15.
w www.gotacanal.se

Gotland's high-speed catamaran service approaching Visby

Road Travel in Sweden

Tourist route sign

DISTANCES WITHIN SWEDEN are huge, and in the rural areas travelling in your own or a rented car is often the only way of getting about. The well-developed road network varies in quality, but the major roads are generally of a good standard. State-run ferries operate a free service in the archipelagos. Although traffic can be heavy in the cities in rush hour, it is never on the same scale as in the UK and on the Continent, and Swedish motorists are generally good-natured. For advice on driving in Stockholm, *see page 334.*

Elk on the road, a hazard for motorists in the forests

ROAD STANDARDS

SWEDEN HAS an extensive road network, with more than 210,000 km (130,000 miles) open for public use. Almost the same again is not accessible, primarily forestry roads which are closed with a boom. The majority of the public roads are sealed and of a good standard. The exceptions can be found in the forested counties of the northwest, where ice and heavy traffic can make the roads difficult to negotiate.

The national road network comprises *europavägar* ("European motorways"), *riksvägar* (national roads) and *länsvägar* (county roads). Motorways such as the E4 and stretches of the E20 and E6 make up less than 1,200 km (700 miles). With the exception of the Öresund Bridge, roads are toll-free.

The three-lane highways require some attention for the uninitiated. The traffic runs in opposite directions along one or two lanes with a wire barrier to separate the flow.

TRAFFIC RULES

GENERALLY, SWEDISH traffic is comparatively well organized and the majority of motorists follow the rules of the road. Road safety is good, despite occasionally dense traffic and severe weather conditions. The number of road fatalities is less than 500 a year, the same level as in the 1940s.

The most common breach of the rules relates to speed limits, despite the presence of speed cameras and radar patrols. The fines are high and there is a risk of losing your licence for serious speeding offences.

The maximum permitted speed on motorways is 110 km/h (68 mph), but the limit is more often 90 km/h (55 mph). On country roads the limit is usually 70 km/h (43 mph) and in built-up areas the limit is 50 km/h (31 mph). The limit is reduced to 30 km/h (19 mph) around all schools and nurseries. Residential areas often have traffic calming measures such

as road narrowing and speed bumps. By law, the driver and all passengers must wear seatbelts. Children up to the age of six must use child seats.

Beware of the strict rules regarding alcohol and driving. A driver is guilty of drink-driving with a blood alcohol level of only 0.2 per mil and gross drink-driving (from 1.0 per mil) is punishable by imprisonment.

Motorists must give way to pedestrians at crossings not controlled by lights. Vehicles must stop at junctions onto major roads, even if there is no Stop sign. At roundabouts, vehicles already on the roundabout always have right of way. Traffic lights with a continuous amber light mean "stop" and there are hefty fines for driving through a red light. Side-lights or dipped headlights must be used even during daylight hours.

Winter tyres must be used from 1 Dec–31 Mar. Studded tyres may be used, but not during the period 1 May–30 Sep, unless the road conditions require them.

CAR FERRIES

STATE-RUN CAR ferries operate free of charge in the archipelagos and across some of the larger rivers. Some places also have private ferries, which do levy a charge. You rarely need to book, but check the timetable carefully as the ferries may not run late at night unless in emergencies. **Vägverket** can provide information.

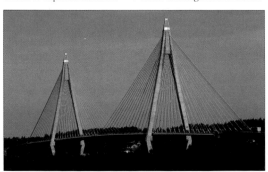

Sunnerstabron on the E6, one of Sweden's many road bridges

ROAD SIGNS

SWEDISH ROAD SIGNS mostly follow the European standard, but the country also has some signs of its own. Signs carrying the symbol for elk, reindeer or deer warn drivers that there is a major risk of colliding with wildlife. Thousands of accidents involving animals occur every year and a collision between a car and a full-grown elk is often fatal. The risk is particularly high in the summer around 5am–8am and 10pm–2am, when visibility is poor. Fences along the roadside are no guarantee that animals won't suddenly appear on the road.

Warning sign for elk

As in the rest of Europe, brown signs with white symbols indicate recommended tourist routes, heritage sites, tourist areas and attractions along the road such as a national park or a historic building.

Individual attractions may be indicated by a sign with a white "pretzel" on a blue background.

PARKING

THERE IS USUALLY a charge for parking in towns and built-up areas, especially in the centre of towns and cities. City car parks and on-street parking are often expensive. Sometimes charges apply 24-hours a day and at weekends, too. Many ticket machines accept credit cards and petrol cards, but they may not always work, so it is best to keep a good number of 10 Kr coins to hand.

Diligent traffic wardens hunt out illegally parked cars and the fines can be high, particularly if you have parked illegally in a space reserved for disabled drivers.

Where parking is free during the night, there is sometimes a parking ban on certain days for cleaning, so it is always important to check the signs – otherwise your

Traffic warden

car may be towed away. Supermarkets and other large stores often have free parking for a few hours, but be aware that sometimes they require a special parking ticket for your windscreen showing your arrival time.

FUEL AND SERVICES

THERE ARE PLENTY of service stations along the major roads and in built-up areas, but they may be few and far between in rural areas. Although some stations are manned 24-hours a day, drivers are often directed to automatic pumps which take cards and notes. It is sensible to fill up before a night drive.

In the event of technical problems, there are few places which can help outside working hours – garages are usually closed in the evenings and at weekends.

Assistancekåren and **Falck** offer emergency roadside assistance. They often have an agreement with motoring organizations and insurance companies abroad.

RENTING A CAR

IN ADDITION TO the familiar international car hire chains, there are a number of local options, including the petrol companies' extensive rental service. Most places will have some form of car rental.

It is possible to pre-book cars at airports and major train stations, often for one-way rental where you leave the car at your destination. Bookings can be made from abroad via the Internet or by phone.

You generally only need a valid driving licence to rent a car, but there may be an age limit of 20, or even 25 for exclusive vehicles. Prices vary considerably, so it is worth shopping around. Special weekend deals are common and considering Sweden's long distances, it is best to opt for offers which include unlimited mileage.

WINTER DRIVING

ROAD CONDITIONS in the winter vary depending on the severity of the weather and the location. Studded tyres are permitted in Sweden and their use is recommended, at least from central Sweden northwards.

Anyone not used to winter driving should not venture out if there is a risk of snow and ice. The major roads are treated with salt, and ploughing is generally good, but even in Skåne in the far south, snow storms can cause traffic chaos and in some years military tracked vehicles have had to be called out.

Getting Around Stockholm

Pedestrians and bicycles

Stockholm is a perfect city for pedestrians. Distances between sights are short, and there is always something interesting to discover among the eye-catching vistas and waterfront scenes. Cycling is popular and there are many cycle lanes throughout the city, although for the visitor a green area such as Djurgården might be more relaxing for a cycle trip. Public transport on buses, trams, underground trains, local trains and ferries is efficient. Apart from Gamla Stan, and during the rush hours, driving a car in Stockholm is relatively easy, although parking can be difficult.

Taking a waterfront stroll along Djurgårdsbrunnsviken

STOCKHOLM ON FOOT

In central Stockholm, walking is the best way to see the sights and get a feel for the place. Road users are more disciplined here than in many other cities. Pedestrians are not allowed to cross a road against a red light, but motorists must stop and give way to pedestrians at zebra crossings without traffic lights.

The clear street signs make it easy to find one's way around, and Stockholmers are always glad to help visitors. There are walking and cycling routes everywhere in the city. Take care not to step out in the cycle lane, which is often marked just with a white line to separate it from the walking lane.

Gamla Stan is a popular area for exploring on foot, and there is always something to see around Kungsträdgården as well. In good weather, nothing beats Djurgården, with its host of attractions set in beautiful parkland only a short distance from the centre.

There are pleasant waterfront walks along the quays, for example from Stadshuset along Norr Mälarstrand and the Riddarfjärden bay.

Walks with multilingual guides are organized regularly, often with a special theme – history, architecture or parks, for example.

CYCLING

The capital's network of cycle paths is increasing all the time, but you need to be an experienced city cyclist if you want to explore the central area from the saddle. Otherwise Stockholm and its surrounding area are tailor-made for cycling. There are plenty of places to hire bicycles and mopeds.

DRIVING IN STOCKHOLM

Anyone familiar with driving in large cities will have no problems in Stockholm. It is relatively easy to get about by car, except during the rush hours (7.30am–9.30am, 11.30am–1pm, and 3.30–6pm). Cars are not really necessary in the city centre because of the short distances between sights and excellent public transport. However, a car is an advantage if you want to explore further afield.

Congestion charges are being introduced on a trial basis during weekdays at the approaches to the city centre.

The speed limit is usually 50 km/h (31 mph), but near schools it is 30 km/h

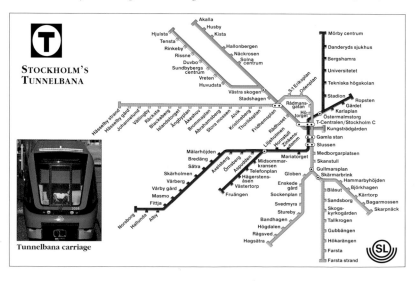

STOCKHOLM'S TUNNELBANA

Tunnelbana carriage

(19 mph). Speeds up to 70 km/h (43 mph) are permitted only on the main roads in and out of the city.

It is often hard to find a parking space. In some areas parking charges apply 24-hours a day, but usually parking is free in the evenings, at night and at weekends. Check for street cleaning times when parking is prohibited.

The city's traffic wardens are diligent. Being wrongly parked could cost you a fine of 450 kr or more. Do not leave valuables in your car, particularly in a car park.

TAXIS

DISTANCES BETWEEN places in the city centre are short and brief journeys by taxi rarely cost more than 100 Kr. There are usually plenty of taxis available, particularly at taxi ranks and major sights, with the exception of the rush hours. You can also hail an empty taxi, indicated by the illuminated sign on the car roof. The best method is to order a taxi by phone or book one in advance. It is always worth enquiring what the fare is likely to be, as many companies charge a fixed rate. Be careful about using unauthorized taxis without a taxi sign on the outside, or a taxi identity card on display inside, especially at night.

PUBLIC TRANSPORT

ALL PUBLIC TRANSPORT in the county of Stockholm is under the control of **Stockholms Lokaltrafik**, but the actual services are run by several companies. An extensive network of local trains, underground trains, buses and ferries carries hundreds of thousands of commuters in from the

Red city bus and blue "feeder" bus

suburbs every day. In the city centre, the Tunnelbana (T-bana) underground system's green, red and blue lines are the mainstay, supplemented by city buses, a few tramlines and ferry routes.

The Stockholm area is divided into five zones, one of which is the city centre. There is a choice of tickets – single trip, one-day, three-day, one-month. It is worth buying a book of 10 or 20 discount coupons if you are planning several trips. Each zone costs 30 kr, but the coupons cut the price to 16 kr. Tickets for a single journey can be bought on departure, while the books of coupons are sold at Pressbyrån outlets, SL stations and T-bana stations.

The network of red city buses is built around a number of blue "feeder" routes

Ferry linking Gamla Stan and Djurgården

which run more frequently. Many streets in the city centre have special bus lanes which speed up the traffic. The best routes for sightseeing are 3, 4, 46, 47, 62 and 69.

Run by **Waxholmsbolaget**, public transport in the archipelago is good all year round, with more frequent services from June to August. An excellent way to explore the archipelago is to take the ferries from Strömkajen, which stop off at countless picturesque jetties along the way.

Other recommended trips include Birka, Drottningholm and Mariefred/Gripsholm *(see pp110–11)*. A popular way of getting to Djurgården is on the ferry from Slussen to Allmänna Gränd. SL's one-day and three-day cards are valid on the Djurgården ferry.

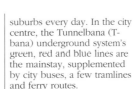

SIGHTSEEING

A PLEASANT WAY of enjoying Stockholm from the water is to take an excursion run by Stockholm Sightseeing (**Strömma Kanalbolaget**). A "Round Kungsholmen" tour departs hourly from the quayside near the City Hall. The "Under Stockholm's Bridges" and "Round Djurgården" tours depart from Strömkajen near the Grand Hotel, and passengers are also picked up from Nybroplan. Tickets can be bought at both these points. A commentary is provided on headsets in several languages. The tours generally run once an hour. Most tours are only available in the summer, but some run until December.

Sightseeing tours by bus include the **Open Top Tours** double-deckers, which run between strategic stops close to attractions in central Stockholm. Passengers can hop on and off along the way.

Page numbers in bold type refer to main entries. The Swedish å, ä and ö fall at the end of the alphabet.

A

Aalto, Alvar 66
ABBA 14, 25
Abelin, Rudolf 174
Abisko 264, 274, 275, 289
Aboda Klint nature reserve 154
Aby Säteri 213
Accommodation see
  Where to stay
Adam of Bremen 129
Adelcrantz, Carl Fredrik 67
  Adolf Fredriks Kyrka
    (Stockholm) 69
  Court Theatre (Drottningholm,
    Stockholm) 109
  Klara Kyrka (Stockholm) 68
  Sturehof (Botkyrka) 137
  Ulriksdal (Stockholm) 97
Admiralitetskyrkan (Karlskrona) 189
Adolf Fredrik, King 52, 54, 57
  Adolf Fredriks Kyrka
    (Stockholm) 69
  Drottningholm 106, 108
  Marinmuseum (Karlskrona) 188
Adventure centres, Boda Borg
  (Dundret) 273
af Chapman (ship, Stockholm) 72,
  74, **77**
Age of Greatness **36–7**, 188, 236
Agriculture 12, 137
Aguéli, Ivan 138
Ahlströmer, Jonas 223
Ahrbom, Per 68
Air travel 328, 329, 330
Aircraft 144–5, 251
Ájtte Fjäll- och Samemuseum
  (Jokkmokk) 273
Akvariet (Gothenburg) 204
Albert Engströmsmuseet
  (Grisslehamn) 127
Albertus Pictor 125, 130, 268
Albrecht of Mecklenburg, King 33
Alby 253
Alcohol 321
Ales Stenar (Kåseberga) 171, **182**
Algotsson, Bishop Brynolf 220
Alingsås 223
Almedalen (Visby) 166
Alnön 254
Alskog 168
Alsnö, Ordinance of 33
Alsters Herrgård 234
Alströmer, Jonas 223
Alvastra Kloster 143, 150
Ammarnäs 274
Amusement parks
  Äventyret Sommarland
    (Leksand) 240
  Gröna Lund (Stockholm) 87
  Lådbilslandet (Löttorp) 156
  Liseberg (Gothenburg) 200
  Parken Zoo (Eskilstuna) 135
  Skara Sommarland **223**, 315
Anckarström, Captain 41
Anderberg, Axel 66, 96
Andersson, Benny 25
Andersson, Dan 236
Andersson, Johan Gunnar 76
Andrée, Salomon August 150
Andrén, Vicke 67
Ånge 253
Ansgar (monk) 130
Anshelm, Klas 177, 179
Anthroposophists 131
Anund Jakob Skötkonung 32
Aqua Nova (Örebro) 239
Aragon, Louis 79

Arboga 123, **137**
Arbrå 27, 248, **252**
Archaeology 31
  see also Bronze Age; Burial
    mounds; Iron Age; Museums and
    galleries; Stone Age; Stone ships
Archipelago Boat Day 27
Architecture 18–19, 24, 75, 76
  see also styles by name
Arendtz, Cornelius 30
Arjeplog 273
Arken (Örnsköldsvik) 255
Armémuseum (Stockholm) 70
Armfelt, Carl Gustaf 259
Art 24
Art galleries see Museums and
  galleries
Arvfurstens Palats (Stockholm)
  64, **67**
Arvidsjaur 273
Arvika 233
Asberget 212
Askersund 236
Asmussen, Erik 131
Asplund, Gunnar 24, 75, **99**,
  105, 197
Asplund (Stockholm) 23, 308
Asschierska Huset (Karlshamn) 187
Astrid Lindgrens Värld
  (Vimmerby) 153
Athletics 15, 315
ATM machines 324
Axel Ebbehallen
  (Trelleborg) 182
Axel Oxenstiernas Palats
  (Stockholm) 50
Axvall 223

B

Babajan restaurant
  (Stockholm) 93
Badande Wännerna 167
Baertling, Olle 66
Balck, Victor 96
Baldersnäs Herrgård 210
Balka, Miroslav 179
Ballet 67, 311, 313
Baltic Aquarium (Stora
  Fjäderholmen) 110
Baltic Sea 36
Bandy 253
Banks 324
Barbecues 21
Barken Viking (Gothenburg) 190,
  195, **196**
Barnens Petes 169
Bassholmen 214–15
Bauer, John 21, 151
Bears, brown 17, 229, 234, 244
"Beauty for All" movement 23
Bed & Breakfast 278, **279**
Beijershamn 155
Bejemark, K G 235
Bellman, Carl Michael 21, 70, 87,
  93, 102
Bengtsfors 210
Bengtsson, Walter 95
Berg 146, 147
Berg, Christer 60
Berga 245
Bergdala 152
Bergeforsen 258
Bergh, Richard 92
Bergman, Ingmar 14, 25, **71**
Bergman, Ingrid 14, 25, 212–13
Bergrum Boliden 267
Bergs Slussar 147
Bergsten, Carl 201
Bergviks Industrimuseum 251
Bernadotte, Jean-Baptiste see Karl
  XIV Johan

Bernadotte Apartments (Royal
  Palace, Stockholm) 55, **56**
Bernadotte dynasty 56, 60
Berns' Salonger
  (Stockholm) 79, 294
Berzelius, Jöns Jacob 25
Bil och Teknikhistoriska
  Samlingarna (Köping) 138
Bildmuseet (Umeå) 266
Billeberga 298
Billingen 222
Biologiska Museet (Stockholm) 87
Birds 16–17
Birger, King 33, 134
Birger Jarl see Magnusson, Birger
Birgersson, Valdemar 32–3
Birka 31, 123, **130–31**
Bjälbo dynsaty 33
Bjälbo Kyrka 145
Bjärehalvön 174
Björk, Oscar 71, 92
Björketorpsstenen 187
Björling, Jussi 25, 237
Björnstierna, Michael 306
Black Death 33
Black Friars 167
Blasieholmen & Skeppsholmen
  (Stockholm) **72–81**, 281, 294
Blasieholmstorg (Stockholm) 79
Blekinge 171, 186–9
Blekinge Museum (Karlskrona) 188
Blom, Henrik 66
Blue Hall (Stadshuset,
  Stockholm) 100
Blå Jungfrun 154–5
Blå Vagen 264, **266–7**
Boat shows 26, 29
Boating 316–17
Boberg, Ferdinand 66, 92, 93
Bocksten Man 226
Boda 23, 153
Boda Borg (Dundret) 273
Boden **269**, 303
Bohlin, Jonas 23
Bohus Fästning (Kungälv) 217
Bohuslän 207–9, 211–19
Bohusläns Försvarsmuseum
  (Uddevalla) 214
Bohusläns Museum (Uddevalla) 214
Bokenäs 214
Boliden 267
Bollerups Borg 182
Bollnäs 27, 252
Bonde, Count Philip 176
Borås **224**, 286, 300
Borensberg 146
Borg, Björn 24, 25, 308
Borgholm **156**, 284, 297
Borgsjö 253
Borgström, Hans 94
Borgviks Bruk 233
Borlänge **237**, 287, 301
Börsen (Gothenburg) 197
Bosjökloster 176
Botanic gardens see Parks and
  gardens
Bothnia, Gulf of 253, 256, 269
Botilsäter 233
Botkyrka 137
Botvidarson, Lafrans 162
Bouchardon, J P 54
Boucher, François 56
Boulognerskogen (Gävle) 250
Böda 156
Brahe, Count Per 150
Brahe, Tycho **174**, 175
Brahehus 140, **150**
Brantevik 298
Branting, Hjalmar 42
Brassworks 138
Breitenfeld, Battle of 36

Bremön (minesweeper) 188
Bridges
  Högakustenbron 256
  Tjörn 216
  Västerbron (Stockholm) 102
  Älvsborgsbron
    (Gothenburg) 205
  Ölandsbron 141, 155
  Öresund 171, 173, **181**
Bro Kyrka 163
Broa 161
Brofjorden 214
Bronze Age 31, 84, **212**
  Gannarve Skeppssättning
    (Gotland) 168
  Jävre 268
  Kinnekulle 221
  Tanum 208, **212**
Brostaden (Malmö) 181
Broström family 204
Brömsebro 187
Brömsehus 187
Brösarps Backar nature
  reserve 183
Bröt-Anund, King 138
Brunflo **259**, 302
Brunkeberg, Battle of 33
Brunkeberg hill (Stockholm) 99
Brunnby Kyrka 174
Bruns Gård pharmacy
  (Hudiksvall) 252
Bunge 162
Bureaux de change 324
Burial mounds 31
  Anundshögen 138
  Ekornavallen 223
  Gammla Uppsala 129
  Gannarve Skeppssättning
    (Gotland) 168
  Hjortsberga Grave Field 187
  Högom 254
  Karleby 223
  Pilane Gravfält (Tjörn) 216
  Skegriedösen 182
Burmeister, Hans 164
Burmeisterska Huset 164
Bus travel 329, 331
Buskgården (Särna) 244
Butterflies 96–7, 222
Byggstam, Per Eddi 255
Bystad 224
Byxelkrok 155, **156**
Båstad 174
Bååtska Palatset (Stockholm) 79
Bäckaskog Slott 186
Bäckaskog Woman 84
Bäckström, Lieutenant Arthur 137
Bärnstensmuseet (Höllviken) 177
Bönhamn 257
Börjesson, John 71
Börsen (Gothenburg) 197
Bünszowska Huset
  (Stockholm) 86

C
Cadier, Régis 77
Calatrava, Santiago 181
Camping 279
Canal holidays 146–7
Cannons 76, 80, 180
Canoeing 124, **316–17**
Capellagården School of Craft and
  Design (Vickleby) 155
Car ferries see Ferries
Car hire 333
Carl Larssongården (Sundborn) 23,
  24, **237**
Carl XVI Gustaf, King 12–13, 54, 57,
  97, 134
Carlberg, Bengt Wilhelm 198
Carlberg, Carl Wilhelm 198, 225

Carlstens Fästning (Marstrand) 216
Carolina Rediviva (Uppsala) 128
Carove, Carlo 97, 98, 106, 108
Carove, Giovanni 106, 108
Casinos 312–13
Castles and fortifications
  Bohus Fästning (Kungälv) 217
  Bollerups Borg 182
  Borgholms Slottsruin 156
  Braheus castle 140, **150**
  Bromsehus 187
  Bulverket (Tingstäde) 163
  Bäckaskog Slott 186
  Carlstens Fästning (Marstrand)
    216
  Citadel (Landskrona) 175
  Eketorps Borg (Öland) 157
  Engsö 136
  Falsterbohus 177
  Gavle Slott 250
  Gråborg 155
  Gräfsnäs Slottsruin and Park 223
  Gripsholms Slott (Mariefred) 122,
    134–5, 136
  Halmstad Slott 227
  Ismantorps Borg (Långlöt) 156–7
  Kalmar Slott 155
  Karlsborg 221
  Karlsvärd fortress (Enholmen)
    162
  Kärnan (Helsingborg) 175
  Kastellet (Karlshamn) 186
  Kastellholmen (Stockholm) 77
  Krapperups Slott 174
  Läckö Slott 209, **220**
  Löfstad Slott 144
  Lojsta Slott 168
  Malmöhus 180
  Nääs Slott 223
  Nya Älvsborgs Fästning 198, **205**
  Nyköpinghus 33, 134
  Oscarsborg (Söderhamn) 251
  Rödbergsfortet (Boden) 269
  Skansen Kronan (Gothenburg)
    201
  Skokloster 123, **127**
  Sofiero 175
  Stegeholm fortress (Västervik)
    154
  Stenhammar 134
  Sturefors 144
  Sunbyholms Slott 135
  Svaneholm 182
  Torpa Stenhus 224
  Torsburgen fortress 168
  Trelleborgen 182
  Trolle-Ljungby 186
  Uppsala Slott 128
  Uraniborg (Ven) 175
  Varbergs Fästning 226
  Vaxholm Fortress 110
  Visby town wall 164, **166**, 167
  Visingsborg Slott 150
  Wanås Slott 186
  Wik 137
  Örebro Slott 237
Cathedrals
  Domkyrka Sta Maria (Visby)
    158, **165**
  Domkyrkan (Kalmar) 155
  Domkyrkan (Linköping) 144
  Domkyrkan (Strängnäs) 135
  Domkyrkan (Västerås) **138**, 311
  Gustavi Domkyrkan
    (Gothenburg) 198
  Karlstad 234
  Luleå 268
  Lunds Domkyrka 177
  Mariestad 221
  St Nicolai (Visby) 167
  St Petri Kyrka (Malmö) 178

Cathedrals (cont.)
  Skara 222
  Storkyrkan (Stockholm) 50, **53**,
    311
  Uppsala Domkyrka 121, **128**, 311
  Växjö 151
Catholicism 13, 34
Caves 163, 169
Cederflychtska Huset (Västervik)
  154
Cederström, Gustav 37, 71, 175
Celsing, Peter 68
Celsius, Anders 24, 25
Cemetery, Skogskyrkogården
  (Stockholm) 24, 99, **105**
Ceramics 226, 308–9
Changing the Guard (Royal Palace,
  Stockholm) 54
Chapels see Churches
Chapman, Fredrik Henrik af 77, 94,
  189, 204
Chinese Pavilion (Drottningholm,
  Stockholm) 108–9
Chirico, Giorgio de 79
Christian I, King of Denmark 33
Christian II, King of Denmark 33–4,
  58
Christian III, King of Denmark 175
Christian IV, King of Denmark 186,
  187, 227
Christianity 31, 32, 123, 130
Christmas 20, 21, 29, 241
Church music 311
Churches
  Admiralitetskyrkan (Karlskrona)
    189
  Adolf Fredriks Kyrka (Stockholm)
    69
  Bjälbo Kyrka 145
  Bro Kyrka 163
  Brunnby Kyrka 174
  Bunge Kyrka 162
  Edestads Kyrka 187
  Finska Kyrkan (Stockholm) 51
  Forshems Kyrka (Kinnekulle) 221
  Fredrikskyrkan (Karlskrona) 188
  Fröjel Kyrka (Gotland) 168
  Frösö Kyrka 259
  Fårö Kyrka 161
  Gårdslösa Kyrka 156
  Gårdstangå Kyrka 177
  Gökhems Kyrka 223
  Gösslunda Kyrka 220
  Hakarps Kyrka 151
  Hedareds Kapell 224
  Helge And (Visby) 167
  Heliga Korsets Kapell
    99, **105**
  Heliga Trefaldighets Kyrka
    (Arboga) 137
  Heliga Trefaldighetskyrkan
    (Gävle) 250
  Heliga Trefaldighetskyrkan
    (Karlskrona) 188
  Heliga Trefaldighetskyrkan
    (Kristianstad) 186
  Herrevadskloster (Klippan) 175
  Härkeberga Kyrka 125, **130**
  Jacobs Kyrka (Stockholm) 65, **66**,
    311
  Kaga Kyrka 144
  Katarina Kyrka (Stockholm) 103
  Kinne-Vedum 221
  Klara Kyrka (Stockholm) 68
  Landskyrkan (Askersund) 236
  Lau Kyrka 168
  Lidens Kyrka 258
  Lojsta Kyrka (Gotland) 168
  Lärbro Kyrka 162
  Nederluleå Kyrka (Gammelstads
    Kyrkstad) 268

Churches (cont.)
  Riddarholmskyrkan (Stockholm)
    60
  Rinkaby Kyrka 186
  Royal Chapel (Stockholm) 54, **57**
  St Jakobs Kyrka (Hudiksval) 252
  Sta Karin (Visby) 165, **166**
  St Nicolai Kyrka (Örebro) 238
  St Nikolai Kyrka (Sölvesborg) 186
  St Olovs Kyrka (Ljusdal) 253
  Sami church (Arvidsjaur) 273
  Sami church (Gällivare) 272
  Själevads Kyrka 255
  Skäfthammars Kyrka (Öregrund)
    126
  Skogskapellet (Stockholm) 105
  Södra Vings Kyrka 224
  Sofia Kyrka (Stockholm) 105
  Stora Kils 228
  Trefaldighetskyrkan (Karlskrona)
    173
  Tronö Kyrka 251
  Tyska Kyrkan (Stockholm) 58–9
  Ulrika Eleonora Kyrka
    (Söderhamn) 251
  Uppståndelsekapellet
    (Stockholm) 105
  Vadstena Klosterkyrka 145
  Valleberga Kyrka 182
  Varnhems Klosterkyrka 222
  Våmbs Kyrka 222
  Älvros 261
Citadel (Landskrona) 175
City (Stockholm) **62–71**, 280–81,
  294
Clarhäll, Lenny 255
Clason, Isak Gustav 71, 86, 88
Climate 12, **28**
Coastline 16
Concert halls *see* Theatres
Conran, Terence 79
Constitution 43
Copenhagen 181
Copper 139, 240, 259
Cottages 278, **279**
Courier services 327
Court Theatre (Drottningholm,
  Stockholm) 109
Cousinet, Jean François 57
Cragg, Tony 179
Crayfish festivals 21, 27
Credit cards 279, 291, 304, **325**
Culture **14**, 40
Currency 324–5
Customs *see* Traditions, customs
  and folklore
Customs House (Sandhamn) 111
Customs regulations 320
Cycling 315, 317, 334
  races 26, 27, 315
Cyrén, Gunnar 306

D
Dacke, Nils 141, 151
Dahlbergh, Erik
  Carlstens Fästning (Marstrand)
    216
  Gothenburg 191, 201
  Karlskrona 188
  Oxenstierna-Soopska chapel
    (Landskyrkan, Askersund) 236
  statue (Uddevalla) 214
Dahlgren, F A 21
Dala horses 241, 306
Dalälvarnas Flottningsmuseum
  (Gysinge) 250
Dalälven delta 250
Dalarna 229–31, 236–7, 240–45
Dalarnas Museum (Falun) 240
Dalby Söderskog 177
Dalén, Gustaf 223

Dalhalla 241
Dalsland 207–11
Dalsland Canal, a tour on 210
Dance 311, 313
Dannemora Gruva (Österbybruk)
  126
Danska Fall 227
Dansmuseet (Stockholm) 64, **67**
Dardel, Nils 78, 99
David Design (Malmö) 23
De Geer, Louis 126, 144
De la Gardie, Jakob 97, 220
De la Gardie, Magnus Gabriel 56,
  98, 220
De Vries, Adrian 106, 109
Defence 15
Delsbo 18, 252
Denmark 33–5, 37, 171
Derkert, Siri 222
Descartes, René 69
Desideria, Queen 93
Design **22–3**, 308–9
Design Torget 23, 308
Desirée, Queen 39
Desprez, Louis Jean 50, 109
Disabled visitors 321
Disagården (Uppsala) 129
Discounts 95, 320–21
Ditzinger, Gustaf Adolf 67
Djurberga 244
Djurgården (Stockholm) 90, 93,
  281, 295
Docksta 256
Dolls' Houses (Nordiska Museet,
  Stockholm) 88
Dolphinarium, Kolmårdens
  Djurpark 144
Domkyrka(n) *see* Cathedrals
Döda Fallet (Jämtland) 258, 268
  (Norrbotten)
Döderhultarmuseet
  (Oskarshamn) 154
"Döderhultarn" (Petersson) 154
Drentwett, Abraham 57
Dress 20, 321
Drinks *see* Food and drink
Driving 332–3, 334–5
Drottningholm 40–41, 56,
  106–9, 137
Dunkers Kulturhus
  (Helsingborg) 175

E
East India Company 194, **198**
Easter 20
Eastern Götaland **140–57**
  getting around 142
  map 142–3
  sights at a glance 143
  where to eat 297–8
  where to stay 283–4
Eastern Svealand **122–39**
  getting around 125
  map 124–5
  sights at a glance 124
  where to eat 296–7
  where to stay 283
Ebbe, Axel 182
Eckstein, Johan Niklas 108
Edestads Kyrka 187
Edmund Skötkonung 32
Eghil, Master 251
Ehrenheim, von, family 136
Ehrenstrahl, David Klöcker von 53,
  61, 108
Eketorps Borg (Öland) **157**, 238
Ekman, P J 197
Ekoparken (Stockholm) **97**, 110
Ekornavallen 223
Ekshärad 234
Eksjö 151

Ekwall, Knut 89
Eldh, Carl 96, 101, 233
Elgström, Ossian 272
Elisabeth Reliquary 85
Elks 17, 21, 217, 317, 332–3
Embassies 323
Emergencies 323
Emigration 12, 39, **151**
Endurance tests 315
Engelbrekt Engelbrektsson 33, 101,
  187, 231
Engelsbergs Bruk (Fagersta)
  123, **138–9**
Englundsgården Cultural Heritage
  Centre (Kalix) 269
Engman, Kjell 153
Engsö 136
Engström, Albert 127
Engström, Leander 92
Enköping 130
Entertainment 310–13
Environment 13
Enånger 253
Erici, Andreas 253
Ericson, Sigfrid 200
Ericsson, John 25, **235**
Ericsson, L M 25
Ericsson, Nils 210, 235
Erik XIV, King 34, 66, 151, 187
  crown 57
  orb 46
  tomb (Domkyrkan, Västerås) 138
Erik Klipping, King of Denmark 227
Erik of Pomerania 33, 180
Eriksberg Vilt- och Naturpark 187
Eriksbergsvarvet (Gothenburg) 205
Eriksson, Amalia 150
Eriksson, Christian 71, 93, 101,
  233, 272
Eriksson, King Erik 32
Eriksson, Gustav *see* Gustav I Vasa
Eriksson, Liss 222
Eriksson, Nils Einar 201
Erixson, Sven 105, 201
Erlandsson, Theodor 162
Erskine, Ralph 196
Eskilstuna **135**, 283
Esrange 272
Etiquette 20, 321
Etnografiska Museet (Stockholm) 93
Eugen, Prince 92–3, 100, 201, 272
Events calendar 26–9
Evert Taubes Terrass
  (Stockholm) 60
Evertsberg 245

F
Fagerberg, Carl 96
Fagersta 138–9
Fahlsten, Lars 68
Fahlströmska Gården (Arboga) 137
Falbygden 208
Falbygdens Museum
  (Falköping) 223
Falkenberg **226**, 286
Falköping 33, **223**
Falsterbo 177
Falun **240**, 287, 301
Farmers' Party 42
Fashion 308–9
Father Christmas 241, 269
Fattighuset (Halmstad) 227
Ferlin, Nils 235
Ferries 329, 331, 332–3
Fersen, Axel von 47, 130
Feskekörka (Gothenburg) 192, **201**
Festivals 20, 26–9, 312–13
Filipstad 28, **235**
Film 14, **25**, 217, 313
Finnhamn 111
Finska Kyrkan (Stockholm) 51

Fish 16, 27, 28
Fishing 21, 317
Fishing industry 186, 215, 216
Fiske- och Sjöfartsmuseet
  (Umeå) 266
Fiskebäckskil 120, 215
Fjaestad, Gustaf 233
Fjäderholmarna 110
Fjällbacka **212–13**, 286
Fjällgatan (Stockholm) 104
Fjärils- & Fågelhuset (Hagaparken,
  Stockholm) 96–7
Flen 134
Flora 17
Flygvapenmuseum (Malman)
  144–5
Fogelberg, Bengt Erland
  195, 197
Fogelström, Per Anders 104
Folk movements 39
Folk music 14, **21**, 311, 313
Folklore see Traditions, customs
  and folklore
Folkung dynasty 32, 141
Food and drink 21, **290–93**,
  307, 309
Football 15, 199
Foreign policy 15
Forests 17
Forsbacka 211
Forseth, Einar 100
Forshems Kyrka (Kinnekulle) 221
Forsmarks Bruk 126
Forsmarks Kärnkraftverk 126
Forsviks Bruk (Karlsborg) 221
Fossum 212
Fotomuseet Olympia (Falkenberg)
  227
Foucquet, Jacques 37
Frank, Josef 22, 306
Franzén, Anders 91
Fredman, Jean 93
Fredriksdal Friluftsmuseum
  (Helsingborg) 175
Fredrikshald, siege of 35, 37, 52
Fredrikskyrkan (Karlskrona) 188
Free Church 13
Fretwork 19
Fridman, Sigrid 99
Friluftsmuseet Fiskartorpet
  (Strömstad) 211
Frostavallen 176
Fröä Gruva 259
Fröding, Gustaf 234
Frölén, Sture 95
Frösö Kyrka 259
Frösö Zoo 259
Frösön 258
Fryken Lakes 120, 229, **232**
Fryksås 244
Fryksdalsbanan 230, 232
Fulufjället National Park 244
Funäsdalen 260
Functionalist style 24, 83, 95, 99,
  105
Furuviksparken (Gävle) 251
Fyrisån river 128, 129
Fårö **161**, 169
Fårösund 162
Fängelsemuseet (Gävle) 251
Färjestaden 155
Färnebofjärden 250

G

Galtström 254
Gamla Haga (Gothenburg) **201**,
  202–3
Gamla Linköping 144
Gamla Stan (Stockholm) **48–61**,
  280, 294
Gamla Uppsala 129

Gamla Örlogsvarvet (Karlskrona)
  188–9
Gammel-Remsgården 261
Gammelgården (Mora) 229
Gammelstads Kyrkstad 263,
  268, 303
Gammelstan (Norrboda) 241
Gammelvala Brunnskog 27
Gammlia Friluftsmuseum
  (Umeå) 266
Gannarve Skeppssättning
  (Gotland) 168
Garbo, Greta 14, 25, **105**, 154
Gate, Simon 153
Gathenhielm, Lars 204
Gathenhielmska Huset
  (Gothenburg) 204
Gegerfelt, Victor von 201
Gene Fornby 255
Gesunda 241
Geunja Lapp 265
Gimo Manor 126
Gjörwell, C C 98
Glaciers 12
Glassware **22–3**, 306, 308–9
  Kingdom of Crystal 27, 121,
    152–3
  Småland 23, 27, 141, 151
Glimmingehus 183
Globen (Stockholm) 29, 105,
  310–11
Gold 267
Gold Room (Historiska Museet,
  Stockholm) 85
Golden Room (Stadshuset,
  Stockholm) 100
Golf 15, 316, 317
Gordon, Willy 60
Gothenburg **190–205**
  boat tours 205
  climate 28
  events 29, 312–13
  getting there 193
  history 191
  map 192–3
  sights at a glance 192
  where to eat 299–300
  where to stay 286
Gotland **158–69**, 187
  events 27, 111, 159
  getting around 161
  map 160–61
  ponies 159, **168**
  sights at a glance 160
  where to eat 298
  where to stay 284–5
Gotlands Djurpark (Alskog) 168
Gotlands Fornsal (Visby) 164, **166**
Gotska Sandön 169
Government 12–13
Grafikens Hus (Mariefred) 134–5
Granbergsdals Hytta 235
Grand Hôtel (Stockholm) 77
Granqvist, Carl Jan 139
Grate, Eric 222
Greenaway, Peter 179
Gren, Gunnar 199
Grenna Museum (Gränna) 150
Grevagården (Karlskrona) 188
Grilska Huset (Stockholm) 58
Grinda 110–11
Grip, Bo Johnsson 134
Gripsholms Slott (Mariefred) 122,
  134–5, 136
Grisslehamn 27, **127**
Grundsund 215
Grut, Torben 96
Gruvmuseet (Falun) 240
Grythyttan 139
Gråborg 155
Gråsten, Viola 66

Gräfsnäs Slottsruin and Park 223
Grängesberg Lokmuseum 236
Gränna 141, 150
Gröna Lund (Stockholm) 87
Grönsöö 136
Grövelsjön **244**, 274
Grünewald, Isaac 69, 92
Gudhems Klosterruin and
  Klostermuseum 223
Gudmarsson, Birgitta see St Bridget
Gudmarsson, Ulf 145
Guillou, Jan 24, 220
Gulf Stream 12
Gullesson, Håkon 253
Gullholmen 215
Gunnebo Slott 207, **225**
Gustaf, Prince 236
Gustav I Vasa, King 30, 34, 58, 60
  Domkyrkan (Strängnäs) 135
  Hagaparken (Stockholm) 96
  Livrustkammaren
    (Stockholm) 52
  Mora 241
  Örnässtugan 231, **237**
  statue (Nordiska Museet,
    Stockholm) 89
  tomb (Uppsala Domkyrka) 128
  Vasaloppet ski race 245
Gustav II Adolf, King 34–5, 36,
  57, 90
  equestrian statue (Stockholm) 64
  statue, Gothenburg 195, 197
  statue (Sundsvall) 254
  Streiff statue 51, 52
  tomb 60
Gustav III, King 24, 38, **40–41**,
  52, 58
  Drottningholm (Stockholm) 109
  Malmö 180
  Museum of Antiquities
    (Stockholm) 55, **57**
  Pavilion (Hagaparken,
    Stockholm) 96
  Royal Palace (Stockholm) 55,
    56, 57
  statue 51
  theatre, Gripsholms Slott
    (Mariefred) 134
Gustav IV Adolf , King 38, 97
Gustav V, King 42, 93, 131
Gustav VI Adolf, King 60, 76, 175
Gustav Adolf Day (Gothenburg) 29
Gustav Adolfs Torg (Gothenburg)
  195, **197**
Gustavi Domkyrkan
  (Gothenburg) 198
Gustavian style 41
Gustavianum (Uppsala) 128
Gyllenhielm, Admiral Karl
  Karlsson 98
Gårdstangå Kyrka 177
Gällivare 263, **272–3**
Gärdet (Stockholm) 26, 83, 95
Gärdslösa Kyrka 156
Gästrikland 247–51
Gävle 247, **250–51**, 288, 302
Gökhems Kyrka 223
Gösslunda Kyrka 220
Göta Canal 141, 142, **146–7**, 221
Götaplatsen (Gothenburg) 120,
  200–1
Göteborgs Maritima Centrum 194,
  197
Göteborgs Stadsmuseum 194, **198**
GöteborgsOperan 194,
  196–7, 311
Götene 221
Götesam, Staffan 86
Göthe, Erik 66
Göteborgsl Itikien 195, **196**
Göthlinska Gården 139

H

Hagaparken (Stockholm) 96–7
Hagfors 234
Hakarps Kyrka 151
Hall, Johan 225
Hall of State (Royal Palace, Stockholm) 54, **56–7**
Halland 28, 207–9, 226–7
Hallands Väderö 174
Hallwyl, Walther and Wilhelmina von 71
Hallwylska Palatset (Stockholm) 46, **71**
Halmstad 208, **227**, 287, 300
Hammarby 124, **129**
Hammarskjöld, Dag 15, 24, 25
Handicrafts 165, 182, **306–9**
Handöl 259
Hanö 186
Hans Hedbergs Museum (Örnsköldsvik) 255
Hanseatic League 32, 58, 166–7, 182
Hansen, Jacob 175
Hansson, Per Albin 42
Haparanda **269**, 289
Harald Blue Tooth 182
Harbour, Gothenburg 205
Harg 126
Harpsund 134
Hasselberg, Per 92
Hasselberg-Olsson, Elizabeth 61
Haupt, Georg 56–7, 67, 80, 106
Haupt, Georg (grandfather) 57
Haverö Strömmar 253
Havets Hus (Lysekil) 214
Hazelius, Artur 88
Health 323
Hebel, Hans 66
Hedareds Kapell 224
Hedberg, Hans 22, 255
Hedemora 236–7
Hedin, Sven 93
Hedvig Eleonora, Queen 97, 107, 108
Heidenstam, Verner von 145, 154
Heineman, Hans-Erland 222
Helags 248, 260
Helénsgården (Skövde) 222
Helge And (Visby) 167
Helgeandsholmen (Stockholm) 49
Hellerström, Alfred 175
Helsingborg **174–5**, 285, 298
Hemavan 264, 267, **274**
Hembygdsparken (Nässjö) 151
Hennen, Jobst 59
Henning, Gerhard 200
Herrevadskloster (Klippan) 175
Hidemark, Ove 103
High Coast **256–7**, 288
Hiking 13, 21, **314**
Hill, Carl Fredrik 92
Hill, Joe 250
Hilleström, Pehr 40, 109
Himmelstalund (Norrköping) 144
Hindersmässen (Örebro) 29
Hirschska Huset (Sundsvall) 254
History plays 21
Hjertén, Sigrid 92
Hjo 27, **222**
Hjorth, Bror 272
Hjortsberga Grave Field 187
Hjortzberg, Olle 68
Hjärne, Urban 145
Hoburgen 159, **169**
Holiday houses 14, 21
Holmöarna 266
Holocaust Museum (Stockholm) 79
Hoppet (schooner) 94
Horn, Gustav 67, 79
Hornborgasjön lake 26, **223**

Hornbrytare, Härjulf 261
Hornsgatan (Jansson) 93
Horse riding 316
Hospitals 323
Hot-air ballooons, Gränna 150
Hotell Knaust (Sundsvall) 254
Hotels **278–89**
  booking 278, 279
  prices 278–9
Hovs Hallar nature reserve 174
Hovstallet (Stockholm) 70
Huberget rural heritage centre 253
Hudiksvall **252–3**, 288, 302
Humlegården (Stockholm) 70
Hunnebostrand 213
Hunting 21, 317
Husaby 32, 207, **220**
Husbyringen 237
Huss, Magnus (Vildhussen) 258
Huså Bruk 259
Huså Herrgård 259
Huts, mountain 314–15
Hydman-Vallien, Ulrika 152
Hydroelectricity 217, 250, 267, 273
Håkon Magnusson, King of Norway 217
Hållö 213
Hårleman, Carl 24
  Drottningholm (Stockholm) 106
  Göteborgs Stadsmuseum 194, **198**
  Jacobs Kyrka (Stockholm) 66
  Klara Kyrka (Stockholm) 68
  Observatory (Stockholm) 99
  Övedskloster 176–7
  Riddarholmskyrkan (Stockholm) 60
  Royal Chapel (Stockholm) 57
  Royal Palace (Stockholm) 55, 56
  Ulriksdal (Stockholm) 97
  Uppsala Slott 128
Håverud aqueduct 210
Hägg, Axel 168
Hällevik 186
Hälsingehambo marathon dance 27, 252, 253
Hälsingland 18–19, 247–9, 251–3
Hälsinglands Museum (Hudiksvall) 252, 253
Härjedalen 247–9, **260–61**
Härjedalens Fjällmuseum (Funäsdalen) 260
Härkeberga Kyrka 125, **130**
Härnösand **254**, 288
Högakustenbron 256
Högbo 251
Högbonden 257
Höglund, Erik 188
Högsbyn Rock Carvings 210
Höör 176

I

Ice Age 31
Ice Globe Theatre (Jukkasjärvi) 29, **272**
Ice Hotel (Jukkasjärvi) 121
Idre 244
Idrefjäll 244
Iggesund 252
IKEA 304–5
Immigration 12, 13, 14
Indalsälven river 258
Industrial revolution 39
Industrimuseum (Mariestad) 221
Industry 12
Information technology 14
Ingrid Bergmans Torg (Fjällbacka) 213
Inlandsbanan 230, 248, 273, 331
Innovatum Kunskapens Hus (Trollhättan) 217

Interior design 308–9
Internet services 14, 326–7
Inventors 25
Iron Age 31
  Bollnäs Museum 252
  Eketorps Borg (Öland) 157
  Gene Fornby 255
  Gråborg 155
  Ljugarn 168
  Lojstahallen 168
  Neptuni Åkrar 156
  Pilane Gravfält (Tjörn) 216
  Seby Gravfält (Öland) 157
  Skäftekärr Järnåldersby (Böda) 156
Isaac, Aaron 98
Ismantorps Borg (Långlöt) 156–7
Iwersson, Gottlieb 67
Izikowitz, Jan 197

J

Jacobs Kyrka (Stockholm) 65, **66**, 311
Jacobsen, Arne 66
Jaenecke, Fritz 199
Jamtli (Östersund) 258, 259
Jansson, Eugène 92, 93
Jarramas (training ship, Karlskrona) 188
Jazz 28, **312–13**
Jewish Centre (Stockholm) 79
Jews 25, 81, 98–9
Joe Hill Gården (Gävle) 250
Johan III, King 34, 66, 68, 138, 157
  tomb (Uppsala Domkyrka) 128
Johannishus Åsar 187
Johannson, Cyrillus 98, 110
Johansfors 153
Johnsson, Ivar 96, 99, 204
Jokkmokk 29, **273**
Jolin, Einar 92
Jonasson, Mats 153
Jonze, Paul 258
Josephson, Ernst 200
Judiska Museet (Stockholm) 98–9
Jugendstil 61, 71, 110
Jukkasjärvi 29, 121, 263, **272**
Julita Gård 124, **137**
Jungstedt, Axel 67
Junibacken (Stockholm) **86**, 87
Jussi Björlingmuseet (Borlänge) 237
Jämtland 27, 187, 247–9, 258–9
Järnvägsmuseum (Nässjö) 151
Järvsö 27, 252, 253
Jönköping **150–51**, 283, 297
Jörgen Kocks Hus (Malmö) 178
Jösse 233

K

Kaga Kyrka 144
Kaitumsjön lake 262
Kaknästornet (Stockholm) 94–5
Kalix 269
Kalixälven river 269
Kallbadhuset (Varberg) 226
Kalmar **155**, 283, 297
Kalmar Union 33, 155
Kalmarsund 141, 154, 155
Kanalmuseet (Mariestad) 221
Kandell, John 23
Kapelludden (Öland) 148–9
Kapitelhusgården (Visby) 165
Karl IX, King 34, 135, 235
  Arvidsjaur 273
  Karlstad 233
  Örebro Slott 238
Karl X Gustav, King 35, 103, 157
  portrait 37
  statue (Uddevalla) 214
Karl XI, King 35, 37, 220

Karl XI, King (cont.)
 Carolus XI (Sjöhistorika Museet,
  Stockholm) 94
 Karl XI Gallery (Drottningholm,
  Stockholm) 108
 Karl XI Gallery (Royal Palace,
  Stockholm) 37, 55, 56
 Karlskrona 173
Karl XII, King 35, 37, 60
 Karl XII's Hus (Ystad) 182
 Karlbergs Slott (Stockholm) 98
 Länsmuseet Varbergs
  Fästning 226
 Livrustkammaren (Stockholm) 52
 statue (Stockholm) 65, 66
Karl XIII, King 13, 65, 66
Karl XIV Johan, King 12–13,
  38–9, 57
 Bernadotte Apartments (Royal
  Palace, Stockholm) 55, 56
 Göta Canal 146
 Karlsborg 221
 Örebro Slott 238
 tomb 60
Karl XV, King 70, 97, 238
Karl Knutsson, King 60
Karlbergs Slott (Stockholm) 98
Karleby 223
Karlevistenen 155
Karlfeldt, Erik Axel 240
Karlfeldtsgården – Sångs i
  Sjugare 240
Karlsborg 221
Karlshamn 186–7
Karlskoga 235
Karlskrona 171, 186, 188–9
 hotels 285
 map 189
 restaurants 298
Karlslunds Herrgård (Örebro) 239
Karlsöarna 168–9
Karlstad 234, 287, 301
Karlsvärd fortress (Enholmen) 162
Kastellet (Karlshamn) 186
Kastellholmen 73, 77
Katarina Kyrka (Stockholm) 103
Katarinahissen (Stockholm) 103
Katthammarsvik 168
Kebnekaise massif 270–71,
  272, 275
Key, Ellen 150
Kil 232
King Chulalongkorn Memorial
  (Utanede) 258
Kingdom of Crystal 27, 121, 142,
  152–3
Kinne-Vedum 221
Kinnekulle 220–21
Kirkeby, Per 179
Kirsten Munk's house
  (Halmstad) 227
Kiruna 272, 289, 303
Kivik 183
Klarälven river 229, 234
Klintehamn 285
Klippan 175
Kloster 237
Klostergränden (Trelleborg) 182
Klässbols Linneväveri 233
Knitwear 224, 307
Kock, Jörgen 178
Kolmården 141
Kolthoff, Gustaf 87
Kommendanthuset (Malmö) 180
Konserthuset *see* Theatres
Konsthall/Konstmuseet *see*
  Museums and galleries
Kopparberg 139
Kosta Glasbruk 121, 152–3, 308–9
Koster Islands 211
Köping 138

Köpmantorget (Stockholm) 51
Krämm, Johann 255
Krapperups Slott 174
Kremberg, Jacob 177
Kreuger, Nils 92
Kristianopel 187
Kristianstad 186, 285, 298
Kristina, Queen of Sweden 35,
  52, 60
 summer house (Stockholm)
  65, 66
 throne 54, 56
Kristinehamn 235
Kristler, Hans Jakob 97
Krok, Olof 104
Kronan (man-of-war) 155
Kronberg, Julius 69, 71
Kronhuset (Gothenburg) 195, 197
Krusmyntagården 163
Kukkolaforsen 27
Kulbackens Museum (Västervik)
  154
Kullabygden 174
Kulturen (Lund) 177
Kulturens Östarp 176
Kulturhuset (Skövde) 222
Kulturhuset (Ytterjärna) 131
Kungajaktmuseet Älgens Berg
  (Hunneberg) 217
Kungälv 217
Kungliga Biblioteket (Stockholm)
  70
Kungliga Dramatiska Teatern
  (Stockholm) 71
Kungliga Konsthögskolan
  (Stockholm) 74, 77
Kungliga Myntkabinettet 51, 52
Kungliga Operan (Stockholm) 64,
  66–7
Kungliga Slottet *see* Royal Palace
Kungsbacka 226
Kungshamn 19
Kungsholmen 83, 281–2, 295
Kungsleden Trail 260, 263, 274–5
Kungsträdgården (Stockholm) 64–5,
  66
Kyllaj 162
Kåseberga 182
Källemo 23
Kämpen rural heritage centre
  (Bollnäs) 252
Käringön 215
Kärnan (Helsingborg) 175

L
Laestadius, Lars Levi 269, 272
Laestadius Pörte 269
Lagerlöf, Selma 24, 105, 233
 Mårbacka 229, 230, 232
Laholm 227
Lallerstedt, Erik 110
Lamberg, Johan Anders 200
Landscape 11–12, 16–17
Landskrona 175, 285, 298
Landskyrkan (Askersund) 236
Landstingsmuseet 238
Languages and dialects 13–14
Laponia 264, 272, 275
Lappland 263–5, 270–75
Lapps *see* Sami
L'Archevêques, Pierre Hubert 64
Larsen, Henning 180
Larsson, Carl 23, 24, 237
 Carl Larssongården (Sundborn)
  237
 Konstmuseet (Gothenburg) 200
 Kungliga Dramatiska Teatern
  (Stockholm) 71
 Kungliga Operan (Stockholm) 67
 Nationalmuseum (Stockholm) 81
 Thielska Galleriet (Stockholm) 93

Larsson, Karin 22–3, 237
Lassekrog 253
Lau Kyrka 168
Laxens Hus (Mörrum) 187
Legends *see* Myths and legends
Leipzig, Battle of 39
Leksand 21, 240
Lerkaka 157
Lewerentz, Sigurd 105
Liberal party 42
Lidens Kyrka 258
Lidingö 24, 28, 95
Lidköping 220, 287
Liljefors, Bruno 24, 87, 92
 Liljeforsateljén (Österbybruk) 126
 Stadion (Stockholm) 96
 Thielska Galleriet (Stockholm) 93
Liljekrantz, Johan 137
Liljevalch, C F 87
Liljevalchs Konsthall (Stockholm)
  26, 87
Lilla Bommen (Gothenburg) 190,
  196, 205
Lilla Karlsö 168–9
Lillhärdal 261
Lilljekvist, Fredrik 71
Limhamn (Malmö) 181
Limtorget (Lidköping) 220
Lind, Jenny 25
Lindegren, Agi 87
Lindgren, Astrid 24, 87, 141
 Fjällbacka 213
 Junibacken (Stockholm) 86
 Lunds By 154
 Vimmerby 153
Lindh, Anna 25
Lindroos, Bengt 94
Lindström, Rune 21, 240
Ling, P H 96
Linköping 141, 144–5, 284, 297
Linné, Carl von 17, 25, 26, 128
 Botaniska Trädgården (Uppsala)
  129
 Hammarby 124, 129
 Naturhistoriska Riksmuseet
  (Stockholm) 96
 Uppsala University 38, 128
 on Västerbotten 263
Linnquist, Hilding 99
Liseberg (Gothenburg) 200
Literature 24
Livrustkammaren
  (Stockholm) 51, 52
Ljugarn 168
Ljungadalen 153
Ljusdal 253
LKAB InfoMine (Kiruna) 272
LKAB's Gruvmuseum
  (Gällivare) 272
Lohe Treasure (Stockholms
  Stadsmuseum) 102
Lojsta 168
Loka Brunn 139
Lost property 322–3
Lovisa Ulrika, Queen 52, 106–7,
  108–9
Lucia 20, 29
Ludvika 236
Luleå 28, 268, 289, 303
Lummelundagrottorna 163
Lund 177, 285, 299
Lundberg, Theodor 71
Lundberg, Willy Maria 252
Lundgren, Per 97
Lundqvist, John 105
Lunds By 154
Lundström brothers 150
Lundstömska Gården (Sigtuna) 130
Luossastugan (Skattlösberg) 236
Lurö 233
Lutfisk 216

Lutheran Church 13, 34
Lycksele 266, **267**, 289, 303
Lysekil 214
Lådbilslandet (Löttorp) 156
Långban 235
Långbryggan pier (Rättvik) 240–41
Länge Jan (Öland) 157
Länge Raden (Stockholm) 75
Långholmen (Stockholm) 102
Länsmuseet *see* Museums and
  galleries
Läckö Slott 209, **220**
Lärbro 162
Löfstad Slott 144
Löka (Gundbo) 252
Lövånger 267
Lövstabruk 126
Lübeck 34, 58, 167
Lützen, Battle of 35, 36, 52, 197

M
M/S Juno 146, 147
Madeleine, Princess 10
Magnus Eriksson, King 33, 151, 238
Magnus Ladulås, King 33, 60, 150,
  227
Magnus, Olaus 128
Magnusson, Arn 21
Magnusson, Birger 32, 53, 60, 145
Malmahed (Malmköping) 134
Malmarna and further afield
  (Stockholm) 82–111
Malmbanan railway 274, 275
Malmköping 134
Malmö 28, 171, **178–81**
  hotels 285
  map 179
  restaurants 299
Malmsten, Carl 101, 155
Mamsell Josabeth's Steps
  (Stockholm) 104
Mankell, Henning 24
Maps
  Dalsland Canal 210
  Drottningholm 108
  Eastern Götaland 142–3
  Eastern Svealand 124–5
  Fryken Lakes 232
  Gothenburg 192–3
  Gothenburg: Inner Harbour 205
  Gothenburg: Västra Nordstan
    194–5
  Gotland 160–61
  Karlskrona 189
  Kingdom of Crystal 152–3
  Mälardalen's castles 136–7
  Malmö 179
  Northern Norrland 264–5
  Örebro 239
  Österlen 183
  Southern Götaland 172–3
  Stockholm 46–7
  Stockholm: Blasieholmen &
    Skeppsholmen 73, 74–5
  Stockholm: City 63, 64–5
  Stockholm: Fjällgatan 104
  Stockholm: Gamla Stan 49,
    50–51
  Stockholm: Malmarna & Further
    Afield 83
  Stockholm: street finder 112–17
  Sweden 8–9, 120–21
  Uppsala 129
  Visby 164–5, 166
  Western Götaland 208–9
  Western Svealand 230–31
Marathon, Stockholm 27, 315
Marcus Wallenberg-hallen
  (Södertälje) 131
Mardsele falls 267
Maré, Rolf de 67

Margareta, Queen of Denmark-
  Norway 33
Maria from Viklau (sculpture) 85
Maria of Pfalz 221
Maria Eleonora, Queen 60
Marie Euphrosyne, Princess 220
Marieberg porcelain factory 137
Mariebergsskogen 234
Mariefred 134–5
Mariestad 221
Markets 27–9, **308**
Marklund, Bror 84
Marstrand 208, **216–17**, 218–19,
  287
Masreliez, Jean-Baptiste 56
Masreliez, Louis 67, 96
Matchsticks 150–51
Mathsson, Bruno 22
May Day 20, 26
Mecklenburg, Duke of 33
Medelhavsmuseet (Stockholm) 64,
  67
Medelpad 247–9, 253–4
Medeltidsmuseet (Stockholm) 61
Medevi Brunn 145
Media 14, 327
Medicines 323
Medieval festivals 21, 27
Mellbystrand 227
Mem 147
Midsummer 20, **27**, 223
Milles, Carl 24, 71
  Boulognerskogen (Gävle) 250
  Europa and the Bull fountain
    (Halmstad) 227
  Millesgården (Stockholm) 24, **95**
  Nike 120
  Nordiska Museet (Stockholm) 89
  Orpheus 69
  Poseidon (Götaplatsen,
    Gothenburg) 120, 193, 200
  Skogskapellet (Stockholm) 105
  Stadsparken (Eskilstuna) 135
  Ulriksdal (Stockholm) 97
Millesvik 233
Miniland (Halmstad) 227
Moberg, Vilhelm 151
Mobile phones 326
Moderna Museet (Stockholm) 47,
  75, **78–9**
Modernism 68
Molin, J P 65, 66
Mollösund 216
Monarchy 12–13, 43
Monasteries
  Alvastra Kloster 143, 150
  Gudhems Klosterruin 223
  Herrevadskloster (Klippan) 175
  Kloster 237
  Klostergränden (Trelleborg) 182
  Roma Kloster 163
  St Nicolai (Visby) 167
Moneo, Rafael 75, **78**
Mora 27, 229, **241**, 245
  hotels 288
  restaurants 301
Moritska Gården (Umeå) 266
Mörrumsån river 26, **187**
Morups Tånge 227
Moskosel 273
Mosquitoes 323
Motormuseum, Skokloster 127
Muddus National Park
  273, 275
Mulen 244
Munch, Edvard 93
Munthe, Ulf 99
Museums and galleries
  agricultural museum (Julita
    Gård) 137
  Aguélimuseet (Sala) 138

Museums and galleries (cont.)
  Ájtte Fjäll- och Samemuseum
    (Jokkmokk) 273
  Albert Engströmsmuseet
    (Grisslehamn) 127
  Alingsås Kulturhus 223
  Alingsås Museum 223
  Amals Hembygdsmuseum 211
  Arbetets Museum (Norrköping)
    144
  Arkitekturmuseet (Stockholm)
    75, **76**
  Armémuseum (Stockholm) 70
  Arvika Fordonsmuseum 233
  Axel Ebbehallen (Trelleborg) 182
  Barnens Petes 169
  Bellman museum
    (Långholmen) 102
  Bergrum Boliden 267
  Bergviks Industrimuseum 251
  Bil och Teknikhistoriska
    Samlingarna (Köping) 138
  Bildmuseet (Umeå) 266
  Biologiska Museet
    (Stockholm) 87
  Birkamuseet 131
  Blekinge Museum
    (Karlskrona) 188
  Bohusläns Försvarsmuseum
    (Uddevalla) 214
  Bohusläns Museum
    (Uddevalla) 214
  Bollnäs Museum 252
  Borås Museum 224
  Borgsjö rural heritage centre 253
  Bungemuseet (Bunge) 162
  Buskagården (Särna) 244
  Båtmuseet (Galtabäck) 226
  Bärnstensmuseet (Höllviken) 177
  Cultural Centre (Steninge Slott,
    Sigtuna) 130
  Dalälvarnas Flottningsmuseum
    (Gysinge) 250
  Dalarnas Museum (Falun) 240
  Dalénmuseet (Stenstorp) 223
  Dansmuseet (Stockholm) 64, **67**
  Disagården (Uppsala) 129
  Dunkers Kulturhus
    (Helsingborg) 175
  Döderhultarmuseet
    (Oskarshamn) 154
  Etnografiska Museet
    (Stockholm) 93
  Falbygdens Museum
    (Falköping) 223
  Falkenbergs Hembygdsmuseum
    226–7
  Falkenbergs Museum 226
  Falsterbo Konsthall 177
  Falsterbo Museum 177
  Fishing museum (Hällevik) 186
  Fiske- och Sjöfartsmuseet
    (Umeå) 266
  Flygvapenmuseum (Malmen)
    144–5
  Forsviks Bruk (Karlsborg) 221
  Fotomuseet Olympia
    (Falkenberg) 227
  Fredriksdal Friluftsmuseum
    (Helsingborg) 175
  Friluftsmuseet Fiskartorpet
    (Strömstad) 211
  Fängelsemuseet (Gävle) 251
  Gamla Linköping 144
  Gammlia Friluftsmuseum
    (Umeå) 266
  Garvaregården (Kåkstan) 131
  Gotlands Fornsal (Visby)
    164, **166**
  Grafikens Hus (Mariefred) 134–5
  Grenna Museum (Gränna) 150

Museums and galleries (cont.)
Grängesberg Lokmuseum 236
Gruvmuseet (Falun) 240
Gudhems Klostermuseum 223
Gustav III's Museum of
Antiquities (Stockholm) 55, **57**
Göteborgs Maritima Centrum
(Gothenburg) 194, **197**
Göteborgs Stadsmuseum
194, **198**
Göthlinska Gården 139
Hallwylska Palatset (Stockholm)
46, **71**
Hans Hedbergs Museum
(Örnsköldsvik) 255
Historiska Museet (Lund) 177
Historiska Museet (Stockholm)
84–5
Hjo Stadsmuseum 222
Holmöns Båtmuseum 266
Huberget rural heritage centre
253
Hälsinglands Museum
(Hudiksvall) 252, 253
Härjedalens Fjällmuseum
(Funäsdalen) 260
Innovatum Kunskapens Hus
(Trollhättan) 217
Jamtli (Östersund) 258, 259
Joe Hill Gården (Gävle) 250
Judiska Museet (Stockholm) 98–9
Julita Gård 124, **137**
Jussi Björlingmuseet
(Borlänge) 237
Järnvägsmuseum (Nässjö) 151
Jönköpings Läns Museum 151
Kalmar Konstmuseum 155
Kalmar Läns Museum 155
Kalmar Sjöfartsmuseum 155
Karlshamns Konsthall 186
Karlshamns Museum 186
Klockarbolet (Odensåker) 221
Kommendanthuset (Malmö) 180
Konstgalleriet (Uddevalla) 214
Konsthallen (Gothenburg) 201
Konstmuseet (Gothenburg) 200–1
Konstmuseet (Visby) 164
Konstmuseum (Uppsala
Slott) 128
Kopparbergs Miljömuseer 139
Koversta rural heritage centre
(Österfärnebo) 250
Kulbackens Museum
(Västervik) 154
Kulturen (Lund) 177
Kulturens Östarp 176
Kulturhuset (Skövde) 222
Kulturhuset and Stadsteatern
(Stockholm) 68
Kungajaktmuseet Älgens Berg
(Hunneberg) 217
Kämpen rural heritage centre
(Bollnäs) 252
Laestadius Pörte 269
Laholms Teckningsmuseum 227
Landskrona Museum 175
Landstingsmuseet 238
Laxens Hus (Mörrum) 187
Lerkaka Linmuseum 157
Lighthouse (Bönan) 19
Liljevalchs Konsthall (Stockholm)
26, 87
Limhamn Museum 181
Livrustkammaren (Stockholm)
51, **52**
Ljusdalsbygdens Museum 253
LKAB InfoMine (Kiruna) 272
LKAB's Gruvmuseum
(Gällivare) 272
Ludvika Gammelgård och
Gruvmuseum 236

Museums and galleries (cont.)
Lunds Konsthall 177
Länsmuseet Gävleborg 250
Länsmuseet (Halmstad) 227
Länsmuseet Varbergs
Fästning 226
Länsmuseet Västernorrland
(Härnösand) 254
Malmahed (Malmköping) 134
Malmö Konsthall 179
Malmö Museum 180
Marcus Wallenberg-hallen
(Södertälje) 131
Mariebergsskogen 234
Mariestads Industrimuseum 221
Marinmuseum (Karlskrona) 188
Medelhavsmuseet (Stockholm)
64, **67**
Medeltidsmuseet (Stockholm) 61
Mining Museum (Utö) 111
Moderna Museet (Stockholm) 47,
75, **78–9**
Museisparvägen (Malmköping)
134
Museum of Antiquities
(Stockholm) 41
Musikmuseet (Stockholm) 70
Näs Gård 224
National Portrait Gallery
(Gripsholms Slott, Mariefred) 134
Nationalmuseum (Stockholm) 23,
47, **80–81**
Naturhistoriska Museet
(Gothenburg) 204
Naturhistoriska Riksmuseet
(Stockholm) 96
Nobelmuseet (Karlskoga) 235
Nobelmuseet (Stockholm) 58
Nordiska Akvarellmuseet
(Skärhamn) 19, **216**
Nordiska Museet (Stockholm) 23,
47, **88–9**
Norrbottens Museum (Luleå) 268
Nostalgia (Fågelfors) 154
Observatoriemuseet
(Stockholm) 99
Orrefors glassworks museum 153
Oskarshamns Sjöfartsmuseum 154
Polhemsmuseet (Stjärnsund) 237
Porjus Expo 273
Postmuseum (Stockholm) 59
Pythagoras (Norrtälje) 127
Rackstadmuseet (Arvika) 233
Railway Museum (Åmal) 211
Railway Museum (Mariefred) 135
Rallarmuseet (Moskosel) 273
Rooseum (Malmö) 179
Roslagsmuseet (Norrtälje) 127
Röhsska Museet (Gothenburg)
23, 199
Rörstrands Museum
(Lidköping) 220
Silurum (Lummelundas Bruk) 163
Silvermuseet (Arjeplog) 273
Sjöfartsmuseet (Gothenburg) 204
Sjöfartsmuseet (Trelleborg) 182
Sjöfartsmuseum (Skärhamn) 216
Sjöhistorika Museet (Stockholm)
27, 94
Skalbankmuseet (Kuröd) 214
Skansen open-air museum
(Stockholm) 27, 29, 47
Skellefteå Museum 267
Skogs- och Flottningsmuseet
(Storforsen) 268
Skokloster Motormuseum 127
Slipstensmuseet
(Mässbacken) 244
Smålands Museum (Växjö) 151
Sockenmuseet (Lövånger) 267
Söderhamns Stadsmuseum 251

Museums and galleries (cont.)
Söderhamns/F15
Flygmuseum 251
Sölvesborgs Museum 186
Sörmlands Museum
(Nyköping) 134
Stadsmuseum (Skövde) 222
Stensjö By 154
Stockholms Stadsmuseum 102
Strindbergsmuseet Blå Tornet
(Stockholm) 69
Strömstads Museum 211
Sundsvall Museum 254
Svenska Skidmuseet 266
Sveriges Järnvägsmuseum
(Gävle) 250–51
Sveriges Sjömanshusmuseum
(Uddevalla) 214
Tändstickmuseet (Jönköping)
150–51
Teknikens Hus (Luleå) 268
Teknikens och Sjöfartens Hus
(Malmö) 180–81
Tekniska Museet (Stockholm) 94
Textilmuseet 224
Textilmuseet (Sandviken) 251
Theatre Museum (Drottningholm,
Stockholm) 109
Thielska Galleriet (Stockholm) 93
Tom Tits Experiment
(Södertälje) 131
Torekällbergets Museum
(Södertälje) 131
Toy Museum (Tidö) 136
Tre Kronor Museum
(Stockholm) 57
Trelleborgs Museum 182
Tycho Brahe Museum (Ven) 175
Ulricehamns Konst- och
Östasiatiska Museum 224
Ulricehamns Museum 224
Umeå Energicentrum 267
Universeum (Gothenburg) 199
Utvandrarnas Hus (Växjö) 151
Vadsbo Museum (Mariestad) 221
Vagnmuseum (Malmö) 178
Vasaloppsmuseet (Mora) 241
Vasamuseet (Stockholm) 47,
90–91
Vattenriket (Kristianstad) 186
Vaxholm Fortress Museum 110
Viktor Rydbergs Museum
(Jönköping) 150–51
Vin- & Sprithistoriska Museet
(Stockholm) 98
Vitlycke Museum 212
Vuollerim 6000 År 273
Vänermuseet (Lidköping) 220
Vänersborgs Museum 217
Världskulturmuseet
(Gothenburg) 199
Värmlands Museum
(Karlstad) 234
Västergötlands Museum
(Skara) 223
Västerbottens Museum
(Umeå) 266
Wadköping (Örebro) 238–9
Waldemarsudde
(Stockholm) 92–3
Wanås Slott 186
Ystads Hantverksmuseum 182
Ystads Konstmuseum 182
Zornmuseet (Mora) 241
Ölands Museum
(Himmelsberga) 156
Örebro Läns Museum 238
Örnsköldsviks Museum 255
Östasiatiska Museet 74, **76**
see also Palaces
Music 14, 20–21, **24–5**, 311–13

Music (cont.)
  festivals 27, 28, 312–13
  shopping for 308–9
  see also Theatres
Muslims 13
Myths and legends 21, 129, 154
Målerås 153
Måltidens Hus i Norden
  (Grythyttan) 139
Mårbacka 229, 230, **232**
Mårtagården (Rydet) 226
Mårten Trotzigs Gränd (Stockholm)
  59
Måås-Fjetterström, Märta 22
Mälardalen 16, 136–7
Mälaren lake 29, 102, 111, 123
  tour of Mälardalen's castles 136–7
Mälsåkers Palace (Selaön) 135
Möja 111
Möller-Nielsen, Egon 95
Möllerberg, Nils 99

N

Napoleon 12, 38, 39
Narke Sameläger 259
National Day 27, 34
National parks
  Fulufjället 244
  Gotska Sandön 169
  Muddus 273, 275
  Norra Kvill 153
  Padjelanta 273, 275
  Sarek 273, **274**, 275
  Sjaunja 275
  Skuleskogens 256
  Söderåsen 175
  Stora Sjöfallet 273, **275**
  Tivedens 208, **221**
National Portrait Gallery
  (Gripsholms Slott, Mariefred) 134
National Romantic style 99, 100,
  105, 241
Nationalmuseum (Stockholm) 23,
  47, **80–81**
Nature reserves
  Aboda Klint 154
  Bassholmen 214–15
  Brösarps Backar 183
  Döda Fallet 258
  Eriksberg Vilt- och Naturpark 187
  Hallands Väderö 174
  Holmöarna 266
  Hovs Hallar 174
  Johannishus Åsar 187
  Karlsöarna 168–9
  Koster Islands 211
  Morups Tånge 227
  Ottenby Naturum 157
  Rogen 260
  Skurugata 151
Naturhistoriska Museet *see*
  Museums and galleries
Nederluleå Kyrka (Gammelstads
  Kyrkstad) 268
Nedre Gärdet 95
Neptuni Åkrar 156
Neutrality 15
New Year's Eve 20, 29
Newspapers and magazines 14, **327**
Nightclubs 312–13
Nikkaluokta 275
Nils Holgersson's Adventure Park
  232
Nilsson, Birgit 25
Nilsson, Christina 25
Nilsson, Lennart 25
Njupeskär waterfall 244
NK Clock (Stockholm) 65
Nobel, Alfred 24, 25, **69**, 235
Nobel Day 29
Nobel Prizes 15, **69**, 77, 100

Nobelmuseet (Karlskoga) 235
Nobelmuseet (Stockholm) 58
Nobility 32–3, 37, 39
Nolhaga Slott (Alingsås) 223
Nora 139
Nordanå Kulturcentrum (Skellefteå)
  267
Nordens Ark (Åby Säteri) 213
Nordenskiöld, Adolf Erik 96
Nordingrå 256
Nordiska Akvarellmuseet
  (Skärhamn) 19, **216**
Nordiska Kompaniet (NK) 65, **66**,
  305
Nordiska Museet (Stockholm) 23,
  47, **88–9**
Nordkoster 211
Nordström, Karl 93
Norra Kvill National Park 153
Norrbotten 263–5, 268–9
Norrbottens Museum (Luleå) 268
Norrköping 141, **144**, 284, 297
Norrtälje **127**, 283
Norse gods 129
North America, emigration to 12,
  39, **151**
Northern Norrland **262–75**
  getting around 264
  map 264–5
  sights at a glance 265
  where to eat 303
  where to stay 289
Norway, union with 39
Nostalgia (Fågelfors) 154
Notke, Bernt 53
Nusnäs 241
Nya Älvsborgs Fästning 198, **205**
Nya Stadens Torg (Lidköping) 220
Nybrokajen 11 81
Nyköping 21, **134**, 283, 296
Nyköpinghus 33, 134
Nynäs Slott 134
Nynäshamn **169**, 283
Nyströmska Gården (Köping) 138
Nämforsen 249, **255**
Närke 229–31, 236, 238–9
Näs Gård 224
Nässjö **151**, 284, 297
Nääs Slott 223

O

Obelisks (Stockholm) 50, 68
Observatoriemuseet (Stockholm) 99
Observatory, Stjärneborg (Ven) 1
  74, **175**
Ohlsson, Olof Thorwald 95
Olav the Holy 162
Olof Skötkonung, King 32, 52,
  207, 220
Olovson, Gudmar 213
Omberg 142, **150**
Opening hours 320–21
  restaurants 290–91
  shops 304
Opera 311, 313
  GöteborgsOperan 194,
  196–7, 311
  Kungliga Operan (Stockholm) 38,
  40–41, 64, **66–7**
Orchids **16–17**, 159, 169
Orrefors 153
Orsa 244
Orsa Grönklitt 244
Orust 214, 215, **216**
Oscar I, King 108, 154, 236
Oscar II, King 56, 67, 70, 213
Oscarsborg (Söderhamn) 251
Oskarshamn **154**, 155, 284
Ottenby Fägelstation 141, **157**
Ottenby Naturum 157
Oxenstierna, Axel 50, 136

Oxenstierna, Bengt Bengtsson 60
Oxenstierna-Soopska chapel
  (Landskyrkan, Askersund) 236
Oxhälja Market (Flipstad) 28

P

Paddan Boats 205
Padjelanta National Park 273, 275
Pageants 21
Painting 24
Pajala 269
Palaces
  Arvfurstens Palats (Stockholm)
  64, **67**
  Axel Oxenstiernas Palats
  (Stockholm) 50
  Bååtska Palatset (Stockholm) 79
  Drottningholm (Stockholm) 24,
  40–41, **106–9**
  Haga Slott (Stockholm) 97
  Hallwylska Palatset (Stockholm)
  46
  Karlbergs Slott (Stockholm) 98
  Mälsåkers Palace (Selaön) 135
  Nordiska Kompaniet (Stockholm)
  65, **66**
  Riddarhuset (Stockholm) 41,
  60–61
  Roggeborgen (Strängnäs) 135
  Rosersberg (Sigtuna) 130
  Royal Palace (Stockholm) 24, 37,
  54–7
  Sagerska Palatset (Stockholm) 62,
  67
  Sollidens Slott 156
  Steninge Slott (Sigtuna) **130**, 137
  Strömsholms Slott 132–3, **136**
  Tessinska Palatset (Stockholm)
  51, **52**
  Tullgarns Slott 131
  Tynnelsö Slott (Selaön) 135
  Ulriksdal (Stockholm) 97
  Utrikesministerhotellet
  (Stockholm) 79
  Waldemarsudde (Stockholm)
  92–3
  Wrangelska Palaset
  (Stockholm) 60
Palme, Olof 25, 43, 69, 222
Palmstedt, Erik 58, 59, 67
Paper industry 175, 247
Paradise (Tinguely/de Saint Phalle)
  47, 74
Parken Zoo (Eskilstuna) 135
Parking 333
Parks and gardens
  Almedalen (Visby) 166
  Astrid Lindgrens Värld
  (Vimmerby) 153
  Berzelii Park (Stockholm) 81
  Bosjökloster 176
  Botaniska Trädgården
  (Gothenburg) 191, **204–5**
  Botaniska Trädgården
  (Uppsala) 129
  Botaniska Trädgården
  (Visby) 167
  Boulognerskogen (Gävle) 250
  Drottningholm (Stockholm)
  106, **109**
  Ekoparken (Stokholm) **97**, 110
  Fredriksdal Friluftsmuseum
  (Helsingborg) 175
  Grönsöö 136
  Gunnebo Slott 225
  Hagaparken (Stockholm) 96–7
  Harpsund 134
  Hembygdsparken (Nässjö) 151
  Humlegården (Stockholm) 70
  Kapitelhusgården (Visby) 165
  Krusmyntagården 163

Parks and gardens (cont.)
   Kungsträdgården (Stockholm)
   64–5, 66
   Liseberg (Gothenburg) 200
   Långholmen (Stockholm) 102
   Miniland (Halmstad) 227
   Nils Holgersson's Adventure Park
   232
   Nordanå Kulturcentrum
   (Skellefteå) 267
   Norrvikens Trädgårdar 174
   Ramnaparken (Borås) 224
   Rosengården (Kristianopel) 187
   Skansberget (Gothenburg) 201
   Skäftekärr Järnåldersby (Böda)
   156
   Slottskogen (Gothenburg) 204
   Sofiero 175
   Stadspark (Hjo) 222
   Stadsparken (Borås) 224
   Stadsparken (Skara) 223
   Stadsparken (Trelleborg) 182
   Sträckleparken (Vännersborg) 217
   Sundsvall Stadspark 254
   Tessinparken (Stockholm) 95
   Tomteland (Gesunda) 241
   Trädgårdsföreningen
   (Gothenburg) 198–9
   Ulriksdal (Stockholm) 97
   Vita Bergen (Stockholm) 105
   Waldemarsudde (Stockholm)
   92–3
   Wanås Slott 186
   see also Amusement parks;
   National parks
Parliament 13, 49, 61
Passports 320
Pataholm 155
Pauli, Georg 61
Pauli, Hanna 164
Peace politics 15, 25, 266
Pernevi, Palle 201
Pershyttan (Nora) 139
Personal security 322–3
Persson, Sigurd 23, 69
Peter the Great 35
Peterson-Berger, Wilhelm 258–9
Petersson, Axel 93, 154
Petes 169
Petri, Olaus 50, 53, 238
Petrus de Dacia 167
Pharmacies 323
Photography 25
Picasso, Pablo 78, 227, 235
Picture stones (Gotlands Fornsal,
   Visby) 166
Pilane Gravfält (Tjörn) 216
Pilo, C G 40
Piper, Fredrik Magnus 96
Piteå 268, 289, 303
Platen, Baltzar von 146
Polhem, Christopher 237
Police 322–3
Politics 12–13, 42–3
Poltava, Battle of 35
Pop music 14, 311
Population 12, 39, 42
Porcelain 220
Porjus Expo 273
Poseidon (Milles) 120, 193, 200
Postal services 327
Postmuseum (Stockholm) 59
Postrodden Mail Boat Race
   (Grisslehamn) 27
Precht, Burchardt 137
Prince's Gallery (Stadshuset,
   Stockholm) 100
Proposal, The (Ekwall) 89
Prästgatan (Stockholm) 48
Public holidays 29
Pubs, music in 312

Pukeberg 153
Punschfabriken (Karlshamn) 186
Pythagoras (Norrtälje) 127

Q
Queen Hedvig Eleonora's State
   Bedroom (Drottningholm) 107
Queen Lovisa Ulrika's Library
   (Drottningholm) 107
Qvarnström, C G 231

R
Rackstadmuseet (Arvika) 233
Rademacher, Reinhold 135
Radio 14, 327
Rafting 234, 316–17
Rail travel 329, 330–31
   Friksdalsbanan 230, 232
   Inlandsbanan 230, 248, 273, 331
   Malmbanan 274, 275
   steam trains (Mariefred) 135
   steam trains (Nora) 139
   Västervik to Hultfred line 154
Railway museums see Museums and
   galleries
Rainfall 28
Rallarmuseet (Moskosel) 273
Ramlösa Brunn 175
Ramnaparken (Borås) 224
Ramsey, Christopher 153
Ramundberget 260
Raoul Wallenbergs Torg
   (Stockholm) 81
Rauchenberg, Robert 78
Rådhuset see Town halls
Rågårdsvik 215
Rättvik 27, 240–41
Refugees 43
Rehn, Johan Eric 55–7, 106–7, 126
Reindeer 17, 247, 261
Religion 13, 43
Rembrandt 80
Residenset (Malmo) 178
Restaurants 290–91, 294–303
   booking 291
   children in 291
   prices 291
Riddarfjärden Regatta
   (Stockholm) 28
Riddarholmen (Stockholm) 49, 60
Riddarholmskyrkan (Stockholm) 60
Riddarhuset (Stockholm) 41, 60–61
Right to Roam 13, 21
Riksdagshuset (Stockholm) 49, 61
Riksgränsen 273
Riksjarl 32
Rinkaby Kyrka 186
Road signs 333
Road travel 329, 332–3
Rock carvings 31, 212
   Himmelstalund (Norrköping) 144
   Högsbyn 210
   Nämforsen 249, 255
   Sigurdsristningen 135
   Tanum 208, 212
Rock music 311
Rogen lake 260
Roggeborgen palace
   (Strängnäs) 135
Roma 163
Romany 13
Romare, Bengt 84
Ronneby 187
Roos, Fredrik 179
Rooseum (Malmö) 179
Rosengården (Kristianopel) 187
Rosenlund Canal (Gothenburg) 192
Rosersberg palace (Sigtuna) 130
Roskilde, Peace of 35, 36, 187
Roslagen 123, 127
Roslagsmuseet (Norrtälje) 127

Roslin, Alexander 81
Rottneros 120, 232
Rovdjurscenter (Ekshärad) 234
Rowing 27
Roxen lake 147
Royal Armoury see
   Livrustkammaren (Stockholm)
Royal Chapel (Stockholm) 54, 57
Royal Palace (Stockholm) 24, 37,
   51, 54–7
Royal Philharmonic
   Orchestra 27, 69
Royal Swedish Yacht Club 111
Rödbergsfortet (Boden) 269
Röhss, Wilhelm and Augustus 199
Röhsska Museet (Gothenburg) 23,
   199
Röks Kyrka 150
Rörstrands Museum (Lidköping)
   220
Rubens, Peter Paul 47, 56
Rudbeck, Olof 128, 129
Rudbeckius, Johannes 138
Runestones 130, 150, 155, 187

S
S/S Blidösund 111
S/S Freja av Fryken 232
S/S Trafik 222
Sachs, Josef 66
Safety 322–3
Sagerska Palatset
   (Stockholm) 62, 67
Saggat lake 264
Sahlin, Gunnel 152
Sahlström siblings 232
Sahlströmska Gården (Utterbyn)
   232
Sailing 14–15, 27–8, 111, 316–17
Saint see also Cathedrals; Churches
St Bridget 141, 145
St Eskil 135
St George and the Dragon
   (Notke) 53
St Martin's Day 29
St Olofsholm 162
Saint Phalle, Niki de 47, 74
Sala 138
Salmon 26, 28, 187, 227
Saloman, Geskel 151
Salvius, Johan Adler 53
Sami 11, 259–61, 263, 272–3
   costume 20
   handicrafts 307
   language 13, 14
Sampe, Astrid 66
Sandhammaren 182
Sandhamn 27, 111
Sandviken 251, 302
Sånfjället 260, 261
Sankta Annas archipelago 141
Sarek National Park 273, 274, 275
Sälen 229, 244–5, 288, 302
Särg, Heikki 196
Särna 244
Scandinavium
   (Gothenburg) 310, 311
Schantzka Huset (Stockholm) 58
Scharinska villa (Umeå) 266
Scheele, Carl Wilhelm von 25
Scholander, F W 79, 97, 178
Schultheis, Jakob 87
Schyler, Jules and Karin 179
Science and technology 25
Sculpture 24
Sea travel 329, 331
Seals 16, 169, 211
Seasons 26
Seby Gravfält (Öland) 157
Sehlstedt, Elias 111
Selaön 135

Self-catering 278–9
Semla buns 26
Sergel, Johan Tobias 24, 67
  Adolf Fredriks Kyrka
    (Stockholm) 69
  The Faun 81
  Gustav III bust 55
  Gustav III statue 51
  Klara Kyrka (Stockholm) 68
  Kungliga Operan (Stockholm) 67
  Life in the Inns 40
  The Priestess 57
Serra, Richard 179
Seven Years War 34, 187
Seyfridtska Huset (Stockholm) 58
Shipyards
  Gothenburg 205
  Karlskrona 188–9
Shopping 304–9
  tax refunds 304, 320
  what to buy 23, 306–7
  where to shop 308–9
Shows 312–13
Sibbe the Wise 155
Sigtuna 130, 283, 296
Sigurdsristningen 135
Silurum (Lummelundas Bruk) 163
Silvergruvan (Sala) 138
Silvermuseet (Arjeplog) 273
Silvia, Queen 13, 54, 57
Simlångsdalen 227
Simrishamn 183
Singing 14, 20–21, 27
Sista Styverns Trappor
  (Stockholm) 104
Sjaunja National Park 275
Själevads Kyrka 255
Sjöberg, Birger 217
Sjöbert, Josabeth 104
Sjöfartsmuseet *see* Museums and
  galleries
Sjögren, Nils 94, 99
Sjöhistorika Museet (Stockholm)
  27, 94
Sjömanstornet (Gothenburg) 204
Sjöström, Victor 25
Sjötorp 147
Skaftö 215
Skagerrak 207
Skalbanksmuseet (Kuröd) 214
Skanör 177, 285
Skansen Kronan (Gothenburg) 201
Skansen open-air museum
  (Stockholm) 27, 29, 47, 92
Skara 222–3, 315
Skarsgård, Stellan 24
Skåne 11, 16, 171, 174–86
Skåneleden trail 172
Skånes Djurpark (Frostavallen) 176
Skänninge Market 27
Skäftekärr Järnåldersdersby
  (Böda) 156
Skäfthammars Kyrka (Gimo) 126
Skärfva Herrgård (Karlskrona) 189
Skärhamn 216
Skegriedösen 182
Skellefteå 263, 267, 289, 303
Skepparhuset (Gullholmen) 215
Skeppsholmen *see* Blasieholmen &
  Skeppsholmen
Skeppsholmsbron (Stockholm) 72
Skiing 15, 316, 317
  races 26, 29, 241, 245
Skogaholm Manor 18
Skogs- och Flottningsmuseet
  (Storforsen) 268
Skogskapellet (Stockholm) 105
Skogskyrkogården (Stockholm) 24,
  99, 105
Skokloster 123, 127, 137
Sköld, Otte 61, 201

Skottsbergska Gården (Karlshamn)
  186–7
Skövde 21, 222, 287, 301
Skule Song Festival 27
Skuleskogens National Park 256
Skultuna Messingsbruk 138
Skurugata nature reserve 151
Slipstensmuseet (Mässbacken) 244
Slottsbacken (Stockholm) 50–51
Slottskogen (Gothenburg) 204
Smoking 321
Småland 16, 141, 150–55
  glassworks 23, 27, 141
Smålands Museum (Växjö) 151
Smögen 213, 287
Smörgåsbord 292
Snowstorm at Sea (Strindberg) 89
Social Democrat party 13, 42–3
Societetshuset (Marstrand) 18
Societetshuset (Varberg) 226
Sockenmuseet (Lövånger) 267
Sofia Albertina, Princess 67
Sofia Kyrka (Stockholm) 105
Sofia Magdalena, Queen
  40–41, 56
Sofiero 175
Soldat-torpet (Limhamn) 181
Sollerön 241
Sollidens Slott 156
Sommarhagen (Frösön) 258–9
Sommerlath, Silvia *see* Silvia, Queen
Sotenkanalen 213
Southern Götaland 170–87
  getting around 173
  map 172–3
  sights at a glance 173
  where to eat 298–9
  where to stay 285–6
Southern Norrland 246–61
  getting around 248
  landscape 248
  map 248–9
  sights at a glance 249
  where to eat 302–3
  where to stay 288–9
Souvenirs 306–7, 308–9
Söderåsen National Park 175
Söderblom, Nathan 251
Söderhamn 251, 289
Söderköping 297
Södermalm (Stockholm) 83, 104–5,
  282, 295–6
Södermanland 123, 131–7
Södertälje 131, 283, 296
Södra Vings Kyrka 224
Sölvesborg 186
Sörmlands Museum (Nyköping) 134
Space centre, Esrange 272
Sparre, Lars 60
Spikarna 254
Sports and outdoor activities 14–15,
  25, 314–17
Sports stadiums 96, 105, 199
Spring Salon (Liljevalchs Konsthall,
  Stockholm) 26, 87
Stadion (Stockholm) 96
Stadsbiblioteket (Malmö) 180
Stadsbiblioteket (Stockholm) 24, 99
Stadsgården harbour (Stockholm)
  104
Stadshuset (Gothenburg) 197
Stadshuset (Stockholm) 46, 82,
  100–1
Stadsmuseum (Stockholm) 102
Stadsparken *see* Parks and gardens
Stadstearten (Gothenburg) 201
Stamps 59, 327
Standing stones 138
State Apartments (Royal Palace,
  Stockholm) 56
Ståhle, Ephraim 56

Steep Backafallen (Ven) 175
Stegeholm fortress (Västervik) 154
Steiner, Rudolf 131
Stenbrohult 26
Stenhammar castle 134
Stenhammar, Ernst 110–11
Steninge Slott (Sigtuna) 130, 137
Stenkil dynasty 32
Stenkyrka Man (Gotlands Fornsal,
  Visby) 166
Stenshuvud National Park 184–5
Stensjö By 154
Stiller, Mauritz 25, 105
Stjärneborg observatory (Ven) 174,
  175
Stjärnsunds Slott 236
Stock Exchange (Stockholm) 58
Stockholm 44–117
  Blasieholmen & Skeppsholmen
    72–81
  City 62–71
  climate 28
  events 26–9
  Gamla Stan 48–61
  getting around 334–5
  history 32–5
  Malmarna & Further Afield
    82–111
  maps 46–7
  population 68
  sightseeing tours 111, 335
  street finder 112–17
  where to eat 294–6
  where to stay 280–82
Stockholm Archipelago 11, 19, 24,
  110–11
Stockholm Bloodbath 33–4, 58, 245
Stöde Kyrkby 253
Stone Age
  Höörs Stenaldersby 176
  Karleby 223
  Kinnekulle 221
  Skegriedösen 182
  Vuollerim 6000 År 273
Stone ships 168, 171, 182
Stoneware 22
Stora Alvaret 157
Stora Hyttnäs 237
Stora Karlsö 168–9
Stora Kils church 228
Stora Sjöfallet National Park
  273, 275
Stora Torget (Visby) 165, 166
Stora Tuna 237
Storforsen 258, 268
Storkyrkan (Stockholm) 50, 53, 311
Storlien 259
Storsjön lake 251, 258, 259
Storsjöyran Festival 27, 312
Stortorget (Karlskrona) 188
Stortorget (Malmö) 178
Stortorget (Stockholm) 50, 58
Stoves, tiled 137
Störlinge Kvarnrad 156
Strand 150
Strandvägen (Stockholm) 86
Strindberg, August 24, 42, 79
  Strindberg Collection (Nordiska
    Museet, Stockholm) 89
  Strindbergsmuseet Blå Tornet
    (Stockholm) 69
  Thielska Galleriet (Stockholm) 93
Strykjärnet (Norrköping) 144
Sträckleparken (Vännersborg) 217
Strängnäs 135
Strömbergshyttan 152
Strömmen channel (Stockholm)
  73, 80
Strömsholm Canal 139
Strömsholms Slott 132–3, 136
Strömstad 211, 287, 301

Sture, Sten, the Elder 33, 53
Sture, Sten, the Younger 58
Sturefors 144
Sturehof 137
Stüler, August 80
Sunbyholms Slott 135
Sundborn 23, 24, **237**
Sundsvall **254**, 258, 288, 302
Sunne **232**, 288
Sunshine 28
Surströmming 247, **255**, 256
Svampen (Örebro) 239
Svaneholm 182
Svea Kingdom 220
Sveafallen 235
Sveg 261
Sven Tveskägg, King 177
Svenska Skidmuseet 266
Svenskt Tenn (Stockholm) 23, 306, 308, 309
Svenskund, Battle of 38, 40, 75
Sveriges Järnvägsmuseum (Gävle) 250–51
Sveriges Sjömanshusmuseum (Uddevalla) 214
Sverker dynasty 32, 157
Sweden
    architecture 18–19
    area 8, 11, 12
    calendar of events 26–9
    climate 12, **28**
    culture 14
    famous Swedes 24–5
    government and politics 12–13
    history 31–43
    image of 15
    landscape and wildlife 11, **16–17**
    languages and dialects 13–14
    location 8
    maps 8–9, 120–21
    population 12, 24
    Swedish design **22–3**, 308
    traditions, customs and folklore 20–21
Swedenborg, Emanuel 18, 38, 94
Swedish Academy 40, 58
"Swedish Grace" 22
"Swedish Modern" style 22
Swimming 15, 27, 46, **315**
Sylvius, Johan 106, 107, 108
Synagogan (Stockholm) 79

T

Taberg 151
Tanum 208, **212**
Taube, Astri Bergman 105
Taube, Evert 21, 60, 105, 215
Taxis 335
Tällberg **241**, 288
Tändstickmuseet (Jönköping) 150–51
Tännforsen 246, 259
Tärnaby 274
Tegneby 212
Teknikens Hus (Luleå) 268
Teknikens och Sjöfartens Hus (Malmö) 180–81
Tekniska Museet (Stockholm) 94
Telephone services 326
Television 14, 327
Tempelman, Olof 96
Temperatures 12, **28**
Tengbom, Anders 69
Tengbom, Ivar 68–9, 223
Tengbom, Svante 69
Terra Nova (Gothenburg) 205
Tessin, Carl Gustaf 24, 52
Tessin, Nicodemus the Elder 24
    Bååtska Palatset (Stockholm) 79
    Domkyrkan (Kalmar) 155

Tessin, Nicodemus the Elder (cont.)
    Drottningholm (Stockholm) 106, 107
    Rådhuset (Gothenburg) 197
    Stockholms Stadsmuseum 102
    Ulriksdal (Stockholm) 97
    Wrangelska Palatset (Stockholm) 60
Tessin, Nicodemus the Younger 24, 50
    Drottningholm (Stockholm) 106
    Fredrikskyrkan (Karlskrona) 188
    Heliga Trefaldighetskyrkan (Karlskrona) 188
    Royal Chapel (Stockholm) 57
    Royal Palace (Stockholm) 54, 56
    Steninge Slott 130, 137
    Stockholms Stadsmuseum 102
    Storkyrkan (Stockholm) 53
    Tessinska Palatset (Stockholm) 51, 52
    Ulrika Eleonora Kyrka (Söderhamn) 251
Tessinparken (Stockholm) 95
Tessinska Palatset (Stockholm) 51, **52**
Textile industry 223, 224, 251
Thaveniuska Huset (Stockholm) 86
Theatre 109, 311, 313
Theatres
    Court Theatre (Drottningholm, Stockholm) 109
    Dalhalla 241, 310
    Dunkers Kulturhus (Helsingborg) 175
    Gävle 250
    GöteborgsOperan 194, **196–7**
    Ice Globe Theatre (Jukkasjärvi) 29, **272**
    Konserthuset (Gothenburg) 201
    Konserthuset (Stockholm) 68–9
    Kulturhuset and Stadsteatern (Stockholm) 68
    Kulturhuset (Ytterjärna) 131
    Kungliga Dramatiska Teatern (Stockholm) **71**, 311
    Kungliga Operan (Stockholm) 64, **66–7**
    Nybrokajen 11 81
    Opera House (Stockholm) 38, 40–41
    Romateatern (Roma Kloster) 163
    Scandinavium (Gothenburg) 310
    Stadsteatern (Gothenburg) 201
    Sundvalls Teater 311
    Theaterladen (Hedemora) 237
Thiel, Ernest 93
Thirty Years War 35, **36**
Tickets, entertainment 310, 313
Ticks 323
Tidö 136
Timber industry 247, 254, 255
    Dalälvarnas Flottningsmuseum (Gysinge) 250
    Skogs- och Flottningsmuseet (Storforsen) 268
Tingstäde 163
Tinguely, Jean 47, 74
Tiveden, forests of 208, 229, 236
Tivedens National Park 221
Tjärnö 216
Tjäro 187
"Tjejtrampet" (Stockholm) 26
Tjolöholms Slott 226
Tjörn 216
Tjugondedag Knut 20
Tom Tits Experiment (Södertälje) 131
Tomelilla 183
Tomteland (Gesunda) 241

Torekällbergets Museum (Södertälje) 131
Torekov 174
Torhamn, Gunnar 105
Torne river 27, 263, **269**
Tornedalen 12, 13, **269**
Torpa Stenhus 224
Torsburgen 168
Tors;hälla 135
Torshälla 135
Tossebergsklätten 232
Tourist information 320, 321
Tours
    Dalsland Canal 210
    Fryken Lakes 232
    Mälardalen's Castles 136–7
    Österlen 183
    through the Kingdom of Crystal 152–3
Town halls
    Rådhuset (Gothenburg) 197
    Rådhuset (Laholm) 227
    Rådhuset (Malmö) 178
    Rådhuset (Örebro) 238
Town walls, Visby 164, **166**, 167
Toys 136, 154, 169
Törneman, Axel 61
Törngrens Krukmakeri (Falkenberg) 226
Trädgårdsföreningen (Gothenburg) 198–9
Traditions, customs and folklore **20–21**, 92
Traffic rules 332
Transport **328–35**
Transport museums *see* Museums and galleries
Traveller's cheques 325
Tre Kronor Museum (Stockholm) 57
Treasury (Royal Palace, Stockholm) 57
Trefaldighetskyrkan (Karlskrona) 173
Trelleborg **182**, 299
Triewald, Mårten 126
Trolle-Ljungby 186
Trollhättan 26, **217**, 287, 301
Trollhättan Canal 147, 217
Trollkyrka 221
Trollskogen forest 172
Tronö Kyrka 251
Tropikcenter (Halmstad) 227
Trosa **131**, 297
Trotting races 26, 28
Trysunda 257
Tullgarns Slott 131
Tundra landscape 16, 17
Turning Torso (Malmö) 181
Tycho Brahe Museum (Ven) 175
Tylösand 208, 227
Tynnelsö Slott (Selaön) 135
Tyska Kyrkan (Stockholm) 58–9

U

Uddeholm 234
Uddevalla 57, **214**, 301
Ullängersfjärden 256
Ullevi (Gothenburg) 199
Ulricehamn 224
Ulrika Eleonora Kyrka (Söderhamn) 251
Ulriksdal (Stockholm) 97
Ulvaeus, Björn 25
Ulvöhamn 255, 257
Umeå 28, 263, **266**, 273
    hotels 289
    restaurants 302–3
Umeå Energicentrum 267
United Nations 15, 43
Universeum (Gothenburg) 199
Universities 128, 177, 266
Uppland 123, 126–31

Uppsala 26, 31, **128–9**
  hotels 283
  map 129
  restaurants 297
Uraniborg (Ven) 175
Utmeland monument 241
Utrikesministerhotellet
  (Stockholm) 79
Utvandrarnas Hus (Växjö) 151
Utzon, Kim 175
Utö 111

V

Vadsbo Museum (Mariestad) 221
Vadstena **145**, 222, 284, 297
Vagnmuseum (Malmö) 178
Valdemar Atterdag, King of
  Denmark 159, 167
Valhallavägen (Stockholm) 95
Valleberga Kyrka 182
Vallée, Jean de la 61, 98, 103, 236
Vallée, Simon de la 61
Vallien, Bertil 151, 152
Vallonsmedjan (Österbybruk) 126
Value Added Tax 304
Vansbrosimningen 27, 315
Varberg **226**, 287, 301
Varnhems Klosterkyrka 222
Vasa, Gustav *see* Gustav I Vasa
Vasa (warship) 47, **90–91**
Vasaloppet ski race 11, 26, **245**
Vasaloppsmuseet (Mora) 241
Vasamuseet (Stockholm) 47, **90–91**
Vatlings Gård 163
Vattenborgen (Karlskrona) 188
Vattenriket (Kristianstad) 186
Vaxholm (Stockholm Archipelago)
  27, **110**
Vega Monument (Stockholm) 96
Vegetarian restaurants 291
Vemdalsfjällen 261
Ven 174, **175**
Ver Weiden, Cornelius 57
Vickleby 155
Victoria, Crown Princess 10, 13, 156
Viking (barque) 190, 195, **196**
Vikings 31, 84
  Ales Stenar 171
  Birka 123, 130
  Gotlands Fornsal (Visby) 166
  Jamtli (Östersund) 258, 259
  Kämpinge Vall 177
  Trelleborgen 182
  Västerås 138
  Årsunda Viking centre 251
  Örebro Läns Museum 238
Viksten, Albert 253
Viktor Rydbergs Museum
  (Jönköping) 150–51
Vilhelm, Prince 134
Vimmerby 86, 87, **153**
Vin- & Sprithistoriska Museet
  (Stockholm) 98
Vingboons, Justus 61
Visby 32, 121, 159, **164–7**
  festivals 21, 27, 167
  hotels 284–5
  maps 164–5, 166
  restaurants 298
Visingsö 150, 222
Vita Bergen (Stockholm) 105
Vitlycke 212
Volvo 12, 191, 217
Von der Lindeska House
  (Stockholm) 59
Von Echstedtska Gården (Västra
  Smedbyn) 233
Vrams Gunnarstorp 175
Vuollerim 6000 År 273
Våmbs Kyrka 222
Våmhus 244

Väddö 127
Vällingby 42
Vänermuseet (Lidköping) 220
Vänern lake 147, 207, 208, 229
Vänersborg 217
Värmland 27, **228–35**
Värmlands Museum (Karlstad) 234
Värmlandsnäs 233
Västerås **138**, 283, 297
Västerbotten 263–7
Västerbottens Museum (Umeå) 266
Västerbron (Stockholm) 102
Västergötland 32, 207–9, 217,
  220–25
Västergötlands Museum (Skara) 223
Västerlånggatan (Stockholm) 59
Västervik **154**, 284
Västmanland 123, 137–9
Västra Nordstan (Gothenburg)
  194–5
Vättern, Lake 27, 142, 229, 315
Vätternakvarium (Hjo) 222
Växbo 252
Växjö **151**, 152, 284, 297

W

Wachtmeister, Admiral-General
  Hans 188
Wadköping (Örebro) 238–9
Wåhlström, Ann 23
Waldemarsudde (Stockholm) 92–3
Walking *see* Hiking
Wallén, Pia 306
Wallenberg, K A 67
Wallenberg, Raoul 25, 81
Wallquist, Einar 273
Walpurgis Night 20, **26**
Wanås Slott 186
Watersports 15, 316–17
Watteau, Antoine 80
Weaving 233
Wendelstam, Johan 58
Western Götaland **206–27**
  getting around 208
  map 208–9
  sights at a glance 209
  where to eat 300–1
  where to stay 286–7
Western Sveland **228–45**
  getting around 230
  landscape 230
  map 230–31
  where to eat 301–2
  where to stay 287–8
Westin, Fredrik 66
Westman, Carl 199
Westphalia, Peace of 35, 36
Where to eat 290–303
Where to stay 278–89
White-water rafting 316–17
Whitefish Festival 27, 269
Wik 137
Wildlife 16–17
  see also Nature reserves; Zoos
  and wildlife parks
Wilhelm, Heinrich 61
Windmills 143, 156, 157
Wines and spirits 305
Winter sports 15, 316, 317
Wooden boats (Strandvägen,
  Stockholm) 86
World War I 43
World War II 25, 43, 79, 81
Wrangel, Carl Gustav 37, 60, 127
Wrangelska Palaset (Stockholm) 60
Wärf, Goran 121

Y

Youth hostels 278, **279**
Ystad **182**, 183, 286, 299
Ytterjärna 131

Z

Zettervall, Helgo 176, 177, 178
Zoos and wildlife parks
  Borås Djurpark 224
  Fjärils- & Fågelhuset
  (Hagaparken, Stockholm) 96–7
  Frösö 259
  Furuviksparken (Gävle) 251
  Gotlands Djurpark (Alskog) 168
  Gunnesbo (Skaftö) 215
  Kolmårdens Djurpark 144
  Lycksele Djurpark 267
  Nolhaga Slott (Alingsås) 223
  Nordens Ark (Aby Säteri) 213
  Ölands Djurpark 155
  Orsa Björnpark 244
  Parken Zoo (Eskilstuna) 135
  Rovdjurscenter (Ekshärad) 234
  Skånes Djurpark (Frostavallen)
  176
  Skansen (Stockholm) 92
  Tropikcenter (Halmstad) 227
Zorn, Anders 24, 92, 93, **241**

Å

Ådalen 255
Åfors 156
Åhus 186
Åmal **211**, 287
Ånge 253
Ångermanland 247–9, 254–7
Åre **259**, 289, 303
Åreskutan 259
Årsta bridge 76
Årsunda 251
Åsnen lake 187
Åstol 216–17

Ä

Älvkarleby 250
Älvros 261
Älvsborgsbron (Gothenburg) 205
Ängelholm 174
Äventyret Sommarland
  (Leksand) 240

Ö

Öhrström, Edvin 68
Öja church (Gotland) 166, 168
Öland 16–17, 141, **155–7**, 284
Ölands Djurpark 155
Ölands Museum (Himmelsberga)
  156
Ölandsbron 141, 155
Örebro 29, 208, 229, **238–9**
Öregrund 126
Öresund 171, 174, **181**
Öresund Bridge 171, 173, **181**
Orm, Edvard 151
Örnässtugan 231, **237**
Örnskold, Per Abraham 255
Örnsköldsvik **255**, 289, 303
Öst, Per Nilsson 252
Östarp 170, **176–7**
Östasiatiska Museet 74, **76**
Östberg, Ragnar 94, 100, 266
Österbybruk 126
Österfärnebo 250
Östergötland 32, 141, 144–7, 150
Österlen 120, **183**
Östermalm **83**, 281, 294–5
Östersund 28, **258–9**, 303
Östhammar 126
Ostindiska Huset (Gothenburg) 198
Östra Granfjället 244
Östra Nordstan (Gothenburg) 194
Övedskloster 176–7
Övertorneå 269
Övralid 145

Acknowledgments

STREIFFERT FÖRLAG would like to thank the following staff at Dorling Kindersley:

PUBLISHER
Douglas Amrine

PUBLISHING MANAGERS
Jane Ewart, Anna Streiffert

SENIOR EDITOR
Christine Stroyan

MAP CO-ORDINATOR
Casper Morris

DTP MANAGER
Jason Little

PRODUCTION CONTROLLER
Linda Dare

DORLING KINDERSLEY would like to thank all those whose contributions and assistance have made the preparation of this book possible.

MAIN CONTRIBUTORS
ULF JOHANSSON has produced Swedish guidebooks such as *Sverigeboken* and *Sverigevägvisaren*. He has also been a publisher and year-book editor at the Swedish tourist association Svenska Turistföreningen.

MONA NEPPENSTRÖM is an editor and travel journalist and has written a large number of Swedish guidebooks, including *Sverigeboken*, *Sverigevägvisaren*, *Turisttoppen* and rail company SJ's travel guide series *Längs spåret*.

KAJ SANDELL wrote the *Eyewitness Stockholm* travel guide. He is a journalist and formerly wrote for Swedish publishers Åhlén & Åkerlunds Förlag and Swedish daily broadsheet *Dagens Nyheter*.

FACTCHECKING
Lena Ahlgren

PROOFREADER
Stewart J Wild

INDEX
Helen Peters

ARTWORK REFERENCE
Svenska Aerobilder AB

PHOTOGRAPHY PERMISSIONS
The publishers would like to thank all those who gave permission to photograph at museums, palaces, churches, restaurants, hotels, stores and other sights too numerous to list individually. Particular thanks go to the Guild of Museum Directors in Stockholm for permitting access to picture archives as well as making additional photographing of objects and exhibitions possible.

PICTURE CREDITS
t = top; tl = top left; tlc = top left centre; tc = top centre; trc = top right centre; tr = top right; cla = centre left above; ca = centre above; cra = centre right above; cl = centre left; c = centre; cr = centre right; clb = centre left below; cb = centre below; crb = centre right below; bl = bottom left; bc = bottom centre; br = bottom right; b = bottom.

Every effort has been made to trace the copyright holders. Dorling Kindersley apologizes for any unintentional omission and would be pleased, in such cases, to add an acknowledgment in future editions.

Commissioned by the publisher, the book's main photographers, Peter Hanneberg, Erik Svensson and Jeppe Wikström, produced the majority of the photographs reproduced in this book. They have also contributed archive pictures which have been listed among the other picture credits. The publisher would like to thank the photographers and all the other individuals, organizations and picture libraries for permission to reproduce their photographs and illustrations:

AMAROK AB:
Magnus Elander 16t, 16clb.

ARMÉMUSEUM:
266bl.

ÁTTJE FJÄLL- OCH SAMEMUSEUM:
Jan Gustavsson 20tr.

©DACS:
Märta Måås-Fjetterström 22br; *Concrete*, Jonas Bohlin 23tr; Hans Hedberg 22tr; Sigurd Persson 23tl; *Breakfast Outdoors*, Pablo Picasso 78tr; *The Dying Dandy*, Nils Dardel 78bl; *Monogram*, Robert Rauchenberg 78crb; *The Child's Brain*, Giorgio De Chirico 79cl; Einar Forseth 100tr; Simon Gate 153tr; *Visby Wall*, Hanna Hirsch-Pauli 164tr; *Altarpiece in Jukkasjärvi Church*, Bror Hjort 272c.

DANSMUSEUM:
64tr.

DROTTNINGHOLMS SLOTTSTEATER:
Bengt Wanselius 109tr, 109bc.

ETNOGRAFISKA MUSEET:
Bo Gabrielsson 93c.

FJÄRILS & FÅGELHUSET:
97cl.

GREAT SHOTS:
Peter Gerdehag 118–119.

GUNNEBO SLOTT:
225tl.

GÖTEBORGS KONSTMUSEUM:
Karin and Kersti, Carl Larsson 237b.

PETER HANNEBERG:
2–3c, 4t, 13t, 16cla, 16cra, 17tc, 17cl, 17br, 19cr, 20tl, 20b, 21cb, 123b, 135b, 161bc, 246, 247b, 248c, 258bl, 259tr, 262, 263b, 268c, 269br, 270–271, 274ca, 275cb, 312b, 314b, 315t, 315b, 318–319.

CHRISTER HÄGG:
East Indiaman Wasa, Jacob Hägg 198b.

IMS BILDBYRÅ:
43tl.

JÖNKÖPINGS LÄNS MUSEUM:
Bianca Maria in Among Elves and Trolls, John Bauer 21bl.

KOSTA BODA:
Ann Wåhlström 23b; Ulrika Hydman Vallien152b; Kjell Engman 153bc.

KUNGLIGA BIBLIOTEKET:
36br, 70b.

KUNGLIGA HUSGERÅDSKAMMAREN:
Alexis Daflos 4b, 56tr, 56clb, 57tr, 107tc; 106cl, 106bl, 107bl, 108tr, 108clb; *The Triumph of Karl XI*, Jacques Foucquet 37tl; 46b; Håkan Lind 54cra, 54crb, 54br; 54tl, 55tc, 55cr, 56cla, 107cr; 135c.

KUNGLIGA MYNTKABINETTET:
51crb; Jan Eve Olsson 52cl, 69tr.

KUNGLIGA OPERAN:
Mats Bäcker 64bc, 67tl, 67c.

KÄLLEMO AB:
23c.

LIVRUSTKAMMAREN:
37bl, 41br; Göran Schmidt 41cla, 51tl; Nina Heins
52bl.

MEDELHAVSMUSEET:
Ove Kaneberg 64cla.

METRIA KIRUNA:
8cr.

MODERNA MUSEET:
Per Anders Allsten 78br.

MUSEUM TRE KRONOR:
56br.

MUSIKMUSEUM:
Nina Heins 70cra.

NATIONALMUSEUM:
22clb; *Flowers on the Windowsill*, Carl Larsson
22–23c; *Gustav Vasa*, Cornelius Arendtz 30; *Ansgar
Preaches Christianity*, Georg Pauli 32bl; *Stockholm
Bloodbath*, Dionysius Padt-Brügge 33t; *The Entry of
King Gustav Vasa of Sweden into Stockholm, 1523*,
Carl Larsson 34t; *Portrait of Erik XIV*, Steven van der
Meulen 34c; *The Fire at the Royal Palace 7th May
1697*, Johan Fredrik Höckert 35tr; *Portrait of Queen
Kristina*, David Beck 35cl; *The Death of Gustav II
Adolf of Sweden at the Battle of Lutzen*, Carl
Wahlbom 36bl; *The Crossing of the Belt*, Johan Philip
Lemke 36–37c; *Karl X Gustav*, Sébastien Bourdon
37cr; *Bringing Home the Body of King Karl XII of
Sweden*, Gustaf Cederström 37br; *King Gustav III
of Sweden*, Lorens Pasch d.y. 38tl; *Portrait of the
Bernadotte Family*, Fredrik Westin 38crb; *The
Coronation of Gustav III*, Carl Gustav Pilo 40cla; *The
Battle at Svensksund*, J T Schoultz 40clb; *A Noisy
Dinner*, Johan Tobias Sergel 40bc; *Conversation at
Drottningholm*, Pehr Hilleström 40–41c; *The Murder
of Gustav III*, A W Küssner 41tr; *Bacchanal on
Andros*, Peter Paul Rubens 47tl; 55br; *The
Conspiracy of the Batavians under Claudius Civilis*,
Rembrant 80cla; *David and Bathsheba*, 80bl; *The
Love Lesson*, Antoine Watteau 80tr; *The Lady with
the Veil*, Alexander Roslin 81tl; *The Faun*, Johan
Tobias Sergel 81cb; *Karl XIV Johan's Visit to
Berga*, A C Wetterling 146t; *Valdemar Atterdag
Plunders Visby 1361*, Carl Gustaf Hellqvist 167b.

NATURHISTORISKA RIKSMUSEET:
Staffan Waerndt 96c.

NORDISKA MUSEET:
47tr; Birgit Brånvall 88tr; Mats Landin 88cl; Sören
Hallgren 88bc; *Snowstorm at Sea*, August Strindberg
89cra; 89tr; *The Proposal*, Knut Ekwall 89tl.

POSTMUSEUM:
59crb.

PREMIUM PUBLISHING:
Anders Hanser 24b.

PRESSENS BILD:
5tr, 6–7c, 10, 11b, 12t, 14t, 15b, 21tr, 24tr, 25t, 25c,
25b, 27b, 43cr; Hans T. Dahlskog 43br; 54bl; Jan
Delden 68br; Gunnar Seijbold 71tl; 87tl; Axel
Malmström 99tr; 105br, 120t, 206, 259b, 304cr,
305tr, 310cr, 316tl.

REDERI AB GÖTA KANAL:
147cra.

LAILA REPPEN:
18–19c.

RIKSANTIKVARIEÄMBETET:
3c.

SJÖHISTORISKA MUSEET:
94c.

SKANSEN:
Marie Andersson 92c.

SKOGSKYRKOGÅRDEN:
105c.

SKYWAYS:
Jonas Kosunen 330t.

INGALILL SNITT:
18t.

STATENS HISTORISKA MUSEUM:
84cla, 84clb, 84bl, 84br, 85tc, 85ca, 85cb, 85br,
85bl, 130b.

STENINGE SLOTT:
130t.

STOCKHOLMS AUKTIONSVERK:
41bl.

STOCKHOLMS STADSBYGGNADSKONTOR:
95c.

STOCKHOLMS STADSHUS:
Jan Asplund 100br, 101tl.

STOCKHOLMS STADSMUSEUM:
32t; *Tre Kronor Palace*, Govert Camphuysen 36cl;
Newspaper Readers, J A Cronstedt 39tl; *The
Regicide Anckarström Punished in Front of the
House of Nobility*, 41cr; 42bl, 43clb.

STRINDBERGSMUSEET:
24tl; Per Bergström 69bc.

SVENSKA AKADEMIEN:
Leif Jansson 40tr.

ROLF SØRENSEN:
16bl, 17bl.

THIELSKA GALLERIET:
Hornsgatan, Eugène Jansson 93tr.

LARS TUFVESSON:
Lars Tufvesson 181b.

INGRID VANG NYMAN:
14c.

VASALOPPSMUSEET:
244t, 244cla, 244cra, 244bl.

VASAMUSEET:
Hans Hammarskiöld 47br, 90tr, 90cla, 90bl, 90br,
91tc, 91cra; 91crb, 91bl.

VIN & SPRITHISTORISKA MUSEET:
98c.

CLAES WESTLIN:
22cla.

JEPPE WIKSTRÖM:
26b, 27t, 29b, 44–45, 48, 52tr, 62, 64clb, 65crb, 65bl,
68tl, 72, 76br, 77ca, 82, 83t, 86t, 87tr, 97br, 99tl, 99b,
100bl, 102t, 103t, 103cl, 103b, 104tl, 110cr, 110cra,
111tl, 111br, 276–277, 290b, 310bl, 329t, 334t.

ÖSTASIATISKA MUSEET:
Erik Cornelius 74cla, 76bl.

JACKET: Front: CORBIS: Freelance Consulting Services
Pty Ltd, bl; DK IMAGES: Jeppe Wikström, br;
WWW.PIXGALLERY.COM: Bo Jansson, main; STATENS
HISTORISKA MUSEUM: c. Back: DK IMAGES: Peter
Hanneberg, tr; ZEFA VISUAL MEDIA: F Damm, bl.
Spine: WWW.PIXGALLERY.COM: Bo Jansson.

Phrase Book

When reading the imitated pronunciation, stress the part which is underlined. Pronounce each syllable as if it formed part of an English word, and you will be understood sufficiently well. Remember the points below, and your pronunciation will be even closer to the correct Swedish.

ai:	as in 'fair' or 'stair'
ea:	as in 'ear' or 'hear'
ew:	like the sound in 'dew'
EW:	try to say 'ee' with your lips rounded
oo:	as in 'book' or 'soot'
OO:	as in 'spoon' or 'groom'
r:	should be strongly pronounced

Swedish Alphabetical Order
In the list below we have followed Swedish alphabetical order. The following letters are listed after z: å, ä, ö.

You
There are two words for 'you': 'du' and 'ni'. 'Ni' is the polite form; 'du' is the familiar form. It is not impolite to address a complete stranger with the familiar form

IN AN EMERGENCY

Help!	**Hjälp!**	*yelp*
Stop!	**Stanna!**	*stanna!*
Call a doctor!	**Ring efter en doktor!**	*ring efter ebn doktor*
Call an ambulance!	**Ring efter en ambulans!**	*ring efter ebn ambewlanss*
Call the police!	**Ring polisen!**	*ring poleesen*
Call the fire brigade!	**Ring efter brandkåren!**	*ring efter brandkawren*
Where is the nearest telephone?	**Var finns närmaste telefon?**	*vahr finnss nairmasteb-telefawn*
Where is the nearest hospital?	**Var finns närmaste sjukhus?**	*vahr finnss-nairmasteb shewkhews*

COMMUNICATION ESSENTIALS

Yes	**Ja**	*yah*
No	**Nej**	*nay*
Please (offering)	**Varsågod**	*vahrshawgOOd*
Thank you	**Tack**	*tack*
Excuse me	**Ursäkta**	*ewrsbekta*
Hello	**Hej**	*bay*
Goodbye	**Hej då/adjö**	*baydaw/abyur*
Good night	**God natt**	*goonatt*
Morning	**Morgon**	*morron*
Afternoon	**Eftermiddag**	*eftermiddabg*
Evening	**Kväll**	*kvell*
Yesterday	**Igår**	*ee gawr*
Today	**Idag**	*ee dabg*
Tomorrow	**I morgon**	*ee morron*
Here	**Här**	*hair*
There	**Där**	*dair*
What?	**Vad?**	*vah*
When?	**När?**	*nair*
Why?	**Varför?**	*vahrfurr*
Where?	**Var?**	*vahr*

USEFUL PHRASES

How are you?	**Hur mår du?**	*bewr mawr dew*
Very well, thank you.	**Mycket bra, tack.**	*mewkeh brah, tack*
Pleased to meet you.	**Trevligt att träffas.**	*treavlit att traiffas*
See you soon.	**Vi ses snart.**	*vee seas snabrt*
That's fine.	**Det går bra.**	*dea gawr brah*
Where is/are . . .?	**Var finns ...?**	*vahr finnss...*
How far is it to . . .?	**Hur långt är det till**	*bewr lawngt ea dea till*
Which way to . . .?	**Hur kommer jag till ...?**	*bewr kommer yah till ...*
Do you speak English?	**Talar du/ni engelska?**	*tablar dew/nee engelska*
I don't understand	**Jag förstår inte.**	*yah fursbtawr inteh*
Could you speak more slowly, please?	**Kan du/ni tala lång-sammare, tack.**	*kan dew/nee tabla lawng-ssamareb tack*
I'm sorry.	**Förlåt.**	*furrlawt*

USEFUL WORDS

big	**stor**	*stOOr*
small	**liten**	*leeten*
hot	**varm**	*varrm*
cold	**kall**	*kall*
good	**bra**	*brah*
bad	**dålig**	*dawleeg*
enough	**tillräcklig**	*tillraikleeg*
open	**öppen**	*urpen*
closed	**stängd**	*staingd*
left	**vänster**	*vainster*
right	**höger**	*burger*
straight on	**rakt fram**	*rabkt fram*
near	**nära**	*naira*
far	**långt**	*lawngt*
up/over	**upp/över**	*EWp/urver*
down/under	**ner/under**	*near/ewnder*
early	**tidig**	*teedee*
late	**sen**	*sebn*
entrance	**ingång**	*ingawng*
exit	**utgång**	*EWtgawng*
toilet	**toalett**	*too-alett*
more	**mer**	*mebr*
less	**mindre**	*meendre*

SHOPPING

How much is this?	**Hur mycket kostar den här?**	*bewr mEWkeh kostar debn hair*
I would like . . .	**Jag skulle vilja . . .**	*yah skewleb vilya*
Do you have?	**Har du/ni ...?**	*habr dew/nee ...*
I'm just looking	**Jag ser mig bara omkring**	*yah sear may babra omkring*
Do you take credit cards?	**Tar du/ni kreditkort?**	*tabr dew/nee kredeetkoort*
What time do you open?	**När öppnar ni?**	*nair urpnar nee*
What time do you close?	**När stänger ni?**	*nair stainger nee*
This one.	**den här**	*debn hair*
That one.	**den där**	*debn dair*
expensive	**dyr**	*dEWr*
cheap	**billig**	*billig*
size (clothes)	**storlek**	*stOOrlek*
white	**vit**	*veet*
black	**svart**	*svart*
red	**röd**	*rurd*
yellow	**gul**	*gewl*
green	**grön**	*grurn*
blue	**blå**	*blaw*
antique shop	**antikaffär**	*anteek-affair*
bakery	**bageri**	*babgeree*
bank	**bank**	*bank*
book shop	**bokhandel**	*bOOkbandel*
butcher	**slaktare**	*slaktareb*
cake shop	**konditori**	*konditoree*
chemist	**apotek**	*apoteak*
fishmonger	**fiskaffär**	*fisk-affair*
grocer	**speceriaffär**	*spesseree-affair*
hairdresser	**frisör**	*frissurr*
market	**marknad**	*marrknad*
newsagent	**tidningskiosk**	*teednings-cbeeosk*
post office	**postkontor**	*posstkontOOr*
shoe shop	**skoaffär**	*skOO-affair*
supermarket	**snabbköp**	*snabbchurp*
tobacconist's	**tobakshandel**	*tOObaks-bandel*
travel agency	**resebyrå**	*reasseb bEWruw*

SIGHTSEEING

art gallery	**konstgalleri**	*konnst-galleree*
church	**kyrka**	*cbEWrka*
garden	**trädgård**	*traidgawrd*
house	**hus**	*bews*
library	**bibliotek**	*beebleeotek*
museum	**museum**	*mewseum*
square	**torg**	*tobrj*
street	**gata**	*gabta*
tourist information office	**turist-informations-kontor**	*tureest-informasbOOns-kontOOr*
town hall	**stadshus**	*statsbews*
closed for holiday	**stängt för semester**	*staingt furr semester*
bus station	**busstation**	*bewss-stasbOOn*
railway station	**järnvägsstation**	*yairnvaigs-stasbOOn*

STAYING IN A HOTEL

Do you have any vacancies?	**Har ni några lediga rum?**	*habr nee negra leadiga rewm*
double	**dubbelrum**	*doobelrewm*
room with double bed	**med dubbelsang**	*med doobel seng*

twin room	dubbelrum	doobelrewm
	med två	med tvaw
	sängar	sengar
single room	enkelrum	enkelrewm
room with	rum med	rewm med
a bath	bad	babd
shower	dusch	dewsh
key	nyckel	newckel
I have a	Jag har	yah habr
reservation	beställt rum	bestellt rewm

EATING OUT

Have you got a	Har ni ett	habr nee ett
table for...	bord för...?	bOOrd furr ...
I would like	Jag skulle vilja	yah skewleb vilya
to reserve	boka ett	bOOka ett
a table.	bord.	bOOrd
The bill, please.	Notan, tack.	nOOtan, tack
I am a	Jag är	yah air
vegetarian	vegetarian	vegetariahn
waitress	servitris	sairvitress
waiter	servitör	sairviturr
menu	meny/	menew/
	matsedel	mabtseadel
fixed-price	meny med	menew med
menu	fast pris	fast prees
wine list	vinlista	veenlista
glass of water	ett glas	ett glabss
	vatten	vatten
glass of wine	ett glas vin	ett glabss veen
bottle	flaska	flaska
knife	kniv	k-neev
fork	gaffel	gaffel
spoon	sked	shead
breakfast	frukost	frewkost
lunch	lunch	lewnch
dinner	middag	middabg
main course	huvudrätt	bewvewdrett
starter	förrätt	furrett
dish of the day	dagens rätt	dabgens rett
coffee	kaffe	kaffeb
rare	blodig	blOOdee
medium	medium	medium
well done	välstekt	vailstehkt

MENU DECODER

abborre	abborreh	perch
ansjovis	ansbOOvees	anchovies
apelsin	appelseen	orange
bakelse	babkelse	cake, pastry, tart
banan	banabn	banana
biff	biff	beef
bröd	brurd	bread
bullar	bewllar	buns
choklad	shooklabd	chocolate
citron	sitrOOn	lemon
dessert	dessair	dessert
fisk	fisk	fish
fläsk	flaisk	pork
forell	fooraill	trout
frukt	fruckt	fruit
glass	glass	ice cream
gurka	gewrka	cucumber
grönsaksgryta	grurnsabks-grewta	vegetable stew
hummer	hummer	lobster
kallskuret	kall-skuret	cold meat
korv	koorv	sausages
kyckling	chewkling	chicken
kött	churtt	meat
lamm	lamm	lamb
lök	lurk	onion
mineralvatten	minerabl-vatten	mineral water
med/utan	mebd/ewtan	still/sparkling
kolsyra	kawlsewra	
mjölk	m-yurlk	milk
nötkött	nurtchurtt	beef
nötter	nurtter	nuts
ost	oost	cheese
olja	olya	oil
oliver	oleever	olives
paj/kaka	pa-y/kabka	pie/cake
potatis	potabtis	potatoes
peppar	peppar	pepper
ris	rees	rice
rostat bröd	rostat brurd	toast
räkor	raikoor	prawns
rökt skinka	rurkt sheenka	cured ham
rött vin	rurtt veen	red wine
saft	safft-	lemonade
salt	sallt	salt
sill	seell	herring

skaldjur	skahl-yewr	seafood
smör	smurr	butter
stekt	stebkt	fried
strömming	strurmming	baltic herring
socker	socker	sugar
soppa	soppa	soup
sås	saws	sauce
te	tea	tea
torr	torr	dry
ungsstekt	ewngs-stebkt	baked, roast
vinäger	vinaiger	vinegar
vispgrädde	veesp-graiddeh	whipped cream
vitlök	veet-lurk	garlic
vitt vin	veett veen	white wine
ägg	aigg	egg
älg	ail-y	elk
äpple	aippleh	apple
öl	url	beer

NUMBERS

0	noll	noll
1	ett	ett
2	två	tvaw
3	tre	trea
4	fyra	fewra
5	fem	fem
6	sex	sex
7	sju	shew
8	åtta	otta
9	nio	nee-oo
10	tio	tee-oo
11	elva	elva
12	tolv	tolv
13	tretton	tretton
14	fjorton	f-yoorton
15	femton	femton
16	sexton	sexton
17	sjutton	shewton
18	arton	abrton
19	nitton	nitton
20	tjugo	chewgoo
21	tjugoett	chewgoo-ett
22	tjugotvå	chewgoo-tvaw
30	trettio	tretti
31	trettioett	tretti-ett
40	fyrtio	furti
50	femtio	femti
60	sextio	sexti
70	sjuttio	shewti
80	åttio	otti
90	nittio	nitti
100	(ett) hundra	(ett) bewndra
101	etthundraett	ett-bewndra-ett
102	etthundratvå	ett-bewndra-tvaw
200	tvåhundra	tvawbewndra
300	trehundra	treabewndra
400	fyrahundra	fewrabewndra
500	femhundra	fembewndra
600	sexhundra	sexbewndra
700	sjuhundra	shewbewndra
800	åttahundra	ottabewndra
900	niohundra	nee-oobewndra
1,000	(ett) tusen	(ett) tewssen
1,001	etttusenett	ett-tewssen-ett
100,000	(ett) hundra-	(ett) bewndra
	tusen	tewssen
1,000,000	en miljon	ebn milyOOn

TIME

one minute	en minut	ebn meenewt
one hour	en timme	ebn timmeb
half an hour	en halvtimme	ebn balvtimmeb
ten past one	tio över ett	teeoo urver ett
quarter past one	kvart över ett	kvabrt urver ett
half past one	halv två	balv tvaw
twenty to two	tjugo i två	chewgoo ee tvaw
quarter to two	kvart i två	kvabrt ee tvaw
two o'clock	klockan två	klockan tvaw
13.00	klockan tretton	klockan tretton
16.30	sexton och trettio	sexton ock tretti
noon	klockan tolv	klockan tolv
midnight	midnatt	meednatt
Monday	måndag	mawndabg
Tuesday	tisdag	teesdabg
Wednesday	onsdag	oonssdabg
Thursday	torsdag	toorsdabg
Friday	fredag	freadabg
Saturday	lördag	lurrdabg
Sunday	söndag	surndabg